The Creation of the Zulu Kingdom
War, Shaka, and the Consolidation of Power

This scholarly account traces the emergence of the Zulu Kingdom in South Africa in the early nineteenth century under the rule of the ambitious and iconic King Shaka. In contrast to recent literary analyses of myths of Shaka, this book uses the richness of Zulu oral traditions and a comprehensive body of written sources to provide a compelling narrative and analysis of the events and people of the era of Shaka's rule. The oral traditions portray Shaka as rewarding courage and loyalty and punishing failure; as ordering the targeted killing of his own subjects, both warriors and civilians, to ensure compliance to his rule; and as arrogant and shrewd but kind to the poor and mentally disabled. The rich and diverse oral traditions transmitted from generation to generation reveal the important roles and fates of men and women, royal and subject, from the perspectives of those who experienced Shaka's rule and the dramatic emergence of the Zulu Kingdom.

Elizabeth A. Eldredge is an independent scholar. She has published *A South African Kingdom: The Pursuit of Security in Nineteenth-Century Lesotho* (Cambridge University Press, 1993) and *Power in Colonial Africa: Conflict and Discourse in Lesotho, 1870–1960* (2007).

The Creation of the Zulu Kingdom, 1815–1828

War, Shaka, and the Consolidation of Power

ELIZABETH A. ELDREDGE

CAMBRIDGE
UNIVERSITY PRESS

University Printing House, Cambridge CB2 8BS, United Kingdom

One Liberty Plaza, 20th Floor, New York, NY 10006, USA

477 Williamstown Road, Port Melbourne, VIC 3207, Australia

314-321, 3rd Floor, Plot 3, Splendor Forum, Jasola District Centre, New Delhi-110025, India

79 Anson Road, #06-04/06, Singapore 079906

Cambridge University Press is part of the University of Cambridge.

It furthers the University's mission by disseminating knowledge in the pursuit of education, learning and research at the highest international levels of excellence.

www.cambridge.org
Information on this title: www.cambridge.org/9781107428027

© Elizabeth A. Eldredge 2014

This publication is in copyright. Subject to statutory exception and to the provisions of relevant collective licensing agreements, no reproduction of any part may take place without the written permission of Cambridge University Press.

First published 2014
First paperback edition 2017

A catalogue record for this publication is available from the British Library

Library of Congress Cataloging in Publication data
Eldredge, Elizabeth A., author.
The Creation of the Zulu Kingdom, 1815–1828 : War, Shaka, and the Consolidation of Power / Elizabeth A. Eldredge.
pages cm
Includes bibliographical references and index.
ISBN 978-1-107-07532-0 (Hardback) – ISBN 978-1-107-42802-7 (Paperback)
1. Shaka, Zulu Chief, 1787–1828. 2. Zulu (African people)–Kings and rulers–Biography. 3. Zulu (African people)–History–19th century. [1. Zululand (South Africa)–History–To 1879.] I. Title.
DT1831.C53E43 2014
968.4039092–dc23
2014014323

ISBN 978-1-107-07532-0 Hardback
ISBN 978-1-107-42802-7 Paperback

Cambridge University Press has no responsibility for the persistence or accuracy of URLs for external or third-party internet websites referred to in this publication, and does not guarantee that any content on such websites is, or will remain, accurate or appropriate.

Contents

Preface		*page* vii
Glossary		x
Map 1 Peoples and Chiefdoms of Southern Africa, c. 1820–1825		xii
Map 2 Chiefdoms of KwaZulu-Natal, c. 1815–1820		xiii
1	Political History in Precolonial Africa: The Case of the AmaZulu Kingdom	1
2	Powerful Chiefs Before Shaka	26
3	Shaka's Early Life: Oral Traditions, Tales, and History	42
4	Shaka as Warrior	59
5	AmaZulu Expansion and Repercussions: Early Conflicts and Migrations	76
6	Chiefs, Chiefdoms, Violence, and Political Reconfiguration	106
7	Challenges and Consolidation, 1824–1827	139
8	Royal Women: Authority and Subservience	172
9	Zulu Voices, Zulu Meanings: Ancestors, Praises, and History	205
10	Shaka's Rule: Social Configuration and Social Control	231
11	Shaka's Ambitions	253
12	The Legacy of Shaka's Reign	276
Appendix: James Stuart Interviewees		298
Notes		325
Bibliography		388
Index		397

Preface

This book is one of two major projects to emerge from research I conducted from December 1993 to November 1994 when I was based in Durban at the University of Durban-Westville and traveled from there for research stints in Swaziland, Mozambique, and Lesotho. The research for this book was supported by a Fulbright Senior Scholar Fellowship, a grant from the Social Science Research Council, and funds from Michigan State University. I am especially grateful to the faculty in the history departments of the University of Durban-Westville, the University of Swaziland, the Universidade Eduardo Mondlane, and the National University of Lesotho. I was proud to be associated with all of the faculty at the University of Durban-Westville during this period of political turmoil and the tremendous historical transition from the apartheid regime to a newly born democracy. Irena Filotova, Mandy Goedhals, and Julie Pridmore were especially gracious and supportive of my research, and my interactions with their students were extremely gratifying. In Durban I spent most of my time at the Killie Campbell Library, and I am grateful for the support I received from the entire staff there over many, many months of daily work with their assistance and support. I am also grateful to the teachers and friends of my children who made their stay in Durban so successful. John Wright, Cara Pretorius, and their family were not only supportive of my research, but also provided my family with unforgettable hospitality as we all hiked through the Drakensberg on several occasions. Thank you all for the welcome and support you provided to my family throughout our stay.

Writing up my previously completed research for my second book on the history of Lesotho has delayed the completion of this work for many years. I nevertheless remain indebted to everyone who assisted me during my yearlong sojourn in southern Africa from December 1993 through November 1994.

This work would not have been possible without the instruction, advice, assistance, and encouragement of many people throughout my career. When I began my doctoral work at Northwestern University, I began my language and linguistic studies with Professor Jack Berry and Professor Wandile Kuse. Dr. Kuse, who was at the University of Illinois at Chicago, taught me isiXhosa intensively, which provided me with the essential linguistic basis for my later field research. I am grateful for the advice and instruction I received at Northwestern University from Professors John Rowe, Ivor Wilks, and Ibrahim Sundiata. My preparation was directed toward research in South Africa, but the cultural boycott for foreigners that had been declared, similar to the sports boycott that was so widely honored, precluded contacting and working with South Africans who were in South Africa and conducting research in the country. On the explicit personal advice of Dennis Brutus whom I met while at Northwestern University, I honored the cultural boycott, and my contact with scholars at South African universities began only many years later after the cultural boycott was lifted in 1992 and I attended a conference that year at the University of Durban-Westville.

For the remainder of my graduate studies, I moved to the University of Wisconsin where I completed my doctoral dissertation in 1986 under the invaluable direction of Jan Vansina. While there, I continued my language studies under the direction of Professor Daniel Kunene with whom I completed advanced language study in isiXhosa, a cognate language of isiZulu that allowed me to make the transition for my later research. Because of my decision to reorient my doctoral research to Lesotho, I also received intensive language instruction in SeSotho from Dr. Kunene in preparation for my fieldwork. As I read S. M. Mqayi's *Ityala Lamawele* in the original isiXhosa and Thomas Mofolo's novels *Pitseng* and *Moeti oa Bochabela* in the original SeSotho under his instruction, I learned not only the nuances of language use but also the idioms of culture expressed through the works of these early twentieth century South African writers.

Finally, I would like to express special thanks to Ibrahim Sundiata, Jan Vansina, Fred Morton, and Hunt Davis for their support and encouragement over the years. I am grateful to David N. Plank for his support and encouragement during the years of research and to my entire family for their constant and continuous support throughout my career. This work would never have reached fruition without the support of Donald H. and Charlotte M. Eldredge, Lucy E. Bailey, Robert M. Eldredge, Barbara D. Eldredge, Michael Eldredge Plank, and James Eldredge Plank, to whom I dedicate this book with love.

Glossary

Only terms used frequently are included in this glossary. For the ease of readers unaccustomed to identifying or searching for words according to their word root without its prefix, the terms below are listed in alphabetical order according to prefix.

Original spellings are retained in quoted passages, including interview notes made by James Stuart. Shaka's name was spelled "Tshaka" by James Stuart in accord with the correct pronunciation of his name according to interviewees born in the nineteenth century. In modern orthography, aspirated consonants are indicated with the letter *h* as in Thukela (Tugela) River; Phakathwayo (Pakatwayo), Bhungane (Bungane). The more commonly used plural prefix for peoples, Ama-, is used in place of the less common prefix *abakwa-* (indicating "people of the place of") for ease of reading.

Aba	plural prefix for people of, or associated with, the root name (i.e., AbaQwabe: "Qwabe people")
abakwa	plural prefix for "people of the place of" followed by the root name
Ama	plural prefix for people of, or associated with, the root name (i.e., AmaZulu: "Zulu people")
assegai	spear; *umkhonto*
idlozi	ancestral spirit; sometimes appears as (embodied in) a snake (pl. amadlozi)
ikhanda	regimental military barracks attached to a royal homestead (pl. amakhanda)
ilobolo	bridewealth given to the bride's family by the groom's family that establishes her children as belonging to the husband's line of descent; usually paid in cattle

Glossary

ibutho	military regiment; men's or women's age grade group (pl. amabutho)
impi	military expedition; army; military force (pl. izimpi)
inceku	personal attendant; servant to a chief (pl. izinceku)
induna	person of authority; principal man/headman in a homestead; commander (pl. izinduna)
inkosi	chief, paramount chief, king (pl. amakhosi)
inyanga	traditional "doctor"; healer (pl. izinyanga)
isibongo	composed and recited praise; praises (pl. izibongo)
isigodlo	secluded women's quarters in the royal homestead; king's quarters located in the women's quarters (pl. izigodlo)
isikhulu	person of importance; great person (pl. izikhulu)
isithakazelo	praise-greetings used for persons according to their ancestral line of descent (pl. izithakazelo)
izwe	*ilizwe* country, territory; *isizwe* nation
ka	by; son or daughter of (used in names)(e.g., Shaka ka Senzangakhona)
uku-giya	to dance with fighting gestures as if in battle
uku-khonza	to offer allegiance and accept a subordinate tributary status to a chief; to offer loyalty and tribute (uku-konza)
umkhonto	spear
umuzi	homestead (pl. imizi)

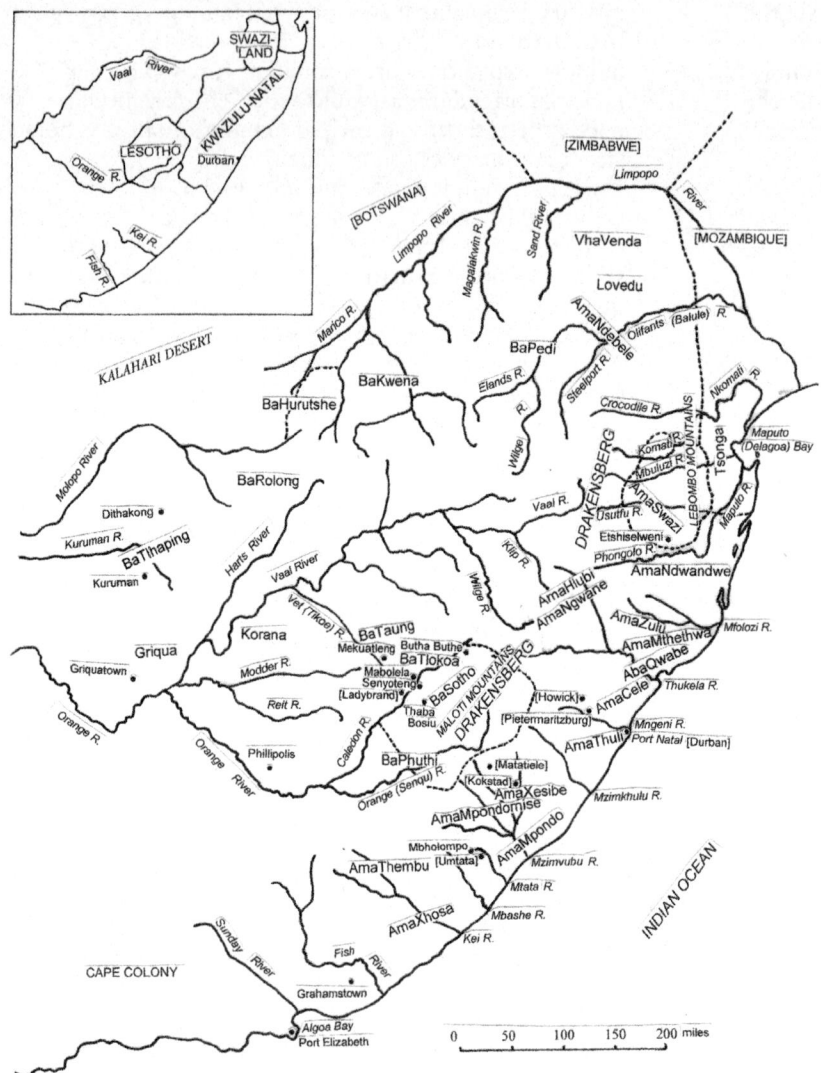

MAP 1 Peoples and Chiefdoms of Southern Africa, c. 1820–1825

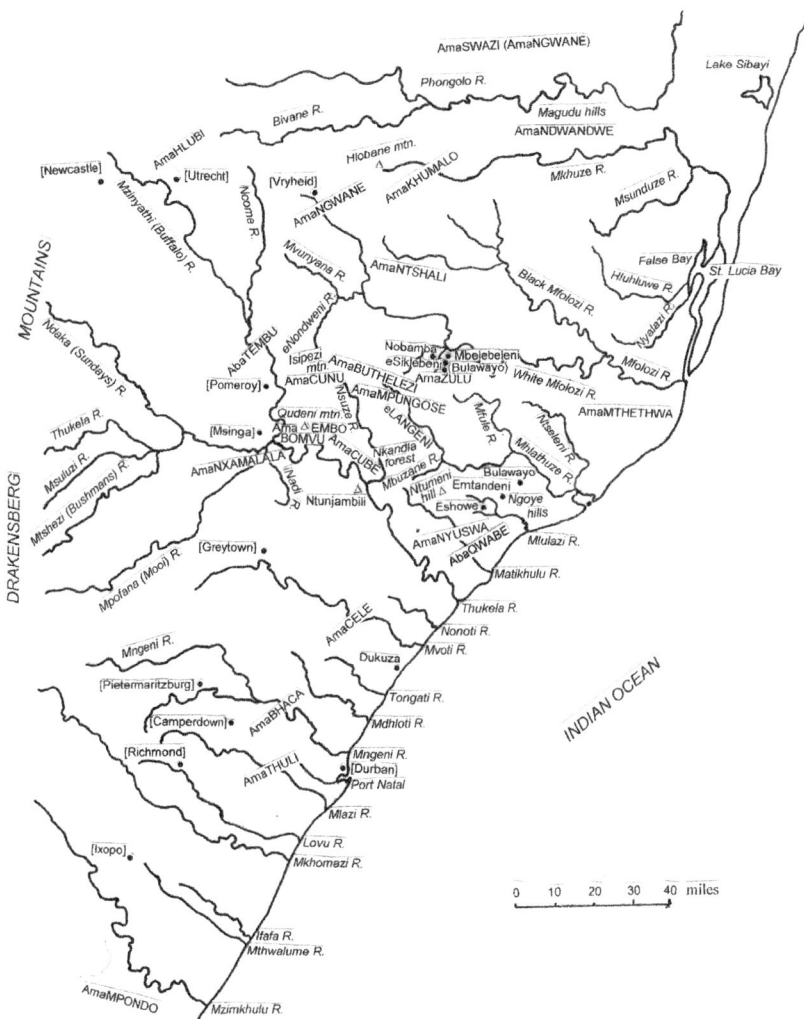

MAP 2 Chiefdoms of KwaZulu-Natal, c. 1815–1820

Chapter 1

Political History in Precolonial Africa: The Case of the AmaZulu Kingdom

Many of the kingdoms of precolonial Africa still exist today in name, in sentiment, in affiliation, and in residual forms of identification. The shifting composition and open boundaries of social and political groups over centuries render their residual names, still found as family names and place names, ambiguous outside of their historical context. Associated with a distinct geographic location, a common political history, and a common culture and language as the result of cultural assimilation that had followed political and social consolidation, the large political units of the past were the so-called "tribes" identified by European western observers. Europeans, by the time of the advent of colonial rule in the nineteenth century, perceived only the primitive aspects of an impoverished material culture rather than the generations and centuries of steadily increasing political sophistication that had finally created institutionalized states in the form of kingdoms. As elsewhere in the world, these large political units had multicultural origins and had been forged by cooperation and warfare, ambition, and submission. These kingdoms were the products of leaders who were chiefs, kings, and military commanders and of their followers or adherents or subjects who produced the food and marched into battle on behalf of their chiefs, kings, ancestors, and children in the name of their chiefdom, kingdom, or empire.

The colonization of most of the African continent by the foreign nations of Europe curtailed abruptly the independence and sovereignty of African chiefdoms and kingdoms. Even where indirect colonial rule allowed the continuation of the forms and functions of precolonial political units, chiefdoms, and kingdoms with chiefs and kings, the political as well as economic prerogatives of surviving chiefdoms and kingdoms were harshly restricted to conform to the goals of the colonizing nations. Now perceived in these residual forms as "tribes" by colonial officials, western ethnographers, and anthropologists, many of these truncated and disempowered chiefdoms and kingdoms of the past survived into the colonial and postcolonial periods as the roots of group identities that had been joined by new group identities or "tribes" forged or fabricated under colonial auspices. With a sense of common group culture and experience from a past common belonging to a chiefdom or kingdom, an institutionalized political unit that had fostered cultural assimilation, the inheritors of these political and cultural memories and traditions retained their sense of common identity in the whirlwinds and turmoil of the colonial era. They created real and functional bonds that came to be perceived as ethnic groups. The mobilization of ethnic bonds for political purposes sometimes generated violent competition over access to resources and authority in the colonial and postcolonial worlds, and "ethnicity" has rightly been condemned as the source of intractable and violent disruptions causing enormous harm in the modern world. In its origins and functioning, *ethnicity* refers to the politicization of sociocultural identity for political and economic gain at the expense of others. Ethnic groups and ethnic identities are not merely imagined, however, and the presence of ethnic identities linked to a common past does not necessarily breed the violence of politicized ethnicity. Cultural assimilation has followed political consolidation or unification and the adoption and promotion of common values and practices for the common social welfare of all. The memory and recognition of multicultural or "multi-ethnic" origins need not inhibit popular and voluntary adherence to and support for new and larger forms and boundaries of political organization. In the modern world, equal access to opportunities, resources, and decision-making processes can prevent the inequalities that breed politicized ethnic mobilization and the violence of ethnicity.

The people of southeast Africa who identified themselves as AmaZulu in the late nineteenth and early twentieth centuries readily recognized their diverse multicultural and political origins from centuries and generations before.[1] Between 1817 and 1828 Shaka, the firstborn son of Senzangakhona, chief of the AmaZulu chiefdom, used war and diplomacy to bring about the submission of dozens of large and small neighboring chiefdoms and, through a process of consolidation, to create the Zulu kingdom of southern Africa. The nature of warfare changed, and the scope of Shaka's military campaigns, or *impi*s, expanded as the size of the military under his command grew from hundreds to tens of thousands of warriors in only a decade. Through ruthless raids, surprise attacks, and battlefield confrontations, war accomplished the goals of compelling the submission of chiefs and chiefdoms to the rule of Shaka and the expanding Zulu chiefdom, the expulsion of defiant and recalcitrant chiefs and their adherents, the expansion of the pool of available men of military age, and the seizure of wealth in the form of territory and cattle. Diplomacy allowed for the voluntary submission of chiefs who might give their allegiance to, or *khonza*, Shaka and become a tributary subordinate ally. Shaka was motivated by personal ambition for himself and for the Zulu royal family into which he had been born. Shaka built a cadre of loyal followers from family members, senior counselors, subordinate chiefs, and military commanders who oversaw the expansion and maintenance of a multitiered sociopolitical unit comprising many large and small chiefdoms from across the region of modern KwaZulu-Natal that lost their independence as they voluntarily and involuntarily submitted to the rule of the Zulu royal family. The once small chiefdom of the AmaZulu people, so named after an early ancestor called Zulu, meaning the sky or heavens, was headed by Shaka, who had seized the chieftaincy by force and killed the heir, his half brother, and a younger but senior son of his father. Shaka pursued expansionist aims until the time of his assassination in 1828. The sociopolitical organization of his kingdom revolved around a military system that incorporated every man as part of a regiment from about age twenty to the time of their death, even as old men. Shaka accompanied many of his most important *impi*s but for his last military campaign had stayed behind, leaving him vulnerable to his half brothers. They returned secretly from the military campaign and succeeded in a long-standing plan to kill Shaka whose violence against his own people had become intolerable even to his closest family members and counselors. Shaka left behind a kingdom that was united by only tentative and fragile bonds, so that his successor, his half brother Dingane by another mother, was left to subdue rebellion and reinforce the political boundaries of the diverse peoples who comprised the new AmaZulu kingdom. The process of forging a new AmaZulu identity that had enjoyed a common political origin under Shaka and reflected growing cultural assimilation took the remainder of the nineteenth century, spurred by the perceived common threat of European intrusion and white settler expansionism. The AmaZulu identity of the twentieth century has multicultural roots stemming from the political and social processes of consolidation that created the Zulu kingdom under Shaka in the early decades of the nineteenth century.[2]

For the region of southern Africa east of the Drakensberg mountains, the longest genealogy remembered in oral traditions is that of the ruling family of the Swazi kingdom that was consolidated in the 1810s and 1820s. The ruling line of descent traces its genealogy back to the ninth century AD based on the number of generations recorded in it, indicating long-standing traditions of socially constructed political units that valued the retention of a genealogical remembrance of their origins. For the region of modern KwaZulu-Natal, evidence of the ancestors of modern Bantu-speaking agriculturalists practicing mixed herding and cultivation has been found dating to about the third century AD, when these societies interacted with ancestral San populations of hunter-gatherers across the area. The fairly good distribution of water resources through large and small rivers running from the Drakensberg to the Indian Ocean allowed the widespread distribution of settlements over the centuries. The practice of ironworking allowed for more efficient cultivation and hunting to support a growing population. Large and small chiefdoms were not new in KwaZulu-Natal at the beginning of the nineteenth century, but it was the chief of a the small chiefdom known as the AmaZulu, descendants of an ancestor named Zulu, who managed to consolidate political control over KwaZulu-Natal and create a political unit with the structural components and size to be considered a kingdom by the 1820s.

Historians of Africa have long recognized the processes involved in the emergence of larger political units through the consolidation or amalgamation of several smaller polities. These sociopolitical and cultural units are appropriately conceived of as *chiefdoms*, defined as the adherents to a political leader or "chief," usually chosen because of his social role that was often inherited. In southeastern Africa, the term *inkosi* has been understood to refer to the person in political authority who ordinarily was also the senior male of the ruling descent line in a sociopolitical unit or chiefdom. That the head of small sociopolitical units in Africa have commonly been the senior male of a ruling line of descent has also prompted historians to perceive of such units as "clans" with the understanding that the family and blood ties defining membership in a clan unit were often blurred with the acquisition of new adherents joining voluntarily in an accepted social process of incorporation. A chiefdom's incorporation of multiple smaller chiefdoms in a subordinate status – marked by symbolic submission and the payment of tribute and taxes and contribution to military functions – has commonly been perceived in western terms as the creation of a kingdom by virtue of its greater size and multiple layers of authority. The accepted understanding that a kingdom ordinarily relied on a legal and political system and process similar to that of smaller chiefdoms but on an expanded scale and with additional layers of overlapping authority has provided historians a term that can be appropriately applied even when a kingdom lacked the complex structure of a formal state with systematic foreign diplomacy and the routine functioning of civil servants from diplomats to tax collectors, operating within well-defined boundaries. Shaka created a kingdom and by extension the term *inkosi* came to refer to the highest authority, commonly referred to as "king" by Europeans at the time.

Modern scholars have assumed that the Zulu kingdom constituted a new and revolutionary political structure in the region. However, as Adam Kuper has observed, there was continuity in sociopolitical structures as represented in the kingdom's royal settlements that "embody some of the same symbolic spatial dimensions as the homestead."[3] These spatial configurations as found in homesteads and royal settlements demarcated "the lines of political affiliation." This was true even as the royal settlements alternatively incorporated other family members or commoners or separated to form independent homesteads that nevertheless remained under the authority of the main "house" of the ruling descent line.[4] In a process of such geographic or spatial expansion,

> The head of the original, core homestead is formally the *umnumzana*, or family head of the whole cluster of related homesteads, but in the course of time, and especially after his death, these relationships of relative authority become attenuated, each homestead gaining greater autonomy, though the original homestead, now under the *uyise wabantu* [the heir of the section of the house which remains in the old homestead to guard the ancestral burial grounds when other sections relocate], retains a ritual pre-eminence.[5]

Larger sociopolitical units falling under the authority of a chief were structured in accordance with "the 'house' system of the reigning chief's family."[6] Women, as Kuper has shown, were central in the creation and sustenance of political structures, because in the "house" system, "[i]ts nodes are female-centred units, clusters of wives and their heirs. These nodes represent the points of impact of marriage alliances made by the homestead head. To understand the political dynamics of the great homesteads, one must therefore pay attention to the pattern of royal and noble marriages, and to the political position of leading women."[7] Kuper further explains, "[a]s the houses of new chiefs succeeded at the apex of the hierarchy, they propelled some peripheral houses of earlier regimes [previous generations] to the very edge of the royal family. After five generations they were extruded from the royal family and became marriageable.... More closely related royal houses did not intermarry, however, heirs were normally produced by wives who had been taken from outside the royal family."[8] In their roles as daughters, wives, and mothers, women created and reproduced important political ruling houses and alliances.[9]

Early European observers were aware of the political basis for the identity of chiefdoms and kingdoms, which did not correspond with cultural differences such as language and ritual practices because known polities comprised peoples of multiple languages and cultures, and people of the same language and cultural practices were dispersed over multiple political units. Nevertheless, these political units, chiefdoms, and kingdoms were elided into the European western concept of "tribe," which in turn was mistakenly presupposed to comprise only a single and entire linguistic and cultural population. Europeans' reification of cultural identities was the result of imperial, colonial, and missionary efforts to understand the people they were confronting, ruling, or proselytizing at that moment in time. These identities corresponded with a widespread European fascination with the pseudoscientific classification of race according to somatic or phenotype characteristics of people who were being encountered across the globe during the era of colonization. The pseudoscientific establishment of categories of race provided ideological support for colonial domination and racial discrimination and culminated in an extreme form: the formal implementation of apartheid policies of modern race-based domination in South Africa. The European definition of culture as timeless and primordial has never been the indigenous understanding of named identities associated with political and social authority and cultural attributes, notably language and ritual practices, that have always been described in oral tradition as changing and in flux. The persistence in South Africa of the misunderstanding and manipulation of reified cultural identities, which has long been discredited, prolonged the acceptance of these false claims of authority and entitlement whose goals were economic control and financial gain.[10]

The people living in the many small chiefdoms of KwaZulu-Natal at the beginning of the nineteenth century recognized that the processes of political amalgamation involved cultural change and cultural assimilation, however obscure these differences have been to modern observers.[11] By the twentieth century, the cultural heterogeneity of the original societies Shaka had incorporated into the Zulu kingdom had given way to strong cultural as well as social and political bonds of affinity and identification. Earlier understandings of and preferences for sociocultural differentiation were becoming lost to historical memory. But in the era of Shaka's reign, cultural assimilation was only beginning, and cultural homogeneity from a local perspective had not yet been achieved and could not serve as the basis for political unity. The Zulu kingdom was not only created but also sustained by force and the threat of force. Violence and fear underlay popular compliance with Shaka's governance and his deviation from past and accepted practices of leadership and rule prompted popular disaffection and discontent.

The association of the Zulu kingdom of the AmaZulu people with warfare has been well-established in the European understanding of the region since the time of Shaka. Europeans blatantly distorted the history of the region as they sought to justify European settlement and colonization in lands once ruled by Shaka. However, the broad picture conveyed by biased European sources of Shaka's use of violence in his foreign relations and his internal governance can be established and confirmed from indigenous AmaZulu historical sources.[12] The military organization established by Shaka persisted beyond his death, allowing the kingdom to survive under the rule of his half brothers Dingane, from 1828 to 1840, and Mpande, from 1840 to 1872. The process of unification was accomplished by means of violence and the threat of violence by Shaka's famous regiments sent on military expeditions, called *impi*s, within and beyond the borders of modern KwaZulu-Natal. During the twentieth century, the unification achieved by Shaka overshadowed the violence of the process and the harshness of his rule. However, a side comment about Shaka made by Magidigidi ka Nobebe to colonial magistrate James Stuart in 1905 reflects the understanding of those AmaZulu who had experienced the reign of Shaka and kept the oral traditions of the past. The AmaZulu of the early nineteenth century had inherited centuries of cultural practices, including laws and a judicial process upheld by chiefs, that embodied an adherence to the rule of law, practices that reflected social respect for life, family, property, and entitlement to land resources. Shaka, however, was remembered as achieving the unification of a kingdom under the rule of the AmaZulu chiefdom only by engaging in illegal acts, earning him the moniker, "the wrong-doer who knows no law."[13] His eventual assassination reflected a widespread discontent with the violence that he had come to inflict upon his own followers in the governance of the kingdom, and with few exceptions the accession of his half-brother Dingane was readily supported.

A primary goal of this book is to reconstruct as accurately as possible a chronological narrative of events surrounding the creation of the Zulu kingdom and the shifting social and political contexts in which those events occurred. In spite of the long-standing fascination of Europeans with the AmaZulu kingdom, in part because of its defeat of the British in battle in 1879, an historical study of KwaZulu-Natal in the era of Shaka's reign has not been previously produced using the entire range of oral and written sources for the era in accordance with current accepted practices in the discipline of history. This may be because an accepted version of the broad narrative of events was established in the nineteenth century that left a false impression that the political history of the AmaZulu kingdom under Shaka was already known and did not need to be revisited. In fact, to date our knowledge and understanding of the events and circumstances surrounding the consolidation of the AmaZulu kingdom by Shaka has been both limited and distorted because of unintentional misunderstanding as well as an inadequate consultation of oral histories and traditions.

In a seminal contribution, Carolyn Hamilton has written an incisive analysis of the transformation of the images and myths of Shaka from the time of his rule through the production of movie images in the 1980s.[14] In tracing both European and African perspectives and presentations of images of Shaka, she has demonstrated how these perspectives diverged widely among Africans who had been incorporated into the Zulu kingdom and how they had changed over the generations among Europeans, whose motives for purveying certain myths shifted with their political goals of colonization. Hamilton demonstrates that in spite of, or because of, the variations portrayed in images of Shaka, it has been impossible to suppress competing perspectives on Shaka in order to convey a single, hegemonic myth, whether positive or negative in its connotations. Literary scholar Dan Wylie has analyzed "white myths of Shaka."[15] The sequence of events associated with Shaka's consolidation of many small chiefdoms under AmaZulu rule has been known from European traders of the time.[16] Unfortunately, a reliance on the writings of missionary A. T. Bryant's work has persisted.[17] Modern scholars have perpetuated to the present day distortions in the European understanding of the history of events of the nineteenth century surrounding the emergence of the AmaZulu kingdom. These distortions have had unfortunate effects on modern politics that draw upon these false assessments of the region's political and cultural history. The outstanding work of Jeff Peires and Philip Bonner in recreating the history of the AmaXhosa and the

AmaSwazi by using recorded oral traditions has not been duplicated for the early history of the KwaZulu-Natal region, although John Wright has studied the region south of the Thukhela River.[18] In their essay, "Traditions and Transformations: The Phongolo-Mzimkhulu Region in the Late Eighteenth and Early Nineteenth Centuries," John Wright and Carolyn Hamilton devoted only a few pages to Shaka's reign.[19] In his more recent work, Wright has made a significant contribution in presenting evidence that the destruction of the region was more limited during Shaka's reign than has been commonly assumed and that it was other chiefs and chiefdoms rather than Shaka and the AmaZulu regiments that inflicted most of the damage that occurred.[20] However, Wright underestimates the damage inflicted on chiefdoms of the Natal region upon the orders and with the support of Shaka himself. Wright reiterates unsupported speculative assertions of an active slave trade out of Delagoa Bay in the late eighteenth and early nineteenth centuries that have been definitively overturned by the work of half a dozen historians.[21] Jeff Guy has raised important issues regarding the productive needs for herding that affected settlement and expansion patterns.[22] His work *The Destruction of the Zulu Kingdom* remains seminal and representative of the more extensive literature on Zulu history in the later nineteenth century and since.[23]

A number of scholars have explored the history of southern Africa in the era of Shaka's reign and after to consider both migrations and conflicts triggered by chiefdoms from KwaZulu-Natal as well as demographic and political turmoil caused by other factors during the same period, events sometimes denoted as the *mfecane* or, in the interior west of the Drakensberg, *lifaqane*.[24] Recent research has demonstrated both that demographic dislocations and sociopolitical consolidation into chiefdoms predated the era of Shaka both east and west of the Drakensberg. The research has also shown that these events were caused by a variety of factors both before and during Shaka's reign, and were not merely a consequence of the consolidation of the AmaZulu kingdom. Taken collectively, this recent scholarship on the eighteenth and early nineteenth centuries emphasizes multiple factors at play in demographic dislocations and social and political reorganization, including environment and trade.[25]

The relative neglect of the precolonial history of southern Africa, except for the historiography of the Cape Colony, has been recently noted by scholars seeking to renew interest in the area, hoping to regenerate interest in the region's early history.[26] John Wright's new contribution,

"Rediscovering the Ndwandwe Kingdom," draws attention to the possibilities for reconstructing a narrative of events but underscores how little has been done in the past three decades.[27] Wright traced the contemporary historical treatment of the AmaNdwandwe kingdom and presented a preliminary narrative of the kingdom based on secondary sources.[28] Wright has also made a close and careful reading of the evidence to establish a narrative of events concerning "The Thuli and Cele Paramountcies in the Coastlands of Natal, c. 1770–1820," which is almost entirely in accord with my reconstruction of these. He suggests, however, a more compressed time period for the events described.[29] Wright's overview of the entire region and period, "Turbulent Times: Political Transformations in the North and East, 1760s-1830s," written for the newly published *Cambridge History of South Africa*, of necessity relies exclusively on publications from twenty to thirty years ago, the most recent source cited being Hamilton's 1998 book on Shaka.[30] A 2009 book on *Zulu Identities: Being Zulu, Past and Present* contains numerous brief contributions by various historians, which provide important summaries and reiterations of the existing scholarship on the subject but do not contain any new contributions for the precolonial era.[31]

Some of the recent work that has been pursued for other areas of southern Africa suggests potential avenues of investigation and elaboration for the region of KwaZulu-Natal. With a focus on the southern African interior, Paul Landau has traced the process by which Europeans constructed the set of their accepted conceptions and misconceptions of "tribes" and of indigenous beliefs about and references to ancestors.[32] As elsewhere in Africa, he points out that "…the passage of successful *chiefs*, to *ancestors*, to *community self-identification*, to *oblivion* formed a kind of ideal cycle."[33] Thus, "…every so often an ancestor, nearer to the [contemporary] chief in time than the ancients, would give his name to a chiefdom, and the ancestral namesake which *had* been invoked would recede in favor of the more germane one."[34] A "500 Year Initiative" of archaeologists and historians studying southern Africa, launched in 2007, has borne fruit in the gradual reconciliation of archaeological evidence with historical evidence that is inevitably recorded oral evidence.[35]

Norman Etherington has produced a masterful reconstruction from an exhaustive range of both primary and secondary sources that covers the wider region. He links the events of the region of KwaZulu-Natal to the rest of southern Africa. However, Etherington is somewhat misled by relying on Bryant, leading Etherington, for example, to question the identity of the "Mbo."[36] Contrary to Etherington's assertion, this chiefdom known by the ruling line of descent did survive into the nineteenth century through its Mkhize branch under chief Zihlandlo and his brother Sambela. The oral traditions from within the region of KwaZulu-Natal collected in the late nineteenth and early twentieth centuries are definite and consistent about the identity of the "Embo" or "AbaMbo." The confusion about their identity derives, however, from Europeans and Africans living outside KwaZulu-Natal to the southwest and who could have been misled by rumors caused by the dramatic military role played by Zihlandlo's Mbo chiefdom in causing widespread demographic upheaval during Shaka's reign. The name of Zihlandlo's chiefdom was known as the Mkhize to distinguish it from other branches of his ruling line of descent that had created separate sociopolitical units, but their common ancestry and identity as Mbo continued to be known.

Because of the fascination with Shaka that has persisted for almost two centuries, studies on the era of his reign have primarily focused on his person and stories about him rather than on historical events themselves as studied by historians.[37] As a result of Carolyn Hamilton's work, we know more about the historical production of images of Shaka, as generated by both Africans and Europeans over a period of 150 years, than we do of the historical reality about him and the history of KwaZulu-Natal during the years of Shaka's rule. In the 1920s, James Stuart published selected individual accounts of oral traditions in children's school readers in the isiZulu language. These schoolbooks have left subsequent generations of African school children with the mistaken impression that the individual versions of oral traditions in these readers reflected an accepted version of the past, whereas Stuart chose for these schoolbooks the more fanciful and embellished versions of oral traditions without regard for whether they were accurate depictions of history traditions in order to engage his young readers. Educated but untrained readers, much less school children, cannot be expected to distinguish the many kernels of truth in these oral traditions from the literary embellishments given them in the spoken transmission of oral history and oral traditions.

In a second book, *Myth of Iron: Shaka in History*, Dan Wylie has produced an imaginative rendition of pieces of many of these oral traditions. However, his work reflects his training as a scholar of literature and mythology and he does not employ careful historical methodology in using oral history and traditions.[38] As entertaining as Wylie's approach may be to readers interested in the mythology of Shaka, unsuspecting readers should be aware of either his lack of awareness of or arbitrary disregard of serious historical scholarship. Evident historical mistakes are found throughout this work. Some of the important historical evidence is found in oral traditions and European records from outside of KwaZulu-Natal, including Lesotho and the Maputo Bay region, which imposes limitations on the research of scholars unable to conduct primary research in multiple languages. However, Wylie's choices of what information to report and what to omit seem arbitrary and capricious, perhaps designed to create a dramatic sense of literary myth, but unfortunately lacking in respect to the careful and systematic recreation of the past from all available sources. For example, in spite of the existence of numerous descriptions of Shaka's person and a full-body sketch portrait of him, Wylie asserts incorrectly that Shaka's appearance is unknown except for a description of his buttocks. Wylie has written an engaging literary interpretation of selected oral traditions, treating them as myth rather than as historical sources. However, Wylie has not succeeded in recreating the historical background and events of Shaka's life, to which he devoted considerable effort but which requires a consideration and weighing of all contradictory evidence with thoroughness. In his work, Wylie demonstrates the same failings for which he has criticized previous amateur historians of Shaka. Some of Wylie's observations about the fictionalized accounts written by A. T. Bryant and the early trader accounts that reflect obvious cultural distortions are incisive, but many are self-evident.[39] Wylie calls his own account of Shaka an "antibiography" because he considers that "[h]istory, in the end, is a creative literary medium. It tries to say something verifiable about the past, but the past is ultimately a construction of language; it's something imagined."[40] He asserts that "[v]irtually all cross-cultural attempts to convey the Zulu 'reality', inevitably inscribe the individual and cultural identity of the writer as powerfully as they describe the subject."[41] Wylie chooses to compare comments from the Stuart interviews describing Shaka's buttocks, to make a mistaken argument that because there is disagreement, information about Shaka's appearance is unknown. Wylie's choice of descriptions of Shaka's anatomy in order to explore problems of historical methodology do not further the project of historical reconstruction. Instead, Wylie's descriptions appear to reveal how his cross-cultural attempt to convey a "Zulu 'reality'" is inscribed by his own individual and cultural identity. Of the numerous comments describing aspects of Shaka's appearance that appear in these recorded oral testimonies, Wylie reveals a fascination with Shaka's sexuality and ignores all of the oral testimony about Shaka's appearance to make the declarative statement that "[w]e do not know what he looked like."[42] His own repeated dismissals of legitimate and valid African oral testimony appears to be implicitly, if unconsciously, derogatory and insulting. Wylie mimicked Bryant's paternalistic imaginative renditions of the AmaZulu and Shaka with fictionalized portrayals such as one of daily life in AD 1300.[43] Wylie conveys false connotations implicitly when he calls an encounter between Shaka and Senzangakhona "an Oedipal Moment" with its obvious sexual and incestuous connotations of the man Oedipus of ancient Greek mythology known for killing his father and marrying his mother. The inapplicability of this reference to Shaka is self-evident because he neither killed his father nor had a sexual relationship with his mother.[44] Wylie's dismissal of history as only something imagined has allowed him mistakenly to accept as true the false speculation that the AmaZulu engaged in slave raiding and slave trading but to deny the events of one of the most famous of the AmaZulu military expeditions, that against the AmaNdwandwe under Soshangane at the Balule (Olifant's) River in 1828 for which there is ample evidence.[45] Wylie presents information as objectively true when it suits his purposes, and arbitrarily dismisses evidence when it does not. He arbitrarily interposes his own conjectures as if they were accepted and factual. Nevertheless, Wylie should be credited for his attempt to go beyond the mere demonstration of the construction of myths of Shaka and to reconstruct an actual history of the events of the era with critical consideration of sources. His open presentation of contradictory evidence and his lengthy discussions of his assessments and reactions reflect the difficulties presented to an historian in attempting to reconcile conflicting sources. My conclusions differ from many of Wylie's about specific historical events because I assume that when multiple independent sources agree about an event and there is no evidence of deliberate distortions or unintentional error in the origins, transmission, or recording of the oral traditions, then the oral traditions are a reliable record with regard to points of agreement. When European sources agree with the oral record that has been independently transmitted, it is assumed that both sources are correct to the extent that they agree, although not in their details. In contrast, when an event has been reported in a written source of European origins but is not found in the oral sources, I do not assume that the European report is accurate unless other independent sources have confirmed it. However, I do not presume that oral traditions have been tainted by the objectionable racist attitudes and assumptions of Europeans who recorded them when there appears to be an accurate record of what they were told and when they do not appear to have had any motive to have altered it for their own purposes or interests.

The earliest European observers left written renditions of events about which they had been told and those events they themselves had witnessed. These reports vary in reliability but are critical historical sources. An English priest and Christian missionary, A. T. Bryant, was based at the Mariannhill Mission in Natal from 1883. He and a colonial magistrate of English descent, James Stuart, each began collecting oral histories that had been told to them in the course of their lives and work in the region of modern KwaZulu-Natal. Bryant's works are well known, and scholars have continued to rely upon them, in spite of the fact that all of his historical writings are from secondary sources that lack substantiation from primary sources. These works contain many assertions, such as his theories of migration, that have been definitively overturned by countervailing evidence. Bryant produced his own amateurish and flawed written histories during the early twentieth century based on the stories he had heard, but he was unsystematic and uncritical of his sources and openly allowed himself "poetic license" to embellish the stories with inventions of his own imagination. He explained this in writing to Stuart, who was appalled by the inaccuracies and distortions in Bryant's work because he was arbitrary in sometimes crediting some sources, and sometimes others. As Bryant himself admitted, his goal was to entertain a western European readership, which explains his use of openly fictional embellishments that are impossible to distinguish without carefully weighing the details of his stories and assertions against other sources. Bryant's short rendition of a history appeared as part of a dictionary in 1905. He later changed and expanded his historical narrative in *Olden Times in Zululand and Natal* that appeared in 1929.[46] The prominent ethnographer N. J. van Warmelo concluded that Bryant's theories of early cultural groups and their migrations were "not even worth repeating here. They are fanciful and do not meet the case."[47] Monica Wilson thoroughly criticized Bryant's work, including the validity of some of his most basic assumptions.[48] More recently, John Wright and Carolyn Hamilton have provided an incisive critique of the weaknesses of Bryant's work with regard to both his methodology and his historical analysis.[49] Wright demonstrated that Bryant did not make any original contribution to the historiography because he relied exclusively on secondary sources that had been already available.[50] Wright's new article, "A. T. Bryant and the 'Lala,'" underscores Bryant's failure to understand the meaning of names that he had consequently misidentified and misrepresented.[51] When James Stuart challenged Bryant about his theories of migration, Bryant conceded that his dictionary history "wants revision."[52] A 1929 letter from Bryant to Stuart provides critical evidence that the historical material in *Olden Times* should not be taken seriously.[53] In describing his newly published book, Bryant conceded to Stuart that his history contained "a dearth of solid historical stuff" comprising "frequent presentations of obvious trifles and historical inessentials with some levity and a sense of humour," a strategy he deliberately employed so "that a book so costly of production and so limited in appeal, should be made deliberately attractive to the great disinterested masses and so be made to sell."[54] Although Bryant used oral traditions as primary sources, his product is a series of secondary sources written by a missionary serving as an amateur historian. The usefulness of the results is undermined by his own arbitrary personal fictional additions, thus eliminating his writings as useful historical sources. Because it is so well known, Bryant's work left a legacy of mistaken assumptions about the early precolonial era that continues to be cited but has been successfully discredited numerous times.

Stuart similarly produced his own written summaries of history based on the oral traditions (passed down through one or more generations) and oral histories (firsthand accounts) he had personally collected. Unlike the case of Bryant's writings, it is not necessary for historians to rely upon these secondary sources because Stuart also left behind his extensive interview notes that are themselves primary sources.[55] Modern historians can therefore bypass Stuart's amateurish historical essays – most of which were left unpublished although some were presented as speeches in England in his later life – and still use the massive collection of interview notes now mostly available, published, and – when necessary – translated, by John B. Wright and by Colin Webb before his death after the first volumes.[56]

James Stuart, who conducted the AmaZulu oral interviews used in my research, was born in 1868 in Pietermaritzburg in the British colony of Natal. Because he was fluent in the isiZulu language, he became interpreter and clerk to the Resident Commissioner and Chief Magistrate in Pietermaritzburg.[57] In 1894, Stuart was sent as interpreter for the Acting British Consul in Swaziland. Within a year, he had become a Resident Magistrate himself and served in that capacity in several places in Zululand and Natal in the following years. Most of the Africans living in the region of Natal, then marked on its northern colonial boundary by the Thukela (Tugela) River, and in the Zulu kingdom to its north spoke dialects similar enough to be considered a single language now known as *isiZulu*.

Stuart's interest in the history of the AmaZulu people he administered arose from his need to understand the underlying circumstances in court cases he handled. He began questioning the man who served as his assistant and servant, Ndukwana, about the customs and history of the peoples of the region. Beginning with a few interviews in the late 1890s, Stuart interviewed more than 150 African men and a few women over the next twenty-five years, meticulously recording everything he was told by hand. This wealth of information remains a font of historical evidence because of his care to record accurately what he heard from the interviewees. His interview notes meet the accepted criteria for historians' use of oral histories and traditions: their origins and points of transmission can be checked from the texts themselves, the written record is an accurate rendition of what Stuart was told, and the evidence can be cross-checked from independent primary sources. Stuart's oldest informants had personal memories of Shaka and events during the rule of Shaka, ending when he was assassinated by his half brother Dingane in 1828. The portrayal of the entire body of recorded oral evidence collected by James Stuart as "tainted" ignores the evidence of the precision and accuracy with which Stuart recorded what he was told in the documents themselves regardless of his own personal racist and colonial biases that were virtually inevitable for a man of European descent born in colonial Natal in the second half of the nineteenth century.[58]

The history narrated in this book also rests on the oral testimony that was recorded in the notes and writings of Europeans ranging from the early traders Henry Francis Fynn and Nathaniel Isaacs to the colonial officials Theophilus Shepstone and James Stuart. The historical reconstruction of each event narrated has been done after the careful assessment of the reliability of each source and point of information. This assessment has been made with reference to other available primary sources passed down independently and to the motives and intentions of the original source and the European transmitter of the oral evidence as far as these can be determined. It has therefore been possible to retrace and write the history of the AmaZulu in the era of Shaka's rule with the detail and reliability found in works following the later history of the AmaZulu, moving well beyond the speculative and flawed theories and allegations of the past.

SOURCES AND THE WRITING OF THE HISTORY OF THE ZULU KINGDOM

Modern historians must rely in part on the writings of early Europeans who recorded their own observations and what they were told in their early travels through KwaZulu-Natal. Beginning in the sixteenth century, the first Europeans to pass through the region were shipwreck survivors, including Portuguese sailors, officers, civilian passengers, and slaves from the Far East on voyages between Europe and the far reaches of the Portuguese empire in India and beyond. These travelers left sporadic, vague, and – to Europeans of the early nineteenth century – tantalizing descriptions of the lands through which they passed and the people they met on their arduous overland travels to reach rescuers at Delagoa Bay or later at Cape Town. European trading vessels, mostly of Portuguese and, from the early seventeenth century, Dutch origins, had plied the Indian Ocean for centuries, and the Dutch settlement at Cape Town dated to 1652. The formal arrival of the British at Cape Town in 1795 and the permanent installation there of British colonial rule after a three-year hiatus in 1803–1806 inspired the interest of British traders in the southeastern African coast. Francis Farewell, having left British military service as a lieutenant, eventually made contact with Henry Francis Fynn, whose earliest trade venture was to Delagoa Bay in 1823. An exploratory voyage set out in early 1824 under their auspices. After an unsuccessful landing at St. Lucia, they found their way by ship to the bay farther south overlooked by white bluffs that they came to call Port Natal, the later site of modern Durban. Farewell was among the early European travelers and traders who published a few letters in the *Graham's Town Journal* before his untimely murder en route from the Cape Colony to Port Natal in 1829, a year after Shaka's death. The best known account of events, however, comes from Fynn, whose original diary was said to have been buried with his brother; he rewrote it a few years later and included additional material with the intention of publishing it.[59] He had not managed to do so by the time of his death in 1862, and his son gave the notes to James Stuart many years later. Stuart failed to finish the job of editing and publishing the manuscript, so D. McK. Malcolm saw to the final editing and publishing of the "Diary" in 1951.[60] At publication, the editors included with Fynn's diary other materials he had written: an "Historical Introduction"; an "Epilogue," taking the narrative of events to 1837; and "Additional Notes on History and Customs," a brief ethnography of the social and cultural practices he had observed among the AmaZulu and their neighbors in colonial Natal. Stuart noted that others had assisted Fynn in writing some of the additional materials. The text indicates that Fynn finished writing the contents of the "diary" section with perhaps the exception of one or two paragraphs between 1831 and 1833 before he received a letter from fellow trader Nathaniel Isaacs encouraging him to "make them [Chaka and Dingaans] out as blood thirsty as you can."[61]

Fynn does not seem to have been much influenced by the comment except for including a couple of sentences condemning Shaka, but his narrative is strongly sympathetic to the ordinary people he considered to be victims of Shaka's repression, reflecting his own strong personal attachment to the Natal African community among whom he informally married and in which he lived out most of his life.[62] In 1852 Fynn, by then the Assistant Resident Magistrate at Pietermaritzburg, having entered government (colonial) service in 1834, provided a statement on the "Ethnology of Natal, or, The History, Condition, and Government of Its Native Population" to a Native Commission hearing.[63] Writing in the first person, he provided both an "ethnology" as well as commentary about labor issues affecting the Cape Colony and Natal. He also stated that he had begun writing his "diary" notes upon his first arrival at Port Natal in 1824 and had completed them in 1834.[64] Fynn also exchanged correspondence with J. Centlivres Chase, who sent him extensive lists of questions in letters from 1829 and the early 1830s and who thanked Fynn for his notes. For his own diary, intended for publication, Fynn wrote that his goal was to provide "an insight into the revolutions the various tribes have undergone and the rise and progress of the Zulu nation" and that he was unable to include sufficient information about the character of Shaka even by citing instances of his atrocities.[65] Literary scholar Dan Wylie has written an excellent textual critique of Fynn's "diary" that examines his overt bias and distortions, notably his use of inflammatory language and exaggerations, which influenced virtually all later negative representations of Shaka.[66]

The presence of Fynn and the other Port Natal traders in this era when the Cape Colony had become part of the British Empire demonstrates that European knowledge about Africans beyond its borders was minimal. It also demonstrates that the demarcation of a temporal distinction between the "precolonial" and the colonial eras for KwaZulu-Natal was artificial in nature. Contrary to caricatures of this early trader found in the work of Wylie and others, Fynn's dealings with Shaka were complicated by Fynn's role in his familial relationships with the Africans among whom he lived and the intimate relations with African women who bore him children.[67] Although he arrived in the region with the sole intention of establishing and benefiting personally from trade networks between the Cape Colony and the region of KwaZulu-Natal, he entered into codependent relations with Africans in Natal who had been victims of Shaka and had fled from his rule. The roles of the Port Natal traders were ambivalent because they maintained permanent ties with the Cape Colony and their families there even as they built large establishments at Port Natal and, in Fynn's case, farther south. At Port Natal they lived as and were regarded as playing the role of local chiefs over those who sought refuge under their homestead-like paternalistic authority. This work employs the term *precolonial* to refer to KwaZulu-Natal before the formal imposition of British colonial rule and the formal creation of the Colony of Natal. That colony was exclusively located south of the Thukela River and did not originally include most of the territory that fell under the rule of the Zulu royal house. The influence of colonial expansion began to be felt in KwaZulu-Natal before the formal imposition of colonial rule, and the response to the colonial presence in the Cape Colony on the part of Shaka and his successor Dingane reflected deep ambivalence. Shaka expressed a desire both to enter into trade relationships with the British at the Cape Colony and to expand his formal authority and control up to and perhaps into the Cape Colony itself. From the perspective of Shaka and Africans living in the Zulu kingdom during his reign, the arrival of the Voortrekkers and future domination by Europeans was virtually inconceivable.

In 1836, Nathaniel Isaacs published his own book about his experiences as a trader based at Port Natal and told Fynn that his intent was to show the "treachery, and intrigues" of the two AmaZulu chiefs.[68] Isaacs first published his "journal" as lengthy contributions to the *South African Commercial Advertiser* between June and October 1832 before its appearance in book form with slight editorial changes.[69] He had traveled with Captain James King to the Cape of Good Hope in 1824 with plans to join him in trading for ivory on the "South East Coast of Africa," which they did in the wake of the efforts of Fynn and Farewell who had not been heard from since their departure from Cape Town. Captain King's boat, the *Mary*, was wrecked at Port Natal upon arrival, so he and Isaacs had to stay long enough to build a small boat for their return. They discovered that Fynn and Farewell were both safe and had begun trading inland; both men provided them their long boat to go seek help from Algoa Bay for the stranded crew. When the rescue vessel, the *H.M. S. Helicon*, arrived at Port Natal to rescue the crew, Isaacs was away on a trading trip to Shaka himself and was left stranded again, "mortified at losing so fine an opportunity to leave the country."[70] King departed but "returned in a few months in the schooner Ann with Mrs Farewell and a suitable present for Chaka and articles for trade" by which time Isaacs "had got quite reconciled to the place," having begun to learn the language. He stayed and proceeded to conduct a successful trade in ivory until the boat for King and Isaacs was completed at the Port in late 1827. At that point and under pressure from Shaka, King and Isaacs transported a mission of Shaka's representatives, headed by Sotobe, to Port Elizabeth. They stayed there for a few months while Shaka's military campaign against the AmaMpondo was launched, causing confusion and distrust among the Europeans in the Cape Colony. Isaacs and James King returned the emissaries safely, but soon thereafter King became ill and died, prompting Isaacs to leave once again because he had heard that Shaka had offered thirty elephant tusks as payment for killing him. After traveling to Cape Town and from there to St. Helena where he recuperated from exhaustion, Isaacs returned to Port Natal in 1830 and rejoined Fynn in the ivory trade, prompting their correspondence and Isaac's efforts to inspire the extension of British colonial rule to Natal through the publication of his journal.

In 1826, the small Port Natal trader community was joined by a young teenage boy, Charles Rawden Maclean, whom they called "John Ross," Fynn's name for him. On Maclean's first trip with Captain King and other members of their trading party to meet Shaka, the group was regaled with ceremonies and by warriors. On the third day, the group requested permission to return to Port Natal. Shaka agreed to this with the exception that the young boy Maclean whom Shaka said "could be of no use in the construction of the *umkhumbi* [boat]. I should remain with him [Shaka] to explain the use and administer the medicine to patients." Later Maclean wrote that on this pretext "[h]e determined on keeping me with him."[71] The young teenage boy stayed with Shaka against his will, but as a result, we have some of the most important insights on the workings of society and governance in Shaka's capital during the later years of his reign. Maclean, who claimed to be fourteen but could have been as young as ten when he arrived on King's ill-fated boat in 1825, spent three years living in the region during which time he developed a strong affection for the Africans among he lived, both at Shaka's capital and around Port Natal. Shaka insisted John Ross be left at the capital, Bulawayo, where he was given free rein to visit even the women's quarters because of his youth and perceived innocence. Fynn noted that when the traders needed to send someone on an overland three hundred-mile return trip to Delagoa Bay for medicine, they sent "John Ross" with an escort provided by Shaka who offered the protection because John Ross had lived for some time, involuntarily, with Shaka.[72] Maclean made the brief overland trip of several weeks to the Portuguese settlement at Delagoa Bay in 1827, when he was between twelve and sixteen years old, leaving him with vivid memories about which he later wrote. He spent his adult life engaged in trade on vessels that made the rounds of Atlantic Ocean ports including those in the United States and the Caribbean where he eventually settled and was buried. His youthful memories persisted. In his later writings, he referred to his "old friends the Zulus" whom he had met when he was thirteen years old, hoping his "old native friends will yet recollect the little Mlungu" (i.e., white child) who had lived among them.[73] Maclean's account therefore carries great credibility, and he related what he had heard from the old men, who "take a pleasure in raking up the memory of the past, and of conversing on subjects that engrossed their attention in their youthful days."[74] The old men had told him about "the early wars of Shaka" in which they had fought as well as the oral traditions they themselves had heard from their own fathers that Maclean feared would not be remembered. He viewed Shaka as "brilliant" in war but an "extraordinary savage" to whose spontaneous brutality against his own people Maclean had been an eyewitness.

The early history of the region was not only told to early European visitors but also passed down within African communities in the form of oral traditions told to their children and grandchildren. Fynn, Isaacs, and Maclean/Ross wrote down the oral traditions they had heard as well as their own personal observations. However, Africans continued to pass down memories of old traditions and of new more recent experiences in the forms of stories. Longer narratives were sometimes remembered and retold without embellishment but sometimes had acquired fictional elements that enhanced their entertainment value to audiences. Praise poetry was always limited in historical value and the explanation of events but emphasized the characters and actions of the people whom they praised in enhanced, embellished, and dramatic forms that appealed to the values and expectations of audiences of that time. They accepted the exaggerations as emphasis rather than fact. But the value of these oral sources and the oral history told by eyewitnesses and participants is enormous in the reconstruction of events and their causes and consequences in early KwaZulu-Natal. The early colonial administrator Theophilus Shepstone had acquired the language skills he needed to converse directly with Africans during his years in the Transkei region before moving to colonial Natal. In the 1840s he focused his attention on learning the early history to understand the identities and histories of peoples in both regions who had been dislocated in the 1810s and 1820s.[75] His summary of the oral history he was told from eyewitness participants and of the oral traditions from earlier periods was based on multiple interviews he and one or two others conducted. The information resulting from those interviews that were eventually published provide a careful assessment of the location of various Natalian families, chiefs, and chiefdoms in the 1830s and 1840s as well as their earlier locations. Limited in scope to the region south of the Thukela River because it was accepted then as the colonial border with the Zulu kingdom to its north, the map he produced is a meticulous reproduction of residency for that period, and the accompanying text, although sparse, appears to be an accurate summary of what he was told and accords with oral traditions from other sources.[76] At the end of this "Historic Sketch," Shepstone signed it as "'Secretary for Native Affairs'" with the designation "Office of Secretary for Native Affairs, Pietermaritzburg, Natal, January 18, 1864." Shepstone wrote his "Historic Sketch" and an accompanying 'despatch' of the histories of ninety-four "tribes" that had inhabited the area of modern Natal (i.e., south of the Thukela River), based on interviews he conducted in 1863, sent to London in 1864, and later published in three sources, the first appearing in the report of a Cape government commission in 1883. Shepstone interviewed at least fourteen individuals who had been born in the late eighteenth or early nineteenth century and had personal memories of events during Shaka's reign. When Shepstone wrote these notes in 1863, documents written by Lewis Grout for an 1852–1853 Natal government commission and by James Perrin, appointed as a clerk in Shepstone's office in 1853, were already available. Perrin had begun collecting information from the time of his arrival in Natal in 1849 and compiled his own interview notes. Grout used evidence from at least thirty interviews of Africans of whom he names thirteen.[77]

These early interviews were of people who had directly experienced the events and circumstances of the 1810s and 1820s with the insights and distortions that participant testimonies can include. From the 1890s to 1920s, Stuart interviewed men and a few women who were primarily the children and grandchildren of people who had lived during Shaka's reign, but some had been old enough to have personal memories of the 1820s. By the time Stuart conducted his interviews, the setting had changed dramatically with the arrival beginning in the 1860s of a strong influx of settlers from Great Britain, sponsored by the colonial government, and indentured servants from India. At that time, the territory and independence of the Zulu kingdom had been slowly whittled away. Stuart's assistant, Ndukwana ka Mbengwana, answered his questions in dozens of interviews between October 1897 and October 1903 and was present at most of the early interviews from those years. Most of Stuart's interviewees were men whom he invited to his home and treated as guests, uncommon for Europeans of that era. These interviewees returned Stuart's evident respect in kind and marveled at the wealth of knowledge he had accumulated about their own history. His notes show evidence that Stuart challenged the interviewees with questions of detail and issues of inconsistency, and they responded sometimes with a defense of their information or long joint discussions of the discrepancies. This form of interview has the advantage of asking those with the most knowledge to reconsider all available evidence and assess it even though this process can lead to "feedback" problems when later generations repeat oral traditions and information provided by someone like Stuart is newly incorporated into an old "tradition." However, a careful reading of the interview notes according to the chronological dates of the interviews reveals the absence of this problem within this corpus of evidence. Stuart's interviewees were very aware and explicit about revealing the sources of their information from persons about the period predating Stuart's earliest interviews. The evidence from two or three interviewees sometimes overlapped because their original sources were the same person or persons, such as a father or a prominent person, but Stuart's occasional interventions in relating evidence from one interviewee to another does not seem to have affected their own adherence to their evidence and narratives learned from within their own communities. Similarly, although a few interviewees had been educated within the small African Christian community, this seems to have had little or no impact on their retelling of indigenous oral traditions as they had been told to them. The men and women who provided the evidence were primarily knowledgeable about their own communities and the chiefdoms from which they hailed as well as the more famous stories about Shaka and AmaZulu military exploits that involved men and regiments from across the region involved in the same sequence of events. Many of Stuart's interviewees were familiar only with the later period of history during the reigns of Dingane, Mpande, and Cetswayo, indicating how critical it was that Stuart recorded the early traditions when he did so that they were not lost to later generations. The history as reconstructed in the chapters that follow is pieced together primarily from these interviews and from the contemporaneous European reports from European eyewitness travelers and traders.[78]

The organization of this book is both chronological and thematic with attention to the political, military, and social changes that emerged during the eleven or twelve years of Shaka's rule. This chapter has surveyed the historiography of KwaZulu-Natal and the era of Shaka's reign and provides evidence about the primary sources of both African and European origin that are used in this study. After a brief survey of historical events in the region prior to the nineteenth century, Chapter 2 examines the most powerful chiefs and chiefdoms in the region of modern KwaZulu-Natal just before Shaka usurped the AmaZulu chieftaincy, providing a context for understanding the many precedents for sociopolitical consolidation in southeast Africa prior to Shaka's reign. Chapter 2 also analyzes the demise of the AmaMthethwa chiefdom of Dingiswayo in 1817 and of the AmaNdwandwe chiefdom of Zwide in 1821, which eliminated the major impediments to Shaka's expansionism. Chapters 3 and 4 explore the oral traditions of Shaka's early life, and his life as a warrior. Chapter 5 considers the early process of the expansion of the AmaZulu chiefdom and the chiefs and chiefdoms of KwaZulu-Natal who engaged in battles and migrations after 1817 that led to demographic turmoil, violent confrontations, and political reconfiguration. The chapter that follows examines the confrontations between the AmaZulu and more powerful chiefs within KwaZulu-Natal, elucidating contests over power and authority and the means by which Shaka expanded political control through both voluntary submission and the use of military force. Chapter 7 chronicles the events of the middle years of Shaka's reign, 1824–1827, including his first major military campaign to the south against the AmaMpondo chiefdom, the arrival of European traders at Port Natal, an assassination attempt against Shaka and the violent repercussions that followed, and two more major military campaigns in 1826 and 1827. Chapter 8 examines the role of royal women in positions of authority. Chapter 9 examines African perspectives found in the oral traditions of the early cultural diversity and variations among the peoples who later were incorporated into the AmaZulu kingdom, and elucidates the use of oral traditions in the reconstruction of history. Chapter 10 includes an assessment of social reconfiguration under Shaka's rule, and considers his methods and actions in governing the people in his kingdom. The chapter explores Shaka's controversial use of violence and executions to support his authority and gain compliance through fear, which explains the popular disillusionment that eventually surfaced and led to his assassination. Chapter 11 examines evidence of Shaka's expansionist ambitions in the direction of the Cape Colony. A diplomatic mission of an emissary from Shaka to the Cape Colony coincided in 1828 with his second major military campaign against the AmaMpondo to the southwest. This was construed as the cleansing or purification campaign marking the one-year anniversary of his mother's death. After creating confusion and havoc in the Transkei region and upon their return to KwaZulu-Natal, Shaka ordered his troops to continue immediately on a second major military campaign into the region of southern Mozambique to the north. The distress of his people, including his half brothers and counselor, led to his assassination in September 1828. Shaka's legacy was an unstable but unified kingdom that endured more stresses under the erratic rule of his half brother and heir Dingane and that developed a reputation for cruelty and ferocity that clung to the people of KwaZulu-Natal thereafter. Chapter 12 therefore concludes with an exploration of early Cape Colony perspectives on Shaka and the AmaZulu, and an assessment of the aftermath of his assassination and Dingane's succession. The chapter also includes an analysis of the levels of mortality that accompanied the creation of the AmaZulu kingdom under Shaka's rule. The analysis ends with an assessment of various historical controversies that have persisted in the historiography of the period and an attempt to lay them finally to rest. The study of the emergence of an AmaZulu kingdom under Shaka provides significant insights into the construction of an AmaZulu identity in the nineteenth and twentieth centuries and the processes by which politics and culture intersect in the formation of modern "ethnic" identities. The contests for control over material resources, wealth, and political authority that were evident in the competition between chiefs and chiefdoms in precolonial southern Africa have persisted in new forms of "ethnic"-based identity and "ethnicity" that are the political and cultural residue of the chiefdoms and kingdoms of the past.

Chapter 2

Powerful Chiefs Before Shaka

The two great chiefs in the old days, just before Tshaka's fusion of the tribes into one nation, were Zwide and Dingiswayo.[1]

The Mtetwa made war over the whole country, and the Ndwandwe too.[2]

In what was to become the Zulu country, there were many chiefs, each ruling on his own. Each lived separated from the others, including Senzangakona. The Mbata, Butelezi, Ntombela, Mtetwa, Ndwandwe, Qwabe, iLangeni, Mpungowe, and eMbo, together with the people of many other territories (*izifunda*) all lived separately. Some chiefs, like Senzangakona of the Zulu and Nkomo ka Tshandu ka Ndaba ka Mbungela of the Mbata had *konza*'d [*ukukhonza*, i.e. submitted, given allegiance and become subordinate and tributary] to Dingiswayo.[3]

Shaka was not the first chief to achieve domination over a large territory in modern KwaZulu north of the Thukela River, but rather he adopted strategies and tactics, including military, from his lesser-known predecessors in the area. In the region north of the Thukela River in the last quarter of the eighteenth century, the largest and most powerful chiefdoms were those of the AmaHlubi of Chief Bhungane, the AmaMthethwa (*abakwa*Mthethwa) of Chief Dingiswayo, the AmaNdwandwe of Chief Zwide, and the AbaQwabe of Chief Khondlo. In the second half of the eighteenth century, the AmaHlubi chiefdom northwest of the Zulu heartland gained fame for peaceful expansion under Chief Bhungane, the AmaNdwandwe chiefdom northeast of Senzangakhona's chiefdom began challenging chiefdoms to the north and south of its base at the Magudu hills, and the AmaMthethwa chiefdom consolidated authority over neighboring chiefdoms, the AmaZulu among them. The young chief of the

AmaMthethwa, Dingiswayo, had usurped the chieftaincy from a brother after years of exile and travel among the AmaHlubi and elsewhere, and had come back and introduced a military system based on the recruitment of all young men into age-based regiments that he used to compel the submission of neighboring chiefdoms to his rule.

Processes of political consolidation had also intensified south of the Thukela River in the second half of the eighteenth century. In about 1750, several AmaThuli chiefs led their followers in a migration from north of the Thukela River across it to the south, accompanied by several smaller groups. This migration was accompanied by considerable violence as remembered in oral traditions of these events, for pre-existing chiefdoms south of the Thukela were attacked, deprived of their wealth, and driven from their lands, and in some cases brutally killed.[4] The AmaMbili and AmaKomo were said to have accompanied the AmaThuli. According to one oral tradition, Chief Dole, who led the initial AmaThuli migration, was remembered as "a Marauder" who "impaled children on posts and drove the occupants of the lands off."[5] Chief Myebu led another branch of AmaThuli south across the Thukela. The AmaThuli are said to have defeated the people they encountered by the use of stabbing spears in hand-to-hand fighting in close quarters; this was more than two generations before Shaka adopted their use after 1815. Among the people the AmaThuli found living south of the Thukela River were the AmaMpofana with a fishing-based economy along the Mhlatuzana and Mlazi rivers. They were among the most prominent groups driven south upon their arrival. Others driven out of the region of modern colonial Natal (i.e., south of the Thukela River) were the AmaJali, AmaNtshangawe, im'Zindhle, AmaKanyawo, ImiTwana, and AmaCi. A section of AbaTembu related to those living north of the Thukela but who were established near the site of modern Durban became tributary to the AmaThuli upon their arrival.[6] The group that came to be called AmaZuba were originally AmaThuli, and the AmaLuthuli are from the same ancestral line of descent.[7]

Shortly after the AmaThuli migration in about 1750, the AmaCele (*abakwa*Cele) chiefs also led their followers from their home near the AmaMthethwa chiefdom south across the Thukela River. The AmaCele migrated under the leadership of their chief Mkokeleli, who was said to have engaged in fighting upon his arrival in the region of modern Natal, but he allowed those he defeated to enter into subordinate tributary relationships with him instead of driving them out. Those who accepted tributary status included the AmaNdhlovu, AmaNgati, AmaMganga,

AmaMbili, AmaTshange, AmaNxamala, AmaNhloko, AmaZomi, AmaNdelu, AmaNlongwa, "and others." The AmaThuli chief near the site of Port Natal also submitted to Mkokeleli's rule, and the AmaCele and AmaThuli chiefly families intermarried.[8] The AmaThuli chief's son Dibandhlela was well-established by the end of the century.[9] Some AmaCele remained behind in the region that became modern Zululand, and those who migrated south of the Thukela entered into close relations via marriage with the AmaThuli there. Two generations later (i.e., about 1800) additional AmaCele segments that had originally migrated north to live near the AmaTembe of the Delagoa Bay area joined their relations south of the Thukela in a second migration.[10]

In the mid-nineteenth century, Theophilus Shepstone summarized what he had learned from many sources and provided an apt description of the sociopolitical setting in KwaZulu-Natal a half-century earlier. Describing chiefdoms as "tribes," he wrote what appears to be a fairly accurate summary that depicts the social and political setting of the time.

Towards the close of the last [eighteenth] century, the two countries at present known as the Colony of Natal and Zululand, were thickly inhabited by numerous Native Tribes closely located together, intermarrying with each other, and living generally in terms of peace and friendship; they possessed cattle, sheep, and a small kind of goat, and cultivated the soil, from which they mainly drew their subsistence.

Each Tribe had its own Chief, who although ruling as a sort of patriarch, possessed and exercised the power of life and death. In those days domestic quarrels were more frequent than inter-tribal ones; arising mostly out of disputes about succession between members of the Chiefs' families.

Tribal quarrels of course also occurred, in some cases periodically; but the wars arising out of them seldom lasted longer than a few days; or as the native describe it, 'an army never slept away from its home,' and never, within the territory now known as the Colony of Natal, did war cause the destruction of a Tribe; one battle, such as it was, usually terminated the dispute; and it not unfrequently happened, that young warriors whose addresses had been paid to girls of the Tribe with which they had been fighting, sent home their shields from the field of battle by their friends, and returned with their late foes to prosecute their love suits; the lives of women and children were respected, prisoners taken in battle were not put to death, but detained till ransomed; and victory, rather than plunder and devastation, seems to have been the great object of these encounters.[11]

Oral traditions retained and retold by the AmaZulu in the early nineteenth century chronicled people and events dating back generations and centuries, showing remarkable continuity in genealogies that indicated lines of descent of chiefly families of southeastern Africa from the fifteenth century AD and in some cases much earlier. The genealogies were accompanied by scanty information about people and events in the early centuries. Fuller narratives and details, however, were retained about the eighteenth century, reflecting an indigenous awareness that there were ample precedents for the more recent and dramatic emergence of a kingdom under Shaka after he usurped the chieftaincy of the AmaZulu in 1817. Shaka's father Senzangakhona absorbed two or three smaller chiefdoms under the AmaZulu chiefdom during his reign from the 1870s until his death in 1816 or 1817 but was himself tributary and subordinate to the chief of the AmaMthethwa, Dingiswayo. Dingiswayo's history has remained well known because of his influence on Shaka, who as a young man had sought refuge with the AmaMthethwa along with a significant group of his maternal eLangeni relatives who had been forced out by a struggle over their own chieftaincy sometime soon after the turn of the nineteenth century. Dingiswayo had by then extended his overrule across a region encompassing the lowlands along the coast inland far enough to include the AmaZulu heartland and south along the coast to the Thukela River to include the AmaCele chiefs and peoples.[12] AmaMthethwa expansion from the Black Mfolozi and their lowland coastal homeland gave rise to their identification as *eZansi*. This expansion was constrained to the north by the strength of the AmaNdwandwe chiefdom centered at the Magudu hills, which was itself in competition with the AmaNgwane proto-Swazi chiefdom with whom the AmaNdwandwe were genealogically related, that was also located in the vicinity of the Phongolo River. Westward of the AmaMthethwa were the AmaNgwane under Chief Matiwane who vied with the AmaHlubi of Chief Bhungane, an even larger and stronger chiefdom of renown that was situated just beyond the AmaNgwane to their west and northwest. Between the territory of the AmaNdwandwe and the AmaNgwane of Matiwane (not to be confused with the AmaNgwane-AmaSwazi) was the smaller AmaKhumalo chiefdom that gained fame under its recalcitrant chief, Mzilikazi, in the era of Shaka's reign, when Mzilikazi rebelled with his people and absconded with captured cattle from a raid instead of sending them to the royal AmaZulu herds. Just southwest of the AmaMthethwa heartland was the capital of the AbaQwabe chiefdom under Chief Phakathwayo at the Ngoye hills. From their home near the White Mfolozi where the graves of their chiefs marked the long duration of their residence in the region, the descendants of an ancestor named Zulu sustained the AmaZulu chiefdom under Senzangakhona, but it remained small during the era of Chief Dingiswayo and his peers, Bhungane, Zwide, and Phakathwayo.

THE AMAHLUBI CHIEFDOM

Chief Bhungane ka (son of) Nsele ka Matshiyi traced his family's genealogy as chiefs of the AmaHlubi to at least 1500 AD.[13] Oral traditions indicate the AmaHlubi chiefdom had originated at the Lebombo mountains of eastern Swaziland. The AmaHlubi had close relations and may have had ancestral links with the AmaNgwane AmaSwazi, who remembered a royal heir named Hlubi many generations earlier when they were also based in the Lebombo mountains. Following a period of food shortages, as the oral traditions recounted, the AmaHlubi chiefs with their adherents migrated to the Newcastle district, and the graves of the early ancestral chiefs were known to be near Alcock Spruit. Nsele himself had been buried at the Mzinyati at eMange. Bhungane was remembered as having had a very long reign, and he maintained a friendly relationship with Dingiswayo and the AmaMthethwa from whom the AmaHlubi purchased grain that they did not grow themselves.[14]

Bhungane's chiefdom encompassed a large enough territory that Dingiswayo was said to have visited him personally to find out how he had "overcome nations," and Bhungane is said in the oral traditions to have provided Dingiswayo with wisdom, including the knowledge of "medicines," or *izintelezi*, to strengthen oneself and weaken one's enemies. By the time Shaka began his rule over the small and still subordinate AmaZulu chiefdom, Bhungane had died. After a contested decision his son Mthimkhulu inherited the chieftaincy and his younger brother Mpangazitha retained his own followers and villages as a strong segment nominally subject to overrule by the senior line represented by Mthimkhulu. This large but peaceful chiefdom overshadowed Dingiswayo's AmaMthethwa at the time Dingiswayo assumed the chieftaincy but could not withstand the turmoil that would ensue following Shaka's accession and expansion.

In 1821, the nearby AmaNgwane chiefdom under Chief Matiwane attacked the AmaHlubi and Mthimkhulu was killed. Each of Mthimkhulu's two brothers led a large segment of the chiefdom to seek a site for resettlement west of the Drakensberg, and Mpangazitha re-established his branch of followers near the Caledon valley. There Mpangazitha's followers raided the local populations until he was defeated and killed in 1824 or 1825 by Matiwane who had led his own followers west in the wake of the recent AmaHlubi migration. Many of the defeated AmaHlubi were absorbed into the AmaNgwane chiefdom after their defeat, but the AmaNgwane chiefdom itself survived only a few years longer before being broken apart after a move to the Transkei. At the time of the original defeat and breakup of the AmaHlubi into several large sections in 1821, however, other members of the AmaHlubi royal family chose to give their allegiance to Shaka, who placed them with their followers in his mother Nandi's village. He allowed them to form a regiment, the Iziyendane, that would become renowned for its ferocity. The subjects of the AmaHlubi chiefs Bhungane and Mthimkhulu were thus dispersed in many directions in the 1820s, and not until after Shaka's death did many gradually return to their original home territory in the northwestern area of modern KwaZulu.

THE AMAMTHETHWA AND DINGISWAYO

The AmaMthethwa had lived since their ancestral memory from territory high up on the Black Mfolozi to as far as the coast and were known as the people of the lowlands. During Dingiswayo's reign, they were centered in the territory south of the Black and White Mfolozi rivers and the territory over which Dingiswayo ruled extended to a boundary on the Mhlatuze river.[15] Probably born in the mid-1860s, Dingiswayo had not been the uncontested heir to the chieftaincy and had spent his early adulthood in exile after conspiring, it was believed, to usurp the chieftaincy from his father Jobe. In Shepstone's version of events, Jobe was said to have chosen Dingiswayo's brother Tana as his heir, and the two brothers conspired together against their father.[16] This account indicates that an heir was not known from the time of birth, that being the eldest did not necessarily confer the inheritance of office to a chief's son, and that the incumbent chief had the power to appoint his successor during his lifetime. This version of events also indicates there had been more than one royal kraal among the AmaMthethwa before Dingiswayo's time, indicating it was a relatively large chiefdom before he expanded it. When the plot against Chief Jobe was discovered, he ordered both sons be put to death, leading to Dingiswayo's dramatic escape, flight, and life in exile until after his father's death. Various stories told by both AmaZulu and Europeans throughout the nineteenth century insisted that during this time when he was still called Godongwana, Dingiswayo had sought refuge from several nearby chiefs before traveling as far as the eastern Cape. Europeans believed that after seeing the bayonets on the end of the rifles of British colonial soldiers there, Dingiswayo conceived the idea of using spears for stabbing rather than throwing.[17] The AmaMthethwa oral traditions also remembered him as having returned at the same time that they first saw a horse, and some stories say it was he who had brought the horse.[18]

According to Shepstone's information, when Dingiswayo, still known as Godongwana, returned from exile to contest the chieftaincy, "the reigning Chief fled with a portion of the people, but Godongwana eventually overcame him and put him to death." In establishing his authority, Shepstone had been told that "he [Dingiswayo] met with opposition from some of his father's tributaries [tributary chiefs], but he at length made himself undisputed master of the Umtetwa power." Other sources agree with Shepstone that at that point, he changed his name to Dingiswayo, said to connote "the Wanderer" or "he who was caused to wander." Fynn believed that Dingiswayo was about 25 years old in 1795 when he began his reign, although he was born in about 1760–1765 and so was probably a little older.[19]

The AmaHlubi chiefdom is one of several places where Dingiswayo is said to have found temporary refuge during his years of exile, and the oral traditions have strong evidence that he visited there at least once – either at the time of his exile or after he had returned and taken over the AmaMthethwa chieftaincy – and then went to seek advice from Chief Bhungane.[20] There is no evidence, however, that Dingiswayo ever entered into a tributary subordinate relationship with Bhungane. Mabonsa ka Sidhlayi commented, "[t]he Hlubis blame themselves now for having educated Dingiswayo."[21]

The AmaMthethwa had already achieved regional dominance under Jobe prior to Dingiswayo's accession to power, so Dingiswayo had to overcome opposition to the re-establishment of AmaMthethwa over-rule and dominance in the region.[22] The men who related the oral traditions to Stuart decades later agreed that Dingiswayo had initiated significant political changes across the region by means of warfare to accomplish the territorial expansion under his rule. One said, "at first Dingiswayo defeated all the country." He explained to Stuart that "his [Dingiswayo's] mode of conquest or warfare was to go, then halt, and so on and on by degrees, following or driving his enemy for many miles; in consequence of this perpetual pursuit the women would 'get tired' and return, whereupon the fleeing people, on account of their women, would be forced to surrender."[23] Dingiswayo did not kill the chiefs who surrendered, however, and his use of armed forces did not result in high levels of violence.[24] Nevertheless, the incorporation of these small chiefdoms under his rule led one man to say of Dingiswayo, "he killed all the nations."[25]

After he returned to the AmaMthethwa and usurped the chieftaincy during the 1790s, Dingiswayo expanded trade with Delagoa Bay that had already begun to bring in beads and other goods in exchange for cattle and ivory.²⁶ Fynn reported that Dingiswayo suppressed previous barbarous customs in war and conceded that

> By means of the strong natural capabilities of which he was possessed, he succeeded in raising himself and his people above all other tribes along the coast, while his ingenuity as a mechanic and the mildness of his rule, although a despotic chief, the ability displayed in the military system he introduced, as well as his universal kindness, so endeared him with the people, that he will be revered by them as long as the Zulu nation exists.²⁷

Fynn listed the chiefdoms conquered by Dingiswayo as the "Qwabe, Langeni, Qadi, Zulu, Ntshali, Buthelezi, Kuyiwane, Thembu, Swazi and the Xhosa," although he must have known this was inaccurate regarding the distant and independent AmaSwazi and AmaXhosa.²⁸ Dingiswayo is said to have sent his forces to attack Malusi of the AmaNxumalo (branch of the AmaNdwandwe) and against Phakathwayo in a battle fought at the Mhlatuze while Shaka was serving in Digniswayo's military. It was on the occasion of this battle that Dingiswayo was said to have called Shaka, who was "then called Sikiti," by the praise name "the axe that surpasses other axes," saying he was one "who is not beaten."²⁹ However, Dingiswayo was also dismayed that Shaka had disregarded his instructions not to enter the battle and that he had used wanton violence in battle.³⁰ Fynn wrote that Dingiswayo "gave his commanders strict orders not to allow the whole of the tribe's property to be plundered, and to destroy no more people than was absolutely necessary. His superior discipline, to which neighbouring tribes were unaccustomed, insured his success."³¹ Nevertheless, he evidently did not tolerate insubordination from chiefs who were considered to be tributary and subordinate. Senzangakhona complied with payment of tribute in the form of cattle, but Dingiswayo was said to have had another subordinate chief, Nkomo of the AmaMbata, put to death "because he did not hold a dance for Dingiswayo or make him a present of cattle," even though he made a formal visit to Dingiswayo in the company of Senzangakhona.³²

> Dingiswayo attacked the Qwabe many times, always driving them into the Ntumeni forests. He also attacked the Nyuswa tribe, chasing them away. Dingiswayo, however, never attacked the Langa people, for reasons best known to himself.³³

The AmaMthethwa would seize goats for food from villages that they passed on military campaigns and would enter peoples' homes to drink the curdled milk from their gourds, demonstrating that "they considered themselves the masters of the countries they passed through."³⁴

THE ABAQWABE AND CHIEF PHAKATHWAYO

Chief Qwabe had established the AbaQwabe chiefdom at the Ngoye hills in about 1600 AD. Because of their location near the coast, "[t]he Qwabe people were spoken of by the Zulus and other northern tribes as those from down-country [*a ba se zansi*]."[35] In addition to their distinction as belonging to a political unit ruled by a member of the founding chief's line of descent, AbaQwabe descendants were still distinguishable as late as the early twentieth century because, as Stuart was told, "[a] characteristic of the Qwabe people is that they *tefula*", i.e., they spoke a dialect characterized by specific uses of consonants in otherwise similar regional languages labeled "Nguni" by modern linguists.[36] By the second half of the eighteenth century, the AbaQwabe were ruled by Chief Khondlo, and in that era, some AbaQwabe under Mnengwa ka Makanya migrated to south of the Thukela River. Since then, the AbaQwabe had lived on both sides of the Thukela.[37] Khondlo was the son of Mncinci ka (son of) Lufuta ka Simamane ka Kuzwayo ka Sidinane ka Mahlomo (or Mahlobo).[38] The royal family remained at the Ngoye hills, and Khondlo married a sister of the AmaMthethwa chief Dingiswayo. She bore his eldest son Nomo, and another wife of Ngadi origins bore his son Phakathwayo. Upon reaching adulthood, Nomo and Phakathwayo engaged in a succession dispute over the chieftaincy.

Mmemi ka Nguluzane, of AbaQwabe origins, told Stuart "[o]ur tribe was a peaceful one, not like the Zulus, who were warlike. The only blood [bloodshed] that began with us [AbaQwabe] was in the time of Nomo, when Khondlo wished to make him his son and heir."[39] Other versions suggest that Khondlo did not support Nomo as his heir, however. Mbovu ka Mtshumayeli told Stuart that a quarrel arose between the Ntoleleni and oDwini villages of Phakathwayo and of Nomo over a small ox with large horns called ULovu. Mbovu commented that the ox named ULovu "may have been the ox of the gourd, of the *tshwama* ceremonies, seeing it was the cause of so great a quarrel."[40] The presentation of a single ox of particular appearance was commonly used to signify the offering and acceptance of an alliance between two chiefs, so the symbolic purpose of the ox used in a ceremony to signify seniority would have indicated that the inheritance to the chieftaincy itself was implicitly at stake. The actual sequence of events was remembered as having been initiated when Phakathwayo's men attempted to raid the cattle of the AbaQwabe under Mnengwa ka Makanya, south of the Thukela River. The Makanya successfully defended their cattle, and subsequently Nomo attacked

Phakathwayo and drove his people from their homes. Mbovu related this story to Stuart:

> A quarrel occurred in Pakatwayo's day. Pakatwayo crossed the Tugela into Natal, the Makanya people being here (having built). The Makanya left behind Sitibane ka Makanya, his eldest son. Pakatwayo came across with troops to attack, saying he would cause the gourd of his place to be filled. He [Phakatwayo] came to seize cattle but failed, owing to resistance. He was defeated and ran off. He might have been killed but for the fact that fighting in those days was different to what it became under Tshaka. This was before Tshaka came to the throne.
>
> Nomo, the eldest son of Khondlo, fought with Pakatwayo and defeated him. Pakatwayo was obliged to take refuge in the bushes, and there stayed till they [Phakatwayo and his followers] were obliged to eat skins. At this point, Khondlo sent to the Makanya people, saying, "What do you mean by looking on? [i.e., how could you let your cousins become destitute?]." The Mnguni "who is like the rays of the sun" (i.e., Mnengwa) armed, and took his forces to Khondlo's assistance, whereupon Nomo was defeated. Pakatwayo then built the Mtanda kraal.[41]

Khondlo's intervention in seeking the aid of the Makanya AbaQwabe on behalf of Phakathwayo suggests that he favored this younger son over his eldest son and heir apparent, Nomo. Some oral traditions indicate there was resistance to the inheritance of the chieftaincy by Nomo because his mother was the sister of the AmaMthethwa's chief Dingiswayo and the AmaMthethwa therefore might attempt to extend their influence and dominance over the AbaQwabe by means of this relationship with Nomo. However, after Khondlo died under suspicious circumstances and Phakathwayo was installed, Dingiswayo is said to then have aided Nomo in an unsuccessful attack against Phakathwayo, causing Nomo to take refuge among the AmaMthethwa. There he would meet and establish a relationship with Dingiswayo's young warrior, the refugee Shaka. Mbovu said,

> I think Nomo went with Tshaka when he was made chief of the Zulus. When Tshaka afterwards defeated Pakatwayo he did not kill him, nor did he seize his cattle. He gave them all over to Nomo.[42]

Phakathwayo's *imizi* "were in land lying south of and adjacent to the Mhlatuze river," and his principal royal *umuzi*, or capital, was eMtandeni (or Mtanda). AbaQwabe homesteads in the era of Phakathwayo's reign included ukuDabuka (where Phakathwayo was buried); oDwini (that belonged to Mncinci); Nomo's *umuzi* eNtoyeyeni that had "contended with" the Mtanda kraal, eyiDedeni; eNdhlekezeni; eMteteni (a section of the Mtandeni); and Nqetho's villages eMaganukeni and eMaganukeni.[43] Regiments were recruited by *umuzi* and district rather than age, and Phakathwayo created regiments for young women and kept a separate women's quarters, *isigodlo*, at his capital, comprising daughters from prominent families. Mbovu named Phakathwayo's regiments as the Izengqana, Izilinda, uBede, and Izinkonde (a big regiment), among others.⁴⁴ Kambi ka Matshobana, interviewed with Mtshwayiza, remembered,

> The Qwabe tribe had regiments of its own. The only one of Pakatwayo's which Kambi and Mtshwayiza can name is the iziNkonde, which was so large a one that if it began in the course of the morning to enter the kraal the process would continue until sunset. Regiments were enlisted according to age and incorporated into the iziNkonde, which then became a huge body of men of different ages.⁴⁵

The Makanya AbaQwabe living south of the Thukela remained subject to overrule by the royal AbaQwabe family of Khondlo and Phakathwayo. Mbovu explained,

> We Makanya did not hold the *Tshwama* or *umkosi* [first fruits or harvest] ceremony. Permission was asked of Pakatwayo across in Zululand. He then held the *umkosi* ceremony, and after finishing would say, "Let my younger brother now hold the *umkosi*; let him cook the gourd, eat it, and lick the drinking pot" – the gourd of chiefship.⁴⁶

The explicit references to symbols and symbolic acts of chiefship and the understood restrictions of their use or practice without authorization from a superior political authority, in this case Phakathwayo, indicated the recognition of the political dispensation of control and the subordinate status of the Makanya branch of AbaQwabe rather than a mere alliance of equals. The AbaQwabe chiefs were also said to exercise control over the use of supernatural means of seeking power. Kambi said the AbaQwabe had

> a very strong objection to *abatakati* [persons using concoctions or "medicines" to achieve personal or political goals or outcomes]. This being so, the greatest restrictions were placed on people becoming doctors. The Qwabe people paid special attention to the matter, and so controlled the keeping of drugs as to confine them to a few well-known and respectable men. Whenever there was a supposed case of *takata*ing [using supernatural means to harm others], the king would call his *izangoma* [diviners] together and have them divine; i.e. the doctors would be encircled by a large body of men etc.; they would leap about inside and, by *bula*ing [divining], proceed to smell out the evil-doers.⁴⁷

The subsequent fate of the AbaQwabe proves that their chiefs were right to be wary of being weakened by poisonous concoctions, which, according to oral traditions, ultimately became their undoing when used against them collectively. Phakathwayo's troops would prove unable to provide for his defense when Shaka's warriors eventually arrived.

ZWIDE AND AMANDWANDWE CHIEFS

Zwide, the Ndwandwe king, was the son of Langa ka Ludonga ka Mabuso ka Pangode ka Sidinane...

We did not come from the Zulus or Besuto; we are said to have originated with the Swazi and Nhlwenga. We are from the coast lands, not Amantungwa or Abanguni. We resemble the Mtetwa...

The Ndwandwe tribe originated at the Gudu (hill overlooking Pongolo). We are spoken of as the Ndwandwe of the Gudu...

There are a number of our former kings buried at the Gudu hill between the Mkuze and Pongolo.[48]

The famous AmaNdwandwe chief Zwide, son of Langa ka Ludonga and Ntombaze, his mother of ill repute, was a contemporary of Shaka's father Senzangakhona and the AmaMthethwa chief Dingiswayo. By the time Shaka was a young warrior under Dingiswayo, Zwide had extended AmaNdwandwe dominance from its base at the Magudu hills. Soon after Sobhuza of the AmaSwazi, still then known as Somhlolo of the AmaNgwane ancestors of the AmaSwazi, succeeded to the chieftainship in about 1815, Zwide drove these AmaNgwane-AmaSwazi from the Magudu hills region south of the Thukela north across the Phongolo River and deep into the area that came to comprise modern Swaziland. The oral traditions of the AmaSwazi shed light on Zwide's militarism and expansionism in the early nineteenth century while Shaka was still living under Dingiswayo and serving in his military. The AmaNgwane-AmaSwazi had ancestral links to the AmaNdwandwe and in the era of Sobhuza's predecessors had migrated from the Lebombo mountains to south of the Phongolo into the vicinity of their AmaNdwandwe kin.

The Swazis were defeated by Zwide and put to flight. They fled into what is now the Transvaal, to the Basutos [i.e. chiefdoms of SeSotho culture of northern Swaziland]. Ncaba, Zwangendaba and Mpakeni fled at the same time. Sobuza's kraals [villages] were burnt by Zwide and the place is now known by the name Etshiselweni... The Swazis fled as far as the Basutos, to Esidhlomodhlomo hill, because Zwide's *impi* followed them.[49]

Zwide came to have about eight large homesteads, *imizi*, or large villages, and about a half dozen regiments in his military.[50] "Zwide lived at Nongoma at his Nomgoma kraal. When he was defeated the hill came to be called Kwa Nongoma."[51] However, "Zwide's main kraal was

Emgazini; it was below Isigwegwe hill, where Ziwedu is now living," and it was at eMgazini that Tshaka finally defeated him.[52] "Zwide's other kraals were Esikwitshini, near Tatiyana, and Kwa Dhlovunga (where Ntombaze lived) at eTokazi hill. Tatiyana are dongas near where Zwide caught Dingiswayo."[53] In addition, "[t]here was also uMgazana; uPunga was another, then Pungana another, also iZulu and iZuywana."[54] Zwide's regiments included the AmaPela, AbaHlakabezi, Isikwitshi, AmaNkaiya, uDhlovunga, Iziboya, Amankayiya, and Mgazi, and his chief *induna* was Noju.[55] Under Zwide's rule, the Nxumalo branch divided into the Manqele and Piseni sections, and he "was the cause of these divisions taking place."[56]

Because Zwide had a personal reputation as a ferocious fighter in battle and for killing defeated enemies, in his praises he was called "The one who crouches over people so that they may be killed; owl of Mkonto and Langa."[57] One of Stuart's informants said that Zwide used his mother's house to purify himself, and that she kept there "human heads" that "were hung on pegs at the back." Shaka himself, referred to by his praise-name Dhlungwana, was said to have burned down the house.[58] This interview is significant in indicating the extent to which the reputation of Zwide and his mother Ntombazi were associated with evil for keeping human skulls in her house was taken for granted and not even questioned in reports handed down for three generations. Zwide's eldest son and heir was Sikhunyana, and his other sons were remembered as Somapunga, Nqabeni, Myomo, Nomahlanjana, Dayingubo, Mpepa, and Nombengula.[59] Zwide's brother or half brother Zikode ka Langa was the father of Soshangana, who led a large branch of the AmaNdwandwe north in 1821–1822 to re-establish an independent chiefdom in the region of southern Mozambique. Soshangana wrought damage across the Maputo Bay chiefdoms of the era through raiding. Shaka would confront the AmaNdwandwe challenge of Zwide more than once and subsequently pursued the remnant chiefdoms of the AmaNdwandwe in his later military campaigns.

THE EARLY AMAZULU CHIEFDOM

North of the Thukela River, the small AmaZulu chiefdom had long been settled near the Mfolozi River. The AmaZulu chief at the beginning of the eighteenth century – one hundred years before the era of Shaka – was Ndaba, and the small chiefdom was subdivided under his sons Xoko, Jama, Ntopo, and Zivalele as it grew. By about 1750, the most prominent chief was Jama, father of Senzangakhona who was born about that time and was to inherit the chieftaincy.

Among the many small family-based chiefdoms in the KwaZulu region in the late eighteenth century were, in addition to the AmaZulu, the AmaButhelezi (i.e., people of Buthelezi, or *abakwa*Buthelezi, people of the place of Buthelezi); AmaQungebe; the people of Imbuyeni; the AmaChunu; the AmaMajola; the AmaXulu; and the AmaSikakane. These small chiefdoms were located near the AmaZulu capital or royal *umuzi* at Nobamba and intermarried with the AmaZulu. Somewhat farther from the AmaZulu chiefdom were the AmaNyuswa (*abakwa*-Nyuswa); AmaMbata; AmaGasa; AmaKhumalo; AmaHlubi; AbaQwabe; AmaDube; AmaLanga or people of eLangeni; AbaTembu; AmaZungu; and AmaMakoba.[60] The eLangeni chiefdom of the AmaLanga, named for an ancestor, was located next to the territory of the AmaZulu, and the two ruling families maintained cordial relations, explaining how the eLangeni chief's daughter Nandi became involved with Senzangakhona as a young unmarried man.[61] The ancestral chief Langa lived nine generations before Mbengi, Nandi's father, but was a contemporary of Senzangakhona's father Jama, dating Langa's approximate dates of rule to the 1500s.[62] Langa's followers were believed to have been related to the AmaZulu of many generations earlier and to the AbaQwabe and AmaChunu chiefdoms to whose people the AmaZulu were known to have been related for many generations.[63]

Senzangakhona, son of Jama, inherited the AmaZulu chieftaincy before he came of age and was allowed to marry, so Senzangakhona's sister Mnkabayi, the elder of twins, ruled until he was old enough to do so.[64] Competition for the inheritance of the small AmaZulu chieftaincy was intense enough, according to oral traditions, to prompt an assassination attempt against Senzangakhona, but he and Mnkabayi were alerted and deflected the attempt at poisoning.[65] Another brother is said to have challenged Senzangakhona for the inheritance of their father's chieftaincy after Senzangakhona had reached his majority, married, and had children.

Among the AmaZulu, marriage was often delayed for the heir to the chieftaincy, although future wives were chosen to be married once permission to the young chief was given. As heir to the chieftaincy, Senzangakhona's legal marriages were delayed by custom. It was during this period, in about 1780–1785, that Senzangakhona encountered the daughter of the eLangeni chief, Nandi, and she became pregnant with his son who would be called Shaka. The oral traditions of these events differ in some details, but most agree that although she was not married to Senzangakhona right away, she was brought into his household after his formal marriage to other wives, and bridewealth was paid for her.[66] Senzangakhona's first legal wife was Mnkabi of the emaBeleni people, who bore his daughter Nozilwana. Nandi was later considered a junior wife and placed in the house of his first wife Mnkabi, but her son Shaka was not considered a rightful recognized heir.[67] Senzangakhona married at least eight wives, and

> Nandi became a wife (*umakoti*) at the place of Mnkabi, the mother of Nozilwana. Mnkabi was Senzangakona's great wife; she was married (*zeka*'d) first. (She was a girl of the emaBeleni people, from the place of the people of Ndhlela kaSompisi, so I fancy. I do not know her father.) The girl of our tribe, i.e. Nandi, was married (*zekwa*'d) and placed (*ngenisa*'d) there, i.e. in Mnkabi's house. (It must be remembered that Mnkabi is a different woman from Mnkabayi – a sister of Senzangakona.) Mpikase [another wife of Senzangakhona] was the mother of Sigujana, following with Dingana. I do not know who [his son] Mhlangana's mother was.[68]

Thus, Senzangakhona married numerous wives, and more than one bore a son who was considered eligible to inherit the chieftaincy.

The chiefdom that Senzangakhona had inherited from his father Jama was small, and he is remembered as having enlarged it through the incorporation of several small neighboring chiefdoms. In one case, the AmaMpungose are said to have assisted Senzangakhona in a fight with his brother, Makasana, who was disputing the inheritance to the chieftaincy. When Senzangakhona's people were forced to flee their village suddenly, one of his small daughters was left behind but was rescued by an uMpongose man to whom Senzangakhona remained ever grateful. The rescuer, Kuba, "...threw in his lot with Senzangakhona and, with the assistance of Ndhlovu (my ancestor), succeeded in defeating Mkasana and putting him to death."[69] As a result, the AmaMpungose chiefdom was said to have been the first small chiefdom to give allegiance to Senzangakhona and enter voluntarily into a subordinate tributary relationship to the small Zulu chiefdom. With that alliance in place,

> Senzangakona decided to fight the amaCunu, so he directed Kuba to get a force together, including his son Ndhlovu, and go and subjugate them. Ndhlovu went and defeated the Cunus, upon which he was given [by Senzangakona] a tract of country at Taleni. He was also given the people who were living there. After this, Senzangakona attacked Xabatshe of the Xulu people. Ndhlovu again joined in this attack. Xabatshe was defeated, upon which Ndhlovu was given the territory and people that had belonged to the deceased. After this, Senzangakona died; so also did Ndhlovu.[70]

A portion of the AmaBhaca chiefdom also joined the AmaZulu under Senzangakhona.[71] He adopted the AmaMthethwa method of recruiting men into regiments according to their age rather than according to their village of origin as had been done previously.[72] Senzangakhona, who had given allegiance, or *khonza*'d, Dingiswayo and the AmaMthethwa, thus persisted in pursuing his own ambitions.[73] Accordingly, "the AmaWombe regiment was Senzangakona's first one; it was enrolled to copy Godongwana [Dingiswayo]."[74]

Senzangakhona fathered at least nineteen children, the most famous being Shaka and his half brothers Dingane, who succeeded him in 1828, and Mpande, who succeeded Dingane in 1840.[75] Shaka spent at least part of his early years living among his half brothers and sisters, and "Ngqengelele used to look after the children, and cooked at the place of the wife Mtaniya (wife of Senzangakona)."[76] Ngqengelele was an important man but not an *induna* [officer] and was remembered as "a man of the locality, was Tshaka's 'father'. Tshaka and his brothers grew up in his charge."[77] But there is general agreement that Shaka spent most of his childhood living among his mother's people because she was the daughter of the neighboring eLangeni chief.

Chapter 3

Shaka's Early Life: Oral Traditions, Tales, and History

The many myths of Shaka's early life, produced by and through African oral traditions and European written sources, obscure the circumstances of his conception, birth, and early life. The evidence of Shaka's parentage is uncontested, however, and the oral traditions indicate what was accepted to be true by nineteenth-century Africans of KwaZulu-Natal. The contradictions found in the various stories leave ambiguity surrounding some of the major circumstances of Shaka's birth and childhood, but their broad agreement lends strong credibility to many aspects of this period of Shaka's life.

CONCEPTION AND BIRTH: SENZANGAKHONA AND NANDI

Nandi, the mother of Shaka, was the daughter of the AmaLanga or eLangeni chief Chief Mbengi and Mfunda, a daugher of the AbaQwabe chief Khondlo and sister of Phakathwayo.[1] She was "known for her good nature in the Zulu country; she was well-liked," and "another name for Nandi was Somqeni, and so Shaka was called 'the one of Somqeni's place' (*wa kwa Somqeni*)."[2] The oral traditions are not in agreement about her first meeting with the young heir to the AmaZulu chieftaincy, Senzangakhona, but the preponderance of evidence supports the widespread understanding that they met while Senzangakhona and his cohort of young men were out herding cattle prior to their recognition by society as adult men. One of James Stuart's informants, Mgidhlana, knew a man who had "herded cattle with Senzangakona in the bush, i.e. where he met Nandi."[3] Ndlovu ka Timuni said, "The story of Shaka's birth was kept

Shaka's Early Life: Oral Traditions, Tales, and History   43

hidden by the *abanumzana* [headmen]. It was not a story common to everybody." He added,

> When Senzangakona was a boy he was in the habit of herding cattle with other boys, and to do so properly rough shelters (*amakhlangala*) were erected for his temporary use. These rough shelters were a short distance from his home. In the neighbourhood of the Zulu tribe was the Langeni one, of which a girl named Nandi was a member. She was the daughter of Mbenge.[4]

According to Ndhlovu ka Timuni, Nandi had the active assistance of her relatives in arranging a meeting with Senzangakhona, who had already been designated as chief of the AmaZulu people. One or more AmaLangeni men and girls accompanied her several times to a place near the temporary shelters where the boys, Shaka and his friends, eventually discovered them.[5] Then "on subsequent occasions, as often as Senzangakhona came to herd cattle, Nandi would come, bringing beer with her for him to drink in his shelter."[6] Jantshi ka Nongila also related that Senzangakhona and other young men herded near the kraal of the eLangeni chief Mbengi where Nandi and her friends hid nearby and watched them.[7] Their hiding place was discovered; Senzangakhona's party questioned them and then brought the girls to the temporary huts where they met Senzangakhona, Zivalele, Sitayi, and others. There Nandi said she liked Senzangakhona and went into his hut.[8]

In 1919, Stuart interviewed Ndhlovu ka Timuni a second time, seventeen years after his first interview, and then published the preceding version of the story in London. We therefore have the opportunity to compare two oral traditions told by the same person, Ndhlovu, many years apart and observe changes in the narrative. The fact that Stuart published his 1919 version made it widely available and familiar, but the intervening years allowed for Ndhlovu to have picked up and introduced apocryphal anecdotes into the narrative, which as recorded by Stuart sounds more authentic because he retained the isiZulu idioms in his 1919 notes. The narrative of events remained mostly the same but with many more details that gave the story a literary flair. In this better-known rendition, Senzangakhona's friends invited the girls to join them. Nandi questioned Senzangakhona, asked for him to become her lover, and then took his arm and led him into his makeshift hut. Nandi had her close attendants (*izigqila*) with her in Senzangakhona's hut; other girls went into huts with other boys. In the hut, Nandi ate meat and drank beer with her attendants, Senzangakhona, and four other boys. Nandi then told the boys to stay there overnight and went home where she arranged for a hut that was being built to be transported to the place of Senzangakhona's hut. His hut was also repaired and he then stayed in it alone; it was where he had sexual relations with Nandi, who became pregnant.[9]

Ngidi ka Mcikaziswa had not heard that Nandi had first met Senzangakhona in the fields, a story he attributed to "Mudhli's people," but provided another that is equally dramatic and credible.[10] Nandi is presented as having been brought into the household of Senzangakhona as a junior wife, as confirmed in some of the oral traditions. According to Ngidi,

> Senzangakona did not like Nandi. Mnkabi [his senior wife] made a fire in her hut and, when she saw that her lord was coming to her hut, put the fire out. Senzangakona then went to sleep with Mnkabi in the hut. When Senzangakona had laid down to rest, Mnkabi admitted Nandi, then a newly married wife (*makoti*) of her house, and placed her alongside of Senzangakona. Senzangakona turned, thinking it was Mnkabi, and had intercourse, and so Tshaka was conceived. Nandi ran off to her home to bear her child because she was not liked. She was not driven away; she went off on her own accord. She felt she was of rank and should be treated properly. When this happened Nandi was a wife of Senzangakona.[11]

Mmemi ka Nguluzane told a similar story regarding how Nandi became pregnant. He said,

> It was widely known that Tshaka [Shaka] was illegitimate (*zalwa'd esihlahleni*). I have heard that Nandi was not liked by Senzangakona. She belonged to his *isigodhlo*. One night a particular girl was summoned to him, but somehow she was suppplanted by Nandi, and although Senzangakona did not care for her he had connection with her and so conceived Tshaka.[12]

It was considered socially acceptable for young unmarried women to engage in external sexual relations with young men as long as they did not consummate the relationship, casting a scandalous light on Nandi's behavior and pregnancy. However, Mangati ka Gogide said it was a well-established custom that unlike other young men, the sons of chiefs did not *hlobonga* [engage in external sexual relations] but only had actual intercourse with girls.[13] Mkehlengana ka Zulu said his father described the circumstances differently, and referred to Nandi as an *ingodosi*, or a woman who is betrothed to be married and for whom bridewealth, *lobola*, had already been paid. He said,

> My father told me that Nandi became pregnant prior to marriage with Senzangakona. She was then an *ingodosi*. When pregnant she went off to her home, being conducted thither by special messengers. Tshaka seems always to have lived apart from Senzangakona. Nandi, however, married and bore Nomcoba, but left for some reason, afterwards marrying Gendeyana.[14]

Narratives about what happened when Nandi's pregnancy was discovered diverge in a number of ways. Madikane ka Mlomowetole agreed with Mkehlengana's assertion that Nandi was already a woman in the household of Senzangakhona when she became pregnant, saying, "Tshaka was not illegitimate. Nandi had come to Senzangakona to marry by becoming one of his *isigodhlo*, and it was whilst she was living there that she had intercourse with Senzangakona and, becoming pregnant, bore Tshaka."[15] But several oral traditions explain that her pregnancy was scandalous because Senzangakhona had not yet come of age or been recognized as an adult eligible for marriage. Mkehlengana said that "Nandi became pregnant before Senzangakona had been circumcised. Tshaka was therefore illegitimate (*o wa se sihlahleni*)."[16] Conversely, Madikane explained,

Tshaka was born at Esiklebeni. He was not born illegitimately. My father told me this. He was driven out from Esiklebeni.

Tshaka was conceived by Nandi before Senzangakona had been circumcised. When it was seen that N. had become pregnant the order was given that Senzangakona should be circumcised. He was circumcised. Nandi came to marry Senzangakona from the Langeni people. She was the sister of Makedama the chief, Makedama ka Mbengi. Mbengi was Nandi's father.[17]

According to Henry Francis Fynn's information, the AmaZulu under Chief Senzangakhona had been "subdued by Dingiswayo," who had postponed all circumcision ceremonies until after he had finished his conquests, which affected Senzangakhona and others under Dingiswayo's domination. Fynn explained that by long custom an uncircumcised chief, although he could collect women in a seraglio to become his wives, until he was circumcised he could not "have any intercourse with them for the propagation of his race."[18] Nandi was said to have been one of the women "set apart by Senzangakona," and she appeared to be pregnant after having been in the seraglio for about six months.

The oral traditions about the reaction to news about Nandi's pregnancy vary widely. Most indicate that she returned to her mother's at eLangeni. Baleka ka Mpitikazi, who received her information from a family member and witness who was in a position to know these intimate details, also related the story of Nandi's pregnancy, and the attribution of her medical condition to a disease commonly known as *itshaka* before she was obviously pregnant. Nandi told her family she had been made pregnant by Senzangakhona. "She then bore the child; she bore it at the home of her Langeni people." Senzangakhona was told and "he admitted that it was he who had made Nandi pregnant. She then married him. She was now his wife."¹⁹ Ndhlovu's narrative explains why Nandi's pregnancy was unacceptable and put her into danger:

Ndhlovu gave in detail the history of Nandi becoming enceinte and re the birth of Tshaka. When it was found she was pregnant, she said she was suffering from *itshati* or *ikambi* (a particular ailment). Mudhli, Ndhlovu's grandfather, secreted her. In those days kings had no sons (all were killed off); consequently, when Nandi was found out to be pregnant, an *impi* was sent to kill her and the child, but warning being received beforehand, Nandi and her child escaped. It was not commonly known the child had been born. The child itself was handed over to its grandmother to bring up so as to allow Nandi's breasts to "dry" as soon as possible.²⁰

Ndhlovu's grandfather Mudhli had been personally involved:

This affair now came to the notice of Mudhli of the Zulu tribe, who gave strict instructions that the child, when born, should be carefully concealed. Care was to be taken that it was suckled by its grandmother, for it was inexpedient for Nandi to do so as her breasts would develop to too noticeable a size. Mudhli, close relation of Senzangakona as he was, warned Nandi's parents of the fact that Zulu kings never allowed themselves to have children, and therefore Senzangakona, as soon as he heard Nandi had a child, would be bent on putting it to death. Nandi's pregnancy was reported to Senzangakona, when he admitted he was fond of the girl. He made this admission when the eLangeni people came to him. It seems Mudhli directed these people thus: "Take care of that for us and cause her to bring out that 'illness' of hers." Nandi's people acted accordingly.²¹

But Ndhlovu then contradicted himself, also saying that the birth of Nandi's child was kept secret from Senzangakhona, and indicating that Senzangakhona had not yet become "king" at the time of the baby's conception and birth. About the baby, Shaka, Ndhlovu said,

unbekhown to its father, it grew under the secret circumstances prescribed by Mudhli. Its grandmother made a string and took a measure of its waist, and by that means was able to judge how it compared with other children. When the child had grown a little, Mudhli expressed a desire to see it and it was accordingly taken to his kraal and there hidden under some mats in the hut. An intimation now reached Senzangakona, by this time king, to the effect not only that he had had a child by Nandi but that this very child was being harboured at Mudhli's kraal. So astounding was this that the king instantly dispatched a body of men to put to death not only the child but Mudhli and his kraal (*umuzi*) as well. But Mudhli, as the *impi* set forth to kill him, had also heard of his danger, and, causing the child to be taken back to the eLangeni, left at once. On getting to the kraal the *impi* found Mudhli absent but killed the inmates thereof.²²

Ndhlovu believed that Senzangakhona did subsequently marry Nandi:

Nandi was sent for, and was duly married to the young king. Nandi, however, left Tshaka at her own home, for she had been directed not to suckle it and only her mother was to do so. I have not heard if Nandi had another child by Senzangakona. When Nandi married Senzangakona, Tshaka was a little boy, perhaps herding. Nandi then took up her abode at Senzangakona's kraal. She was *lobola*'d.[23]

Madikane insisted that "Nandi had come to Senzangakona to marry by becoming one of his *isigodhlo*, and it was whilst she was living there that she had intercourse with Senzangakona and, becoming pregnant, bore Tshaka."[24] Madikane specified,

Nandi did not have a marriage ceremony. The Langeni came to ask for cattle from the Zulus. It was then arranged that Nandi should be given. She was put in the *isigodhlo* [women's quarters]. This happened after Jama's death. Mnkabayi was reigning then. The *isigodhlo* in question, into which Nandi was put, was Jama's. Tshaka was as a child concealed by Mnkabayi. Senzangakona's circumcision wounds had healed up in the river. Mnkabayi went to see her brother Senzangakona and told him that the illegitimate child that she [Nandi] had, had been brought forth. Senzangakona was told that it was a boy. Senzangakona said, "How can a person my age be said to have a son?" Mnkabayi said, "When I saw it was a boy I gave him poison." Senzangakona said, "My sister, you did well." Mnkabayi said to Nandi at Esiklebeni that she was to run away to the Langeni people and hide the child. Nandi tied up her belongings and returned to the Langeni. Tshaka grew up there.[25]

In this narrative of events, Mnkabayi is said to have secretly saved Shaka as a baby from her brother Senzangakhona.[26] Moreover, "Mnkabayi afterwards caused the man who had made the report to Senzangakona to be put to death."[27]

Jantshi insisted that Shaka's birth was not kept secret from Senzangakhona but he was called to come see the child and did so. Jantshi was very certain of Senzangakhona's intention to have Shaka killed when he was very young and hiding at Senzangakhona's mother's.[28] Jantshi also believed that the child's paternal grandmother, Senzangakhona's mother, not Mudhli, had taken the initiative and made the decision to rescue the child, to whom Jantshi says the birth had been reported. Jantshi did not believe that there were any orders to kill her in addition to the child.[29]

Ndhlovu's 1919 narrative continues essentially the same as his 1903 version but with the addition of dialogue.[30] The use of such techniques to emphasize the entertainment effect of the story is evident throughout and is just as likely to have been part of the isiZulu tradition of storytelling as the result of Stuart's expansiveness for publication purposes. However, some of the narrative and dialogue stands out as having been manipulated. For example, there is a change in the story about the attempt to discover Shaka in his paternal grandmother's hut.

This time the rumor is said to have been that she was hiding an "*impaka*," a possessed cat controlled by a malevolent spirit, in her hut.[31] This change in the telling heightened the dramatic tension in an idiom familiar and appealing to an AmaZulu audience in a fairy-tale style. This was almost definitely a change introduced into the narrative by Ndhlovu because of the care with which Stuart recorded such idioms with the original isiZulu words and metaphors, even in his earliest interviews in 1902–1903. Ndhlovu either kept that detail back from Stuart then because it reveals old Zulu beliefs and superstitions that were so unpalatable to Europeans and therefore injudicious to speak of in 1902–1903, or added the change himself in the intervening years of telling the story because a new generation of his own Zulu listeners did not demand accuracy and appreciated poetic license in these stories, which had by then acquired more and more of a mythic quality and value in Zulu society.[32]

In Ndhlovu's later rendition, we are told what Mudhli (supposedly) thought, and that Senzangakhona had ordered that his own mother be put to death, and told the names of the women who are said to have prevented it, including Mnkabayi. Mudhli is presented as pursuing a plan with regard to protecting the baby Shaka from birth, and Mnkabayi is also portrayed as having played a crucial role in preventing the execution of Senzangakhona's order to kill his mother. Mnkabayi also is said to have protected the secret of the young child Shaka. In 1902–1903 and in 1919, the roles of these people in the early history of the AmaZulu were politically significant because they had a bearing on the status, position, and credibility of their descendants in contemporary twentieth century AmaZulu society and politics. Ndhlovu's grandfather was later killed by the order of Shaka. This fact would have suggested to later generations who were mobilizing all aspects of Zulu history, especially Shaka stories, that there had been political reasons for the death. It also would have suggested that Mudhli and, in guilt by association, his descendents were disloyal to Shaka and to the AmaZulu nation he built. This story therefore serves to exculpate Mudhli and his descendants from disloyalty because the young Shaka would never have been born or lived through childhood to later effect political unification had it not been for Mudhli's heroic plan as this narrative depicted. Similarly, Mnkabayi, Senzangakhona's sister and Shaka's aunt, is later remembered as playing a role in trying to prevent her nephew's atrocities and ultimately in condoning his assassination and approving Dingane as his successor, again suggestive of disloyalty to the AmaZulu nation as symbolized by the mythical Shaka of the twentieth century. Ndhlovu's 1919 narrative explicitly portrays

Mnkabayi in a heroic role with regard to the royal AmaZulu family, including when Senzangakhona threatened the lives of the young Shaka and of his grandmother. This positive portrayal of Mnkabayi had the effect of rehabilitating the reputation of the many people associated with Mnkabayi's villages where she had remained influential through the rise and fall of the mythically heroic Shaka.[33]

Jantshi said, "Now as regards the name Tshaka, I took care to question my father specially about it." Jantshi was explicit that his father Nongila said Shaka "got the name from the ailment from which his mother Nandi was at first said to be suffering, before it became evident she was pregnant, viz. *itshaka*." He continued,

My father said *itshati* [a disease] by some was called *itshaka* by others in those early days. My father Nongila said that if a person had what is now known as *ikambi*, she was spoken of as having *itshaka*. The same expression was used in regard to a girl who had by accident, become *enceinte* [pregnant] before marriage. The illegitimate child she had produced was also spoken of as *itshaka*. My father drew my attention to the fact that we come from the north and that our dialect is different from what it used to be. He also said that some spoke of *itshaka* as *itshati*. He himself used the word *itshaka* and it was from the circumstances under which Tshaka was conceived that he was so named.[34]

Thus, according to Nongila, this ruse was commonly used to politely cover for the pregnancy of an unmarried girl, and at the time, the reference to illness from *itshaka* and its equivalents were widely understood without explicit reference to the pregnancy.

Ndhlovu told Stuart,

My father did not say the motive for hiding Tshaka was because Senzangakona had not been circumcised when he [Tshaka] was born. Munyana (aged about Mavalana age) says that the custom of the leopard is, when say three young are born, one of them a male, the male is taken away and hidden by its mother and suckled where hidden, for fear lest the father should kill it. Ndhlovu says the lion does the same thing. Thus the Zulu kings were following this practice. Timuni said, "A Zulu chief does not father children" i.e., he is not supposed to father children; he takes precautions not to father children. That was the reason for hiding [Tshaka].[35]

At the time of Nandi's pregnancy, a competitive tension existed between the AmaZulu and eLangeni chiefdoms. Many stories of the meeting between Senzangakhona and Nandi reflect a belief not only that the meeting had been prearranged and deliberate but also that she had seduced the heir to the AmaZulu chieftaincy. Many tales say that she had her family's deliberate and carefully considered assistance to do so.

he people of eLangeni would gain a foot in the door of
[Z]ulu chiefdom through such a connection, so too might the
[Zulu] eventually gain leverage over their eLangeni neighbors. The
[use of ma]rriage to forge and reinforce political alliances was common;
there were perceived advantages to both families when important
marriages took place across political boundaries between chiefs and their
sons and daughters.

Not all of Stuart's interviewees believed *lobolo*, or bridewealth, had
been paid for Nandi to make her son Shaka legitimate.[36] On being
questioned, Jantshi asserted:

Tshaka was illegitimate. I feel quite sure on this point. Nandi never became
Senzangakona's wife, nor did he ever *lobola* her. Had she been his wife, how
came she to marry Gendeyana and have children by him? I will not allow [agree]
that Senzangakona chased her away for having a bad temper. Nandi never went at
all to Senzangakona to be his wife.[37]

Jantshi was certain that Nandi had later married another man,
Gendeyana, and argued,

Had *lobolo* been given for Nandi, and had the incident happened, about
Mbikwana rescuing Tshaka when the dust was up, she [Nandi] could never have
gone and married Gendeyana. She would have been forbidden by ancient custom
to do this even if she had been chased away. She would have returned to her
parents.[38]

Similarly, Stuart wrote that "Mkebeni is firmly of the opinion that Nandi
never actually married Senzangakona" and was explicit that after she
became pregnant and gave birth, "he [Shaka] was illegitimate (*o wa
sihlahla*)."[39]

Baleni ka Silwana claimed Shaka was illegitimate but that Nandi was
subsequently married to Senzangakhona.[40] Baleka ka Mpitikazi did not
know whether bridewealth was ever paid for her but was explicit that
"Nandi bore Tshaka out of wedlock. Tshaka is therefore illegitimate.
My father told me this."[41] Mmemi concurred that "it was widely known
that Tshaka was illegitimate (*zalwa'd esihlahleni*)."[42]

An equal number of Stuart's informants stated just as emphatically,
however, that Nandi had been legitimately married to Senzangakhona
with *lobola* having been paid, making her son Shaka a legitimate son and
heir. Ngidi ka Mcikaziswa said

Nandi became a wife (*umakoti*) at the place of Mnkabi, the mother of Nozilwana.
Mnkabi was Senzangakona's great wife; she was married (*zeka*'d) first. (She was a
girl of the emaBeleni people, from the place of the people of Ndhlela kaSompisi,

so I fancy. I do not know her father.) The girl of our tribe i.e. Nandi, was married (*zekwa*'d) and placed (*ngenisa*'d) there i.e. in Mnkabi'e house. (It must be remembered that Mnkabi is a different woman from Mnkabayi – a sister of Senzangakona.)[43]

Mayinga ka Mbekuzana agreed that Senzangakhona gave *lobolo* for Nandi and noted that "[t]he name which Tshaka was given by Senzangakona was Sikiti."[44]

SHAKA IN HIS YOUTH

The oral traditions disagree about where Shaka grew up and how long he lived with his mother Nandi. We know that she lived with him after he was installed as AmaZulu chief following Senzangakhona's death, but the intervening years remain something of a mystery, including her putative marriage to the man named Gendeyana. Mayinga said that Nandi bore three of Senzangakhona's children, who were Shaka, Nomcuba (a sister), and Ngwadi, and insisted,

Nandi never became intimate with Gendeyana. She is being slandered by saying she did. Nomzinhlanga [known as Nomcuba] followed Tshaka in age, and Nandi bore her by Senzangakona. Nandi never married Gendeyana. Ngwadi was not the son of Gendeyana but of Senzangakona. Ngwadi was killed by Dingana.[45]

Mayinga was certain that Nandi was a legitimate wife of Senzangakhona and persisted, saying, "no wife of Senzangakona ever married again. Nandi did not marry. She did not marry when she got to the Mtetwa."[46] Mayinga also explained that the rumor had been started because "succession disputes cause slanders to be spread; that is why Nandi was said to have married Gendeyana, and yet that was not so. Ngwadi followed in age after Nomzinhlanga, whose other name was Nomcoba."[47] Gendeyana was identified as of AbaQwabe origins, and it is not clear where he lived or what his relationship with Nandi was. Henry Francis Fynn, misidentifying Gendeyana as "a commoner of the Langeni tribe," believed that Nandi had married him and he was the father of her son Ngwadi.[48] Stuart believed that Mkebeni was mistaken in assuming that Nomcoba was the daughter of another wife of Senzangakhona and hence was Shaka's sister only by a different father. The point was contentious.

In his more embellished 1919 narrative, Ndhlovu said that Senzangakhona believed the infant Shaka had been killed at the attack on the homestead that he had ordered until some years later a rumor reached him that the child was alive. Then cattle for *lobola* were driven to the eLangeni for Nandi, and Ndhlovu depicted Mudhli as speaking directly with Nandi's mother (i.e., Shaka's maternal grandmother). Shaka appears to have spent his early years at eLangeni with his mother's family. According to Mkehlengana, Shaka's presence was known to senior Ama-Zulu men for "whilst Tshaka was an infant, the Zulu indunas used to send sticks to measure the exact height of the child."[49] Madikane believed that Nandi returned to Senzangakhona with Shaka once he was old enough to walk but was warned off by Mnkabayi. He said that Shaka was known to be Senzangakhona's child "and the one which had caused him, Senzangakona, to be circumcised."[50] This indicates why the circumstances of Nandi's pregnancy and Shaka's birth would have become widely known and raises doubt about whether the pregnancy could have remained secret as claimed by others. Madikane said that, therefore, "Tshaka grew up among the Langeni."[51] Speaking from information originating among the AmaLangeni themselves, Ngidi said that "Tshaka spent the greatest portion of his youth in the Langeni country, at the place of Mfunda, his grandmother, namely at Ngugeni kraal."[52] Even though Baleka said that Senzangakhona had acknowleged his paternity of Shaka and married Nandi so that Nandi was his wife, Baleka also said, "Tshaka stayed with his grandmother Mfunda (Nandi'a mother). He eventually became an *insizwa* [young man]. When he had become an *insizwa* he went away to the Mtetwa, and became a great warrior. Dingiswayo, the Mtetwa chief, made him an *induna* [commander], and he became a commander of the Mtetwa army."[53] Mayinga said that "Tshaka grew up in the Zulu country, but became something of a wrong-doer (*itshinga*). Senzangakona used to chase him off, and he went to the eLangeni country."[54] But these events appear to have occurred somewhat later in his childhood and youth.

The most widely told story about Shaka's youth involved Makedama, his first cousin by his mother's brother Mgabi when Shaka lived at eLangeni. Makedama was evidently not much older than Shaka, and they spent time together at Ntengweni, where, as Mkando ka Dhlova said, Shaka was treated badly "and that is why he killed Makedama – for that grudge," years later.[55] Mkando said, "Tshaka killed him because he fed him with hot curds poured into his hands. Tshaka had gone there as a boy."[56] None of the oral traditions about him portrays Makedama in a favorable light, and as a young man, Makedama introduced brutal and cruel fighting tactics before Shaka did. The oral traditions include stories of confrontations between Makedama and Shaka during Shaka's youth, but some evidence has been wildly misconstrued in later European accounts in trying to explain Shaka's personality. Ngidi said that "the 'stone' incident occurred between Shaka and Makedama at Ngugeni kraal, belonging to Mbengi," and later explained,

> The fight about the "stones" took place between Tshaka and Makedama, who was Tshaka's cousin (umzala), and not with Mgabi [Makedama's father]. They were making imaginary kraals with stones, with cattle kraals of dry dung, on flat rocks out in the open.[57]

The story was well known. Ndhlovu interrupted his narrative chronologically to tell the story of Shaka herding with the eLangeni chief's son Makedama, making bulls from stones, and "setting them against each other." His 1919 version is longer and has more dialogue than the earlier version. Makedama explained to others that his hand had been hurt as they played, pretending stones were bulls, and Shaka is said to have overheard the reply in which Makedama was shamed: "Hau! So this little nothing [Shaka] that has been in hiding has killed [defeated] the son of our chief? So the son of our chief has been killed by a little Ntungwa that has been in hiding?" Shaka is said to have allowed Makedama to win in their next contest with their stone bulls, which this time were evidently bulls modeled from clay, after which Makedama is said to have crushed Shaka's toy bull. After this happened a second time, Shaka is said to have overheard Makedama boasting of his victorious bull and the other boys responding, "Ho! So the little Ntungwa thought his little bull would overcome ours?" In this story, after Makedama crushed Shaka's third toy bull, Shaka is said to have taken an *assegai* (spear) and stabbed a cow. This incident was reported to Chief Mbengi, who was also told of the earlier events. When Mbengi heard that Shaka had never crushed Makedama's toy bulls after his had won a contest but that Makedama had done so, Mbengi is said to have stated of Shaka, "[t]hen he did well to stab the cow." These events are used to later explain Shaka's hostility toward the people of eLangeni.[58]

In his 1919 narrative, Ndhlovu depicted similar events involving Phakathwayo, the chief son of the AbaQwabe chief. He was also reported to have complained to some men when Shaka broke off the horns of his toy clay bull. The men are reported as having said, "Hau! What has done this? A little Ntungwa, a little nothing in hiding, with a little penis that points upwards? Has he been troubling the son of the chief, then?"[59] These insults, misconstrued as being literal in popularized stories of Shaka in the twentieth century, were consistent with the prevailing idiom of insulting language and refer to an early Zulu progenitor, who had come to be called "dog's penis" by his enemies. Because this man had prevailed as a commander in battle, he had embraced the insulting name. Moreover, references to identifying styles of clothing among men, such as the penis cover, were also commonly used derogatorily and are implied in these insults.[60] Later generations, and certainly Europeans, would not have understood that the penis sheath, made earlier of leather and later from certain plant leaves, was designed with ties that pulled the penis to one side or the other, hence the reference to a penis that points upward. There is ample evidence that the AmaTsonga, who wore this sheath habitually, were recognized and identified by this article of clothing when traveling south. The insulting term *AmaHlengwa* was one of the names by which the AmaTsonga were known south of the Pongola. Moreover, these insults were meant to be understood and were understood by Shaka to indicate his socially inferior status among the people to whom he had been sent, first the eLangeni and then the AbaQwabe. The former regarded him and treated him as a dependent servant as indicated by the references to eating milk curds from his hands like a dog rather than as an equal, much less the son of a chief, Senzangakhona. The emphasis on the insults and his response are classic features of dramatic narratives, used to foreshadow his later life and actions as he is portrayed as an unfairly humiliated victim who overcomes adversity to achieve greatness. That the same story was told about young Phakathwayo and then about Shaka's treatment first at eLangeni and then among the AbaQwabe only underscores the prevalence of the use of these insults among youth and young men taunting each other. By 1919, Ndhlovu appears to have been cultivating the myths of Shaka, whereas in 1902–1903 he, like Stuart, appeared to be more interested in arriving as closely as possible to the historical truth. In 1919, the imperatives of narrative drama took precedence for Ndhlovu.[61]

The fact that Shaka was upset because the insults of Makedama and the others were affronts to his status as the AmaZulu chief's son rather than ones referring to his personal appearance is obvious in the evidence. Maziyana ka Mahlabeni had very specific information to this effect, saying,

Mande was the one who insulted Tshaka by saying, "The little Ntungwa with a penis-cover made from the tongwane tree; could he ever get here to our place at Emgakuceba?" He spoke of Tshaka as an umNtungwa.[62]

There is also evidence that Makedama's eLangeni friends were stirring up trouble deliberately between Makedama and Shaka. Ngidi ka Mcikaziswa said, "Nsindwane was an inceku to Tshaka and Makedama.... He took up the stones belonging to Tshaka and threw them into Makedama's imaginary cattle kraal."⁶³ Baleka explained,

> Tshaka complained of the way in which he was treated by Makedama: he complained, whilst still a boy, (a) of Makedama's objecting to Tshaka drinking water higher up a stream than where he [Makedama] was drinking; (b) of his [Makedama] picking out the best of Tshaka's stones, which represented cattle in the games they played, whereby kraals of cowdung were built and stones selected and put inside.⁶⁴

Baleka also said that "Makedama was later on killed by Tshaka for having bullied him when a boy whilst he was staying at home among his mother's people."⁶⁵ This eLangeni version of the story lays the blame for their later bad treatment by Shaka firmly at Makedama's door and portrays Shaka as a victim when he was living among them.⁶⁶

Some of the oral traditions portray a common and more likely relationship between Chief Senzangakhona and his son Shaka in which Shaka was treated in much the same manner as Senzangakhona treated his other sons. Ngidi said, "Senzangakona's name for Tshaka was Mandhlesilo. He was called Tshaka because he was a hero." If Senzangakona had a name for Shaka, the implications regarding what Senzangakona knew and when he knew it about Shaka are significant.⁶⁷ Ngidi provided the significant information that "Tshaka, whilst in our tribe, was *butwa*'d [recruited] with Makedama into the Amananana regiment by Mgabi, Mbengi being now dead. Tshaka was in this regiment *before* he went to the Mtetwa country."⁶⁸ Mmemi said, "Tshaka belonged to the Wombe regiment but this was Senzangakona's regiment. The Sipezi and ama-Wombe did not take wives; they were not allowed to do so." Ngidi said that one of Nandi's brothers, Mbikwana, was of the iWombe regiment like Tshaka.⁶⁹ This means that Shaka, as a young man eligible to be inducted into a military regiment, did so with his brothers while still living in the AmaZulu chiefdom during the reign of his father Senzangakhona. Ngidi further explained, "Dingana followed in age after Sigujana, the son and heir, and so, though of the iWombe, was a good deal junior to Tshaka."⁷⁰ Ndukwana also portrayed a more normal relationship between Senzangakhona and Shaka. He said,

> It seems Senzangakona built Siklebeni kraal for Tshaka and Sojisa [a brother of Senzankhona]. They went out then and this kraal was built at Mahlabatini. When Tshaka was at Siklebeni it was then that Senzangakona wanted to put him to death, as it was said, "He is a scoundrel (*itshinga*); he does all sorts of unacceptable things" – Ndukwana does not know what. Tshaka ran off to the Mtetwa

tribe and *konza*'d Dingiswayo. At this time he must have been a young man, for he had, of course, left the home of his mother's people. His boyhood and childhood was passed in the Qwabe country, at the home of his mother's people. Senzangakona did not put Sojisa to death; it was said Tshaka had got away by means of their strength (*amandhla*), and therefore, though Sojisa was originally to have been killed, he escaped because Tshaka had succeeded in getting away. Hence the origin of the name of Zibebu's people, Mandhlakazi.[71]

In relating his evidence to related information, in this case about Zibebu's people, Ndukwana lent weight to the reliability of what he said. This information also agreed with what Mruyi ka Timuni told Stuart:

I think Tshaka ran away at the time the well-known Siklebe kraal separated off. The chief's wives muttered and grumbled; they became very jealous, and a rumour sprang up that Tshaka was to be put to death. It was such a rumour, possibly without any good foundation at all, which led to Tshaka's running away. There is a definite statement to the effect that Tshaka was born at his mother's home.[72]

According to Ngidi, Shaka was not singled out by his father, but rather his father drove all of his sons who might contest the chieftaincy with the designated heir, Sigujana, out of the chiefdom. Again, Ngidi was specific:

Mfihlo, Somajuba, Mdungazwe, Ngqojana, Sopana, Dingana, Mhlangana – all these sons of Senzangakona ran off to konza Pakatwayo, on the ground, as Senzangakona alleged, that they hlobonga'd with girls, for this was not allowed in accordance with custom.[73]

Ngidi said,

Tshaka herded at the Langa tribe, then went to Senzangakona. Here he remained till Senzangakona wanted to kill the sons mentioned, when Tshaka ran off, not to the Qwabe tribe like the others, but back to his own people [at eLangeni], whereupon Nxazonke, Mbikwana and others went off with Tshaka to konza Dingiswayo. Nxazonke was sent away from the Langeni tribe by Makedama on account of the chiefship, when the latter became chief, for Nxazonke had been regent for him.[74]

Madikane attributed Shaka's decision to move to the AmamMthetwa to Makedama's hostility toward him:

Makedama made war with an *impi*. He attacked with Tshaka and the other two men, and succeeded in winning. Tshaka also killed people. Makedama then *lungisa*'d [set in order] the warriors who had stabbed. He left Tshaka alone; he did not *lungisa* him [put him into the line of honored warriors]. Tshaka questioned him [Makedama] saying, "Is not the *impi* [for which] I stabbed [fought] yours?" Makedama replied, "You do not belong to us." Tshaka became angry and left his uncle. At this time Nandi had married among the Qwabe people. Tshaka then ran off to the Mtetwa. He was with Silwane and Nomleti. He went to the place of the *induna* Ngomane. Ngomane questioned the men Tshaka was with and they told him. Ngomane then reported him to Dingiswayo.[75]

Ngidi cited an alliance between Mfundeko and Shaka in opposition to Makedama, and explained Shaka's later attack against his mother's people as actually directed against Makedama personally because Shaka evidently remained on good terms with most of the eLangeni people. Ngidi said that Nxazonke had become chief while Makedama was away among the Xulu people "for some time" and that Makedama returned and chased away Nxazonke and Shaka, who both went to the AmaMtetwa.[76] Makedama earned a reputation for brutality:

When Makedama returned from the Culu (Xulu), his mother's home, to assume the [Langa] chieftainship, he is said to have put men to death in a most cruel manner... Nxazonke got angry at this, and decided to leave and go to the Mtetwa, which he did, taking Tshaka with him.[77]

Makedama killed any potential rivals to the eLangeni chieftaincy, which he took by force. Ngidi said, "Makedama killed the *izikulu* [great or important people] of the Langeni. Nxazonke, seeing this, feared being killed and so left. He was put out at not being permitted to reign longer."[78] According to Ngidi, Makedama introduced the use of the spear to stab at close quarters rather than throwing it, usually harmlessly, from afar. This method is usually attributed to Shaka while he served in Dingiswayo's regiments, but it may well have begun with Makedama:

The using of only one assegai began with Makedama when he came from his mother's place (among the Xulu). He said, "People are afraid. Are people like buck that they should be stabbed at a distance? They must come to close quarters and so have only one assegai."[79]

Ngidi explained also how Shaka would have learned brutal methods of warfare from Makedama:

When Makedama came back from the Xulu he impaled people with barbed assegais (*izinhlendhla*), laying them flat on their backs, driving these assegais in... This was his mode of killing...

This, Ngidi says, is the precedent that was subsequently followed by Tshaka when he introduced the single assegai, for it occurred *before* he went to the Mtetwa... It was Makedama who taught him.[80]

This passage indicates that Shaka's move was the choice he made as a young man who had already reached adulthood and served in military campaigns, going in company with other adult men with whom he retained a voluntary family association. Ngidi's narrative concurs that

Shaka had aligned himself with Makedama's uncle and subsequently left with the uncle. Ngidi had firsthand information about this because his own family was involved, and he told Stuart,

> Mgabi, Makedama's father, was dead, and Nxazonke was acting as regent on behalf of Makedama. As soon as Makedama was considered old enough to assume the position of chief, Nxazonke was ousted from being regent by his life being threatened. He withdrew with Tshaka, Mfundeko, Gaqa ka Mendameli, Mbikwana and others to Daleni (my ancestor), where he was pursued and attacked by the members of the Isiwa kraal, namely that which chiefly supported Makedama. Daleni's faction was known as that of uBane of oBaneni. A fight took place in which Daleni's section proved successful. No sooner did this occur than Nxazonke asked Daleni what he should do under the circumstances. Daleni advised his going off with his party to *konza* Dingiswayo. Nxazonke, accepting the advice, acted accordingly. Upon arrival at Mtetwa, Nxazonke, Tshaka and others were placed under the immediate supervision of Ngomane. In the meantime Daleni picked out cattle and sent them as a peace offering to his "grandchild" Makedama, whilst Makedama did the same towards him, and there was peace as far as those two were concerned.[81]

Ngidi also knew that "[w]hen Tshaka went to the Mtetwa he went with Nxazonke, his uncle, and Mbikwana, also a large number of followers," and that they all returned with Shaka later. Ngidi said in a tone of certainty, "it should be remembered that of the Langa people who went to Dingiswayo, all, when Tshaka went [returned] to become king, went with him."[82]

Chapter 4

Shaka as Warrior

When Shaka went to give his allegiance to the AmaMthethwa [*abakwa*Mthethwa] chief Dingiswayo, he was merely one of several of the AmaZulu chief Senzangakhona's sons who might later try to claim their father's chieftaincy. He was among people who were more powerful and important, members of the AmaLangeni [*abase*Langeni, or people of the place of Langa] ruling family.[1] There has been considerable disagreement about who went with Shaka to the AmaMthethwa, but Ngidi was able to identify these people specifically:

Nxazonke, Mbikwana, Mfundeko, Mendameli, Ngceba ka Nodanga (Nodanga was *induna* of Kangela). When they left [eLangeni] they went and slept at my ancestor Daleni's kraal. They were fleeing, for Nxazonke had installed Mfundeko but the majority objected in favour of Makedama, hence his (Nxazonke's) flight. He fled with Tshaka and the others named. They were attacked at Daleni's. The *impi* of the great house (*ya ko mkulu*), of the eSiweni *ikanda* (*umuzi*) [homestead], was defeated by the uBane (kraal) section. Nxazonde asked Daleni what he was to do, seeing that, after trying to hide in this way, he had been followed up. Daleni then said, "Go to the Mtetwa." Nxazonke thereupon went off with the above named and a number of other Langeni people. Nandi did *not* go to the Mtetwa; she had married Gendeyana of the Mbedu section of the Qwabe peoople. I certainly do not think Nandi went to the Mtetwa. Nomcoba may have gone but I have not heard she went.[2]

Evidently his AmaLanga companions stayed with Shaka as he gained fame as a warrior, for when they arrived among the AmaMthethwa, "Tshaka was given to Ngomane [and] he was given as Nxazonke's dependent, for he had left the Zulu tribe."[3]

Ndhlovu ka Timuni and his brother Mruyi disagreed over the details of what happened to Shaka when he arrived at Dingiswayo's. Ndhlovu claimed that Shaka's presence there was concealed from Senzangakhona and explained why Mudhli took an interest in Shaka's welfare even though he was Senzangakhona's *induna*. According to Ndhlovu, "Tshaka was a young man when he got to Mqombolo's. Mudhli did not appear much in all these proceedings, and the part he took was purposely concealed. He was anxious that Tshaka should not die. Tshaka was of his main house (*indhlunkulu yake*), and this is why he displayed so great an interest in the matter. He concealed his close relative as he was afraid lest they should put the boy to death."[4] Contradicting him, Mruyi said that "Tshaka's presence at the Mtetwa tribe was well enough known to Senzangakhona and his other sons, of whom there was a large number (a great collection of his brothers, i.e. Tshaka's). Tshaka was not concealed from his father, but from, or on account of his brothers."[5] Mruyi added, "At Dingiswayo's, Tshaka was kept by Ngomane ka Mqombolo of the Caya people." Ngomane later returned to the AmaZulu chiefdom with Shaka.[6] Shaka had his first homestead among the AmaMthethwa, and the people of his homestead there, called *Nogqogqa*, later followed Shaka on his return to the AmaZulu chiefdom. There they were re-established as the Mkandhlu *umuzi* known as Shaka's first royal settlement.[7] Ngidi believed that Shaka had not gotten his name as an infant but rather from Dingiswayo. Stuart wrote in his notes that "Dhlungwana is evidently a regular name for Tshaka, for I heard Ngidi use it several times. He does not know the derivation." Later Ngidi repeated that Dingiswayo had given Shaka his name as a praise-name and that he was previously called Mandhlesilo.[8] Moreover, Ngidi said that Shaka's experience living among the AmaMthethwa may have remained evident in his pattern of speech, saying, "Tshaka seemed to have a defect in his speech; he mouthed his words, maybe due to his having learnt the Mtetwa dialect."[9]

Magidi, Ngomane's son, explained Dingiswayo's reaction to the arrival of the son of his subordinate chief, Senzangakhona:

Dingiswayo called Ngomane, who lived at Yengweni, and said, "Ngomane, son of Mqomboli, look after this child of the chief for me." Ngomane agreed to do so. Tshaka built at Kwa Nogqogqa in the Mtetwa country. Tshaka had come with his mother Nandi and sister Nomcoba, also Ngqengelele, father of Mnyamana. He came with him from Zululand. Tshaka came, being a youth.[10]

According to Ndhlovu, "At Dingiswayo's, Tshaka, still unknown to his anxious father, served in the army. He became distinguished as a warrior, was a noted warrior (*iqawe*)."¹¹ According to Jantshi, Shaka had earned a reputation as a warrior among the Mthethwa, which drew Senzangakhona there. He said, "Tshaka was known by Dingiswayo as 'He whose fame spreads even while he is sitting; the *ilembe* [hoe, meaning 'axe'] which surpasses other amaLembe."¹² Ndhlovu told several stories that were intended to demonstrate Shaka's strength and success as a warrior, and Jantshi noted that "I do not know if Tshaka became an *induna* to Dingiswayo. Probably not. He was a favourite there because he was a great warrior."¹³ Ngidi said that "Tshaka was one of the Isifazana regiment of Dingiswayo," and that while he was a warrior in Dingiswayo's regiments, the AmaMtetwa fought against the chiefdoms of the AbaQwabe, the AmaNyuswa (*abakwa*Nyuswa), the AmaNdwandwe, the AbaTembu under chief Mlunjwa, and the *abakwa*Dube under Nzwakele ka Kutshwayo.¹⁴ While serving under Dingiswayo, according to Ngidi,

Tshaka had the reputation of fighting fiercely (*hlabana*ing). In former times (*endulo*), before he came, people used to fight by hurling assegais at one another. He learnt the practice of stabbing from us Langeni; among us, people used to stab one another. This mode of fighting in our tribe began in Makedama's time, Makedama being about the same age as Tshaka.¹⁵

Ndhlovu's 1919 narrative included stories about Shaka among the AmaMthethwa that he had not previously related regarding militarization under Shaka's rule.¹⁶ He said,

It was there at oYengweni that Tshaka learnt about war. When they went out to fight, the order was that they should hurl their assegais at the enemy with whom they were fighting. They fought, and the enemy fled. They were ordered to leave off, and return, as the enemy had run away. The next day the enemy *impi* would return to fight again. Men were killed who had survived the fighting of the previous day. Then Tshaka said, "Wo! This is a bad way of fighting. No sooner have we routed the enemy than we are ordered to leave off fighting. They then return and kill our men. If we continued to pursue them, we would finish them off." He said, "Wo! It would be better if we did not let them go." He said this to Dingisayo's son. Dingiswayo's son agreed with him. After this they would stab the enemy; they would press the attack without withdrawing. With this method of fighting they were always victorious. They caused Dingiswayo to be a great chief who overcame the nations.¹⁷

Shaka lived with and was treated exactly the same as was Dingiswayo's son, and the change to a brutal style of fighting by stabbing (to death) instead of throwing assegais (in order to wound) is attributed to the initiative of Shaka with the agreement of Dingiswayo's son. Ndhlovu believed Dingiswayo gave his approval when it was explained to him.[18] However, other versions depict Dingiswayo as rebuking Shaka for using this style of fighting and killing so many people, including women and children (i.e., unarmed innocent bystanders). Ndhlovu's narrative moved into a heroic epic style: "This is what made Dingiswayo a great chief, a feared one, for his people were now stronger than all the other nations (*izizwe*) with whom he fought; he overcame them all. We Zulu, too, were as nothing to Dingiswayo; we feared him."[19] Mandhlakazi ka Ngini said similarly,

My fathers (Ngini and Zulu and others) said that Tshaka found fault with the practice of carrying a number of assegais. This was when he was still among the Mtetwa with Dingiswayo. He said, "Wo! If these men were mine I would cut a single assegai for each of them. I do not want them to bear wounds behind. A good many should have his wounds on his chest." So when he came back to the Zulu country he [Shaka] ordered that only one assegai should be carried, and this was done.[20]

Madikane said that Dingiswayo subsequently disapproved of the brutality of Shaka's fighting and explicitly chastised him on the basis of a more humane policy to which Dingiswayo adhered. Madikane said,

Dingiswayo sent Tshaka out with a body of troops to attack the amaMbata people whilst he went to war against the amaNtshali. Tshaka not only defeated the amaMbata but pursued them, killed them off and returned with their cattle etc. Dingiswayo, who had expected Tshaka to return sooner and had been waiting for him, reproved him for his drastic measures, it being against Dingiswayo's policy to exterminate any tribe.[21]

Dingiswayo's practice of retaining subordinate chiefs in their positions after they had tendered their submission, as in the case of Senzangakhona, is well established historically as is his policy of limiting bloodshed in military engagements. Mayinga provided an alternative explanation for Dingiswayo's disapproval that it was meant to be protective of Shaka:

Dingiswayo sent out a force to attack Malusi of the Nxumalo peopole. Tshaka went on this occasion, and that is where he began the battle. On this occasion he rushed forward along into the enemy and started stabbing about. Dingiswayo reproved him; he said that being a chief's son he should not go forward alone.[22]

Shaka was a warrior in Dingiswayo's army when the AmaMthethwa fought against the AbaQwabe. Mayinga ka Mbekuzana's tesimony about Shaka's early life diverges so significantly from that of Stuart's older generation of informants as to cast doubt on his information, but because it is a version of oral tradition that has been passed down, it is worthy of consideration. Moreover, Mayinga's father had served as Shaka's *inyanga*, or doctor, before serving as *inyanga* to Mpande, that may have given Mayinga's father access to information not known by others. One of the unique pieces of testimony Mayinga offered related to this battle fought at the Mhlatuze. According to him, Dingiswayo had sent his warriors to attack the AbaQwabe chief Phakatwayo and after defeating him, "Dingiswayo found out that Pakatwayo's impi ran off because of Tshaka, [who was] then called Sikiti. Dingiswayo now named him Tshaka by saying 'Tshaka who is not beaten, the axe that surpasses other axes, the impetuous one who disregards warnings' (for he was warned not to throw himself into the battle, but disregarded the instructions)."[23] Mayinga was certain that Shaka had previously been called Sikiti, and that "[t]he name Tshaka arose because of his deeds as a warrior of the Mtetwa chief. The name Tshaka was given by Dingiswayo, not owing to the *itshati* which the girl Nandi may have said she was suffering from."[24] He provided other details about Shaka's daily habits, suggesting his father as the source, such as that Shaka "was always talking of war," and "he snuffed a good deal."[25] He also referred to the regalia by which Shaka came to be known:

The feather of Madolwane, the long one. It was called Madolwane because of its length, i.e. the blue crane feather worn by Tshaka.[26]

SENZANGAKHONA'S VISIT TO DINGISWAYO

The next important story that has some consistency in the oral traditions is about a visit Senzangakhona paid to Dingiswayo after Shaka had become a warrior and the subsequent events that led to Senzangakhona's death. Ndhlovu began one of his tellings of the tradition by saying,

Tshaka lived years among the Mtetwa tribe; he became a youth (*insizwa*), and took an active part in Dingiswayo's military enterprises.

The rumour that a child of Senzangakona's was among the Mtetwa people came to be circulated. Senzangakona then said, "I will myself go down and court girls,' i.e. look about himself for what he has lost and cannot otherwise find. He went to Dingiswayo's, where he was given a splendid welcome.[27]

By contrast, Mkebeni later told a more complicated told a story about the events that led to Senzangakhona's visit to Dingiswayo. Like others, Mkebeni reported that it was at Dingiswayo's invitation that his subordinate chief Senzangakhona came to visit. In this narrative, Shaka overcame a mad man who had been terrorizing people and killed him;

this was the first time he had killed a man and Shaka then drew Dingiswayo's attention by barring the entrance of the *isigodlo* to prevent food being carried into the women, and threw stones at some warriors. This prompted Dingiswayo to invite Senzangakhona to come for a visit to an *injadu* dance.[28] The story implies that this is when Shaka was recognized as an adult and that it was then that the events surrounding Senzangakhona's visit to Dingiswayo and his subsequent death occurred. Shaka was already an accomplished warrior who had achieved fame among the AmaMthethwa and their enemies. Dingiswayo recognized Shaka's status formally, and Magidi ka Ngomane, son of Shaka's great *induna*, said, "He *tunga*'d [put on the headring signifying adulthood] at Mtetwa – was *tunga*'d by Dingiswayo."[29] According to Ndhlovu's version of events,

> Senzangakona was once more worried by hearing a rumour to the effect that his supposed son was hiding among Dingiswayo's tribe. He resolved himself to go down and see if he could not find him. Such search had, of course, to be disguised, and so he said he was going down to court the girls, no doubt with the view to getting a wife.[30]

The telling of the story in such detail is in itself notable, suggestive of the importance of these details in the transmission of the story by those who had told it to Ndhlovu, because Stuart did not think Ndhlovu had added any embellishments of his own in the telling.[31] To emphasize the accuracy of his narrative Ndhlovu identified his source: "Sipika says he accompanied Senzangakona when he went to oYengweni, to court the girls as Senzangakona said, whereas in truth he was going to look for Tshaka."[32] The reference to participants and eyewitnesses to the events that interviewees, in this case Ndhlovu, related to Stuart underscores the importance of their evidence in reconstructing historical events, not merely literary mythology. However, Ndhlovu's narrations later became so embellished with the flourishes of epic storytelling that the core events may mistakenly appear to have been invented.

According to Ndhlovu, the initiative for the visit was from Senzangakhona, not at the invitation of his superior, Dingiswayo.

> Hearing of the intended visit, Mudhli dispatched a messenger to Dingiswayo, warning him. Senzangakona, on arrival, was treated with great respect. Mats were laid on the ground many yards from the door of the hut (*ilawu*) he was to occupy. In the meantime Dingiswayo had apprised Tshaka of his father's coming. Unseen, Tshaka himself looked on his father. Dingiswayo gave Senzangakona quantities of meat and beer, and treated him with every mark of civility. He directed that Tshaka, with others, should go very early to the pond where people usually

washed and wash himself, it being his intention afterwards to conduct Senzangakona there for a similar purpose. The intention was that Senzangakona should wash in water already soiled or dirtied by Tshaka's having washed in it.[33]

The use of supposedly supernatural concoctions, in this case the water soiled by Tshaka, was commonly practiced well into the twentieth century, making this scenario credible. Dingiswayo himself had been "doctored" by Bhungane's *inyanga* when he went to the AmaHlubi chiefdom seeking advice on how to unify a chiefdom, and there is ample testimony that Dingiswayo was among the chiefs at the time who attempted to employ the potions made by his *izinyanga* to disempower and destroy his political rivals. Ndhlovu continued,

Tshaka followed his guardian's instructions, and Senzangakona himself, with all his followers, except two who were left behind to mind the hut, went to the river to wash. Dingiswayo, who remained at home, then sent for the two men left in charge, caused them to be taken into a hut, and there supplied both with meat and beer in large and inviting quantities. The men, however, at first demurred, but, on two others in the employ of Dingiswayo (being his men) saying they would remain in charge [of Senzangakona's hut], eventually consented to go.

Whilst the two men were engaged eating and drinking, Dingiswayo and Tshaka entered the hut. Dingiswayo took a mat, a sitting-mat belonging to Senzangakona – that on which that king himself sat – and made Tshaka stand on it. He [Dingiswayo], moreover, drew an assegai from the bundle belonging to Senzangakona and gave it to Tshaka, who held it, while standing, in both hands as Dingiswayo applied various drugs not only over Tshaka but the mat and assegai as well, the intention being to enchant or bewitch the king, cause him to become sick and die, when Tshaka would succeed him. This done, the two left the hut, Tshaka, of course, taking the assegai with him.[34]

This story sheds light on what the oral traditions came to portray about the relationship between Shaka and Dingiswayo and the use of tricks and "medicines" for evil purposes by a king, Dingiswayo. It indicates that Shaka learned these practices, including the implementation of a deliberate conspiracy with long-term goals, from Dingiswayo's example. Ndhlovu's version of what followed next is perhaps the most detailed and varies with other, shorter versions: "Next day Dingiswayo caused a lot of girls to be brought into Senzangakona's hut and himself went in to converse with him."[35] This part of the story is consistent with Ndhlovu's earlier assertions about Senzangakhona's ruse; Dingiswayo would have sent in the girls to fulfill Senzangakhona's stated intention of having come to find another wife. Then the plot unfolds:

Senzagakona whiled away the time pleasantly enough, then, in pursuance of a preconcerted plan, Dingiswayo ordered the girls to leave, as he wished

Senzangakona to see what he called his great warriors. It might be observed here that Tshaka's identity was practically unknown at Oyengweni (Dingiswayo's kraal). Dingiswayo, Mqomboli and Mudhli (with some others living at a distance) were the only ones who knew his exact whereabouts. Whilst sitting on the *taka*'d mat, the young men passed in one by one, Dingiswayo, as they did so, singing their praises by way of introducing each individual to his distinguished visitor.

It was so arranged that Tshaka should be the last to come in, and as it had been arranged so it was done – and in this way. By the time Tshaka had to come in, that side of the hut on which Dingiswayo sat – he sat in a particular position – was chock-a-block with men whose bodies were in contact with one another's. With large curling horns poised on either side of his neck, dressed from top to bottom in –[sic]. Tshaka entered. Finding that side of the hut on which, according to custom, he ought to sit, full of men, he stood still a moment, immediately opposite his father so that his (Tshaka's) shadow completely covered him, and, glancing at him but once face to face, proceeded to a short distance and there sat down, not on the ground but raised up. No sooner did the shadow fall on the king [Senzangakona], their eyes meet, and Dingiswayo asked if Senzangakona knew who that was, than great trembling came over the latter.[36]

Ndhlovu prefaced some of his comments with the words, "report says," indicating he was consciously passing on what he had heard as if it were commonly accepted and without imposing his own judgment about the accuracy of the story. Senzangakhona did not answer Dingiswayo's question:

Report says he gave no reply to the interrogation. The drugs had evidently done their fatal work. Senzangakona got ill and decided to return home on the following day. He was accompanied by several of Dingiswayo's followers, who brought back the news that it was very doubtful if the king would recover of his illness, seeing it was already of a serious character.[37]

Later on the same day, Ndhlovu added new details of this, saying, "The question put by Dingiswayo to his visitor after the young men had entered the hut they sat in ran somewhat as follows; 'Do you see the beast of your people among these cattle?' Senzangakona then pointed to Shaka but was overwhelmed with fear as he did so."[38]

Ndhlovu's 1919 version of the story of Senzangakhona's visit to the AmaMthethwa is shorter and differs significantly from his earlier 1902–1903 telling of the story, but the explanation of the motive and pretext remain the same. This later version placed more emphasis on the details of encounters, seeing, and recognition that raised the level of dramatic tension in telling the tale. Hence, twice Senzangakhona failed to recognize Shaka, and a visual imagery is sustained through the mention of these encounters that foreshadowed the coming dramatic events. In this version, the details of a conspiracy against Senzangakhona contrived and executed by Dingiswayo, with Shaka as his instrument, were more elaborate than in the 1902–1903 Ndhlovu narrative. The importance of the oral performance stands out at this point because of the dramatic use of foreshadowing in the text that was absent in the earlier Ndhlovu version:

Dingiswayo then took Senzangakona's sitting-mat, made Tshaka stand on it, and doctored him with medicines. He then smeared it with medicines; he rubbed it with the fat of many types of fierce animals, so that when Senzangakona saw Tshaka, his neck would "break" and Tshaka would be foremost. Senzangakona would bow down; his neck would bend; he would no longer be able to look upon Tshaka; he would hold him in fear; he would be overcome by fear. Dingiswayo finished doctoring him, then pulled out two of Senzangakona's assegais which were bound round with the tail of an elephant. He doctored Tshaka with them, and then placed them back with the others.[39]

In this version two assegais, not just one, were doctored, but Shaka did not take it; he was given it later in the hut by his father. This scene is similar, with Dingiswayo's sons called in before Shaka. Dingiswayo praised them, and then Shaka came in as Dingiswayo said his praises, "The one whose fame spreads even as he sits, the son of Menzi, the axe which surpasses other axes." Shaka allowed his shadow to fall on his father who was overcome by fear. "His neck 'broke' on the spot; it went snap! His eyes stared fixedly." When Dingiswayo saw him collapse he called out, "Hau! Does the chief see the beast from the place of his people?" Senzangakhona was not dead but merely frozen in terror, and Ndhlovu says he replied, "Hau! I see it." Shaka then asked his father for an assegai and chose one of the doctored ones, but Senzangakhona said it was one that belonged to another of his sons, so Shaka took the second doctored spear and left with the other warriors to *giya*, dance, with his father's assegai.[40]

Ndhlovu added a new scene in the 1919 Shaka narrative, in which a dance was held that Senzangakhona, then feeling ill, was unable to attend, but Mudhli and Dingiswayo attended it. Ndhlovu's extended tale provided dialogue associated with the event, and he added a scene in which a crane feather fell off of Dingiswayo's ceremonial dress to the ground where it stuck and stood upright. The dance ended as Dingiswayo refused to allow his *izinduna* to retrieve the feather. Ndhlovu added a piece of dialogue, attributed generally to the spectators, explaining the meaning he intended to be attached to this symbolic scene: "Dingiswayo has been overcome; he has been overcome by Mudhli!" Unlike the Stuart record of Ndhlovu's 1902–1903 Shaka narrative, Stuart recorded in 1919 that

Ndhlovu had repeatedly refered to Mudhl as "my grandfather, Mudhli." Mudhli is portrayed as having a final conversation with Dingiswayo on behalf of Senzangakhona, making his farewells. Dingiswayo is said to have asked Mudhli to remain behind, which he did while Senzangakhona left with his attendants. In this conversation, Dingiswayo refers to Shaka as "your [Mudhli's] son, [i.e. Mudhli's responsibility]" and tells Mudhli, "I shall now return him" but Mudhli requested that he "not do it today" because, Mudhli explained when asked why, "I fear the Zulu." Mudhli then elaborated, "Nkosi, they will put me to death." When Dingiswayo asked why the AmaZulu would put Mudhli to death, Mudhli responded, "They will say, 'So you have been put in charge of two people at once? You have been put in charge of Senzangakona and of Tshaka?'"

Dingiswayo is said to have remained silent, and after Mudhli left, an extended and obviously invented conversation is attributed to Dingiswayo and his men:

"Why does he do this, when it was he who caused Tshaka to come here to me? It was he who caused Tshaka to be here, and now he is refusing to return him to his country. It seems that he wants to make Nomkwayimba chief. My men, take Tshaka to his country. Go with him this very day; take him after his father." The men agreed, saying, "Yes. Let him be taken back." He [Dingiswayo] then said to Tshaka, "When you see this man [Mudhli] put him to death. You will not be chief if you leave him alive. You yourself saw how, when I was dancing with him, my feather fell to the ground. If you do not kill him you will not be chief."[41]

Magidi ka Ngomane knew some of these details and told Stuart, "'A man cannot serve two masters,' as was said by Mudhli to Dingiswayo when directed to protect Tshaka as against Senzangakona."[42]

Mruyi's narrative deviated from that of his brother Ndhlovu.[43] In his version, when Senzangakhona arrived at Dingiswayo's,

a large number of young men of Dingiswayo's tribe entered the hut by pre-arrangement. Tshaka also came in, unknown at the time to Senzangakona. He stood as if there were no place for him; he did this on instructions from the Mtetwa chief (i.e. according to a preconcerted plan). Tshaka had on horns about his neck and the *iziqu* amulets of a man who had killed in battle; he was, moreover, one of Dingiswayo's heroes.[44]

Shaka's shadow fell on Senzangakhona, "a silence fell upon all in the hut," and Dingiswayo asked, "Do you see your calf here?" Senzangakhona identified Shaka, and Dingiswayo sang Shaka's praises. Then Shaka asked Senzangakhona for an assegai "and he was presented with one." This 1903 narrative does not contain the dramatic elements of sudden fear or illness on the part of Senzangakhona but describes elaborate ploys by both Dingiswayo and Mudhli. The next day at the dance, when a feather fell from Dingiswayo's head and stuck into the ground, he prevented his *izinceku* (servants) from retrieving it, but the dance continued for a while, after which the feather was picked up.[45]

Mruyi included an element of impending doom in his narrative of the events of the following day when Senzangakhona left Dingiswayo's "feeling somewhat uncomfortable; evil forebodings haunted him." Mruyi also described a conversation between Mudhli and Dingiswayo before Mudhli's departure in which Dingiswayo told Mudhli, "Here is Tshaka. I am bringing him to you." As in Ndhlovu's version, Mudhli demurred, saying, "How can you expect me to look after and protect Tshaka, seeing I already have his father, Senzangakona, to see to?" In language typical of Stuart's early written records of these interviews, Dingiswayo has a dialogue with Shaka in which he tells Shaka to kill Mudhli: "This man Mudhli refuses to have anything to do with you, saying he has to take care of Senzangakona. It is manifest, therefore, he does not care for you. Don't spare him. He is the leading and responsible head of the Zulu tribe. Put him to death or you can never reign." Shaka accordingly "summoned to his side numbers of Mudhli's own followers, and they joined him." This particular statement provided an explanation for why the family of Mruyi and Ndhlovi (i.e., Mudhli's son Timuni [their father]) and others should not be regarded as having betrayed the interests of Shaka but had in fact become his earliest adherents upon his return to the AmaZulu. It indicates a clear break within the family of Mudhli, for Mruyi continues, "Mudhli was then surrounded, when both Mudhli and Zivalele were put to death."[46]

Jantshi's tale is dramatic and entertaining: the dance was held the day after Senzangakhona's arrival and after his party had "danced," Dingiswayo dramatically announced the entrance of Shaka, who had heretofore remained hidden, by calling out, "Where is the hoe that surpasses other hoes?" Dingiswayo thus used the same metaphor and praise or *isibongo* previously employed to refer to Shaka. As Dingiswayo recited more of Shaka's praises, he came out and *giya*'d, that is, performed the ritual dancelike warrior's performance; Jantshi described his shield and skin clothing in detail. Rather than a hostile encounter, in Jantshi's narrative, Shaka said to Senzangakhona, "Father, give me an assegai, and I shall fight great battles for you!" When Senzangakhona had his assegais brought to him and told Shaka to take one, Shaka said "No, let it come from your hand; I cannot take it myself." Senzangakhona made the choice carefully, taking each of his assegais one by one before selecting one and giving it to Shaka. The dialogue and description included in this version would have helped to hold an audience to this oral narrative spellbound. The dramatic tension rose further as Shaka *giya*'d with his new assegai in the direction of his brothers Dingana, Sigujana, Mhlangano, Ngqojana, Mpande, and Maqubana. Shaka proceeded to approach Sigujana and tap him on the head with his assegai, whereupon they greeted each other and "conversed a little" before Shaka joined the rest of his companions in more dancing. This portrayal of a casual encounter broke the narrative tension, but the symbolic mention of tapping his brother on the head with an assegai foreshadowed conflict between Shaka and his rivals for the inheritance of the AmaZulu chieftaincy.[47]

Jantshi's more common version of the story portrays Shaka as having gone to Senzangakhona's hut at night after everyone had retired and gone to sleep, and going on top of the hut.[48] There above his father, in accordance with Zulu chiefly rituals used to attain power over an enemy, Shaka washed himself with special medicines designed for this purpose. Jantshi said that Senzangakhona "woke and at once roused those in the hut and told them to go out and see what that was on the hut which appeared to be washing itself there. As they opened the door they heard a person jump off the hut and run away. It being a moonlight night, they saw the person running away. They saw it was Tshaka."[49] The narrative reflected and took advantage of AmaZulu beliefs in the supernatural, which revived the dramatic effect of the storyline: "Senzangakona was then overome by fear. He became sick in the night. The next day he was ill."[50] Senzangakhona sent a message to tell Dingiswayo he was leaving because he was ill, and the latter came with Shaka and others "to bid him goodbye"; at this point, Senzangakhona told Dingiswayo about the previous night's incident but without reference to Shaka. Dingiswayo's conversation with Mudhli took place in front of Senzangakhona and Zivalele as well as Shaka. Dingiswayo pointed to Shaka and told Mudhli, "Take good care of this person for me." Jantshi reported a collective reply, in which "they" (unspecified) said, "Au, *nkosi* [chief], must we look after him too, while we are still caring for this one [Senzangakhona]?" With this, the story ended and Senzangakhona's party returned home. With dramatic license, Jantshi said that after their return, an AmaZulu party of warriors (*impi*) was sent to fight against the AmaKumalo under chief Donda, and there Shaka's brother Sigujana was struck and killed by an assegai, hit in the very spot where Tshaka had tapped his head.[51]

Madikane's less dramatic version nevertheless includes magical elements:

> That night Tshaka got on top of the hut in which Senzangakona was asleep. In doing this he was gaining ascendancy over his father, according to the ways of the black people. He was following the customs of his own people, not the Mtetwa's. Tshaka washed etc.⁵²

Madikane said that Senzangakhona arrived home alive from Dingiswayo's, contrary to other versions. The next part of Madikane's narrative is also unusual: "He [Senzangakhona] heard that he would not recover." This is consistent with a role of Senzangakhona's own *izinyanga* in conspiring with Shaka against Senzangakhona. It would not have been difficult for the *izinyanga* to have controlled Senzangakhona on his deathbed after they had sufficiently weakened him with their very real poisons. Madikane's story of events surrounding Senzangakhona also would certainly explain Shaka's own fear of, hostility toward, and killing of the AmaZulu *izinyanga* after he came to power. Once Senzangakhona had been told he would not recover, "[h]e then issued an order in the Zulu country. He proclaimed, "Let this matter that we were talking about not be discussed' (viz. appointing Sigujana); 'let it be avoided, because Tshaka is at Mtetwa where we are ruled.'"⁵³ There is logic in this version that attributes Senzangakhona's appointment of Shaka not to an argument of legitimacy as his heir but to the political power of the AmaMthethwa chief Dingiswayo to whom they were subject. According to Madikane's version of AmaZulu history, Shaka came to power as chief of the AmaZulu not because Senzangakhona or the AmaZulu people accepted him as heir to Senzangakhona, or preferred him to Sigujana or other more legitimate choices as heir, but only because Shaka was Dingiswayo's protégé and Dingiswayo had the political power over the AmaZulu sufficient to override their legitimate choice and impose his own choice, Shaka.⁵⁴

Ngidi was quite certain that "Senzangakona died of fear. He died on the way, viz. among the abakwaMakoba people (chief: Joko), and was then carried home to be buried. I believe he was dead before he reached home, and was dead when carried."⁵⁵

Sivivi had heard that at Dingiswayo's,

> After *giya*ing, Tshaka concluded by leaping over (*eqa*ing) his father. Senzangakona then went home to the Zulu country. He said to his men, "Look here, Zulu, you had better allow Tshaka to reign after me, for I have seen he is one who does harm (*itshinga*); he jumped over me." Senzangakona had nominated Uzikatshana [Sigujana] as his heir, but Uzikatshana did not reign.⁵⁶

Mkebeni's 1921 stories portray Shaka as being a madman and so had been declared to be one by his own father Senzangakhona, who nevertheless is said to have ordered Shaka be made chief after his own death.[57] Mtshayankomo's version, told in 1922, reflected storytelling practices that had allowed altering the oral traditions of the events surrounding Senzangakhona's visit to Dingiswayo and encounter there with Shaka for the sake of drama at the expense of historical accuracy. Mtshayankoma related that at Senzangakhona's, groups of youth were brought three times and Dingiswayo asked Senzangakhona to point out his son, and the third time he pointed out Shaka. "The *amakosikazi* [royal women or queens], Tshaka's mothers, then called him. They kissed him."[58] But Bibi ka Nkobe, the sister of Ndhlela, did not. Shaka left and went to the *isigodhlo* where Dingiswayo had gone and asked him for medicine because Bibi, his father's wife, had not kissed him. After dark, the *izinyanga* "doctors" gave advice to Dingiswayo who called for Shaka to come to his own hut where they made the medicines. Then Dingiswayo's *inceku* (servant) went with Shaka to where Senzangakhona and his wives were asleep. According to Mtshayankomo, "Tshaka then climbed up onto the hut where his father and the *amakosikazi* were sleeping. He thrust a stick through the thatch above the place where his father was sleeping. The *inceku* passed the medicine up to him. He took it, pulled out the stick, and proceeded to wash himself with the medicines there on top of the hut. The water ran down through the hole made by the stick and dripped onto Senzangakona as he lay asleep. Senzangakona was startled." He exclaimed and asked what the water was but they saw nothing outside, and then he asked, "what is urinating on me, then?"[59]

The next morning the incident and that Senzangakhona was in pain were reported to Dingiswayo. He sent to ask the diviners what had happened, and they said the ancestors had caused Senzangakhona's illness. He slaughtered oxen to appease the ancestors, saying it was on Senzangakhona's behalf, but Senzangakhona was still in pain when he left the next day. Dingiswayo had him followed "up-country" by a spy who returned to say that Senzangakhona was still very ill, and after going to check several times, finally returned with the news that Senzangakhona had died.[60]

SHAKA'S RETURN TO THE AMAZULU CHIEFDOM

Oral traditions described the circumstances under which Shaka returned to the AmaZulu chiefdom and the events surrounding his accession to the chieftaincy of the AmaZulu, which was still subordinate to Dingiswayo's rule. The AmaMthethwa *induna* Ngomane who had, on Dingiswayo's instructions, taken in Shaka when he arrived in Dingiswayo's chiefdom years before, accompanied Shaka back to the chiefdom of the AmaZulu and remained with him for the rest of Ngomane's life. Ngomane's son Magidi said,

> Dingiswayo directed Ngomane to bring up Tshaka, the child of a chief. Ngomane proceeded to do so. Ngomane went to the Zulus with Tshaka, together with those with whom Tshaka had come from the Zulus. He did not take soldiers. Tshaka arrived in the Zulu country whilst Senzangakona was still living. Senzangakona was overcome by fear and died, and Tshaka disputed the succession with Sigujana. The people accepted Tshaka as soon as he arrived, so he was able to contest successfully against Sigujana. Tshaka at this time had no wives.[61]

In Sivivi's rendition, "Senzangakona then died. Tshaka then went up-country to rule, Dingiswayo sending him up and presenting him with cattle. He came with many cattle, driven up by Dingiwayo's *amabuto* [regiments]. Tshaka asked the names of all the *izikulu* [senior, great men] of the place, and the names were all given him, for he had left the tribe whilst still young. He distributed the cattle he had come with among the men. He then began destroying the peoples (*izizwe* [nations, chiefdoms]), and captured their cattle. He also killed uZikatshana [Sigujana]."[62]

The different narratives do not agree about whether Senzangakhona was still alive when Shaka returned to the AmaZulu chiefdom. Jantshi believed that "when Tshaka arrived in the Zulu country, Senzangakona was certainly dead. I have not heard that Senzangakona declared Tshaka to be his legitimate son."[63] The preponderance of evidence supports the commonly held view that Sigujana (Dingane's elder brother) was still considered to be Senzangakhona's heir at the time of his death and that Shaka took his position as chief by force. He may have had local support, however, and Stuart noted, "Ndukwana has heard that Mkabayi ruled a little after Senzangakona's death, so she may have done so to allow Tshaka to come up."[64] Jantshi did not believe that Sigujana, the designated heir, was widely supported, and said,

> Senzangakona had no one who stood armed by his grave as his successsor. Sigujana did not stand thus, for when Tshaka got up, people accepted him without a fight. No one was ousted by Tshaka. It is probable then that Tshaka was offered the position of king.[65]

Ndhlovu gave the longest versions of events.[66] The involvement of his family members lends his account credibility.

Mudhli then sent to ask Dingiswayo when he was going to instate Tshaka as king, begging him not to attempt to do so then, seeing the part Mudhli had taken in bringing up Senzangakona. He [Mudhli] was afraid lest Senzangakona would kill him. Dingiswayo however advised Mudhli should be put to death. As Tshaka proceeded on the way to his father's kraal to assume the government, he killed all at once four prominent men, their names being as follows: Mudhli himself, Zivalele ka Jama [Ntombela], Sijisa ka Jama, and Nobongoza ka Jama.... No sooner did Tshaka arrive than his coming was reported to Senzangakona, when the man so long in search of his son came by his death from fear because Tshaka had come to see him.[67]

Ngidi said that when Shaka went up-country with the men he specified it was because he had been called back by some of his own people:

Tshaka was called by Menziwa ka Coko (Xoko) of the Biyelo people in the Zulu country, Mnkabayi, Mawa, and Mmama. They objected to Sigujana being king on the ground that his mother Mpikase was not a woman of rank, and that Nandi, the daughter of Mbengi, was. Hence Tshaka's selection.[68]

Ngidi believed that Sigujana did become chief and that Shaka was called back because his own people disliked Sigujana, indicating that Ngidi believed Senzangakhona died before Shaka's return. Ngidi said, "Sigujana, son of Mpikase, succeeded his father until deposed by Tshaka." However,

The Zulu people (uZulu) objected to Sigujana being made the heir, seeing that his mother was Mpikase, whereas the chief wife was Mnkabi, and Tshaka's mother Nandi had been put into her house. The Zulus wanted to know what the objection was to Tshaka's being the heir. Menziwa ka Cogo, Mudhli ka Nkwelo, Sojisa ka Jama, Renqwa and others, also Mnkabayi and Mmama ka Jama, also Mawa, objected to Sigujana being appointed.

Zivalele and others wished Sigujana to be chief.[69]

This would explain popular acquiescence to Shaka's seizure of the chieftaincy from his younger half brother Sigujana and to Shaka's killing him.

The widely known historical narrative of Henry Francis Fynn fundamentally agrees with these later versions told to Stuart.[70] Fynn says that while living among the AmaMthethwa, Shaka distinguished himself in battle and was known by the name Sikiti and by the honorary title given to the heads of regiments, *Sidlodlo sekhanda*. Fynn wrote that Shaka stayed with Dingiswayo until the year 1816 when Senzangakhona died. According to Fynn, Shaka had approached Dingiswayo for help in taking the chieftaincy from Sigujana after Senzangakhona had died, but Dingiswayo had refused on the grounds that Sigujana had the right as designated heir.[71] However, Dingiswayo is said to have promised aid if Sigujana was "out of the way," prompting Shaka to send his half brother

Shaka as Warrior

Ngwadi to kill Sigujana and another brother who was with him at the time. Then, according to Fynn, Dingiswayo sent Shaka with men dressed in war attire, singing a song composed by Shaka for this occasion.[72] Ngidi said, "Senzangakona really foreshadowed Tshaka's subsequent rank by calling him Mandhlesilo. There was a man Mandhlesilo (among the Langeni) ka Ncumela, chief of the Langa tribe. Senzangakona selected this name for Tshaka."[73] Shaka was praised as "*amandla wesilo*, which means 'strength of the wild beast.'"[74]

Chapter 5

AmaZulu Expansion and Repercussions: Early Conflicts and Migrations

> During the *umkosi* [first fruits harvest] ceremony a regiment would fetch Tshaka from the *isigodhlo* [women's quarters] and bring him to the men's assembly in the cattle kraal, and a chant they sang which Baleka's father told her was "Come Down! bird which devours others; come Down! you who overcome the chiefs; come down! come here!"[1]
>
> War has in the past had its seat in Mnkabayi's Mahlabaneni kraal. When the men of that place take the field, it is generally known that war has broken out in the land in earnest and will be universal in character.[2]

Shaka's AmaZulu chiefdom at the time of his accession to the chieftaincy in 1816 was still only a small subordinate chiefdom to the larger AmaMthethwa kingdom that had been consolidated by Chief Dingiswayo. But within a few years, Shaka had become the "bird which devours others;" you, the chief "who overcome the chiefs."[3] Shaka had gained considerable experience as a warrior while he served in Dingiswayo's AmaMthethwa army. During that time that he was in Dingiswayo's, Shaka was a warrior for the AmaMthethwa, fighting against the AbaQwabe, AmaNyuswa, AmaNdwandwe, AbaTembu of Chief Mlunjwa, AmaDube under Nzwakele ka Kutshwayo, AmaMbata, AmaNtshali, and the AmaNxumalo under Chief Malusi.[4] It is impossible to establish with certainty the chronological order in which Shaka achieved the voluntary and involuntary submission of neighboring chiefdoms to his authority and AmaZulu rule, which he accomplished by various means. The territory and people of the immediate vicinity were absorbed into the expanding AmaZulu chiefdom very quickly following Shaka's accession to the chieftaincy in 1816.

The Butelezi, amaQungebe, Imbuyeni, amaCunu, Majola, Xulu, Sikakane, are all tribes which were quite close to Nobamba. There was intermarriage with them. Tshaka attacked and killed off these tribes; he crept up on them in the night. Tribes further off were the amaMbata, Gasa, Kumalo, Hlubi, Qwabe, Dube, Langeni, Tembu, Zungu, Makoba.[5]

The fates of these chiefdoms of various sizes and strengths varied, however, and the terminology used in this oral tradition can be misleading, and in some cases, the information appears to be incorrect. When an oral source said that a chiefdom was "killed off," the meaning implied was not the actual killing of people but the disruption and overthrow of the chiefdom as an independent and unified political unit. When a chiefdom was broken apart, sending some or most of its people and its chief into migration, it was said to have been "killed off," even if many of the remainder stayed behind and gave their allegiance to Shaka and the AmaZulu. Only one specific instance of a surprise night attack, against the AmaNdwandwe, was reported, and the confrontations between Shaka and other chiefs were reported to have been open and in daylight.[6] Many chiefs submitted to Shaka's authority and were allowed to retain their chiefdoms and positions in a subordinate status, owing Shaka allegiance, submission, and obedience in a layered system of political authority.

Shaka used his military to impose the rule of his AmaZulu chiefdom over other chiefdoms across the region, including that of the AmaMthethwa to which the AmaZulu themselves had formerly been a subordinate tributary chiefdom. He accomplished this through a combination of political strategy and the use of more effective technologies and tactics of warfare. Over time, warfare and its purposes had changed:

Indulo ya i ngenzi luto, i.e. the people of olden times were not actively inclined. They would throw assegais at one another and afterwards visit one another; i.e. when a quarrel arose the two sides would arm and, as soon as they got within range, would throw their assegais at one another, and after the battle, such as it was, had been concluded, the two parties would forget their differences and be on visiting terms as before. The fighting moreover used to take place in one locality; there was no pursuit. Stabbing was introduced by Tshaka. In view of this mode of existence, fighting etc., it became easy for even a small tribe, like the Zulu, to retain its autonomy.[7]

Stuart was told,

Tshaka's policy at first was to attack one tribe at a time and take care not to embroil others. He would take special pains to warn adjoining tribes that he was not attacking them in any way, and so his enemies would be reduced to clearly defined limits.[8]

Shepstone wrote that by the time Shaka became chief of the small AmaZulu chiefdom after the death of his father Senzangakona, all the neighboring chiefdoms had adopted the military system that Dingiswayo had introduced. This would have meant that the military system itself could not have conferred any advantage to the AmaZulu in any fighting against these neighboring chiefdoms. The AmaNdwandwe were the most powerful neighboring major chiefdom or "kingdom" to have adopted Dingiswayo's military system, and "between this Chief Zwide and Dingiswayo, many battles took place." Thus, as a military commander of Dingiswayo's before succeeding to the subordinate chieftaincy, Shaka had ample experience of the tactics and technologies of warfare then used.[9]

The militarization of society in KwaZulu-Natal through the enrollment of all young men first as boys serving as baggage carriers and then as young warriors linked the communities and people of the entire region to Shaka's regiments and barracks. Later generations remembered the roles their own family members, fathers, uncles, or brothers, had played in various military expeditions as well as the stories about the most famous of Shaka's warriors. The warrior whose name appears most often in oral traditions about the AmaZulu in the era of Shaka is Komfiya ka Nogandaya, known by his popular honorary name, Zulu.[10] He was born among the AbaQwabe, and, still known as Komfiya, he met Shaka there when Shaka was visiting his maternal uncle "in the Qwabe country."[11] Because of their earlier meeting, Komfiya/Zulu decided sometime after Shaka had become chief of the AmaZulu chiefdom to *khonza* or give his personal allegiance to him with three other men including Situnga, the father of Stuart's informant Mandhlakazi whose mother was Zulu's daughter.[12] Shaka appointed Komfiya as an *inceku* in his own household, where Komfiya was to smear the floors of the hut.[13] The story of how the servant became the warrior and earned the name "Zulu" was widely known; although only an *inceku*, he had taken up a challenge posed to the warriors, and upon succeeding, was allowed to go into battle where he fought so valiantly that Shaka gave him the honorary name Zulu.[14] Thereafter, he became *induna* of the *amakhanda* military barracks of one of the most formidable regiments.[15]

Only Nqetho – one of Kondhlo's sons and half brother to Pakatwayo who was Shaka's rival and chief of the AbaQwabe – rivaled Zulu in fame as a warrior. Nqetho of his own accord left the AbaQwabe to join Shaka and give him his allegiance while Shaka was a very young chief, early in his reign. Nqetho and his uncle, Sopane ka Mncinci, made this move at the same time because within their own community they were not allowed to marry the women they wished to wed.[16] Receiving the submission and allegiance of two royal princes from a rival chiefdom was a significant accomplishment for Shaka, who accepted them without hesitation. According to stories about Nqetho in residence at the AmaZulu royal capital, Shaka did not at first treat him with favor but was unable to wound Nqetho's pride and finally treated him as a "prince."[17] He was given a homestead site at oDibini along the Thukela River and was allowed considerable independence of action by Shaka there.[18] Nqetho remained loyal to Shaka throughout his life, and, Stuart was told, "Nqeto greatly regretted Tshaka's death, the only one probably who did so. There was no mourning for Shaka. Nqeto accordingly fled from Dingana."[19]

Shaka did not go to war unprepared but gathered intelligence using spies sent to enemy territory. Numerous stories from Dingiswayo's and Shaka's era told of individuals being sent to gain the confidence of an enemy in order to gain information or advantage. An example is Dingiswayo's reputed use of his daughter in marriage to Zwide to acquire his bodily fluids that might be used in "medicines" designed to weaken him and strengthen Dingiswayo and by *izinyanga*, "doctors," in similar capacities. The most explicit explanation of the duties of a spy in Shaka's employ came from the son of Shaka's spy Nongila, and it sheds light on Shaka's strategic thinking and practices. He said, "[m]y father was a spy and so had to go before any expedition left to see the country about to be attacked. He himself therefore had to accompany the forces to act as guide. He once got as far as the 'Cape' (Kibi), saw the white people, and reported what he had seen to Tshaka."[20] Nongila was in Shaka's confidence as expeditions were planned and knew why Shaka targeted a given chiefdom for attack, either in retaliation, for purposes of political expansionism, or to raid for cattle. Jantshi explained,

> he used to precede by going to see what the country to be attacked was like. He spied out the country's forces... He used to go out alone when on a tour of preliminary inspection. Tshaka used to doctor him on each of his trips, before his setting forth.[21]

Shaka selected spies "from the old Zulu heartland" and a few others such as Jantshi's father. When he was called with others to Shaka's, "[m]y father was created *induna* [commanding officer] of all the spies."[22]

Both European and indigenous sources indicate that Shaka sometimes authorized "total war" that allowed the killing of civilians, including women and children, during a military campaign, but historical evidence also indicates that this rarely happened.[23] The son of Shaka's subordinate ally, AmaCele chief Magaye, said that

> Tshaka, when giving instructions to his *impi*, would direct them to make away with everything, even a dog or a hearthstone (what a pot stands on in the hearth). "Let no one remain alive," he used to say – every soul to be killed, even a child being nursed on the back.[24]

Indicating the common awareness that this represented a distinct and deliberate deviation from previous accepted conventions of warfare, Mbovu told Stuart,

> There is a law or recognized custom among the natives regarding warfare, a law transgressed by Tshaka, to the effect that the victors must not spoil and seize the country of their foes, nor kill women and children.
>
> This was the rule prior to Tshaka's day, and corresponded in a way to the agreement of Geneva re explosive bullets and other cruel acts.[25]

However, Fynn's account suggests that the outcome of Shaka's military conflicts was incorporation rather than killing of the populations that his troops conquered. Fynn also implied that specific accounts of high mortality may well be accurate but also unusual rather than characteristic of Shaka's common *modus operandi*.[26] Fynn's evidence, if accurate, also helps to establish a chronology of events with regard to military expeditions and the incorporation process. According to him, after Shaka had incorporated the AmaQwabe chiefdom, he "next attacked Mahlungwana, the chief that had promised to assist him on the death of his father. He [Shaka] defeated him, upon which many of the tribe gave their allegiance."[27] Shaka evidently betrayed the trust of this chief but also appears to have readily incorporated them. From a strategic point of view, Shaka had reason to believe these people would just as readily give him their faithful allegiance. Lugubu explained more fully that

> In the fights that took place in former days, the men would hurl assegais at one another. They did not approach closely. If one side was defeated and a man was left exhausted, he would say, "Mo! I am defenceless!" He would be taken captive, but never killed. When the fighting was over his family would come and ransom him with a beast [head of cattle]. That was the custom in former times. Chiefs had not yet begun putting people to death, even if they had done wrong. Women were not killed in war, nor was a man who was running away, for he was like a woman. Only a man who was engaged in fighting was stabbed. The practice of stabbing a man who was running away, or one who was left wounded, was begun by Tshaka. Small boys, children, used not to be killed. The practice of killing even women was one begun by Tshaka.[28]

Mayinga said that in warfare, "[e]veryone was taught by Tshaka what true bravery was. He made them throw away their many *assegai*s and ordered that each man was to carry only one *assegai*. Tshaka said the old system of hurling *assegai*s was bad; it caused cowardly behaviour."[29] The spear itself was altered for use in warfare, however. Stuart learned further details of this technological innovation:

> The *assegai* [spear] which Tshaka introduced was a short-handled one. He gave his troops the *isijula assegai*, i.e. with a shank (*umsuka*) to it. There was, however, a second one, called *iklwa*, for use after the enemy had begun to flee. They would then be spoken of as "stabbing the *ibece* melon," for they were stabbing people's backs as they ran. The *izijula* by this time would have been bent by stabbing and covered with blood. *Assegai*s were manufactured in the Nxumalo country, also in the Cunu country (chief: Sigananda) at the Nkandhla.[30]

Baleni confirmed that

> It was Tshaka who proclaimed that only one *assegai* was to be carried by each warrior. He said that there was to be no throwing, but every warrior was to stab at close quarters. All his troops accordingly carried only one *assegai*, viz. the *isijula*, with a nine-inch blade and about a 14-inch shaft. Should a man break his *assegai* when in conflict, he was to grip the other [man] with his arms and fight for the one carried by his assailant.[31]

Before departing for battle, the troops were "doctored" by an *inyanga*, who sprinkled over them "medicines" from a "medicine horn" derived from a variety of ingredients, including animal, herbal, and human.[32] To meet the enemy, Shaka "taught his men to do as he used to do when among the Mtetwa. He taught the attack to take place by running sharply. They were to run to the attack, with shields tucked under the arm."[33] The names of military commanders who led the warriors into battle were remembered with reference to specific military campaigns, and they "led the fighting after the plan of battle had been discussed in the ordinary way."[34] In a typical battle formation strategy, "[w]hen an *impi* fights, the right *hlangoti* [wing] begins the attack; the *isibay'esikulu* [great encircling force] remains behind, and when it attacks the fighting becomes grave."[35] Shaka accompanied most of the major military campaigns, and "'*Isibiba*', refers to the *izinsizwa* forces [of young men] who closely support the king, i.e. remain with the king until the fight is turning; then they follow on."[36] The son of the famous warrior Zulu ka Nogandaya, who fought at the "Kisi" battle against the AmaNdwandwe, said "[t]he Zulu *impi*, on going to the attack, shouted, 'Here is Mabope!' i.e. on beginning the attack. When driving off evil with *intelezi* medicines the doctors said, 'Here is *umabope*.' *Umabope* is a red-root plant used as *intelezi* medicines for inspiriting the forces."[37]

The Kisi battle was not typical because the AmaZulu attempted to take the AmaNdwandwe by surprise at night, and "[t]he fight began in the dark, and after a while the moon came out."[38] The Kisi battle had this name because "Kisi" was the password adopted to prevent AmaZulu warriors from mistakenly attacking one another in the dark.[39] Oral traditions about specific battles suggest that Shaka changed his tactics when he faced his formidable foe Zwide and the AmaNdwandwe, launching this surprise attack. This was unlike previous military campaigns when the targeted chief received an announced warning from Shaka. This allowed chiefs who expected an attack to submit and offer allegiance and prevent any actual fighting.[40] It was self-evident that Chief Zwide would never submit to Shaka's rule, and after this battle, the use of surprise may have become common. Stuart noted that "Tshaka's tactics were to attack unexpectedly, says Socwatsha. Any *induna* [commander] coming back and reporting that so-and-so had remained behind (i.e. deaths) [killed in battle] would cause the king to be very angry and kill the *induna*."[41] Stuart was told that under Shaka, "the army used to close in on the enemy at this time of day [just before daybreak] so that daylight would soon come and they would not kill one another."[42] In another unusual battle against the AmaMpondo, Shaka's warriors were reported to have thrown poisoned spears at the AmaMpondo warriors, "so that even if they did not penetrate, even if they simply cut a person, he would die." The AmaZulu are said to have successfully "scattered" the AmaMpondo in this instance.[43]

Shaka's early military expeditions from about 1817 to 1821 were designed to subdue and incorporate smaller chiefdoms in the region and were conducted with the military resources he had at the time. He had fewer and smaller regiments than were available to him later in his rule because he incorporated into his own military the men of the chiefdoms whose chiefs gave him willing allegiance without resistance or whom he had defeated. Even during the middle years of his rule, from about 1822 to 1826, his more powerful subordinate chiefs who kept and commanded their own regiments retained considerable latitude to conduct raids and inflict violence without Shaka's prior orders or knowledge. Shaka was then still consolidating his military organization and control over areas considered to be part of his domain. His major military campaign against the AmaNdwandwe chief Sikhunyana in 1826 marked a turning point when Shaka's allied chiefs brought their regiments and participated under his direct command (he was present at the battle) only to find themselves more tightly controlled (and in some cases eliminated) thereafter. By this time, Shaka had extended his sociomilitary organization to young unmarried women who were, like young men, enrolled in regiments according to their age grades. The descriptions pertaining to these regiments reflect only the last major military campaigns of the era but were described to Stuart generations later. The tales of tens of thousands of personnel who accompanied this 1826 *impi*, including not only warriors but also civilians – among whom were the senior royal women – gave rise to the stories and myths of Shaka's military strength. On the one hand, "Girls used to carry mats as carrier-boys (*udibi*) did, in time of war (Tshaka's day)."[44] On the other hand, there is some evidence that the young women in regiments also carried weapons, were trained to fight, and sometimes themselves engaged in the fighting during battles:

Tshaka used to go out to war with the *amakosikazi* [royal women, queens] as well as girls. Girls were, like men, collected into regiments. They cut shields (*izihlangu*) and carried assegais, and had to fight when required to do so. Girls were sometimes to be seen wearing *iziqu*, showing they had killed people.[45]

Probably in response to a question about women, Stuart was told,

Tshaka never *juba*'d [*duba*'d, ignored or treated harshly] girls: [This corresponds with what Socwatsha told me a few days ago – 17.4.1916.] The regiments *butwa*'d [enrolled into women's regiments] by Tshaka, with the corresponding men's age-grade regiment, were: Mcekeceke (Sipezi), Ntshuku (Mgumanqa), Mbutwamini (Fasimba), Cenyane (Mbonambi); the first girls' regiment *butwa*'d by Dingana was the Inzawu, etc.[46]

But the presence of these regiments of young women was indicated only with specific reference to the late (second) major military campaign against the AmaMpondo in 1827, when

with the Amampondo *impi* went the *girl* regiments, the Ntshuku, Mcekeceke and Mvutwamini. Each of these carried war-shields (*iziHlangu*). Their indunas were Magaye ka Dibandhlela and Zihlandhlo.[47]

MILITARY REGIMENTS

Fundamental to the sociopolitical reorganization of the region as well as the military strength and capability of the emerging AmaZulu kingdom were the recruitment of men into military regiments and the incorporation of the regiments of subordinated chiefs and chiefdoms into the military organization. When the AmaCele chief Magaye, having witnessed Shaka's growing power through the incorporation of chiefdoms close to the AmaZulu heartland, voluntarily gave his allegiance (*khonza*'d) Shaka, Shaka took from him his best military regiment to relocate and serve directly under his command. However, Shaka allowed Magaye to raise and keep other regiments for his own use and for combined military operations. All of the men of military age, whether in his own regiments or in regiments that had been enrolled by his subordinate allies, fell under Shaka's authority and putative command unless their own chief rebelled. This was well understood:

> The reasons why Tshaka had so many regiments was because he conquered people in all directions, and so got regiments [from the "conquered" or subordinated chiefdoms] at a quicker rate, and more of them, than if he had reigned quietly like Dingana and Mpande.[48]

These regiments were remembered because they became a primary form of identity for men who built their reputations on the basis of their military careers and because they were the primary basis of social organization for men during their years of military service. Moreover, these regiments retained their significance for identifying men throughout their lives, indicating a primary form of age grade group identity with those to which they had been originally enrolled or recruited by order.[49] The identity of regiments was sometimes confused when they were subdivided or if surviving members renamed them as the result of some members' disgrace and punishment (and even execution).[50] Identification by regiment was critical and compulsory:

> It was a great offence for a man not belonging to a particular regiment to carry a shield of the colour proper or reserved to that regiment. The reason was, "How could such a man be distinguished as to what he was if he carried a shield of a colour used by a particular regiment?", i.e. he was behaving as an imposter if he carried a shield of a regiment to which he did not belong.[51]

The recruitment of young adult men into military regiments according to their age rather than place of origin became the basis for a fundamental reordering of the military that had previously placed all men of military age from the same district into a single regiment. Like his peers in other chiefdoms, Shaka's father Senzangakona had begun to formalize his military by recruiting men into distinct regiments rather than on a contingent basis in time of war. He disbanded older regiments, but their members retained their regimental affiliations. They could be called up in time of war even after they were no longer part of the standing army. Thus, regiments from a previous generation recruited by a former king retained their identity and organization into the reign of later kings. The village where a regiment was stationed was often but not always called by the same name as the regiment. Sometimes a regiment was popularly referred to by the name of the village where it was stationed. Some regiments acquired a new name or came to be known by a popular name that referred to an event in which they had participated. In addition, during most of Shaka's reign, the strongest subordinate allied chiefs were permitted to recruit and keep their own regiments. The names of these were less likely to be known or remembered beyond the locality of that distinct subordinate chiefdom.

The narrators of the oral traditions from this era understood that Shaka used his *impi*, or military expeditions, not to destroy and kill people randomly and on a large scale but to incorporate them into his kingdom with or without their chiefs' compliance. According to one account,

It was Tshaka who forced all the less significant peoples to submit. His father Senzangakona did not do so. After conquering them, he [Tshaka] caused them to fight for him.[52]

Thus, later generations also understood this practice to have been a process of subordination and unification under Tshaka.

EARLY MILITARY CAMPAIGNS

Among the nearest neighbors of the small AmaZulu chiefdom were the AmaLanga people at eLangeni with whom the AmaZulu had long had friendly relations:

The Zulus were not good at composing songs, consequently Senzangakona used to ask the Langas to compose them for him, and these he used to sing when dancing with the Amambata, Butelezi and other northern tribes he lived on friendly terms with. As for the Zulu and Langa, they were so close to one another that they brought fire for one another (*okelana*'d *umlili*).[53]

During the rebellion against the rule of Makedama, Shaka had left eLangeni with his AmaLanga maternal relatives just as he was reaching warrior age. Thus, it is not surprising that he and the accompanying warriors and villagers who returned with him were determined to suppress Makedama's authority. Evidently, the people at eLangeni were among the first neighboring chiefdoms to be subdued by Shaka.[54] Two generations later, one man remembered only the hostile relations that had been generated between the people of eLangeni and the AmaZulu. Ngidi said, "[w]e [the eLangeni people] had a strong hatred (*itambo*) for Tshaka, though we gave birth to him."⁵⁵ Evidently in reference to the turmoil of the years of Shaka's rule, the man said that "[p]eople from all parts were given protection (*tolwa*'d) by the Langa tribe – a most hospitable one." Ngidi did not seem to recognize Makedama as a legitimate chief, presumably because of the disputed inheritance of the chieftaincy after Mbengi's rule, when his son, the father of Makedama, was unable to establish his authority. Thus, Ngidi said,

> Our tribe was broken up owing to having no chief, Lubango, Daleni and Mbengi died, leaving no chief...We were killed off by Tshaka, but especially Dingana, and this was on account of our being preferred by the girls whom he ordered to marry into other tribes...No tribe could defeat us by resorting to an *assegai* [spear]. Tshaka succeeded only by combining with others against us.⁵⁶

Shaka sent raids against Makedama twice, but the AmaZulu troops were unable to seize any cattle. He then arranged for a coordinated attack with the AbaQwabe and AmaNyuswa against eLangeni and Makedama, but Makedama managed to hold out in a fortress. Makedama then returned with his followers to his lands only to leave soon after to give allegiance to Zwide and the AmaNdwandwe. This arrangement was unsuccessful, and Makedama then returned home to eLangeni and submitted to Shaka, who allowed the AmaLanga who had followed Makedama to return to their original homes.⁵⁷ Makedama appears to have had a long-standing relationship with the Embo chief Zihlandhlo, who also *konza*'d Shaka and thereby remained powerful even during Shaka's reign.

Military campaigns marked Shaka's early years of political consolidation. One account specified,

> He began with Macingwane, chief of the Cunu, calling him "Fellow who troubled my father", for Senzangakona's nation had been small. After this he went to attack Pungatshe, chief of the Butelezi, and also attacked other chiefs.⁵⁸

> He then attacked all the peoples, conquering them. He finished off all the peoples on the other side [north of the Thukela river]. After this he crossed over [to south of the Thukela river] and came against those on this side, the Baca people. He killed them; he finished off the Baca in this country, and the Lala. The Baca fled; they now live beyond the Mzimkulu.⁵⁹

Another account indicates that Shaka indeed accomplished the submission of all of the smaller chiefdoms in the region of KwaZulu during his first year of rule. This was before Dingiswayo's death about a year later in 1817, although the sequence of conquests remains contested in these various versions of events. According to one oral tradition,

AmaZulu Expansion and Repercussions

Tshaka first attached the Ntshali people. His *induna* at this time was M⸤ (After this man came the *induna* Mqamama.) He [Tshaka] routed them. It w⸤ that occasion that Kondhlo [the AmaNtshali chief] died. After this, Hlangab⸤ the chief son of Kondhlo, left and went up-country; he was pursued by Tshak. Tshaka must have killed them, for Hlangabeza could not have gone far up-country; the land was still in a bad state (*izwe la li nga ka lungi*). Subsequently to this, Tshaka made war on all the small chiefs, and forced them all to submit. When he had conquered and subordinated the various tribes, Dingiswayo was killed by Zwide.[60]

Fighting between chiefdoms had become prevalent during the decades when both Dingiswayo and Zwide had been consolidating their authority over more territory and people. Therefore, Shaka was not the only source of conflict and violence when he first usurped the AmaZulu chieftaincy in 1817. Among the earliest chiefdoms to be set into flight collectively was that of the AmaNgwane under their chief Matiwane, but in their initial migration "Tshaka did not trouble the Ngwane people and did not make war on them. It was Zwide or Zide who did that."[61] Shaka did not refrain from attacking chiefdoms out of magnanimity but was forced to wait to attack larger and stronger chiefs such as Matiwane until he had incorporated more of the smaller chiefdoms and through the accession of manpower had increased the size of his military. Then his battles became more destructive because he engaged more often with chiefs who would never submit to his authority. Shaka's goal was to break apart existing sociopolitical units – descent-based chiefdoms – as far as necessary to ensure their submission and prevent their consolidation into larger chiefdoms that would compete with him for regional political control.

ZWIDE AND DINGISWAYO'S DEATH

During the period that Shaka was serving in Dingiswayo's military, Shaka was sent with troops to attack the AmaNyuswa (abakwaNyusa) and settle a dispute.[62] According to later oral traditions,

> the amaNyuswa also were attacked by Tshaka. There were troubles among them. They went to Dingiswayo to ask for an *impi*, for Sirayo ka Mapoloba was being troubled by Mgabi ka Mapoloba. Dingiswayo then sent Tshaka to settle their affairs. Tshaka went and built the iNtontela *umuzi* [village] among them. All the Nyuswa became iNtontela. At this time Tshaka was still an *induna* of Dingiswayo.[63]

During this same period, Dingiswayo's AmaMthethwa forces occupied AmaNdwandwe country and seized all of their corn several times.

body fluids and then provide them to Zwide to be used to make "medicine" to weaken, subdue, and defeat the unwitting Dingiswayo, which she reportedly did.⁷⁰ Dingiswayo was said to have ordered his troops to prepare for war precipitously and to have personally set out with a small advance guard without waiting for adequate preparations. Thus, perhaps influenced and "weakened" by Zwide's potion, Dingiswayo used poor judgment and made himself vulnerable to capture with insufficient protection, and he fell into Zwide's hands. Zwide performed the symbolic ceremony of jumping over his captive Dingiswayo to signify his victory and Dingiswayo's defeat, and some narratives report he jumped over him many times. Dingiswayo died in Zwide's custody soon thereafter, but the oral traditions differ in reporting the circumstances. Some attribute Dingiswayo's death to Zwide's mother, who insisted he not be released, and at least two narratives describe his murder at the hands of Zwide. One version of the story that does not match others related that "Nombona (Zwide's great *induna*) and Ntombaze opposed the killing of Dingiswayo, but Zwide insisted on it and did so, cutting off his head."⁷¹ According to another story, Zwide had Dingiswayo staked to the ground and drove cattle over him, trampling him to death, prompting a retaliatory attack by Dingiswayo's ally and subordinate, Shaka.⁷² Other narratives agree that Shaka attacked Zwide in retaliation for his having killed Dingiswayo, and agree that Zwide had weakened Dingiswayo by the use of *izidwedwe* "medicines."⁷³ Fynn believed that Shaka had betrayed Dingiswayo by giving information about his whereabouts to Zwide and was therefore complicit in his capture and death, but this allegation of treachery on Shaka's part is not found in any other sources. Fynn also reported that Zwide had killed Dingiswayo cruelly and then removed his gall and drank it in a symbolic act of victory and "medicine"-based power, a doubtful story not found anywhere else in the sources.⁷⁴ The sources agree that Shaka sent forces to pursue Zwide to Zwide's village at eMlandwaneni where they engaged in battle but Shaka's troops were unable to defeat the AmaNdwandwe and withdrew.⁷⁵

According to Mandhlakazi, Dingiswayo's widows and the royal women went to mourn him where he had died at Zwide's village:

On Zwide putting Dingiswayo to death, Dingiswayo's wives (*umdhlunkulu* [women of the royal house]) all left their tribe and went to where their husband was, i.e. Zwide's kraal. They there got up onto the top of the huts and wailed and lamented. They there struck up a chant (this chant is quite well known). It was suggested that they should be put to death, but Zwide refused, saying, "They are widows. I won't put them to death. They have come merely to lament their husband's death." Hence they were allowed to go free, after being brought down. Their doing so at all was regarded as uncanny and mysterious.[76]

Mandhlakazi concluded, "That was how Zwide overcame the Mtetwa people. I have not heard anyone say that they went to war again after Dingiswayo's death. People say that it was only Tshaka who continued to feel hatred."[77] Thus, Dingiswayo's death and Shaka's retaliatory military attack against Zwide fostered sociopolitical confusion in the region. Some AmaMthethwa gave their allegiance to the victor Zwide, as commonly occurred after a battle, and others left under the leadership of Dingiswayo's son Somveli, who "went off to Sotshangana with a section of the Mtetwa tribe."[78] Nhlekele told Stuart,

It is not known where Dingiswayo was killed by Zwide. He was simply caught and carried off. After Dingiswayo's death, part of the Mtetwa *konza*'d [gave allegiance and submitted to] Zwide, who then lived near Ndunu and Nongoma, and part went off with Somveli. I do not know if Somveli is still living.

Tshaka, after defeating Zwide, took over the Mtetwa.[79]

A large segment recognized Dingiswayo's successor Mondisa who had initially accepted subordinate tributary status in submission to Shaka and the AmaZulu. Shaka is said to have had killed Mondisa later in an act of planned treachery during an *umjadu* dance meant to symbolize an alliance.[80] According to one account,

When Dingiswayo died, Tshaka held an *umjadu* dancing competition, and invited [Dingiswayo's successor] Mondisa to do the same. Mondisa came up to the Zulus with his party. Tshaka danced first; Mondisa and his party followed. Tshaka had however hidden his *impi* in the bushes. It suddenly rushed on Mondisa and his dancers and killed Mondisa and others, this, as Tshaka said, being punishment for their having deserted their king Dingiswayo when fighting with Zwide, and allowing him to be captured by Zwide. After this, Tshaka became king over the Mtetwa people. His plan was to kill the king of a tribe and then take his people and make them *konza* [give allegiance and submit to] him. He did the same afterwards in regard to Zwide.[81]

Stuart was told that "Mondisa ruled for a short time after Dingiswayo's death." Then, however, "Mondisa was killed by Tshaka at Bulawayo for making up a song while dancing was taking place," because Shaka, believing the song alluded to him, was offended and so caught and killed Mondisa during the dance. As a result,

Many of Mondisa's followers, of the *indhlunkulu* [senior branch], were killed at the same time; the *ikohlo* side [junior branch] under [the junior AmaMthethwa chief] Tshangane escaped, for they were not dancing. Those followers of Mondisa that remained over ran off after Somveyi (to Soshangana's country), leaving Tshangane as head of such of the Mtetwa tribe as remained.

Thus it is that Tshangane's section came to rule. Mondisa's followers tried to induce them to go off to Sotshangana's, but they refused on the ground that they had already *konza*'d Tshaka.[82]

Shaka's first attack against the AmaNdwandwe was thus made in retaliation for Dingiswayo's death in 1817 or 1818. He again attacked the AmaNyuswa under Chief Paboloba ka Mbele, a branch of the AmaNgcobo, defeated them, and seized their cattle. After this, the AmaNgcobo tendered their submission to Shaka. The AmaZulu troopos then defeated the AmaNtshali and killed their chief Kondhlo ka Magalela. The heir, Kondhlo's son Nkubu, rallied his people and returned to attack the AmaZulu, but they were again defeated. AmaZulu troops were sent against several other important chiefdoms that put up resistance and then then submitted under their chiefs who were allowed to remain as Shaka's subordinates. These included the junior AmaCele chief Mande ka Dibandhlela, the Embo chief Zihlandhlo ka Gcwabe, the Makanya chief Duzi, and the Dube chief Kutshwayo, all of whom paid tribute to Shaka after they tendered their submission and allegiance.[83]

Conflicts and demographic dislocations affected the chiefdoms of the region of modern KwaZulu north of the Thukela River prior to Shaka's accession to the AmaZulu chieftaincy and during his first year of rule. The practice of migrating en masse to seek a new site for settlement had been common for centuries. Either the senior or junior members of ruling families led a portion of followers away from their old homes that were left in the hands of a remaining branch of the chiefly family and its adherents. Sometimes the leader of the migration was the senior chief, and sometimes a junior chief relocated with his own followers, as occurred in the case of Mpangazitha after he lost his challenge against his brother Mtimkulu for the rule of the AmaHlubi chiefdom. This occurred after the death of their renowned father Bhungane. As in this case, the junior branch normally did not go far and remained subject to the senior ruling line of descent and honored the senior chief's prerogatives according to accepted rules of inheritance as confirmed by leading members of the community. Once a process of amalgamation of different, formerly independent and sovereign chiefdoms had begun, however, subordinate chiefs were no longer connected through ties to the ruling family and showed their obeisance by paying tribute and performing ceremonial acts such as attending their superior chief on formal visits to the capital village.

In Shaka's expanding chiefdom and emerging kingdom, subordinate chiefs were obliged to comply with his orders to perform raids on other recalcitrant or foreign chiefdoms and return the acquired booty in cattle to the royal herds. In principle, failure to do so was an act of rebellion and incurred retaliation in the form of Shaka's punitive expedition to retrieve the booty forcibly and kill the rebellious subordinate chief, bringing his followers under a compliant chief of Shaka's choosing. Falling out of compliance with Shaka's orders and demands on the part of a chief also brought the prospect of punishment to all of his followers. To avoid Shaka's *impi*, it was not uncommon for small chiefdoms to migrate collectively under the leadership of their rebellious chief and seek refuge from Shaka's rule in new, more distant lands. Sometimes these chiefdoms survived as they re-established themselves elsewhere, but sometimes they suffered a military attack by Shaka's pursuing army and were completely broken apart and dispersed. These chiefdoms lost their existence as identifiable and independent social and political units. This latter fate suffered by many small chiefdoms was part of the period referred to as *izwekufa*, the "killing of nations," although most people might indeed survive by scattering among other chiefdoms wherever they could find refuge.

NGOZA AND THE ABATEMBU

Chief Ngoza of the AbaTembu chiefdom of KwaZulu-Natal was a formidable rival for Shaka when he assumed the AmaZulu chieftaincy and began his expansionary military expeditions. The oral traditions about Ngoza make it obvious that the stronger chiefs of the region communicated with each other and hoped to be able to resist the expansion of AmaZulu dominance. Not surprisingly, those in the area of central KwaZulu-Natal recognized that they would be early targets of the AmaZulu military and would have to choose to submit, fight, or flee. Stuart's main informant about the history of the AbaTembu chiefdom under Ngoza told him,

> It so happened that Ngoza had sent to conspire with Macingwane of the Cunus with a view of resisting the Zulus. The Zulus, anticipating something of the kind, sent another section of their army up the Tugela to attack Macingwane.
>
> It was under these circumstances that Ngoza judged it best to leave Zululand for the south.[84]

Stuart heard two versions of the oral tradition about the factors leading to the flight of Ngoza and his followers from the same man, Lugubu, a few years apart, in 1909 and 1916. In the 1909 narrative, Shaka's motives are explained as jealousy of a powerful chief whose leadership and abilities might exceed his own. Shaka therefore sought a personal confrontation, cloaked in an innocent invitation, but Ngoza was neither fooled nor entrapped by him. According to this oral tradition,

> The Tembus were a big tribe and actually fought against Tshaka. It occurred in this way. Tshaka, proud of his growing power, asked his people if there was anyone like him, anyone who was so great a hero and who led his men to battle. They said Ngoza ka Mkubukeli, the Tembu chief, was such an one, that he was in the habit of leading his men, and had on various occasions been wounded in battle and could show the scars. Tshaka thereupon sent four messengers to Ngoza to invite him to come on a visit to Tshaka and to sit with him, i.e. as his equal. As soon as Ngoza got this invitation he sent men to go and cut some reeds. When they had brought them, he ordered two men to take a small portion of these reeds, go along to Tshaka and, on coming before him, to stick a reed in the ground before him by way of defiance. This the men did, whereupon Tshaka got into a rage and had it in mind to put the men to death, but they did not swerve, whereupon Tshaka (who talked with a kind of lisp, mouthing his words) commended them for sticking to their chief. He said he had no quarrel with them, for they were only messengers, but with their master. He thereupon ordered the men to be supplied with three oxen, one to be slaughtered on the spot and two to be for food on their way back. They were told to go back and to tell Ngoza that he would be attacked at the next new moon, for when that moon began waxing it would be Tshaka himself that was appearing.[85]

Shaka, as the story was told to Stuart in 1909, sent a warning to Ngoza that the AmaZulu would be coming to attack the AbaTembu in response to Ngoza's deliberate provocation. In the 1916 version (which Stuart recorded in isiZulu verbatim), Lugubu said that when Tshaka's three messengers conveyed his offer of an alliance of equals with Ngoza, Ngoza consulted with "his men's assembly." "The Tembu said, "Mnguni [Shaka] is deceiving you. He will kill you and take your people." This indicates the agreement of Ngoza's people to his subsequent actions, as well as the expected process of consultation practiced at the time.[86] Ngoza's messengers were told to provoke Shaka deliberately with a signal of defiance, sticking the reed into the ground in front of him. Ngoza said to these men, "Go to Tshaka and tell him to fix a handle to his assegai."[87]

The story in both versions continues the narrative with a description of the encounter and conversation between Ngoza's messengers and Tshaka. The AbaTembu had time to prepare for the expected attack and successfully repelled the AmaZulu forces:

> The men [messengers of Ngoza] left. Whilst on their way back, the Zulu army caught up to and passed them on their way to attack Ngoza. The men pushed on at

once to give the alarm, traveling through the night. Ngoza at once warned his tribe and all crossed over into the Umsinga division. The Zulus followed and an action took place at the Umbe hill near Pomeroy (where Gwalagwala used to live). The Tembus fought well and defeated the Zulus, driving them back into Zululand.[88]

Ngoza attempted to recruit assistance and to send his people and cattle into hiding.[89] Lunguza ka Mpukane agreed that the AbaTembu had successfully defended themselves in the first attack from Shaka's forces. He said "Ngoza was attacked by Tshaka's Bekenya regiment. Owing to his mode of fighting, whereby he put men first, then a group of women in their immediate rear (including his own wives) [to inspire the men to fight], they succeeded in defeating the Bekenya."[90] Lugubu said that then, however, "[t]he Zulu went off along the Tukela. They discovered where the cattle and women of the Tembu had been hidden; there were very many of them. They seized the cattle and killed all the women and children."[91] The assertion that all of the women and children were killed is contradicted elsewhere in this narrator's various versions of events, but the AbaTembu did suffer losses and were forced to migrate.

The collective migration of the AbaTembu chiefdom under Ngoza disrupted numerous smaller chiefdoms in Natal. Lunguza explained,

> The Mpumulwana hill is on the south side of the Tugela prior to its junction with the Buffalo, and is near the drift where the punt is. Nomagaga lived at Mpumulwana. Ngoza fought this tribe and dispersed it. Nomagaga was killed. Ngoza then went up to about Mhlumba mountain. He fought another Nomagaga ka Mpumela, of – tribe (I forget name). He killed him and scattered the people.[92]

Lugubu's 1916 narrative provides more details of these events after Ngoza and the AbaTembu were set into flight and crossed to south of the Thukela River.[93]

> After seeing this, Ngoza crossed the river. The Tembu sing a song that goes: "Did we not say that the Cunu are dogs? They ran away, child of the elephant." He crossed over and came into the country of Nomagaga of the Kuze people of Dhlomo. Nomagaga blocked his way, saying, "Do not come here. If you cross here, I shall fight you." Ngoza said, "I shall pass; I am running away from Tshaka." Nomagaga said, "Do not pass. Stay there and stand against Tshaka." Ngoza replied, "I am coming." He crossed over. Men of the Tembu said to him, "Give us the opportunity to fight, otherwise what will we have to eat? You always let the regiments fight, while as for us, we do not take part. Then you give the captured cattle to the fighting men." For when Ngoza overcame a chief and seized his cattle he would give them all to those who had been in the fighting; he kept only the oxen for himself.[94]

Ngoza agreed to this. He crossed the river and let the men of the Tembu go into battle. He himself remained at the river with all the womenfolk who had escaped.

Nomagaga's force was on the hill called Mduna. He sent his force into the attack, and they joined battle [against Nomagaga]. The Tembu force was defeated by the Kuze and driven back to where Ngoza was. Ngoza cried, "What? Are you running away after asking to be allowed to fight?" They answered, "Nkosi, we haven't done yet." He cried, "Into it!" They joined battle, and again our force was defeated and driven back to Ngoza. He said, "What? Are you running away again?" They answered, "Nkosi, we haven't done yet." He said, "Into it!" Again they joined battle, and again the Kuze drove them back to Ngoza. Ngoza asked, "How is it now, Tembu?" They said, "Nkosi, we are defeated."[95]

Ngoza had with him two regiments, the Izinkwenkwezi and the Nonyenge...They joined battle, and the Tembu regiments drove the enemy up the hill to where Nomagaga was positioned on the summit. They drove the enemy force past him, and killed him... At that place died my father's younger brother, Nketo of the Mbata people. They stabbed him here in the small intestine [low down on the right side]. My father left the battle because his brother had died.[96]

This testimony establishes the local and regional perspective of events that have been distorted and debated in the historiography of the era. According to indigenous oral traditions, Ngoza and his AbaTembu followers did indeed cause widespread destruction as they fled from Shaka's rule and AmaZulu territory. That these narratives were remembered and conveyed by the descendants of participants lends them great credibility with regard to the narrative of events, if not to all of the details that tend to be distorted over time. After he defeated one chief named Nomagaga, Ngoza was soon to encounter another of the same name before moving on and defeating and killing several chiefs in the area.

After climbing the hill, Ngoza went off towards Mhlumba. There he came upon another chief Nomagaga – I don't know of what line. He [Ngoza] at once killed him, in the country where the Cunu are living today. He then came to the Pata. He encountered Ndawonde of the Gozini people who was living at the Pata, and killed him. He [Ngoza] went on, and crossed the Mpogana river. Ngoza's people did not yet know the country well, and were heading back the way they had come, towards the Zulu country. They found they were going back to the country of the Nguni. In the country near the Ngome, (i.e. where Bambata recently lived), they encountered Mbemba of the Mdhletsheni people. Here they took fright, saying, "We are close to the Zulu country. There is Pisweni" (a hill opposite Qudeni). So they turned back. (There was a chief killed by him [Ngoza] at the Mpofana river where the Pata joins it.)

Then he [Ngoza] came to Mrolweni.[97]

Ngoza and his followers proceeded southwards, and "Ngoza dispersed the [AmaBhaca] tribe under Macibise living about Pietermaritzburg, and went southwards to Pondoland where he was put to death by the Pondo king Faku."[98] Although upon Ngoza's death many of his AbaTembu followers "remained in Pondoland," not all did, and "[a] number of the Tembu people now determined on going back and giving their allegiance to Tshaka. When they got to Tshaka, he commended them for their loyalty to their chief, which made them cling to him as far off as Pondoland. He was glad to have them as his adherents, for men who had proved they could be so devoted to their chief might be expected to become devoted to him. He put them under the immediate supervision of Sojiyisa, son of Jama."[99]

Lunguza's narrative indicates Ngoza's role in wreaking destruction as remembered by those who suffered from it, and it explains evidence of the proximity of women in battles in this time and region, similar to what happened at Lithakong where women were caught in the field of fighting.[100] The evidence of the high level of destruction Nogza caused before his death is clear:

> He [Ngoza] then came on to the Mpofana (Mooi river). He there found Mahlapahlapa ka Siyoto – I do not know his clan-name – said to be a cannibal. This Mahlapahlapa is not the same man as that attacked by Dingana at the Ndaka (near Ladysmith) and driven off to Basutoland. Ngoza killed the former Mahlapahlapa. He went down to the forests on the north side of the Umgeni. He there found Dhlepu ka Ngcwanekazi – I do not know his clan-name. He fought with and killed this petty chief. Ngoza then passed by Mbubu (near Pietermaritzburg), and went to the Mkomazi and found, on this side, Ciki of the Amawutshe. He fought with and killed him... Ngoza then crossed the Umkomai and went right off to Pondoland.... He was there killed at once by the Pondos. He was attacked the day after his arrival. The battle continued all day. The Pondos withdrew and renewed the attack the following day, when they succeeded in putting him to death.[101]

Lugubu commented, "[t]here were many chiefs killed or who had cattle seized during his [Ngoza's] flight," and said, "Ngoza broke up her [Macibise's AmaBaca] people when flying towards the amaMpondo" before providing more details of the trail of raids and battles.[102]

> In his course he [Ngoza] killed many chiefs indeed; I no longer remember their names. He went down into Macibise's country, and broke up her people. I do not know whether he killed her or not. Then he went up towards Howick, where he encountered a strong chief, Sondaba ka Patwa. This man fought against those two regiments, the Izinkwenkwezi and the Nonyenge.... When they had defeated Sondaba's *impi*, they made towards the Nhlosana hill and then went down to the Nzimga. They crossed the Mkomazi and passed beneath Marwaqa hill [on the site of Bulwer]. Then they went off into the Mpondo country, and there the chief [Ngoza] died.[103]

Other remembered oral traditions told to Stuart related Ngoza's exploits and depicted him as continually fighting with those he encountered.[104]

Before describing the battle of Ngoza and the AbaTembu against Nomagaga and the Kuze, one man said,

Ngoza ka Mkubukeli and Nomagaga ka Dhlomo ka Nsele ["of the Dhlamini people"] had been fighting alone. For Ngoza made war while on the march; he was passing by on his way to the Mpondo country. He was fleeing from Tshaka.[105]

The AbaTembu peoples remained dispersed across the region. Two chiefs of the AmaMbata section, Manyosi ka Dhlekezele and Diyikane, headed the portion of the AbaTembu who had already given their allegiance to the AmaZulu during the reign of Jama or Senzangakhona or earlier in Shaka's reign and had not followed Ngoza in his flight southward.[106] Most of those living at Malakata, where Ngoza's main village was at Ukadada (Ekudadeni), and at Qudeni, had been forced to leave as a result of Shaka's attack on Ngoza.[107] However, one of Ngoza's followers, Jobe ka Mapita ka Mnyanda, remained at Qudeni with a group of followers, and they *khonza*'d Shaka after Ngoza's departure. Those AbaTembu who had refused to emigrate with Ngoza and Sondaba had remained under Mtsholozi ka Matomela, a brother or half brother of Sondaba. Sondaba was among the AbaTembu who returned to the Nxamalala district after Ngoza's death with a younger brother Lugaju, but Mtsholozi ordered their deaths. Sondaba was killed but Lugaju escaped death because the messengers (including another brother) had not received explicit instructions to kill Lugaju, only to lure him back to Mtsholozi's. Lugaju survived after Mtsholozi was later killed by Dingane and eventually collected some remnants of their followers. After subsequent attacks against his people, Lugaju sought refuge from Baleni.[108]

MACINGWANE, PHAKADE, AND THE AMACHUNU

The AmaChunu neighbors of the AmaZulu were among the strongest chiefdoms in the region at the time Shaka usurped the AmaZulu chieftaincy in about 1817 and were a natural threat to his ambitions. Magidigidi believed the AmaChunu chief Macingwane was probably born at the place of his father at eNgonyameni and said that his heir, Phakade, of Shaka's generation, was born at the village of eLangeni.[109] When Shaka took up a position on the Isipezi mountain in the Nqutu district to watch the AmaZulu regiments attack Ngoza, Macingwane and the AmaChunu had already suffered an attack by Shaka's forces. However, it appears that Ngoza and the AbaTembu were the first to uproot themselves and migrate southwards, and the AmaChunu under Macingwane followed in their path sometime afterward.[110] Lunguza believed "Ngoza and Macingwane were in league with one another," and noted that unlike Ngoza, who went as far as AmaMpondo territory, the AmaCunu "only got as far as Nsikeni hill, on the south side of the Mkomazi."[111] Lunguza also noted that the AbaTembu had destroyed many chiefdoms as the AmaChunu discovered in their wake. Baleka agreed that Macingwane had been attacked first, however, and stated that when Shaka "began to make war," he first sent military campaigns against the AmaChunu chief Macingwane and the AmaButelezi people of chief Pungatshe, and then against other chiefs and chiefdoms.[112] Another informant associated the migration of the AmaChunu to that of the AmaBhaca and linked it to that of Matiwane's AmaNgwane, saying, "Macingwane ran off from Zululand. The Bacas ran off with him, under Ncapayi ka Madikana. Matiwane ka Masumpa of the Ngwane people also ran off."[113] Mqaikana provided a lengthy narrative of the history of the AmaChunu under Macingwane's leadership. They were a logical target for an attack early in Shaka's reign when he was determined to expand AmaZulu territorial rule because "Macingwane's original district was in Zululand and quite close to that of the Zulu tribe."[114] It is therefore not surprising that the AmaChunu and AmaZulu had fought in earlier generations and that Shaka considered them to be troublesome neighbors, for "Macingwane, the Cunu chief, used to fight with Senzangakona and his people, though the fighting never went further than burning one another's kraals."[115]

Macingwane's attempt to avoid AmaZulu forces under Shaka's command set in motion the AmaChunu migration from the AmaZulu heartland to south of the Thukela River in about 1818 or 1819, for "[w]hen Tshaka, however, appeared on the scene, Macingwane saw he was no match for him, so he decided to quit Zululand."[116] The strength in numbers of the AmaChunu is indicated by their villages under Macingwane's rule, the main towns named as Engonyameni, eLangeni, eNkanini, eNkomba, dNkaulweni, eMdakeni, eMbandwini, and Ebatweni. Macingwane's regiments were the Ingagu (the oldest), abaTwa, Izinkwenkwezi, uMungu, and amaTshanga (the youngest), and "[t]he Ingagu and abaTwa had kraals of their own. The Izinkwenkwezi were stationed at Ngonyameni. Umungu was at eLangeni, and the amaTshanga were also at Ngonyameni."[117] Macingwane's son and heir Phakade was in the Inkwenkwezi regiment, which was composed of men of the same age as Shaka's and his brother Dingane's AmaWombe regiment of the AmaZulu, making Phakade approximately the same age as Shaka.[118] AmaChunu history was well remembered because Phakade lived until "about 1882" when he was about 93 or 94 years old. Stuart's informant Magidigidi knew well Phakade and his mother, Macingwane's wife Ndabakajwayele, who died only a month or two before her son Phakade, giving her a memory extending over a hundred years into the past.[119] Phakade had additional AmaChunu *imizi*, royal homesteads – at eMxweleni, eMxwelaneni, ekuLingeleni, ekuNgengeleni, ekuBukeni – and his regiments were the Izipunzi (men of Phakade's age), Isicanula, Isangole, uMngwempisi (Magidigidi's regiment), iMbungulu, uMatinikwana, abeSutu, iNyandezulu, and abaTwa (i.e., the same name as Macingwane's older regiment), Isixwazi, Izimpisi, iMbukuzane, and uKongolo.[120]

The AmaChunu fought against various people they encountered. Among the chiefs Macingwane defeated – said to have been accomplished by "doctoring" to weaken his resistance – was Mpongo ka Zingelwayo.[121] Mqaikana traced other conflicts as well:

He [Macingwane] made his way to where Pietermaritzburg now is, and attacked the girl Macibise and her [AmaBaca] people. But Macibise offered so stout a resistance that Macingwane was obliged to give up the idea of capturing her cattle. He turned his attention northwards to Cinso, an induna of Macibise's tribe living up the Little Nsunduze, who however was a petty chief. Macingwane killed this man and seized his stock. Macingwane now made across the Mkomazi to the high land south of the Mkomazi, where he attacked the amaNtambo people and defeated them. He then occupied their lands. He had his kraal at a hill and forest called iGqunu, in open country. He built about the Ifafa river and established his uMungu regiment in the same district.[122]

Mahaya, of the Mtwana (Imitwana) chiefdom in the region of the Kei River, remembered that the AmaChunu had raided across the Transkei region with the AmaBhaca under chief Madikane, and said

[t]he amaMboto were, whilst we were being killed off, being killed off where the Ibisi enters the Mzimkulu, at the Isantombe forest. This was their stronghold. Macingwane (of the amaCunu) and Madikane (of the amaBaca) were in league and were the two who attacked the amaMboto and killed them off. We all ran off, also the amaMboto, to the abeNguni, but eventually came back in peaceful times.[123]

It appears that Shaka left the AmaChunu alone for some time, perhaps even a year or two before the chiefdom was forced to migrate once again.

This time they took refuge at Insikeni mountain, hiding the women in the nearby forest, and were attacked there by AmaZulu regiments who soundly defeated them. Mqaikana narrated these events as follows:

> Later on, Tshaka appeared on the scene with his army, which he personally accompanied, taking up a position on the Pateni hill as the army went forward to attack Macingwane. Macingwane, finding he was no match for Tshaka, immediately moved off with his stock, women and children across the Mzimkulu and Ingwagwane to a district about Insikeni mountain, where there was a forest. The cattle and children, also the *impi*, took refuge in the forest. Before the mountain was a plain on which the Zulu army drew up and where it was given its instructions. Macingwane himself went and took up a position on the very top of a mountain, going to a point, and from there he observed Tshaka's tactics. Tshaka himself was with his forces – for he never failed to accompany them in person until the occasion of his assassination, when the army was away in the north-east. The Zulus then move forward and *tshaya'd ingomane*, i.e. simultaneously struck their shields loudly, and so loudly that the cattle in the forest became terrified and emerged into the open. This was the signal for closing in. The Zulus entered the forest, fought and defeated the Cunus, killing off even women and children without exception. In the meantime, Macingwane, seeing the game was up, came down the mountain and fled to Pondoland. Thus Tshaka got the whole of the Cunu cattle. It was in this battle at Insikeni that Ludaba, father of Ngoza, Sir T. Shepstone's induna, was killed.[124]

With a handful of followers, Macingwane fled toward the northeast where he was killed when he sought protection from the abakwaMadongo people who refused to give him refuge because he was a chief.[125] It appears that Mqaikana's assertion that the AmaZulu killed off the women and children is a false exaggeration because a portion of AmaChunu did survive this battle with the AmaZulu and returned to give allegiance to another of Macingwane's sons, Mfusi, who had long since given his allegiance to Shaka and who had remained in AmaZulu territory where the returning AmaChunu were allowed to resettle.[126] Macingwane's heir Phakade followed his father's instructions and gave the royal insignia of the AmaChunu to Mfusi but, as instructed, then went personally to give his allegiance to the Embo chief Zihlandhlo, perhaps because Zihlandhlo's mother was from the AmaChunu people.[127]

VIOLENCE AND THE DISRUPTION OF SMALLER CHIEFDOMS

The territory of mid-KwaZulu-Natal deserted by Ngoza remained in turmoil after his departure. Before leaving to seek refuge to the south in AmaMpondo territory, Ngoza and his relative Sondaba repeatedly attacked Xesibe. Xesibe was the AmaMpumuza chief, distantly related to Nomagaga's AmaKuze people, whom Ngoza's AbaTembu also attacked and defeated.[128] Mqaikana's narrative of Ngoza's attacks against the AmaMpumuza chief Xesibe provides considerable details about these conflicts and their political ramifications. After Xesibe was eventually killed, Mqaikana's father Yenge was put in charge of the AmaMpumuza (Zondi) people (linked about ten generations earlier to Dhlamini, the AmaSwazi ancestor) as a regent because the heir, Jingose, and Nobanda, head of the junior section of the AmaMpumuza, were sent to stay with the AmaNxamalala. The man who had killed Nomagaga in the fight against Ngoza was Mdingi. He had found Chief Nomagaga along with the women and cattle, and when they learned of his death, Nomagaga's AmaKuze followers had fled, causing their defeat by Ngoza.[129] Ngoza had attacked Nomagaga to seize his cattle for food, but Mdingi, mistakenly thought by Ngoza to be friendly, kept the cattle himself and "entered into a treaty, with Baleni (father of Sikoyi), Nombewu (father of Fodo), and Yenge (my father)." Ngoza and the AbaTembu moved on, and "Nomagaga's son Mmiso *konza*'d in the Zulu country."[130]

Mqaikana's testimony reveals the confusion during Shaka's early military campaigns of expansion to and across the Thukela River. Mqaikana explained that the treaty between Baleni, Nombewu, and Yenge created a confederacy designed to defend these chiefdoms from AmaZulu aggression and conquest. He also said that the agreement was made after Shaka had defeated Zwide and turned his attention southward. There was evidently no ambiguity about the alliance's political and military goal of defense, for "[i]t was quite plain to the confederacy that the Zulus were about to attack them all, all the way down the Tugela to the amaNgcolosi people, their chief then being Nkuku."[131] Mqaikana said specifically,

It was two, three or more years after the flight of the Cunus and Tembus that the confederacy in question was formed, and the reason for its formation was because by that time Tshaka had defeated Zwide and the rest of the Zululand tribes, and was contemplating a direct attack on the tribes south of the Tugela.[132]

His narrative includes details of the fate of the followers of chief Xesibe when attacked by Shaka's AmaZulu forces, which explains why the AmaMpumuza entered into the confederacy treaty:

Tshaka's *impi* did actually attack Xesibe in his original tribal lands. Xesibe and his people got into a natural fastness and successfully defended themselves for a whole day, morning till night. When the Zulus had withdrawn for the night, Xesibe said to his people, "It is impossible for me to fight two and three more days with the

Zulus; they are much too powerful." Upon this he quitted his stronghold. It so happened that just before attacking him, the Zulus had seized a large number of cattle from the Nadi tribe (i.e. the sister tribe of the Mpumuza people). Xesibe came across these and, seizing them, put them with his own. His people remonstrated, saying that he ought to give them back to the Nadi people, but he said, "No, I have only captured what had already been captured by the Zulus; therefore they are rightly my property." However he was afterwards, though on the same day, prevailed on to give them back to the Nadi people, then in hiding in the adjoining forests. All were given back, although Xesibe had intercepted them when actually being driven off by the Zulus.

No sooner did Xesibe quit his district with his people, than he made for that of the Nhlangwini under Nombewu and Baleni, where the Cunus are now located. It was then that the three agreed to enter into a league as stated. When, on the following morning, the Zulus came to renew the attack against Xesibe at the stronghold, they found it completely deserted.

Xesibe, Nombewu and Baleni induced Mdingi (who by that time had killed Nomagaga) to join them, which he did. He lived then in what is Umsinga division. As soon as the confederacy was formed, they moved south to Mrolweni, where they plundered Mbangambi's cattle as stated, and where Xesibe was killed.[133]

The collective migration of these chiefs with their followers is documented in this oral tradition, which depicts them moving into the Mrolweni district near Howick, only two or three years after Ngoza and the AbaTembu had been there. There Xesibe met his death:

Mdingi, Baleni, Nombewu and Xesibe, finding themselves exposed to the Zulu attacks, entered into an alliance, with the object of forcing their way through towards Pondoland. They left their respective tribal lands in the thorns. (Nombevu and Baleni up to that time had lived on the lands now being occupied by the Cunu people.) Leaving those parts, the confederacy made their way to Mrolweni (near Howick), where a chief, Mbangambi, of the amaBele people, was living. They decided to loot their [the AmaBele] stock. The *impi* dispersed for the purpose. Xesibe, then happening to be alone, saw a few calves being herded on a hill. He went towards the hill in order to seize them, but there were some of the enemy there who immediately began to chase him. He ran hard until [sic] but one kept up with him, and this man, drawing in closer, flung his assegai and struck him [Xesibe] a deadly wound in the back, after which, perceiving some of our tribe nearby, he [Xesibe's attacker] ran off and fled. Xesibe died almost at once and was buried.[134]

None of the small chiefdoms of this small confederacy remained settled on the land they had held before the migrations prompted by Shaka's expansionism. Describing the process of intrusion by one chiefdom upon another, Yenge's son told Stuart, "[w]e pushed them on; they went on further, i.e. we Zondis, pressed by Tshaka's impis, pushed or drove or shoved them, the Bacas [Macibise's people], further on. They formerly lived about Cedara and near Pietermaritzburg, i.e. land we now have."[135] As they migrated south, they were joined by the AmaBhaca.[136] Chief Xesibe, by whose name some of these people came to be known as AmaXesibe, "was killed at Mrolweni" in a battle one of Shaka's *impi*s. His death prompted flight by the survivors to AmaMpondo territory where they were turned back and thus forced to live at eMrolweni.[137] Nombevu's people suffered a retaliatory attack from the AmaBhaca chief Ncapayi son of Madikane, and Nombevu himself was killed after Mdingi's people pretended to be those of Nombevu when they attacked and killed the AmaBhaca chief Sonyangwe.[138] Mdingi was later killed by the AmaCele chief Magaye when he returned to Natal.[139]

The raids and attacks of AmaZulu troops continued as well. The ferocity of some of Shaka's early battles is reflected in an account of the AmaNgidi under chief Mnguni. Stuart collected a lengthy oral narrative about "Tshaka's attack on Mnguni, chief of the Ngidi tribe, and how that tribe came to flee from Zululand."[140] Shaka sent his army to the Mhlatuze river, and the AmaNgidi chief Mnguni assembled his regiments in response after sending the women and children, old people, and cattle across the Thukela river to avoid the *impi*. Using a small remaining herd to lure Shaka's army, the AmaNgidi were attacked at the Nsuze River where they fought two full days until dark when the AmaZulu army pulled off for the night. Shaka and Mnguni then prepared both their armies to fight that night, and the fighting continued for a third day. Shaka's warriors were reportedly under orders "to return with Mnguni's head." In a statement meant to convey the high level of mortality, Stuart was told "[t]he Nsuze and the Mhlatuze [rivers] were red [from blood]. On the fourth day they fought to a finish. They began in the morning, and fought until the sun went down." Emphasizing the courage and determination of the AmaNgidi, the narrator said that "[i]t was the darkness which caused them to draw off; there was no one who ran away." Nevertheless, the AmaZulu killed Mnguni's son Mnteli and took his head to Shaka, and Chief Mnguni determined that they could not defeat the AmaZulu there and so ordered a complete withdrawal to Hlobane mountain. There the AmaZulu forces caught up with them two days later and the fighting resumed. After a night and day of fighting, "the country at Hlobane mountain was red." Mnguni ordered his men to escape, fetch the civilian population and cattle, and migrate as a chiefdom beyond the reach of the AmaZulu. They went first to a location west of the Mnambithi river and then again farther southwest, along the Drakensberg range, until they reached the Orange River where they settled safely away from the fighting.[141]

The AmaBomvu, who generations before had been a branch related to the AmaNgwane of Matiwane but had long since been living separately, also fled their home at Qudeni in KwaZulu and crossed the Thukela.[142] According to one account, the AmaMbomvu were attacked by the AmaZulu at their mountain stronghold at oPisweni mountain. In the night attack, the AmaZulu used ladders to scale the mountain, release the cattle through the gate, and take the men by surprise. The women and cattle were captured without a fight, and although their chief was killed, most remained in their own territory as subjects of Shaka.[143] According to another narrative, however, some AmaBomvu moved to south of the Thukela River where they drove the AmaNxamalala from their lands, forcing them to migrate, and the AmaBomvu fought the AmaKabela and AmaSithole, even though they had in the past intermarried with all three of these chiefdoms. Their chief, Somhashi, returned the cattle they had raided to those men who had married AmaBomvu women but did not desist from raiding in the area.[144] These AmaBomvu remembered that

> It was Tshaka who chased our tribe out of Zululand. [Chief] Zombane was killed by Tshaka. Tshaka killed Zombane because he was so handsome that it seemed as if he should become the chief of the Zulu country. Tshaka said that when he looked into the water (our fomer looking-glass [mirror]) he found himself ugly and not so handsome as Zombane who had a nice long neck, whereas Tshaka's nose was so large that it filled much of his face – was as big as a toad. Tshaka said that on looking on Zombane it seemed as if he, Tshaka, should salute (*kulekela*) him. Tshaka sent for Zombane, his object being to kill him, which was done at the eMateku.[145]

Zombane's son Somhashi took his followers, including his uncles, and was given refuge by Chief Jobe of the AmaSithole in Natal for the remainder of Shaka's reign. Not until Dingane invited those who had been forced into exile during Shaka's reign to return did one of Somhashi's uncles take him back to *khonza* Dingane. They were allowed to reoccupy their old territory but were forced to flee back into Natal when Mpande succeeded his half brother as king.[146]

It is difficult to trace the effects of early battles and the disruptions of chiefdoms because when they broke up into separate segments under more than one chief, the fate of each segment might differ dramatically. One segment of the AbaTembu known as the AmaBomvana resettled more than once before finding refuge and living among the AmaMpondo of Chief Faku in the Transkei region. Eventually, they came to live between the Kei and Mtata rivers, having left their stronghold after an attack at their home on the Mtwalume River.[147] Similarly, various branches of the AbaTembu suffered different fates. After Ngoza's death, Shaka welcomed those of Ngoza's followers who returned to give allegiance to him, and they were resettled among the Mandhlakazi.[148] Because of their long prior history of migration and warfare, however, and the death of their most prominent chief Ngoza, the survival of other AbaTembu could be easily overshadowed and overlooked. Stuart was told that "there are no more Tembus left; they were killed by the Zulus in Tshaka's day," but this interviewee was referring only to the followers of a single recalcitrant chief, Mangete, who had gone into hiding in Natal and been killed off by bandits over time.[149] Those of Mangete's followers who had left their chief and "run off to Pondoland," however, had not suffered the same fate.[150] The breaking up of chiefdoms was known as the "death of nations," but the peoples composing these chiefdoms often survived as new adherents to Shaka's AmaZulu chiefdom or as refugees beyond the reach of AmaZulu troops.

Chapter 6

Chiefs, Chiefdoms, Violence, and Political Reconfiguration

Shaka's early military campaigns, although still limited in size, had successfully expanded the territory and people that fell under AmaZulu control. This allowed him to increase the size of his military strength accordingly because the men of the chiefdoms he had incorporated were enrolled in AmaZulu regiments. Much of the dispersed AmaMthethwa chiefdom, including its subordinate chiefs and chiefdoms, had fallen under Shaka's rule, but several large rival chiefdoms retained their dominance in the territories surrounding the growing AmaZulu chiefdom. As he had done with the smaller chiefs, Shaka continued his strategy of seeking the voluntary submission of larger chiefs as his subordinate allies, and he sent *impi*s to impose AmaZulu rule when they refused. The confrontation between the AmaZulu and larger chiefdoms was to bring increased resistance and violence to a larger region, and broke apart more than one large chiefdom, setting some segments of chiefdoms into flight and migration under the leadership of their chiefs. The political configuration of the regions of modern KwaZulu and Natal changed dramatically as a sweeping process of consolidation under AmaZulu dominance was imposed by the use of military campaigns. After Dingiswayo's death, Shaka was confronted with the challenges posed by the other major chiefdoms of the region, including the AbaQwabe of Phakathwayo, the AmaCele and AmaThuli south of the Thukela River, the AmaHlubi and AmaNgwane toward the west, the Embo of Zihlandlo southwest of the AmaZulu heartland, and the formidable AmaNdwandwe of Zwide to his north. The process of incorporation did not always involve violence because some chiefs gave their allegiance to Shaka voluntarily and became tributary to him, and others offered their submission after minimal fighting involving few casualties. In the many battles that were fought, large and small, thousands of lives were lost. But the wages of war included the loss of life following the destruction of crops and loss of livestock taken as booty and in raiding and affected civilians as well as warriors. Some chiefs chose to flee with their followers to seek land for resettlement beyond the reach of Shaka's authority and in so doing sometimes inflicted violence on the areas through which they passed. The process of demographic dislocation was considerable and disrupted food production, causing hunger and sometimes famine for the peoples involved and driving them to raid from others in desperation. Over the course of these processes of dislocation and sociopolitical reconfiguration during the era of Shaka's rule, thousands of lives were lost across the region of KwaZulu-Natal and bordering regions in all directions.

PHAKATHWAYO AND THE ABAQWABE

Phakathwayo, who was Khondlo's son, had succeeded to the AbaQwabe chieftaincy during the reign of Shaka's father Senzangakhona. According to oral traditions, early in Shaka's reign, Phakathwayo's behavior toward Shaka proved insulting to the AmaZulu and Shaka. During a period of food shortage and famine, Shaka was said to have asked for grain from Phakathwayo, who sent a refusal and a verbal insult. Subsequently, Shaka is said to have provoked conflict with Phakathwayo by having one of his military regiments build their barracks, *ikhanda*, on territory claimed by the AbaQwabe. After the AbaQwabe burned down the Mbelebele *ikanda* Shaka's regiment rebuilt it. Phakathwayo decided to tolerate it, according to oral tradition, because he did not consider the AmaZulu to be strong enough to pose a threat.[1]

The AmaZulu and AbaQwabe maintained a formal relationship, however, that was reflected in the holding of the ceremonial warriors' dance, the *umjadu*. Mmemi knew that Shaka had once attended an *umjadu* warriors dance with the AbaQwabe, a sign of alliance because Shaka stayed at Mmemi's father Mbokazi's village, Emkiwaneni, while other men and the women of Shaka's *isigodlo* stayed in neighboring homesteads.[2] Mmemi told a story that Stuart recorded as "Origin of the Quarrel between Tshaka and Qwabe which led to the death of Phakathwayo."[3] This story may explain the AbaQwabe's reputation for not tolerating the use of medicines and associating their use with the evil deeds of *abatakati*. In a long narrative, Mmemi related that an *inyanga* ["doctor"] named Mqayana had been driven away by the AbaQwabe for having used *ikatazo* medicine. Mqayana sought refuge with Shaka for whom he offered to use his skills.[4] Shaka was said to have tested Mqayana's skills as an *inyanga* by having him "doctor," or strengthen, Shaka with the blood of a black bull, and "[w]hen he had finished, Tshaka said, 'Could you kill Pakatwayo, as you say you are a doctor?'" Thus, according to this oral tradition, Shaka employed Mqayana to help in killing Phakathwayo. To provide the opportunity to confront Phakathwayo, Shaka planned an *umjadu* dance. During the course of the *umjadu*, the AbaQwabe are said to have insulted the AmaZulu as too small and insignificant for the AbaQwabe to hold a dance with them.[5] One UmQwabe was said to have compared the numbers of the AmaZulu to a necklace too small to fit around the head, saying "Are we as insignificant? What makes them think they can dance with us?"[6] It was then that Nqetho ka Khondlo ka Mncinci and Sopane ka Mncinci were said to have left the AbaQwabe and *khonza*'d Shaka, and they are said to have reported these insults to Shaka. Mqayana was able to concoct *intelezi* "medicine" with dirt from where the AbaQwabi had danced mixed with other toxic ingredients such as animal feces to be used against the AbaQwabe. This *intelezi* concoction was used to pollute the spring from which the AbaQwabe took their drinking water. It was also conveyed by means of frogs, toads, and cockroaches.[7]

At least one version of the narrative about these events relates that immediately after the joint *umjadu* dance, the AmaZulu warriors attacked the AbaQwabe. The AmaZulu, having hidden their weapons nearby, retrieved them and returned, taking the AbaQwabe by surprise.[8] The attack may have occurred on a later occasion, but the stories agree that the AbaQwabe were taken by surprise. When Shaka and an AmaZulu *impi* invaded AbaQwabe territory and arrived by surprise at Phakathwayo's ekuDabukeni homestead, the small contingent present with Phakathwayo was unarmed and became ill as they tried in vain to mount an effective defense, and Phakathwayo was captured after very little fighting. One person asserted that "[w]hen Tshaka arrived the Qwabe ran away, fleeing into the palm trees. The people whom the Zulu found in their homes were stabbed."[9] A victory ceremony was performed in which Shaka repeatedly jumped over, or *eqa*'d, the defeated chief, who was seated in the middle of a semicircle, but Shaka did not kill him.[10] Instead he told his troops to "take him and look after him," but Phakathwayo had also been made ill by the drugs and was said to have died having been overcome by the powerful drugs, and in some versions, by fear.¹¹ Evidently, it was believed widely that Shaka had used *intelezi* to overcome and subdue Phakathwayo and the AbaQwabe, and therefore the AbaQwabe retained their formidable reputation in spite of Shaka's success. Thus, the AmaZulu king Mpande paid tribute to AbaQwabe courage generations later with reference to Phakathwayo's death and their submission to Shaka. Stuart was told,

> Mpande once asked Mapita in the assembly what people were braver than the Qwabes. Mapita remarked that the Zulus had defeated them at Kwa Hlokohloko (i.e. the name of the hill where the Qwabe king Pakatwayo was taken). Mpande said, "Yes, but that was an occasion only where they were overcome not by our valour but by our drugs (*izintelezi*)", or, as Mpande, said, "our *intonga*." Mpande maintained that the Qwabes were always the first to go to the attack.¹²

Shaka saw that Phakathwayo was properly buried, and "[a]fter this the Qwabes surrendered to Tshaka, whereupon our cattle were seized."¹³ With their chief dead, "[i]t was at this stage that a large number of Qwabes went to *konza* [offer allegiance to] Dingiswayo," i.e. Shaka's superior.¹⁴ However, many tendered their submission and allegiance directly to Shaka, who allowed them to return to their villages but live under his authority.¹⁵ The royal family, now subordinate tributaries to Shaka, survived with their followers and identity intact but had lost the unity and strength to remain prominent. Phakathwayo's brother Nqetho had already become a loyal follower of Shaka, under whom Nqetho kept his own villages with a high degree of autonomy. His brother Nomo, who had known Shaka from their time together living among the AmaMthethwa, was also allowed to re-establish himself, but other sons of Khondlo were said eventually to have been killed by Shaka.¹⁶

Three of Phakathwayo's brothers, Godolozi, Godide, and Vubukulwayo, went to give their allegiance to the AmaNdwandwe chief Zwide. Mmemi told Stuart,

> After this, Godolozi, the younger own-brother of Phakathwayo (Godolozi ka Khondlo was the father of Musi), Godide ka Khondlo (Godide is the father of Mamfongonyana), and Vubukulwayo ka Khondlo (Vubukuluwayo was still young, a minor son of Khondlo) – these three went to Zwide. When they got to Zwide he asked them, "Seeing there are two principal ones here, which is the bigger? Who is the one who should be recognized by me as chief?" Those Qwabes who accompanied these to go and *konza* the Ndwandwe king said, "The proper chief of these, Sir, is one who is still young, namely Vubukulwayo." When they said this Zwide demurred and said Godolozi was the principal man, especially as he was the eldest son of Khondlo. "This is a person of high rank."

Even though Zwide decided thus, it did not suit Godolozi to remain among the Ndwandwe. He therefore returned to the Zulu country. He was moved to doing this owing to the action of the Qwabes in pointing out not him but a child when questioned by Zwide. Godolozi then said, "Let me go and be killed once only, by Tshaka."[17]

Godolozi therefore returned to *khonza* Shaka, but many AbaQwabe remained behind with Zwide and the AmaNdwandwe.[18] Shaka allowed Godolozi to marry and bear heirs to the AbaQwabe chiefly line of descent, so that generations later Mmemi said "[a]fter this these people settled down under Tshaka. The Qwabe people would not have risen again but for this order by Tshaka."[19] Eventually, however, "Godolozi was killed by Tshaka."[20] Some AbaQwabe remained living among the AmNdwandwe under Zwide, and some are said to have fled and migrated into Swaziland.[21]

MAGAYE AND THE AMACELE CHIEFDOM

Shaka remained attentive to affairs south of the Thukela River where early in his reign he found assistance and refuge for his chiefdom when they were driven from their homes by Zwide's AmaNdwandwe. There the AmaCele chiefdom under Dibandhlela had come to overshadow both the AmaThuli chiefdom, then under the rule of a regent, Matubane, and the Makanya AbaQwabe who had lived in the area for two generations. Dinya related to Stuart a lengthy account of the succession dispute between Dibandhlela's sons, Mande, elder but junior, and Magaye, younger but the heir. Magaye had been sent away by his father Dibandhlela, who "hid him among the people of his mother's brother, Pakatwayo." There,

Magaye grew up. He was fetched and came back when an *insizwa* [young man]. He was then installed as chief of Nikela kraal [homestead, *umuzi*]. Mande roused himself and resisted his portion of people being swallowed up by Magaye. Mande gained as adherents many large kraals of Dibandhlela's [who was a very old man]. The result of this separation was that only three of Dibandhlela's kraals remained with Magaye, viz. Nikela, Ngwazi (of Zwana ka Mkokeleli), and Lwasi (of the people of Mpalazi ka Dibandhlela).[22]

As Mande "took to arms," his father Dibandhlela became angry and called back the Nkungu and Amabola *imizi*, his senior royal homesteads, on the grounds they belonged to Nikela (i.e., Magaye's homestead).

Chiefs, Chiefdoms, Violence, and Political Reconfiguration   111

Mande complained, "I refuse to have appointed as chief over me a mere child," but as Dinya explained, it was well known that Magaye was the legitimate heir:

> They failed to see that the reason for this appointment was because Magaye's mother was Dibandhlela's *inkosikazi* [queen], who at her marriage was danced for (with genet tails tied to sticks) and she was *lobola*'d [had bridewealth cattle paid for her] with tribal cattle, indicating she was [from the time of her marriage] the *inkosikazi* [great wife designated to bear the heir]. These ceremonials had not occurred in regard to any other of Dibandhlela's wives."[23]

Dinya related further events surrounding what he termed this "civil" war fought among the junior AbaQwabe chiefs early in Shaka's reign. In the war, the senior kraals supported Magaye as directed to do so by Dibandhlela.

> Whilst fighting was still going on Tshaka crossed over to Dukuza. He then mediated by calling all the chiefs, viz. Nzwakele ka Kutshwayo of the Dube tribe, Nqeto ka Khondlo, Mepo ka Ngwane of the Ngcolosi, Zihlandhlo ka Gcwabe, Duze ka Mnengwa of the Makanya, and Nodokwana ka Dibandhlela ka Lubeleni of the Mapumulo (not Dibandhlela, son of Mkokeleli), Nodokwana having been appointed by Tshaka over the Mapumulo tribe in succession to Mtimkulu ka Dibandhlela ka Lubeleni. All of these had *konza*'d Tshaka; all had paid tribute.[24]

Dinya told Stuart he had heard the story of the events from an eyewitness, Mazangane ka Mfaniswa ka Dibandhlela ka Mkokeleli, who had been present when Shaka heard the case and passed judgment.[25] Dinya continued,

> All these assembled at Dukuza. All the Celes arrived at Dukuza too. Dibandhlela was still living but too feeble and old to attend. The meeting took place on the flat outside the kraal.[26]

Dinya's narrative of Shaka's hearing of the case was elaborate, and he told it well. Shaka questioned Mande and heard his objection to being subject to a younger brother. Shaka asked him what he had said when Magaye's mother had been married as great wife, presumed to be future mother of the heir she would conceive, which had occurred when Mande was already a grown man. Dinya's narrative relates the conversations at length. Shaka preempted a response from the other men there by saying, "Let me speak first. Has a chief ever been made? A chief is not made; a chief makes himself. It is the calf of the cow which is picked out and has its place assigned to it."[27]

With this statement, Shaka indicated that although inheritance of position was assigned according to the choice of the senior wife, this did not necessarily lead to the actual accession to the chieftaincy of that designated heir. Quoting Shaka thus had the effect of foreshadowing favoritism and deciding the case according to demonstrated success, which seemed to suggest that Shaka would have favored Mande. Magaye, when questioned, pointed out that although his brother had defeated him twice in battle, it was only because Mande had had more followers, and that once the men from the senior villages had deserted his brother and rejoined him, Mande had been unable to defeat him. Shaka sent Mande away and discussed the case with the other influential AmaCele men who had been called to hear the case. Here there is a twist in the narrative, for first, as Dinya narrated, Shaka expressed his admiration for Mande, the older but junior brother: "I stand in awe of this man Mande; he is a chief indeed. When he looks at me, though I am Shaka, my eyes drop to the ground and give way before him." With this indication that he believed Mande had earned the position, Shaka proceeded to decide against him and in favor of the younger but senior brother Magaye, saying, "Let me and Magaye rule alone. I shall remove this man Mande of Mfakuceba, and this man Duze ka Mnengwa, and take their two followings and join them to Magaye, and we shall hold dances together." This was done, and "Mande and Duze were thereupon put to death, I do not know if at Dukuza or their own homes."[28] Shaka had made the practical decision of putting to death the more formidable son of Dibandhlela who posed the greater threat to him and upholding the inheritance rights of the apparently less ambitious man, Magaye.[29]

After telling the story, Dinya gave his own interpretation that Shaka "was likening Mande's position to his own when saying, 'A chief is not made.'" Dinya specified the next day, "The decision come to by Tshaka in regard to the case Mande vs. Magaye was remarkable for the pronouncement that kings are not born, they make themselves. From this it seems he had in mind the method by which he had risen to the throne. He therefore secretly approved Mande as the de facto 'king' or chief of the Cele tribe and, because of his having made himself king, feared he might in time have designs on Tshaka himself."[30]

Melapi ka Magaye said that during Shaka's reign, the AmaCele, linked by marriage to the AbaQwabe chiefdom north of the Thukela, were so closely identified with Shaka that they came to be referred to by other Africans in Natal as themselves being AmaZulu. Not all of the Natal chiefs south of the Thukela accepted the terms offered by Shaka, however, of becoming subordinate allies, and Melapi stated that "Tshaka attacked the Qwabe on this side of the river after killing Pakatwayo."[31] According

Chiefs, Chiefdoms, Violence, and Political Reconfiguration 113

to this version of events related by a royal family member of mixed AmaCele and AbaQwabe heritage,

> Tshaka sent a man to go to the chiefs across the Tukela and say, "Tshaka is coming." He [the man] began at Emfeni; he reported Tshaka's word to Mande. Mande said, "Weu! He comes to us here? The umNtungwa who wears the *tongwane* fruit as a penis-cover?" The messenger then traveled westward and went to the various chiefs in Natal. He came to Nzala, chief of the amaNdhlovu. When he left Nzala he came to Magaye.³²

This report is important for establishing chronology. It indicates that Shaka's *impi* or military campaign against the AbaQwabe chiefdom, which resulted in Phakathwayo's death, had preceded Shaka's subordination of the chiefdoms of the AmaCele and AmaThuli south of the Thukela River. The story also reflects the common use of insults as a means of provocation. The AmaCele chief was Magaye, the son of Dibandhlela and of his senior wife who had come from the AbaQwabe royal family. When Shaka's messenger arrived, Magaye treated him cordially and slaughtered a head of cattle for him, and when the messenger returned to report, "Shaka asked his messenger what the various chiefs had given him to eat."³³ The messenger told Shaka that he had been fed at each of the kraals he had visited. When Shaka heard that Magaye had slaughtered a head of cattle for the messenger, he is said to have replied, "[t]here, then, is one who is our people, one who saw that you came from a chief." The messenger also reported to Shaka the insulting response of Magaye's brother Mande, who had also made a defiant gesture by striking the ground with the stick of his *assegai* (spear).

> Tshaka then assembled the Zulu because Mande had insulted him. This was the year when the country this side of the river (Natal) was going to be destroyed. Tshaka crossed over at the time of the new moon. He then attacked. He crossed the Tukela with his forces. He camped between the Mhlali and Tukela. He then sent the same messenger to Magaye to say, "Tshaka says you are to cook for him." The messenger delivered the message. Magaye asked some of the old men of Mkokeleli's what was the proper thing to do. They said, "Why do you ask? Do as he says." Magaye then took a lot of cattle off to Tshaka and cooked for him with them. They [Magaye's men] came to him [Shaka]. Men of the Cele tribe were sent with the messenger and cattle to Tshaka. They returned and said he gave praise "for your cooking for him."³⁴

Magaye's narrative provides details about Shaka's motives and the deliberateness of his actions, including specifically targeting those who had openly defied and challenged him and protecting those who *khonza*'d him, including from unintentional military depredations that resulted when warriors seized provisions to feed themselves as they passed through territories. Shaka tested chiefs before determining whether to attack them. Thus, "[a]fter a while Tshaka's troops seized a beast belonging to the Makanya section. He was provoking them, to see if they would take action. The Makanya people however refrained from taking action."³⁵ Shaka had already decided to punish Mande but did not want inadvertently to attack Magaye's people, and asked Magaye to mark their boundaries with bundles of wood set on fire so they could be seen at night. When Mande attempted to flee with his cattle,

> Tshaka's troops attacked Mande and chased him north. This attack all arose out of the insult. Mande then went off to Nzala among the emaNdhlovini people. Tshaka attacked both, surrounding them. Tshaka gave orders for his troops not to go beyond Nzala, and not to go along the coast, as Magaye's people might get hurt in the absence of the troops. They must turn back by the way they had come down. Mande was defeated at Nzala's place. He, Mande, returned to the Tete stream [from Pondoland?], to his kraal sites. His women and children had hidden, and now returned to their homes. Finding he had returned, Tshaka then directed his Iziyendane regiment to go and kill him. He was then killed. The people of Mande's household then returned to Magaye.³⁶

According to this oral tradition, although Mande himself was killed, his people were allowed to live and rejoin the chief who had *khonza*'d Shaka (i.e., Magaye). Magaye was then invited to visit Shaka, who held festivities for him and reassured him of his intentions:

> "Among the peoples here," said Tshaka, "a fire will burn at two doors – among our people (the place of Nandi), and among your people (the place of Siwetu). Both will be ours, so that when the fire of our people's place goes out, it will be made at Siwetu's place, and when the fire goes out at your people's place, it will be lit at Nandi's place."³⁷

Thus, Magaye entered into a subordinate alliance with Shaka. As a result, Shaka provided him the temporary command of an AmaZulu regiment. With it, Magaye attacked across the Mkomazi and took the cattle of Ngoyi ka Nomakwelo of the AmaMbili, and then he formed his own regiment, first known as the Njanduna ("Dog chief"). Subsequently, Shaka was so impressed by these warriors of Magaye that he took both them and their name, the Njanduna. Magaye renamed the village and regiment the "uRodi" into which he placed a new cohort of men to serve as warriors under his own command.³⁸

The evidence of the relationship between Magaye and Shaka is somewhat ambiguous, however. Dinya said that relations between Shaka and Magaye were cordial. He explained: "Tshaka entertained great affection for Magaye, and spoke even of taking him onto his lap. He was, however, afraid of doing this on account of the ill-feeling that would be given rise to."³⁹ Dinya explained the complicated relations whereby Magaye's men might desert Shaka in favor of their own chief if called upon to do so. Dinya continued,

It seems that Tshaka and Magaye used to hold dances together. At these, on one occasion, Magaye's men sang a chorus about "The one who is choked with meat" and "The circle of men will turn round." Tshaka could not understand what was implied by these phrases. He was apprehensive lest Magaye meant that the time would come when Tshaka's own men (circle) would leave him and join Magaye, presumably in the same way that Mande's men had come round to him. Tshaka did not like this, especially as, with the recent additions referred to, the tribe had become a very large one, and questioned Magaye, who thereby became frightened. Tshaka would have put him to death but for an oath he [Shaka] had taken in the presence of Nzwakele, Nqeto and other neighbouring chiefs to the effect that Magaye should come by no harm at his hands "until he were [helped to] to drink milk." ("Not until you are helped to drink milk" is an expression meaning "never" or until he reached second infancy [senility].)⁴⁰

Shaka was savvy enough to know that he could not safely alienate Magaye as long as Shaka also faced threats north of the Thukela River and because Shaka harbored designs to extend his authority even farther south, over the AmaMpondo and AmaXhosa chiefs. Beginning in 1824, European traders operated out of Port Natal, so it was even more imperative that Shaka retain control over the region of Natal. Hence, Shaka forbade his men to ""help themselves" to Magaye's property as they were passing through, the way they did in Zululand" and on *impi*s (military expeditions) sent outside of Zululand. Shaka also "gave Magaye the right to protect himself," (i.e., his property). "This Magaye did, and occasionally put offenders to death, reporting thereafter to Shaka what he had done."⁴¹ Maquza ka Gawushane said, "Tshaka used to get on very well with Magaye, and called him 'my younger brother.' The two were of the same age."⁴² He told Stuart that "Tshaka only came once to see Magaye. When Tshaka came to Dukuza he ordered Magaye to bring his own hut and build it inside Dukuza. This was his hut for *konza*ing [demonstrating obeisance]. Tshaka came to Magaye when he [Shaka] had [already] come [moved and rebuilt his capital] to Dukuza."⁴³

Magaye's son Melapi was one of Stuart's oldest informants and an eyewitness to this period. He told Stuart, "I was born before Tshaka had become known among our people. I distinctly remember people running away when he fought south of the Tukela."⁴⁴ Melapi related oral history from his own personal experience:

I saw Tshaka when he visited Emkhlazi to see his "younger brother" (*umnawe*), my father. He was with the Dibinhlangu (still unmarried – *izinsizwa*) and Gibabanye (still unmarried – *izinsizwe*) regiments. We peeped out at him through the hut-coverings while dancing was taking place. Tshaka himself danced. He sang:

> "The kraal of Nzala ka Mangqatshi
> Will no more be mentioned,
> Ask among the Nsomi people."

And:

> "Kukuluku, the cock crowed,
> Who placed it there? Vutani and Gubetuka praised him,
> The husband enters,
> You must carry *imincwazi* berries,
> I am not a goat to be made terrified in the kraals,
> I am not a gate-keeper such as is selected by kraal-owners
> I am a great warrior there in the Zulu country, I am foremost in the place of headrings."⁴⁵

Melapi's testimony is a key descriptive narrative for understanding politics in the area south of the Thukela during the early part of Tshaka's reign, before 1824. Melapi stated, "I only saw Tshaka once. An *umjadu* dance was going on at my father's kraal." As the heir to the principal chief, Magaye, Melapi would certainly have known of all the occasions of Shaka's visit to the kraal there. This indicates the probability that Shaka went there only once (before 1824), which would explain why Fynn and the other early European traders did not know about Shaka's visit to Natal before moving his headquarters to Dukuza. "He carried no warshield for he had come for an *umjadu* dance."⁴⁶ Everyone remembered a warrior's warshield because it became part of his identity and indeed identified him individually and by regiment, so this is probably an accurate memory from Melapi as an eyewitness even though he had been young. The observation also indicates the level of real trust between Shaka and Magaye at that time.

Shields are only carried in war-time. The regiments had decorated themselves with the *umkoka* plant and the *isundu* palm – about the head and some about the knees. The men so dressed stood round in semi-circle fashion whilst others, also belonging to Tshaka, danced in the centre. These I noticed had no *umkoka* or *isundu* leaves but they had strings of calf-skin round the limbs. They also had girdles (*imitsha, umahlanyana*)."⁴⁷

In his notes, Stuart drew a sketch of a man's *imitsha* on his lower body from behind, revealing his buttocks with the wide belt above and ornamental danglings on each side. "Assegais" (i.e., spears), "were not carried."[48]

The events as Melapi remembered reveal the sociopolitical relationship that had been established by the two chiefs as Magaye publicly took on the subordinate role:

> Magaye danced first – he must do so in order to *tshaya*, that is, prepare the ground for the king. Magaye's [warriors] had put on their *imitsha*. His regiments were the uSoka, uRodi, ukuMangala, also the Mdhlazi (his main kraal). The izinduna of Mdhlazi were Lucunge ka Nodinga of the Sitole people, also Nhlasiyana ka Nomunga ka Mkokeleli. Lucunge is the person who went to report on the arrival of the white people to Tshaka. The Sitole people are a section of the Cele tribe.[49]

Further indicating the content of the dance, Melapi commented there were "Stamping feet – causing the ground to thunder; then shout, 'Tshwe!' and say, 'He is called to Faku in the Mpondo country.'"[50]

Melapi remembered that

> Tshaka made up songs for himself. He was dark-brown (*nsundu*) in colour. His buttocks looked as if they were drawn in. That is, his buttocks were small. He wore a bunch of loury feathers. I did not see him close so I cannot describe his face. He was not tall; he was of medium size (*isidhlodhlo*).[51]

Melapi was certain that Shaka had composed his own songs and related that "[w]hen Tshaka built Dukuza he said to my father he was to make up songs and that they would hold dances together. My father [Magaye] did so. Those given above are Tshaka's [songs]."[52] It was Maquza who related the unexpected result of Shaka's visit to Magaye in a passage Stuart began with a presumptive notation concerning the visit itself, "Tshaka's coming to Magaye etc.":

> Tshaka came at breakfast to Mdhlazi. He sat on the hill above the homestead, at the track made by the cattle. He had many people. Magaye then gathered his men to perform a dance for the chief Tshaka. He assembled the Njanduna. They danced for a long time. Tshaka then came to the Mdhlazi kraal. He entered the cattle enclosure, and went up to Magaye's *isigodhlo*. Tshaka asked, "Are these your men?" Magaye said, "Yes." Tshaka said, "They are handsome; they have long legs. They must become my regiment." Magaye agreed, not having anything to say. Tshaka thereupon took the regiment which Magaye had assembled [enrolled]. Tshaka then built them a kraal up the Mdhloti in their own country. He did not take them to Zululand.[53]

Magaye's well-trained and disciplined warriors thus came under the direct command of Shaka's own *induna*s, available for service to the AmaZulu king in the region south of the Thukela. Melapi remembered,

"My father was a great favourite with Tshaka."[54] The AmaCele became so closely associated with Shaka that Melapi told Stuart, "[d]uring the *Izwekufa* ["death of nations," i.e. era of Shaka's wars] we ran off into the bushes. While we were there, people pointed us out, saying, 'There are Zulu!'"[55] The Makanya section of the AbaQwabe was "dispersed, and *konza*'d Magaye. Tshaka agreed to this."[56] Magaye's son Melapi remembered that the AbaQwabe had been stealing the food that the AmaCele kept stored in their gourd. Magaye reported the problem to Shaka, who responded promptly:

Tshaka said, "O, they are doing things they shouldn't do behind my back. Why do they do this? Let these wrong-doers perish!" The gourds were then hidden. Tshaka proclaimed a warning to the wrong-doers and the annoyance ceased, whereupon the gourds which had been hidden away were once more used openly. The country then became quiet.[57]

According to this narrative of events, Shaka continued to intervene until the problems were solved. His first threat succeeded in deterring the theft of food from gourds, and "[a]fter this, this wrong-doing came to an end, but bandits emerged":

Cattle were stolen by them [bandits] at night, and found missing in the morning. The thieves had gone off with them into the bushes and killed them there. Tshaka said an announcement should be made to the people in the bushes, for he thought he might be the cause of their behaving in this lawless fashion. So the proclamation was made in the bushes to the effect that all were to return to their homes and resume their natural ways of living. They thereupon returned home. Tshaka did nothing to them.[58]

Melapi's testimony thus sheds light on Shaka's style of governance early in his reign when he used diplomatic measures rather than force to achieve the ends of peaceful social adjustment.[59] In 1827, Shaka was drawn southward by the presence of the European traders at Port Natal (Durban) and selected a site for his new capital in the territory of the AmaCele who had long lived there. Thus, "[a]t Dukuza Tshaka built on an old site of Dibandhlela's. I do not know its name."[60] It is also significant that "[e]ach of the [AbaQwabe] chiefs – Mepo, Nqeto, Nzwakele etc. – had a hut set apart for his occupation in the royal kraal, Dukuza."[61] The AmaCele chief Magaye remained Shaka's primary representative in dealing with the Europeans as they arrived in the region. Only Dingane questioned Magaye's loyalty after Shaka's death, even though he had declined an offer to join in a rebellion against the royal house.[62] Melapi remembered about Magaye,

Chiefs, Chiefdoms, Violence, and Political Reconfiguration 119

"My father's songs for singing when dancing was going on (these are what my father made up):

> 'With what nations are you going to make war?
> The elephant took what belonged to it,
> You people refused it.
> It had been challenged by Matiwane,
> How great is Matiwane who challenges the elephant?
> How big is your assegai, Matiwane?
> For we took that of the Ndwandwe
> Broke it in pieces, and drove it into the ground.'"[63]

SHAKA AND THE AMANDWANDWE OF ZWIDE

During the early years of Shaka's reign, his military remained vulnerable to the more powerful chief Zwide of the AmaNdwandwe to his northeast. Zwide was renowned for his ambition and brutality. Shaka first attempted to rout the AmaNdwandwe after Zwide had captured and killed the AmaMthethwa chief Dingiswayo in 1817. When Shaka sent regiments to avenge Dingiswayo's death, he was no doubt also motivated by his own ambitions. He did not dare engage in open battlefield warfare but planned a well-known night attack, the Kisi battle, in which his regiments did kill many AmaNdwandwe but were driven off after their own significant losses. According to one narrative of these events,

> I know Tshaka cut reed whistles (*amavenge*) when he fought with Zwide, so that, in a night attack, the Zulus would know one another. The instructions were that, when two met, the Zulu was to blow his whistle. If he got no answer he was to blow a second time, and if the other did not blow a whistle, the other was to conclude he was confronted by an Ndwandwe man, whom he was forthwith to stab. This battle took place at kwa Denge (country), at the White Mfolozi. They *tshayelana*'d, i.e. separated and went home.[64]

This would have been in about 1818, or a year after Dingiswayo had assisted Shaka in usurping the AmaZulu chieftaincy. Zwide in turn had led his troops on more than one occasion to retaliate against the AmaZulu, burning their villages and driving them out. This forced Shaka to retreat with his people and troops farther south temporarily. There he devised a strategy to lure AmaNdwandwe troops on a long meandering trail of pursuit devoid of food for their consumption to tire them out before any battle confrontation. Seeking a decisive victory in unfavorable circumstances, Shaka implemented his plan to lure Zwide's troops across a long and tiring trail of pursuit deeper in AmaZulu territory. He also had "medicines" spread along the path to weaken the enemy before battle.

Then at a preplanned location of Shaka's choice, the AmaZulu attacked Zwide's pursuing forces at the Mhlatuze near Mandawe hill. According to Mangati's narrative, in this 1821 battle, both sides suffered heavy casualties before the AmaNdwandwe began their retreat. He related,

> The Ndwandwe came down the Gcongco ridge, passed Empandhleni, and reached the Tukela at Ndondondwana. They then turned about, climbed up the Madungela, and went down to Maqonga, below the Komo; they went along the Mvuzane towards the Mhlatuze, where they turned about and set up camp. The Zulu watched them. The next day the Zulu approached, coming from Tshaka at eTshowe. In discussing the plan of action with Tshaka, Hlati ka Ncidi and Ndhlela ka Sompisi said, "Do not be agitated; do not be afraid. When the enemy come to take you they will do so only after having defeated us men of the Ntontela *ibuto*. We shall scatter them." Indeed at dawn the next day the armies met at Nomveve. The two men fought fiercely with the enemy. As the enemy began to give way they both fell, severely wounded. They were as if dead. The enemy retreated, then broke and fled. The Ndwandwe were routed by the iNtontela and driven towards the Mhlatuze. But the two men [Hlati and Ndhlela] were lying badly wounded where the fight had taken place. The Ndwandwe were utterly defeated. Ndwandwe and Zulu corpses were lying across one another where the armies had met.
>
> Those who could do so returned to Tshaka, those with wounds and those without.[65]

The AmaZulu roundly defeated Zwide's troops and pursued them to and beyond their own villages to the north. The hungry, tired, and perhaps sickened AmaNdwandwe fled in retreat being then pursued by AmaZulu troops. Another battle was fought at the entrance to Zwide's village at Esikwitshini, and many soldiers from both sides were said to have died there as Zwide escaped and fled.[66] The AmaZulu were also said to have engaged in atrocities against women and children found at Zwide's capital. They were said to have been impaled on posts in response to a reported order from Shaka that no women be allowed to survive.[67] Most of the AmaNdwandwe, however, both men and women, survived, and only "those who refused to throw down their shields were stabbed. Those who obeyed were collected into Tshaka's army; those who resisted were killed."[68]

Shepstone's interviewees told him similar narratives of these events, and he concluded that most of the AmaNdwandwe gave their allegiance to Shaka after their defeat and the flight of their chief Zwide.[69] Shaka incorporated AmaNdwandwe into his chiefdom after both this victory and the later AmaZulu impi against Zwide's son Sikhunyana in 1826. However, many left under the leadership of subordinate AmaNdwandwe chiefs to re-establish chiefdoms farther north, never to return. Luzipo told

Stuart "Zwide is said to have died beyond Mtolo. I don't think Zwide rejoined Sotshangana. Mtolo is well to the north."⁷⁰ Madikane said "[m]any customs or practices were 'taken' by Tshaka from Zwide whom he defeated. The salutation 'Bayete' may have come from him [Zwide]. The royal ceremonial song came from Zwide ka Langa, who in his turn had taken it from [AmaSwazi king] Sobuza ka Ndungunya."⁷¹ Zwide's final defeat in 1821 broke apart the AmaNdwandwe, who were forced to retreat and resettle north of the Phongolo River in several branches under the rule of several different chiefs. The arrival of migrant segments of the AmaNdwandwe chiefdom in the vicinity of Delagoa (Maputo) Bay led to attacks and depredations against the Bay chiefdoms that the Portuguese colonial officials – whose fort the AmaNdwandwe threatened more than once – had first reported in early July 1821. The defeat of the AmaNdwandwe marked the end of the older powerful chiefs, paving the way for Shaka's consolidation of authority across the entire region after 1821.

MATUBANE AND THE AMATHULI

The AmaThuli chiefdoms were also located south of the Thukela River and in the vicinity of Port Natal but were weakened by the inheritance of a young royal while still in his minority, requiring rule by two successive regents until he came of age. The AmaThuli chief Mabonsa died before the era of Shaka's reign, and "[a]fter Mabona's death Dhlemula ka Mzucu was established as chief. Dhlemula only ruled on behalf of Mnini, like Matubane, and when Dhlemula died, Matubane succeeded as guardian [of the heir, Mnini]."⁷² However, Matubane became the de facto regent even before Dhlemula died:

> Dhlemula was a mature man but not of Matubane's age. Before the "*Izwekufa*", when the tribes were disturbed by the Iziyendane and others with them, Dhlemula was the acknowledged tribal guardian. Matubane, after the depredations of Tshaka's troops, *konza*'d Tshaka. Tshaka took a fancy to him and gave his orders to him; he spoke to him direct and not to Dhlemula. As Matubane was in favour with Tshaka, so he superseded Dhlemula and became the *de facto* guardian of the tribe and responsible to Tshaka for its good behaviour.⁷³

Shaka chose to recognize Matubane as AmaThuli regent because he appeared to be the more effective leader, although Dhlemula lived throughout his reign and even "went on the uBalule campaign and died there. Matubane did not go on this campaign. He remained with Tshaka."⁷⁴ Shaka must have highly trusted Matubane to have allowed him to stay behind from this last major military campaign to the north against Soshangane in 1828, just prior to Shaka's assassination, when Matubane might have himself attacked Shaka while he was undefended. The oral traditions merely remembered,

> After the *Izwekufa* [death/scattering of nations/chiefdoms] Matubane went with Dhlemula to Tshaka to *konza*. Tshaka was attracted by Matubane, and spoke to him. Tshaka said nothing to or about Dhlemula. He proceeded to negotiate with Matubane as representing the tribe. Matubane had been in charge some years when the Europeans first arrived at Port Natal.[75]

Shaka's respect for Matubane, who was "the age of the Fasimba [regiment]" and therefore "not as old as Tshaka," was evident, for "Tshaka used to speak direct to Matubane and not through his *izinduna* as in the case of other people."[76] Matubane's fate became entangled with that of Lukilimba, one of Shaka's commanders of the Mdadasa regiment before Zwide's defeat when Shaka had moved his people south to take refuge from AmaNdwandwe raids and destruction. Shaka had sent his *induna* Lukilimba into Natal as punishment for having inadvertently drawn an attack of the AmaNdwandwe under Zwide far into AmaZulu territory. This had happened when the AmaZulu were still relatively vulnerable and could not defend their own villages, forcing them into flight before Zwide was finally defeated in 1821. As one of Shaka's indunas, Lukilimba had already earned Shaka's high regard before this time (i.e., before he fell out of favor).

> When the Ndwandwe impi under Zwide invaded Zululand, Tshaka withdrew, burning and destroying everything as he went. The Mdadasa regiment under Lukilimba, however, came into conflict with Zwide's forces and was repulsed. Tshaka at a later date, having heard of this occurrence, was dissatisfied with Lukilimba's conduct, for by opposing the invaders and allowing them to make a feint on him, he thereby drew Zwide's forces onto the Zulus. Zwide was still living at this time. Tshaka now said to Lukilimba, "what were you doing, drawing the enemy on? Go and die in the wilderness, so that you will be removed from my sight" (i.e. he would be destitute, and would be killed by anything that might chance to come in contact with him.) Lukilimba went off to eNtumbankulu, on the north side of the Mzimkulu, in the Port Shepstone magisterial district. He went off simply with the section (*isigaba*) of the Mdadasa which he commanded, not the whole regiment.[77]

When Shaka sent a military expedition south on the *Amabece* campaign against the AmaMpondo (and AmaXhosa), he gave the instruction to seek out Lukilimba's whereabouts. Shaka then sent Matubane to bring him back. Matubane convinced Lukilimba of Shaka's good faith and successfully returned with Lukilimba without engaging in a fight. Upon their return, Shaka gave both Lukilimba and Matubane a large number of cattle.[78]

Another royal AmaThuli descendant, Mcotoyi ka Mnini, remembered that Matubane fell out of favor somewhat later and met his death, and his people's villages were broken up and dispersed. Mcotoyi explained,

Matubane [ka Jombela ka Mzoywane ka Dole] *konza*'d in the Zulu country. Tshaka killed him. He [his theft of cattle from Shaka] was reported by Msekelo to Tshaka. He [Msekelo] said [to Shaka], "He eats cattle; he kills them." These cattle were Tshaka's. They had been put out among all our [AmaThuli] kraals [south of the Thukela River], and our people were herding them for the king [i.e., in Natal]. Matubane was killed at Tshaka's great kraal, Dukuza or Bulawayo. Msekelo said to Tshaka, "There is a kraal of his maternal uncle's people." Tshaka then sent and killed Matubane's relatives. Amabikwane was the name of the kraal killed off – this was a Tembu kraal. (Kupela, my [Mcotoyi's] informant, belongs to this.) After this the people came out of the forests. The section then began to *konza* the white people, for these protected them. When Febana [Farewell] was killed Jana (Cane) looked after the tribe. Kamu Kengi (Captain King) then received the people and protected them.[79]

CHIEFDOMS AND RAIDING IN THE NATAL REGION

Often warfare and battles in the early years of Shaka's reign were caused by conflicts between chiefs whom Shaka and the AmaZulu had not yet subordinated or had offered their allegiance but retained considerable independence and latitude in pursuing their own ambitions. The peoples of the Natal region became subjected to systematic raiding by Shaka's subordinate chiefs and commanders with regiments Shaka had sent there after he had reigned for several years.

Some of the peoples of the Natal region who had suffered from these disruptions and predatory raids remembered narratives about them. Like the AmaThuli whom they had accompanied on a large-scale migration in the mid-eighteenth century into Natal from north of the Thukela, the AmaMbili, AmaKomo, AmaBhaca, and AmaTshaba or Tshabeni peoples were settled across Natal long before Shaka's reign. They were among descendants of the earliest inhabitants of the area who had been there since about the third century AD.

The amaMbili built south of the Mkomazi and as far as the Mzimkulu. The amaKomo extended from the Ngilanyoni to Camperdown. The Bacas were above them. The uTshaba people of Gwayi lived along the banks of the Mzimkulu, on the north side. These last are still living there. Tshaka attacked them.

The Tshabeni chief was Kofiyana ka Mbangana ka Bwayi (Gwayimbili – i.e. showing union with the amaMbili). When Tshaka attacked them he merely seized their cattle. They, like the Tulis, hid in the forests and retained possession of their lands. Fynn brought out all who were in the bushes, including the Tulis, the Xolo, and the Tshabeni. He brought the latter two tribes to Port Natal. Kofiyana was made an *induna* by Febana [Farewell] on the present site of Durban. He became induna of eSinyameni.[80]

The AmaThuli, who dominated the other peoples residing south of the Thukela River, had long engaged in infighting between branches within the ruling family, so that "[t]he Tulis had a reputation for ferocity inasmuch as they were always fighting." Then,

When Tshaka appeared on the scene all the domestic quarrels ceased and the various sections scattered. Some were killed during the general lawlessness that prevailed; some were eaten by hyenas; some went to the Xozas; some went to find protection in Zululand; and later on some crossed over into Natal with Mpande.[81]

The sources agree that forces that Shaka sent into Natal caused significant demographic dislocation and misery among the pre-existing populations there. His goals were to eliminate any potential political or military threats from chiefs and to raid for cattle as booty to be taken to the royal herds or later kept at cattle posts established in Natal. The AmaCele under chief Magaye submitted immediately to Shaka's rule and became one of his most loyal allied subordinates. Other AmaCele did not cooperate and came under attack by the AmaZulu along with lesser chiefs and smaller chiefdoms. By the time Shaka sent military expeditions into Natal, his army had grown by acquiring the regiments of chiefdoms he had incorporated. These included warriors from the AmaHlubi (the Iziyendane regiment), the AmaMthethwa, and others who therefore were then perceived of and identified as AmaZulu by the peoples they raided and attacked. Thus,

The Iziyendane, Mtetwa, amaNganga, amaPumulo etc. were those who attacked the tribes south. They adopted a Zulu chant, and if any stranger should hear them chanting thus he would dash off and jump into a swamp or other hiding place. These men therefore were transformed into Zulus and were regarded as such by the tribes south.[82]

It was the Iziyendane and the others mentioned that attacked along the Natal coast as far as the Mzimkulu – on Tshaka's behalf – and scattered all the tribes. They are the ones who, without special instructions, caused people to flee in the way referred to by Fynn, who in July 1824 found only a few kraals of Tulis on the Bluff [above modern Durban].[83]

Makedama, the eLangeni chief and Shaka's first cousin, who was known for his violence and arrogance, was also among those Shaka sent to raid in Natal. After one of these raids, which provoked what he regarded as the rebellious act of a chief seeking to be regarded as independent, Shaka finally had Makedama put to death.

Another of Shaka's commanders who engaged in predatory raiding in Natal was the chief Lukilimba who had established some dominance in the region of modern Natal. He had fallen out of favor with Shaka but by virtue of distance retained his status and authority. Because Shaka blamed him for drawing the AmaNdwandwe under Zwide south in their attacks, Shaka had ordered Lukilimba to leave. He had good reason to assume that Shaka was no longer friendly toward him. Lukilimba therefore re-established himself in Natal. The relocation of the regimental section of the Mdadasa under Lukilimba to the Port Shepstone area north of the Mzimkhulu brought raiding and destruction to the area. A man from the Transkei region whose people, the Imitwana, had lived in the region between Lukilimba's domain and the AmaMpondo farther southwest described the unfortunate result for his chiefdom.[84] Referring to the disruptions of warring and population dislocations and migrations as experienced by the Imitwana people, the chiefdom to which he belonged, Mahaya ka Nongqabana said,

> Sojingi was killed on the occasion of the Imitwana being hemmed in by Nombeu, Mdingi, Baleni, Ngoza, and Mcwana, as already described. With these five the following also combined in the attack: the amaLanga, amaNdelu, amaDhlala, amaDunge, and Lukwilimba. On that occasion members of the Imitwana tribe scattered and fled south, indeed wherever they could find a refuge.[85]

Lukilimba constructed an *isigodlo*, separate quarters in his main village for the women of the chiefly family. This marked his intention to be recognized as being independent of Shaka, but Lukilimba and his adherents had obvious origins as AmaZulu and were remembered as such by the people they preyed upon. After moving south but before being fetched back to Zululand by Matubane, Lukilimba "went and seized the cattle of the amaMpofana, amaVundhle, Mgayi, Tshobeni (at the umZumbe river). He also crossed the Mzimkulu but the amaNgutshana tribe (Pondo one) defeated him."[86]

The Imitwana were among the victims of his constant raids:

> Lukwilimba fought with us Imitwana for two years but did not succeed in defeating us. Five other tribes then joined Lukwilimba, hemming us in at Ntumbankulu. This took place during the winter. We were then set on to and dispersed. We crossed the Mzimkulu near where Ndongeni lives, and went to Bobeni, i.e. to deep precipices, and thereafter lived near the Msimkulwana. We were not killed much.[87]

Chiefs from the territory of the AmaMpondo to the south also attacked the Imitwana, however, demonstrating the futility of their seeking refuge in the borderlands between southern Natal and the Transkei region:

> Our chief Ntuma ka Ngwadhla refused to *konza* [submit to Lukilimba or Shaka]. He stabbed us [punished or killed his subjects] for *konza*ing. The five chiefs from Pondoland, viz. Nombeu, Mdingi, Ncwana, Baleni, and Ngoza (of the Tembus) attacked us in the rear. We were not expecting this, especially as we thought the enemy was in front. They entered when there was no look-out. They came upon us at dusk and started stabbing women, children, and cattle – and this is the occasion when we were really killed off and broken up. This was in Tshaka's day. Those who escaped went and *konza*'d in the Nguni and Mpondo countries.[88]

The AmaLanga, AmaNdelu, AmaDhlala, AmaDunge, and Lukilimba also joined in this attack, and "[o]n that occasion members of the Imitwana tribe scattered and fled south, indeed wherever they could find a refuge."[89] There is no doubt from oral traditions that turmoil afflicted everyone across this area on both sides of the Mzimkhulu River. The Imitwana chief, Ntuma,

> was not killed. He escaped, and when he got out had to contend with cannibals. The amaMboto were, whilst we were being killed off, being killed off where the Ibisi enters the Mzimkulu, at the Isantombe forest. This was their stronghold. Macingwane (of the amaCunu) and Madikane (of the amaBaca) were in league and were the two who attacked the amaMboto and killed them off. We all ran off, also the amaMboto, to the abeNguni, but eventually came back in peaceful times.[90]

The predatory actions in the Natal region of the Iziyendane regiment and its adherents formed from AmaHlubi who had given allegiance to Shaka eventually brought about their own demise and dispersal. They incurred Shaka's wrath for acting independently of him, for

> The Iziyendane used to go out on their expedition south by Tshaka's order. They used to hand over the cattle to him, but many no doubt were stolen by *izinduna* before reaching the king. It was the fewness of the cattle received which caused Tshaka's displeasure against the Iziyendane.[91]

There is no question that many families and small chiefdoms took refuge in the Transkei region, although many returned to the Natal region after Shaka's death. A man of the small AmaNcwabeni chiefdom related, "[o]ur people formerly lived at the eNyamvubu, a small stream at the eMpafane (Mooi River), on the river, between it and the Estcourt river, and near where the railway line runs. When Tshaka attacked Macingwane, our people, hearing of the fame of Sikiti [i.e., Shaka, one of his praise names], a name by which the Zulus were known, left, and fled to

Matatiele in the Cape Colony. Some later on returned, and built at the eMkuzana stream (enters the Umlazi)."[92]

MIGRANT CHIEFDOMS TO THE WEST: THE AMANGWANE OF MATIWANE AND THE AMAHLUBI OF MPANGAZITHA

The AmaNgwane under their chief Matiwane were neighbors of the AmaHlubi chiefdom under Bhungane and his sons, including the most famous, Mthimkhulu and Mpangazita. Before they migrated as a chiefdom, first within modern KwaZulu and then west across the Drakensberg mountains, "[t]he amaNgwane tribe lived on the northern side of the white Umfolozi, about the neighbourhood of Vryheid."[93] AmaHlubi territory covered almost all of the modern Utrecht district, all of the Klip River country except the Msinga division, and extended to the upper reaches of the Phongolo River.[94] Upon the AmaHlubi chief Bhungane's death in about 1815, Mthimkhulu prevailed against an attempt by his brother Mpangazitha, based at Magoloza, to seize his inheritance of the chieftaincy. Mthimkhulu's village became the AmaHlubi capital at oDidini, "at the eZimbutu, three hills which were closely similar and arranged like hearthstones, not far below Newcastle and near the Mzinyati."[95] Mpangazitha, who retained a following but remained a subordinate unit of the larger AmaHlubi chiefdom under Mthimkhulu, built a new village at the site of modern Newcastle. In about 1815–1816, the AmaNgwane in their territory around Hlobana and Vryheid were attacked by Zwide and the AmaNdwandwe. Then they suffered a joint attack launched by Dingiswayo and the AmaMthethwa along with the AmaZulu troops of Shaka in the first year of Shaka's reign (while Dingiswayo was still alive), 1816–1817. As a result of this attack, the AmaNgwane migrated as a chiefdom from their home to the Newcastle district under the Drakensberg mountains in the vicinity of Mpangazitha's AmaHlubi followers.

A few years later, in about 1821, the AmaNgwane sent three companies of soldiers to attack Mthimkhulu's AmaHlubi capital and managed to kill the chief. The AmaNgwane surrounded Mthimkhulu by surprise in the fields where he was undefended. He was said to have been lured there to meet a young woman and was immediately killed. Apparently after killing Mthimkhulu, the AmaNgwane troops did not proceed to attack his capital at oDidini nearby but instead raided the cattle and returned to their homes.[96] This may have been enough to break up the chiefdom into several sections led by several of the princes who each took their followers in different directions, although at least one oral tradition states that the AmaHlubi were also attacked twice by the AmaZulu under Shaka's command.[97] Maziyana reported, "[s]ome Hlubis, at the time of the scattering of the peoples (*ngezwekufa*), i.e. in Tshaka's day, were broken up and were given protection by us [AmaZulu]."[98] Some went to give formal allegiance to Shaka, who formed them into the Iziyendane regiment and placed them at Nandi's village. Others followed Mpangazitha west across the Drakensberg in 1821 where they re-established themselves in proximity to other AmaHlubi who had preceded them there before the AmaHlubi dispersal after the AmaNgwane attack.[99] The fate of the different sections of the AmaHlubi thus diverged. Of those who *khonza*'d Shaka, "Makata was the *induna* of the Iziyendane. Zwayi ka Mbombo ka Makata ka Ndhlukazi of the Tshabalala people, Mndebele, Mananga, Ntambama, all Mthimkhulu's sons went and *khonza*'d Tshaka."[100] Not all of Mthimkhulu's brothers *khonza*'d Shaka, however.

When Mtimkulu was murdered, Maranqa, who followed Mtimkulu in age, fled off to the Mhlongambula mountain. He was with his following – a large one. There was fighting with Mate ka Ndaonde (not Ndwandwe) ka Langa, who was Maranqa's maternal uncle. Mate was defeated and took refuge on Mhlongamvula mountain. Maranqa went down the Igwa and when he got near the Mpama hill he went up to Kwa Tsetse. He then returned to his father's country at the Mzinyati.[101]

Thus, although Mpangazitha led a large following to the Caledon River valley, it was only part of the AmaHlubi chiefdom of his father, for "[a]fter Mtimkulu's death, Maranqa looked after the people when they came back from where they had fled to. The greater number did not return."[102]

In 1821, after Shaka had already subdued and obtained the submission of the people of eLangeni and the AbaQwabe and after the AmaNgwane had attacked the AmaHlubi, Shaka attacked Matiwane's people at their new Newcastle district location.[103] According to an oral tradition,

Matiwane lived about the White Mfolozi, i.e. Vryheid. Tshaka attacked him, possibly with the Iziyendane. Makata (already referred to) and Mdhleleni ka Ndhlela of the Hlubi were izinduna of the Iziyendane. I cannot say if it was Tshaka's friendship for the Hlubis that caused him to attack Matiwane, or if he attacked Matiwane with the Iziyendane (probably he did).[104]

As a result of the attack by the AmaZulu, the AmaNgwane migrated a second time as a chiefdom, this time west across the Drakensberg, along the path through the mountain passes that the AmaHlubi under Mpangazitha had taken not long before.[105]

The first chiefdom to suffer an attack from Mpangazitha's AmaHlubi after they crossed the Drakensberg were the BaTlokoa under Queen Regent 'Mantathisi and her son Sekonyela, just then coming of age. By July 1822, these AmaHlubi had defeated the BaTlokoa and driven them from their homes, had attacked the BaHlakoana under chief Tseetse at Mabolela, and had prompted the BaFokeng under chief Patsa and a BaTaung chiefdom to flee in the wake of the BaTlokoa.[106] The AmaNgwane under Matiwane had also arrived in the area by July 1822. The BaTswueneng under chief Khiba suffered one of the first attacks of the AmaNgwane and in turn migrated and unsettled other chiefdoms in the Caledon valley region. Both the AmaHlubi and AmaNgwane in succession attacked some chiefdoms, such as the BaRamokhele branch of the BaTaung of Montueli (also known as Ramokhele), and drove them out of their homes near Mekuatleng. These chiefdoms that had been driven out by the AmaHlubi and AmaNgwane in turn disrupted the small chiefdoms of BaPhuthi and BaSotho to the south where they moved from place to place. Matiwane, in the pursuit of his primary threat Mpangazitha, also took the abandoned crops of the BaTlokoa and destroyed those of other chiefdoms they encountered. That same year, the AmaNgwane attacked the small BaSotho chiefdom of Moshoeshoe and took about two thousand head of cattle from him but left those of Moshoeshoe's father at Menkhoaneng untouched. Fearful of another attack, Moshoeshoe became renowned for his conciliatory gesture in sending six more head of cattle to Matiwane as a symbolic payment of tribute, an act welcomed by Matiwane who by then was reportedly engaged in a battle with Mpangazitha.

Within a year, the AmaNgwane re-established the chiefdom at a capital at Senyotong in the Caledon River valley from which they used raids to establish their dominance. Not far from there, the AmaHlubi under Mpangazitha also began to reconsolidate from a base at Mekoatleng, and the two chiefdoms fought several battles in competition over control of the territory and peoples of the Caledon River region. In 1824, Moshoeshoe led his small chiefdom from Butha Buthe in the north to a mountain stronghold at Thaba Bosiu that was closer to the center of modern Lesotho and somewhat farther from the site of the turmoil of the previous two years. Matiwane's capital, however, was not far from Thaba Bosiu, and Moshoshoe continued to pay him tribute. Thus "[e]ven Basuto, broken by war and starvation, in their eagerness to find a strong protector, joined Matuoane, and were marked with the distinguishing mark of the AmaNgwane – that is to say, a short piece of reed was thrust through the lobes of their ears, which served at once as an ornament and a receptacle for snuff."[107] Between 1822 and 1824, the AmaNgwane and AmaHlubi engaged in several major battles with each other and continued to raid the neighboring chiefdoms of the BaMonaheng, BaKubung, BaRamokhele, Batsueneng, and other Caledon Valley residents for their cattle and crops.[108]

The sources agree that in 1824 or 1825 Matiwane launched a final major attack against Mpangazitha at Mabolela in which Chief Mpangazitha himself was killed, and after which his AmaHlubi followers were dispersed. Some were incorporated in a subordinate status among the AmaNgwane, and some fled north with Mpangazitha's son Mahlomaholo where they took refuge for about two years with Mzilikazi's AmaKhumalo/ AmaNdebele kingdom.[109] One oral tradition related that Mpangazitha's son Setenane returned to Tshaka "who had him killed."[110] The AmaNgwane stayed only about three more years along the Caledon River, however. First they were weakened by an attack from an AmaZulu *impi* that succeeded in raiding thousands of head of cattle from the AmaNgwane in villages along the Caledon River in spite of offering strong resistance in the battle of Ladybrand, when the two sides fought to a standoff, after several hundred warriors had been killed. Then the AmaNgwane were attacked by warriors sent by Mzilikazi. Under pressure from his counselors, Matiwane allowed an AmaNgwane attack against the BaSotho at Thaba Bosiu, and they suffered another decisive defeat. Having previously sent troops to scout and raid in the Transkei region south of the Orange River, Matiwane decided the chiefdom should once again migrate to new territory and in 1827 led his followers to the Transkei.[111] There they raided successfully and began to plant crops, but about a year later the AmaThembu, assisted by a small British contingent, recaptured many of the cattle they had previously lost to the AmaNgwane in a small engagement in late July 1828. With their many large herds, however, the AmaNgwane remained the target of a planned joint counterattack by the joint forces of the three major chiefdoms of the region. In the famous battle of Mbolompho on August 29,1828, armies from all three chiefdoms, assisted again by a small British colonial unit with its devastating cannon fire, attacked the AmaNgwane. The migrant chiefdom of Matiwane finally fell apart for good, and the fate of the AmaNgwane was known in AmaZulu oral traditions because Matiwane himself later returned to *khonza* Shaka only to find he was dead. Dingane had Matiwane put to death.[112]

For their part, the Iziyendane regiment of AmaHlubi warriors had played a major role in the systematic raiding and devastation of the small chiefdoms south of the Thukela River. There they established their own village barracks from which to raid. So harsh was the Iziyendane regiment's raiding that one oral source related that it had depopulated "the whole of Natal."[113] However, they dispersed after Nandi's death in 1827. The Iziyendane feared for their lives because she had been their patroness.[114] Shaka had become incensed not by the Iziyendane's raiding but because they kept the cattle instead of sending the booty to join the royal herds. Thus, he sent other regiments to attack the Iziyendane who dispersed, some raiding in Transkei before eventually finding their way back to their original home territory in the northwest of modern KwaZulu-Natal.[115]

ZIHLANDHLO AND THE EMBO

While Shaka was serving in Dingiswayo's AmaMthethwa military, he fought in a battle against the Embo chiefdom located in the central area of KwaZulu-Natal.[116] The battle is remembered in the oral traditions because Shaka was said to have engaged in hand-to-hand fighting with an Embo warrior, Bacwali, and to have fallen into a ditch (*donga*) during the fighting. Bacwali taunted him, but Shaka climbed out of the ditch on the other side so they did not continue fighting. Remembering the name Bacwali had used in swearing as they fought, Shaka tried after he assumed the AmaZulu chieftaincy to learn the man's identity from the Embo (or Mkhize) chief Zihlandhlo ka Gcwabe. Zihlandhlo, claiming ignorance, was able to forewarn Bacwali that Shaka planned to kill him, so Bacwali who moved away with a number of families as his followers and resettled "at esiHlutankungu hill, Ixopo division."[117] Similarly, another branch of the Embo left the area during Shaka's reign:

> Nqume ka Nzangwini ran off to the amaXozas; he was afraid of Tshaka. He was chief of a section of the abaMbo. He had come from the Manyane in Zululand with these. He afterwards returned from the Xozas and settled at Ntumbankulu on the Mzimkulu.[118]

Shaka evidently feared Zihlandhlo's military potential and decided to test it by insisting that he engage in a battle against the AmaNxamalala, another small chiefdom near the Thukela River not far from the AmaZulu heartland. Mandhlakazi told Stuart, "Tshaka on one occasion set on the Embo and Nxamalala people to fight one another" Mandhlakazi later insisted, "These people did not formerly quarrel with one another in any way. Tshaka just simply set them on to fight."[119] Another of Stuart's informants, Mbokodo, told him essentially the same story about these events and even knew the names of Shaka's commanders who were sent to witness the battle:

When Tshaka set Zihlandhlo and Mtsholoza on to fight each other, he brought *izinduna* [officers, commanders] to watch. These *izinduna* accompanied the *impi*. Among them were Nsizi and Sikunyana.[120]

According to Mbokodo, Zihlandhlo ordered his brother Sambela to hold back his regiment, the Umngenela, and instead sent only his larger regiment, the Simahleni (Isimahla), into battle. This regiment crossed to the south of the Thukela River and, unable to detect the location of Mtsholoza's AmaNxamalala forces, were easily surrounded on all sides before they even had time to unroll their shields. Thus, the AmaNxamalala "stabbed the Isimahla and scattered it," also killing its chief commander.[121] Upon hearing that his larger regiment, the Isimahla, "had been defeated and dispersed," Kombe, the commander of the Embo regiment that Mngenela had insisted carry out its own plan of attack, crossed the river overnight to take a hilltop position. When the regiment met with the AmaNxamalala army the next day, Kombe ordered two units (*amabandhla*) to stop in the center while the remainder of his forces circled around in a horn formation to the right and the left. The strategy succeeded, and this Embo regiment drove the fleeing AmaNxamalala forces "twelve or fifteen miles," burning their villages and seizing their cattle as booty.[122]

Mandhlakazi said that "Sambela fought the day after Zihlandhlo's fight. Sambela defeated the Nxamalalas unaided by Zihlandhlo of his people, and set about burning the Nxamalala kraals." Then the Nxamalala cattle were sent to Shaka. But events took a tragic turn, for "[o]n this occasion, the amaNxamalala, on being defeated and chased, got caught in traps that had been set for game, when they were easily killed. Although not many could have been killed in that way, the incident was never forgotten or forgiven by the Nxamalalas, who regarded the traps as intentionally set to catch them."[123]

Shaka evidently saw the battle as a way to select a strong ally and eliminate a weaker one. Mbokodo said that when the victorious Embo regiment returned, their commander found that "Nsizi, Tshaka's *induna* had put on his war-dress. He had threatened to set on the *impi* on seeing that the greater section of Sihlandhlo's *impi* (Isimahla) had been defeated, but Zihlandhlo said, 'Wait a bit,' the carrying-skin has not yet arrived,' i.e. the Umngenela. So after seeing the Umngenela succeed, Nsizi set them free, i.e. refrained from setting on his *impi* and killing off Zihlandhlo's people."[124]

It is not surprising, then, that "Tshaka got Zihlandhlo to co-operate with him when he was building up his power and conquering tribes. Owing to this, Tshaka took a fancy to him."[125] Zihlandhlo and the Embo troops aided Shaka in his major military campaigns against the AmaNdwandwe chief Sikunyana, Zwide's son, and against the AmaMpondo. Shaka took one or two regiments of warriors from Zihlandhlo to serve directly under his own command and to build "in Zululand."[126] Before Shaka went on the famous 1826 military campaign against the AmaNdwandwe chief Sikhunyana, he is said to have invited Zihlandhlo to an *umjadu* dance, signifying their alliance.[127] In stylized narrative, Mbokodo said that after a dance and mock battle, Shaka explained the war preparations and expedition planned against Sikunyana, and then told Zihlandhlo, "[a]s for you, my *mnawe*, you shall guard me. I'll send the whole of the Zulus to Sikunyana."[128]

Shaka's evident confidence in Zihlandhlo, or perhaps fear of him, left Zihlandhlo relatively free to pursue his own interests. After Zihlandhlo assisted Shaka in the *impi* against Sikunyana, he returned and "attacked Macingwane in the Cunu country, but he failed to kill him."[129] Mbokodo continued,

He killed, however, Sondonzima (ka Luboko), brother of Macingwane. On returning from there, Zihlandhlo attacked Matomela ka Ndhlovu in the Bomvu country. He killed his chief, Zipundulu. He killed also Sotshenge ka Ndhlovu, a man of high birth. Zihlandhlo then made Nzombane ka Matomela chief. On returning from this, he [Zihlandhlo] attacked Tshitshi near the country of the Pepeteni. He [Zihlandhlo] killed him [Tshitshi], and returned. He [Zihlandhlo] attacked Nomagaga of the Nadi people, and ate up their cattle. Dibinyika was Nomagaga's heir, of the Zondi tribe. He [Zihlandhlo] next attacked Dhlaba of the Inade (Zondi) tribe, and ate up [confiscated] his cattle. He attacked Voyizana living higher up, and ate up his cattle. He attacked Nguza of the Dhlamini people. His [Nguza's] father was Ngonyama. He [Zihlandhlo] killed him [Nguza]. He [Zihlandhlo] attacked Bodeyana of the Dhlamini people. The *amakubalo* medicines were eaten by Mmiso of the Kuze people. He attacked Nzombane ka Matomela. He [Zihlandhlo] captured him [Nzombane], but did not kill him. He however seized his [Nzombane's] stock.[130]

Zihlandhlo attacked Sali ka Sibenya, and killed him. He attacked Sibenya of the Wutshe people living in the vicinity of Cedara and Mbubu, and killed him. He killed Mbonjeni. He attacked Nomagwayi of the eMazolweni people, and killed him. Zihlandhlo also killed the isikulu Mnqundu ka Mzaula of the Ndhlovu people. He killed Ngebe ka Mzila of the Ngcongo. He killed Madonjeni of the left-hand house, among the Embo people. He [Zihlandhlo] caught Nsele ka Gcwabe of the Embo people, but did not kill him, for Zambela objected. He [Zihlandhlo] ate up [confiscated] his [Nsele's] cattle. He [Zihlandhlo] killed Ntiti ka Gcwabe and took his cattle.[131]

Zihlandhlo's brother Sambela was known as "a man of temper" who put people to death and who "always wanted to be attacking and fighting other tribes."[132] However, Zihlandlo allowed Sambela to build his own following. He was popular because he frequently ordered cattle to be slaughtered and the meat widely distributed to people, including "the common crowd" and people "belonging to tribes other than his own" so that people "all liked him."[133] Sambela was able to provide so generously to his adherents because of the cattle he raided from others, however. He led a dozen or more raids against neighboring chiefdoms to raid their cattle, but Shaka left him alone as he incorporated the followers of the small chiefs he killed in numerous battles.[134] One oral tradition includes details of these events:

> Sambela's *impi*s. In a climate of peace Sambela gathered his *impi*, saying, "I am going to attack Nomanaka ka Ngcongo (amaPambuka – their *isibongo* [praisename]). He killed him [Nomanaka] and took over his people. These are the people that at this day [1913] are so numerous a section of Mqolombeni's kraal.
>
> He [Sambela] attacked Mandaba of the Vezi people, killed him, and took over his people. It is they who are there with Mqolombeni. He [Sambela] returned. He attacked Mpongo ka Zingelwayo of the Ndhlovu people. They fought and fought until both sides retired. Mpongo then attacked Sambela. They fought. Both retired. There was a period of peace. The next thing that happened was that Sambela attacked Mpongo. He killed him [Mpongo] and also his brother Ntiti. He then took over a portion of Mpongo's people.
>
> Next, Sambela attacked Majiya ka Mapinda of the Emapepeteni people. He seized their cattle and burnt their homesteads.
>
> Sombela killed Mziki ka Toza (I don't know his *sibongo*). He also killed Mkubane ka Mpoko of the Manyana people. He also killed Pakatwayo ka Mpoko (his *sibongo*) of the Manyane people. He killed Nosongolwayo ka –, [sic.] of the Hlele people; he killed Nombombo ka –, [sic.] of the Hlele people; he killed Zisangwana ka Langana of the Mguli people (his [Zisangwana's] *sibongo*). He killed Mande ka Dibandhlela of the Cele people.[135]

Sambela is said to have tried to get Zihlandhlo to conspire against Shaka, but Zihlandhlo disapproved. Not surprisingly, "Tshaka wanted to kill Sambela because he was so strong, and also because he had fame as a warrior. Sambela made the suggestion in the assembly of his people that Tshaka should be killed." Dingane later had both Zihlandhlo and Sambela killed.[136]

NORTHERN DISRUPTIONS

Shaka's defeat of Zwide and the AmaNdwandwe in 1821 also created commotion in the northern reaches of KwaZulu territory. Some of Zwide's followers chose to *khonza* Shaka rather than migrate away. The small chiefdoms in the vicinity of the AmaNdwandwe were faced with the same choice, and many also gave their allegiance to Shaka at this time.

When Tshaka drove out the Ndwandwe tribe, and with them Zwide, Mgudhlana was living near land occupied by the Ndwandwe tribe, but he and his people had not up to that time *konza*'d [submitted or given allegiance to] Tshaka. After Zwide's rout he, Mgudhlana, *konza*'d. Tshaka then built the Empangisweni kraal, placed Nquhele in charge, and permitted Mkosi to rule and, as already remarked, directed that the rib-meat was to be presented to him.[137]

Some AmaMthethwa had *khonza*'d Zwide after he had killed their chief Dingiswayo and now again faced the choice of submitting to Shaka's rule or migrating away. After Zwide's death, Shaka sent *impi*s against two of Zwide's recalcitrant subordinate chiefs Beje and Mlotshwa, who were forced to submit to AmaZulu rule.[138] Other chiefdoms that had been under AmaNdwandwe rule chose at that time to join the AmaNdwandwe chief Soshangane who moved with many followers into the region of Olifant's River and Delagoa Bay in modern southern Mozambique. Zwide's son Sikhunyana took his followers north to the Transvaal region, where a branch of the small AmaKhumalo chiefdom was also being rebuilt by Chief Mzilikazi, a former subject chief of Zwide.[139]

One of the most famous kingdoms of southern Africa, the AmaNdebele chiefdom of Mzilikazi had its origins as a small branch of the AmaKhumalo chiefdom located not far from the heartland of the AmaZulu kingdom.[140] Because this small AmaKhumalo chiefdom emerged as a kingdom and incorporated local populations at two locations in the Transvaal region and then in the area of modern southern Zimbabwe, its history was mostly played out well beyond the area of modern KwaZulu-Natal. Oral traditions include little about the origins of Mzilikazi's chiefdom. Some information was retained, however, and one man told Stuart,

I think Mzilikazi was the first to go off north, before Nxaba. Mzilikazi was an *inceku* [servant] at esiKlebeni, responsible for milking. He was Tshaka's *inceku*.[141]

Mzilikazi ka Matshobana was the chief of a branch of the AmaKhumalo, who lived in territory neighboring the AmaZulu, and who had become tributary subordinate chiefs to Chief Zwide of the AmaNdwandwe. After Shaka defeated Zwide, he expected the chiefdoms formerly subordinated to the AmaNdwandwe to submit to AmaZulu rule. From his villages at eNkungwini and eMhlahlandhlela, Mzilikazi was expected to give cattle that he had raided to Shaka to join the royal herds. According to one oral tradition, Shaka is said to have asked Mzilikazi to become his *induna* at the capital of Bulawayo. Mzilikazi refused to do this on the grounds he was an independent chief, but he did take an *impi* to attack chief Maconi of the AmaNtshingila on Shaka's orders. Mzilikazi put the chief to death and raided the cattle successfully, but his failure to send the cattle to Shaka afterward put him in open rebellion and forced him to migrate with his followers away from KwaZulu and relocate in the region of the Transvaal.[142] One source said,

> I know that Mzilikazi left Intumbane hill when he fled from Tshaka. I know this from our speaking of his people as "those beggarly people from Ntumbane". This Ntumbane hill is low down the Bivana and near Dumbe mountain.[143]

In addition to those AmaKhumalo who joined him, "a number of Zwide's people accompanied Mzilikazi in his flight to the northwest, also the abakwaZikalala, formerly defeated by Zwide."[144] Mzilikazi's former territory became that of Shaka's brother and later of king Mpande and his Mfemfe village. The branch of AmaKhumalo who emigrated from the KwaZulu-Natal region established a militarized sociopolitical system that preyed upon and incorporated the local peoples they encountered in the Transvaal. The AmaKhumalo branch raided across a wide area of the Transvaal and became the dominant political authority across a wide region. These AmaKhumalo remained the focus of Shaka's fears and later Dingane's military expeditions until the branch finally relocated farther west in the Transvaal. Ultimately, the AmaKhumalo went across the Limpopo River to re-establish their kingdom in the vicinity of modern Bulawayo, Zimbabwe.

Other chiefdoms also fled northward when Shaka threatened their chiefs. Two of Zwide's *indunas*, Soshangana and Zwangendaba, each led followers into southern Mozambique and subsequently into Zambesi River region and modern Zimbabwe.[145] Nqaba, or Nxaba, chief of the Msane or Msene chiefdom, did not originally intend to leave and instead went with Lubedu ka Masondo to give allegiance to Shaka and pay tribute after Zwide's defeat. At the ceremonial dance, Lubedu is said in the oral traditions to have laughed at a comment made by Shaka without any intention of offense. However, Shaka responded with the comment,

"So the small, fat toad is laughing at me!" and had him seized and put to death "for laughing at the king, and yet he was only laughing because he approved what the king did."[146] Nxaba, who had arrived in Lobedu's company, was alarmed but gave Shaka the women he had brought for Shaka's *isigodlo* and accepted a gift of one hundred head of cattle from Shaka. According to the oral tradition, the young women one by one became ill and had to be sent back to Nxaba, who realized he would soon be attacked by Shaka. "When the last girl got ill and returned to Nxaba, he at once did up his things and fled to the north."[147]

Thus, Nxaba or Nqaba ka Mbekane led his Msene chiefdom into southern Mozambique in the wake of the AmaNdwande indunas Soshangana and Zwangendaba where Nxaba was temporarily allied with the small Maseko chiefdom led by a chief named Ngwane.[148] The fate of these two small chiefdoms resembled that of their better-known counterparts under Zwangendaba and Soshangane. The two chiefdoms were forced to migrate and resettle several times in the course of the next decade. Nxaba's success brought Shaka's attention. An *impi* was sent to seize the cattle Nxaba had himself captured and accumulated in the Delagoa Bay region from the chiefdoms of that vicinity whose people were known as "AmaNhlwenga":

An *impi* of Tshaka's went to fetch Nxaba and the cattle he had taken at eCwebeyeni, i.e. in the amaNhlwenga country. Makasane, the Tonga king, ordered his troops out, seeing Nxaba fleeing with cattle, and wanted them [Makasane's own troops] to seize the cattle. They [Makasane's troops] replied, "Leave us alone, son of Mwali ka Tembe; we shall fetch them at dawn, when there is dew." They [Nxaba's *impi*] did not go [leave the area], so the Zulus came up and seized the cattle. These were Tshaka's troops.[149]

The famous warrior known as Zulu ka Nogandaya went on this military expedition against chief Nxaba after Nxaba had led his chiefdom into southern Mozambique, and Zulu's son had been told about these events:

The Nxaba ka Mbekane campaign. Tshaka sent my father in charge of a regiment to attack this man. They traveled a whole day and night, and got there. My father got tired and lay down to rest in a forest near a sheet of standing water. Nxaba's *imbongi* [praise-singer] was then heard declaiming the praises of his chief. On hearing this my father jumped up and attacked the *imbongi*, killing him and another. Nxaba was defeated and his short red cattle were seized. Tshaka presented my father with 150 head of cattle on account of what he did on this occasion. Although an *induna* [commander], he always dashed straight into the fight, beginning it himself.[150]

The Msane turned west and migrated into southern Zimbabwe. They eventually came into conflict with Sebetoane's AmaKololo chiefdom that had originated in the Transvaal and then had relocated to southern Zambia. There the Msane subsumed the pre-existing Lozi kingdom under their putative rule. Nxaba there met his demise in battle. For their part, the Maseko continued northward into Tanzania where they, like the followers of Zwangendaba, became known as "Ngoni," and where they incorporated various peoples under their rule.

Chapter 7

Challenges and Consolidation, 1824–1827

By 1824, Shaka had consolidated his authority and control over the region of KwaZulu-Natal sufficiently to feel confident enough to send his troops beyond the territory of at least putative AmaZulu rule. The survivors of the AmaNdwandwe chiefdom of Zwide following the battle of 1821 had broken into several major sections, all of which had moved to north of the Phongolo River, reducing threats from the north. Various regiments of the AmaZulu army had been established in the region of Natal (i.e., south of the Thukela River), where the AmaCele and AmaThuli chiefs acquiesced to their subordinate tributary status as other smaller chiefdoms were raided, broken apart, or fled farther south to the Transkei region. There some found refuge with the AmaMpondo chief Faku, whose chiefdom lay in territory between KwaZulu-Natal and the AmaXhosa chiefdoms of the Ciskei and Transkei regions. By 1824 Shaka had heard about the large AmaXhosa chiefdom of Hintsa and about the European settlement somewhere even farther to the southwest. His curiosity as well as his ambition prompted him to send a major military expedition into the region of the Transkei in February or March of that year. He could not have predicted that just as his troops were returning, the first boats bringing the first Europeans with ambitions to trade would land at the white bluffs in the small inlet that came to be called Port Natal or later, Durban. The years 1824 to 1827 were years in which Shaka sought both to reinforce his authority internally and extend the reaches of his influence in territories and over chiefs to the north, south, and west. The first Europeans did not witness Shaka and the events surrounding his early consolidation of the AmaZulu kingdom, but they were eyewitnesses to his efforts to maintain and extend his authority in the first years of their settlement in what would later become the British colony of Natal.

THE *AMABECE IMPI* AGAINST THE AMAMPONDO, 1824

Tshaka went twice south – two campaigns. On the *"amabece"* campaign the Zulu were cut up by the Mpondo, for three Zulu units (*amabandhla*) were finished off. But the Zulu got the better of them and succeeded in seizing some of their cattle, but not many. Tshaka did not accompany this *impi*. This force got to the end of their cattle (meat supply) and suffered from hunger. They were obliged to eat melons (*amabece*) and wild plants. The melons were eaten at the Umzinhlamvu, this side of the Umsimvubu but high up from the sea.[1]

Early in Shaka's reign the AmaBhaca chief Madikane had led his people from their territory at Emkambatini (Table Mountain) near modern Pietermaritzburg, an area where Shaka was extending his authority through military action, to resettle farther to the southwest. The AmaBhaca eventually found refuge in the Transkei territory of the AmaMpondo under Chief Faku. A few years later, in early 1824, Shaka deployed his regiments on a military campaign to Chief Faku's territory on the pretext of hoping to find and defeat Madikane and accomplish the submission of the AmaBhaca. The AmaBhaca retreated as far as AmaXhosa territory, however, and the AmaZulu forces, sweeping around the edge of the Drakensberg inland and then turning toward the coast, never encountered the AmaBhaca on this campaign.

AmaZulu oral traditions remembered Shaka's motives for this major military campaign into the Transkei region differently, however. He had already exhibited ambitions for expansion southwestward where chiefs in Natal nominally subordinate to him had imposed their regimental followings over the local population. Much of the population had therefore retreated even farther into AmaMpondo territory. One man told Stuart that "[w]hen the *amabece* campaign took place, Natal had been already denuded of inhabitants, north as well as south. [Chief] Mnini and his small following along remained about the Bluff."[2]

Shaka's attention had been drawn to the southwest by the flight of Ngoza's AbaTembu and then was said to have been aroused by a provocative message sent to him by Chief Nguboyencuga of the AmaThembu. The message claimed to Shaka that Chief Nguboyencuga had superior forces, but Nguboyencuga's followers then fled farther west into the domains of the AmaXhosa chiefdoms. The AmaMpondo Chief Faku himself posed a possible threat because his AmaMpondo forces had defeated the formidable AbaTembu of Ngoza. The evidence of the oral traditions suggests that when Shaka's regiments arrived in AmaMpondo territory on the *amabece* campaign, they spread word that as tributaries to him, the AmaMpondo would not be attacked. The AmaZulu forces passed unchallenged until, pursuing Madikane's AmaBhaca, the regiments found themselves deep in AmaMpondo territory and bordering that of the AmaXhosa Chief Hintsa. There Shaka's forces were attacked, and lost three units (*amabandhla*), and faced starvation so that they were forced to eat *amabece* melons to survive. On their return homeward, they seized large herds of AmaMpondo cattle, so as a cattle raid the military expedition was a success in spite of the heavy military losses they had suffered.[3]

The sources are in agreement that the AmaZulu engaged in fighting and suffered heavy losses and that they successfully raided many AmaMpondo cattle, but the identity of the enemy they fought in the Transkei is not clear. One source referred to the *amabece* campaign as an *impi* against the "abeNguni," a term used by the AmaZulu to refer to the AmaXhosa chiefdoms, and another said explicitly that the *amabece impi* "attacked Hinsa," the AmaXhosa Chief. The evidence that Shaka had ordered his forces to try to reach Hintsa's territory is certainly credible, although it may not have been Hintsa's AmaXhosa forces whom Shaka's regiments engaged in battle. He had begun to accumulate knowledge about the AmaXhosa chiefs in the Transkei region beyond Faku's territory and was jealous of their reputations. According to one Zulu narrative,

Tshaka attacked twice in Pondoland. First Nhlamba (Hlambamanzi) told him Hintsa had a regiment called the Indonyane which, on starting, would be in the act of moving off all day – it moves off company by company. Tshaka was surprised at this and wanted to see this regiment. He sent out spies and an army past Howick, above Pietermaritzburg. This army merely seized cattle belonging to the Pondos [i.e., did not get as far as Hintsa's]. The army entered Siyoyo's district, emaCwereni. The people, seeing Tshaka's *impi* as large as a forest, ran off, leaving many of their cattle to be taken.[4]

Another account was similar:

Tshaka first sent an *impi* to Hinsa, as it was said he had an *ibuto* [regiment] so large that it would take all day rising. This regiment was known as the Inkonyane of Hinsa. Tshaka's forces went, failed to find Hinsa, and came on European houses. Mdhlaka turned back as there were no instructions to attack Europeans, and in turning, discovered some of Faku's cattle, which the Zulus seized.[5]

Stuart's informant was quite certain that Shaka's forces had traveled far enough to see European houses, and elsewhere in his interview reiterated, "Tshaka sent his forces to attack Hinsa. They took an up-country route.

Failing to find him, they came on Europeans houses. They turned back, seizing some Pondo cattle. Mdhlaka was in charge."[6] But the warriors' hunger was also distinctive of this campaign, giving it the name "*amabece*" and ensuring that these circumstances were remembered. The famous warrior Zulu ka Nogandaya told his son about both major campaigns against the AmaMpondo:

> The *amabece impi* went forth first. It attacked Hinsa. The *amabece* were eaten when there was no other food to eat. They were eaten uncooked, in Pondoland and beyond. My father went with both these *impi*s.[7]

This is the only account that asserts the AmaZulu actually attacked the AmaXhosa of Hintsa, and this source may have been mistaken and confused part of his father's narrative. However, the AmaZulu sources agree that as the AmaZulu forces turned back homeward, they entered the territory of the AmaMpondo and decided to raid their cattle. The AmaMpondo chief Faku, however, was prepared for a defense, and the first AmaZulu regiment sent to attack, the Mkandhlu, were roundly defeated. The commander of the AmaZulu forces, Mdhlaka, then sent in reinforcements and turned the battle, accomplishing the defeat of the AmaMpondo and the seizure of their cattle.[8]

According to another account,

> The Pondos were attacked by the Mkandhlu [AmaZulu regiment], who were killed off by the Pondos by a shower of *assegai*s [spears] – small *assegai*s thrown by the Pondos and coming down on to their heads. After this the Nomdayana came to the rescue and the Pondos were repulsed.[9]

The return of the AmaZulu troops brought ignominy to the Mkandhlu regiment. Shaka eventually killed many Mkandhlu warriors for their supposed cowardice, inferred from their defeat. However, the troops also returned with the AmaMpondo cattle they had successfully raided after their eventual victory over Faku's forces.[10]

THE ARRIVAL OF EUROPEAN TRADERS AT PORT NATAL

In early 1823 two British officers, Lieutenant George Francis Farewell and Lieutenant James Saunders King, both of the Royal Navy, began their plans for a commercial voyage to St. Lucia Bay, and in June 1823 set sail from the Cape Colony.[11] After some early trading ventures, Farewell had returned to Cape Town, found accommodations at a boarding house, and married the proprietor's daughter. Then Farewell chartered the brig *Salisbury* commanded by Lieutenant James Saunders King who like

Farewell was now retired from the Royal Navy. Farewell also chartered a smaller boat, the *Julia*, to explore the prospects of buying ivory at St. Lucia.[12] Before they left the Cape Colony, Farewell and King stopped at Algoa Bay where they collected information about the coast from Captain Owen and hired two African interpreters named Fire and Jacob. The boats encountered bad wind conditions at St. Lucia Bay, forcing Farewell and King to leave several sailors with Jacob on shore for five weeks where they were well treated until the *Salisbury* and *Julia* could retrieve them. Thus, unsuccessful at opening communications from the St. Lucia Bay with ivory traders from the interior, the two boats returned to Algoa Bay for resupplying and proceeded to the Port of Natal for the same exploratory purpose. There

The Julia, commanded by Armstrong, entered the port, the Mary [sic, Salisbury] remaining at the outer anchorage.

Armstrong, though a heavy and most unfitted man for such an enterprise, was selected to open up a communication with the natives. He walked north-east to the Umngeni River in search of natives and, meeting none on that side of the port, he passed over to the south of the Bay, where a few had been seen. These, however, fled at his approach. All prospects of establishing communication were now abandoned and the two vessels returned to the Cape.[13]

A few days after the return of the *Salisbury* and *Julia* on December 3, 1823, to Cape Town, Henry Francis Fynn arrived there on the *Jane*, traveling with the *Mary*, from Delagoa Bay. Although King and Farewell had sustained losses on their 1823 trips to St. Lucia and Port Natal, King left for England to pursue a partnership for establishing trade at Port Natal. Farewell prevailed upon his father-in-law, only identified as Mr. Peterson, and a Dutch gentleman named Mr. Hoffman to join the partnership seeking to trade in ivory from Port Natal. Farewell invited Fynn to join the party to manage the trading operations, for which he would receive a percentage of the profits in lieu of salary; it was to be a six-month venture. Farewell, Peterson, and Hoffman induced thirty to forty others to join the party, and Farewell hired two boats, the brig *Antelope* and the sloop *Julia*.[14] On March 10, 1824, the *Julia*, the first of the boats, with Fynn and part of the company, landed at Port Natal. With him were "three mechanics, Ogle, an Englishman, a Prussian, and a Frenchman, also Michael, a Hottentot servant, and Frederick, a Kaffir interpreter, from the Cape frontier."[15] They began building on their first full day ashore, having warded off wolves overnight; they did not encounter anyone until their third day there and used beads to entice him to speak to them.

His name was Mahamba. He and my interpreter understood very little of each other's dialect, though speaking in the same language. My enquiries as to where Shaka resided were unsatisfactorily replied to. All I could learn was that their nation [unidentified] had been destroyed by Shaka and that he was a powerful chief living to the northward, and that I would have to travel 30 days before I reached him. I was sure this was incorrect as I had seen kraals only 30 miles north of the port, when our vessel had been driven past it. But such was their fear of him [Shaka] that they durst not accompany us or leave the bush at low tide to get fish, their only sustenance."[16]

Fynn left almost immediately with "Frederick, 'my Kaffir interpreter,' Jantyi Michael, 'my Hottentot servant' and Mahamba." Fynn hoped to see Shaka and went as far as Siyingila's village about twelve miles away. En route the first day, Fynn wrote later, they stopped to rest and while he was sitting on the beach,

I saw on my right a dense mass of people coming fast from the direction I had come. My view extended over several miles of the beach, but I could not see the rear of this immense black and continuous mass of natives, all armed and in their war-dresses. Our surprise was great and had I known the character of these people and the danger I was in, as I now know it, it is a question if I would have stood my ground, though an attempt to run away would not have saved me.[17]

Fynn mistakenly assumed they had already killed the rest of his party at the port. Mahamba disappeared at once, and Jantyi and Frederick urged flight, but they had already been seen. "On the approach of the head of the column I was struck with astonishment at their appearance, for it was sufficient to terrify. Evidently they were equally surprised at mine, and looked at me with a kind of horror." Unable to speak with them because his interpreter had fled, he tried saying Shaka's name, but after talking among themselves the men leading the warriors continued past him. Fynn noted that as he watched, "this dense mass of natives continued to pass by me until sunset, all staring at me with amazement, none interfering with me." He later concluded "that my coolness, for I certainly felt no fear, saved me from instant destruction. In the passing of this force I could not but remark that they moved in divisions, the leader of each showing me the immense control they had over their followers; they frequently struck at them at the slightest appearance of disorder." Fynn said the armed forces at that time which passed him were "not less than 20,000 strong."[18]

The next day Fynn continued with his men except for Mahamba who had deserted and used beads to allay the fears of the people at a small village where Fynn's party was then presented with a cow for slaughter and watched as a second column of warriors, like the first, passed them by. This was the return of Shaka's army from the AmaMpondo campaign. As he watched the endless columns of armed men, Fynn learned "they were Shaka's army returning after having attacked chief Faku, who was said to live a great distance to the southward."[19] Fynn noted that some of the passing troops pillaged the village, sending the women screaming into the countryside with their children to hide. The chief of this small village, Siyingila, sent word to Shaka and asked Fynn to wait until they had a response, which came several days later in the form of a party of about thirty men under chief Mbikwana from a village about ten miles to their north.[20] Fynn was taken to Mbikwana's, where he waited fourteen days before hearing from Shaka. According to Fynn's *Diary*, on his third day at Mbikwana's, he used his medical supplies to treat a woman who was dying of fever. Fynn wrote that they were preparing to carry the woman into the field to die at the time he treated her, and when she recovered, the rumor started that he had "raised this woman to life after having been already dead."[21]

A later report of the AmaCele chief Magaye's son Melapi recorded the reaction of Shaka and his subordinate chiefs upon the arrival of Europeans:

They came from the Isibubulungu [white bluffs above Durban (Port Natal)]. Matubane [AmaTuli regent] was at the Isibubulungu. He said that their arrival should be reported to the chiefs. A report was sent to [AmaCele chief] Magaye [a loyal subordinate of Shaka]. To report to Magaye was as good as to report to Tshaka. Magaye referred the matter to Tshaka. He [Magaye] sent Lucunge, his induna of Ndhlazi. He said to Tshaka, "*Nkosi*, I have come to report that some people have arrived as if sprung from the earth. But I cannot tell you more; their speech is not understandable." "Go, then, Lucunge," said Tshaka, "and fetch them. Say to my brother (*umnawe*) [i.e., Magaye] to fetch them. Bring them to me so that I may see them."[22]

Eventually thirty men arrived from Shaka to meet Fynn and present him with forty head of oxen and milk cows and seven large elephant tusks. They gave these to Fynn "with the assurance that Shaka was much pleased at my coming to his country, but that he would not be prepared to see me until after his army had rested after their return from their recent war with Faku."[23] Shaka provided a man to take care of Fynn's wants in the interim, whom Fynn promptly offended by saying he looked like a murderer he was so fierce, which amused everyone. A letter arrived reporting that Farewell's party had reached the port.[24]

After a delay of about fourteen days at Mbikwana's, Fynn returned to Port Natal (Durban), where the combined group of men now numbered about thirty-five, including men of Dutch, German, French, and Danish origins. Fynn wrote, "Farewell, Ogle and I were the only Englishmen."[25] When Shaka finally sent word via Mbikwana accompanied by one hundred followers, Hoffman stayed behind at the port and Farewell, Petersen, Fynn, Frederick, and the three "Hottentots" went to meet Shaka for the first time. At the Umngeni River, Farewell delayed them to look for signs of gold. Then Petersen, who was sixty-three years old and in poor shape, rolled over with his horse in a bog, so it was after dark when they arrived at Siyingila's village where they were expected. Fynn described the journey: messengers were exchanged several times a day between Mbikwana and Shaka, and "frequently" his group passed large gatherings of people watching a grotesquely-dressed man "smell out" or detect "evil doers" who were put to death. It took the party thirteen days to go the distance of what, by the indirect route they took, was two hundred miles. When they arrived at Shaka's main village Farewell and Fynn were invited to proceed with Mbikwana and twenty of his followers, and they entered "the great cattle kraal." Here Fynn says they found "about 80,000 natives in their war attire," although elsewhere Fynn said it was "about 12,000 men in their war attire" and regiments of girls, women, and servants.[26] Among the events they witnessed, Shaka had a man standing near them killed "for what crime we could not learn, but we soon found this to be a very common occurrence."[27] They were given a hut to stay in and two oxen were slaughtered for them. Fynn joined Shaka at his request, with the African interpreter Jacob, in "the seraglio, where I found him [Shaka] seated in a carved wooden chair and surrounded by about 400 girls, two or three chiefs and two servants in attendance."[28] This must have been about the beginning of May; Fynn, Farewell, and Davis stayed behind when the others returned to the port.

Melapi reported that his father the AmaCele chief Magaye was present at Bulawayo, Shaka's first capital village between Eshowe and Empangeni. Shaka spoke directly to Magaye after seeing the Europeans, and Melapi's narrative reported Shaka's words as follows: "My brother, you are clever indeed, for you have shown me these people. See them; though we are chiefs we are beneath their feet. Go, Magaye, take back these people of yours to the place from which they came, at the Isibubulungu."[29] These reported words of Shaka are important for understanding Magaye's perspective and what he wanted to convey to his son and his own people about the situation, whether accurate or not. Melapi said, "There were other visits to Tshaka. They [the 1824 white traders] went via Magaye and so became regular subjects of Tshaka's."[30]

THE FAILED ASSASSINATION ATTEMPT AGAINST SHAKA

On his first visit, Fynn was present when an attempt was made to kill Shaka by stabbing him while he was dancing. After the first day of dancing, Fynn was watching the dancers when suddenly "I heard a shriek and the lights [bundles of lighted dry reeds] were immediately extinguished."[31] When Fynn learned what had happened, he and his companions went to Shaka's hut in the palace grounds, struggling to get through the crowds, until he and Farewell were guided to Shaka who had been taken to another hut where he would be less easily found. According to Fynn, "he had been stabbed with an assegai through the left arm, and the blade had passed through the ribs under the left breast. It had made the King spit blood." That Shaka's death was anticipated is evident in the chaotic shrieking that persisted, and Fynn described the scene as being similar to the one said to follow the death of Nandi soon thereafter. Fynn was overwhelmed by the number of people killed in the immediate aftermath of the attempted assassination during the hours and days that Shaka's survival remained uncertain. He wrote that over the first night, the crowds of thousands shrieked unbearably, and "morning showed a horrid sight in a clear light." After a night in which the crowds had pushed and pulled against each other and fainted from exhaustion, "They had now begun to kill one another. Some were put to death because they did not cry, others for putting spittle into their eyes, others for sitting down to cry, although strength and tears, after such continuous mourning and exertion, were quite exhausted."[32] He continued,

> It was not till the fourth day that cattle were killed for the sustenance of the multitude. Many had died in the interval, and many had been killed for not mourning, or for having gone to their kraals for food.
>
> On the fifth day there were symptoms of improvement in the King's condition; these favourable indications were also noticeable on the day following.
>
> At noon on that day the party sent out in search of the would-be murderers returned, bringing with them the dead bodies of three men whom they had killed in the bush (jungle). These were the supposed assassins.[33]

According to his own account, Fynn stayed to nurse Shaka while Farewell left to send for medicines. Two of Shaka's regiments were sent out to pursue the supposed assassins whom Fynn mistakenly says were believed to have been sent by Zwide, "King of the Ndwandwes."[34] The AmaZulu oral traditions all agree, however, that after the attempted assassination, Shaka blamed the AbaQwabe and used the event as an excuse to kill them off. Ngidi ka Mcikaziswa told Stuart, "Tshaka was stabbed in the arm at Siklebeni kraal; it was alleged that Sikwayo, a man of the Qwabe tribe, had stabbed him. It was said the assegai was a Qwabe one."[35] Later Mcikaziswa elaborated, saying that Shaka's mother Nandi openly disapproved of some of Shaka's violent actions against people she said provided protection:

Nandi asked, "Why are you taking off your covering, the one of your mother's people? Why are you killing them? Where will you run away to? What people will you fly to?' This question was asked of Tshaka after he had caused the Qwabe people to be put to death because of the assegai being [taken as] proof that one of them had stabbed him. The Zulu regiments were formed into a semi-circle (*umkumbi*) at Bulawayo (not Siklebe), when the Qwabe people were picked out and all found were forthwith put to death.[36]

The attempt to assassinate Shaka in 1824 was a momentous event, but the identity and purpose of the assassin or assassins was almost immediately obscured, and European sources are vague on this subject. The son of the AmaCele chief Magaye provided several details, suggesting his father may have been an eyewitness to the events.[37] He related:

The man who stabbed Tshaka was trembling. The assegai did not penetrate. Tshaka took out the *assegai* [spear]. Next day Tshaka asked where this had come from. The Zulus said, this is a Qwabe *assegai*. They saw it by the butt end, the way of carving it. Tshaka asked how the Qwabes had come to pass by the Zulus with this *assegai*. What were they doing?[38]

It seems self-evident both that Shaka would have recognized the make (i.e., style and origins) of the assegai without asking and that no hostile umQwabe warrior should have had access to him with an assegai. This in turn indicates that Shaka knew there was Zulu complicity either in allowing an armed umQwabe man to get near him, or that he knew it had not been an umQwabe man who had stabbed him. These details are important because this incident became the pretext for a slaughter of many AbaQwabe who had given allegiance and submitted to Shaka, some of whom were in residence there at Bulawayo. Other versions, without these details, represent the killing of AmaQwabe as deliberate retaliation on the part of Shaka, but Melapi's version suggests Shaka's knowledge and motives were more complicated. Makewu stated,

Tshaka built his principal Natal kraal where Stanger now stands and called it Dukuza. The reason for the name is that when he was at Gibixegu kraal in Zululand he was stabbed by Ntintinti ka Nkobe. The assegai, which he drew out, he recognised as belonging to Sipezi where his brothers lived (he had distributed to them this kind of assegai). It struck him high up on the arm (right, I fancy) above the elbow and therefore penetrated the arm and just touched the side. It was prevented by his arm from entering his person or side – i.e. it dakuza'd. After this incident he [Shaka] left Zululand [i.e., the AmaZulu heartland north of the Thukela River], calling it Empakeni... and lived at Dukuza [at his new capital built south of the Thukela River] until he was assassinated by his *inceku* Mbopa, who was avenging his mother's death at the hands of, or by the direction of, Tshaka."[39]

Shaka retaliated violently against the AbaQwabe population, thereby threatening those who had aspired to assassinate him, whoever they were, and his extreme reaction suggests that he believed the attempt on his life was the result of a conspiracy of more than one man. As Melapi told it, Shaka said, "'As you say it is a Qwabe assegai, you will now go and do what needs to be done.' An *impi* then went and killed the Qwabe and filled a *donga* [ditch] with them. They were put into a *donga* when killed. That is where they were killed, namely in a gully. I was a young lad at this time and heard men speaking of the incident at the time."[40] Identifying Shaka's *induna* or commanding officer Mbopha as one of the assassins four years later (September 1828), one informant explained, "Tshaka, it was said, was stabbed the first time as well by Mbopa, and yet it was openly stated that Sikwayo of the Qwabe people had done so, and forests were encircled by men in the hope of catching him."[41] He was nevertheless certain that "[t]he *assegai* as a matter of fact was not Sikwayo's or even a Qwabe one, but belonged to the princes (abantwana), Dingana and Mhlangana; they had given it to Tubelisa, alias Mbopa, who, I fancy, actually tried to stab him."[42] Ndukwana said, "the Qwabe tribe were 'all killed off' by Tshaka."[43] Mbovu ka Mtshumayeli told Stuart,

> It was in respect to the great massacre of the Qwabe people that Tshaka is said to have caused dongas to be filled with corpses. So vast was the massacre that the whole people left Zululand to settle in Natal, Pondoland and elsewhere. There is nowadays no section of the Qwabe tribe in Zululand. On seeing a member of the Qwabe tribe in Zululand, some old woman of the amaCunu is said to have expressed great surprise, believing, as the slaughter was so thorough, that every one [of the AmaQwabe] must have been killed.[44]

According to Fynn, when Farewell returned with the medicine, the king granted Farewell land covering a territory that was 25 miles long at the coast and fifty miles long inland and included Port Natal. Fynn quoted the document, and said it bore Shaka's mark "X," as well as the native witnesses' marks, "X," of Umgequaru (Mbikwana), Umsega (probably uMsika), Cuntelope (Mhlophe), and Clambamaruze (Jacob, the "interpreter").⁴⁵ Fynn wrote that this was when Shaka sent out an *impi* against the AmaNdwandwe, and Fynn believed they had been blamed for the assassination attempt. Observing the preparations, Fynn, Farewell, and Davis promptly departed for Port Natal and covered the 125 miles in six days.⁴⁶

The Europeans were told that the AmaNdwandwe had initiated the failed assassination attempt. Fynn wrote, "We then understood that six men had been wounded by the assassins who wounded Shaka. From the road they took, it was supposed that they had been sent by Zwide, King of the Ndwandwes (Ndwandwe tribe), who was Shaka's only powerful enemy. Two regiments were accordingly sent off at once in search of the aggressors."⁴⁷ On the day before the *impi* departed, "[a] speech was made by Mbikwana in which he showed what the aggravating cause was that called for revenge, namely, the attempt on the life of their King. The order to march was given, and they were directed to spare neither man, woman, child nor dog. They were to burn their huts, to break the stones on which their corn was ground, and so prove their attachment to their King. The command was given to Benziwa, an elderly chief."⁴⁸

When Fynn, Farewell, and Davis reached Port Natal, they learned "... that Petersen and the Afrikanders, who comprised nearly the whole of our party, intended to return to the Cape." This had to be done in two voyages since the *Julia* was too small to take them all in one trip. After two days, Fynn went back to visit Shaka with a present from the party and stayed three days with the King. "During this time the army that had been sent out against Zwide returned, bringing with it several droves of cattle. It had, moreover, destroyed a number of kraals."⁴⁹ Fynn stayed three days at Shaka's, returned to Port Natal, and then after "not many days" set out on a trip to find the AmaMpondo to the southwest.

FYNN'S EARLY ENCOUNTERS

On Fynn's earliest attempts to reach the AmaMpondo chief Faku, he observed both poverty and fear in the small homesteads he visited. His encounters were marked by suspicion but hospitality. At one small homestead, the only food was honey and roots because the small "patch of Indian corn" was but ten yards square and their chief, they said, "had ordered it to be reserved for his own use," and if any were eaten, he "would put all of them to death."⁵⁰ When they were thirty miles from the resident of the AmaMpondo chief Faku, Fynn sent word to this "king" to explain his visit and avoided all reference to Shaka. He wrote later, "as I was aware that they had recently been defeated by Shaka, I though it wise to appear to know nothing about him, for had I admitted knowing their great enemy nothing I could afterwards say in self defence would have convinced them I was not one of his spies." Fynn told the people of the village near Faku's capital, "that the object of our coming was to open a trade in ivory with their people."[51] He returned to Port Natal without continuing on to meet Faku but left word that he would return.

While Fynn was away, the first group of traders including Peterson had left the port in the *Julia* to return to the Colony. Fynn received a request from Shaka to visit him. "I accordingly proceeded to his residence, where I found that a number of natives of Delagoa Bay had recently arrived with tribute for the King. It turned out that one of them knew me very well, having seen me at Delagoa in 1823."[52] This is one of the few pieces of remaining testimony of the early direct links between Shaka and the Tembe and Maputo chiefdoms at the Bay. When questioned by Shaka about his trip to the AmaMpondo, Fynn attempted to dissemble, but he realized that Shaka remained distrustful.[53] On his second trip to the AmaMpondo, Fynn arrived without difficulty at the AmaNtusi tribe where he stayed two days before proceeding on the King Faku's kraal; there he was presented with an ox for food.[54] However, the next day Fynn discovered that the representatives of the nation had been arriving because he was "to be put on trial under what appeared to me difficult and dangerous circumstances. I was accused of being employed by Shaka as a spy."[55] Their evidence was the direction from which he came, that he used salt that they thought was found only at the Thukela River in Shaka's country, and that they thought Shaka was of white extraction and therefore Fynn was probably related to Shaka. Fynn expected to be condemned because every person had the right to question him and they repeatedly asked the same questions, but "at length, the charges were dropped and, after Faku had received from me a present of beads, I proceeded to the particular business I had come upon."[56]

Fynn wrote, "After this second visit to Faku, which lasted two days, I returned to the amaNtusi tribe to set up there a trading station for the purchase of ivory."[57] Among other events, Fynn stayed briefly with an AmaBomvana chief. There he met the son of the blacksmith from the *Grosvenor*, a ship that had been wrecked there decades earlier; the descendants of other European survivors from this wreck; and several runaway slaves from the Cape Colony.[58] After four months in the region, Fynn received word from Farewell that Shaka had been enquiring about him, that Shaka's spies were about in the area, and that an attack against the AmaMpondo was anticipated. The correspondence itself aroused the suspicions of the AmaMpondo against Fynn. This was enough to prompt Fynn's return to Port Natal.[59] By this time about one hundred people had attached themselves to Fynn as dependents and supporters, as if he were a local chief.[60]

From Port Natal, Fynn proceeded on to see Shaka in the hope of preventing misunderstanding and conflict, and upon his arrival he learned that "nothing of importance had happened in Shaka's country during my absence, except the death of Zwide, King of the Ndwandwes – Shaka's principal enemy; his son, Sikhunyana, had succeeded him."[61] Shaka offered sixty men to help Fynn get the ivory he had acquired from the amaMpondo back to Natal, which took several journeys to carry all the goods for the trip of two hundred miles.

During this time, Fynn heard that the *Mary* had been wrecked at the port with Lieutenant King aboard. King allowed some of the crew to take one of the boats to return to Port Elizabeth and decided to build a vessel for himself at Port Natal. Shaka also heard about the wreck and invited the crew to come see him; Farewell, King, Isaacs, a friend of King's, and Fynn went with the ten remaining crew members to Shaka's about 140 miles away. Shaka gave them a four-horned bullock (formed by splitting the horns in a calf) and two oxen to slaughter. Shaka had Fynn come to talk with him in the evenings at his "seraglio," and on this visit, Shaka sent the European traders out with their guns to shoot an elephant, thinking they would fail. The elephant dropped dead when it was shot, and "Shaka's consternation was great, and he admitted that our weapons were superior to his own." It turned out that the bullet had penetrated the elephant's ear merely by chance.[62] While they were there, Shaka's grandmother died.

The European traders were constantly made aware that their continued safety was contingent upon maintaining a positive relationship with Shaka, but Fynn established himself south of Port Natal at the Umzimkhulu River, where people were "distressed and famished," many being refugees from Shaka. These Africans sought Fynn's protection and lived around him. By about 1832 or perhaps a few years earlier there were some four thousand Africans settled around the Natal traders.[63]

The shipwrecked *Mary* had brought more traders to Port Natal. In 1832 the *South African Commercial Advertiser* published in its pages the "Journal" of another trader, Nathaniel Isaacs, in a series of issues and noted he was attempting at the time "to communicate with the local Government respecting the utility of a settlement being formed at

Natal."⁶⁴ Isaacs stated that his intentions in 1824 were to trade in ivory and he had joined Captain King on the *Mary* for this purpose. He accompanied Fynn on a visit to Shaka at the time that the H.M.S. *Helicon* had come to the port to retrieve those who had been shipwrecked and desired transportation back to Algoa Bay. Isaacs says that he decided to stay while the schooner was rebuilt and set himself up as an ivory trader at Port Natal. From Isaacs and from a boy named Charles Rawden Maclean, later known by the pseudonym John Ross, we have contemporaneous accounts about Natal, KwaZulu, and Shaka to supplement Fynn's eyewitness accounts. It is obvious that the European traders were motivated by the attraction of trade and profit in ivory when they invested their time and money into establishments at Port Natal.

Maclean, or John Ross, was an unfortunate youth who had lied about his age in order to be taken on as a ship's boy and had ended up stranded at Port Natal while only about ten or twelve years old.⁶⁵ From his experience, we know that the overland trade route from KwaZulu to Delagoa Bay was arduous, a three hundred-mile journey that they accomplished in the matter of a few weeks. He was sent to the Portuguese settlement and fort at Delagoa (Maputo) Bay in the company of an AmaZulu escort provided by Shaka in order to procure medicine, and they accomplished the 300-mile journey in the matter of a few weeks.⁶⁶ Maclean's account provides a sympathetic perspective, and from commentary provided by the editor Stephen Grey in the introduction to the published volume, it is evident that as an adult Maclean devoted himself to the antislavery cause and employed free blacks on his own trade vessels.⁶⁷ Maclean stated unequivocally his perspective with regard to the AmaZulu, a sympathy imbibed as a child: "I owe them a debt of gratitude that leads me to wish and to hope my countrymen, whosoever they be, will exercise that mercy and kindness toward them which I experienced at their hands in the day of their rule. Those are yet living to whom I am indirectly indebted for my life, and I trust their goodness will meet a just reward by kindness and forbearance at the white man's hands."⁶⁸ Before proceeding with his narrative of events, Maclean told the reader and reminded the AmaZulu, hypothetical listeners as he wrote, that he had always spoken to them about God and salvation.⁶⁹ Maclean's experience of the region began in September 1825. Soon thereafter, according to him, "Farewell and his party had been called on to assist the Zulus in the contest with the Sikhunyana, for their safety depended on the Zulus being victorious, as the hostile chief was not considered friendly to the white man, but no compulsory measures had been adopted to enforce the white men to join the *impi* (war or army)."[70] Maclean wrote that the security of the Europeans themselves depended on the AmaZulu defeat of Sikhunyana's AmaNdwandwe.[71] Farewell brought a message from Shaka that the newly arrived white men should visit him, but Maclean stayed behind when Captain King and several others left to take Shaka "beads, bugles, and a few blankets."[72]

Later James King told Maclean that Shaka had focused the conversation on determining the strength of peoples who might be a threat to him. Shaka wanted to know how large King George's dominions were, how wealthy he was, and how strong his military was. These were questions for which he would have been using spies and interrogations to discover about his African neighboring chiefdoms and kingdoms routinely. Shaka approached the question of Europeans in the same way. The nature of Shaka's concerns as revealed in his conversations is one of the important areas on which Maclean's account sheds light. Evidently told by King, Maclean reported that Shaka told King and the others, "I wish," he added, "that there should be only two great kings in the world; that King George should be king of the whites, and I king of the blacks."[73] One of Shaka's main sources of information was the interpreter Jacob who had been arrested in the Cape Colony for cattle theft and imprisoned on Robben Island. Captain King had later arranged his release so Jacob could travel with them as interpreter on their 1823 exploration of Saint Lucia Bay and River. After a quarrel, he fled from King and Farewell's exploratory party and made his way to Shaka's where the explorers later found him. Maclean concluded that "from him [Jacob] there is no doubt the Zulu chief first learnt the white men's strength and numbers at the Cape Colony."[74]

There is evidence that Shaka was truly worried about the Europeans at the Cape Colony as a threat to him. Previously, he would have learned from Dingiswayo everything that he knew about Europeans, whether in the Cape Colony or at Delagoa Bay, via African traders who frequented the area. This information gave Shaka forewarning of the possible dangers of European weapons, about which he was obviously worried. Jacob was undoubtedly not his first informant about European weapons and soldiers. His direct eyewitness testimony to Shaka about Cape Town and British forces and military strength evidently heightened Shaka's anxiety about this threat as his conversations with the European traders showed. According to Maclean, Jacob withheld from Shaka information about the cause of his imprisonment by white men, "telling him that he had been made a prisoner or war, his countrymen having been vanquished by the whites, and that the latter never killed the enemy that fell into their hands, but shut them up in dungeons or in some solitary island, where they were detained for life."[75] Jacob, who had his own village and took the name Hlambamanzi, remained a source of calumny about the Europeans individually as well as collectively. He deliberately fomented trouble between Shaka and the traders. Maclean said, however, that Shaka did not believe all he was told nor adopt Jacob's perspective, for "in Shaka's reasoning, if they spared the lives of their enemies, how much more then ought he to protect them as friendly and unfortunate strangers."[76]

Shaka told Maclean that he had often been advised by his council "to kill you wild beasts of Mlungus" (i.e., white people), but he called Maclean, whom he insisted stay with him, "Jackabo." Shaka used his conversations with the boy to try to manipulate the traders with the constant implication that their very lives were in his hands and they should not forget it.[77] The observations of Maclean, Fynn, and others indicate that Shaka commonly used the strategy of appearing to take Europeans into his confidence in order to gain information from them and to let them know what he wanted them and their people – as far abroad as King George – to know. Everything written about Shaka from eyewitnesses indicates that he was very self-conscious about everything he said and did around white people as well as his own people and regarded every encounter as an opportunity for manipulation.

Maclean shed further light on Shaka's intentions, indicating that from the moment that Captain King notified Shaka he was going to build a boat to return to the Cape Colony, Shaka began his plan for what was eventually the Sotobe embassy to the Cape Colony.[78] King portrayed Shaka's intentions as solicitous of a friendly alliance even though he was aware of Shaka's history of violence that he attributed to a desire "to enrich himself with cattle of the conquered tribes."[79]

Maclean wrote the memoire of his direct experiences with Shaka that shaped his later perceptions, beginning with his first visit to Bulawayo. If he had any illusions about Shaka they were dispelled before he even met the chief. Maclean's descriptions are more revealing than others with regard to the ambiance of the vicinity of Shaka's capital at Bulawayo. He wrote that "on the evening of the fourth day's travel we encamped at the foot of the mountain range of Bulawayo, on attaining the summit of which we could view the termination of our weary journey."[80] They had not been taken on the long route of fifteen or so days used to first lead other Europeans to the capital, but the group had arrived quickly, having "passed through comparatively depopulated country where nought was left us to contemplate but the perishing remnants of humanity that were, indeed, thickly strewn in the way."[81] He was impressed that he and his companions were being passed "by numerous pedestrian warriors, decked in their full war costume, wending their way to headquarters," who were all "exceedingly civil and even respectful in their deportment to us."[82] A man whose life Farewell had saved by rescuing him from a fall off a precipice and nursed him to health, was particularly solicitous. Not only Fynn, but also Farewell thus gained a reputation as an *inyanga* or doctor.[83] Commenting on the regalia of the warriors, Maclean wrote that they wore strings of small pieces of wood as necklaces and bracelets, and

> the Zulu warriors set great value on these apparently useless trifles, and that they were order of merit conferred by Shaka on those who had distinguished themselves by daring deeds of bravery on the field of battle. Each row, whether round the neck or arm, was the distinguishing mark of some heroic deed, and which the wearer had received from Shaka's own hand. These were principally gained in the last amaMpondo war, from which Shaka had returned with a large booty.[84]

That Maclean retrospectively confused his various experiences is evident because he later explains that his party was entering the gates not of Bulawayo, but of Dukuza.[85] The first capital at Bulawayo was where Maclean spent most of his time, and he described the group's conversations with Shaka and how he learned with despair that Shaka had insisted that he stay behind when the rest of the Europeans, all adults, returned to Port Natal.[86] Several major events occurred before Shaka removed his household from Bulawayo to a newly built "kraal" south of the Thukela River, near modern Stanger, that was called Dukuza.

From his trading post on the Mzimkhulu River, Fynn developed a thriving ivory trade; he wrote,

> I had not long been established there before natives from the surrounding country, because of their distressed and famished state, flocked to me for protection from that death which those who had joined me in my former expeditions had escaped. It was not long before the remains of four tribes, with their chiefs – amounting to more than 2,000 of both sexes – came to live under me. Many of them were people who had made their escape when at the point of being put to death by the Zulus. By merely notifying such arrivals to Shaka, the refugees were allowed to reside with us, a favour contrary to all former custom.[87]

Challenges and Consolidation 1824–1827

The situation was similar at Port Natal, where the European settlement would become permanent and eventually grow into the modern city of Durban. In about 1830 Fynn wrote,

> Messrs. Farewell, King, Isaacs, Cane and Ogle, as well as myself, have in this manner been the means of saving the lives of hundreds of people. The country for 25 miles round Natal was uninhabited except by the few previously mentioned. There are now more than 4,000 inhabitants under our protection, and our departure from the country would be the signal for their immediate destruction.[88]

Fynn's narrative provides considerable insight into regional economic and political interactions among chiefs and chiefdoms. His situation as a trader who established his main ivory trading post on the border of Faku's territory to trade with the AmaMpondo was inevitably insecure because he and his partners depended on Shaka's tolerance for their operations at the port, which were essential for their trade. However, the AmaZulu of Shaka and the AmaMpondo of Faku were implacable enemies, and Shaka was bound to exploit Fynn to make political and military inroads into Faku's territory. Fynn had immediately become aware of AmaMpondo fears of Shaka, so he was careful in his conversations with Shaka. Shaka asked Fynn about his trip and "laughed heartily on hearing the account." He also warned Fynn that he could not expect to travel without his help: "I could only expect to be murdered by them or poisoned by bush Kaffirs." Fynn tried to explain to Shaka that "it was customary with my countrymen to try and become acquainted with the manners and customs of other natives with a view to self improvement, and in return, to strive to benefit those with whom they come in contact by teaching them something of British manners and customs."[89] From this it is evident that Fynn went to great lengths to dissemble and placate Shaka. In the nineteenth century there were no Europeans, including British who expected to learn how to improve themselves from natives anywhere. That Fynn nevertheless told Shaka this is certainly credible given Fynn's character and personality, and the verbal survival instincts he exhibited often. However, he also evidently realized there was no chance he could influence Shaka, for he commented in the text, in one of his very direct judgments of Shaka, "But I might have saved my breath on this occasion as well as on many others, for I found I had to deal with a king [Shaka] who had no idea of any limit to his powers, and who was confident his commands were both lawful and strictly reasonable."[90] Fynn did not further attempt to justify to Shaka his actions in visiting people without Shaka's assistance or consent.[91]

THE 1826 *IMPI* AGAINST SIKHUNYANA AND THE AMANDWANDWE

Shaka's 1821 defeat of the AmaNdwandwe under Zwide had been decisive, and although Zwide survived, the leadership of a large segment of his chiefdom devolved onto the shoulders of his son and heir, Sikhunyana. Zwide's nephew Soshangane had led a large section north to re-establish a chiefdom near the Olifant's (Balule) River north of the AmaSwazi chiefdom of Sobhuza. The area was just northwest of the chiefdoms of Delagoa Bay who were raided and in some cases devastated by AmaNdwande depredations. When the old chief fled north after his defeat, "Zwide never reached Sotshangana's; he died from illness on the road."[92] According to oral tradition concerning Zwide, most of his followers left with his son who was determined to recover AmaNdwandwe strength and return to fight the AmaZulu again:

> When Tshaka defeated Zwide, the latter fled to the Ezindololwane hills, down the uSutu, near Mampontsha's. Zwide went off towards Sotshangana's for Sotshangana was of the Nxumalo (Ndwandwe) tribe, the chief being Malusi (father of Sotondose). Sikunyana would not follow his father. He said, "Tshaka has, as you say, defeated you, because you are an old man. I am his own age, and mean to try and see what I can do." Sikunyana thereupon returned and subsequently met Tshaka at Umhlongamvula, where he was defeated.[93]

Sikhunyana led his followers northwest where he believed they would be out of range of Shaka's military expeditions, and they resettled there for several years and recouped their strength. Shaka did not send an *impi* against him while Sikhunyana was that far afield, although later AmaZulu expeditions were sent as far as the Transvaal region in pursuit of Mzilikazi and his AmaKhumalo or AmaNdebele chiefdom. With Mzilikazi, the AmaNdwandwe found temporary respite:

> Sikunyana did not go after Sotshangana as his father did on being defeated; he went off towards Mzilikazi. He built at the Nhlabangekanda, the name of a stream, near the Nzwabuhlungu, another stream, both in Mzilikazi's district, where we got to on our expedition in Dingana's day.[94]

Not much is remembered in the oral traditions about the AmaNdwandwe during these years, but in 1826 Shaka received word that Sikhunyana had led his chiefdom back toward the Phongolo River area and was there reportedly planning an attack against the AmaZulu.

Shaka mustered a defense, including the aid of Zihlandhlo's regiments, and in May 1826 a huge military campaign set out to attack Sikhunyana's AmaNdwandwe pre-emptively north of the upper reaches of the

Phongolo.⁹⁵ Shaka hoped to attack Sikhunyana's AmaNdwandwe before they had a chance to secure their cattle and women at the Phongolo and start south on a campaign against the AmaZulu. Shaka made a decision to send "the whole of the Zulus" against Sikunyana, indicating his determination to use all available force to eliminate what he perceived as a formidable threat – the returning Ndwandwe forces who had defeated him in the past.⁹⁶

It was May 1826 when Fynn next visited Shaka and encountered Sikhunyana's brother Somaphunga, who had "come to tender his allegiance to Shaka" because he feared being put to death by his brother, now king of the "Ndwandwe tribe." "He [Somaphunga], moreover, gave such information to the King as could not possibly have been obtained by means of spies."⁹⁷ A few days later when he was back again at Port Natal, Fynn and the other traders received a messenger from Shaka calling up "all hands, white as well as black, to resist an attack, which was momentarily expected on Shaka's kraal."⁹⁸ Wary of violating the laws of the Colony but also of refusing Shaka, the European traders went together to Shaka's residence and two days afterward learned that the whole nation had been called to arms. Shaka told Fynn it was necessary for them as able-bodied men to accompany him, and the European traders explained their duties not to do so according to their own laws, which "caused him to make some very unpleasant observations." Shaka threatened to massacre them, saying that should the English seek to avenge such an action, they would be terror-struck by Shaka's army. "Shaka then remarked that there would be no necessity for our taking part in the actual fighting; all he wanted us to do was to accompany him, i.e. give him our moral support."⁹⁹ It is evident that Shaka had wanted not moral support but rather to be seen with white European support, an implicit threat to his enemies.

Shaka's army departed overnight, and Fynn with his party caught up with them at Nobamba, about sixty miles away, where the regiments were organized, spies were sent out, and they waited two days. Fynn recalled, "[e]very man was ordered to roll up his shield and carry it on his back – a custom observed only when the enemy is known to be at a considerable distance. In the rear of the regiments were the baggage boys, few above the age of 12, and some not more than 6 [years old]. These boys were attached to the chiefs and principal men, carrying their mats, headrests, tobacco, etc., and driving cattle required for the army's consumption. Some of the chiefs, moreover, were accompanied by girls carrying beer, corn and milk; and when their supply had been exhausted these carriers returned to their homes."[100] Fynn's description suggests the formidable appearance of AmaZulu forces on a military expedition, for he said that "[t]he whole body of men, boys and women amounted, as nearly as we could reckon, to 50,000. All proceeded in close formation, and when looked at from a distance nothing could be seen but a cloud of dust."[101] They were on the road several days, camping at night, and Fynn described their meeting with remnant AmaHlubi who were by then referred to as Iziyendane.

The large numbers of people traveling together inevitably created some chaotic conditions, and Fynn reported that when crossing a river, some people were trampled to death in the mud.[102] Passing through the territory of a remnant of the AmaHlubi chiefdom, they engaged some as spies and guides "as these people had a perfect knowledge of the country."[103] Fynn's partner Farewell was injured en route when he was attacked by an ox and stayed behind, but Shaka ordered Fynn to join a detachment that was sent ahead to Hawana's Fastness, Inqaba ka Hawana, about twenty miles east of modern Utrecht. When Shaka and the remaining troops caught up, Shaka's forces went together into a forest and waited two days for the spies to return. When the *impi* eventually proceeded and came in sight of the enemy AmaNdwandwe, it found the AmaNdwande cattle and women secured on a mountain surrounded by military regiments. Fynn, unable to find Shaka, "Being a stranger to their [AmaZulu] mode of attack I determined to ascend the mountain and be a spectator of passing events." He had a view over an extensive valley, an immense mountain, the enemy forces surrounding all their cattle, "and above them the women and children of the nation in a body. They were sitting down, awaiting the attack."[104]

Then a major battle involving tens of thousands of warriors arranged in formal regiments on both sides was engaged.[105] Ndukwana said the battle occurred at Endololwane hill, near Ingcaka mountain and Mhlangambula.[106] Watching from a nearby mountain, Fynn observed the meeting of the AmaZulu forces with the AmaNdwandwe enemy, the AmaNdwandwe women and children in the mountain above them, and their cattle surrounded by the warriors.[107] Fynn estimated the total AmaNdwandwe population there at 40,000 or more.[108]

Among the various reports of this battle, Mbokodo told Stuart that Zihlandhlo's Embo forces and Shaka's AmaZulu forces were used as two different wings or "horns" sent to surround the enemy and at first did not recognize each other as allies and mistakenly fought each other at the outset when the "two horns met." This did not last long, however,

Challenges and Consolidation 1824–1827 161

and they did succeed in hemming in the enemy forces, Sikhunyana's AmaNdwandwe.[109] The AmaNdwandwe warriors were not able to withstand the AmaZulu regiments in the hand-to-hand fighting that ensued.

Fynn described the battle. Shaka's troops approached to within twenty yards of the enemy, and a servant of Cape Colony Khoi origins working with the European Port Natal traders fired off three shots, which was a signal to attack. The warriors from the two armies clashed and stabbed each other for about three minutes and then fell back a few paces; they engaged in fighting again for a few minutes and again fell back from each other. This time the enemy's (i.e., AmaNdwandwe's) losses were seen to be greater. Fynn later wrote,

> This urged the Zulus to a final charge. The shrieks now became terrific. The remnants of the enemy's army sought shelter in an adjoining wood, out of which they were soon driven. Then began a slaughter of the women and children. They were all put to death. The cattle being taken by the different regiments were driven to the kraal lately occupied by Sikhunyana. The battle, from the commencement to the close, did not last more than an hour and a half. The numbers of the hostile tribe, including women and children, could not have been less than 40,000. The number of cattle taken was estimated at 60,000. The sun having set while the cattle were being captured, the whole valley during the night was a scene of confusion.... Many of Shaka's wounded managed to crawl on hands and knees in the hope of getting assistance, but for the enemy's wounded there was no hope.[110]

Other evidence, including his own contradictory testimony, indicates that Fynn was incorrect when he wrote that all of the women and children were put to death, and these contradictions reflect his hyperbolic style of exaggeration.[111] However, the outline of events seems to be approximately correct. According to Fynn, Shaka inspected the regiments the next day and had put to death men selected as having been cowardly. Of this Fynn commented astutely, "Many of these, no doubt, forfeited their lives only because their chiefs were in fear that, if they did not condemn some as being guilty, they would be suspected of seeking a pretext to save them and would incur the resentment of Shaka."[112] Ceremonies were held by the *izinyanga* (doctors) to purify those who had killed in battle, a reminder that killing a person even in battle was taken so seriously that purification of the surviving warrior was necessary.

Maclean recounted the events of the expedition against Sikhunyana that Farewell's party had accompanied as told to Maclean at the time. The publication of Stephen Kay's *Travels and Researches in Eastern Africa* provoked Maclean to defend the Europeans at the port from Kay's accusations of cruelty against innocent Africans. Maclean stated unequivocally that "the battle was fought in the night, so that the services of the fire-armed men [i.e., Farewell and his party] on that occasion were not called into requisition."[113]

Maclean wrote:

The enemy fought with great obstinacy and bravery, equal in every respect to the Zulus, but the superior discipline and practice of the latter in war prevailed over the more uninitiated forces of the Sikhunyana [Izeecanyana]. The latter were beaten and almost totally annihilated, no quarter being given or received. The brave fellows, even when wholly discomfited, scorned to seek safety in flight, and even the women stepped into the ranks and filled up the gaps occasioned by their falling husbands; the old chief alone, at the earnest persuasion of a handful of devoted followers, saved himself when the field was irretrievably lost.[114]

Maclean had been told that 3,000 AmaNdwandwe men and women were killed in the battle, and half of the 5,000 AmaZulu warriors were killed. He saw the battle site two years later because it straddled the route between Bulawayo and Delagoa Bay. Maclean wrote that the devastation of homes and fields had been so complete that "there it remains a barren and desolate wilderness, there the bleaching bones of the slain now blanch the plains, and present to the traveler the painful evidence of a field where one of the most fearful conflicts that ever took place between savage hosts was decided."[115] Returning to his defense of the Port Natal traders who stood accused by Stephen Kay, he reiterated that in this battle, the only gun fired was that of a "Hottentot," who was about to be killed by an AmaZulu warrior because of "an old standing grievance that existed between them."[116]

An estimated 60,000 cattle were captured.[117] According to one oral tradition, Sikhunyana was seen escaping during the fighting and was not caught by warriors sent to capture him. According to another tradition, Sikhunyana was caught during the fight and put to death.[118] Thus, "Sikunyana was defeated at the Mhlongamvula – this is a stream which enters the Usutu river."[119] The AmaZulu forces learned that Sikunyana had escaped death and was among those who fled to the north.

Magojela ka Mfanawendhlela told Stuart that his grandfather Manzini's troops had assisted Shaka, and because Shaka had witnessed how strong they were in the battle against Sikunyana's AmaNdwandwe, Shaka later had Manzini put to death as too strong a threat.[120] In stylized narrative form, Mbokodo provided considerable details about the march of the troops northward, camping along the way, and the battle itself during which Sikunyana escaped. According to Mbokodo, after Sikunyana's warriors had been routed, "'Kill off every soul,' said Tshaka, 'women and child.' He wanted nothing of Sikunyana's to survive."[121] This narrative is important as an example of stories of Shaka ordering the killing women and children as well as warriors. The AmaNdwandwe were old enemies who had defeated him more than once, and he was now fighting against a second generation of this chief's family, explaining why he did not want any of Sikunyana's possible heirs to survive. Furthermore, the circumstances of the attack indicate the vulnerability of the AmaNdwandwe civilians to Shaka's soldiers because Shaka had achieved a surprise attack from long distance. Shaka had come to eliminate a threat. "The *impi* went in and finished them all off. Tshaka then directed the troops to follow after Sikunyana, but they failed to overtake him."[122] Mbokodo then said that after their return, Shaka ordered his troops to kill any men who had failed to go on the *impi* on the grounds that they had been malingerers. Maziyana told Stuart this was the expedition that had been accompanied by the Port Natal traders, saying that "when Tshaka fought Sikunyana he called on Europeans to assist. They did so. Fynn went. 'Usutu' cattle were seized. Mbulazi [Fynn] got a share of these and brought them back and established his Insimbi kraal with them."[123] But the reports of the carnage may have been exaggerated. After Sikunyana's death, several of Zwide's other sons and their followers came to give their allegiance to Shaka, and the younger men were enrolled in AmaZulu regiments under Shaka and later his successors, Dingane and Mpande.[124]

European witnesses said that the AmaNdwandwe women stepped forward to fill the ranks of the men and fight, thus providing an explanation for why women were killed in the battle. These witnesses also reported a total AmaNdwandwe mortality of 3,000 men and women killed (combined, including warriors).[125] A staggering number relative to other battles, this was nevertheless far short of the total population of 40,000 estimated by Fynn to have been killed, and it appears the vast majority of these AmaNdwandwe did manage to escape death as the AmaZulu turned their attention instead to gathering the herds of cattle as darkness fell.

Shaka had observed the battle and the subsequent seizure of tens of thousands of cattle as night fell from a nearby mountain overlook. According to Fynn, however, "[e]arly next morning Shaka arrived, and each regiment, previous to its inspection by him, had picked out its cowards and put them to death."[126] Ceremonies were held to purify those warriors who had killed in battle. Fynn witnessed Shaka question a woman and child about Sikhunyana who had escaped and then order that they to be killed. This prompted Fynn to ask Shaka to spare the life of the child, although Fynn comments that he knew it was too much to ask Shaka to spare both lives.[127] The Europeans accompanied Shaka on the return journey and reached Port Natal just after the arrival of another trading vessel on October 6, 1826.[128]

That most AmaNdwandwe survived this terrible battle is self-evident because after Sikhunyana's death several other of Zwide's sons and their followers returned to give their allegiance to Shaka. After they came to *khonza* the younger AmaNdwande men were enrolled in the AmaZulu regiments both during Shaka's reign and during the rule of Dingane and then Mpande.[129] Ndukwana provided a description of the absorption of the remnants of Zwide's people who had returned from the north with an explanation of their incorporation that was evident to future generations. He said,

After Sikunyana's death, Somapunga ka Zwide (Somapunga is Mankulumana's father) came to Tshaka and tendered his allegiance. Nqabeni ka Zwide, Mlomo ka Zwide, and others also came and tendered their allegiance. These two, however, were still young, for they enrolled in the Zinyosi regiment.[130]

This information from Ndukwana provides insight into the process of political consolidation under Shaka, which contradicts common assertions of destruction. Thus, some of Zwide's followers pursued their fate in migrations to the north, some died in battle, and some gave their allegiance to Shaka and were scattered, but survived, among the AmaZulu alongside whom they then fought. The fate of both the chiefs and the people of chiefdoms attacked by Shaka was in large part determined by their response to his attack. The survival of at least a portion of a chiefdom intact was important, and ensured the continued honoring of both ancestors and descendants of the ruling family and their adherents.

After Zihlandhlo had assisted Shaka in this *impi* against the AmaNdwandwe under Sikunyana in October 1826, Shaka gave him free rein to conduct his own further military expeditions. Mbokodo listed these *impis* at length, giving a chronology of the attacks and their results. Mbokodo's terminology is ambiguous, however, because it was common to say that a chief had been "killed" when he had merely been defeated and his cattle stolen as booty. As a consequence, his chiefdom would not survive independently without offering submission to the victors. According to Mbokodo, after Zihlandlo assisted Shaka in the *impi* against Sikunyana, Zihlandlo "attacked Macingwane in the Cunu country, but he failed to kill him. He killed, however, Sondonzima (ka Luboko), brother of

Macingwane." Mbokodo then listed eighteen chiefs who were attacked and raided or "killed" by Zihlandhlo's forces. The details of the differences between these various attacks with regard to their purpose, outcome, and what they achieved, indicate that this piece of testimony is a straightforward description of factual events by Mbokodo, who carefully differentiated these aspects of reports on the various attacks.[131] Zihlandhlo's Embo were eventually themselves attacked by Shaka and driven off to south of Natal.

The strength and threat of the AmaZulu were by then obvious, and other chiefdoms that had been subordinate to the AmaNdwandwe gave their allegiance to Shaka at this time, and he sent troops to attack those that were recalcitrant.[132] Chiefs who offered their allegiance to Shaka could hope to be spared as long as they did not pose a threat to him. Thus,

When the Ndwandwe tribe (there was no king of this name) was broken up by Tshaka, Mkosi ka Mgudhlane withdrew, and crossed the Sikwebezi river, and when he got to Ngome he remained there. He then submitted to Tshaka; he did so by *Konza*ing, and paid nothing (tendered his submission though he in fact paid nothing). Tshaka said, "They have done well to come, the sons of Mgudhlane." He then went down with them to the Black Mfolosi on the far side of Cesa. Tshaka then built Mpangisweni kraal, saying, "They have come hurrying (*pangisa*) to *konza*; we have poured them together in one place with the Ndwandwe." Nquhele ka Mgudhlane was made induna of the kraal; he followed in age after Mkosi who was the chief son.[133]

After the battle against Sikhunyana, Shaka ordered two of three columns to proceed and attack two other small chiefs who had been tributary to the AmaNdwandwe under Zwide, Mlotshwa, and Beje. Shaka suspected these chiefs of treachery even though they had already *khonza*'d him.[134] After defending themselves in a mountain stronghold until their stores ran out, Mlotshwa's people again offered their submission, which Shaka accepted. However, Beje's people, according to Fynn, managed to "cut to pieces" a regiment of Shaka's of two thousand men, and Shaka had the AmaZulu survivors of that defeat put to death by their own chief.[135] Fynn later wrote:

[Beje] too, had a strong position among the rocks, and succeeded in cutting to pieces one of Shaka's regiments, raised only two months previously, and numbering two thousand men. This regiment had the name of the regiment of "Warmth," or in the Zulu "Motha." A few escaped and came to the army, now on its return homeward; but orders were given to put them to death at once, as men who had dared to fly.[136]

By this time in 1826, Shaka's troops seldom suffered defeat, and various details of their eventual success against Beje's people were later remembered.[137] Shaka had to send another *impi* against Beje's stronghold some months later, and in February 1827 – after two Khoi men in the traders' party had committed adultery – raged in anger and used their offense as a pretext to demand that the Europeans join an attack against Beje with their firearms. Fynn reported that

> Mr. King saw the necessity of acceding to his wishes to prevent his avenging himself on the whole of us. After some deliberation, Messrs. Cane and Isaacs, together with part of the crew of the Mary, also two Hottentots, and several natives (with guns) volunteered to go. They succeeded in completely defeating Beje's tribe and killing the chief himself.[138]

Fynn was not himself an eyewitness, and his account left ambiguous the roles actually played by any of the men with firearms who had been compelled to accompany Shaka's troops against Beje. Maclean, in his account of events written decades later, conflated the hearsay accounts of the battle against the AmaNdwandwe of Sikhunyana, and the second against Chief Beje months later, that he had heard.[139] Maclean disputed Stephen Kay's allegations that the Europeans and their armed servants had used their weapons to kill twenty to thirty refugees from Shaka who had taken up a position on a mountain, an apparent reference by Kay to Chief Beje's people.[140] Kay's account is not supported by the limited oral narratives of these events remembered and told to Stuart generations later, nor does it agree with Isaac's account as a participant. It is the trader Nathaniel Isaacs who left a reliable account of these events.[141]

According to Isaacs, he, John Cane, a sailor named Brown, and their Khoi and African servants, motivated solely by the threat of Shaka against their lives should they decline to participate, had joined the encampment of five thousand AmaZulu warriors who had been at the site about two miles from "the enemy," AmaBeje, for three months. That the AmaZulu were themselves reluctant to carry out Shaka's orders to subdue the AmaBeje is therefore self-evident because the latter were engaged in routinely herding their cattle, coveted by the AmaZulu, on the rich plains of the area without being molested by the fierce amassed warriors. Isaacs stated that none of the AmaZulu commanders wanted to fight but that nevertheless they deterred Isaac's party from opening communications for negotiations with the AmaBeje by making "false representations."[142] Instead Shaka's military commanders wanted Isaacs' party to "strike a terror by the application of our fire-arms in the attack, and thus at once subdue the tribe opposed to us," intending to set the AmaBeje into flight in a "want of courage," resulting in their submission.

Challenges and Consolidation 1824–1827

In the end, this is indeed what happened. Without consulting Isaacs, the other men in his party of ten, only two besides Isaacs being European, had decided to take the AmaBeje cattle when they were brought out to pasture. This action precipitously launched the confrontation that the AmaZulu commanders had been so assiduously avoiding. Only then did the AmaZulu warriors prepare for fighting with their ceremonial "doctoring" by the *izinyanga* ("doctors") as the AmaBeje herders abandoned their cattle to run for help. The AmaBeje took up "their positions in small detachments on the several heights," so that the AmaZulu had to approach up a hill. As the traders' party advanced, however, the AmaZulu fled to the far side of the river, leaving the traders' party to advance on their own toward the "large rugged rocks" behind which the AmaBeje "had taken shelter."[143]

Isaacs wrote that his party attacked and defeated about fifty men, but because the report of the shots fired caused such panic, the enemy "shouted and ran in all directions," allowing this victory almost without bloodshed. Isaacs shot and killed a man in self-defense, and the others wounded a few of the "enemy." Dodging the stones being thrown at them, even by women and children, Isaacs' party burned the huts they reached "in order to induce them to surrender without further bloodshed."[144] The AmaBeje men then reassembled for battle, but when their chief led the advance to fight they failed to follow him. The chief was shot by a Khoi man from the traders' party just as the chief was about to kill him with a thrown spear. Isaacs had also fired at the chief but then was himself struck in the back by a barbed spear that was difficult to remove, leaving a painful wound that eventually healed.

The AmaZulu expected to fight the following day, but while they were debating among themselves, messengers from the AmaBeje arrived to negotiate their surrender and submission to Shaka, for which they were required to surrender their "half-starved cattle and goats."[145]

The oral traditions of the AmaZulu do not report that there had been a major battle, much less many fatalities. In a report that includes details suggestive of an eyewitness participant and therefore is very credible, one man told Stuart,

At the Ngome, when Beje and his people were attacked by the Zulus, my uncle Nomnanzi entered Beje's stronghold after the whole of the Zulu had attempted and failed. He [Nomnanzi], however, entered and succeeded in killing two men. Tshaka's *impi* entered the stronghold on the following day and saw the men dead.[146]

Shaka's famous warrior Zulu ka Nogandaya had told his son similar details of the AmaZulu infiltration into the mountain stronghold by means of ropes, providing them access. These events were remembered in a folk song about the events:

"Beja is in the Ngome, Beja is in the Ngome", is another chant – sung at the *umkosi* [first fruits ceremony] in Tshaka's days. Women and boys sing this. Beja of the Kumalo people had gone into a stronghold. The Zulu descended by means of *zungulu* creepers and went to the *impi* – only one entrance. The men groaned.¹⁴⁷

This song indicates that the AmaNtshali of chief Beje held out until after Shaka's death, and Dingane is said to have finally managed to subdue them. According to one account,

Beje's people held out in a stronghold in the eNgome. Tshaka eventually left them alone; they successfully resisted him. They were subsequently routed by Dingana, who besieged them and so starved them out. This place was a great natural fortress; the gate or entrance was completely closed in, so much so that the attacking forces did not know where it was. When the besieged surrendered, the position of this gate was discovered, and only then; it turned out to be "on top", "above."¹⁴⁸

This expedition returned to Shaka's new capital at Dukuza on March 18, 1827.¹⁴⁹ Fynn in the meantime had returned to his trading post on the uMzimkhulu river where two thousand people under four chiefs settled around him, just as some four thousand people settled for protection near the Port Natal traders.¹⁵⁰ Maziyana, who commented extensively about the earliest European residents of Natal/Port Natal, said that after Farewell, known as "Febana," gave presents to Shaka, he "then returned and cut down trees and built his establishment and called it Isinyama. The site of it is where the courthouse at present stands. Those who had hidden away by ones and twos in the bushes about Port Natal came out of their places of refuge on seeing food available."¹⁵¹ Preoccupied with building their new boat, the traders asked Shaka to send an escort with Maclean, then estimated by Fynn to be about fifteen years old, on a journey to Delagoa Bay where the traders wanted Maclean to buy medicine. This trip was successful, and he returned after only a few weeks. King and Isaacs surveyed the mouths of the Mhlathuze and Mlalazi Rivers, and visited Bulawayo and Dibinhlangu.¹⁵²

By the end of 1826 Shaka had successfully widened the territory under his control both to the south and to the north. He remained worried about the threats far to the north and northwest posed by Soshangane's AmaNdwandwe chiefdom and by Mzilikazi's emerging AmaNdebele kingdom. But Shaka's attention remained focused on the southwest where the AmaXhosa chiefdoms and the European Cape Colony drew his expansionist ambitions.

EYOBUTSHINGA IMPI: THE 1827 RAID IN THE CALEDON RIVER VALLEY

Dingane led an AmaZulu military expedition in 1827 into Lesotho and the Caledon River area without authorization from Shaka. His military fought a major battle against the AmaNgwane near modern Ladybrand as independent oral traditions from the AmaZulu, AmaNgwane, and BaSotho confirm.[153] After the AmaNgwane defeat of the AmaHlubi, "Matiwane was presently attacked by the Zulus, just as if they had come to interfere in the fighting going on. Matiwane was then chased by the Zulus via Basutoland; he was caused to cross the Isangqu [Orange River], but the Zulus did not cross."[154] These place references indicate that the passage refers explicitly to the AmaNgwane migration from Lesotho south to the Transkei in 1827. Fynn's evidence also appears to confirm that the AmaZulu attacked the AmaNgwane while they were based in the Caledon River region.[155] According to him the AmaNgwane while living on the southern highveld near the Caledon River, were "again attacked by the Zulus, who took from them immense droves of cattle, which all died from the change of country."[156]

The AmaZulu oral traditions say little about this battle, probably because Shaka did not authorize it; that is, he did not hold ceremonies seeking ancestral approval and assistance, and the thousands of cattle seized as booty are said to have all perished on the long return journey. But the campaign is remembered by name as the *eyobutshinga impi* and identified as the one that had raided the AmaNgwane. The officers who commanded the troops were remembered by name as well with reference to the regiment under their command.[157] The BaSotho oral traditions remember these events also with reference to the names of those known to have been killed, including the prominent wives of several chiefs. BaSotho traditions agree with those of the AmaZulu that Dingane was among those who led the *impi* and suggest that it had been initiated in response to a message sent to Shaka by the rising chief of the emerging BaSotho kingdom, Moshoeshoe.[158]

Shaka's regiments appear to have crossed the Drakensberg at the end of 1826, and engaged in one of their first attacks at Clocolan in February

1827.[159] The primary goal appears to have been to raid for cattle, but in at least one place, civilians were said to have been put to death in an attack against a village.[160] Some oral traditions claimed that an AmaZulu regiment crossed to south of the Orange River before turning back to continue their attack and raid against Matiwane's AmaNgwane.[161] The locations and participants in the ensuing fights along the Caledon River valley were remembered by the AmaNgwane, who watched their cattle being swept away by the AmaZulu regiments.[162] Perhaps because one of the oral traditions originated from an eyewitness participant, an UmNgwane warrior, a major battle near Ladybrand involving several regiments from both sides facing off against each other is among the best documented of the conflicts that were fought in this AmaZulu military campaign. The same eyewitness also reported that Dingane was wounded in battle, stabbed in the chest with an assegai (spear), which might account for the suppression of later AmaZulu accounts of these events.[163] He also provided evidence of the high mortality suffered in the Ladybrand battle, for "[m]any warriors of both sides fell on that day, and, for years afterwards, the Basuto used to pick up fragments of weapons among little piles of human bones."[164] This was one of only two fights in the region of Lesotho during the 1820s said to have resulted in mortality figures that were counted in "the hundreds," other battles usually reported to have resulted in the death of no more than one or two dozen, and sometimes less.[165] The BaSotho and AmaNgwane witnessed the AmaZulu warriors driving off the cattle by the thousands. An AmaZulu source maintained that all of the cattle died of disease, so the AmaZulu may have returned without any booty from this *impi*. The European trader Isaacs witnessed their return and wrote, however, that the cattle were distributed by Shaka "among his people."[166]

The distribution of cattle as booty was indeed Shaka's primary means of maintaining the loyalty of his troops and ensuring their compliance with his commands as he sent them on military campaigns. Shaka had by then held the chieftaincy for about eleven years, but his rule had remained very tenuous until about 1824, by which time he had eliminated most of his potential rivals. Between 1824 and 1827, he had eliminated the threat of the AmaNdwandwe, as well as that posed by his main rivals who had been his subordinate chiefs paying tribute to him. But a vast number of people living over a wide territory had fallen under his rule without their voluntary consent, and his arbitrary and violent methods of rule would ultimately lead to the disaffection and alienation of even his own family, who had long provided him with loyal support. The new social and political configuration of the region of KwaZulu-Natal, in place by the last years of Shaka's reign, would not ensure his own continued rule. Nevertheless, the enrollment of almost twenty military regiments, the promotion of brave and successful soldiers, and the construction of major villages the size of small towns, would create an enduring legacy from the middle years of Shaka's reign.

Chapter 8

Royal Women: Authority and Subservience

In their contests over power and authority in the kingdoms and chiefdoms of precolonial KwaZulu-Natal, men relied on the assistance and support of their mothers, sisters, daughters, and wives. The interactions of royal women and royal men could and often did determine important historical events, including the survival and selection of the royal heir to the chieftaincy. Royal women were sometimes entrusted with significant roles of authority by their male kin, but they remained subject to the authority and control of royal men. Like other women, royal women operated in circumstances of women's subordination to men across society. Women's subordination was supported by dispensations in the allocation of decision making and authority in politics, in control over land and material resources, and in legal status and access to the courts, which privileged men exclusively and were denied to women. Insofar as royal women gained positions of authority, they did not enjoy autonomy and independence from royal men who maintained control over wealth and military forces. The women achieved their authority only upon its allocation to them by royal men, who retained the option to rescind women's appointments and privileges.

The evidence about women in the early precolonial history of KwaZulu-Natal is scant because when it was recorded in writing in the nineteenth and early twentieth centuries, it was done primarily by men of European origin seeking and recording information from African men. The most thorough description of events and conditions in Shaka's era with some evidence collected about the preconsolidation era is found in the writings of the British Port Natal traders Fynn, Isaacs, and Maclean (John Ross), and from the British administrator Shepstone, whose information is important in spite of the evident Eurocentric distortions. The scarcity of information about women in the recorded oral traditions is largely the result of a failure of the interviewers – whether Fynn, Shepstone, or Stuart – to ask about women individually or collectively, with the obvious exception of Shaka's mother Nandi. Women rarely appear in the oral traditions of precolonial KwaZulu-Natal, and only when their role at a given moment in history was important to the social and political dispensation, especially the birth, survival, or succession of an heir to a chieftaincy. Moreover, the success of the former AmaZulu chiefdom in consolidating control and achieving domination over the other chiefdoms and kingdoms of KwaZulu-Natal gave primacy to the retention and collection of information about the AmaZulu ruling family and followers while the histories of the families and women of incorporated kingdoms and chiefdoms were neglected. This situation leaves modern historians with an incomplete body of evidence about the precolonial women of KwaZulu-Natal, including royal women from other royal families whose historical roles and contributions were never recorded.

Studies of women in South African history have been extremely limited for the precolonial era.[1] Jeff Guy's studies of gender relations in precolonial KwaZulu-Natal remain important in drawing attention to the complicated ways in which gender relations intersected with socioeconomic divisions and stratification in society.[2] His seminal work, however, uses the misleading and exaggerated terminology of "oppression" to overstate a theoretical argument of gender-based precolonial class divisions.[3] Nevertheless, the evidence supports his important point that women were dependent upon and subordinate to men.[4] Guy also underscored the value of women's labor in crop cultivation, which created an incentive for male control over women's labor.[5] Sean Hanretta has made a valuable contribution to the study of women in precolonial KwaZulu-Natal. He shows that the consolidation of the Zulu "state" did not lead to the uniform lowering of women's status but rather generated much greater degrees of social, economic, and political stratification among women, as some women benefited from the positions of status and authority allocated to them by virtue of their attachment to the ruling family.[6] A recent article by Sifiso Ndlovu indicates the difficulties of reconstructing women's history when it has been entangled with and distorted by modern literary productions that blend history with fiction.[7] Dan Wylie's literary interpretation of Shaka and his era includes fragments of information about women, but his struggle to use and interpret the evidence with the inclusive and systematic methodology of historians has led him to various conclusions that the evidence does not support, including in his narratives about royal women.[8] Nevertheless Wylie, not an historian himself, is to be credited for attempting to reconstruct this era with an inclusion of the roles of women in a way that historians had not yet attempted.[9] Adam Kuper's study on bridewealth and marriage in southern Africa is indispensable; it includes an excellent presentation and analysis of historical evidence in case studies of Lovedu, Venda, Swazi, and Tsonga women and marriages.[10] Kuper's analysis demonstrates the conscious manipulation of marriages for social and political ends, and how women in public positions of authority nevertheless remained subject to their male relatives.

WOMEN IN PRECOLONIAL KWAZULU-NATAL

The control over women by chiefs was evident in their maintenance of separate and protected sections of the royal village for royal women and women sent as tribute to the chief. Among chiefs who kept these *izigodlo* before Shaka's reign were Senzangakhona himself, the AbaQwabe chief Phakathwayo, and the AbaTembu chief Ngoza, while the AmaHlubi chiefs, including Bhungane a contemporary of Dingiswayo and Senzangakhona, and his sons, did not keep *izigodlo*.[11] Chiefs before Shaka were said to have kept *izigodlo*, but the practice became formalized under Shaka and with the new creation of separate villages for military regiments, *amakhanda*, Shaka attached *izigodlo*, under the supervision of royal women, to these. During Shaka's reign, senior chiefs and important men were allowed to keep an *isigodlo* of their own, as could only be done by men who were wealthy and could demand the provision of women by their own subordinates.[12] This was a privilege that could only be awarded by Shaka himself, however. Even his subordinate chiefs who had formerly been independent could not presume to keep an *isigodlo* because doing so was presumptive of extremely high status and could be taken as a challenge to the king.[13] The provision of daughters was required of important men and served as a symbol of allegiance and form of tribute. When these women married, the *lobola* from the husband's family was first paid to the chief or king, but was then sent back to the woman's male kin.[14] The young women who were sent to Shaka lived either in the king's own *isigodlo* or in the women's quarter's that were attached to military villages, *amakhanda*. There they were overseen by a female relative of Shaka, and they cultivated fields to provide food for the men in the military barracks.[15] Baleni said, "[t]he girls used to leave the isigodhlo, three and four at a time, to cultivate the fields. When there was *amabele* [sorghum] to be carried from the gardens one might see a large number of girls going out to fetch it. They used to be accompanied by say an *inceku* [male servant of high status]."[16] At the capital, a hierarchy governed the status and work of women of Shaka's *izigodlo*; the women born and married into the royal house held a higher status and were not subjected to the tasks assigned to women brought in either as a form of tribute from important families or as captives taken after the defeat of their fathers or husbands.[17]

Social conventions afforded protection to women, although they were not always enforced. Shaka and his half brothers were forced into exile from AmaZulu territory for having sexual relations with young women, although this was generally viewed as a pretext for ridding the heir of his rivals.[18] Senzangakhona had a man killed for engaging in sexual relations with a woman of his *isigodlo*.[19] Shaka's most famous warrior, Komfiya "Zulu" ka Nogandaya, came from the AbaQwabe chiefdom with four other men to offer their allegiance because they feared for their lives at home after they became suspected of planning to meet some women secretly.[20] Two other AbaQwabe men – the famous warrior Nqetho and Sopane – had eloped with women with whom they had fallen in love but were forbidden to marry and "deserted" to the AmaZulu chiefdom.[21] The men married the AbaQwabe royal women after they *khonza'd* Shaka.[22] The story indicates the restrictions placed on royal women and the lengths both royal men and women would go to for the sake of a marriage of love and choice as they left the protections of family and gave up the perquisites of royalty.

In spite of protective social conventions there were many stories of Shaka's personal abusive treatment of women, such as catching and raping them when he was a young man still living among the AmaMthethwa.[23] It was reported that while on a trip to visit his eLangeni maternal relatives, Shaka "*hlobonga*'d with the girls. He caught hold of one and penetrated her, causing her to be pregnant. It was reported to Dingiswayo, who said, 'What can I do to this Zulu wrongdoer (*itshinga la kwa Zulu*)?' and took no further steps in the matter."[24] Generalizing about Shaka's behavior toward young women, Ngidi told Stuart, "[I]t is said that Shaka used to catch girls (whilst he was living with Ngomane), girls belonging to commoners, and have intercourse with them. When he met a girl in the path he would catch her and make her pregnant."[25]

All women were vulnerable in warfare although Dingiswayo was said to have avoided violence against women and children in military campaigns.[26] When chiefs resisted incorporation by Shaka in a tributary status, however, they had to migrate with their followers to seek refuge beyond the reach of his military, and the entire migratory population remained vulnerable if an attack were launched against them. After a battle against the AbaTembu under chief Ngoza, when AmaZulu troops were pursuing Ngoza's people in flight, Shaka's warriors are reported to have found and killed many of the women and children.[27] The AbaTembu reached the territory of the AmaMpondo where the latter were said to have cut off the hands of "all of Ngoza's *isigodhlo* girls" to remove their brass arm rings. This indicates that the members of the royal household had survived their earlier battle with the AmaZulu only to suffer an appalling fate somewhat later.[28] When attacked by the AmaZulu, the AmaChunu were unsuccessful in securing the women and children, some of whom were reportedly killed after the defeat of the AmaChunu warriors.[29] The occasion of the greatest battlefield fatality of women occurred when Shaka led a huge military expedition of about fifty thousand people in May 1826 against the AmaNdwandwe. At the enemy encampment, the AmaNdwandwe warriors surrounded the herds of cattle while their women and children were placed in security in the mountain above.[30] The AmaZulu and their allies secured a rapid military victory, however, and many of the women and children, along with the wounded defeated AmaNdwandwe warriors, were killed after their defeat, although the numbers were exaggerated and many also survived.[31] During Shaka's reign, women whose fathers or husbands had been defeated in battle were treated as booty and given by Shaka as rewards to men who had proved their courage in battle and demonstrated their loyalty to him.[32]

Women also sometimes accompanied military expeditions in their individual capacities or as members of regiments of young women. Girls, like boys, served as mat carriers for the warriors.[33] The expedition against the AmaNdwandwe was accompanied by women and girls carrying beer, corn, and milk, who each returned home as soon as the food they carried had been consumed.[34] Shaka recruited women, including royal women, into their own regiments as the AbaQwabe had done under Phakathwayo.[35] Some of the women may have been trained to fight and given weapons. According to oral reports even royal women accompanied military campaigns:

Shaka himself went with his *impi* to Pondoland on what is known as the "*ihlambo* of Nandi" *impi*, and took Mnkabi, one of Senzangakona's greater *amakosikazi*, mother of Nozilwane. This woman was taken ill at the Mtamvuna, across the Mzimkulu, and died there. Her corpse was carried back to Zululand and buried either at Siklebeni or Dukuza.[36]

In the oral traditions, the presence of these regiments of young women was indicated only with specific reference to the late (second) major military campaign against the AmaMpondo in 1827, when "with the Amampondo *impi* went the girl regiments, the Ntshuku, Mcekeceke and Mvutwamini. Each of these carried war-shields (*iziHlangu*)."[37]

The sociopolitical organization of the region into chiefdoms under the rule of the head of a ruling family created opportunities for royal women to influence politics in important ways. For hundreds of years the maintenance of accurate oral traditions of genealogies and the relations between different lines of descent had been vital for maintaining knowledge and claims of legitimacy to rule over small and large chiefdoms. Lines of descent were used to determine eligibility for marriage in a strictly exogamous society, which discouraged deliberate inventions and distortions of genealogies. The practice of patrilineal inheritance and polygamy presumed that the senior wife of a chief, who presided over his senior "house," would produce the male heir, but other members of the ruling family, including brothers or junior sons, remained eligible to succeed to the chieftaincy and an heir was selected by the senior members of the family following the death of a chief. The payment of *lobola* or bridewealth upon marriage transferred rights over the children of the marriage to the father's line of descent while the wife retained her membership and affiliation with her paternal line of descent and associated symbolic greetings and praises, the *izibongo*.[38] This continued relationship of a married woman with her paternal family made marriage alliances an important source of building social and political, and consequently military, alliances, between families and, in the case of royal families, between their chiefdoms. Marriages were therefore a key means of establishing and reinforcing political alliances between ruling houses of different chiefdoms as well as between chiefs and the most important men of their chiefdoms, such as their counselors, appointed officials or *indunas*, and prominent wealthy men under their authority. As wives, mothers, sisters, and daughters, in their marriages women reproduced lines of descent and forged and reproduced social and political bonds and alliances in a form of political reproduction.[39] A chief or king could call upon the political or military support of the men and families to which he was related by marriage.

ROYAL WOMEN: MARRIAGE ALLIANCES AND SUCCESSION

The earliest royal woman claiming a place in the oral traditions that were still told at the end of the nineteenth century was Nozidiya, said to have been the wife of Chief Malandela and mother of the AmaZulu progenitor, Zulu himself and his elder brother Qwabe.[40] Oral traditions were in accord that although Qwabe was her elder son, Nozidiya favored Zulu such that Qwabe took offense and migrated away with his own followers, to form his own separate chiefdom. The story is significant in what it reveals about the prerogatives of an early woman of a ruling chiefdom. Nozidiya is said to have cultivated and sold enough sorghum [*amabele*] that "people used to come and buy from her."[41] In exchange for the sorghum, Nozidiya acquired her own cow and then a small herd of cattle, some of which she gave to her favored son Zulu, although not to Qwabe who thus moved away with his followers. This portrayal of a woman who was able to produce surplus grain and then gain her own property in cattle to dispense with as she chose indicates a high degree of autonomy for a royal wife. The praises, *izibongo*, of the mother of the early Zulu chief Ndaba, who was Mtoniya daughter of Zingelwayo, express the respect she commanded that was compensate with the role she was said to have played in ruling matters during her son's reign.[42]

From the oral traditions it is evident that chiefs often chose their wives from the royal houses of other chiefdoms, thus creating or reinforcing political alliances. After the AmaCele chiefdom migrated under Chief Mkokoleli from the coastal region of the AmaMthethwa chiefdom to south of the Thukela River in the mid-eighteenth century, his followers intermarried with the AmaThuli who had preceded them to the area. The AmaThuli tendered their submission and allegiance to Chief Mkokoleli. He married a daughter of the UmThuli Chief, Masivuba, and she became the mother of his heir Dibandhlela.[43] When Dibandhlela inherited the chieftaincy, he married an UmQwabi wife, Siwetu, who was the daughter of the AbaQwabe chief Khondlo, and she bore Dibandhlela a son, Magaye.[44] Dibandhlela designated Magaye as his heir while the latter was still a child and to protect the heir sent him to be raised among his mother's people, the AbaQwabe, by his mother's brother, chief Phakathwayo. The decision to send the heir of a chief to be raised by his maternal relatives while a child is remembered in the oral traditions about numerous southern African chiefs in this period, including most famously Shaka himself. The commonly understood reason was that the maternal family would protect the heir, whereas at the home of the chief the heir was in constant danger because there were many other contenders to the inheritance who would benefit from his death.[45]

Wives and daughters of the royal family also became involved in controversy over succession to the AmaMthethwa chieftaincy. Chief Jobe's sons by two different wives – Godongwana, born about 1765 and later known as Dingiswayo, and his half brother Mawewe – came into conflict after Mawewe's mother informed her husband Jobe that his son by another wife, Godongwana (Dingiswayo) planned to assassinate him, perhaps with the aid of another son Tana. This oral tradition suggests the means by which royal women might conspire to ensure the succession of their own son at the expense of another potential heir, although it is also possible the conspiracy was real. Dingiswayo and Tana were forced to flee, and Tana was killed. In the elaborate version of this oral tradition collected by Shepstone in the 1840s said that Dingiswayo was said to have been stabbed in the back by a double barbed *assegai* at the same time that Tana was killed and sought help from his sister to save his life. She reportedly extracted the spear and gave him provisions and a leather blanket that allowed him to disguise an attendant who helped him make his escape from the search parties who still sought to kill him.[46] After Dingiswayo escaped with the aid of his sister, he found temporary refuge with his mother's relatives before going farther afield into exile.[47] This man who would inherit the AmaMthethwa chieftaincy and achieve fame for his expansion of the authority and rule of the royal AmaMthethwa house over a wide region, including over the small AmaZulu chiefdom, survived to do so only because his royal sister had long before saved his life from their father's vengeance.[48]

Several royal families intermarried with the AmaSwazi royal family of Sobhuza. Sobhuza's own mother was a daughter of Chief Simelane from what became northern Zulu territory, so Sobhuza allowed members of the Simelane family and their followers to settle in the south of Swaziland. Sobhuza asked the AmaHlubi chief Mthimkulu to send him one of his daughters to become his wife and sent 140 head of cattle as *lobola* for her. Later AmaHlubi Chief Langalibalele married a daughter of Sobhuza's in return.[49] AmaSwazi oral traditions remember that Shaka sent to Sobhuza to ask for his daughter in marriage and that the Swazi king sent his first-born daughter, Mpandeze. She was then, according to these AmaSwazi traditions, put to death when she became pregnant, an event that shocked the AmaSwazi and ensured that no future AmaZulu kings were sent women of the AmaSwazi family for marriage.[50] The information is credible because it came from a member of the AmaSwazi royal family and indeed one of Sobhuza's own sons, Giba ka Sobuza. He told Stuart,

> King Shaka asked Sobuza for one of his daughters in marriage. Sobuza acquiesced and gave him his first-born daughter named Mpandeze. It appears that this girl became enceinte, whereupon Shaka, without in any way consulting Sobuza, caused her to be put to death. The Swazis were much surprised at this arbitrary action and regarded it as an insult...No Swazi princesses or others were given in marriage to any of the subsequent Zulu kings, although marriages took place between Swazis and the Zulu indunas Masipula, Mnyamana, and Seketwayo.[51]

The AmaSwazi royal family did continue to intermarry with other important families of *induna*s of KwaZulu-Natal. The AmaNdwandwe chief Zwide also sent his youngest daughter Thandile to marry Sobhuza, where she became the Swazi queen Lazide, known after her father's name, and bore Sobhuza's heir Mswazi.[52] This marriage alliance between Sobhuza and Zwide's daughter later secured the survival of a portion of the AmaNdwandwe chiefdom, for after Shaka defeated Zwide, his son Madangala sought protection with his sister, Sobhuza's wife and the Swazi queen, and he was received and given land by Sobhuza.[53] One of Sobhuza's daughters was married to Mgazi, a royal member of the Maseko chiefdom, but Sobhuza drove the Maseko away after they tried to kill her.[54]

The AbaQwabe chief Khondlo married a sister of Dingiswayo from the AmaMthethwa chiefdom in the mid-eighteenth century, which was given in the oral traditions as the reason Khondlo never fought against the AmaMthethwa.[55] Dingiswayo's sister was the mother of Nomo, a prominent half brother of Khondlo's designated heir Phakathwayo. Phakathwayo's mother was Zunguse, of Ngadi origin, and therefore he was considered to be less likely to be influenced by powerful outsiders, the AmaMthethwa of Dingiswayo, than would Nomo.[56] Khondlo originally nominated Nomo, one of his elder sons, to be his heir, but his people challenged this choice on the basis that Nomo would have divided loyalties and be overly influenced by his UmThethwa mother, Dingiswayo's sister.[57] After the chiefdom refused him as heir, Nomo went off to the AmaMtetwa and took refuge among his mother's powerful relatives. Some time later Kondlho's sons, including Phakathwayo, visited Dingiswayo to have him settle their dispute over the inheritance of the chieftaincy, but his pronouncement was ambiguous.[58] When Khondlo died and Phakathwayo was installed, Nomo's mother's people, Dingiswayo's AmaMthethwa, provided Nomo with warriors to attack Phakathwayo and contest the AbaQwabe chieftaincy, but Phakathwayo's forces defeated them, and Nomo lived out his life among the AmaMthethwa.[59] In this inheritance dispute, the maternal relatives of one potential heir to one of the largest chiefdoms of KwaZulu-Natal, themselves of a different and equally powerful royal family, provided him refuge and protection as needed and helped him try to secure the chieftaincy, but in the end, their attempt failed.

Aside from information about royal marriages, and the AmaZulu ruling family, little was recorded about individual women. An exception was the AmaNdwandwe queen, Zwide's mother Ntombazi, who was remembered because of her influence over him. Ntombazi was said to keep the skulls of defeated enemies in her house and to use various magical means to enhance her powers and her influence over her son.[60] When the AmaMthethwa chief Dingiswayo was captured and Zwide hesitated to kill him, he is reported to have then done so on the insistence of his mother Ntombazi. Shaka was said to have burned down her hut during the decisive AmaZulu attack of about 1821.[61]

Macibise was identified as a chief in her own right, although she was probably serving only as queen regent during the minority of a male heir to the chieftaincy. Her chiefdom was a branch of the AmaBhaca who lived originally near Pietermaritzburg, although many subsequently resettled to the south. Macibise was also remembered for successfully defending her chiefdom and her cattle from the attack of the AmaCunu chief Macingwane. Her followers also were attacked by Ngoza and the AbaTembu on their migration route to the south.[62]

The relationships established by marriage alliances between royal families of different chiefdoms were not always friendly. After the AmaNdwandwe chief Zwide was unable to defeat his AmaMthethwa rivals militarily, he sent his daughter to marry the AmaMthethwa chief, Dingiswayo. On Zwide's instructions, his daughter is said to have secretly collected her new husband's semen and sent it back so that her father could use it to make a concoction that would weaken Dingiswayo through magical means, and it was believed to have been successful.[63]

The vulnerability of women to the demand of a chief is evident in the oral traditions about women associated with Shaka's maternal cousin Makedama, himself an heir to the eLangeni chieftaincy before it was consolidated into Shaka's expanding AmaZulu kingdom. In attempt to escape Shaka's authority Makedama led some eLangeni followers to seek refuge among the AmaNdwandwe under Zwide. After they arrived and had built their new settlement, the AmaNdwandwe king demanded as wives some of the women who had accompanied Makedama. These eLangeni women insulted Zwide and refused to marry him on the grounds that he was too old, and his own AmaNdwandwe royal women are also said to have scolded him. Zwide issued a threat against the lives of the eLangeni women, and Makedama led them and the young men to seek refuge with the AmaMthethwa living under Dingiswayo's brother, Sigewu.[64]

SENZANGAKHONA AND ROYAL WOMEN

During the reigns of Senzangakhona and Shaka, the women who were born into and married the AmaZulu ruling line of descent gained in stature and authority as the men of the AmaZulu royal house came to rely on them increasingly in the administration of an expanding territory and subject population. The influence and formal authority of these women, known as *amakhosazana*, daughters of the royal house, and *amakhosikazi*, chiefs' wives or queens of the royal house, was nevertheless always subject to the superior decision-making authority of the men of their royal line. During the nineteenth century different branches of the ruling line of descent of the AmaZulu chiefdom came to be known by several different names, arising out of events that occurred during the reign of Shaka. These nominal distinctions did not, however, diminish the central roles of all men born into the royal descent lines. During the reigns of both Senzangakhona and Shaka the male uncles, cousins, and nephews of the chief played decisive roles in protecting the interests of the AmaZulu ruling family and administering the region that fell under their rule, moderating and overshadowing the roles of the royal women. The familial relationships created the context in which the *amakhosikazi* gained certain levels of position and authority, both individually and collectively.[65] Jama's children included at least fourteen sons and four daughters.[66] Senzangakhona's half brother Zivalele was said to have been herding with Senzangakhona at the time Senzangakhona met Shaka's mother Nandi and played a leading role throughout his reign.[67] Senzangakhona's half brother Sojisa and his sons Mapita and Tokotoko remained leading royal members of the Zulu kingdom in the nineteenth century as *izikhulu* ruling their own territories under Shaka and his successors. Senzangakhona's elder brother Nkwelo was born into the "left-hand" house of Jama and therefore was not entitled to inherit the chieftaincy. His son Mudhli, however, served as regent upon the death of Jama (Mudhli's grandfather) until Jama's designated heir Senzangakhona came of age. Even after Senzagakona assumed the chieftaincy, Mudhli continued to be "the leading and responsible head of the Zulu tribe" and took an active role in the affairs of the ruling family throughout Senzangakhona's reign.[68] Jama's brother Coko (Xoko) headed what came to be known as the Biyela branch of the royal family, and his son Menziwa ka Coko, Senzangakhona's first cousin, was consulted in the inheritance dispute after Senzangakhona's death.[69] The son of Zivalele (Sitayi) was Mbopha, who was Senzangakhona's nephew and first cousin to Shaka, and became a leading counselor to Shaka and later his assassin.[70] Shaka's great military commander was Mdhlaka ka Ncidi, whose genealogy places him in a junior line of descent of Jama's father Ndaba.[71] As influential as the *amakhosikazi* became, some achieving the influence and authority of male *izikhulu* of the royal house, like individual royal men, they remained subject to the collective decisions of the senior men of the ruling family.

The first dramatic story involving women of the AmaZulu royal house is found in oral traditions about Shaka's father Senzangakhona as a young man early in the second half of the eighteenth century. Because Jama had died before his heir Senzangakhona had come of age, Jama's grandson from his left-hand house, Nkwelo's son Mudhli, became regent. Coming from Jama's left-hand house, Mudhli was a safe choice as regent because he could have no claim or pretentions to the chieftaincy himself. In addition, Jama's daughter Mnkabayi is said to have served as regent after her father's death, presumably because she was Senzangakhona's sister by the same mother.[72] Mnkabayi's position as an *umkhosazana*, a princess born into the royal house, and as a sister of the heir by the same mother, had a vested interest in protecting him and the interests of the royal house. Her first appearance in the oral traditions depicts her as literally saving the life of her brother, the heir Senzangakhona, fulfilling her duty as regent and thus his protector. A convoluted oral tradition that may be apocryphal indicates that Vubukulwayo, a son of Jama, was allowed to take Senzangakhona's mother, Mntaniya, as his wife according to the custom of *ukungena* normally allowed to a deceased man's brother.[73] This gave Mntaniya's new husband, himself a royal son and potential heir, additional interest in the inheritance of the chieftaincy for his own son by Mntaniya. She is said to have conspired with her new husband to murder her own son Senzangakhona. The two sent him a container of poisoned beer, which Senzangakhona's sister Mnkabayi intercepted and prevented him from drinking. She was suspicious, and to confirm her suspicions, poured out a portion of the beer and refilled the vessel with fresh beer, which was then returned to Mntaniya and her new husband.[74] According to this telling of the story, both conspirators drank the mixture of fresh and poisoned beer and died of their own poison. However, Mntaniya appears in oral traditions after Shaka's birth, so if the story is true in any part, it is probably mistaken in its outcome with regard to Senzangakhona's mother.[75] No matter how much of this oral tradition was true, it reflects a belief that Mnkabayi had loyally served the royal house as queen regent after Jama's death in saving the life of his heir Senzangakhona.

Senzangakhona married at least nine or ten wives. His first and senior wife was Mnkabi ka Sodubo, and Shaka's mother Nandi was said by some traditions to have been placed as a junior wife in her house.[76] Mnkabi's daughter Nozilwane married a member of the eLangeni royal house, a son of Nandi's brother.[77] Mpikase was the mother of Senzangakhona's heir Sigujana (also known as Mfokazi) and of Dingane. Songiya was the mother of Mpande, Nzibe, and a daughter Ntikili.[78] Mpande was said to have been born of a ceremonial union in an *umsizi* hut, supposedly making him ineligible for the inheritance of the chieftaincy although exceptions could be made in the absence of any other legitimate claimant.[79] Senzangakhona married Mudhli's daughter Zitshungu, and made her his chief wife at the royal *umuzi*, eNgwegweni, where she still presided "when the Zulu war was fought."[80] Senzangakhona's other wives included Langazana, daughter of Gubetshe, whom he placed at the ceremonially important village of Siklebeni; she was known to have many followers, Her villages were eZembeni, eNkonjeni, eNdhlwayini, and eNtonteleni.[81] Senzangakhona's favorite wife was said to have been Bhibhi ka Nkobe (Sompisi), sister of the great *induna* Ndhlela ka Sompisi, and sometimes mistakenly identified as Sigujana's mother. Senzangakhona's wife Nomawaru (Nomahawu) became "chief wife at Dukuza," although this was presumably during Shaka's reign.[82] Senzangakhona also married Nozibuku of the Nxumalo branch of the AmaNdwandwe, Ngcaka ka Mncinci, Magulana ka Ntshongolo of the AbaQwabe, and Bandile.[83]

Senzangakhona's many sons made up the ranks of the next generation of the AmaZulu royal family. Their numbers are significant in indicating the strength of the royal house through the reigns of Senzangakhona and Shaka and the wider context in which AmaZulu *amakhosikazi* found themselves. Of at least twenty-four sons of Senzangakhona, Shaka,

Dingane, and Mpande ruled after him, and Sigujana as his designated heir succeeded him briefly before being killed by Shaka. Another son, Mahlangana, later assisted in the assassination of Shaka.[84] Senzangakhona's sons Mfihlo, Nqgojana, Mqubane, and others lived throughout Shaka's reign, only to be later killed by Dingane.[85] A number of his sons entered into important marriage alliances with other chiefdoms, including the AmaMthethwa.[86] Many of Senzangakhona's daughters were also remembered by name, and their marriages indicate Senzangakhona's strategies of building alliances through royal marriages. Nozilwane married into the nearby eLangeni royal house, and Mantongela married a man of the nearby Buthelezi chiefdom. Sikaba married a man of the Mbatha chiefdom, Zayi married an Mdlalose man, and Mtembazi married a man of the Mgazini branch of the Zulu royal line of descent. Senzangakhona was in a subordinate tributary relationship to the AmaMthethwa chief Dingiswayo, and his wife Bhibhi's daughter Nomqoto married among the AmaMthethwa, as did Ntikili, Nomanqa, Matejwase, Nomzinhlanga, and Maqukazi. Senzangakhona's other daughters included Ziwelile, Noziqungu, and Mndibili.[87] Senzangakhona's daughter Mafungwase, known as Nomcoba, and said to be a full sister of Shaka, married Myandeya ka Mbiya, brother of the AmaMthethwa chief Dingiswayo himself. Another daughter, Nomqoto, married Dingiswayo's brother Tshangana.[88]

Senzangakhona's most famous wife was Shaka's mother Nandi, who herself was the product of a royal marriage between two chiefdoms. Her father Mbengi, chief of the neighboring chiefdom of eLangeni, married Mfunda, daughter of the AbaQwabe chief Khondlo, and sister of AbaQwabe chief Phakathwayo.[89] When Mnkabayi is said to have secretly saved Shaka as a baby from her brother Senzangakhona by lying to Senzangakhona and warning Nandi to flee, this role was in accord with Mnkabayi's duties as a regent. As regent, she was to safeguard an heir to the position of the chieftaincy and not merely to oversee her brother Senzangakhona's personal affairs.[90] Senzangakhona's mother Mntaniya, said to have tried to have poisoned Senzangakhona, was also portrayed in one version of this story as saving his child and heir Shaka. When Mnkabayi had the man who had reported to Senzangakhona the presence of the baby Shaka at the village put to death, it was an indication of her authority as regent.[91] However, Mudhli is said to have been the senior male family member who made the decisions regarding Shaka from the time the eLangeni first informed the AmaZulu royal family of Nandi's pregnancy.

ROYAL WOMEN DURING THE REIGN OF SHAKA

After Senzangakhona died, Shaka led his maternal relatives home and killed his father's heir Sigujana to assume the chieftaincy himself.[92] There is some evidence that the AmaZulu royal family, or at least his paternal aunt Mnkabayi, preferred Shaka to assume the chieftaincy upon the death of Senzangakhona. Some oral traditions reported that Mnkabayi ruled temporarily herself, and the symbolic role of the heir was denied to Sigujana at Senzangakhona's funeral, supporting this contention.[93] Mnkabayi may have even sent for Shaka and used delaying tactics before his arrival.[94] According to one report, the royal women, Mnkabayi, Mawa, and Mmama favored Shaka because his mother was royal and had been in the house of Senzangakhona's chief wife Mnkabi (not to be confused with his sister Mnkabayi), whereas the mother of Sigujana and Dingane held no rank.[95]

It would be a mistake to exaggerate the roles of the *amakhosikazi*, and Mnkabayi in particular, with regard to these events, however. Ngidi said Shaka had been called back by some of his own people, and he specified:

> Shaka was called by Menziwa ka Coko (Xoko) of the Biyelo people in the Zulu country, Mnkabayi, Mawa, and Mmama. They objected to Sigujana being king on the ground that his mother Mpikase was not a woman of rank, and that Nandi, the daughter of Mbengi, was. Hence Shaka's selection.[96]

Ngidi believed that although Sigujana had been installed as chief following Senzangakhona's death, Shaka was called back because Sigujana was disliked by his own people. This sentiment was widespread among the men as well as the women of the royal family, so Mnkabayi was voicing and supporting a popular opinion when she favored Shaka. Although Senzangakhona's uncle Zivalele supported Sigujana as chief, the royal men supporting Shaka included not only Coko's son Menziwa – Senzangakhona's first cousin – but also Mudhli and Sojisa, Senzangakhona's influential uncle. Ngidi said,

> The Zulu people (uZulu) objected to Sigujana being made the heir, seeing that his mother was Mpikase, whereas the chief wife was Mnkabi, and Shaka's mother Nandi had been put into her house. The Zulus wanted to know what the objection was to Shaka's being the heir. Menziwa ka Cogo, Mudhli ka Nkwelo, Sojisa ka Jama, Renqwa and others, also Mnkabayi and Mmama ka Jama, also Mawa, objected to Sigujana being appointed.[97]

Mudhli, who had served as regent during Senzangakhona's minority, had ensured that Shaka survived his infancy and had overseen his care before he went as a young man to live under Dingiswayo but was not rewarded for his efforts on behalf of Shaka. On Dingiswayo's advice, Shaka had several senior men of the AmaZulu royal house in addition to the heir Sigujana put to death upon his return. Shaka is said to have sent *impi*s of men to kill Mudhli and his uncles (Senzangakhona's half brothers) Zivalele, Sojisa, and Nobongoza as he entered the country.[98] Shaka would continue to rely instead on the royal women of the older generation, including Mnkabayi, as well as his brothers, from the AmaZulu royal house.

The sociopolitical organization of the AmaZulu chiefdom persisted after Shaka assumed the chieftaincy and amalgamated subject chiefdoms into a new composite kingdom. In his extension of authority over a wider territory and vastly larger population, Shaka made use of his female as well as male relations. Shaka's paternal aunts continued to wield significant influence in the royal family. Senzangakhona's sisters Mnkabayi and Mmama retained authority in their respective villages of Baqulusi and Esisebeni near Nobamba (Lobamba), the former capital, and Mnkabayi "had charge of the people of a district and used to stay there, at ebaQulusini."[99] Another sister, Mawa ka Jama, "belonged to" the Intontela village and stayed with it when it moved to a new site under *induna* Sotobe.[100] Sikile (Sizikile) ka Jama remained the *inkhosikazi* of the royal *ikhanda* of Ndabakewombe.[101] Shaka continued to honor his paternal grandmother (who had rescued him as an infant). Her death in 1824 was marked by dramatic public scenes of mourning that were expected upon the death of a royal family member.[102] Shaka's maternal eLangeni relations who had gone into exile with him among the AmaMthethwa and then returned with him were placed at Gibixegu, which then became known as Bulawayo, his first capital.[103] Shaka built separate villages for his mother Nandi and for her two other children whose paternity was disputed. Nandi's village was only a few kilometers from Bulawayo, and the Iziyendane regiment made up of former AmaHlubi men who had given allegiance to Shaka, including members of the AmaHlubi royal family, were placed there with her as her protection.[104] The fate of Nandi's reputed second husband Gendeyana was not known, but he did not accompany her when she returned to the AmaZulu chiefdom.[105] Shaka built villages for his sister Nomcoba, who lived at eSiklebeni and had a village called eKuhlupuzeni.[106] Shaka's brother Ngwadi was also given "authority over a large number of people" and "a large impi" (i.e., regiment).[107] Shaka's half brother Dingane, who had also been in exile among the AbaQwabe, returned to give allegiance to Shaka and was given authority over the AmaZulu territory north of the Thukela River, including over the royal women to whom positions of authority over districts in this region had been given.[108] Shaka treated Dingane as his presumptive heir, but Shaka also built a special village for his half-brother Mpande, through whom he hoped the royal succession would be ensured.

Shaka's royal household occupied an estimated forty-five to fifty huts, with an additional 1500 huts in the later capital of Dukuza. To reach Shaka's quarters, hidden by fenced walling and surrounded by "courtyards and housing of increasing size and elegance," required passing through several gates.[109] In a special protected section of his quarters, Shaka kept women in seclusion in their own *isigodlo* quarters. The women of his *isigodlo* numbered an estimated 150 to 200 and were not allowed contact outside of their living quarters where they were kept sequestered.[110]

The girls of the *isigodhlo* were presented as tribute (*isitulo*) to the Zulu king. The *izinceku* [men servants] used to go out, and when they saw any good-looking girl they would report and the girl would be taken. The king would send for her. All persons of importance would present daughters to the king. All great men would do this. And whenever any person should be killed, all the children would be taken to enlarge the *isigodhlo*. Up to the Zulu War this practice obtained, and very large numbers came by it to be in the *isigodhlo*.[111]

It was well known that Shaka had sexual relations with the women of his *isigodlo* at the capital who were the daughters of the prominent men of the kingdom. Subordinate and tributary chiefs and their royal male relatives as well as wealthy men of the kingdom were required to make lengthy stays themselves at the capital and to provide a daughter to live in the women's quarters there. In addition, however, the lives of these women served to guarantee the loyal behavior of their influential and powerful fathers and brothers across the kingdom because the women remained subject to Shaka's arbitrary favor or wrath and were sometimes put to death. Ordinarily a woman's paternal relatives were able to protect her from abuse even after marriage, but such protections were not available to the women of Shaka's *isigodlo*. In one incident, Shaka is said to have killed a young woman who refused to have sexual relations with him on the ground that he was ugly and she preferred death.[112] Another story related that Shaka sent home a young woman after she urinated in her bed, and on Shaka's specific order, her own father was said to have put her to death.[113]

Unlike previous AmaZulu chiefs and other chiefs and kings of the region, Shaka never formally married any women following his succession to the AmaZulu chieftaincy.[114] According to an oral tradition, however, before he returned to assume the AmaZulu chieftaincy, Shaka did marry one or more wives while he was still a military commander living among the AmaMthethwa. One of these wives was said to have borne a son, Shaka's biological child, but he recognized neither her nor the son.[115] This child would not have been eligible to inherit the AmaZulu chieftaincy because the AmaZulu royal family and their subjects did not pay the *lobola* to her family as was required for a chief's wife. In addition, Shaka had not yet been recognized as a chief or as designated heir at the time of the marriage and the birth of the child. Sometime after Shaka had left AmaMthethwa territory to become AmaZulu chief, the village of this wife was dispersed and Shaka's purported young son, Zibizendhlela, was said to have found refuge with his mother under chief Faku of the AmaMpondo.[116]

Although as chief, Shaka did not marry any women, he took many concubines, *izixebe*.[117] Although he did not marry them nor pay bride-wealth, *lobola*, for them, Shaka had sexual relations with the women of the *isigodlo* in his compound in the capital; their influential fathers and brothers were subject to his rule. Shaka did not pay *lobola* for them because the payment would have transferred the rights over any children they bore to the AmaZulu royal line of descent and would have thus given any sons from these relations a legitimate claim to the chieftaincy as Shaka's successor.[118] Shaka did not take precautions against impregnating his *izixebe*, however, and they relied upon medicinal solutions provided by doctors to terminate their pregnancies.[119] The doctors, *izinyanga*, provided the pregnant *izixebe* with herbal *umxubuzo* medicines, *izimbiza* herbs that induced abortion.[120] Those women who did not abort their pregnancies were reportedly put to death by a man named Ngozingozi, referred to in insulting terms by Stuart's informant.[121]

The oral traditions are in agreement that women who became pregnant by Shaka were put to death.[122] Evidently some were successfully secreted away to bear their child safely as long as secrecy was successfully maintained.[123] According to one explicit oral tradition,

Shaka had no children. Any girl getting in a family way by him would be got away to the outlying districts to her home on the plea that she was ill. There she would be treated in order to bring about an abortion. When the abortion had occurred and she was well again she would return, her entire absence being attributed to illness and not to pregnancy, or she would surely have been put to death.[124]

As reported by the young European observer Maclean (John Ross), who spent two years from about age fourteen living in Shaka's compound with full access to the women of the *isigodlo*, Shaka may well have spared the life of his half brother Dingane with the understanding that he would become his successor. For that reason and to prevent a direct claim against himself, it was understood that Shaka would not allow the birth of a legitimate heir, a son born to a wife for whom *lobola* had been paid.[125] Because even a son not legitimated through the payment of such bridewealth might also make a claim or use force to seize the chieftaincy, only preventing the birth of any biological son of Shaka would have ensured the succession of one of his half brothers such as Dingane.

Maclean knew that "when any of these women who were called umntwana (princess) showed symptoms of pregnancy, they were sent away from the court, and afterwards lived in great retirement and obscurity."[126] He further explained,

This was carrying out a part of the compact with his brother Dingane to have no heirs to interfere with his [Dingane's] succession. The writer was in a position to know that these women were not put to death on account of being *enceinte* [pregnant], having had the opportunity of meeting two of them after their banishment, as well as the children. But it was never hinted the latter were of the royal blood. The reader will not be disposed to doubt the correctness of this statement when I tell him that I enjoyed the extraordinary privilege of associating with these women in the very interior of the palace, where the foot of a male subject never pressed the floor, and that their habits and their history was as familiar to me as to themselves. So far from their dreading such a contingency, it was rather looked forward to with pleasure, as a relief from the dull monotony of their secluded life.[127]

NANDI'S DEATH

Most of the AmaZulu men and women who spoke to Stuart at the beginning of the twentieth century agreed that Shaka had killed his mother Nandi, or that he had ordered her to be killed.[128] In addition, most indicated that "he killed his mother for hiding one of his own children."[129] Baleka had been told Shaka stabbed her in the armpit, but Mabonsa said "he caused her to be put to death by having a rope tied round her neck then struck, she being strangled."[130] Melapi told Stuart that after Shaka found Nandi "holding in her arms a child which she stated was his," he reacted immediately and "[h]e then stabbed her in the stomach with a sewing awl – he may have got this awl from his mother's hut, for women might sew mats with such an instrument."[131] Melapi chose his words carefully to indicate that the story was hearsay but added that "[n]umbers whispered that Tshaka had himself killed his mother. Dinya does not credit the story." Stuart's efforts to trace the story and the joint effort of his interviewees to consider the evidence carefully are reflected here as elsewhere in these interviews, for Melapi also added, "I heard the story about Tshaka stabbing his mother with an awl from various people. The story arose during the mourning for Nandi."[132] Four of Stuart's interviewees dissented and believed Nandi had died from illness.[133] One said only the child had been killed on this occasion, and another said he was present at the time of her death, but as a child he would not have recognized any signs of a hidden wound previously inflicted, so his statement is not conclusive.[134] But Mabonsa was certain that Shaka had been responsible because after a large section of the AmaHlubi chiefdom had joined Shaka, he had made them into the Iziyendane regiment, also known as Nandi's regiment, and "those who *konza*'d Tshaka returned [to their original homes and left Shaka] on his killing his mother Nandi; they could not approve his killing his mother."[135] Later in the interviews, Mabonsa provided more details, saying "[o]n Nandi being murdered by Tshaka, many of the Iziyendane deserted from Tshaka and fled away through the Transvaal or Orange River Colony down along the Igwa [Vaal River] so as to be beyond his (Shaka's) reach. They feared they would be killed now Nandi, their patroness, had been murdered."[136]

Fynn, who saw Nandi on her deathbed, also was unaware of a wound, but in the most detailed explanation of events, Lunguza said the wound had been deliberately hidden:

Tshaka caused his own mother to be put to death on account of her having harboured his child. It was one of the *umdhlunkulu* [woman from the *isigodlo*] that went and told tales about Nandi having the child. "Go", the girl said, "to your mother. You will find her with something beautiful." Tshaka went there stealthily, for the evidence he wanted, then came back and sent an *inceku* [servant] to go and stab his mother and afterwards to cut the leather skirt and tie up the wound so that it could not be seen. The skirt was cut in the shape of a band. It was then said, "The *inkosikazi* [queen] is sick." No-one of course could go and see her. The child in question was also killed by the *inceku*.[137]

Lunguza referred to the source of his information, and both the details and his confidence in the sources lend credibility to this version of events. It is evident that this oral tradition originated in the inner circles of the AmaZulu capital at the time of Nandi's death. Her *inceku*, Mqumbela, was killed a few days later on Shaka's orders after he cried too much. Lunguza continued,

The child had been borne by one of the *umdhlunkulu* [woman of the *isigodlo*]. I do not know what the girl's name was. The child was a boy; even if it had been a girl the same thing would have happened. I heard, after Tshaka's death, and at Mgungundhlovu, that Tshaka had directed the *inceku* [servant] to go and kill Nandi, that he did not himself stab her. I know the wound was a small one, and may have been caused with an awl or small *assegai*.[138]

A member of the royal house, a son of Chief Mpande, discussed the possibilities with Stuart and with Mandhlakazi who was also present at the interview:

There is a rumour that Tshaka killed his mother for secreting a child of his. But she was not killed by him. He may have set an *inyanga* ["doctor"] on her. And this *inyanga*, adds Mandhlakazi, may have given her medicine made from the *umdhlebe* bush which causes blood to flow from one's nostrils as well as from the ear. The story goes that he went off to hunt elephants at the Mfolozi; this would support the theory, for whilst away the doctor would find a way of administering the deadly *umdhlebe* medicine or other virulent poison. Mgidhlana knows nothing of the stabbing theory, and thinks Tshaka would not have taken that course.[139]

Ngidi, who did not believe that Shaka killed Nandi, nevertheless did believe that she had showed him a child and identified it as his. He also said that the story Shaka had stabbed her was widely known and believed among the AmaZulu from the time of her death. Ngidi's narrative includes details of the conversation said to have been held between Shaka and Nandi, information that few people would have ever heard, but one of Ngidi's sources was Nandi's brother, who lived until late in the nineteenth century and who was with her at her death.[140] Nandi, according to this chain of testimony, is said to have provoked Shaka while holding a small child by saying to him, "Nongqaba, mother's Nongqaba! Your little seeds are spilling over, Whoever doesn't like them can just cook *izinkobe* [bread]."[141]

Ngidi continued,

Tshaka asked her where the child came from Nandi said "You ask me where it comes from? Don't you have a penis, then? Tshaka then left the hut. It is alleged he himself went for an assegai, returned, and forthwith stabbed his mother to death, after remarking to her that she knew he had disapproved of anything of this kind, i.e. having a child.[142]

The AmaZulu oral traditions, then, supported many aspects of Fynn's narrative of events surrounding Nandi's death, even though he was aware only that she had become gravely ill while Shaka was away. From Fynn's memoire the time of Shaka's move from Bulawayo can also be established as occurring at this time: "Shaka, now, for the first time having begun to hunt elephants with his whole force, Mr. King, Myself, and several other Europeans, being out on an excursion, met him on his return from one of these hunts."

Fynn continued,

Shaka insisted that I should accompany him to the kraal where he was going to reside.

After traveling slowly for two days, we passed his usual residence, Bulawayo, closely adjoining which was the kraal of Nandi, his mother, and, proceeding forward, arrived about nine at night, at the place Shaka intended to fix his residence, that is, the one he had come purposely to rebuild. This work was begun on the following morning.[143]

Fynn's evidence is critical in that it establishes where Shaka was for three days prior to Nandi's death, but it also provides evidence of consciousness of guilt on the part of Shaka, who chose this very moment to change his residence, away from that of Nandi.

Messengers now arrived to announce that Nandi was very unwell. Doctors were immediately dispatched, and also some European medicines which Shaka had been made a present of, and had by him, having first asked their uses. As messengers continued to arrive with accounts of the invalid [Nandi] getting worse, Shaka decided to return to her kraal accompanied by his forces.[144]

Fynn accompanied Shaka back to Bulawayo, traveling at night six hours from nine o'clock in the evening until three the next morning, and Shaka asked Fynn to attend to Nandi. Almost choking on the smoke in the hut that was "filled with native doctors and nurses," Fynn merely noted that "her complaint was dysentery" and if she had been stabbed in the anus – a customary form of punishment – as reported and was the bleeding from her bowels, this would have shown the same symptoms as dysentery. Fynn and Shaka rejoined the regiments until word was brought that she had died; then they all retired to put on their war attire as did Shaka. Everyone else, however, immediately removed every form of ornament from themselves as the observance of mourning began.[145] After Shaka "broke out into frantic yells" the people who were assembled at the capital, estimated by Fynn at fifteen thousand men and women, also began yells as lamentations. As news spread, the people from surrounding villages arrived to mourn, so that Fynn believed the crowd had reached 60,000 by the next day, when after a war song was ordered several men were executed and, "as if bent on convincing their chief of their extreme grief, the multitude commenced a general massacre." Fynn also believed this gave those present "the opportunity of revenging their injuries" against anyone else present, and that any sign of a person failing to mourn with tears was used as a pretext by others "mad with excitement" to beat them to death. As a result he calculated that seven thousand people had died around the capital village by the end of the afternoon, so that the stream was choked with bodies and the grounds were "flowing with blood."[146] From the description, these killings were as bad or worse than any field of battle on which the AmaZulu regiments had ever fought. Not until nightfall did Shaka give the orders that ended the killing.[147] The mourning continued, however, for several more days, and Shaka's subordinate chiefs, according to Fynn, sent out bodies of armed men to kill anyone who had failed to come to the mourning ceremonies, so that the killing went beyond the vicinity of the capital.

The AmaZulu oral traditions similarly remembered that many people were killed in the wake of Nandi's death, so that Fynn's descriptions are credible. Jantshi, who did not believe Shaka had killed her, said, "[t]here was very general mourning on her account. Tshaka himself cried. Many people were killed in the mourning for the *inkosikazi* [queen or chieftainess]."[148] One man said, "[p]eople's eyes were examined; if no tears, killed. The purification rituals after the death of his mother Nandi – many killed. Ngunuza of the eLangeni people ran away to the Mpondo country because afraid of being killed in the rituals."[149] Ndukwana remembered a comet appearing at the time of Nandi's death when he was about five years old, so he would have been born about 1822, making him the same age as others of Stuart's informants and his recollection therefore very probable. His evidence indicates that Nandi was buried with the ceremony accorded members of a royal family:

At the death of Tshaka's mother Nandi, everybody had to cry, and in order to pretend to be crying many used to put snuff into their eyes. There was a burial (*umgqibo*) for Nandi. A number of people were killed, three old women, three women, *izinceku*, as well as girls, to cook for her down below. They were included in the burial, for Nandi or persons of her rank cannot die alone. Whom would she be with down below? Tshaka killed his mother. When Nandi died dirges were chanted. At night an *ubaqa* [comet] appeared in the sky. People took pieces of burning wood and threw them at it. Ndwukana has a slight recollection of it; he was still very young, say five or six years old.[150]

So Fynn's information that several people were buried with Nandi's body is also credible. He believed they were buried alive. He wrote that Nandi was placed sitting in her grave near where she had died. He was not permitted to be there for the interment but was told by several eyewitnesses that ten girls of the kraal were buried alive with Nandi's body. As was appropriate for the daughter of an eLangeni chief, now a subordinate chiefdom within the AmaZulu kingdom, Nandi's royal brothers presided at the burial and stayed to watch over her grave for three months along with the eLangeni people themselves:

Nandi was buried by Tshangane, Nxazonke, Bantwana and Mbikwana. They remained three months at her grave at Bulawayo. Nandi died at Bulawayo. They watched over the grave. Manqondo and Sikawu were there, also all Langeni people. The proper persons to keep watch were members of the deceased's tribe and any others selected by Tshaka. I do not know where she was buried, inside or outside the Bulawayo kraal.[151]

Then the chiefs who were present considered whether "further sacrifices should be made" and at the suggestion of Shaka's counselor Ngomane, for three months no cultivation was allowed and no milk was to be used but rather poured out onto the ground. Furthermore, for a full year, all women found with to be pregnant were put to death along with their husbands.[152] These prohibitions and the harm they caused were also remembered by Stuart's informants:

I know Nandi's death – when the *amagula* [calabash milk containers] were buried in the *umbuga esibayeni* [thick woven walls of the cattle kraal] and the order was no cattle were to be milked. The cattle were milked by stealth late at night. It was said the cows too were to *kal'isililo se nkosikazi* [cry for the queen]. *Amasi* [milk curds] were *butshwa'd ebusuku* [taken out only at night]. I was kwa Kangela kwa Dingana when Nandi died.[153]

The mourning observances were a hardship because they were imposed on everyone who was a subject of the AmaZulu and Shaka's rule, and it was ordered that everyone observe them for a full year by. Ordinarily, similar prohibitions would be observed by the members of a family homestead for a month, and for six months to a year for a widow or widower. However, the other members of the household would be able to continue with the household production and consumption of food after their initial, much shorter period of mourning. Because Shaka also prohibited planting as well as harvesting of crops, the mourning prohibitions created food shortages that would last even beyond the prescribed year. Although this could not have been enforced beyond Shaka's territory among the AmaMpondo as Ngidi claimed, nevertheless he remembered the strictures and their reasons. He said that after Nandi's death,

People were forbidden to eat curds everywhere, even in Pondoland; only we eLangeni had milk. Because Tshaka had no mother, so all must stop having milk.

Ordinary people ate *incumbe* porridge, which is ground for children. The calves were fit to burst, there was so much milk.

The country was destroyed; it was destroyed by lack of food. Those who did not come and mourn were killed, and those who did not weep.[154]

But to avoid famine, people risked milking their cows and eating the milk curds at risk of punishment by death. Stuart was told,

Tshaka killed his own mother. After her death he caused the whole country to go into mourning. Cattle were not allowed to be milked; where an *igula* [calabash milk container] was found full of or with *amasi* [milk curds], all the inmates of the kraal were to be put to death; women were not allowed to become pregnant (*mita*) as no *zala*ing [bearing children] was allowed; *lima*'ing (hoeing) was forbidden; where *umbil'o ne kaba* [newly grown fresh cobs of maize or sorghum] was found inmates of kraals to be put to death; nor were *im'fino* [green vegetables] to be *ika*'d [picked and gathered]. Tshaka said all have mothers to *ika imfino* for them, but who was to do so for him?[155]

Another man remembered Nandi's death when he was very young because he remembered eating the meat from the cattle that had afterwards been ceremonially "smoked" to strengthen or "doctor" them, as was done in various ways to both people and food. He remembered that for a year no one ate milk curds, and "[g]ourds that year throughout were hidden in the bushes."[156] One of Shaka's subordinate chiefs was killed after his brother reported to Shaka that food had been taken to him during the period of mourning.[157]

Another man reported his own memories about the mourning period after Nandi's death:

Nandi died sometime after I was born, for I recollect the kind of food we ate after her death. Those who ate amabele were killed; it was said only milk and curds could be taken. There were people who used to go about inspecting, and if they saw faeces at any kraal, as they would do after a grass fire by their [the burning faeces] continuing to smoke, they would know that they had had *amabele* [sorghum, grain]. The people of such kraal would be put to death, for Tshaka said, "So he is living in a state of contentment" – i.e. he is satisfied with life; he is in a condition of prosperity and comfort, living in a state of enjoyment – "whereas I am lamenting because of my mother's death!"[158]

People also remembered that the prohibition on bearing children was enforced by the punishment of pregnant women. One man knew that his own mother had been hidden because she had become pregnant with his younger brother, whom she successfully bore; he believed that so many pregnant women were killed that Shaka had filled a "donga" (deep gully or ditch) with them, thus repeating the reference to a mass killing that had been used in other contexts and may have been a confused conflation from several distinct and unconnected stories.[159] At the time of Nandi's death, this informant was already a big enough boy to carry around his newborn brother. Another man told Stuart that although Shaka "gave orders that no children were to be borne throughout the country," the prohibition did not last long because "[a]fter a time, seeing that the strength of his army would be seriously affected by such an order, he rescinded it."[160] According to another story remembered among the AmaZulu, the country eventually had become so devastated by famine that a brave man, knowing he was risking his life, went to Shaka to ask him to end the food proscriptions:

[a]fter awhile a man Gala ka Nodade ka Mgutshwa ka Mutsha ka 'Zoko/Ndaba, of the Biyela tribe, having made up his mind that he would be killed for doing so, went to Tshaka, finding him at his Bulawayo kraal and acted as follows: He began by bongaing Jama, Senzangakona and Tshaka himself and then spoke to the king in these terms: – "What are you killing your country for?"[161]

Having thus invoked Shaka's ancestors, his father and grandfather, Gala ka Nodade asked Shaka if he meant to kill people, and how this appeared in the eyes of his ancestors. He asked how Shaka thought he could govern in this way while his people ate nothing and cattle were not milked, and he actually told Shaka he should "*fak' itsh'esisweni,*" meaning "pluck up" his "courage" and "be a man."[162] In an unexpected response,

Tshaka at once showed his approval of these bold sentiments for giving expression to which Gala had expected to lose his life. He [Shaka] called his *izinduna* Mdhlaka and Ngomane and said to them: Give ear to this man. Here is one who fills (inspires) me with courage. What kind of men do you fancy yourselves to be?[163]

He scolded his *induna* Mbopha who, like the other men, had not been able to dress respectably because he could not cut and retwist his hair-ring, so that it now hung long because the hair had grown out. Then Shaka gave Gala two head of cattle and told him, "you are a man" (*u yi ndoda*). According to this oral history, "after this the whole country experienced relief" and everyone restored their appearance and the mourning came to an end.[164] Instead of observing the traditional ceremony – washing the spears or *ihlambo* – to end the mourning period, Shaka ordered a military campaign against the AmaMpondo that came to be known as the *ihlambo* campaign.

Shaka's guilt in the death of his mother seems certain from the evidence. Shaka told Fynn his plans to move to Dukuza while he was out hunting, supposedly in ignorance that his mother lay dying, but as if he knew she were going to die. One man remembered, "Tshaka left Zululand for Dukuza after his mother's death, saying, 'It is the place of the *impaka*' [a possessed cat working for an evil supernatural being]."¹⁶⁵ Fynn wrote that this move occurred after the year of mourning and that when Shaka told Fynn he intended to prolong new mourning at Dukuza, Fynn pleaded that Shaka prohibit any killings. According to Fynn, Shaka laughed but agreed to comply, and Fynn then watched the ceremony in which Shaka was cleansed and purified at the new capital.¹⁶⁶

"AMAKHOSIKAZI", AUTHORITY, AND THE STATUS OF WOMEN

The lives of royal woman, even those with authority held by virtue of their birth into the royal house, were always insecure. The fate of many royal women was violent death upon the orders of the king, as evident in the deaths of Nandi during Shaka's reign and of various important *amakhosikazi* and *amakhosazana* on the orders of his successors Dingane and Mpande.

The women of the AmaZulu royal family held prestigious social roles as the heads of royal *imizi*, villages, and *izigodlo* attached to the barrack towns that housed military regiments, *amakhanda*. However, the women received their authority from royal male kin, and their decisions were always subject to the oversight of the senior men of the royal family.

The subordination of women to men institutionally was evident in customs of marriage, bridewealth, and the *izigodlo*. Dingane reportedly said, "I do not want an *isigodhlo*. That is what is destroying the people."¹⁶⁷ Nzobo objected because, as he said, "You can't be called a king if you have no *isigodhlo*. How, without one, can you be a king?" The centrality of the *isigodlo* was more than symbolic, for in it were the women who had been sent as tribute from subordinate chiefs and important, powerful families. Dingane explained, according to this oral tradition, that he did not want an *isigodlo* because "[i]t is the *isigodhlo* which is the cause of people always being put to death. It is a bad institution." Nzobo objected that "the killing of people is a proper practice, for if no killing is done there will be no fear."¹⁶⁸

The construction of this tradition with its inclusion of such specific dialogue suggests that parts of it may have been invented for political purposes at some point in its transmission, but it is significant in expressing the nineteenth century understanding of this strong sociopolitical institution, which Dingane and his successors maintained. The story was remembered because soon after this conversation with his advisor

Nzobo, Dingane was reported to have enticed by direct invitation the senior male members of the royal family into having sexual relations with members of his *isigodlo*. He then had all of the men who had done so picked out and killed. It was obvious to Jantshi that it had been a trap that became a pretext to put to death royal men who might challenge him for the chieftaincy. Jantshi's father had desisted from going "because he felt he was being trapped."[169] Among the royal men killed on this occasion were Dingane's half brothers Mfihlo, Nqgojana, Mqubane, and others.[170] Even more than Shaka, Dingana would need to rely on royal women to administer the kingdom.

Sivivi's observations indicate the extent and limits of *amakhosikazi* authority during Dingane's reign. The royal Queen Nomahawu, "chief wife" at the royal village of Dukuza that had been Shaka's capital, sent Sivivi three times to carry messages to the new royal capital at Mgungundhlovu.[171] The first time she reported to Dingane through Sivivi that some Africans from south of the Thukela River and therefore in her vicinity appeared to be preparing an attack. Sivivi carried the message first to Mpande, whose hut was near the gate at Mgundgundhlovu, and then accompanied Mpande to take the message to Dingane himself. Dingane sent Sivivi back with orders to Nomahawu that she "send out spies to watch them" and gave his brother Mpande the same orders at that time. The second time Sivivi went to the capital on Nomahawu's orders, it was to report the death of two oxen, and the third time it was to supervise seven young men who were carrying bags of sorghum (*amabele*) from Queen Nomahawu to another royal princess, Senzangakhona's daughter Mndibili.[172] Mndibili, an *inkosazana*, or royal daughter born into the royal house, "had a kraal of her own called eGumeni which was quite close to Mgungundhlovu." On this occasion, Sivivi personally gave the bags of grain to girls at the *isigodlo* and then saw Mndibili who sent praises as thanks to her aunt Nomahawu. Sivivi then had to report these events to Dingane, however, which he did after first reporting to Mpande. Sivivi was taken by Mpande to see the king himself. Sivivi explained that "Nomahawu had been asked for *amabele* by Mndebili, and it became necessary for the former to report giving some to the latter because Dingana had told off [ordered] boys to go and cultivate them [the *amabele* fields] for Nomahawu, and they therefore were Dingana's property."[173]

Although the royal women who supervised royal villages and the *izigodhlo* at *amakhanda* administered daily affairs, all of their actions were subject to oversight and approval from the king himself. Their work included cultivating and preparing food as well as brewing and distributing beer, and they performed tasks also assigned to royal men holding similar or parallel positions of authority. They did not, however, derive significant independent power by virtue of the limited perquisites and prerogatives of their positions.

The *amakhosikazi* had tremendous prestige as was recognized in ceremony and ritual, but this did not allow them to transcend the overriding power and authority of the senior men of the royal house, especially the king. The evidence does not support the conclusion that the roles of the *amakhosikazi* gave them significant power or authority beyond very circumscribed arenas. Even there their decisions were always subject to the oversight of their male kin without consultation, and the location of the king's quarters in the center of the *isigodlo* did not empower the women who lived there. The decisions made within the confines were with counsel from the powerful and influential men of the kingdom. When men arrived to meet with the king, the women were sent away.[174]

The royal women retained their assigned roles as heads of homesteads and districts, assisting in the administration of the kingdom, only as long as they did not pose a threat to the king's authority. Mnkabayi's influence appears to have increased under Dingane's reign, when she was allowed to preside at ceremonies giving praises to the ancestors before the army went out to war, *ukuthetha*. But the king Dingane also *thetha*'d the army at the capital before it went to Mnkabayi's village at eMahlabaneni.[175] This ceremonial role reflects the highest esteem accorded to Mnkabayi, and later generations of praise-singers, *izimbongi*, composed and sang her praises following those of the kings.[176] A later generation exaggerated that "the Zulu kings were placed by her," a reference to her participation in succession decisions.[177]

Not all of the royal women fared as well, however. The *amakhosikazi*, like royal men, could easily be put to death by the king when they fell out of favor. Nozilwane lived through the reigns of both Shaka and Dingane and was said to have fled and been killed with her half brother Dingane after his defeat by Mpande.[178] Dingane had allowed Senzangakhona's favored wife Bhibhi to retain her position, as "a woman of great importance at Mgungundhlovu," but Mpande was persuaded she should be killed because the favoritism she had enjoyed was resented by other *amakhosikazi*. She and a brother fled, and were killed when the party of armed men sent out by Mpande discovered them hiding in ditch.[179] A woman born to the royal house, Mnkabayi's sister Mawa ka Jama, also fled to safety south of the Thukela River, referred to as "crossing over" from her village at Entonteleni because she was to be killed. Mpande's brother Gqugqu ka Senzangakhona was caught and killed for accompanying her.[180] The regiment from her own *ikhanda* at Entonteleni, the Izingululu, pursued her and her followers and killed many. Their deaths demonstrated that the life of an *inkhosikazi* was always at risk from the same military regiment for which they had had local oversight in everyday affairs but who received their orders from the king.[181]

The evidence of women causing or influencing the events and circumstances of the past, individually and collectively, sheds light on gender relations that shaped and constrained their roles and actions. In precolonial southern Africa, women's social and economic roles and activities served to empower them individually and collectively. These roles allowed them decision making and control over their own lives and affairs as well as those of others in spheres of activity assigned to women in the family, household, and production. For these reasons women, were not powerless in the context of inequality in gender relations and women's subjection to male decision-making and control over resources. In limited arenas and conditions, women were allowed a voice, i.e., the opportunity to speak and have their opinions or decisions heard, in their own households and sometimes beyond. Women also exercised their influence over society, economy, and politics in hidden and incalculable ways in African settings. Women had important indirect effects on the direction of history but with no certainty of success in their efforts. Insofar as women achieved decision-making powers, the scope of women's empowerment is evident in whether their decisions extended only over their own household or over the larger social communities of family, lineage, village, district, chiefdom, or kingdom.

The evidence of women holding offices of authority in the public sphere as well as controlling the resources and decision making of their households in the private sphere has led women scholars from non-Western societies to question the paradigms established by western Marxist-feminists, which seem to deny women any significant self-conscious and independent roles in determining their own lives and history.[182] Scholars have often used the term "oppression" to describe gender relations. This term, which implies unremitting overt forms of repression accompanied by lack of respect or even contempt, and a complete lack of choice, opportunity, and initiative on the part of the oppressed, does not accurately represent gender relations in precolonial southern Africa. There is no question that women in precolonial KwaZulu-Natal were respected by men, and their personal relations were often characterized by love and affection.

Young men and women fell in love and eloped to evade social restrictions that prevented their marriage; fathers and mothers risked their lives for each other and for their children. Insofar as oppression was experienced, both men and women experienced it in the terrible arbitrary acts of violence inflicted by Shaka when he executed people or massacred entire villages on momentary impulses or as acts of personal retaliation. Their vulnerability to such overt acts of oppression only strengthened the bonds between men and women within families and communities.

Gender-based status was moderated by generational considerations, and young men were controlled by their elders as Guy argued.[183] All men were subject to involuntary military enrolment and control, to the orders of their chiefs, and, after the consolidation of the kingdom, to Shaka. Men as well as women negotiated the lives of their families in the context of severe forms of control maintained through violence and the threat of violence. Men valued the lives and contributions of women and accorded them both respect and honor. It is important to recognize the many facets of gender relations and their ramifications on the lives of women. Women did not remain powerless in the context of their subordination to men, and men were constrained by their motives to maintain and protect the social and political organization that sustained their communities.

Women in precolonial southern Africa exerted considerable control over their own lives and affairs within the private sphere and influence over public affairs in various realms. Some individual women achieved pre-eminent positions of authority and power. Sifiso Ndlovu correctly points out that "precolonial Zulu women" were not "barred by tyrannical patriarchs from the inner circles of Zulu power and monarchy" and that "Zulu women" functioned "as important actors in the *amakhanda* [military villages], *izigodhlo* [women's quarters] and Zulu royal family."[184] However, Ndlovu ignores the permanent inability of women to own wealth and their lack of legal status and access to courts and mistakenly concludes from this that "precolonial Zulu women were neither [not] automatically subordinate to Zulu men."[185]

Recognition of the critical historical roles played by women individually and collectively and acknowledgment of their indispensable contributions and the respect and honor accorded them by men on those accounts are important. However, it is simplistic to ignore the complex interface of gender relations with socioeconomic and political status.

Royal Women: Authority and Subservience

The experience of royal women, who held positions of authority over other women and superior social status to many men, cannot be projected to the experience of women across the societies of precolonial KwaZulu-Natal. The power that individual royal women derived from positions of authority and their influence within royal circles did not allow them to alter the legal and social status, and associated political status and economic circumstances, of women across society. Moreover, the authority and power of royal women were conferred upon them by men, who retained the right to rescind that authority and the power it conveyed. Even when women served in roles that gave them power and authority, gender relations determined the extent of and limits to that authority.

The degree to which women, like men, gained decision-making authority at higher levels of social and political organization varied individually. The achievements of royal women did not always reflect, nor did it necessarily mitigate or modify, inegalitarian gender relations across society and could instead serve to reinforce inequality between men and women through class-based assignments of positions of authority to women as well as men. When women achieved positions of authority, their ability to implement decisions (i.e., wield power) remained dependent and conditional upon male approval or support. Even in their administrative positions of authority, royal women remained subservient to the king and the men of the royal house. Senior royal women such as Nandi and Mnkabayi used their influence to curb Shaka's abuses in order to protect the men, women, and children who had become subjects of the Zulu kingdom. In their positions as queens and queen mothers, however, royal women did not overturn the systemic means by which women were subordinated to men. In their positions of power and authority, these women also perpetuated socioeconomic stratification and the political survival of the AmaZulu ruling family.

The royal women of early precolonial KwaZulu-Natal gained access to resources and to positions of authority and power via their male relations: their fathers, husbands, brothers, or sons. The dependence of women on men was structured economically as well as legally. Women controlled the resources of their households, but could not inherit, dispose of, or bequeath property separately from or without the approval of her husband, sons, or other male relatives, who remained the controlling and legally recognized owners of the property.[186] Women did not have legal status as adults and could not participate in legal proceedings, giving them no legal recourse to courts except through their male relatives.[187]

When women were appointed to high office or served as queens and queen regents, they did so to ensure the succession of the male heir to the ruling line of descent, and they received their appointment and approval from senior powerful men. In precolonial southern Africa, access to resources and authority was structured socially and legally to ensure male inheritance of political position, male ownership of wealth, decision making by men, and the control and subordination of women to men. That some women temporarily gained appointment to high office did not allow them to overturn the inherited laws and processes that guaranteed and perpetuated male authority and control. As Kuper concluded about the Lovedu Queens and demonstrated in other contexts as well, "[t]he female rulers had the glory, but the substance of power remained with their male councillors: half-brothers, husbands, or lovers."[188] Although women enjoyed wealth and status and did not always experience their lack of such power and control as oppressive, their subordination by men in the precolonial era was evident in social, economic, political, and ritual regulations and practices across the region of southern Africa. Women's choices and initiatives made critical contributions historically, but it was in the context of men's control of the economy, social organization, and politics.

Chapter 9

Zulu Voices, Zulu Meanings: Ancestors, Praises, and History

Neither the AmaZulu kingdom of the nineteenth century nor the AmaZulu identity of the twentieth century reflected a homogeneous "primordial" cultural constant of unknown origins. In spite of the tendency of anthropologists who study culture to flatten cultural history into an imagined unchanging past, in order to present a rich image of culture as an "ethnographic present," it is historically inaccurate to project the cultural elements of a recorded moment of time into the indefinite past. The testimony of the people who became subjects of the AmaZulu kingdom in the era of Shaka and therefore were identified subsequently as being AmaZulu indicates the multicultural origins of the dozens of small and large chiefdoms that were amalgamated into the consolidated political unit ruled by the AmaZulu chief. Individuals remembered their own paternal lines of descent, by which they could recognize the relationships of various small and large descent groups, commonly denoted by anthropologists as lineages and clans. Peoples belonging to various lines of descent came to belong over time to various chiefdoms scattered across the region, so that chiefdoms reflected heterogeneous populations in terms of genealogical origins, or lineages and clans. The common daily greetings used in social interaction reflected and reinforced knowledge of these diverse family-based origins within a community and social and political unit, since they were the praise-greetings, or *izithakazelo*, of the person being greeted and their ancestors. Each person retained an awareness of the appropriate praise-greeting for themselves and others because of their common use, and these also embodied political history insofar as they were often the names of founding rulers of the line of descent and its associated chiefdom.

The progenitors of the modern AmaZulu valued evidence of their ancestors that was preserved in oral traditions passed down through generations. These traditions include myths of origins and the genealogies of families and of ruling chiefs. Personal identity remained tied to a person's distant paternal genealogical ancestry or line of descent. As leading members of a line of descent became geographically dispersed over centuries and incorporated into many distinct political units, or chiefdoms, identity came to be linked secondarily to the chiefdom and its chief's genealogy.

Identifiers of families' ancestry, including ruling lines of descent that held political authority over genealogically diverse adherents, included verbal and literary evidence, such as *izithakezelo*, or praise-greetings, and the praise poems of individuals, notably of chiefs. In addition, nineteenth century oral traditions categorized the peoples comprising the large and small chiefdoms of KwaZulu-Natal into three larger cultural-linguistic groups. Each of them comprised many chiefdoms and was recognized according to its cultural characteristics, myths of geographic origin, and distinct speech patterns (i.e., language and dialect). The peoples who came to comprise the AmaZulu kingdom of the nineteenth century were diverse, reflecting their multicultural origins.

Genealogies of the ruling line of descent of the modern AmaSwazi nation date its founding ruler to the ninth century AD, assuming twenty-five years per generation. The ruling descent lines of numerous chiefdoms found in KwaZulu-Natal in the eighteenth and nineteenth centuries can be traced through back to circa 1400 AD and sometimes earlier. Inheritance was governed by patrilineal descent, and because rules of exogamy were observed in marriage, intermixing was necessary for people from numerous "clans" i.e., those claiming descent from a common distant ancestor, a larger and deeper descent group of related lineages.

There was broad agreement in the oral traditions of the peoples of modern KwaZulu-Natal that the peoples of the region could be grouped into three cultural identities with distinctive dialects: AmaNtungwa chiefdoms that had immigrated from "the north" or "up-country," AmaLala groups who had been living on both sides of the Thukela River valley from time immemorial, and AbaMzansi chiefdoms that were from "down-country" coastal areas. A fourth identifying term, AbaNguni, became common only in the nineteenth century and was ambiguous in its reference but denoted a higher social status than the others. Shaka, suppressing earlier insulting reference to his origins as AmaNtungwa, adopted the term Nguni in its place, a praise-name referring to the

Zulu Voices, Zulu Meanings: Ancestors, Praises and History 207

grandfather of his ancestor Zulu, and also widely accepted as a reference to the AmaXhosa peoples of the Ciskei and Transkei.

In the recent historiography, John Wright and Carolyn Hamilton's 1990 article, "The Making of the AmaLala: Ethnicity, Ideology and Relations of Subordination in a Precolonial Context," makes the convincing argument that the era of Shaka's rule marked a significant turning point in the intensification of socioeconomic stratification following upon the amalgamation of various chiefdoms under varying conditions and on differential terms.[1] The central contribution of Wright and Hamilton's article is their analysis of the complicated process through which the AmaZulu kingdom emerged and the structural changes that took place as a result of consolidation. More recently Wright has traced early European uses of and explanations for the term *AmaLala*, identifying A. T. Bryant as a key source for twentieth century misunderstandings of this term of identity.[2] The joint article by Wright and Hamilton provided an important corrective to earlier studies that relied on the flawed interpretations of Bryant. His mistaken identification of "Mbo" and "Lala" as precolonial identities continues to plague the historiography and archeological interpretations of the past.[3] Their article, based on unsupported assertions made in Hamilton's master's thesis, is, however, seriously flawed in its assumptions and analysis. The evidence of indigenous oral traditions and oral history collected in the late nineteenth and early twentieth centuries directly contradicts many of their assertions and conclusions. There are two central errors in Hamilton and Wright's analysis of early precolonial KwaZulu-Natal: their assumption that genealogies had been fabricated for political purposes, and their assumption that the identities of AmaLala and AmaNtungwa were invented in Shaka's era.[4] The only evidence presented to support their assertion that the genealogies of the peoples of KwaZulu-Natal were the product of invention are the presence of discrepancies that are commonly found in oral traditions subject to human memory and error. Wright and Hamilton make the assertion that genealogies had been fabricated based purely on the assumption that there was an incentive to do so in order to claim genealogical links to the lines of descent of the ruling AmaMthethwa and Zulu royal houses and thereby gain royal favor.[5] Hamilton repeated this faulty assertion in a recent article. Again repeating this unsustainable assertion that genealogies were fabricated, in a later article Wright and Hamilton wrote that "the tendency for ruling groups and certain of their adherents to seek to link their traditions of origin" occurred because "[f]or ruling groups this was a means of binding adherents to them more closely; for the latter it opened the way to their being able to make claims on their chiefs for favourable treatment."[6] The authors argue that Shaka invented two new categories of identity to achieve ideological control over the subordinated population: a favored status of "AmaNtungwa" that included the earliest groups incorporated, and invented for them a common origin, and a lower status of "AmaLala" that included groups later incorporated who did not share the origins of the AmaNtungwa and the royal favoritism it provided.

However, the evidence from the oral traditions does not support their assumptions or conclusions, which Hamilton has repeated in her recent article.[7] The genealogies and associated historical traditions of the AmaZulu and associated family lines of descent of the KwaZulu-Natal region meet the criteria for reliability that historians of Africa have long since been accepted in that the oral traditions had at the time of recording been passed down independently for generations and confirm each other with strong correlations in the evidence. Furthermore, there was no incentive to alter genealogies to invent links to the Zulu royal line of descent prior to the 1820s, and no opportunity to do so, undetected, afterwards. The alteration of genealogies systematically would have required the unlikely widespread collusion in invention of the new and suppression of the old because these genealogies were repeated to the public on regular ceremonial occasions several times a year and hence were widely known. Moreover, the oral traditions told of grave punishments that would be inflicted for violations of ceremonial traditions. In addition, an alteration of a genealogy might bring about drought, famine, or disease as forms of ancestral punishment. In fact, the genealogies remembered independently by peoples who had been both voluntarily and involuntarily incorporated into the Zulu kingdom hold up under scrutiny and there is good reason to believe that they preserve fairly accurately ancestral lines of descent. The grave sites of the important royal AmaZulu ancestors, including Zulu himself, were well known and protected, and Hamilton concedes that Makhosini, the "place of kings," was "invested with a very strong sense of the continuity of the Zulu ruling lineage, its 'sacredness' and its antiquity. In particular, the Makhosini served to emphasize the proximity of the Zulu ruling lineage, and the king, to the ancestors on whom the well-being of the nation depended."[8] The explanations of the "AmaNtungwa" and "AmaLala" identities provided by indigenous AmaZulu oral traditions are contrary to those provided by Hamilton. Her interpretations do not support the argument that an ideology based on falsified origins undergirded AmaZulu royal rule. As has long been understood, the cohesion of the emergent AmaZulu kingdom was the result of periodically mustering new regiments from across the population and socializing them into a military command structure upon which the royal house depended. Hamilton herself analyzes this process successfully.[9]

The strength of the evidence regarding the genealogy of the ruling line of AmaZulu chiefs and their associated adherents comprising a chiefdom lies in the retention of independent genealogies and oral traditions and histories passed down, independently, among many subsequently separate lines of descent and their associated political chiefdoms. All peoples of the region of modern KwaZulu-Natal retained knowledge of their genealogies through the use of oral traditions such as praises, remembered in the form of single phrases and in longer praise-poetry associated with individual chiefs. A chiefly family history embodied that of the larger sociopolitical group whose ancestral ties bound them into social and cultural communities. The knowledge of genealogies was considered essential because the ancestors, *amadlozi* (sing. *idlozi*), were believed to be able to affect the fate of the living and could be called upon for assistance in times of need. At the same time, the ancestors were propitiated with rituals and ceremonies to avoid incurring their anger that could bring about destructive consequences among their living descendants. Praises of the ancestors were therefore a prominent and indispensable part of formal ceremonies. Everyday knowledge of one's own ancestors was important because of the belief that the ancestral spirits could visit the homesteads of their living descendants embodied as snakes, and it was necessary to propitiate the ancestor believed to have appeared. Those present were reminded of the names of the ancestors of that particular homestead because everyone would gather for ceremonies to honor those ancestors. These rites involved the performance of praises and dances and the slaughter of cattle by the owner of the homestead where the snake had appeared.[10] "The *dhlozi* [ancestor] is a harmless snake. If it should be seen entering a cattle kraal a beast is killed or *tshwala* is *peka*'d [beer is brewed] and the *amadhlozi bonga*'d [the ancestors are praised]."[11] These practices were communal and common:

> The *amadhlozi* [ancestral spirits] are prayed to as well as praised, i.e. *kulelelwa*'d and *bongisa*'d. They are prayed to when a beast has been killed and when the family and relations are gathered together. All are called on as far as can be remembered. The prayer is that those praying as well as those absent who belong to the same family i.e. near relations may be looked after and protected.[12]

Any instance of illness and misfortune was attributed to an *idlozi*, and succor was sought from a "doctor" who would "address the *idhlozi*; they give praise to it with a beast [head of cattle] etc." The belief in *amadlozi* was central and vital to every individual because "[t]he *idhlozi* is what gives a man his vital force (*hambisa's umuntu*)."[13] It was understood that "all [people] live with the *amadhlozi* [deceased ancestors] of their own people," and that an *idlozi* would stay with its own descendants because it would not be recognized or honored at another village.[14] These ancestors were therefore evoked by name in important ceremonies, such as the rites performed especially at funerals, before going to war, and to bring rain in times of drought. Both ritual specialists associated with the ruling or royal house and those who attended and heard the rituals that were repeated frequently would remember these genealogies with praises attached to each of the ancestors. Because the neglect of an *idlozi* was believed to generate anger and punishment, ancestors were not intentionally omitted from genealogies and praise ceremonies.

The second critical reason for accurately remembering the genealogical relationships between separated sociopolitical groups was the strict prohibition against intermarriage between blood relations and lines of descent groups that were genealogically linked. Several instances were remembered when two genealogically linked groups prohibited to intermarry were declared separate on the grounds that so many generations had passed that they could be considered distinct and intermarriage could be allowed. Not surprisingly, these instances are remembered with reference to specific chiefs who had fallen in love and wished to marry a specific woman otherwise forbidden to them. These were known exceptions, and the genealogical links were nevertheless remembered. Rules of exogamy in marriage were strictly observed because endogamy such as practiced among the peoples of Sotho-Tswana cultures was as repulsive as and considered to be incest. To prevent the marriage of two people from related lines of descent, the knowledge of every person's ancestry was both carefully kept and widely known. For these reasons, the accurate memory of genealogies was so important that the idea of deliberately altering them was virtually unthinkable.

The social and political organization of people in chiefdoms, defined in terms of adherence to the authority of a chief from a ruling descent line, was therefore understood to be distinct from the multiple genealogical and ancestral identities of the chief's subjects. People retained knowledge of the past and their family's genealogical origins with its associated cultural identity through the use of oral traditions such as praises. Praises were remembered in the form of a single phrase, *isibongo*, and longer praise-poetry of important chiefs. The term *isibongo* (pl. *izibongo*) from the verb meaning *to praise* (or *thank*) referred to the collective praises of descendants of a common line of descent, and the culturally correct way to thank someone was to say one of their ancestral praises. The component parts of the *izibongo* of a descent group were used as their *izithakezelo* (sing. *isithakazelo*), or praise-greetings. Because greetings and conferring thanks to ancestors were of daily occurrence, the common praises were known and used, and people remembered the correct praises associated with individuals according to their community of ancestral origin. Thus,

> The *isibongo* identifies all people according to their tribes. It is the name which indicates the origin (*ukudabuka*) of people. People are all known by their *isibongo*, and they retain this even though they may be living at a kraal [village] with people of a different *isibongo*. The word is connected with *bonga*, meaning to praise, because when one is praised, one is praised by means of it. It indicates one's clan (*uhlobo*) of origin – So-and-so, of such-and-such a people. There was no person but he or she had an *isibongo*. In the case of the Zulu, otherwise the Ndabezita, the word "Zulu" is the *isibongo*. The people belonging to any particular tribe are not necessarily all of one *isibongo*.

> All chiefs, without exception, have, as members of their tribe, persons of different *izibongo*. If a chief, having persons of various *izibongo* in his tribe, marries a woman of his tribe of *isibongo* different to his own, children of the marriage would bear the father's *isibongo* and, if one of the children is a girl and marries, she will not lose her *isibongo*, but her children will bear their father's and not their mother's.

> People go by the customs obtaining not to the tribe to which they belong, save when such is the original one from which they derive their *isibongo*. And so, under a single chief there may be many sections of people with *isibongo*s differing from his own, and who will not all act in unison (or uniformly) as far as the various customs are concerned. They have their ancient customs; those remain with them.[15]

Names and phrases derived from praises were also used as exclamations in daily conversation, and in swearing oaths, providing other common uses that reinforced both the memory of names included in praises and the genealogical links they implied. Nursery "rhymes" used to quiet babies included ancestral names, and one man explained that these were used to "hush" babies because "[t]hese are our *isitakazelo*, our *isibongo*, which makes a child happy. *Takaza* [*uku-thakaza*, to show kindness or speak praisingly] is to make happy."[16] Other songs or chants included the *irubo* for ancestors used before eating meat and that for the king used at the first fruit harvest ceremonies. One interviewee asserted with regard to the use of such songs and customs, however, that "[o]nly the

Zulus retained their old laws and customs. Other tribes were made to relinquish many old customs by the Zulus."[17]

In fact, the practice of the rituals and ceremonies of some subordinated and incorporated chiefdoms persisted, but for many, only the oral traditions, not the practiced rituals, could be safely retained and passed down.[18] The oral traditions were susceptible to loss or unintentional partial corruption upon the deaths of those entrusted to remember them and relate them on ritual occasions, the praise-singers (*izimbongi*) and chiefs, many of whom inevitably lost their lives in the violence that accompanied the consolidation of the Zulu kingdom.

According to numerous independently transmitted oral traditions, the AmaZulu chiefdom took its name from the person of a chief named Zulu, son of Malandela. Zulu headed a branch of his father Malandela's chiefdom in the latter half of the seventeenth century. He ruled six generations before the renowned chief Shaka, son of Senzangakona, who consolidated the Zulu kingdom in the 1820s. There is strong agreement between genealogies collected in the nineteenth century as to the line of descent as far back as Malandela, and some genealogies also identify Malandela's predecessors for three generations before him.[19] The genealogy of the AmaZulu chiefly line of descent according to these genealogies was (from oldest to recent) as follows:[20]

Bekapezulu
Mntungwa
Nnja (Lufenulwenja)
Malandela
Zulu (brother of Qwabe, founder of the Qwabe ruling descent line, and
    Chunu, founder of the Chunu royal line)
Mageba
Punga
Ndaba
Jama
Senzangakona
Shaka

In addition to more formal oral traditions, memory of the genealogy of the AmaZulu ruling line of descent was retained in a line of nonsensical "doggerel" linking the names of the chiefs and contained seemingly derogatory references because of an early ancestor. After defeating some enemies in battle, the early chief Nnja ("Dog"), reported to have been Malandela's father and Zulu's grandfather, had earned the "praise-name" of Lubololwenja (penis of a dog) given to him by a people he had defeated. Unless this was understood to refer to the heroic victory of an honored ancestor, the phrase seemed insulting. One man said: "Aba kwa Ntontontwana, or aba kwa Lufenulwenja ["Penis of a dog"], i.e. the Zulu people. Tshaka caused two things to die out, (a) the name Lufenulwenja, (b) circumcision."[21] Another explained, "[t]he *isibongo* at the time of our originating was bakwaLubololwenja ["Penis of a dog"]. Tshaka rejected this name, and substituted that of 'Ndabezita' in its place."[22] After he assumed the chieftaincy of the AmaZulu in about 1817 and expanded rule over subordinate chiefdoms, Shaka prohibited the use of this praise reference and chose another for the AmaZulu:

The praise-name 'Ndabezita', applied to the Zulu people, was a name of the Mbata people. The Zulus were known as Lubololwenja; Tshaka considered the word a bad one and changed it to 'Ndabezita.'[23]

The address form of greeting "Ndabezita" was associated with more than one chiefdom that became subordinate to Shaka's rule, and various reasons were given for its use by Shaka. There was agreement among Stuart's informants that when Shaka "appropriated" the term for people of the original AmaZulu chiefdom, he prohibited its use by others:

As regards the word "Ndabezita" the Zulu people when under Tshaka they acquired power appropriated it [Ndabezitha] for themselves and tabooed it in respect to the Kumalo, Emambateni [AmaMbata] and emaCunwini [AmaChunu] tribes who had previously used the term. The Zulu *sibongo* was also kwa Lubololwenja this afterwards became obsolete and frequently the words *a ba kwa sibongo sibi* ["those of that (unmentionable) praise name"] were substituted.[24]

The descendants of both Zulu and his brother Qwabe retained independent oral traditions that confirm them as having been brothers, both sons of Malandela. AbaQwabe traditions provide correlations and corroborations of the genealogical links between the AmaZulu and AbaQwabe, as well as with the AmaChunu, through a third brother named Chunu or Mcunu.[25] AmaChunu traditions also confirm their genealogical links to the AmaZulu and AbaQwabe through these three sons of Malandela. Magidigidi stated definitively, "Zulu, Qwabe and Ncunu were the sons of Malandela," and recited, "[t]he Cunu chiefs are Silwane ka Gabangaye ka Pakade ka Macingwane ka Luboko ka Dibandhlela ka Nyanda ka Jama ka Ndaba ka Mcunu ka Malandela." He was sure of the genealogy, however, only to Nyanda; he was also sure that "Jama is the son of Ndaba" and that Mcunu was the son of Malandela.[26] As tentative as the genealogies are prior to Malandela's rule, his son Zulu was the founder of the AmaZulu royal house.

The peoples of the various chiefdoms of KwaZulu-Natal were understood to belong to three different cultural groups that were marked by their early geographic ancestral origins and could also be recognized in variations of dialect.[27] Many descent groups were defined as "Amantungwa (those from up-country – *a ba senhla*)," but there was not complete agreement on whom this encompassed.[28] The genealogically related AmaZulu, AbaQwabe, and AmaChunu were all known as AmaNtungwa. A man of the AmaChunu said, "[t]he amaCunus are amaNtungwa just as the Zulus are; so also are the Qwabes, but as they lived down-country near the Mtetwa they *tefula*'d [spoke with a different dialect]."[29] The man also reported, "[t]he amaCube are amaNtungwa like us [AmaChunu]," but this was contradicted by another informant, who may have been confused because the AmaCube were known as ironworkers, the word for which is *amalala*.[30] In addition, Stuart was told, "[t]he Ndhlovu, Mdhlalose, Buthelezi, Nzuza, and Ntuli are tribes that I hear came from the north and are amaNtungwa. The Kumalo and amaMbata, especially the former, are amaNtungwa, Kumalos being nowadays addressed as amaNtungwa."[31] Another informant reported that "the Kumalo, Butelezi, Ndwandwe are all called amaNtungwa because they are in the north – also the Mabaso people."[32] Mkehlengana, son of Shaka's famous warrior Zulu ka Nodangaya who was of the Ncwana section of the AbaQwabe, said about this AbaQwabe section that "[t]radition strongly urges a descent from the north, and this is supported by the fact of their being amaNtungwa and has having 'come down with a grain basket' (*ehla'd nesilulu*). Had they, like the Mtetwa, been an old coast tribe, they would have been known as 'those from down-country' (*abasenzansi*) like the Mtetwa."[33] In spite of their AmaNtungwa origins, the AbaQwabe were sometimes called "*Mzansi*" along with the AmaCele and AmaMtetwa because of their similar coastal dialect.[34]

Mruyi explained several important sources of and references to the origins and identity of the Zulu royal house:

We are amaNtungwa, or abeSutu. We *ehla'd ne silulu* ('came down from the north in a large round basket'), and separated from what is now the Qwabe tribe. We came from the north. Qwabe and Zulu were both sons of Malandela. Qwabe came down into what is now Zululand before we Zulus did. We followed them. I do not hear that Qwabe and Zulu ever quarreled with one another, nor do I know what caused our all coming south.[35]

The identity of the ancestry of the Zulu royal house was explained in terms of migration from the north where the distinct and different speakers of the Sotho-Tswana languages were to be found: "It is often said that the Zulu came from the abeSutu and descended the Drakensberg. 'They rolled by means of a grain basket' merely means they came down from up-country."[36] The historical reference to the AmaZulu and other groups in terms of their immigration from outside of KwaZulu-Natal, bearing distinctive baskets woven of the Ntungwa grass, was not meant to be complimentary, however. As one man explained to Stuart, "It is an insult to say, 'Little Ntungwa who came down by means of a grain basket', just as it is an insult to say a person is an iLala or Inhlwenga."[37]

The most common explanation about the AmaNtungwa that set them apart from other chiefdoms was that they had come with or by means of a grain basket.[38] One person specified,

The grain basket belongs to the Mabasa, the amaMbata, the amaNtshali, Ndaba, Kumalo, Radeba (of the Hlubi), the amaNgwana (Matiwana's people), Dlamini (amaSwati), Tembu, Nxumalo (Ndwandwe) etc.

The word *isilulu* [grain basket] is used to indicate rolling, i.e. towards the south, for all people came from the north.

People from the north came and settled in these parts. At a later period others followed from the north, finding others of similar customs and tongue already in occupation, on also settling down to occupy the upper parts – chiefly where the sources of the rivers of Zululand and adjoining countries are – they spoke of themselves as having come down with the grain basket, meaning that as compared with other inhabitants they were not aboriginals or ancient occupants but had come from the north. And yet as a matter of fact all at some time or another came from the north.

They say, 'We rolled by means of a grain basket', meaning that they rolled from the north to the south where the country is wide, and there settled, just as a grain basket rolled down a hill eventually rolls onto the flats below and its contents empty themselves there.[39]

This person believed that the expression had come into use during his youth, but this may have merely been when he first became aware of it since the grain basket myth was also related by the AmaSwazi, although they were not themselves considered to be AmaNtungwa, therefore the myth must have dated to back a much earlier period.[40] Thus, "[i]t is often said that the Zulu came from the abeSutu and descended the Drakensberg. 'They rolled by means of a grain basket' merely means they came from up-country."[41] The most direct and obvious explanation for the name "AmaNtungwa" was that those called by the name had been the first to introduce the *isilulu*, a large storage grain basket, for use in the region of modern KwaZulu instead of the alternative storage of grain underground in large covered pits.[42] This is credible because, as a member of the Swazi royal family explained, the term came from the species of grass, *intungwa*, used to thatch roofs and to make the grain basket (*isilulu*) associated with the AmaNtungwa by the people living in the region of modern KwaZulu.[43] A son of the Zulu King Mpande told Stuart with certainty that the AmaZulu were AmaNtungwa, saying, "I know Zulus are called amaNtungwa. We, I think, were named Zulus after Zulu ka Malandela. We are said to have come down with a grain basket (*ehla'd ne silulu*)."[44]

Praises and other verbal traditions contained references that confirm a cultural association with origins for AmaNtungwa who arrived, according to myth, from the north, the up-country, and by means of a grain basket. For example, the praise greetings, *izithakazelo*, of the AmaMalunga branch of AmaHlubi were "Hush, Malunga! Hush, Mntungwa! (*Tula*, Malunga! *Tula*, Mntungwa!)."[45] A man from the AmaNcwana branch of the AbaQwabe chiefdom said, "'[t]his little Ntungwa who came down at Kwa Luzipo' – our mothers swore at us in this way."[46] Still in the early twentieth century, "Khumalos [were] nowadays addressed as ama-Ntungwa."[47] The AmaKhumalo chiefdoms, the most famous of which migrated under chief Mzilikazi and became known as the AmaNdebele (or Matabele), were closely identified with the term: "I know the Khumalo people only as being the amaNtungwa....When one of the Kumalos gave one food one originally said, 'E! Mntungwa!' Now of course many tribes are amaNtungwa."[48] The term was still used as a praise-greeting, or *isithakazelo*, in ordinary conversation: "the Khumalo people are the real abaNtungwa, for they say 'Mntungwa' to one another."[49]

AmaNtungwa were also known by their use of a particular phrase: "'Ho! Ofe!' is equivalent to 'Ho! Wenzani!' and is said by the amaNtungwa when they head off anything [e.g., in herding cattle]."[50] As one informant explained, "The amaHlubi people are amaNtungwas. They are those who used to say, 'Ofe, Mkozi!'"[51] Another informant did not know the meaning of the phrase but asserted it was said by "'people of the olden days'/ 'ancient Zulus'..."[52] There was agreement that among the AmaZulu,

> In the old days we made use of this expression, "Ofe Mkozi", i.e. amaNtungwa used it. The amaNtungwa means "those from the north". I do not know what "Ofe Mkozi" means.[53]

Among those listed as being AmaNtungwa according to these various definitions were the "amaBele (upon the Buffalo river), Kumalo, Amabaso, Ntuli, Sitole, Tembu."[54] Two informants disagreed about the AmaNgwane, who had lived in close proximity to the AmaKhumalo in the north. One said they were not AmaNtungwa as far as he knew, but the other said they were.[55] In addition to the AmaKhumalo, numerous other peoples and chiefdoms were also associated with the grain basket myth told by Stuart's informants: the abakwa Zondo, abaseMangweni, abaseMantshalini (of chief Khondlo), AmaHlubi, Malunga, AmaNgwane, AmaBele, AmaHloko, AmaNcwana, AmaChunu, AmaZulu, AbaQwabe, AmaNdhlovu, AmaMdhlalose, AmaButhelezi, AmaNzuza, AmaNtuli, and AmaMbatha.[56]

The oral traditions distinguished between AmaNtungwa and a broad category of peoples living in the chiefdoms in the area of modern KwaZulu-Natal who were generally referred to as *AmaLala*. Because the verb *ukulala* means to go to sleep, the reference was usually understood to refer to the tongue "lying down" in the mouth during speech. In this way, the harsh click sounds were made, although as a noun the term *amalala* refers to ironworkers.[57] The AmaLala were understood to be the peoples of the oldest chiefdoms and ruling lines of descent who were considered indigenous to the region of KwaZulu-Natal, for whom there was no knowledge of any earlier site of origin or any migration. One person told Stuart the AmaLala "originated in the middle [midst] of the nations [*izizwe*, chiefdoms] and first dwelt on both sides of the Tugela extending to the Mhlatuze [river]." He identified as AmaLala: the AmaCube, abakwa Hlabisa, abakwa Cele; abasemaLangeni, Emansomeni (or Emasomini); abaseMaQadini; abakwaNgcobo or Ngongoma; and abakwaNyuswa (of the amaNgcobo tribe); abaseMbo (Embo or AmaMbo, AbaMbo). This list did not include "those [numerous] amaLala tribes living on the south side of the Tugela."[58] Another said that "[t]he amaLala are the inhabitants of Natal in the coast districts."[59] Similarly another man told Stuart, "[t]he people who occupied land in the neighbourhood of what was afterwards called Dukuza were the Amalala. There are none of these now in this part; they have all removed across the Umgeni."[60] But the chiefdoms identified as AmaLala lived up the Thukela river as well, and one man said, "[t]he Nxamalala tribe originated (*dabuka*'d) at the eLoza river in the Zulu country. They are a real Lala tribe."[61] An UmQwabe man identified as AmaLala the Cele, Nyuswa, Qadi, Embo (who he said came from the Swazis), iNhlangwini, Swazis, and Baca.[62] Another informant listed: "Amalala.

Among the tribes that are amaLala are the Nyuswa, Ngcobo, Qadi, Cele (originally Mtetwa), Tuli, amaDunge, amaPumulo, amaPemvu, Hlongwa, Bombo, Malangeni, amaNgcolosi, Mpumuza, Zondi." He added, "[t]here were no amaLala [remaining] in Zululand [i.e. north of the Thukela river] except such as happened to be given protection (*tolwa*'d)," i.e. they had migrated farther south or had been fully incorporated into the AmaZulu kingdom and were no longer independent and identifiable as AmaLala.[63]

Dialect was the means by which people identified AmaLala groups. One man identified a number of peoples from chiefdoms in Natal and the area of Durban were as AmaLala who "spoke a Lala dialect," including the AmaNqondo or AmaNxondo, the AmaJali, the AmaKanyawo, and his own people, the AmaNdelu.[64] On the basis of their speech one person listed as AmaLala, "The amaNgcolosi, amaTshangase, amaQadi (amaNyuswa), amaKhlala, amaPumulo, and amaHlongwa all speak the Lala dialect."[65] The AmaLanga referred to the people of the AbaMbo or Embo and AmaNyuswa chiefdoms as AmaLala.[66] The AmaNyuswa were known as AmaLala, and Stuart was provided with the genealogy of their chiefs.[67] The name of the Embo or AbaMbo derived from an ancestral chief of the name Mbo; a later chief was named Mkhize so that the Embo were also known as the people of Mkhize, but they were presumed to be closely linked to the AmaSwazi because they both spoke the AmaLala dialect.[68]

Oral evidence about interaction between AmaNtungwa and AmaLala groups indicated the earlier displacement and subordination of some AmaLala by some AmaNtungwa chiefdoms. One interviewee who identified his people as AmaLala referred to their original independence, free from overrule, dependence, subordination, or tribute, as evident in their ownership of their own herds without obligation: "Now Socwatsha says he belongs to the Amalala people, these people ba *bezi fuyile* [owned stock], i.e. [were] their own masters."[69] The correlation between people's ownership of property in stock with being their own masters and free of obligation to pay tribute is clear in this characterization of the AmaLala from a man well versed in the traditions of his own people. However, the status of those previously known as AmaLala on the basis of their cultural identity changed with the extension of AmaZulu dominance, and as it did, the implication of the designation *AmaLala* changed, so that another man said, "We Zondi are amaLala, having been so called by the Zulus who defeated us. By so speaking they insulted us."[70]

Thus, the definition of what it meant to be AmaLala appears to have gained a new derogatory connotation. A man of Luthuli descent knew that his people "are Amalala," and specified that they were "not Amantungwa who came down with a grain basket." His ancestors had been settled in the region for as long as the oral traditions could remember, but this man noted the destitution that had befallen them, saying "We do not know where the Amalala came from. This name arose in Tshaka's time because they went about hiding and eating *imihlakanya* woodborers (insects). Dhlozi [his friend] saw the Emakabeleni people near Greytown eating *imihlakanya* after roasting. Amalala ate these [insects] – [it was] those who [in their dialect] said '*Ku tite*.'"[71] Significantly, the meaning of the appellation "AmaLala" changed after the consolidation of the AmaZulu kingdom to refer to a person of lower social status, for as one man commented, "[t]he name amaLala came from the Zulu, for they conquered the land. They then called us amaLala, just as you Europeans call us *amakafula* ['kafirs,' a derogatory term for Africans used by Europeans in South Africa], for people that defeat others insult them."[72] Confusion arose from intermixing between chiefdoms of later "AmaNtungwa" arrival and those of original "AmaLala" communities, as well as the subsequent migrations of chiefdoms. By the end of the nineteenth century, it was only the oral traditions and differences of dialect that distinguished the two:

In comparing amaNtungwa with amaLala the latter are said to *Tekela* [speak a specific dialect]; the building of huts is the same with both peoples; their customs are the same as regarding marriage, burial and construction of headring. The differences between the two classes are now practically nil.[73]

The *a ba Mzansi* were the third cultural and linguistic group that was clearly distinguished from the AmaLala who were the ancient original inhabitants from the midst of the entire region and from AmaNtungwa people and chiefdoms who had originated "up-country." Chiefdoms identified as belonging to this third group were designated by means of another geographic reference, "down-country" (*a ba Mzansi*). The most famous chiefdom representative of the cultural or linguistic group referred to as "down-country" (sometimes called uMzansi) was that of the AmaMthethwa with whom Shaka spent his early adult years as a warrior. The AmaMthethwa, to whom the AmaZulu were subordinate during Senzangakona's reign, spoke "of themselves as merely those from down-country (*aba sezansi*)."[74] As Stuart was told, "'Mtetwa ka Nyambose [an ancestral name], *wena was'ezansi*' [you who are from down country] is an Umtetwa tribe *sibongo* [praise-name]."[75] The AbaMzansi and the AmaNtungwa commonly insulted each other: "The people known as *umzansi* viz. Mtetwa, Qwabe and Ndwandwe tribes *bati* [*bathi*, say] to the Ntungwa '*I ngati na shiy'e lenu na, nehla ne silulu, neza kwe la kiti?*' ['you who came down from the north with a grain basket,' i.e., mocking their status as immigrants, and] amaNtungwa say to Mtetwa '*nina ni nga maNhlengwa a se zansi*'['you who are from the coast and lowly AmaNhlengwa people']. The Mtetwa, Qwabe and Ndwandwe tribes *tefula* in their speech and may be called amaTefulo. Their proper collective name is *umzansi*."[76] The southern AbaQwabe neighbors of the AmaMthethwa, originally AmaNtungwa, had taken on the AmaMthethwa dialect, and their northern AmaNdwandwe neighbors, with common genealogical origins with the AmaSwazi ("AmaLala") to their north, had also acquired the AmaMthethwa dialect. They were all known "as *umzansi*" and all spoke the dialect in which they were said to *ukutefula*. They also all used the same insulting language to the AmaNtungwa, who in turn insulted the AmaMthethwa by calling them "maNhlengwa" or amaHlengwa, a reference to peoples from around Maputo (Delagoa) Bay thought to be distinctly inferior socially and culturally.[77] Another interviewee confirmed, regarding the AmaNdwandwe of chief Zwide: "...we are said to have originated with the Swazi and Nhlwenga [Maputo Bay peoples]. We are from the coast lands, not Amantungwa or Abanguni. We resemble the Mtetwa."[78] This dialect difference was evident between the AmaZulu, located inland, and their ancestral cousins the AbaQwabe, who had long since lived separately from them in the lowlands.[79]

At the turn of the twentieth century, the men who spoke with Stuart were still able to describe differences in dialect associated with the various chiefdoms that had been incorporated into the AmaZulu kingdom in the 1820s by Shaka.[80] Summarizing the three dialects understood to reflect sociopolitical as well as cultural origins, one of Stuart's interviewees explained,

The amaNtungwa were said by the Zulu etc. to *qotshamisa* the tongue, whereas the amaLala were said to *ratula* or *tekeza*. We see then that 1) *tefula*, 2) *tekeza* or *ratula*, and 3) to *qotshamisa* the tongue were the three great dialects, viz the uMzansi (alias *uMzansi we nsimu*), the amaLala, and the amaNtungwa or umuNhla.[81]

With regard to the AmaNtungwa dialect, Magidigidi's grandmother, a woman from a branch of the AmaKumalo (i.e., AmaNtungwa in origin) told Magidigidi that they "belonged to the amaNtungwa from up-country who speak with their tongues in a low position.[82] In the AmaLala dialect, the verb *ukutekeza* (or *ukutekela*, the prefix "uku" indicating the infinitive form) referred to the manner of speech in the dialect used by AmaSwazi, AmaLala, and the AmaBhaca (who migrated as a chiefdom from the KwaZulu region and resettled in the Transkei in the 1820s).[83] The aspirated *t* written as *th* was instead spoken as *ts* and the consonant *z* was spoken as *t* or (as still found in SeSwati spelling), *dz*. Because of the harsh sounds used in these dialects, speakers were said to *ukuradula* or *ukuratula* (or *ukuhadula*, the consonant *r* reflecting a guttural sound). Stuart noted that "Socwatsha was of the AmaNgcobo chiefdom and therefore spoke a Lala dialect, saying *amagxolo* instead of *amaxolo*, the consonant 'x' denoting a click sound that is more guttural (as written in combination with a 'g')."[84] Among prominent chiefdoms of AmaLala origins were the Embo (or AbaMbo). One of Stuart's Embo interviewees, after saying proudly "I am a Lala" explained "[t]he Abambo are amaLala, not amaNtungwa or abeNguni. They say not '*Wenzani?*' but '*Wentani?*' [what are you doing?]."[85] This typical example of a common dialect difference, the use of the pronunciation with *t* instead of *z* also provides evidence of the longstanding relationship between the Embo and the AmaSwazi far to the north. Many other distinctly different chiefdoms were found between them. The common dialect of the Embo and the AmaSwazi led one interviewee to comment, "[t]he Swazis are also real Lalas, also the Abambo."[86] One man provided examples of dialect differences such as "We are called amaLala; we are so called because we say 'Kutite' and not 'Kutile' and 'AmaCwabe' instead of 'amaQwabe.'"[87]

Dialect differences were also used to distinguish people labeled as being "from the lowlands," *a ba Mzansi*, notably the AmaMthethwa. One man provided as examples of dialect, "AmaLala *tekeza*, e.g. '*Wendani?*' People from down-country (*aba se zansi*) *tefula*, e.g. *inkonyane* becomes *inkonana*, and they say *yoku*, not *loku*'" (i.e., *y* is substituted for *l*).[88]

Because the AbaQwabe were said to have migrated south many generations before to the lowlands near the coast and the AmaMthethwa, Stuart heard confused reports identifying the AbaQwabe as AmaNtungwa. This confusion was the result of the contradiction between their known AmaNtungwa ancestry and northern origins but their distinction from the AmaNtungwa on the basis of their longstanding settlement near the coast among *a ba zansi* chiefdoms. This confusion could also have arisen because in their speech, the AbaQwabe were said to *ukutefula*, a term used to refer specifically to the AbaQwabe dialect. A man of AbaQwabe origins explained that "*Yeyeya* is to *tefula* – we are [therefore] called amaTefula or amaYeyeya" (i.e., the people who "*tefula*"). The man of AbaQwabe origins indicated how this speech was viewed by others when he quoted the chief of the AmaChunu as having referred to the AbaQwabe (i.e., speaking with their harsh sounds), saying "you Qwabes are abaNguni of the place of the people of Yeyeya (lelela) – who would destroy a person by beating him down with words."[89]

With a simple explanation of the contradictions between genealogical origins and dialect difference, another informant said, "Zulu and Mcunu are the sons of one and the same person. The amaCunus are amaNtungwa just as the Zulus are; so also are the Qwabes, but as they [AbaQwabe] lived down-country near the Mtetwa they *tefula*'d."[90] On the basis of their dialect but not their genealogy or ancestry, the AbaQwabe were therefore associated with other *ezansi* lowland chiefdoms who were neither AmaLala nor AmaNtungwa:

I hear the Qwabe, Mtetwa, Mgonambi, Mpukunyoni, and Dube all originated in the lower country (*ezansi*). The Qwabe are generally spoken of as those from down-country (*umzansi*), but I have heard them called amaNtungwa.[91]

These differences in dialect, still evident in the twentieth century, were readily identifiable, but people recognized that they were not definitive with regard to origins because sometimes people changed their speech patterns. Language use and practices retain historical influences and are suggestive of historical events and changes. Because changes in language and dialect occur easily in only a single generation, however, they are suggestive but never conclusive. Several informants explained their knowledge of the changing use of dialect by entire chiefdoms. Their knowledge of the circumstances associated with intermarriage and close social interaction indicated a conscious awareness of the historical factors involved and the malleability of even language use.[92] The AmaThuli, who had migrated from north of the Thukela to resettle in the region of modern Natal in the middle of the eighteenth century, remembered their origins as AmaLala and knew that they had retained their AmaLala dialect: "We arrived in this part of the country (Natal) speaking this dialect. It was not a dialect which we adopted or learnt from others – neighbours." The dialectical differences were retained because "[t]he womenkind keep up the old dialects."[93] By contrast, the AmaCele chiefdoms who had migrated south in the wake of the AmaThuli in the eighteenth century were originally from the lowland *ezansi* chiefdom of the AmaMthethwa and had brought with them this *tefula* dialect "of the lowlands." They had modified their speech to the AmaLala *tekeza* dialect during their long interaction with the AmaThuli.[94]

Wright and Hamilton were correct in identifying a new use of the label "Lala" as a reflection of the intensification of socioeconomic stratification during and after Shaka's rule, 1817–1828. However, the identification of people culturally and linguistically as AmaLala long predated this period. The change from a cultural and linguistic connotation to a lower socioeconomic status is explicitly explained in the oral traditions. Hamilton and Wright's argument that the term "Ntungwa" also emerged under Shaka associated with an inner circle of privileged incorporated chiefdoms is also not convincing. The evidence does not sustain Hamilton's assertion that "the claims of these groups to be fellow *amantungwa* and to have a common origin were manufactured during the reign of Shaka to serve as the basis of their unity and to legitimate their privileged position."[95] She argues that "their identity as amantungwa was fabricated during the reign of Shaka" and "[i]t was their common identity as *amantungwa*, which provided the ideological basis of the social cohesion of this otherwise heterogeneous group."[96]

The commonly known and accepted identification of peoples within the KwaZulu-Natal region among themselves according to linguistic (i.e., dialectical), differences, as well as ancestral and geographic origins, is incontrovertible. Hamilton and Wright's hypothetical arguments are not in accord with this local understanding and knowledge that predated the Shakan era and persisted into the twentieth century. Wright recapitulates Bryant's mistaken arguments about the meaning of the label "amaLala" and compares it to evidence from other European writers and scholars who made alternative observations with reference to linguistic or dialectical differences.[97] Although Wright fails to credit linguistic explanations for the terminology, they were indeed identified as salient by Stuart's interviewees in the oral traditions he recorded. Wright's critique of Bryant is incisive but fails to explore the alternative indigenous understandings.

In her recent article, Hamilton has reiterated arguments and incorrect assertions made in her unpublished master's thesis from 1985 and in the earlier article she coauthored with Wright. Contrary to Hamilton's assertion, the term *AmaNtungwa* was not a carefully reserved identity because it carried a connotation of privilege and genealogical connection to the Zulu royal house. Shaka did not impose it as an identity on others such as the AbaQwabe as an attempt to co-opt their support. As Wright has noted previously, "the Ntungwa seem to have been regarded as of lesser status by those who, by the early 20th century at least, were calling themselves Nguni. By these latter the word Ntungwa/Mntungwa was sometimes used as an insult."[98]

Contrary to Hamilton's arguments, indigenous oral evidence supports Wright's assertion here that "the appropriation of Mnguni as an appellation of the Zulu kings, and Nguni as a designation of the ruling Zulu lineage, was consciously initiated by Shaka and the Zulu royal house as a means of legitimizing the lineage's newly achieved political dominance."[99] Hamilton's assertions and theories regarding the identities subsumed under the names "AmaNtungwa" and "AmaLala" are not in accord with indigenous Zulu understanding of the meaning and reference of these terms or identities. The oral evidence decisively contradicts Hamilton's assertion that AmaNtungwa was perceived to be a privileged status. Even Shaka himself considered it shameful to be "Ntungwa" and suppressed knowledge of the AmaNtungwa origins or associations of the Zulu royal house. Shaka and the AmaZulu royal house did not have the motive, means, or opportunity to invent an AmaNtungwa identity to achieve ideological hegemony, as asserted by Hamilton. Similarly and contrary to Hamilton's insistence that AmaLala was invented as a subordinated class of people, the term originally referred to the rather honored groups of people who were considered to be the original inhabitants of the Thukela River region on both sides of the river. However, after the Thukela River chiefdoms became incorporated into the expanding AmaZulu kingdom, they were indeed perceived to have been subordinated by Shaka and the term came to have negative connotations. Neither term nor identity was new under Shaka, however, as Hamilton mistakenly claimed.

In her unpublished master's thesis and later work, Hamilton questions and doubts the integrity, authenticity, and independence of the oral sources. Her entire argument rests on the assumption that the genealogies of the peoples who were incorporated into the Zulu kingdom were fabricated. She cannot demonstrate but only assumes this because of discrepancies found between independent sources of the genealogical information. She concludes that these discrepancies reflect a deliberate attempt by Shaka to alter the genealogies. The purported purpose of this was to create a fictive relationship between the AmaZulu royal house and selected incorporated chiefly families and their followers to achieve ideological hegemony (i.e., convince them to acquiesce to a supposedly natural genealogically-based system of dominance). Hamilton's master's thesis fell short of its goal to demonstrate ideological manipulation by means of the invention of genealogies, and misrepresents the cautions of scholars who advocate the cautious use of transmitted oral traditions and of oral history (i.e., eyewitness testimony), but who would not accept that discrepancies are per se evidence of fraud and fabrication. To the contrary, most important is establishment of the presence or absence of independent sources that can be compared and do not share the same origins or chain of transmission. Discrepancies found in independent sources that are largely in accord with one another indicate the relative reliability of information for which there is concurrence. In contrast, evidence that does not appear in multiple independent sources must be treated as unsubstantiated and unreliable.

It is striking, however, that in her major published work on Shaka, Hamilton presumes that the integrity, independence, and genuineness of the diverse sources reflect divergent opinions about Shaka, perhaps the most controversial subject of all.[100] In spite of her acceptance of and reliance on the oral evidence in her earlier analysis of the varied and shifting indigenous perspectives of Shaka, her recent article has reverted to her previous unsustainable theory of the fraudulence of the oral traditions of genealogies. She asserts that the oral traditions were invented during Shaka's reign along with new identities that Shaka invented. The oral evidence conclusively disproves these theories that she has nevertheless reiterated.[101] In her book on Shaka and the construction of his image from oral and European sources, Hamilton acknowledges that the oral traditions collected by Stuart were remembered and transmitted by people who hailed from all geographic areas, family lines, and political chiefdoms. She also recognizes that the people creating these oral traditions had been openly opposed to Shaka as well as supportive of him. She fails, however, to acknowledge that these independent origins of the transmitted oral traditions and the variations found in them are evidence of the failure of Shaka and the Zulu royal house to impose or achieve ideological hegemony. Her arguments about the creation of new categories of AmaLala and AmaNtungwa, however, rest squarely on her unsupportable assertion that they were part and parcel of Shaka's project of imposing ideological hegemony. The oral traditions conclusively show otherwise.

It was not possible to suppress the oral traditions from before Shaka's reign. That the oral traditions record and remember Shaka's attempts to manipulate praises is evidence of the resilience of knowledge and its transmission throughout the nineteenth century. This was a century in which dissent and resistance to any attempts to impose "ideological hegemony" as well as political authority persisted. The diversity of opinions and perspectives still evident at end of the nineteenth century and beginning of the twentieth century when Stuart conducted his interviews demonstrates the absence of ideological hegemony. Indeed, the many civil conflicts of the nineteenth and early twentieth centuries show that even within the ranks of the privileged there was no ideological consensus established or preserved.

Hamilton and Wright's argument that the AmaZulu royal family and the chiefdoms initially subordinated by Shaka believed that there were benefits from both the fabrication of ancestral ties and the invention of a common myth of origin is unsupportable. People who had been subordinated both voluntarily and involuntarily would never have accepted a false genealogical attachment to an AmaZulu line of descent because it would have meant betrayal of their own ancestors who continued to control their fates. These people pursued the success of their descendants and would not have arbitrarily and consciously omitted or excised their forebears from rituals that honored and propitiated them.

It was necessary for later generations to continue to remember, honor, praise, and propitiate their own ancestors to ensure their own success and protection and to avoid severe forms of ancestral punishment. Substituting someone else's ancestors in rituals would have been fruitless because the ancestors would take an interest only in their actual living descendants. Conversely, from the perspective of the AmaZulu royal family, suggesting that they had a false genealogical connection to groups such as the AbaQwabe in an attempt to impose ideological control would have been unacceptable. The perquisites of worldly political and military success attributable to their ancestors were jealously guarded and not voluntarily extended to formidable royal families such as that of the AbaQwabe chiefdom. In the case of the AbaQwabe, the ties of true genealogical kinship are evident in oral histories independently remembered and related to Stuart by AmaZulu, AbaQwabe, and outsiders. Hamilton's evidence of inconsistencies does not amount to the "systematic adulteration" of the genealogies and oral traditions, as she asserts.[102] The relationship between the AmaZulu and AbaQwabe royal families and their adherents remained contentious and violent throughout Shaka's reign. This argues against a self-conscious and voluntary fabrication of a genealogical link by Shaka to the AbaQwabe royal line. His violent suppression and execution of recalcitrant AbaQwabe indicates he did not seek nor rely upon "ideological" means to dominate them, as argued by Hamilton. The genealogical link between the AmaZulu and AbaQwabe royal families appears to be genuine and legitimate, not an invention as Hamilton argued.[103] The compliance and collusion required for such artificial genealogical invention across all sectors of both royal families and all of their followers was not possible. These families had heard genealogies related on ritual occasions all of their lives and across generations. Ultimately, there were powerful religious, social, and political constraints preventing the manipulation and fabrication of genealogies as Hamilton and Wright posited.

Moreover, the indigenous oral traditions do not support Hamilton's presumption that an "Ntungwa" origin carried a universally favorable connotation and was a desirable identity to claim. She and Wright are correct that the AmaLala were the targets of insults. One man said, "We were laughed at by the Zulus because of our dialect. 'You can hear he's a Lala.'"[104] Dinya explained: "The amaLala were so called by the Zulus and Qwabes because they speak in the *tekela* dialect and thereby speak with their tongues lying down (*lala*)." Furthermore, he supplied the more derogatory version, "It is also said that it is because they sleep (*lala*) with their fingers up their anuses." Nevertheless, the AmaLala were defiant and proud and, he added, "[t]hey don't care for the name and ask, 'When we are asleep, what do you yourselves do at night?'"[105] Thus, the AmaNtungwa were themselves the targets of insults by others who reminded them of their arrival by means of a grain basket, an insult being thereby implied, a point explicitly acknowledged previously by Wright.[106] One man said the "Zulus" who greeted people by saying 'Hofe Mkozi!' were "laughed at and called *amantungwana* [little amaNtungwa]."[107] Another man explained about the AmaNtungwa, "'I hear they rolled by means of a grain basket. The peoples they came to insulted them by saying, 'You come down by means of a grain basket.'"[108]

Perhaps most vague among the labels of identity related to origins is the indigenous definition for the term *Nguni*, which Western linguists later adopted to identify the language group composed of the mutually intelligible languages found south and east of the Drakensberg mountains.[109] *Nguni* had different and narrower connotations in the nineteenth century among the people to whom it came to refer more broadly. It evidently became common only in the nineteenth century.[110] References to AbaNguni were ambiguous, and the name was sometimes understood to be another name for the AmaNtungwa, which generally accorded higher status to the former.[111]

The same people [AmaNtungwa] are called Abanguni, these are the people who *qokot'ulimi* i.e. don't *tefula*, in other words speak pure Zulu. The Amalala are more numerous than the Amantungwa. The word Inzula [i.e., AmaZulu] would be a collective name for all inhabitants of Zululand.[112]

Because of his origins in the (small) AmaZulu chiefdom, Shaka had been subject to the insulting references used for AmaNtungwa both when he was a boy living among his maternal eLangeni (i.e., AmaLala, relatives), and again when he lived for years as a young man and warrior among the "downland" or coastal AmaMthethwa. Both groups commonly used insulting language with reference to people identified as AmaNtungwa, including the AmaZulu. As John Wright has previously noted, to be denoted as or identified as "AmaNtungwa" was perceived as insulting.[113] Shaka deemed these insults to be inappropriate for his ruling house. This is directly contrary to Hamilton's assertion that identification as "AmaNtungwa" conferred a favored status that Shaka used to bind other important royal houses "ideologically" to the Zulu royal house. Contrary to Hamilton's claime, as a result of its insulting connotation Shaka suppressed the use of the term AmaNtungwa to refer to AmaZulu:

> The amaNtungwa speak of themselves as being abaNguni. Tshaka however put an end to this as he said he was umNguni. He was addressed as "Mnguni, Mnguni of our people!" The amaNtungwa [i.e., people of other AmaNtungwa chiefdoms] thereupon became afraid of applying this word to themselves.[114]

Mnguni was identified as the father of Malandela, who had lived in the "far north," and his name may have been a praise name of Malandela's father, identified in the genealogies as Nnja (i.e. "Lufenulwenja").[115] The common ancient origins between not only the AmaZulu and AbaQwabe but also the AmaChunu were assumed because of their common use of the term *Mnguni* from which the appellation AbaNguni was derived:

> The term "Mnguni" originated among the Zulu and Qwabe; they call one another "Mnguni." The Cunu also say "Mnguni!" The older maCunu used to make an oath thus, "Mnguni ka Luboko!" when swearing by Macingwane, who was son of Luboko.[116]

One of Stuart's oldest informants also explained the legitimacy of *Nguni* as a term of reference for the AmaZulu because it was found in their praise poetry:

> According to Mruyi the Zulu people are known by these names: abeSutu, abaNguni, amaNtungwa, abakwaZulu. There is, in support of the second name, an old verse used as a chant or chorus at the *mkosi* [first fruits or harvest] feast, to this effect: "Mnguni, arm yourself and go and seize them", i.e. cattle. The word mNguni or umNguni is merely the singular of abaNguni. The people were called abeSutu because they lived up-country (*enhla*), i.e. north.[117]

Evidence about people associated with the term *Nguni* was found in other praise-greetings that were still remembered at the turn of the twentieth century. One man noted, "We Qwabes speak of ourselves as abaNguni of Kwa Mnyangombili, i.e the hut of the chief Lufuta."[118] Similarly, "Socwatsha says he hears the Nzimela people speak to one another as 'Umnguni'; they live in Zululand."[119]

The identification of those who might legitimately refer to themselves as "AbaNguni" was uncertain and somewhat controversial.[120] More than one of Stuart's informants indicated that the AmaZulu and AbaQwabe were both AmaNtungwa and AbaNguni, and one explained, "the Qwabes and Zulus, who are really amaNtungwa, speak of themselves nowadays as abeNguni."[121] But a man of the AmaChunu, said to be related to the AmaZulu and therefore AmaNtungwa from the north, observed that the use of the name in praises was not exclusive, for "among the amaLala chiefs the phrase umNguni is commonly used."[122] There was common agreement that the term *Nguni* was correctly applied to the AmaXhosa peoples of the Ciskei and Transkei, so it was believed they also shared some common origins with the AmaZulu and other people identified as "Nguni" in the region of KwaZulu-Natal.[123] In a lengthy explanation, one of Stuart's interviewees indicated that Shaka had been the first to use the appellation "abaNguni" for the kingdom and kings of the AmaZulu, and that it seemed to have originally applied to earlier residents, "already here when the Zulus and Qwabes arrived" from the north. However, he explained the legitimacy of "Nguni" as a term of reference for the AmaZulu because it was found in their praise poetry, a form of oral tradition passed through the generations.[124]

> Certain it is, whatever may be thought of this theory, that the name umNguni is a precious one to the people of Zululand, being used as one of the profoundest and most reverential salutations to the Zulu kings, who conquered all the tribes of these parts. Tshaka was the first to appropriate the appellation among the Zulu chiefs.[125]

In the face of the new challenges brought by European settlers over the course of the nineteenth century, the peoples of all of the chiefdoms that had come to be subordinated and incorporated into a kingdom under AmaZulu royal house rule came to be called AmaZulu as well. The progenitors of the modern AmaZulu who hailed from many different houses, descent lines, and chiefdoms, continued to value evidence of their origins that were preserved in oral traditions passed down through generations. These included myths of origins and the genealogies of families and of ruling chiefs. The preponderance of Zulu oral testimony directly contradicts Hamilton's theories and assertions that the AmaZulu royal family manipulated genealogies to achieve assimilation and that the people who were incorporated, including members of subordinated royal houses – both those who were incorporated by force as well as voluntary submission – not only acquiesced in this but actually suppressed knowledge of their actual ancestry. This conspiracy theory was simply impossible to accomplish and was contrary to the interests of everyone involved whose primary concern was to recognize, honor, propitiate, appease, and conciliate their real ancestors who they believed had the power to help or harm them in life. The rituals that honored family ancestors could neither be altered deliberately nor be completely suppressed. The oral traditions kept alive knowledge of deep genealogies stretching back in some cases a millennium, and in others hundreds of years. This was the one element of identity that was inflexible and sustained by ceremony and rituals of religious significance that bound the living to their ancestors.

Chapter 10

Shaka's Rule: Social Configuration and Social Control

> There were many people to whom Tshaka caused great sorrow, as he did by killing off people of various tribes.[1]
>
> It was common for communities to be broken up by war, for in Tshaka's time clans who were settled in their own lands were all broken up.[2]
>
> Dukuza was built after the conquest of Natal, after establishing friendly relations with Magaye, and after the assegai incident. During the *Izwekufa* we ran off into the bushes. While we were there, people pointed us out, saying, "There are Zulu!"[3]

Shaka accomplished the consolidation of power and authority over the territory and people who had been initially incorporated into the expanding Zulu kingdom voluntarily and by force, through pre-existing sociopolitical practices, through intimidation, and through the extreme use of collective punishment. The sociopolitical dispensation of the expanding AmaZulu kingdom during the era of Shaka's reign reflected the process of consolidation and amalgamation of formerly independent chiefdoms that were now subject to new patterns of settlement, land use, and the distribution of wealth in the form of cattle. Maclean ("John Ross") wrote that "[t]he several bloody and exterminating wars of Shaka appear to have had no object in view other than to enrich himself with cattle of the conquered tribes; to obtain these was a sufficient incentive to engage in the most daring and arduous enterprise."[4] Booty and cattle were inextricably linked to the economy, regiments, and settlement in enlarged *imizi* (homesteads or "villages") and barracks, to form a new demographic and sociopolitical configuration in the era of Shaka's rule. The king enjoyed the privilege of allocating all land, but within a given district that prerogative was usually left to the local chief or *induna* who held authority in the area. As Shaka accumulated massive herds of cattle, he used the young warriors to manage them, moving them seasonally between ecological zones with the grasses that could support them. He built cattle posts in the territories of responsible subordinate chiefs both north and south of the Thukela River. As the young Maclean first traveled from Port Natal to Bulawayo in 1826, he observed that the Mngeni River was difficult to cross because of huge alligators there, and the Thukela was dangerous because of the huge hippopotami. Otherwise, the rivers were easily forded, unlike in the rainy season when the waters were very high. He later wrote,

> Our track lay through a fine country, rich in wood and pasture, and well watered by numerous never failing streams, although we were now in the height of the dry season. Here and there, the nearer we approached the mountains of Bulawayo, beyond which was the site of Shaka's residence, we met with large *ithanga*s containing many hundred head of cattle, and where we were invariably regaled with a plentiful supply of rich and excellent milk. These *ithanga*s are but temporarily constructed, for the convenience of removal, when the pasture fails, to a more favourable district. They are under the management of a number of juvenile warriors, who are enjoined by stringent regulations to a life of celibacy, no females being admitted within the precincts of these establishments, and any breach of these regulations is visited by death to the offender. The government and direction of these again are confided to a chief, who, however, seldom resides on the spot, but delegates his authority to resident officers under him, who may be considered as captains of these bands of warriors.[5]

The military establishments interacted with local homesteads that provided food for them. Maclean explained,

> Each of these establishments constitutes a regiment. They live principally upon the milk from the cows, with occasional contributions of Indian and guinea corn, levied on the inhabitants of the kraals [villages] in their vicinity. Those we saw were certainly a fine specimen of savage warriors, all you, active, cheerful fellows, apparently from eighteen to twenty years of age. They appeared to consider themselves much above the common herd, and a somewhat privileged class. Being, moreover, trained to arms, they seemed to despise their more humble brethren whose pursuites were those of peace and utility.[6]

During Shaka's reign, the flight of chiefdoms left their territories available for reallocation by Shaka, and

> Whenever any land, through any cause, was vacated by a tribe, the king would probably cede it to some *isilomo* [an important man not serving in any official capacity]. Should two tribes quarrel with one another, one of the disputants would be taken away whilst his land would be given to an *isilomo* or some other person.[7]

The laws, rights, and privileges of the AmaZulu chiefdom came to prevail across the territory of Shaka's expanding kingdom without distinction.[8] Old patterns of land use continued, and new homestead clusters were created as needed according to the initiatives of local families.[9] The practices of settlement and the allocation and use of land were governed by the same customs and laws that had prevailed for generations. Patterns of land occupation and settlement reflected the aphorism, "'a stick belongs to the one who cuts it.' This principle operates in land matters, especially where a man is encroached upon by some newcomer."[10] From the time of Shaka, it was considered that "[t]he whole land is the king's. No one objected to its being lived on. Members of any given tribe might separate from the tribe and live on land they fancied, even though at a distance."[11]

A small family-based group requesting an allocation of land from a homestead head would receive a designated homestead site, grazing ground, and "garden lands" suitable for cultivation. No taxes or payments were paid for land use, but service to the king was required in the construction of the royal homestead including homes, enclosures, and fences.[12] Natural resources other than land allocated for homesteads, cultivation, and grazing were shared without restrictions:

Red ochre (*isibuda*) and iron could be dug out and taken without permission; and anyone could cut what wood he wanted anywhere he liked, wattles, poles, etc., for forests came under no restrictive law. The land of the kingdom was under no restrictive law (*izwe la li nge na mteto*). Everything [in theory] belonged to the king.[13]

The specific practices and procedures regarding land allocation during Shaka's reign allowed him to develop a system of patronage that ensured loyalty from important men who might otherwise challenge his authority. Because the allocation of land for settlement and sites for building, gardens for crops, and pastures had always been the prerogative of the head of the ruling family of a chiefdom, the chief, the creation of a new layer of authority in the person of the king with comparable prerogatives was not disputed. Thus, it was accepted in Shaka's era that

The land of Zululand belongs to Tshaka, he who unified all of it. Tshaka would take a fancy to a man and then, having conquered some chief's land, would say this man might go and build at any spot he (Tshaka) might indicate. Men used to be given land by Tshaka, and a man might be given permission to occupy land even though other people might be living on it at the time. The old resident would not be called on to quit. If later on, a quarrel were to arise, it might end in the two going to Tshaka, who would generally cause the old resident to move to some other locality which would be indicated to him. The land at all times, all of it, belonged to the king, i.e. since Tshaka's federating or unifying the small, previously existing *amakosi* [chiefs]. Any man who speaks of land as belonging to him means it is his because [it was] given him by the king. Those who were conquered were not required to ask permission to remain. There was no necessity; they merely continued to occupy as before. If, in any particular locality chosen by the king for some man to live in, there should happen to be a man, say an *isilomo* [wealthy important man] with half a dozen kraals of followers, such person and followers would not be turned off to make room for the new arrivals, but simply left alone; nor would he [the original *induna*] be required to *konza* the new man, even though he [the new chief] might be of greater standing.[14]

The setting aside of some land for the use of king for patronage alone, however, was a new practice developed by Shaka. In his era, "[i]n Zululand some land was set apart for the special use of the king's *izilomo*; it resembled Crown Land, which in fact it was. The *izilomo* are those 'made' by the king (*ezenziwe inkosi*)."[15] With these lands thus set aside, "[w]hen given permission to reside on such land, an *isilomo* might take his followers with him, and other *izilomo* might do likewise." But these "Crown Lands" were also a way for Shaka to provide for any man who came to offer his allegiance and presented him with a head of cattle, and "[i]n Tshaka's and Dingana's times any man might, without obtaining special permission, go and live on this land; nor would he in doing so be obliged to *konza* any of the *izilomo*, for the land was the king's."[16]

HOMESTEADS AND SOCIAL ORGANIZATION

The heartland of the AmaZulu kingdom was the area around Nobamba, a cluster of homesteads that made up a neighborhood, "village," or *umuzi*. It had existed since the reign of Shaka's grandfather Jama. Jama had also built the *umuzi* of Siklebe, which "*puma*'d" (broke away) from Nobamba when it became too large. Nobamba was believed to be ancient and was probably built by Jama's father Ndaba. It was Senzangakhona's great "kraal," a term referring to the centralized cattle enclosure that was later used by Europeans to describe these clustered homesteads they likened to villages. Nobamba was "where the nation was born," and there had been five sites of Nobamba within the same general locality.[17] Explaining the shift of this *umuzi* from one location to another, while retaining its name, population, and identity, one man told Stuart,

> I was born at Nobamba *umuzi* [village] while Tshaka was still ruling. We had been given refuge in the Zulu country as our nation had been broken up. After a time Nobamba removed and was rebuilt on the other side of the valley: it was in a low-lying, waterless tract of country. The Mqeku *umuzi* remained behind.[18]

Shaka's father Senzangakhona had not only kept his father's two "villages" at Nobamba and Siklebi but also built the *imizi* of Mbelebele, Ntontela, amaWombe, and probably uMnkangala, although the latter might have been built by Shaka.[19] Other *imizi* identified as having been present in Senzangakhona's reign were Sipezi and uMlangongwenya or uMahambehlala that had separated from Siklebi (Siklebeni), Emahlabaneni (later Mnkabayi's *umuzi*), and Eklobeni (later Gqugqu's *umuzi*).[20]

When Shaka returned from the AmaMthethwa chiefdom to usurp the AmaZulu chieftaincy, he brought with him the eLangeni villagers with whom he had originally sought refuge with Dingiswayo. They had lived in an *umuzi* among the AmaMthethwa. Thus, Shaka placed them as an *umuzi* upon their return with him: "Tshaka arrived with the Mkandhlu alias KwaNogqogqa kraal from the Mtetwa – this was the first kraal he established."[21] An *umuzi* named Kwa Gibixegu, place of old men, was then renamed Bulawayo and became Shaka's capital, and "[t]his was the kraal he disturbed the land (*cita*'d) with."[22] The strength of a chief had always been measured by the number of *imizi* (villages or "kraals") under his authority. These numbered thirty or more under Shaka's rule. Confusion sometimes arose because once a regimental system of military organization had begun under Senzangakhona, regiments were commonly but not always known by the same name as the *umuzi* where they were stationed. However, more than one regiment might be associated with the same village of more than a thousand people in number. Sometimes regiments established their own military barracks that did not have a prior existence as an *umuzi* of civilians. One man explained,

> My father was killed on the Balule campaign. He was simply of the "uNobamba regiment"; he was one of the "white" regiments, for he had put on the headring and had wives and children. The unmarried regiments were called the "black." The men stationed at Nobamba, Mbelebele, Siklebe, Nzimazana etc. were called "Nobamba" etc., i.e. after the name of the kraal, not after their regimental name.

> The Ihlaba [regiment] was stationed at Nobamba. Even though this regiment was there it would be called "Nobamba", or better, the Ihlaba of Nobamba.[23]

In addition to the old AmaZulu homesteads at Nobamba, Siklebi (Siklebeni) and Mbelebele, the most famous royal homesteads or royal*imizi* during Shaka's rule were his Great Place or capital at Bulawayo and his later capital at Dukuza, built in what had been AmaCele territory.[24]

Shaka's building of large *imizi* numbering a thousand or more residents, and his creation of military barracks located near civilian homesteads constituted an unprecedented restructuring of social organization.

His capitals at Bulawayo and later at Dukuza were the largest, and thousands or even tens of thousands of warriors would sometimes be called to gather there. They camped on the outskirts and lived on slaughtered cattle in preparation for war or for ceremonies designed to unify the kingdom and reinforce Shaka's authority. By the time Shaka moved his capital to Dukuza in 1827, he had come to exercise tight control over the territory and people of the AmaZulu kingdom. All important men of the kingdom were expected to maintain residence at the capital at least part of the year. They were also expected to provide young women from their families to live in the women's quarters, *isigodlo*, subject to becoming Shaka's concubines or *izixebe*. Maclean described the size and layout of Dukuza:

> including the external and internal fence-work for the protection of the dwellings and cattle, the diameter might have been about half a mile, and it contained about 1500 huts exclusive of those immediately occupied by the king's household. These latter were of a superior description, and entirely hidden from observation by a close and compact fencing very neatly arranged. They were about forty-five or fifty [huts of the king's household] in number, and were built on sufficiently elevated ground to command a view of the whole village.[25]

To reach the king's quarters required passing through several gates, behind which were courtyards and housing of increasing size and elegance. In the innermost area "the floor of this enclosure is of glassy smoothness, with a polish that reflects the image like a mirror."[26] One hundred and fifty to two hundred women lived with Shaka in the women's quarters, *isigodlo*, and were not allowed any contact outside these quarters. The fifty huts of the king's household were enclosed in a space about four hundred yards in length and fifty to sixty yards across. Within the entire "kraal" (i.e., Dukuza) there lived on a permanent basis about three thousand people, and at the time of Maclean's first visit there were another three thousand camped outside its woven walls.[27]

Shaka used his family to oversee the royal homesteads and *amakhanda* throughout the territory that was incorporated into the kingdom. His paternal aunts Mnkabayi and Mmama both had their own *imizi* built near Nobamba, Mknabayi's at Baqulusi and Mmama's at Esisebeni near Nhlazatshe mountain.[28] In addition, "Mawa was a daughter of Jama, like Mnkabayi and Mmama. I do not know whom she married, if she was married. She built on the Ntonteleni kraal site, i.e. in the district round about that kraal [during Dingana's reign]."[29]

> Mnkabayi used to rule at Nobamba. Mmama was also there. Mnkabayi had charge of the people of a district and used to stay there, viz. at ebaQulusini. I have frequently seen Mnkabayi.[30]

Shaka also built a homestead for his mother Nandi next to the capital at Bulawayo, and she was treated with honor after he was installed as chief. Shaka also had a sister, and "Nomcoba [Shaka's sister] used to live at Siklebeni with Langazana, the *inkosikazi* [queen (i.e., woman of the royal family)]."[31]

Shaka also maintained the positions of his brothers, both the royal sons of his father Senzangakhona and the other son of his mother Nandi, also of royal heritage because she was the daughter of the former eLangeni chief:

> When Tshaka got to the Zulu country he sent for his mother Nandi, also Ngwadi and Nomcoba, who then came and lived with him. Tshaka, after a time, built a kraal for this half-brother Ngwadi, its name being Kwa Wambawa [which was attacked by the Zinyowi regiment, says Tununu, 14.6.1903]. Nomcoba did not, I think, marry. Kraals merely were erected for her by Tshaka.[32]

> Tshaka liked Ngwadi and gave him authority over a large number of people. He had a large *impi*. It was afterwards almost forgotten that Ngwadi and Nomcoba were Gendeyana's children; they were spoken of as Senzangakona's for fear of arousing Tshaka's anger.[33]

As his two successors, Shaka's brothers Dingane and Mpande, younger sons of Senzangakhona by other wives, were the best known of Senzangakhona's many children. They had different mothers, therefore "Dingana was dark brown; Tshaka light, and Mpande black in colour. Dingana was of medium height, whilst Tshaka was slight and rather tall."[34] Shaka's other paternal brothers by other mothers included Ngqojana, Mfihlo, Mqubana, Mhlangano, Sigujana, Nzibe, and Sankoye. Except for Sigujana, Senzangakhona's heir who was killed when Shaka usurped the chieftaincy, all these brothers appear to have been allowed to keep their own homesteads after Shaka became the AmaZulu chief and therefore evidently remained loyal.[35] When Shaka returned to the AmaZulu chiefdom, Dingane, who had left at the same time about ten years before but had taken refuge among the AmaQwabe, also returned and placed himself under Shaka's authority.[36]

Mpande was also considered a favorite of Shaka's, and through him, Shaka took measures to ensure the inheritance of his ruling family. Although Shaka did not want a legal wife who might bear him an heir, creating a challenge to his own status as king by any ambitious family member, he entrusted Mpande with raising an unrecognized heir. Prevailing custom provided that if a man failed to have a son, a son of his brother's could be produced as his own as long as the man, not his brother, paid the bridewealth that ensured recognition to the line of descent to which any children would belong. According to oral traditions,

> Tshaka gave over a girl (engaged to himself) with a large number of cattle and a specially-built kraal to Mpande, asking him to raise up seed to him as he was afraid of doing so himself because he might have been killed. Mpande accordingly married the girl and she bore Mbuyazi who afterwards fought Cetshwayo at Ndondakusuka. Mbuyazi was therefore regarded as Tshaka's successor.[37]

Another son of Mpande similarly remembered this information about his elder brother Mbuyazi:

> Mbuyazi ka Mpande. This was the eldest son in Mkungu's own house. There were eight children in all. Mkungu was the youngest, and is now the only surviving male child. The name was given by Tshaka. Tshaka kept on seeing a kraal near where he lived and asked whose it was. He was told it was his brother Mpande's. Tshaka said to Mpande that the Zulu nation would not allow him to marry and have children. This being so, he gave Mpande a girl in marriage and said that the child she should bear him would be called Mbuyazi. He was named after H. F. Fynn, Mbuyazi we Teku. Tshaka said such a son would restore the land (*buyis'izwe*) and represent him. In course of time Mbuyazi was born and got the name. He was also known as Mbuyazi we Teku, thereby taking part of H. F. Fynn's praise-name.[38]

Some traditions remembered that Mbuyazi's mother Monase had actually been from Shaka's *isigodlo* and that she was bearing was Shaka's child when she was sent to live as Mpande's wife, bearing him more children including Mkungu, who was interviewed by Stuart.[39] Therefore, "Mbuyazi is believed to be really Tshaka's son. I do not know Monase's father."[40] He may not have been Shaka's only biological son, for according to some oral traditions, "Tshaka had wives at Dingiswayo's; one of these had a son, Zibizendhlela, who, when Tshaka broke up (*cita*'d) his kraal, fled to Faku in Pondoland. Zibizendhlela *konza*'d there and refused to return at a subsequent period."[41]

Shaka's kingdom was therefore tied together in part through conventional sociopolitical means, the adherence of ruling family members to the accepted head of their family and chiefdom, and the propagation of the family's rule through new generations. He also gave offices and land to men who proved their courage in battle and who proved loyal. These men were also sometimes given wives, women whose husbands or fathers had been defeated.[42]

Shaka also distributed royal herds to cattle posts established in the territory of trusted subordinate chiefs and indunas. Cattle posts were established not only in AmaZulu territory north of the Thukela River but also in chiefdoms south of the Thukela that became subordinated to and absorbed by the new expanding kingdom. The AmaThuli chief regent Matubane, from south of the Thukela river, went to *khonza* Shaka after the defeat of Zwide in 1821.[43] Then,

> Tshaka first all sent oxen to Matubane to look after for him. Tshaka sent the Ndabenkulu regiment down to cut poles for the cattle posts where the cattle were to stop and where people were to stay and look after them. This establishment was erected at the place of Mcasimbana. No sooner did the regiment construct the kraal than it returned to Tshaka, leaving Matubane to look after them [the cattle] with his own people. The regiment did not stop at all. They merely "placed" the cattle and then returned. When this kraal was erected the amaBece *impi* had returned from its campaign.[44]

Details about these cattle posts and the arrangements for the royal herds there were well remembered.

Ndukwana explained, "All people, like the land they lived on, belonged to the king." He also told Stuart that "[t]he boundaries of the country were determined by the *izizwe* (tribes [chiefdoms]) defeated, i.e the lands occupied by them. Tshaka defined no boundaries, for the territories he conquered and whose occupants tendered their allegiance to him were already sufficiently defined and known."[45] The king held the first fruits or harvest-time *umkhosi* ceremony before which time no foods could be harvested. This reinforced the authority of the king and the symbolic role of his office; chiefs who had previously performed the ceremony within their own chiefdom were no longer permitted to do so. Just as a chief had always been presented as belonging to the people, who provided the cattle for important ceremonies related to the chieftaincy such as circumcision or marriage, the king was now accorded the same symbolic support by the provision of tribute from across the kingdom. Although Shaka never entered into a recognized marriage, the earlier traditions adhered to his position for future generations, and

> To *kunga* is to present a king or chief with cattle; the whole tribe does so, as when he reaches puberty, is circumcised, puts on the headring, and marries. When he gets married he *lobola*'s [pays bridewealth to the woman's family] with them.[46]

Shaka ensured compliance with his authority by imposing extreme punishments for even the smallest sins of disloyalty or disobedience. Many stories of Shaka's actions found in the recorded oral interviews of James Stuart indicate that these atrocities were remembered and passed down among witnesses and victims of the events described for almost a hundred years after his death. In addition to the terrible acts Shaka committed that were remembered, the oral traditions also record acts of kindness and generosity from which he gained loyalty. He staged tests and challenges in the hope of exposing the weaknesses of possible challengers or opponents and of enhancing the appearance of his own superiority in the eyes of witnesses.

With regard to written and oral testimony about information concerning Shaka, including personal incidents, atrocities, and references to his personality and character, it must be assumed that some may be apocryphal or severely distorted in the telling.[47] Each story must be viewed with scepticism, but some reflect actual events as told. Most of the information about Shaka's character and personality comes from evidence about his years as chief. One man said that Shaka was very strong physically, and had a bad temper, such that "Only Ngomane ka Mqomboli ever dared to answer him back among the Zulu."[48] The daughter of a famous praise-singer or *imbongi* told Stuart,

My father said Tshaka was a tall man, dark, with a large nose, and was ugly. He spoke with an impediment, (i.e. mouthed his words, as if his tongue was too big for his mouth and pressed on his teeth).[49]

Another interviewee remembered,

Tshaka was a Zulu and was an umNtungwa. He spoke their dialect, a dialect which I speak. The tongue lies flat (*qotsheme*) in the speech of the Zulu, e.g. "*Kona lodu,*" instead of "*Kona yoku.*"[50]

Perhaps because he had lived among the AmaMthethwa for his early adult life, however, his accent appears to have changed. An elderly man interviewed in 1903 explained that "Tshaka spoke the Mtetwa dialect when he became king. He consequently always *tefula*'d. He is said to have lisped or stuttered, or pretended to do so."[51] With regard to his personality, in 1905 Stuart was told that "Tshaka was a self-assured person (*igagu*), i.e. a man who could make up his own song – not afraid of singing out loudly in public – no nervousness."[52] People remembered that Shaka had a praise-singer to compose and recite his praises and that he wrote his own praises and proclaimed his own praise-names.

Tshaka used to call himself "*uSikiti, uSikit'omnyama!*; 'Let there appear the man,' he once exclaimed, 'who will call me Tshaka! Do I shake (*tshakaza*) the gourd of his people?" [i.e., to *tshukuza* a gourd is to shake it up.][53]

Among the many praises composed about Shaka, the *imbongi*'s daughter remembered only that Shaka was praised as "[t]he violently unrestrained one who is like the ear of the elephant."⁵⁴ Shaka's self-assurance was mocked even while he was still alive. It was remembered that among the AmaCele whose chiefdom had become subject to Shaka's rule,

> Tshaka sometimes declaimed his own praises, Dinya says. Hearing him doing so, the Celes, whispering among themselves said, "The madman is praising himself." Of course this never came to his ears.⁵⁵

Shaka was said to appreciate and reward kind actions and show his gratitude for assistance or loyalty. According to one oral tradition, on an occasion when "it is said Tshaka was caused to be in want by his father Senzangakona," he went to the AmaKuze chief Nomagaga who gave him food in a clean pot, and afterwards Shaka is said to have remembered how well he had been treated there.⁵⁶ Another story was remembered that after Shaka encountered "a woman, dirty and without a good skirt to wear," he learned that her husband had given allegiance to him, so Shaka sent her with two heifers for herself and an ox. He instructed her to take the ox to her husband at his military kraal where he was to kill it and make her two leather skirts. This done, her husband came to give praises to the king who admonished him, "I want women to bear the looks becoming the wives of those who *konza* me."⁵⁷ A man who committed socially unacceptable acts was nevertheless favored by Shaka because, it was explained, "Tshaka had a special liking for cripples, idiots etc."⁵⁸ An early European trader who stayed with Shaka while in his early teens referred to Shaka as an "extraordinary savage chief," but also observed it was known "that courage had always been a sure passport to Shaka's favour and esteem."⁵⁹

The few remnants of Shaka's verbal interactions reported by oral traditions and Europeans make evident Shaka's attention to the importance of signs, signals, and metaphors. Also obvious is his self-conscious use of statements and conversations to manipulate his listeners. Metaphors were commonly used in important communications. The *imbongi*'s daughter Baleka told Stuart a story of Shaka going off to attack the small chiefdoms of the AmaNganga and Mapumulo peoples. In stylized form, she related that Shaka announced he was going to ask for snuff, and did not say he was going to war. The metaphorical reference to a request for snuff was widely understood to mean that the speaker was asking for or threatening a fight. In the same meeting Shaka told the assembly at Dukuza that it was "painful to be like an antbear which digs a hole and doesn't live in it, being driven out by a porcupine."⁶⁰

Fynn recounted his first conversation with Shaka, in which Shaka began by telling Fynn he was angry that Fynn had given medicine to

Shaka's "dogs." This referred to a woman Fynn was said to have nursed back to health. Shaka repeatedly challenged Fynn directly and argumentatively. He challenged Fynn to count a large herd of cattle and was surprised at his accuracy. To provoke Fynn, he philosophized that the greatest of all gifts was a black skin because white skins were unpleasant to the eye and had to be covered. Also to be provocative, Shaka asserted that his weapons were better than Europeans' muskets. Unable to argue through his interpreter in these early encounters, Fynn merely acquiesced to Shaka's statements. Fynn was frustrated because "[w]hilst in the presence of his people he placed the worst construction on everything, ridiculing all our manners and customs, though in perfect good humour. When none of his subjects were present he would listen with the greatest attention and could not help acknowledging our [European] superiority."[61]

Shaka may have made the white traders privy to some of his personal and private thoughts, although it is impossible to assess his honesty or sincerity. For example, Fynn recounted that Shaka told Farewell that he was troubled after having a dream in which his chiefs were in a boat that had been damaged. This occurred when one of Shaka's main advisers, Sotobe, was away on a mission to the eastern Cape Colony. After telling Farewell of his fears because of this dream, Shaka had an ox slaughtered on behalf of his emissary Sotobe who with the others arrived safely from their mission a few days later.[62]

Shaka was a master at using conversations with individuals to send messages to their broader communities as is evident in many stories about him. Fynn's evidence often supports these stories, and from the writings of Maclean ("John Ross"), it can be seen that Shaka interacted with the boy John Ross, whom he called "Jackabo," as a means to manipulate the Port Natal European community. According to Maclean, Shaka repeatedly reinforced the message, or implicit threat, that the Europeans were indebted to him personally and should be grateful. In so doing, Shaka imposed on them an implied but huge obligation that he considered should extend to their British government. Shaka is said to have remarked, "How happy [grateful] King George must be, as king of the white men, to me. I see and feel that you are a good and a superior people; a strange, a wonderful people. If I understood writing, I would write to King George, and tell him all that I feel, and what I think of the Mlungus [white people]."[63]

Shaka appears to have been very self-conscious about everything he said and did and to have regarded every encounter as an opportunity for manipulation. Captain King and his party said that Shaka publicly shunned their gifts, but in private, he thanked the captain for them and asked about the mirror that was among the articles they gave him. Shaka asked Captain King about medicines used by Europeans and if there was anything that could prevent his hair from turning gray, as it had begun to do. During their stay, King and his party were well provided with food, including beer made from malt of the Guinea corn. On their return, Shaka gave them fifteen head of cattle, including five good milk cows with their calves.[64] Shaka showed Europeans hospitality and generosity as was expected of chiefs in their behavior toward visitors, knowing these relationships could be useful to him later.

Shaka posed public challenges to Europeans to learn the effectiveness of their firearms and to discredit Europeans more generally as inferior in front of his AmaZulu audience. Shaka decided to find out how to manufacture guns, which was his motive for trying to send ambassadors not only to the Cape Colony but also farther to England, according to Stuart's informants three quarters of a century later.[65] One man told Stuart,

Tshaka used to have European guns tested by setting them cattle to aim at various distances. He was fond of seeing the power of a gun, and his intention was to send a regiment of men to England who there would scatter in all directions in order to ascertain exactly how guns were made, and then return to construct some in Zululand.[66]

Among the best-known stories about Shaka involves a challenge he posed to diviners, whom he hoped to expose as frauds by means of a staged "test." He challenged the *izangoma*, who supposedly had the ability to "smell out" people who were referred to as "evil-doers" (i.e., who engaged in harming others through supernatural means), and had all but three killed when they failed his test.[67] Shaka also believed in omens. The son of Shaka's servant Noradu had been told about a "feather incident" and related it to Stuart:

It happened when Tshaka was going down the uGcongco, to sweep away the people, when he was still on his way. He drew up his force into a semi-circle. At that point the king's plume fell to the ground; it came loose from his headband and stuck into the ground, where it stood quivering. Msongane ka Mahlobo of the Nzuza people made [prepared] to pick it up, but the king had him stabbed for doing so. Don't you see that we will stab the enemy? Indeed his *impi* did so.[68]

On another occasion, Shaka had all his men throw sticks into the sea to determine their fates, whether one of them were to be sent to the Europeans. Shaka's never came back, so he could not go himself. The sea was perceived as a cleaner or purifier of all things, casting out what is impure. Makuza said he thought Shaka's stick had not returned because he had not confessed his misdeeds, such as killing off girls who became pregnant by him.[69]

The oral traditions reflect a perspective that in failing to allow for hearings and trials, Shaka was arbitrarily imposing his personal will at court. The son of the prominent chief Magaye told Stuart in 1905, "Tshaka did not hold trials. He simply killed a man off."[70] This appears to have been considered acceptable in the case of cattle thieves. Fynn explained that before Shaka's rule, the inability to punish cattle theft with a death penalty had caused the crime to increase, so that "during the life of Dingiswayo thefts of cattle from one another were not infrequent." Shaka introduced the use of the death penalty for thieves and ended "that description of plunder," so that according to Fynn, "during the 12 years of my residence in the Zulu country not a single instance occurred of cattle stealing."[71] Details of an instance of cattle theft by three men indicate that Shaka used an *impi*, or body of armed warriors, to track the thieves and cattle where they surrounded their mountain hideout and captured the three.[72] After conventional greetings in which the thief Gcugcwa identified himself, Shaka ordered him to be laid across the entrance to the cattle kraal and killed by having the cattle driven over him, which then occurred. The seriousness of the crime of cattle theft was evidently considered sufficient reason for the death penalty in this instance.

Shaka also imposed other punishments, sometimes resulting in death. Baleka's father had told her, "[t]hree of our Qwabe people, Matshongwe, Nhlanganiso, and Mpezulu, had their eyes taken out by him while they were still alive." They were then left to die at the bottom of a cliff.[73]

Baleka's father became a target of Shaka for sending a warning to the eLangeni people that an attack was imminent:

He [Shaka] sent out an *impi* [body of armed warriors] to kill my father. Mpitikazi had already heard that the king was going to kill him, so he fled. But there was then no place to run away to. A person would simply wander about in the land until he was eaten by wild animals, for in those days there were many wild animals which ate people. Father climbed into a tree. The *impi* searched for him; he could see it while sitting up in the tree. It searched and searched, but did not see him, and gave up. He ate filth from the river; he no longer knew food. He slept in the forests.

He then went to the place of Mbopa ka Sitayi, not to any relations of his (Mpitikazi's) but to Mbopa's, and did not appear at the Great One's [Tshaka's] place. Then he was sent by Sitayi to the king himself. And he went, because he had been found, and was afraid to refuse. He saw that there was no help for it, for

Sitayi would kill him. "If I refuse, if I say I am not going to the king, he says he will kill me." So he went off, traveling alone. He did not set off in the belief that he would return; he simply went knowing that he was going to die.

He [Mpitikazi] arrived, and went into the cattle kraal to the *izinduna* [officers], to Ngqengelele. He walked forward reluctantly and limply to the upper end of the cattle kraal; the *izinduna* were sitting inside.

Tshaka came out of his hut. He said, "I think I know this person, my Zulu. Look at this red-skinned fellow; I would say it is Mpitikazi." Then his mother Nandi came out. Reciting Tshaka's praises, she said to him, "Surely you will not kill Mpitikazi? What is Mpitikazi that you should kill him, he who is just a dog?" Tshaka said, "Go, fellow, you with the little red ears. Your 'mother' has saved you, go. Go, genet of the wilderness that outwitted the dogs' (the force that had been searching for him)." "The genet became green in colour while sitting up in the tree" [i.e. Mpitikazi remained well hidden from Shaka's forces by climbing a tree.] That is the story of Mpitikazi's escape.

He escaped because Nandi was his mother's sister [i.e., he was Tshaka's first cousin].[74]

Some of the executions ordered by Shaka were politically motivated killings, such as those of chiefs or warriors. But Shaka was also said to have killed sections of his own *impis* if they became too proud.[75] The oral traditions suggest that when he ordered mass killings and the killing of women and children, it was seen as being prompted by personal motives that his people neither understood nor accepted. The most famous of these occurred following the attempt to assassinate him. This attack was attributed to the AmaQwabe on the grounds that a spear of AbaQwabe manufacture had been used to stab Shaka. In 1903, Jantshi gave Stuart his account of the incident that includes details suggestive of an eyewitness account from his father Nongila, lending it strong credibility. Jantshi said that on that day in 1824,

I know Tshaka was stabbed in the left arm, the *assegai* slightly entering his left side. He drew the assegai out himself and ran into a hut. Looking at the assegai he found it had a shaft blunted at the top, and so concluded it belonged to the Qwabe people, whereas it was one of his own people's. After this there was an order that the Qwabe people were to be killed. Having already *konza*'d, they, like the Zulus themselves, lived at Tshaka's kraal at Bulawayo. Those members of the Qwabe tribe found at the king's kraal were killed, a search was made for fugitives at their homes, and the saying arose that members of that tribe would be known by a habit men had of always placing wood on the hearth with the right arm. When caught, they were to be stabbed in the left side. Many members of the tribe were accordingly killed. The people scattered in all directions to hide themselves.[76]

In another report, Stuart learned,

> The main reason why the Qwabe tribe left Zululand is because, when in July 1824 Tshaka was stabbed in the arm and side, it was found he had been stabbed with a Qwabe assegai. This could be seen by the shape of the wood at the end of it, and thereupon Tshaka sent bodies of men out to massacre all members of the tribe. The punitive expedition were told that a characteristic of the people was for them to be always pushing wood further into the fire. Assisted by this and other information, many of the Qwabe people were killed and the majority of the people came south of the Tugela. Many came and lived on a plain known as Kwa Davati near Makanya, not far from Isipingo.[77]

This report is significant in reflecting local AmaZulu knowledge of the event. It suggests that Shaka did indeed attempt to eliminate people of the AmaQwabe chiefdom six or seven years after he had incorporated them following the death of their chief Phakathwayo in the custody of AmaZulu warriors. There are also stories that on one occasion, Shaka killed so many people at one time that he tried to fill a *donga* (i.e., a huge ditch created from erosion), with the bodies, and one person asserted that "Tshaka was dealing with the Qwabe people when he filled or endeavoured to fill a donga with corpses!"[78] Baleka, the *imbongi*'s daughter, had also heard the "donga" story and told it with reference to a motive only of curiosity and experimentation. She did connect this, however, to the AbaQwabe people when she said, "Tshaka said that the Qwabe people should be picked out and all put to death (i.e. hunted out from all parts of the country)."[79] In Baleka's version of this Shaka story,

> Then he saw a *donga* [ditch] as deep as a house, and said, "I wonder if this *donga* could be filled – filled with people?' Then people were tumbled in, and were piled up in the *donga* until it was filled."[80]

Mangati reported the location of the large and deep donga where people were killed "in the bush country on a ridge running towards the Nhlatuze."[81] Taken together, these oral traditions about Shaka's behavior suggest widespread knowledge among the people who came to comprise his AmaZulu subjects that he had engaged in mass killings of people who were killed only on the basis of their identity as AbaQwabe. They came to know it as a form of collective punishment for the crime of an individual or several people engaged in a conspiracy to assassinate him. The evidence seems to suggest that several thousand people may have been killed. However, the evidence also indicates that enough people received warning that they were able to successfully scatter and collectively flee from the area. The majority of the AbaQwabe successfully resettled beyond Shaka's territory where they survived his attempt to eliminate them. The level of mortality can only remain a matter of speculation. It is the best-remembered event of a mass killing of civilians directly ordered by Shaka except for the events associated with the death of his mother Nandi.[82]

A number of stories about Shaka killing warriors survived, and the evidence concerning the collective killing of many at one time is credible with regard to several incidents. The restriction on sexual relations between unmarried men and women was a longstanding tradition, but the regimentation of young men in barracks made it harder for young people to engage in premarital courtship and easier for them to be detected in any violations of the social prohibitions. According to one explanation, "[I]n Tshaka's day no *hlobonga*ing [engaging in external sexual relations] was allowed. The result of this was that girls used to go to their lovers at night time."[83] However, Baleka was told by her father and was certain that Shaka allowed girls to visit their lovers and stay with them, but "what was an offence was if a man spoiled that girl. For she belonged to the king in her regiment, as did the youth. He would now be spoiling a member of a regiment. They would die; they would be killed."[84] The evidence is vague and inconclusive that a large number of young men and women were killed for this offense on one occasion.

More credible are the accounts that Shaka once had an entire regiment killed for contumacy (i.e., resisting authority). The regiments were segregated into their own homesteads or barracks and lived off the food and cattle brought to them by boys and girls from the surrounding areas. The regiments were able to accumulate cattle rewarded to them as booty after a successful raid or expedition. Cattle were the warriors' livelihood, and according to the oral traditions "Tshaka was very liberal with his cattle. He gave the young men (*izinsizwa*) many cattle."[85]

But Shaka also is said to have a warrior tied to a tree and burned to death after he asked Shaka for a greater reward of cattle for his regiment, the Mbonambi.[86] Ngidi explained that Shaka also slaughtered the entire Mbonambi regiment for this reason and had their cattle seized. Ngidi also provided details including names that lend strong credibility to his report. He believed the account was factual and later repeated it with even more details including that of a man, Ndimindwane ka Msweli, who was so loyal to the regiment that he asked to be killed with them, and Shaka accordingly had him also killed. On the other hand, it also appears that not every man was killed, for although

"Tshaka killed the Mbonambi," Ngidi added that "[t]hose remaining were called the Zibolela."[87] The name of a regiment was carried with pride, so in this case, the narrative blurs the distinction between the regiment known by the name Mbonambi and the men who composed it. The dispersal of the survivors makes it impossible to actually know how many men were killed on this occasion, assuming the account was true. Given the ordinary size of a regiment at two to three thousand men, one or two thousand of Shaka's own warriors may have been killed on this occasion.

Shaka was reported to have had the warriors of the umKhandlu regiment put to death after they suffered a defeat on the campaign against the AmaMpondo. He accused them of cowardice and had them "killed off," but at least some of these warriors were allowed to live, and the numbers killed is unknown.[88] Shaka also had warriors killed after they had acquired so many cattle as to pose a threat of overshadowing him.[89] Another of Stuart's interviewees confirmed that "[v]ery frequently did Tshaka cause people to be put to death."[90] He said that, for example, if a man was found with wounds in his back, Shaka had him put to death because he must have been wounded while running away in battle.[91]

Thus, Fynn's description upon first visiting Shaka's capital at Bulawayo that it was a "place of killing," is credible. He later wrote,

On the first day of our visit we had seen no less than ten men carried off to death. On a mere sign by Shaka, viz.: the pointing of his finger, the victim would be seized by his nearest neighbours; his neck would be twisted, and his head and body beaten with sticks, the nobs of some of these being as large as a man's fist. On each succeeding day, too, numbers of others were killed; their bodies would then be carried to an adjoining hill and there impaled. We visited this spot on the fourth day. It was truly a Golgotha, swarming with hundreds of vultures. The effects of this together with the scenes of death made Mr Petersen decide at once to dissolve the partnership and leave for the Cape.[92]

Fynn also described one incident in which "I witnessed 60 boys under 12 years of age dispatched [put to death by Shaka's orders] before he [Shaka] had breakfasted." Fynn said that Shaka's ordering the death of persons in his audience "was a daily occurrence." He described the method of killing and the site where the bodies were taken about a mile away where they became prey to vultures.[93] Fynn's testimony is most credible when it refers to specific events to which he was an eyewitness even if his generalizations were often exaggerated. Such generalizations about Shaka's cruelty could also be found among AmaZulu oral traditions and cannot be dismissed out of hand. One of Stuart's oldest interviewees summarized the stories of Shaka's purported atrocities:

> A man too would be castrated so that he might be an ox. Woman and man would die. If vultures hovered over the kraal he used to cause people to be killed and given to them, as they were hungry and they too had come to attend the *ibandhla* or council. He used to cause a person's eyes to be taken out of his head in order that it may be observed how he managed to walk and adapt himself to the new circumstances. If a man showed a wound in his back, Tshaka would say it was plain he had been running away, and then order him to be pricked with an *assegai* so as to feel what it was like, and then to be stabbed to death and thrown away. People who had been sent to kill others were themselves met when returning and killed in order to know what death was.[94]

This early interview suggests that stories of atrocities committed by Shaka had been long retained in oral traditions and retold throughout the nineteenth century by the AmaZulu. They also remembered that Shaka glorified some of these acts in his own praises:

> "You do not ask the askers for us to agree with them,
> We went and took out their eyes,
> They went floundering about, falling into dongas."

This is one of Tshaka's songs, made up by himself, for he used to do so. People's eyes were taken out with an awl, and sap of the euphorbia was rubbed in the eyes (white stuff from this tree and is very pungent in the eyes). Regiments used to sing this song. It was a hunting song.[95]

Maclean (John Ross) also reported witnessing executions when he first arrived at Shaka's capital. He said that they watched the men and women dance and sing together, but on their first day, the Europeans were to observe three people carried to the site of execution and killed there, reportedly for violating the corn law, i.e. for eating the harvest prior to the first fruits ceremony. Maclean described the means of execution, in which the victims are stunned by a blow to the head and then stabbed with a stake up the abdomen and left to die.[96] Shaka had ensured that the Europeans witnessed every aspect of his power, including the power to inflict a death penalty. Like the other Europeans, Maclean was horrified but remarked at the bravery usually exhibited by those marked for death and during their execution. He claims that he had such extraordinary influence over Shaka that he was able to stay the hand of execution, although he does not indicate if this was on one or numerous occasions.[97] Maclean's testimony is important because he was allowed such open access to the forbidden inner reaches of the capital, including the women's quarters, and because he retained a lifelong affection for the AmaZulu at the same time that he abhorred the violence he witnessed being perpetrated by Shaka himself. Maclean provides a more balanced perspective on the last years of Shaka's rule after 1825 than is commonly found in other European accounts. For example, Maclean denied some of Stephen Kay's statements about Shaka, including Kay's portrayal of an incident in which Shaka is said to have ordered seventy or eighty children to be killed, which Maclean says never happened.[98] Maclean expressed his outrage at the falsehoods regarding the crimes of cruelty Shaka was said to have committed even though Maclean was aware of the executions that took place at the capital. He also testified to the internal politics of Shaka's inner circle to which he attributed much of the violence:

I have indeed witnessed many blood executions of innocent victims prompted by degrading superstitions, and I know too that many victims were immolated at the instance of a cringing and cowardly scoundrel named Mbopha, a confidential servant; so much so, that he was the only individual in the Zulu nation who was permitted to carry a spear in the presence of and within a limited distance of the king. Availing himself of this privilege, he subsequently stole behind and assassinated his master, an arrangement having been previously entered into with the murdered Shaka's brother, Dingane, whose ambition it appears became weary of waiting for the removal of his brother, Shaka, in the ordinary course of nature.[99]

Stuart was told a detailed story about how "Tshaka on one occasion set on the Embo and Nxamalala people to fight one another." The long narrative included dialogue about the planned fight in which the AmaNxamalala defeated the Embo of chief Zihlandhlo and were subsequently defeated by Zihlandhlo's brother Sambela. The AmaNxamalala were tragically caught in animal traps and killed by the warriors when they could not escape. Mandhlakazi told Stuart not only that before Shaka arranged the battle, the two chiefdoms had no reason to fight each other, and "[a]lthough not many could have been killed in that way, the incident was never forgotten or forgiven by the Nxamalalas, who regarded the traps as intentionally set to catch them."[100]

The AmaZulu oral traditions also remember that Shaka ordered the killings of women and children. Not surprisingly, it is the testimony of women who provided the best evidence of the perspective of women during Shaka's era. Baleka, who said, "Tshaka did many evil things to people," told Stuart a story she had heard that Shaka's maternal grandmother, Nandi's mother, Mfunda, once called out to Shaka, "Tshaka! Do you think, because you kill people, that you are now going to kill

Shaka's Rule: Social Configuration and Social Control 251

Mfunda too?"[101] Several people, men and women, told Stuart that Shaka once had a living pregnant woman cut open in order to see the child inside.[102] Maziyana believed Shaka had cut open "a number of women" like this while their husbands were away on the Balule military expedition to the north and that "that was one of the reasons why Dingana put Tshaka to death. These women had done no wrong; he behaved thus as part of his policy of government."[103] Questioned by Stuart at their joint interview, both Melapi and Maziyana indicated that they believed this had actually happened to one woman who was identified by name, but only Maziyana further suggested that more than one woman suffered this form of murder on Shaka's orders.

To indicate disapproval for Shaka's actions could be a death sentence to anyone who so dared. According to oral traditions, Shaka's mother Nandi was willing to reproach Shaka for his atrocities. She is said to have openly disapproved of some of his violent actions, and

Nandi remonstrated on two occasions with Tshaka about "throwing off his covering (*ambulaing ingubo*)" by killing his relations. One was when Makedama was killed. The other occasion was when the Qwabe were massacred consequent upon Shaka's being stabbed in the arm at Siklebeni, when the *umkosi* ceremony was being held, by a man whose name was said to be Sikwayo, of the Qwabe people.[104]

Nandi asked, "Why are you taking off your covering, the one of your mother's people? Why are you killing them? Where will you run away to? What people will you fly to?"[105]

Nandi thus foresaw popular rebellion against Shaka as a result of his oppressive rule. Shaka's half brothers may have had their own ambitions, but when they assassinated Shaka, they were expressing widespread popular discontent with Shaka's rule. His use of arbitrary violence through executions and mass murders served to intimidate any who might wish to oppose his rule or depose him from the chieftaincy. In committing unforgettable atrocities, he had sown the seeds of his own destruction.

As the oral sources confirm, the achievement of political consolidation reflected in ceremonial grandeur and the display of wealth and authority came at great cost for many people. Many lives had been lost in the early struggles that had set small chiefdoms into migration, and more were lost from hunger as crops were destroyed and cattle seized from their owners to be added to the royal herds. Even as a youth, Maclean had noted that before the the arrival of the trader's party en route to Bulawayo, "we had passed through comparatively depopulated country where nought was left us to contemplate but the perishing remnants of humanity that were, indeed, thickly strewn in the way."[106] On their journey, Maclean's party encountered men called Maphisi whose sole occupation was hunting. The hunters were treated as a subject, inferior people; using spears they hunted hippopotami as well as elephants. Maclean wrote,

The heaps of human skulls and bones blanching the plains were sad monuments of the fearful conflicts that had annihilated whole tribes, while these Maphisi were but the wretched remnants.[107]

Chapter 11

Shaka's Ambitions

The death of Shaka's mother in 1827 prompted him to remove his capital from Bulawayo to Dukuza and pursue his ambitions for the expansion of his authority to the southwest, even beyond the territory of modern Natal. Nandi's death was momentous, and its repercussions left the AmaZulu of the kingdom's own heartland reeling and weakened socially and politically. But Shaka demonstrated his sense of having been emboldened by the victories and raids of 1826 and 1827 and made his ambitions clear with two major military campaigns planned and launched in 1828, one to the south and one to the north. At the same time, Shaka became gradually aware of the growing discontent that might threaten him most from the people closest to him, his own family and counselors. Only in the last month of his life would he demonstrate his sense of vulnerability by which time plans were already in the making for his assassination.

SHAKA AND EUROPEANS: THE SOTOBE MISSION AND THE CAPE COLONY

Shaka knew quite a lot about Europeans, the Cape Colony, and Cape Town before he ever met with Europeans the first time. According to one of Stuart's earliest interviewees, "Tshaka liked Europeans, who were first reported to him as people white in colour who had come out of the water and whose hair was like maize tassles....He called the white people *abakwetu*."[1] Shaka was determined to gain as much information as possible about the Europeans at the Cape Colony in order to deter their territorial expansion and pursue his own expansionist ambitions. Fynn wrote, "[d]uring his four years' knowledge of us, Shaka, from the incessant enquiries made of his interpreter, Jacob, and of myself, (who had by this time acquired a knowledge of the Zulu language), received so much information respecting Europe and our sovereign (whom he called umGeorge) that he expressed a desire to send chiefs to visit both the Colony and England."[2]

That passage is important for establishing that Shaka's impressions of Europeans was strongly influenced by two groups. He learned from direct contact with the traders from Port Natal and with those Portuguese who passed through (the ship-wrecked Portuguese who traveled from Port Natal to Delagoa Bay), but also gained information from traders coming and going to Delagoa Bay, from Fynn and Maclean in answer to questions, and from Jacob who had experience of the Cape Colony including imprisonment on Robben Island. These people served as the filters that determined what Shaka heard, and they shaped his impressions and influenced his decision making. This situation gave Jacob, the most constant influence on Shaka with regard to his relations with Europeans, a great deal of power. The evidence of Shaka's questioning multiple independent sources to test the accuracy of information given to him indicates that he was not unaware of the potential problems of being purposely deceived. The evidence also suggests that Shaka tended to disregard information that did not accord with his own explicitly expansionist agenda. The year 1828, prior to Shaka's death, marked a clear turning point in history as a result of Shaka's specific decisions that were consciously linked to his relationship with the Cape Colony. Fynn's evidence about this entire period is critical for understanding Shaka's motives and the extent and limitations of his knowledge and understanding. Jacob's historical role was tragic but was perhaps not the deciding factor as all evidence regarding the situation suggests. Shaka would have proceeded with his plans in any event.

Two important AmaZulu men, Sotobe and Mbozamboza, and their wives were sent with the duplicitous ex-slave interpreter and convicted criminal Jacob and the trader James King via the latter's newly built boat from Port Natal to Port Elizabeth at Algoa Bay. There they were to meet with British colonial representatives and try to continue on to Cape Town.[3] Jacob had been hired as an interpreter on the traders' exploratory voyage to St. Lucia Bay before the first settlement of traders at Port Natal in March 1824. He appears in numerous early European narratives and was probably the earliest source of information about Europeans for Shaka. According to Maclean, Captain King had arranged Jacob's release from prison so he could serve as interpreter and he had fled from King and

Shaka's Ambitions

Farewell's exploratory party in 1823 after a quarrel at St. Lucia Bay. Maclean concluded that "from him [Jacob] there is no doubt the Zulu chief first learnt the white men's strength and numbers at the Cape Colony."[4] Shaka made Jacob, called Nhlamb'amanzi or Nhlamba, into an *induna* with land and people allocated to him from the AmaCele chief Magaye. Stuart was told,

> Tshaka never divulged what Nhlamba [Jacob] told him about what the white people did and were. The only occasion on which he [Shaka] did so was when he directed Kam' Kangi [James King] to build a boat to take his people [the Sotobe mission] to go and see the white people's king (i.e. to see the people Nhlamba had been telling him so much about).[5]

Shaka's main ambassador on this mission was Sotobe ka Mpangalala. The son of Shaka's counselor Ngqengelele referred to Sotobe as "the great prime minister" to Stuart's assistant and informant Ndukwana.[6] Makewu said, "Sotobe was sent by Tshaka over the sea to go and find out what the English people's home was like" but mistakenly believed that he had not returned before Shaka's death.[7] Ndukwana believed that "Tshaka wanted to go himself to the British government and conduct his negotiations with them in person." Ndukwana presumed that Shaka's intentions were amicable toward the British because his positive intentions toward the British were given as the reason that an AmaZulu regimental commander gave his allegiance to the British before the battle of Ceza against Dinizulu ka Cetshwayo in June 1888.[8] The evidence suggests, however, that Shaka was deeply worried about the threat to the AmaZulu posed by Europeans at the Cape Colony. His exposure to firearms confirmed to him the superiority of European weaponry.

Maclean's experiences provide some insight into Shaka's conflicted reactions to Europeans. He called the young teenager "Jackabo" and spoke often with him, perhaps because he was less a threat than the grown men who composed the rest of the European traders' party. In one conversation, Maclean notes that Shaka referred to "an *umfokazana*" ["umfogasann"], which Maclean defined as "a common man, or an expression for the lower order of the natives" This comment indicated that Maclean had distinguished and recognized the clear evidence of socioeconomic differentiation and stratification in Shaka's Zulu society. Shaka claimed that every *umfokazana* wanted him to kill the white people and said, "I have been often told by my Indaba (Council) to kill you wild beasts of Mlungus [white people]." Thus, Shaka was telling this boy, and through him the entire white trader community at Port Natal, that they depended entirely on him alone for their lives because both the commoners and the people of highest rank wanted him to have them all killed. In this conversation Shaka also said, "I see and feel that you are a good and a superior people; a strange, a wonderful people."⁹ Maclean believed that from the moment that Captain James King notified Shaka he was going to build a boat to return to the Cape Colony, on his very first visit, Shaka began his plan for what was eventually the Sotobe ambassadorial mission to the Cape Colony. In his memoirs, Maclean wrote,

> Shaka seemed to entertain an absorbing interest in this mission, and appeared anxious and solicitous to have some certain and tangible proof from the British government of its friendly alliance. I feel assured he would have made a sacrifice of any minor consideration for this. His penetration convinced him of the vast superiority of the white man's mode of warfare in the use of fire-arms, and though his military genius had effected great improvement in the Caffrarian mode practised by his predecessors, he saw with all his improvements its disparity when brought in contrast with the musket.¹⁰

Maclean's memories confirm what the AmaZulu testimony collected by Stuart asserted: that Shaka's real motive was not to have a "friendly alliance" with the British but to gain access to European weapon technology, firearms. Jantshi was explicit: "Tshaka used to have European guns tested .... at various distances. He was fond of seeing the power of a gun, and his intention was to send a regiment of men to England who there would scatter in all directions in order to ascertain exactly how guns were made, and then return to construct some in Zululand."¹¹ Jantshi's father had served as a spy for Shaka, and as such had been sent to scout out the Cape Colony where the Europeans were living. Jantshi told Stuart that "[m]y father was at Dukuza when Tshaka sent off Sotobe. I do not know if any other Zulu went with Sotobe ka Mpangalala. Sotobe's instructions were that he was to go to England to see the white people, and if Tshaka had lived he would have sent more people for he was very anxious to see how guns were made."¹² Part of Shaka's inner circle, Nongila had told his son Jantshi that Shaka had foretold to the men in his Dukuza courtyard as Sotobe's mission was leaving in the boat to go to Port Elizabeth that after his death the country would be "ruled by white men."¹³

Sotobe was "of the Sibiya people" lived "near Ntunjambili – on the Inadi stream," and had territory and adherents both north and south of the Thukela River.¹⁴ One of Sotobe's subjects told Stuart, "Sotobe ka Mpangalala, under whom I lived, had many followers. He occasionally killed people, no one going to report to the king," meaning that during Shaka's era, Sotobe retained the perquisites and prerogatives of a somewhat independent chief.[15] According to this testimony, Sotobe must have been very elderly, for he was said to have claimed he was "of the age-group of Jama," Shaka's paternal grandfather, and had herded cattle "before Senzangakona was born."[16] This is not impossible because Shaka was born while Senzangakona was still a herdboy, perhaps in his late teenage years, so that Sotobe may have been about thirty years older than Shaka, or in his seventies at the time of his mission, and his stature as a chief of this age and importance would explain Shaka's belief he could both impress the Europeans and be trusted to gain important information from the trip.[17]

Ngidi said that far south in Natal, bordering on the territory of the AmaMpondo, "Tshaka built two kraals in these parts, viz. Ndabenkulu near Bellair, i.e. Mcasimbana's (Stainbank's), and the other, Tshoyisa, just across the Umzimkulu (near the mouth) and near the large wagon drift. There is no doubt that Tshaka wanted to go on building until he came into touch with the Europeans, he being on friendly terms with them."[18] Nathaniel Isaacs was among the Europeans who traveled with the Sotobe mission aboard Captain James King's newly built vessel and wrote that Shaka had invested in Sotobe "ample power to negotiate a friendly alliance with His Britannic Majesty," but added that Fynn, left behind, was perceived as a hostage for the safe return of the Sotobe party.[19] Isaacs acknowledged his indebtedness and that of King's party for Shaka's assistance after their original shipwreck in Natal. Isaacs was unnerved, however, by Shaka's behavior and regretted that he had missed the first opportunity to leave Natal because he had been away from the port on a trading expedition. Isaacs and Captain King returned with the Sotobe party in the *H.M.S. Helicon* after about three months at Algoa Bay because of their obligation to Fynn. The tragedy of Jacob's involvement became evident upon their return, for he convinced Shaka of the hostile intentions of all of the traders, inflaming his sentiments against them. It was Shaka's ambitions to expand his territorial control over the AmaMpondo and beyond. That plan was to direct the *Ihlambo* campaign and lead to his assassination soon after.

CLEANSING NANDI'S DEATH: THE 1828 "IHLAMBO" CAMPAIGN AGAINST THE AMAMPONDO

As explained in AmaZulu oral traditions, "[t]he *impi* sent to Pondoland by Tshaka was an *ihlambo* one on account of the death of his mother."[20] But Shaka had already planned that while the Sotobe mission was away, he would lead a military expedition against the AmaMpondo on the pretext that they were part of the cleansing ceremonies related to the death of his mother Nandi. Shaka's attention was drawn again to Faku's territory by the potential wealth and military power to be derived were the AmaMpondo to submit to his rule. The occasion for sending a second campaign in 1828 arose as the final stage of a year of mourning for the death of Shaka's mother, giving it the name "*Ihlambo*" to signify "washing of the spears" and purification. The ceremonial occasion for the second major *impi* into AmaMpondo territory was a pretext, however, as Shaka had planned and prepared for it well beforehand:

When the [*amabece*] *impi* got back its experiences were related before Tshaka, who directed Matubane (Tuli chief) to go and spy in the Mpondo country. He went, and returned with one beast – a black heifer.[21]

Having proved that he had been among the AmaMpondo by virtue of the black heifer he had seized, Matubane provided Shaka the intelligence he needed to plan a campaign. Thus, "[t]he later expedition was a deliberate attack on Faku." The new AmaZulu fighting techniques were used, and "Tshaka's forces did not hurl their assegais but Faku's did." Thus, "[t]he [AmaMpondo] country was not taken."[22]

The timing of Shaka's activities indicates careful planning on his part. Fynn wrote: "Only three days after the vessel's departure, messengers arrived from Shaka to Mr. Farewell and myself, requesting that all blacks in our respective services be sent the following morning to follow up a party that had stolen some cattle. As the situation we were in compelled our compliance, they went. I proceeded to my residence at the Umzimkhulu, a distance 80 miles from the port."[23] This passage establishes how and why the AmaMpondo believed and began rumors to the effect that Europeans, Fynn in particular, were assisting Shaka in his planned attack against the AmaMpondo, and the terms in which these rumors filtered down to British officials and the *Graham's Town Journal* notices in the eastern Cape and in Cape Town. Fynn's people had been called to appear for military service by Shaka and had complied with the order to appear, although they did not join or accompany the regiment subsequently. Fynn was explicitly and Farewell was implicitly hostage to Shaka's toleration of their trading activities that in turn required their compliance with his orders. Defiance of these orders could be expected to result in their deaths. Fynn's residence in proximity to the AmaMpondo had been established precisely because of the access it provided to trade in that direction. The AmaMpondo saw his return to the Umzimkhulu just as

Shaka traveled there to oversee military operations against the AmaMpondo only as evidence that Fynn was an active and willing participant in Shaka's military action against them. This was far from the truth, but Shaka did impose himself upon the unwilling hospitality of Fynn in southern Natal. From there Shaka oversaw the military campaign. Fynn's account of the events surrounding Shaka's 1828 attack against the AmaMpondo and his own actions during this time are very revealing of Shaka's intentions. His commentary also sheds light on the sources of confusion that led to misleading reports about Fynn himself at that time and about the extent and limits of the knowledge and understanding of colonial officers and commanders in operations east of Grahamstown as far as the Bashee and Umtata Rivers. Fynn had only just returned to his residence on the Umzimkhulu River when he heard "that Shaka was near at hand on his way to attack the amaMpondo."[24] The collecting and "doctoring" of such huge regiments for this expedition required considerable advanced planning in calling for and collecting the regiments, giving orders, and sending them out. However, Shaka's troops were on the move within a week or less after the departure of the Sotobe mission. The timing was not coincidental but the result of Shaka's careful planning. Sotobe and Mbozamboza were suspected by colonial officials in the eastern Cape of being Shaka's spies, so it was reasonable for officials who did not know Fynn to suspect his willing complicity with Shaka's military plans. Fynn's relationship with Shaka had put him into what appeared to be an intimate relationship of trust because they stayed up late at night habitually and Fynn provided Shaka with information, including about his trading operations in AmaMpondo territory. This would only have been confirmed, mistakenly, in the minds of the AmaMpondo from subsequent events.

Upon Shaka's arrival, Fynn went out to meet him at one of the villages under his protection and, under implicit threat of his life, Fynn offered Shaka one hundred muids of Indian corn for the use of Shaka's army. Shaka accompanied Fynn back to his own home where, as an unwilling host, Fynn told Shaka to take what he wanted from Fynn's herds of cattle. Fynn could not have anticipated what happened next, but he was not in a position to refuse as his life and the lives of his people were all at risk: "He [Shaka] selected 17 [head of cattle] and thereupon made my place his headquarters. The army, after resting three days, marched toward their destination, some 120 miles further on to the south-westward. Shaka himself remained behind with only a small division, to act as circumstances might dictate."[25] Shaka deliberately led his army via Fynn's home kraal and made it his headquarters so that it would be perceived that Shaka controlled Fynn and the Europeans and that they supported Shaka's military actions, the conclusion to which the AmaMpondo and Hintza and British commanders came.[26] On the colonial frontier, a white man believed to have been Fynn was reported to have accompanied Shaka's troops and to have been fighting with them, having shot and then treated a man.[27]

Fynn, who by his own account was fluent in the isiZulu language, recorded the events and speeches as he observed them when the "doctors" used ceremonies and "medicine" to "strengthen" the troops and Shaka exhorted them in a speech before they left for battle.[28] Most importantly, Fynn wrote that Shaka told the warriors that in mourning for Nandi, "they must, therefore, exterminate the whole of the tribes between him and the Colony." But then Shaka revealed his real object: "He wished, he said, to open a road, and, for that purpose, had already sent chiefs in order that he might be on good terms with the white people."[29] He sent the army out in two divisions, each subdivided and headed by its own commanders, but after they had started, Shaka called them all back so he could order them "not to proceed further than [Chief] Hintsa's [AmaXhosa] people" and not to engage in any hostilities with white people.[30] These orders indicate that the AmaXhosa of Hintsa, as much as the AmaMpondo of Faku, were targets of the attack. According to Fynn, eight days later, daily reports began arriving through messengers of "repeated successes" and that the troops had crossed the Umthata River and were well into Transkeian AmaXhosa territory.[31] The intent to go beyond the AmaMpondo is evident from these reports, heard by Fynn, of the army's advance.[32]

According to his own account, Fynn engaged in frequent arguments with Shaka, who then publicly ridiculed white people in front of the chiefs who were present only to apologize privately later. Shaka's demonstration was as much for the chiefs as for Fynn because it showed the chiefs that Shaka could insult Fynn and white people to their faces with impunity. It also served to enhance the impression that he was more intelligent and more powerful than Europeans. This would dissuade anyone from abandoning Shaka and seeking aid from white people. Many had already done so, finding refuge from Shaka among Farewell, Fynn, and the other traders. However, by then Shaka had been able to call those who had fled to the white traders back to serve in his army. Shaka had good reason to think his reputation of being the most powerful king was secure among his own people. He did not perceive a threat from within his own ranks but from Europeans and understood that the threat came from their superiority of weapons rather than any other factor. He did not wish to become European or be like Europeans; he wanted Europeans to see how his superior people, represented by Sotobe, Mbozamboza, and their wives, dressed. Shaka did not know how Europeans perceived him and his people; Fynn and Farewell had been so successful in dissembling that Shaka concluded that his own power and culture would command the Europeans' respect.

Taking Shaka's claims to be seeking friendly relations with the Europeans at the Cape Colony at face value, Fynn warned him that his attack against the "frontier tribes" (i.e,. the AmaXhosa) would only convince them of the reverse. Shaka deflected this criticism by telling Fynn that Europeans were wrong to trust their frontier neighbors:

"How is it," he observed, "they [the AmaXhosa] attempt to play on your superiority of force and arms? You know they steal your cattle and kill your countrymen. By destroying a tribe entirely, killing the surviving chiefs, the people would be glad to join you on your own terms. You could then seize all the ivory and horns without paying for them, and give me the beads."[33]

In this conversation as reported by Fynn, Shaka also explicitly revealed his perception of the superiority of European "force and arms," which explains why he did not want to engage directly in warfare against any Europeans and wanted to expand trade opportunities with the colonists.

Fynn then used Shaka's dependence on him for information to the benefit of the AmaMpondo. He explained: "Owing to the knowledge I had of Faku, Shaka asked me one morning if I thought, were he to withdraw his army, Faku would consent to becoming his tributary. I replied in the affirmative and recommended, as an inducement, the return of the girls who had been captured and sent to him by the army, and refraining from destroying more corn."[34] These details are important in understanding what was going on in the zone of fighting.

Female captives were taken and food supplies were destroyed, which is what the AmaMpondo were experiencing at the time that Sotobe was on his "mission." Shaka took Fynn's advice. Chiefs formerly tributary to Faku now came to *konza* Shaka in person, and he accepted their allegiance to and subordination to him. Faku's response is not explained. Fynn reported that Shaka

> accordingly sent messengers to Faku with proposals for peace, at the same time returning the females as proof of his bona fides; he, moreover, directed his army to withdraw and to stop destroying the corn. Several chiefs of petty tribes in Faku's

neighbourhood, with messengers from Faku, returned with the army to thank him [Shaka] for his liberality in thus sparing their lives. They were rewarded with presents of cattle, selected from those that had been taken from them."[35]

Several of Faku's subordinate chiefs responded by offering their submission and allegiance, but they did not hear from Faku himself.[36] Orders were sent to end hostilities against the AmaMpondo, but when messengers arrived saying the troops were returning, Shaka had the messengers beaten. According to Fynn, "Shaka wanted to know why they had not reached the Colony and defeated the tribes according to his orders. In consequence of this the army could not approach him; they, therefore, remained three days on a plain four miles away, in a starving state, although amidst droves of cattle they had taken, to the amount of 30,000."[37] The only mortality reported with regard to this entire military campaign that resulted in the capture of these valuable herds was one uMpondo man having been shot as the cattle were being taken. The lack of fighting was given as one reason why Shaka immediately sent his forces north on another campaign against Soshangane at the Balule river.[38] According to Fynn, Shaka arranged an elaborate scheme so that it would appear his orders to mount the Balule campaign had been in response to a request by some subordinate chiefs to do so.[39] The day after the warriors were "doctored" and sent to wash in the sea to purify themselves, Shaka composed and sang a song that Fynn included in his memoires, depicting the fate of several small chiefdoms who had resisted submitting to Shaka's authority. In the song Shaka referred to the AmaZulu chiefs' dilatory action that had allowed the AmaMpondo to retreat safely with some of their cattle.[40] Fynn acquiesced to Shaka's insistence that Fynn return with the troops to Dukuza, where he stayed only a night, and Fynn soon heard that the troops had all been sent on the new Balule campaign only two days later.[41]

Relating these events, Fynn wrote that "about this time Shaka composed the following song" about himself: "Why do they not kill him as they did his father? The calf of the hated one, like his father, They hate him." This appears to reflect Shaka's perception of himself and about how he was regarded, although he did not show this recognition consistently. Nevertheless, Shaka perceived his own vulnerability at this point in time, and he formed a new regiment of boys and youth to protect himself after his Balule *impi* had set out.[42]

Zulu ka Nogandaya's son listed these major military campaigns, naming those sent against the AmaMpondo, and that sent to the north:

Two *impi*s [military campaigns] went from Tshaka to the south: (1) the *impi* of the melons (*amabece*), (2) the *impi* for his mother's *ihlambo* [purification at the end of a period of mourning], followed by (3) the *Kukulela ngoqo impi* [north] to the Balule [Olifant's River]."[43]

Although "the impi sent to Pondoland by Tshaka was an *ihlambo* one on account of the death of his mother," Nandi's death may have merely determined the timing and pretext for this military campaign.[44] The 1824 "*Amabece*" campaign against the AmaMpondo had left Shaka ambitious to return and subdue the AmaMpondo in the 1828 "*Hlambo*" campaign.[45] Stuart received a very cogent Zulu account of the *iHlambo* campaign that showed strong agreement with the lengthy account of events related by Fynn, who was unwillingly drawn into the events. Maziyana told Stuart,

> In the *Hlambo* campaign, Tshaka commanded in person. He crossed the Mzimkulu and took up a position there whilst the *impi* went on ahead under the command of Mdhlaka. Faku directed his men not to attack but to allow the Zulus to seize cattle. The force accordingly proceeded far away south as far as Esikaleni se Nyoka in the country of the Bomvana people. On their way thither the Pondos made no attack at all on them; they did not molest in any way. Tshaka himself stayed in Mbulazi's [i.e., Fynn's] *kraal* [village] a short distance across the Mzimkulu. The *impi* seized cattle and returned with them. The Pondos kept out of sight. Faku went off to the Drakensberg. His own cattle were not seized. He [Faku] took off [hid] his father Ngqungqushe's cattle too. The cattle taken were those of his [Faku's] people, light-brown ones (*ezimdubu*). Tshaka remained with the Nobamba regiment at the Mzimkulu. There was also a regiment of girls [on this *impi*], the uNkisimana. There were also girls of the king's *mdhlunkulu* [great house (i.e., royal women)]. The Nkisimana was *butwa*'d [called up, enrolled] at Dukuza. The Mcekeceke and Ntshuku were collected in Zululand [i.e., north of the Thukela River].[46]

Madikane, whose father "fought against Zwide and Sikunyana," reported that after the iHlambo campaign, Faku's messengers "came to Tshaka at Dukuza to pay tribute."[47] The campaign to end the mourning for Nandi was well remembered, especially with reference to the famous indunas in command of the regiments and the presence of women's regiments on this *impi*.[48]

The oral traditions remembered and retold at the beginning of the twentieth century indicate that Shaka's brothers were already at the time of the *iHlambo* campaign planning to assassinate him and that Shaka was aware of their plotting. In a bizarre and detailed story, Dinya told Stuart about an incident that occurred on the return trip following the *iHlambo* campaign when Shaka reached the Mkomazi River.

> Dingana, Mhlangana and others accompanied him. The *impi* crossed higher up. It seems that this occasion was one which other princes and Mbopa – also

present – were going to utilize for assassinating Tshaka. It is said the princes knelt, leaning on the butt-ends of their *assegai*s [spears] as if in a position of humiliation.⁴⁹

At this moment another warrior appeared, and Shaka had him cruelly punished for the inadvertent interruption of his meeting with his brothers which had nevertheless saved Shaka's life:

> This simple incident [Shaka's cruel punishment of another man] was a means of diverting attention and causing the princes to sacrifice the opportunity of killing Tshaka [because they were no longer alone with him], as they afterwards did. They were afraid that the troops would have killed them had they killed Tshaka.⁵⁰

Dinya explained, "[m]y father died in the Balule campaign (Tshaka's). My father also went through the Pondo campaign. He was of the Dukuza regiment. On the troops' coming from Pondoland to the Mkomazi, the princes wanted to kill Tshaka. Dingane and Mhlangana wanted to kill Tshaka, but were afraid of the forces [presumed loyal to Shaka]."⁵¹ One account reported,

> The Pondos were defeated and their cattle seized. On the way back Tshaka directed his forces to go off to Balule. Faku followed him up to pay tribute to him, and was in the act of doing so when he [Shaka] was assassinated.⁵²

By early 1828, Shaka's expansionist ambitions toward the eastern Cape region were evident, but he was also aware of the growing strength of the AmaNdwandwe chief Soshangane to his north. Mkehlangana provided more details that indicate the information from his father Zulu ka Nogandaya reflected Shaka's intentions when he sent the troops on the Balule impi, which were more rational than later believed. Some rumors reported Shaka had "gone mad by giving such an order" to proceed immediately on a second *impi* without rest. This narrative explains, "Tshaka sent forth this impi to the north because there had been no actual fighting with the Pondos, only a seizure of their cattle."⁵³ This is why the Balule campaign followed the *iHlambo* expedition so quickly. Mcotoyi said,

> Nandi then died. A further *impi* was then sent out, this time to the amaMpondo, also in charge of Mdhlaka. On their return the *kukulele ngoko impi* went forth to the north, Tshaka returning home with the cattle seized. The forces were not allowed to go home.⁵⁴

Shaka insisted that Fynn accompany him home, so Fynn was witness to the fact that they had been back only for two days before the army was again sent on an *impi*. Fynn said they were ordered first to attack two tributary chiefs who had not complied satisfactorily with mourning observances for Nandi and then were to go and attack Soshangane, north of Delagoa Bay.[55] Cane, a trader, took the news to the Cape Colony that

The Portuguese settlement is friendly towards the tribes of Omchumquan, and have armed them with a few muskets, it is therefore supposed Chaka's army will be defeated.[56]

At the same time, Sotobe returned with information that reduced Shaka's fear of a threat from the Cape Colony. Fynn wrote:

Expecting to see castles, cities, soldiers and ships, they [the Sotobe mission to Algoa Bay] saw only a village and oxen which they were in the habit of seeing in their own country. The place could not impress them with any idea of British greatness, but materially served to eradicate those ideas of Britain's grandeur and power we had all striven to inculcate.[57]

When the Sotobe mission returned, Mr. King was sick, so Isaacs went in his stead to Shaka with a present from the colonial government and one from Mr. King. "The description given by the chiefs of their reception differed very much from what Shaka had expected, and they represented everything to the greatest disadvantage to escape being punished by death for not proceeding to England." Shaka was dissatisfied with the results of the mission and turned his anger against the Port Natal traders but would not live long enough for them to suffer the consequences of his wrath. Mr. King died of illness, and the traders were required to participate in the ceremony to purify Shaka. After this, Shaka ordered Cane to undertake another mission to the Colony to complain that the previous embassy had been ignored, and to take a present of ivory tusks.[58]

THE 1828 BALULE CAMPAIGN: THE "KUKULELA NGOQO IMPI" TO THE BALULE (OLIFANT'S) RIVER

The Balule campaign was Shaka's undoing.[59] It was referred to as "*kukulela la ngoqo*" because Shaka had ordered that every man should go, "even *ungoqo*, a man who never *konzas* or attends hunting parties or assists in building kings' kraals," as Stuart learned from Makewu, who knew men killed on the campaign.[60] Dinya's father was among the warriors who had died on this campaign, and he explained that Hlangabeza ka Mabedhla had absconded with his people and cattle to Soshangane's so that the goal of the *impi* was to overtake them and retrieve the cattle before proceeding on to attack Soshangane himself.[61] The *impi* was successful in finding these AmaNtshali people, who were put to death according to Dinya, but at this point "the princes had returned to Tshaka at Stanger, their object being to kill him."⁶²

An *impi* [army, military campaign] was sent to Balule [the Olifant's River], to Sotshangana. Tshaka's order was that every soul should go – "*kukulela ngoqo*" (i.e., take every one, even *ungoqo*, a man who never *konzas* or attends hunting parties or assists in building king's kraals etc., one who is never seen at the king's kraal. It was in this expedition that Maruyi's father Sonyanga was killed. Tshaka was at Dukuza when this *impi* went, and it was during its [the *impi*'s] absence that Tshaka was assassinated by Mbopa, acting in concert with Mhlangana, Tshaka's brother, who really instigated the murder.⁶³

In a long narrative that is partly confused, Mtshapi said that Shaka heard an ox bellow during the night and called up the army immediately, saying that everyone, even the "riff-raff" was to be called up, "let no one remain behind, not even old men with bad knees."⁶⁴ The certainty with which the oral traditions remember this major military campaign is explained both because of memories of the individual warriors from many prominent families who led, fought, and died and because of the terms of deployment reflected in the name, the *Kukulela ngoqo impi*. The term *ngoqo* refered to a person who was an invalid or considered to be of low class or indigent.⁶⁵ The name for this military campaign that forced even invalids and the indigent to mobilize with the well-trained forces of the standing army thus became the term used to mean wholesale mobilization and by extension devastation or total destruction, *khukhulanqogo*. When the troops, including the invalids, were assembled, Shaka allowed the old men to remain behind as his guard while "the army duly went off to the Balule."⁶⁶ The campaign is also well remembered because after sending off the regiments, Shaka suddenly realized he was not personally well defended, so he called back the young men who were not yet warriors and who served as baggage carriers to create a new regiment, the *Izinyosi*, or "Bees." The circumstances of the creation of a new regiment was always remembered, and this young regiment was tasked with protecting Shaka on the occasion of the "Balule" campaign, the *Kukulela ngoqo impi* to the Balule (Olifant's) River.

One account indicates that Mdhlaka, who had commanded the iHlambo campaign against the AmaMpondo, was also in command of the *impi* sent against Sotshangane. According to this narrative,

> The Zulus went on the campaign against Sotshangana in an angry mood, as they had not been allowed to rest and passed by their homes. This *impi* Tshaka divided in two at the Mkomazi, at Dududu (a hill near the sea and the Mpambanyoni). One body was sent past Pietermaritzburg and Pasiwe, passed through the Cunu

country, and made for the amaNkamane hill (in Jobe's country, Msinga division) to join the other body sent up the coast. I fancy the two bodies met across the Pongolo, north of it.[67]

Dinya told Stuart one of the longest and clearest narrative of events associated with the Balule or *Kukulela ngoqo* campaign. From Dinya's explanation, it appears that Shaka was not always kept fully informed of the actions of some of his subordinate chiefs, presumably because of a residual sympathy for them on the part of those who might otherwise report to him.[68] About the initial actions of the troops, Dinya said,

> It was not reported to Tshaka that Hlangabeza ka Mabedhla of the amaNtshali tribe had deserted and gone northward after Sotshangana, with people and cattle. The *impi* went on with Mdhlaka. Dingana and other princes went too. The object was to "bring back" Sotshangana, though the more immediate object was to overtake Hlangabeza.
>
> The Zulus accordingly pursued Hlangabeza, and eventually found out where he had temporarily erected his kraals. He built alongside a forest. Mdhlaka's *impi* divided into two after being prepared for action at night-time. One division advanced on the far side of the forest, whilst the main body came on before daybreak to make a frontal attack. The forces closed in simultaneously, followed by their mat-bearers. Every member of the amaNtshali tribe was put to death, and cattle seized. Hlangabeza himself escaped and got to a pond where he tried to conceal himself by getting into the water up to his neck. He was, however, observed by the mat-bearers, who thereupon attacked and put him to death. Prior to this attack, the princes had returned to Tshaka at Stanger, their object being to kill him.[69]

This attack against Hlangabeza and the AmaNtshali was obviously not part of Shaka's plan since because he is said not to have known about Hlangabeza's defection, and the large AmaZulu army proceeded from Hlangabeza to other targets. The AmaZulu army passed through the territory of the AmaSwazi under Sobhuza (Somhlolo) but did not engage in any fighting with them because they had taken refuge in inaccessible caves. Mayinga ka Mbekuzana told Stuart,

> When Tshaka's forces returned from the iHlambo campaign in Pondoland, Tshaka ordered the whole force north to attack Sotshangana. The whole force went along the Drakensberg on its way up past Swaziland. It met Nhlanganiso and some Ntungwa in the north and killed him [them]. Tshaka in the meantime went home and turned out all the old men to go and fight. Many persons took refuge in the bushes. This force followed the other. He started it off himself and then returned. Dingana, Mhlangana, and other relatives – except Mpande and Nzibe who went north, Nzibe dying of fever (*imbo*) in Sotshangana's territory – returned, having decided to kill Tshaka. I do not know what tribe Nhlanganiso belonged to. Nqabeni was also killed by Tshaka's Sotshangana forces. I do not

know what tribe Nqabeni belonged to. Magonondo escaped, so also Madhlangampisi, and Mlambo ka Mavundhla (got onto a hill and kept watch and so escaped). Putile also escaped. The Swazis escaped by going into caves underground.[70]

While the army proceeded from Swaziland north to the Olifant's (Balule) River where Soshangane's AmaNdwandwe chiefdom had resettled several years before, Shaka's brothers proceeded with their plans for his assassination.

Ezimbizaneni, at the place of Mampontsha (chief's name, of Swaziland) and Matshekana (at the Mbuluze, river of Swaziland) – this is the place where Tshaka's *impi* was *tetwa*'d [ceremonially prepared for battle] in Swaziland, for the Balule expedition. It was from this spot that Dingana and Mhlangana returned to kill Tshaka.[71]

The rest of the campaign was a disaster. Madikane provided details of the routes that the troops, "divided into two at the Mkomazi," took.[72] From the evidence of events at Delagoa Bay, we know that they did succeed in attacking Soshangane and the reverberations were felt at the Bay. But on the route home, many became ill and died of fever, presumably malaria, and others died of starvation. So bad was their condition that Melapi said, "the Balule *impi* moreover had no shields, for most of them, having no food, had been obliged to soak them in water and eat them!"[73] Mtshapi described the problems of the army, which camped in a wood of *umdhlebe* trees and became ill. The advanced section retrieved the cattle they had been sent for and began their return, leaving the sick behind. According to this account, during their raid, they had encountered swarms of red locusts, and the locusts poured into Zulu country as the *impi* returned, finishing off the grass and crops there.[74] The disease and starvation suffered by the troops and their losses as a result made the Balule campaign unforgettable for lamentable reasons. This was the last campaign ordered by Shaka:

The *impi* arrived from Sotshangana ill with fever (*imbo*). It was told of Tshaka's death. Magaye was then living. Nqeto escaped and ate [stole, absconded with royal] cattle. He was pursued by a small force that had remained behind with the king, i.e. with Tshaka.[75]

According to Ngidi, Dingane and Mhlangana had turned back to return and kill Shaka when the troops were passing through Swaziland on their way north.[76] Mayinga said, "Dingana, Mhlangana, and other relatives – except Mpande and Nzibe who went north, Nzibe dying of fever (*imbo*) in Sotshangana's territory – returned, having decided to kill Tshaka."[77]

Melapi told Stuart, "the *impi* arrived from Sotshangana ill with fever (*imbo*). It was told of Tshaka's death."⁷⁸

In one of his earliest interviews, Makewu told Stuart one story of these events,

> Tshaka was at Dukuza when this impi went, and it was during its absence that Tshaka was assassinated by Mbopa, acting in concert with Mhlangana, Tshaka's brother, who really instigated the murder. It seems Tshaka went into the cattle kraal to see his cattle. Whilst there, Mbopa began driving about and beating the cattle. Tshaka said, "Why are you beating the cattle?" and as he turned his back to Mbopa, Mbopa threw an assegai at him which struck him. He pulled the assegai out as he ran out of the kraal, but at the gate of the kraal another man lay in wait. This man snatched the assegai Tshaka carried and stabbed him dead on the spot. The *impi* from Balule returned to find him dead.⁷⁹

SHAKA'S DEATH

Shaka's death came just as he had achieved his ambition of receiving the submission of the AmaMpondo chief Faku. One of Stuart's informants said that his father had been wounded "in the Pondo campaign, the second one, when the Pondos were conquered." According to him, the AmaMpondo then "came to Tshaka at Dukuza to pay tribute."⁸⁰ Another man reported that "[t]he Pondos were defeated and their cattle seized. On the way back Tshaka directed his forces to go off to Balule. Faku followed him up to pay tribute to him, and was in the act of doing so when he [Shaka] was assassinated."⁸¹ Mahaya ka Nongqabana was able to name these AmaMpondo men who had come to Dukuza to submit to Shaka on Faku's behalf Faku because one of the men had been Mahaya's maternal uncle. Mahaya said, "[t]hese were the Pondos who had come to *konza* and were present when Tshaka was killed." He continued, "I know nothing about crane feathers being brought on this occasion. I know Dingana, after Tshaka's death, called these Pondos back, and they *konza*'d."⁸² Yet another man told Stuart that the motive for his assassination was linked to the Balule campaign: "[w]hy are we being sent away to another campaign? We shall not have time to build our own kraals. This is why Tshaka was killed. The Balule campaign."⁸³ Another informant similarly told Stuart,

> Tshaka's decision to send the troops on to the Balule (Olifant's) River to the north, in a campaign against the AmaNdwandwe chiefdom of Soshangane, a nephew and former commander of Zwide, was seen as precipitous and some believed it was a sign Shaka had gone mad because he did not allow the troops to rest between these two major military campaigns. Thus [a]fter this *impi* [against

Soshangane (i.e., the Balule campaign)] had gone, Dingana and the other princes said, "When shall we rule and enjoy peace and contentment? This man Tshaka after all appointed himself. He is not the true or hereditary king."[84]

Shaka was assassinated on September 23, 1828, by his personal attendant Mbopha ka Sithayi and Shaka's half brothers. The AmaZulu sources are in accord that the assassins were Shaka's *induna* Mbopha and his brothers, by other mothers, Dingane and Mhlangana.[85] Fynn says that Shaka received the visiting ambassadors at a small "kraal" named Nyakomubi that was about fifty yards away from the palisaded capital of Dukuza. He added that according to Mbopha's information, Shaka's brothers secretly approached him there. Fynn had heard that Mbopha had chased away the visitors by throwing a stick at them. As Shaka asked why Mbopha had done so, Mhlangana and then Dingane stabbed him. Fynn wrote that two former chiefs who happened to be approaching with Shaka's old counselor Ngomane were also killed, and another was wounded but allowed to live.[86]

Ndukwana explained to Stuart that "Mbopa actually stabbed Tshaka; Mhlangana also was said to have stabbed. Mbopa hid Tshaka's assegais [spears] before killing him."[87] Jantshi also described Shaka's death and the roles of his brothers in planning and executing his assassination. Jantshi said that Shaka was alerted to the threat against him because his brothers returned from the military campaign, contrary to his orders:

It was just after Tshaka had sent his forces on after Sotshangana that he was put to death. For, after going some way, all Tshaka's brothers returned home. Tshaka asked, "So you are returning on your own?" It was then that they plotted and killed him, the *impi* at the time being away at Sotshangana's. It returned to find Tshaka dead and it returned dying too along the way, for it was attacked by malaria. The men returned in ones, twos, fives etc. at a time.[88]

The historical accuracy of this part of the narrative is evident because Jantshi's father Nongila participated in these events. Jantshi continued, "[m]y father (Nongila) left the Sotshangana campaign, and returned ill with malaria and nearly died." This information is important because it places Nongila with the troops who were heading to their destination north of Delagoa Bay, a long way, and into malaria-infested areas. This disease did not plague KwaZulu home territory farther south. The testimony indicates that Nongila returned early because he was ill, not because he was a co-conspirator, and he gained direct knowledge of the ensuing events. Jantshi related,

Tshaka's brothers, as already stated, did not accompany this impi and they made no reply to Tshaka's question, "Are you returning on your own?" My father told me about the death of Tshaka, though it was what he had heard from others, for he was not present. Dingana, Mhlangano, Mpande, Ngqojana, Mfihlo, Mqubana and other brothers of Tshaka decided to assassinate him. Mbopa too joined the "brothers." The plan decided on was that Mbopa should stab him. Tshaka was stabbed by Mbopa. He was seated outside at the time of his assassination. I cannot, however, speak accurately on this matter.[89]

Jantshi reiterated that "Mbopa stabbed Tshaka. Senzangakona's sons directed him to stab." He explained, "Mbopa was in the plot to kill Tshaka. The part he took was to hide Tshaka's assegais, which were in his hut. He did this by direction of Mhlangana and Dingana when Tshaka had gone out to wash. It was Mhlangana who stabbed first; Dingana only took hold of Tshaka, and so on."[90]

Dinya related the events of Shaka's death in a narrative that, as Stuart noted, corresponded closely to Fynn's version. In a shorthand style rather than verbatim record, Stuart wrote in his notes of the interview with Dinya,

He says, however, the Pondos had come from Faku with a small drove of oxen in order to tender their chief's allegiance; that some of these cattle were killed in order to be eaten; that Dingana, Mhlangana and Mbopa arrived at night-time; that seeing the messengers from Faku the following morning talking to the king (seated on his "throne" or seat of kingship), he ran up to them and struck them with the stick end of his assegai; that he did this to rouse Tshaka's anger, Tshaka being of course helpless without his forces; that the Pondos ran off at once for their homes, leaving their assegais and the meat which was cooking for them unconsumed; and that those who buried Tshaka probably never survived, for in accordance with custom they were "stones for burying the king."[91]

Socwatcha retold the events as had been related by an eyewitness named Matingwana. A boy at the time, Matingwana had survived the massacre of his kinsmen and then escaped near death several more times before he was eventually taken in by one of Shaka's adult servants, where he came to Shaka's notice.[92] Several months after the military regiments had returned from the AmaMpondo campaign and had left for "Enzakato," Delagoa Bay, Shaka summoned Matingwana.[93] According to this account, Mbopha entered the courtyard with Shaka's own assegais in hand, surprising Shaka, who questioned him but received no response as Mbopha passed by him. At the same time, many of Senzangakona's sons, Shaka's half brothers, entered the courtyard, "each of them carrying a bunch or handful of assegais." According to Matingwana's story told to Socwatsha, "[t]here were many of them [Senzangakona's sons]. No further questions were asked. Mhlangana *gwaza*'d [stabbed] him, and Dingana [did also]." The boy remained seated and saw that "Tshaka ran towards the gate of the kraal, as he did so he fell to the ground, within the cattle kraal."[94] Socwatsha told Stuart that "all this time Matingwana remained seated there. Tshaka had not even told him what he was wanted for." When Dingane turned and saw the boy, he sent him back to his own household.[95] While Shaka lay dying of the wounds, the assegais still in his side, a black ox was sent for.[96]

Not surprisingly, Shaka's last words became the subject of legend. Maziyana included one version of Shaka's reported last words in a report of his assassination that varies from others in asserting it took place after dark. Maziyana told Stuart,

Matubane was present at Tshaka's assassination. The assassination took place at night-time when Tshaka was speaking to amaMpondo. He sat in an open space. Torches [izihlanti] were alight. "Leave me alone, sons of my father, and I shall be your menial [umfokazana, female servant]" said Tshaka when being stabbed. They, Dingana etc., said, "Leave you, the evil-doer [itshinga] who kills the wives of men who are away?" – i.e. away on war (Balule).[97]

Maziyana's report was close to that of Socwatsha, who reported what the eyewitness Matingwana had told him directly. Matingwane said that Mbopha had thrown the first assegai at Shaka, and it stuck into Shaka's back between his shoulder blades.[98] Then Matingwane watched as Mhlanga, Dingana, Ngqojana, and Sopane came forward and also threw assegais at him. Moving toward the gate as he was struck by their spears, Shaka then turned and cried out, and in his last words referred to the manner in which he was killed. Socwatsha told Stuart that Shaka's last words, after he had been stabbed and when he turned and saw his brothers, were "*Ni ngigwaza nje ba ntaba ka baba, ngenzeni? Sebete hlabani uhlanya lwa kwa Mtetwa, o lu bulal'izwe, llu zinigeni,*" i.e., "You stab me like this my father's sons, what have I done? You would strike and stab thus the wild beast of Mtetwa who shatters and destroys the nations he invades!".[99] Ngidi told Stuart that when he was being stabbed Shaka said, "[t]he land will be overrun by the swallows, the white people; you kill me but the land will be destroyed; the sky will be white with stars."[100] He perpetuated a story, then, of a metaphor of swallows applied to Europeans by Shaka at his death. Elements of Dinya ka Zokozwayo's version has also persisted in modern day renditions. According to him,

Tshaka said when stabbed, "Is it the sons of my father who are killing me? How is this, seeing I never put to death any of my brothers ever since I became king? You are killing me, but the land will see locusts and white people come." He then fell.

True enough locusts and Europeans subsequently came. This is evidence of Tshaka being a prophet.[101]

This passage shows how the transformation of oral history into literary traditions about Shaka had already begun by the time Dinya spoke with Stuart. Similarly, Lunguza ka Mpukane tried to provide a sense of authenticity to his characterization of a prophetic Shaka by pointing out that he was a little boy at the time of Shaka's death and was neither an eye witness nor did he say where his story came from. He told Stuart,

When Tshaka was put to death I know the words he used: "Children of my father [brothers], are you killing me, I who am of your house and king of the Zulu? Your country, children of my father, will be ruled by white people who will come up from the sea." I often feel how true this prophecy was. I was a boy capable of carrying babies pick-a-back at that time [September 23, 1828].[102]

By the end of the nineteenth century, the attribution of Shaka's prophecy of what subsequently happened was appealing politically and for its literary value to listeners. From these Shaka stories of the early twentieth century, we can state with certainty only that in September 1828 Shaka was assassinated, stabbed in his own courtyard by a counselor and at least two of his brothers while he was unattended, unarmed, and accepting tribute from the messengers of a powerful chief.

Fynn's report corresponds to these AmaZulu descriptions of events in the identification of the assassins. He believed "[t]here is little doubt that the intention of killing Shaka had been long in contemplation. As I have since understood, it was intended to have taken place at my residence during the attack on the amaMpondo, at which time both brothers remained behind with Shaka feigning sickness, when an opportunity was wanting to effect their purpose." Fynn also believed that when the brothers finally got their chance to carry out their plans later at Dukuza, Shaka was receiving foreign visitors, identified by Fynn as "Bechuanas" but by AmaZulu traditions as Faku's AmaMpondo representatives. Fynn's account relates that Mbopha drove off the visitors, giving Mhlangana and Dingane the opportunity to approach from behind the fence where they had been waiting and stab Shaka, who exclaimed "What is the matter, children of my father?" as Dingane struck the second blow, and Shaka fell dead near the gate. Fynn's account of these and the ensuing events are neither more nor less credible than any other accounts but was derived from others and cannot be assumed to be accurate in its details.[103]

Shaka's body lay there while "[a] black ox belonging to Tshaka and the Nyakamubi kraal was fetched and killed," and the usual ceremonies were performed using its entrails for purification. Then Socwatsha said,

[a]nother black ox was got for the purpose of providing a skin for Tshaka to be tied up in. At first Mhlangana suggested tying Tshaka with strings and dragging the corpse to the Mbozama where it would be thrown into an *isiziba* [pool] & be eaten by the alligators there. Dingana objected to this & said as he [Shaka] was *inkosi* [chief] he must be buried as such. It was then the ox was got, killed & Tshaka's body done up in it according to custom – after the *assegai*s still sticking in the corpse had been extracted by the Nyakamubi people.

The corpse was then removed to a hut in the kraal and as is usual was tied to a post – in a sitting posture. The hut at night was occupied by relatives, including women but not those who *ncelisa*'d [were nursing babies]. The funeral rites were performed by the Nyakamubi people. Dingana insisted he should be buried in a way that became his rank, as had been done to Senzangakona, Jama etc. I do not know if a hole was dug for him [Maziyana says he was buried in a *mabele* (maize storage pit) hole in the *sibaya* (cattle kraal)] – The *izinceku* [servants] were *lahlwa*'d [buried] with him.[104]

Fynn had been told that a piece of cloth was put in Tshaka's mouth to repress his anger as an ancestor whose brothers (understandably) still feared him. Fynn wrote that Tshaka's possessions were buried with him. The earth was then thrown in and a hut built over it. The people employed at the burial were posted as guard over him, having cattle and corn given them for their subsistence. They were now isolated from their countrymen, not being allowed to associate with anyone or to go out of the place, and everyone entering the kraal was subject to the same restrictions of strict isolation and confinement on pain of death.[105]

The youthful eyewitness Matingwana was lucky to escape with his life because other servants were killed to be buried with Shaka, but Dingane rejected him as too young. Everything that had ever belonged to Shaka or had been used or worn by him was collected from everywhere across the kingdom and burned at Dukuza, and not until this had been done was Shaka's body buried.[106] Socwatsha also said that after Shaka's *izinceku* (servants) had dug his grave, some were killed to accompany him as his servants in the sky (*ngapezulu*, or heavens). Ngidi was able to identify the important attendants killed to be buried with Shaka and explained that some targeted for death managed to escape and flee abroad to safety.[107]

Dingane then sent men to bring all of Shaka's possessions that were in his villages north of the Thukela River to the burial site at Dukuza, where they were all burned and buried with him, and "[t]he body remained unburied until the things referred to had been got from Zululand."[108] According to Socwatsha, Shaka was buried at Dukuza rather than Emakosini, the traditional burial grounds of the AmaZulu chiefs, because "there were none to carry him" there with the *impi* still being away. People were ordered to mourn for Shaka. Fynn reported that the personal property collected and buried with Shaka included "several tons of beads, brass and various other objects," a fortune in wealth at that time. Fynn was not present at the burial, but he was told that Shaka's head was placed on a carved headrest, a blanket was placed over him, and his property was placed by his side before he was covered with dirt. Fynn did not mention and may not have known that Shaka's servants were buried with him according to custom. Ngidi named three indunas who were killed at the same time and buried with him, according to the customary funeral of a chief or king.[109] A hut was placed over Shaka's gravesite, to be guarded by his relatives.[110]

Chapter 12

The Legacy of Shaka's Reign

After Shaka's death, his assassins were left to compete for the inheritance of the chieftaincy. According to Ndukwana, "[i]t was general knowledge that on Tshaka's dying Mhlangana would rule," and Lunguza said that "[w]hen Tshaka was killed Mhlangana jumped over him, as he looked on himself as successor; Dingana did not jump over him," signifying an understanding that Mhlangana was the rightful heir.[1] Not long after Dingane's men killed Mhlangana and Mbopha, the other co-conspirator, leaving the AmaZulu chieftaincy in the uncontested hands of Dingane. Ndukwana explained that Mhlangana was known to have stabbed Shaka whereas Dingane was not believed to have done so:

Mbopa [Shaka's personal attendant] was put to death for having killed the king. A discussion arose as to who should succeed, Dingana or Mhlangana. This discussion took place before Ngqengelele, the first man (*unkulunkulu*) of the Zulu country. Nomcoba, sister of Tshaka, as also Mkabayi, another sister [aunt] of Tshaka, were present. The result of this inquiry was that Mhlangana was not allowed to reign, on the ground, as stated by Nomcoba and Mkabayi, a man may not rule with a red *assegai*, one which has stabbed a king. Dingana was declared king, for it was found that, though participating in the assassination, he had not used a lethal weapon, but merely laid hold of Tshaka. Mhlangana was killed, i.e. by Nomcoba and Mkabayi together (by their order).[2]

The oral traditions remembered the consultative process that took place to choose the new king after Shaka's death. The consultation included both the senior member of the royal family, in this case a woman and Shaka's paternal aunt, and other senior men of the kingdom. Their decision gave the appointment of the new king legitimacy and broad support because it was in accord with past practices and traditions.

Senzangakona's sister Mnkabayi had been coregent after the death of their own father Jama before Senzangakona came of the age to govern. She had facilitated Shaka's return to assume the chieftaincy and then, after his death, helped to guide the decision to install Dingane.[3] When called to the capital following the assassination, she disguised herself as a man carrying a shield and spears, and upon arrival, began reciting the praises of the AmaZulu chiefs.[4] Also present to consult in the decision about the inheritance of the chieftaincy following Shaka's death were the senior counselor and senior man of the kingdom, Ngqengelele, who had served Senzangakona, Mnkabayi's sister Mmama, and Shaka's sister Nomcoba.[5] One tradition asserts that the decision was referred to Mnkabayi, paternal aunt to the claimants, and she selected Dingane by referring to his mother, saying, "Is the child of Myiyeya's daughter not the child of someone important?"[6] According to this oral tradition, Mnkabayi cited uSigujana as her brother Senzangakona's legitimate heir whom Shaka had killed. Then she proclaimed that the son of Senzangakona's wife Mpikase should rule. This was an implicit endorsement of Dingane through reference to his mother.[7] This explicit reference that links Mnkabayi's understanding of the legitimacy for inheritance of the chieftaincy by Sigujana to that of Dingane by reference to Mpikase indicates that the two were full brothers, for the heir to Sigujana would have been his full younger brother if Sigujana had died without an eligible son as heir. Both Nomcoba and Mnkabayi, Shaka's sister and aunt, respectively, are said to have asserted the principle that Mhlangana could not rule because he had actually stabbed Shaka. They asserted that by custom, "a man may not rule with a red assegai, one which has stabbed a king."[8] By this reasoning, "Dingana was excused and allowed to govern because, though he had assisted in the assassination, he had not actually used an assegai; he merely caught hold of his brother whilst the others stabbed him."[9] These two senior royal woman are also said to have given the order that Mhlangana be put to death.[10] Mhlangana was then killed, reportedly by Dingane and on their orders.[11] Dingane and Mbopha also had Shaka's brother Ngwadi killed because he had always been considered by Shaka to have been Senzangakona's son, even though some doubted his paternity.[12] Dingane also had his other half brothers, Senzangakona's sons by other mothers, put to death, with the exception of Mpande. He was not considered a threat to the inheritance because he was ineligible to inherit on the grounds that he was of the *umsizi*, a reference to how he was conceived as part of a purifying ceremony.[13] Such a child was still acknowledged as a child of the king, however:

Strengthening with medicines (*iqungo*) – the small hut of the *umsizi*, where the king takes medicines and is doctored. It would be said, "You are the discarded thing (*isikubana*) of the king's medicines. Of the king's children you count as nothing. They will not talk to you because you are of the *umsizi* hut." But, for all that, such child is rightly regarded as a child of the king.[14]

Mmemi explained that because of the circumstances of his conception, Mpande was not eligible to inherit the chieftaincy, and said:

Ndhlela ka Sompisi said to Dingana, "Why do you concern yourself about this scrofulous little thing (*umcobokwana*)? What is there in this thing of Songiya, this thing of the *umsizi*?" This caused Dingana to desist from killing Mpande. Dingana then took 100 cattle (the umqeku steers) and ordered Mpande to go and establish an umuzi. He was presented with the cattle. He was told to build his own *ikanda*. He accordingly went off with Ngqumbazi. The cattle came from Kangela.[15]

The perspective of later AmaZulu generations was that

Dingana then ruled. He killed all the children of this father Senzangakona. Mpande remained. He was saved by Ndhlela ka Sompisi, who said to Dingana, "Surely you are not going to kill Mpande, one who is just a simpleton? You are not going to kill this idiot, Nkosi?" So Mpande was left. All the children of the chief Senzangakona died.[16]

Dingane claimed that "he [Dingane] had intervened between the people and the madness of Tshaka," but as it was later perceived, Dingane "he himself then killed all the children of his father. Tshaka, though, did not kill the children of his father."[17]

Dingane also worried about Shaka's illegitimate son as a potential rival and claimant to the chieftaincy and took measures to ensure that no one gave him refuge or even spoke about him. Ngidi said, "Tshaka had a son, Zibizendhlela. This boy and his mother escaped the year Tshaka went up from the Mtetwa country, and went to Faku in the Mpondo country."[18] Similarly, Magidi told Stuart,

Tshaka, it is said, had a son Zibizendhlela, but he died in the country of the Nguni, i.e. among the Pondos etc. in the Cape colony. I do not know where Zibizendhlela was born. Dingana killed Nzwakele on account of Zibizendhlela. It is certain he was a son of Tshaka by a sweetheart. Didiza ka Lupahla is said to have gone away with Zibizendhlela. Zulu ka Nogandaya died at the Mkomazi. He went off with Zibizendhlela. We say Zibizendhlela is with the Europeans. Zulu ka Nogandaya escaped with cattle. He was afraid of being accused of having concealed Zibizendhlela. He escaped in Dingana's time. Nzwakele was killed by Dingana for having concealed Zibizendhlela.[19]

Although he believed Shaka's biological but illegitimate son had taken refuge to the north rather than the south, Mkebeni confirmed that

"Sibisendhlela [Zibizendhlela] (Tshaka's son) is said to have existed away north of Mzilikazi's country, far up, and to have had descendants there – many still living. Mkebeni heard of this from a missionary from those parts, as also, in especial, from Lurubu, an umTshopi, the son of Matandeni."[20] The knowledge of his existence appears to have become widely known by the time of Dingane's rule, and he was willing to have someone killed for referring to Zibizendhlela. Ndhlovu's comments, in Stuart's shorthand notes, are convincing evidence that Shaka did have a son who long survived him and who posed a threat to Dingane's inheritance of the chieftaincy:

Zibizendhlele called son of Tshaka. Rumours of his coming in Dingana's and Mpande's reign. Mpande married Monase to raise seed for Tshaka. "Making provision for a house (*eqisw'indhlu*)" – given medicine – cut up. Went to the ebuNguni – to the amaXoza – told to go away. Was of the main house (*mdhlunkulu*) [sic] of Tshaka – not known where Zibizendhlela was born. Nzwakele, father of Habana, was killed by Dingana for saying Zibizendhlela was living. He said he was at his mother's kraal.[21]

Dingane tried to suppress any knowledge of the paternity of Shaka's biological son Zibizendhlela and to prevent his return to claim the chieftaincy.[22] He had gone, it was said, to live with his mother among the AmaMpondo, where Shaka's famous warrior Zulu kaNogandaya is reported to have joined him when he fled from Dingane after Shaka's death. Because he was out of reach, Dingane instead had Nzwakele killed on the grounds that he had concealed Zibizendhlela, or that he had revealed his existence. Shaka's son is said to have died among the AmaMpondo, but rumors he might return to claim the chieftaincy persisted through the reigns of both Dingane and Mpande.[23]

Shaka is also said to have made provision for the inheritance of the chieftaincy through Mpande. In accordance with the custom of the levirate, whereby a man's brother impregnated his wife to bear him a child considered to be legitimate, "Mpande married Monase to raise seed for Tshaka."[24] Ngidi explained, "The same year Shaka gave a sweetheart of his called Monase to Mpande. By this woman Mpande had a son, viz. the famous Mbuyazi."[25] Because Monase had been Shaka's concubine and lover, however, the child born of that relationship, Mbuyazi, was widely believed to be Shaka's biological son, explaining the strong support to Mbuyazi's subsequent claim to the chieftaincy.[26] Mbuyazi's challenge for the inheritance culminated in civil conflict and his death in a famous battle in 1856, leaving his half brother Cetwayo to succeed as king following Mpande's death in 1872.[27]

CAPE COLONY PERSPECTIVES

The events of 1828 irrevocably shaped the perspectives of the European settlers and colonial officials of the Cape Colony with regard to the AmaZulu kingdom. They were just becoming cognizant of the kingdom of Shaka's death. In 1823 and again in 1827, the Cape Colony had become alarmed by the reported approach of large armies from north of the Orange River. The first instance was associated with the migrant chiefdoms of SeSotho and SeTswana origins and the battle of "Lattakoo," or Dithakong. The second involved the relocation of the AmaNgwane chiefdom of Matiwane to the territory north of the AmaThembu chiefs who were friendly with the Cape Colony. This incident had led to raising an alarm in October 1827 when Major General Bourke reported "the invasion of the country of the Tambookies," or AmaThembu, by "a tribe of Caffre origin." He wrote to Cape Town seeking instructions and recommending a policy to maintain those "tribes" on the colonial boundaries. He reported, "[t]he invading tribe, called Massoutas, or, when out on marauding expeditions Fetcanie, occupy a country some days march to the north-west of that of the Tambookies."[28] At that time, colonial officials were already discussing the need "to cultivate a good understanding with Chaca [Shaka] by every means short of the grant of money or warlike stores, with the view of prevailing upon him to desist from his hostile projects."[29]

Less than a year later, the arrival of Shaka's ambassadorial mission at Port Elizabeth under his emissary Sotobe was reported to Cape Town in a dispatch dated June 19, 1828. Bourke believed Shaka's emissaries were going to deliver a message relating to a proposed attack by "Chaka" on the "Caffre and Tambookie [AmaThembu] tribes residing on the frontier of the colony." Therefore, Bourke directed military arrangements be made on the frontier and sent Major Dundas, former Landdrost of Albany, to meet with the "caffre chief" Hintsa to "stimulate" him "to a resolute resistance." Dundas was also instructed to try to meet with Shaka or some of his principal chiefs to inform him the colonial government intended to "support the Caffres" in the event of any attack.[30]

In response to reports of the advance of a large AmaZulu ("Soola") force to about eighteen miles from the "Bashee" (Mbashe) river, (i.e., "the northeastern frontier of the Caffre territory" and that "some of the most powerful Caffre and Tambookie [AmaThembu] chiefs were assembling their forces to oppose the Zoolas," Lt. Col. Somerset was sent to meet what was believed to be the invading forces of Shaka. Somerset had a force of about one thousand regular troops and armed burghers and three pieces of field artillery.³¹ In the end, he had only two dozen men with him, and on July 26, Somerset, "chiefly by means of the musketry of his small party of 24 men, drove the Zoolas [sic] off the field with the loss of 60 or 70 killed, and enabled the Tambookies to recapture a very large quantity of cattle." His party began to return from the frontier only to hear on August 4 "that the Zoolas were again advancing." Somerset turned back to proceed to the Mbashe River and reached it on August 21. Cape officials remained alarmed by the presence of Shaka's emissaries whom they believed were bringing an announcement of an attack, and Sotobe himself became both discouraged and alarmed by the colonial officials sent to talk to him. On August 9, 1828, the Sotobe mission embarked on its return trip by sea from Port Elizabeth, never having delivered its message or gone to Cape Town. The mission also took a return message from the Cape Colonial government to Shaka in which "[t]he views of the Colonial Government with respect to the invasion of Caffreland by the Zoolas have been explicitly declared. They have been given to understand that this Government is anxious to remain on friendly terms with the Zoola nation, but that it cannot permit the Caffres to be plundered and driven in upon the colony; and that to avert so disastrous an occurrence, the colonial troops will oppose by force the progress of the Zoolas."³²

In the meantime, the small contingent of Cape Colony troops met thousands of AmaXhosa, AmaThembu, and AmaMpondo forces that had already amassed and were planning a joint attack against the AmaNgwane under chief Matiwane. The battle of Mbolompo was fought on August 27 with disastrous consequences for the AmaNgwane chiefdom of Matiwane. It was defeated and broken apart even though casualties were not high. Not until a dispatch sent in January 1829 were officials at Cape Town formally notified of the identity of the invaders, i.e., the AmaNgwane, whom they had attacked with the massed armed forces of the AmaXhosa, AmaThembu, and AmaMpondo. This was the first they heard that the alarm on the frontier had not been caused by Shaka's army.³³

A second mission sent by Shaka arrived in the Cape Colony at the beginning of October 1828. The trader John Cane, who had been compelled to accept Shaka's "appointment" as his representative, escorted the mission. He did so because Shaka was effectively holding Fynn hostage at Port Natal until the message was taken to Cape Town. Unaware of Shaka's death, John Cane and Shaka's messengers arrived in Cape Town on October 5, 1828, and delivered the following message to Sir G. Lowry Cole:

The substance of the communication which Cane was directed by Chaka to make to me is as follows. Chaka expressed himself anxious to maintain friendly relations with the white people, and willing to comply with their wishes when he fully comprehended them; but that from Mr King having told him one thing and Mr Farewell another, he could not believe either; he therefore requested that an accredited agent from this Government might be sent to him, in order that he might clearly and fully understand the desire of the Government, to which he was perfectly ready to conform, but which he might from ignorance oppose, unless conveyed to him in the manner stated. Chaka added that he was not disposed to molest the frontier tribes of Caffres, provided they did not provoke him by insulting messages (which he alleged Hyntza had done) and would permit him to have free intercourse with the colony, an object which he had much at heart, and which he was determined to obtain at all risks. He particularly requested that a seal, some medicines, clothing and other articles, might be sent to him.[34]

The news of Shaka's death on September 23, 1828, reached the Cape Colony quickly. Fynn wrote that after Shaka's death,

[d]uring the night the news spread over the country, and [AmaZulu] messengers were sent to inform the Europeans at Natal of the event that had taken place, assuring us, as well as all they were sent to, that Shaka had intended our deaths, but which [plans] they had been fortunate enough to frustrate.[35]

Cole sent some men from the Cape Mounted Rifles frontier forces to escort Cane and the messengers back to Shaka, but upon hearing of Shaka's death when they reached Grahamstown, the escort mission was canceled. Cole was inclined to trust Cane and distrust Fynn and Farewell. He wrote,

I find it impossible to attach any credit to the contradictory statements of Lieutenants Farewell and King, the latter of whom died a few days previously to Chaka's being put to death, as these persons seem to have had in their intercourse with Chaka no other object in view but their own personal advantage, and as far as I can judge from their proceedings, do not appear to be very respectable characters.

Lieut. Farewell is now in Cape Town and inclined to return to Port Natal, where he is very desirous to induce this Government to form a settlement; but even in his own interested statement he shows no ground whatever to make it appear desirable in any point of view. The harbour is insecure and fit only for small craft, and scarcely any article of trade is to be procured there except a scanty supply of elephant's teeth.[36]

The initial report of Shaka's death was attributed to former Lieutenant George Francis Farewell, who had arrived with the news in December 1828 that Shaka had been assassinated on September 23 "by one of his chiefs, as an act of retribution for excessive atrocities committed."[37] Cape

Colony officials received reports of the disastrous military campaign of Shaka's forces, said to number about thirty thousand troops, many of whom were killed in battle at the Oliphants (Balule) River. Many more died from famine and disease on their return route homeward. These were the troops that Shaka had sent as an *impi*, a military expedition, north into Mozambique. They were in pursuit of the AmaNdwandwe remnant chiefdom under chief Soshangane who had fled with there with followers after the AmaZulu defeat of the famous AmaNdwandwe chief Zwide in 1826. According to reports received at the Cape, while his troops were away on this expedition, Shaka had been stabbed by one of his chiefs as countenanced by his brothers. One of these brothers had also been put to death. However, one official concluded, "as the brother likely to succeed him is described as of mild and peaceable disposition and he is stated to be desirous to live on friendly terms with his neighbours, I trust the bordering countries may enjoy a state of tranquility which Chaka's restless and cruel ambition has so long denied them; a more bloodthirsty tyrant never, I believe, having existed."[38]

Readers of the *Graham's Town Journal* were informed from a letter written by Fynn's father, who lived in the Cape Colony but had heard from his son, that at the time of his death, Shaka

was sitting with a few of his chiefs and people when his chief personal servant came and with a stick drove his people away, then stepping forward with a hidden assegai [spear] and Mamtshlongam [Shaka's half brother Mhlangana] with another, they struck him in the back, and he almost immediately expired, having only time to say:-"What is the matter, my father's children?"

The custom is for the nation to decide which mother's son has the greatest right to the throne. There being a brother of Chaka's by the same mother, (not in their confidence) and expecting opposition, they dispatched [killed] him also, took his cattle, and sent them to relieve the army which was wandering to the eastward in great distress – fearing to return without plunder. There now remained no opposition to the advancement of Dingaan, (Chaka's youngest brother) to the throne; and before my son left, messengers had been sent to the chiefs of the tributary nations inviting them to his installation, when they will each receive back part of their captured cattle, with a declaration "that they would not have molested them, but were compelled by Chaka."[39]

Colonial officials had no intention or inclination to extend their authority to Port Natal and the surrounding territory, no matter how much the traders lobbied for the extension of colonial rule there. However, these officials were extremely concerned about maintaining peace and stability along their existing frontier borders and preventing any disruptions among the AmaXhosa and AmaThembu to the east that Shaka might cause. The officials therefore maintained an intense interest in the affairs of Shaka and the AmaZulu. Cole had reported that among other things Cane had told him, "Chaka's people are represented as dissatisfied and disposed to revolt, in consequence of his cruelty and constant wars."[40] Cape Colony officials were relieved to receive the news of Shaka's death.[41]

Some sources suggest that Dingane had planned to dismantle some of the new practices that Shaka had been initiated, such as the maintenance of all adult men in regimental barracks, and arbitrary executions, but then continued them during his reign. The AmaZulu oral traditions also remember the continued practices of "great executions known as 'iDili'" and the perpetration of numerous atrocities by Dingane against his own people, just as had occurred during Shaka's reign.[42] The people of the AmaZulu kingdom did not find the relief they hoped for after Shaka's death, and many remained opposed to the accession of Dingane to the AmaZulu chieftaincy.[43]

DINGANE AND THE "SCATTERING OF THE NATIONS"

Dingane could not assume the loyalty of Shaka's former loyal counselors, *indunas*, and allied subordinate chiefs because they might be expected to pursue their own interests and withdraw support from the new AmaZulu king. Not surprisingly, some did rebel, and Dingane had others put to death to prevent them from doing so. Most disruptive was the rebellion of Nqetho, the AbaQwabe royal who had personally *khonza*'d Shaka early in his reign. He had remained loyal even as Shaka had subsequently conquered and subordinated the AbaQwabe chiefdom under Phakathwato. Nqetho's flight with his large following and many cattle from the AmaZulu royal herds caused widespread dislocations across Natal and the region of Transkei, in the most dramatic incident of the "scattering of nations" following Shaka's death.[44] After Dingane's succession, Nqetho made a traditional cry of rebellion in the courtyard one night. Taking many of the royal cattle with him, he was followed by many people who joined him in rebellion against Dingane. They crossed the Thukela River and moved southwards, raiding and driving people from their homes along the way. The disruptions and destruction caused by Nqetho's revolt was therefore widespread across the region.[45]

The sources regarding the exact chronology of events leading to the death of the AmaCele chief Magaye differ, but all associate it with the aftermath of Nqetho's flight. Fynn wrote that on their return from

The Legacy of Shaka's Reign 285

their battle against Nqetho's troops, the AmaZulu commanders invited Magaye to select his cattle from among the captured herds, but this was merely a ruse to lure him. They put him to death on the grounds that he had communicated with the rebel Nqetho.[46] Magaye's son Melapi recounted that in spite of demonstrating their loyalty by recapturing from Nqetho the cattle they kept on behalf of Dingane, the AmaCele were accused of complicity with him. Melapi said,

When the *impi* that attacked Nqeto returned, it killed my father Magaye. The reason why Magaye was killed was because it was alleged he intended following his uncle Nqeto. My father however did not intend doing this. Nqeto, as he passed through our tribe, seized some of our cattle. We followed him up and recaptured them, and as we returned to our district we passed the Zulu forces then on their way after Nqeto. We passed the iNanda. Nqeto got the better of the Zulus at the Ezimbokodweni.[47]

Some sources state that Magaye was killed immediately upon the return of the AmaZulu *impi* from their battle against Nqetho; others report that he was not killed until after Nqetho's final defeat by the AmaBhaca when some stragglers sought refuge with Magaye, giving Dingane cause to put him to death. As Dinya explained, "Magaye, chief of the Cele people, was closely related to Nqeto. (His mother Siwetu, one whom the Cele people always swore by, was 'own sister' of Nqeto.) It was therefore natural that Nqeto's men should take refuge with him."[48] Dinya said, "Magaye secretly received some of these stragglers, whereupon he was attacked by the Zulu forces and routed, he himself, after being killed, being eaten up by his own dogs."[49]

Dingane did not allow any prominent chiefs from Shaka's reign to survive except for Zulu kaNogandaya. Maziyana ka Mahlabeni told Stuart that

Dingane killed Magaye first, then Zihlandhlo, Sambela, then Matubane, Nzwakele ka Kutshwayo of the Dube people, DubekaSilwane. Matubane was killed before the Boers came to Natal. Matubane might have been killed about 1830. Fynn was still here.[50]

The segment of the AmaMthethwa chiefdom that had originally *khonza*'d Shaka had moved away from the coast, and Shaka relocated them to the north at the site of their Impangiso "kraal." Mgudhlana had been left as their chief under Shaka's rule, and Ndukwana's father Mbengwana was living there at the time of Shaka's death. Ndukwana told Stuart,

My father's death at Sikota's hands occurred after Tshaka's death and when Dingana was king. Sikota informed against the whole house of Mgudhlana, saying that they were weeping for Tshaka, for he used to present them with large numbers of Izimbedu beads. After this Dingana said Sikota was to put these people to death. It was in that way that my father's death came about. All the Impangiso people were taken and were all thrown over the cliff at KwaNganga. (There are two hills opposite one another and on opposite sides of a stream that enters the Black Mfolozi. One hill is called Nganga, the other is Barwana.) My father was thrown over the Nganga precipice.[51]

Dingane engaged in killing civilians just as Shaka had. The pretexts used were similar. For example,

Sikota killed off the whole of Mgudhlana's kraals in Dingana's day by reporting to Dingana that the people complained, saying that in Tshaka's day the grievances they suffered from did not exist. Dingana then caused the whole of the followers of Mgudhlana, including women, to be put to death.[52]

After describing several atrocities committed by Dingane, Baleni ka Silwana remarked,

We used to say Tshaka was the king for he did not kill his father's son. Dingana was a bad king for he killed his own relations. Mpande escaped Dingana as it was said, "He is a little fool." Dingana killed off all the others.[53]

At the time of Dingane's accession, "most of the Natal population had actually been incorporated with the Zulus, and that the remnants who preferred not living immediately under Zulu rule, had found it safest to acknowledge the Zulu King, by paying some periodical tribute in feathers or skins, by these means their condition was much ameliorated."[54]

DINGANE AND THE EUROPEAN TRADERS AT PORT NATAL

The Europeans' purpose and presence of at Port Natal was to create and expand trade links with the Cape Colony and thereby derive commercial profit. In establishing themselves far beyond the boundaries of European settlement in the Cape Colony, the traders nevertheless maintained strong family and social as well as commercial ties with the colonists. The Port Natal Europeans became advocates for the extension of British colonial rule into the region of KwaZuluNatal bordering on or encroaching into the Zulu kingdom. A number of traders came and went early in Dingane's reign, but all found themselves in an ambivalent situation relative to the Zulu king. Dingane deployed his troops to drive out or subdue chiefs who had remained relatively independent as Shaka's voluntary subordinates. The new king also employed threats and violence in an attempt to control the conduct and ensure the obedience of the European traders at Port

Natal. From their arrival during Shaka's reign in 1824, each of the traders had built his own homestead or settlement modeled on the villages or "kraals" of subordinate African chiefs. The traders took in refugees from Shaka and Dingane's destructive attacks against insubordinate chiefs and villages from both north and south of the Thukela. Fynn estimated that in about 1835, "the number [of Africans] now under the management of the Europeans at Port Natal amounts to nearly 6,000 souls."[55]

After Dingane became king, he appears to have tried to establish the same terms of obedience and loyalty from these European traders as were expected of subordinate African chiefs. Dependent on his good will and approval for carrying on their trade, primarily in ivory collected in large elephant hunts the king and his chiefs organized, the traders were not in a position to resist Dingane's demands. After the death of James King and Farewell's departure for Cape Town, Dingane initially restricted trade to that with Maputo (Delagoa) Bay and declined "presents" from the Port Natal Europeans.[56] Dingane offered to open commercial enterprise again with Europeans at Port Natal only after the trader Nathaniel Isaacs returned from an absence of a year (March 1829 to February 1830) because of ill health. He arrived just after Nqetho's ("Kato's") so-called "revolt" that Isaacs wrote had "put the country in an unsettled state."[57] He and Fynn proceeded to Dingane's new capital at Gungundhlovu on the latter's explicit invitation, and Isaacs commented that Dingane "would not trade but [only] give and receive presents, which amounted nearly to the same thing." Dingane sent out a party of men to collect ivory and told them he appointed Fynn, as his "agent," insisting Fynn was also "King of Natal," over Fynn's explicit objections. Fynn and Isaacs formed a partnership to commission and bring the trade goods desired by Dingane for which he would give them the ivory from his country.[58]

When Dingane wanted to open relations with the Cape Colony, he appointed the Port Natal carpenter John Cane as his personal ambassador and representative. In late 1830, Dingane sent him to the Cape Colony in that capacity.[59] Dingane appears to have been attempting to open up direct relations with colonial officials, and sent Cane with four tusks of ivory that he expected to be given to colonial officials as a token of friendship. Cane went only as far as Grahamstown, where he passed Dingane's message through the Civil Commissioner for Albany and Somerset, with whom he met on November 21, 1830.[60] Instead of proceeding on to Cape Town, Cane sold the four tusks of ivory which he had brought "as a present from the Zulu Chief Dingaan to the Colonial Government, and for which he [Dingane] expects a present in return."[61]

Dingane had further expectations that a missionary would be sent and that "a traffic between his people and the colony" would be expanded. Cane, however, proposed "to dispose of the ivory, and to procure with the proceeds thereof a sufficient present for the chief, as well as provision for his [return] journey, by which he will be enabled to set out in the course of a few days."[62] The Civil Commissioner wrote that "Cane has this day stated to me his desire of returning immediately to Natal, as the rainy season is about to commence; and if he should delay his journey he will be unable to proceed thence for several months."[63]

Dingane's attempt to establish diplomatic relations with the Cape Colony through the Port Natal trader John Cane had been rebuffed. When Cane failed to appear at Dingane's capital in person, Dingane sent two regiments to destroy Cane's settlement at Port Natal. The attack took place on April 18, 1830. Cane received warning the day before, so he and his followers took refuge in the "bush" while the homestead was destroyed and did not lose their lives or their cattle. The very presence of these hostile forces, however, also sent Fynn and his followers into flight until they determined that they were not being pursued as well. The troops were led by the famous warrior Zulu kaNogandaya, who had orders to take Cane's cattle, destroy the homestead, and kill Cane.[64] Fynn sent a letter of warning to Isaacs and to his brother, who were at Dingane's at the time, but they were unharmed. After the regiments withdrew, Fynn and the others returned to Port Natal on April 24.[65]

However, this was only the first of two "scares" at Port Natal in 1831. After the first in May, Fynn went to see Dingane to trade for ivory, and it became clear to Fynn that Dingane was conspiring against him. By the time he arrived back at Port Natal, Fynn heard that Dingane had raised troops for a military expedition to be sent either against Mzilikazi and the AmaNdebele to the north or against Faku's AmaMpondo and the Natal traders to the south. Fynn, his brothers who had recently joined him, his followers, primarily Africans of KwaZulu-Natal origins, and the other traders including Cane left their settlements at Port Natal to escape the expected attack.[66] The mobilized troops were in fact sent north against Mzilikazi, but when Fynn and his followers fled south from KwaZulu-Natal, they were pursued by regiments led by Dingane's main commander south of the Thukela River.[67] Cane's people went into hiding in the bush in Natal, but Fynn fled with his people to seek refuge with the AmaMpondo chief Faku. Seven days into their journey while camped at night, they were suddenly attacked without warning by Dingane's troops who killed five men, twenty women, and fifteen children and wounded seventeen. Thirteen of Dingane's men were also killed in the fighting. Devastated by the loss of some of his own immediate (African) family members and exhausted after a twenty-five day journey, Fynn arrived at the Umzimbuvu River with about seventy survivors from the brutal attack. There at the mission station at Bunting, they recovered before returning to Natal in September, but any residual trust in Dingane on the part of Fynn was permanently broken.[68]

Fynn finally left the Natal region for good in 1834 and was appointed to a colonial post in the Cape Colony where he lived among the AmaXhosa.[69] Other traders tried to open up trade in Port Natal, including the Cawoods who were initially welcomed by Dingane. By January 1833, the Cawoods had decided that Dingane had fixed prices so high that trade could not be profitable there, and announced they were withdrawing from Port Natal on that account.[70] Cape Colonial officials were not encouraged by trade prospects in the KwaZulu-Natal region. The Cape papers had extensively covered the fate of Dr. Cowie and Mr. Green, who traveled as far as Delagoa Bay and died on their return trip before reaching Natal.[71] Both Farewell and Fynn had argued to colonial officials that unless a formal British presence was established at Port Natal, it would not be safe for traders or settlers.[72] Fynn's and Farewell's experiences had borne this out and controvert the argument that until 1835, Dingane was not hostile to the Port Natal traders but courted their presence.[73] The killing of forty of the men, women, and children of his followers by an *impi* of AmaZulu warriors and the confiscation of his cattle convinced Fynn that they were not safe at Port Natal as long as Dingane was king.[74] In the surprise nighttime attack, Fynn's brother had barely escaped with his life. He wrote, in response to rumors that he had fled for no cause, "I nearly lost my life and, in the end, quite all my cattle."[75] In his 1852 testimony, Fynn observed,

Of the remnants of the tribes dispersed by Chaka, many sought an asylum with the frontier Kafirs, and unitedly they were termed "Amafengu" supposed by the colonists to mean a particular tribe, instead of regarding it as a name of derision, which it really is, given to them by those to whom they fled. Many of these proceeded to the old colony and entered service [labor] there. In the war of 1835, when Sir B. Durban released the greater portion of the Fingoes (Amafengu) from their service condition with the Frontier tribes, a fair supply of labourers was secured to the whole colony. Many of the frontier Kafirs also have entered into the service of the old colonists from time to time.[76]

Twelve years after Shaka's death, his half brother and successor Dingane was driven from his kingdom by his half brother Mpande, who defeated him with the aid of Dutch-speaking Boer allies. Dingane died at the hands of a Swazi warrior who found him hidden in the hills, his own men having left him undefended at the end. By then, the 1837 murder of Piet Retief and his party, which had complied with Dingane's demand that they retrieve stolen cattle from the BaTlokoa chief Sekonyela before he would grant them permission to settle, had persuaded settlers of both Dutch and British origins that Dingane was an intransigent enemy of Europeans, be they traders, missionaries, or farmers. Retief's murder, witnessed by a recently arrived missionary living on an adjoining hill, indicated to the Cape colonists that Dingane was beyond redemption. The futile efforts of the thousands of AmaZulu warriors to check Boer expansion at the 1838 Battle of Blood River set in motion events that would lead to the king's flight and death in 1840. Contrary to common modern perceptions, Europeans who explored, traded, settled, and farmed in early South Africa did not mistakenly assume that all Africans were irredeemably ignorant, primitive, and hostile; the interactions between Africans and Europeans across cultural and geographic boundaries were complex mediated by the individuals who were involved at each encounter. The many years of upheaval caused by Shaka's warriors followed by Dingane's oppressive rule, however, created in Europeans an indelible image of savagery associated thereafter with the AmaZulu kingdom, the legacy of Shaka's rule.

Many of the generalized condemnations of Shaka's rule can be traced to the influence of Henry Francis Fynn, whose opinion was influential throughout the nineteenth century even after Fynn's death. The publication of his *Diary* almost a hundred years later perpetuated his ideas and perspectives about the early AmaZulu through the rest of the twentieth century and have not yet been entirely put to rest. Fynn believed that

> Shaka having, after much opposition, overcame the neighbouring tribes, in order to prevent a repetition of revolt, put to death the chiefs and principal families of the conquered, selecting, however, the younger men, whom he attached to his regiments, forming together a body of 50,000 effective followers: these he governed with despotic severity. Having, with the exception of Matiwane, who fled to the north-west, brought under his dominion all chiefs and tribes between Delagoa Bay and uMzimvubu, he determined to continue his wars, so long as any body of people could be found to stand in opposition to his force.[77]

The strength of Fynn's opinion, exaggerated and unreliable but influential, is evident here:

> To fight or die was his [Shaka's] maxim, and certain was the death of any man or body of men who retreated before the enemies. The countries to the north-east, as also the coast southward, were separately invaded. Those who attempted to

withstand him were overpowered by numbers, and ultimately exterminated, neither sex nor age being spared. Many were burned to death, their huts being fired at night; while the barbarous cruelties he practised struck terror into many who had never seen his force and fled at his name.[78]

These passages by Fynn are themselves contradictory. In the first, he says both that Shaka put to death chiefs and members of royal families of conquered chiefdoms but enrolled the young men into his military regiments. This indicated that the numbers of people put to death were limited according to specific criteria, allowing for most people to survive after their chief's family had been killed and the chiefdom ceased to exist independently. In the second, he reverted to exaggeration, claiming that everyone from chiefdoms that chose to resist was "exterminated," including women and children. The estimation of mortality from raids and battles during Shaka's era is complicated by this type of contradictory reporting, and by the many unknown deaths that may have occurred when a village was burned and its inhabitants set into flight. The oral traditions, however, do not remember or relate stories of deaths from the burning of villages, suggesting that these were limited even as the destruction of villages and food supplies, crops as well as cattle, caused widespread hunger among those who did not subsequently give their allegiance to Shaka so they could regain access to these resources. The oral traditions indicate that there was very limited mortality from fighting even during the time of the "death of nations," *izwekufa*, and often even the lives of chiefs were spared. Their chiefdoms were broken up as independent sociopolitical units and their people either dispersed or incorporated into new villages and regiments during the dozen years of Shaka's rule. Many chiefs submitted to Shaka without putting up any resistance, and others did so after only a token fight.

The conflicts with heavy fighting were remembered and passed down in oral traditions, but even then the numbers killed were usually counted in the hundreds, not the thousands. Thousands appear to have been killed on a limited number of occasions that were nevertheless memorable and became the source of the fierce reputation of AmaZulu warriors.[79] Major defeats, such as the capture and defeat of Dingiswayo and the breakup of the AmaMthethwa by Zwide and the AmaNdwandwe and the AmaZulu defeat of the AbaQwabe under Phakathwayo, occurred after only very limited fighting. Few died on these two occasions except for these prominent chiefs themselves.[80] As the strength of Shaka's *impi*s in numbers and capability increased, submission or flight without resistance became more common, so that mortality levels appear to have declined rather than increased.

The exceptions are well remembered in the oral traditions. The defeat of Zwide and the AmaNdwandwe in 1821 was the culmination of periodic AmaNdwandwe attacks and AmaZulu resistance. Many people from Zwide's capital, including women and children, were said to have been killed in retaliation and to eliminate this royal house. Nevertheless, most AmaNdwandwe survived this famous defeat and withdrew under major chiefs to resettle farther north in several major segments. On this occasion, the AmaZulu were said to have spared every enemy warrior who laid down his arms. Many of these AmaNdwandwe were not only spared but incorporated into the ranks of AmaZulu regiments. Similarly, when Zwide's son Sikhunyana returned with his followers in a plan to attack the AmaZulu in 1826 and met with a pre-emptive attack by Shaka's major military campaign, although several thousand people, including women who were present at the battle, were said to have been killed. Thousands of others survived to either flee north once again or give their allegiance to the AmaZulu.

The first campaign against the AmaMpondo in 1824 resulted in the deaths of three units of AmaZulu troops, perhaps several thousand men total, with no reported mortality among their enemy. Because Shaka's forces returned with thousands of raided cattle, this military campaign was deemed a success. Upon their return, however, Shaka ordered many men of a regiment perceived to have been cowardly to be put to death. The *eyobutshinga impi* to the Caledon River valley region, where the AmaZulu fought several skirmishes against the BaSotho and AmaNgwane while raiding their cattle and then fought a well-known battle near modern Ladybrand against the AmaNdwandwe, was said to have resulted in total losses of several hundred of the AmaZulu, BaSotho, and AmaNgwane combined killed.

There was no actual fighting on the second major *impi* sent by Shaka against the AmaMpondo in 1828, and only one person was reported killed from the entire military campaign. The AmaZulu troops sent to attack the AmaNdwande under Chief Soshangane at the Balule or Olifant's River in 1828 reportedly annihilated a small chiefdom that had recently absconded, killing perhaps a thousand people en route to attack Soshangane. He was forewarned before the attack was launched so that it was the AmaZulu rather than the AmaNdwandwe who suffered losses from this battle that counted several thousand as dead. The troops were said to have become lost on their return from this expedition, and several thousand more are said to have died from fever, presumably malaria, never making it home. Thus, the total mortality from all of the battles fought during Shaka's major military expeditions, contrary to common perceptions still prevalent today, may have been as few as ten thousand dead, most of these being AmaZulu warriors rather than enemy troops. In combination with the fighting and raids from earlier and small *impi*s sent out by Shaka, the total mortality from fighting amounted to probably no more than twenty thousand people, including both warriors and women and children on those occasions where civilians were killed.[81] Many more people died from the aftermath of battle, however, whether from displacement or loss of food resources that resulted in hunger and famine.

Nor is it possible to assess the destructiveness of Shaka's rule without considering his frequent arbitrary killing of his own people – warriors and civilians – individually and sometimes in incidents of mass execution. Europeans reported that the execution of individuals occurred on a daily basis at the capital, although sometimes this would have been the accepted punishment for a known criminal offense. The oral traditions also confirm many atrocities ordered by Shaka that resulted in the deaths of thousands of people during the years of his rule. The reported collection and execution of people from the subordinated and incorporated AbaQwabe chiefdom following the attempted assassination of Shaka in 1824 may have resulted in several thousand being killed. Similarly thousands of people were reported to have died following the death of Shaka's mother Nandi, many executed summarily by Shaka's troops for failing to mourn properly.

The reports that Shaka had large portions of military regiments executed for reputed cowardice or failure in battle suggest that several thousand of his own troops were killed on Shaka's orders. The destruction wrought by Shaka in terms of people killed during his reign, including probably twenty thousand from his *impi*s, may be reasonably estimated at thirty to forty thousand dead. This was a high cost for the consolidation of the peoples of KwaZulu-Natal under AmaZulu rule, leaving a kingdom of perhaps two hundred thousand willing and involuntary subjects at the time of Shaka's death.

The atrocities of cruelty in punishments and executions remembered in the oral traditions indicate Shaka's ruthlessness and vindictiveness that was not considered acceptable even by his own people. Both European reports and indigenous oral traditions confirm the atrocities that occurred on Shaka's orders; they refer to a personality that was eventually described as "mad" by his own subjects. This may have been the result of the medicines that the European traders first gave Shaka when Fynn treated him with chamomile, an opiate, after the assassination attempt in 1824. The boy "John Ross" (i.e, Maclean) later wrote that he and Shaka's own subjects at the capital only felt free to move around and enjoy themselves only during afternoons when Shaka appeared to be in a drug-induced sleep. The opium of India may have made its way to Shaka's capital by that time in 1826, or he may have indulged in smoking *dagga*, hemp, as was common in the region; either would help to account for his growing ruthlessness and seeming paranoia at the time of his death. This assessment of Shaka's reported personality, and possible causes of his irratic behavior, however, can only remain speculative.

It is also possible that the disregard for human life was a fundamental flaw in Shaka's character that accounted for his early military success and violent usurpation of the AmaZulu chieftaincy and the murder of his half brother at that time. The AmaZulu oral traditions relate evidence of Shaka's ambition and the planning and implementation of long-term strategies designed to extend the reaches of the AmaZulu kingdom and his authority. The Europeans who met him recounted his ability and willingness to use both hospitality and generosity as well as threats and violence to manipulate the actions of others. There was neither widespread popular rebellion against Shaka's assassins after his death nor widespread grieving after his death as normally accompanied the death of a chief or member of his family. One of his assassins, Dingane, was rewarded with appointment as his successor. Few people appear to have regretted Shaka's death, but they did not foresee that Dingane's reign would very soon become equally ruthless.

Processes of political consolidation had been underway for at least a generation before Shaka rose through the ranks of Dingiswayo's AmaMthethwa military and then usurped the AmaZulu chieftaincy. Severe droughts and food scarcity appear to have intensified competition over land and water resources between chiefdoms during the first few years of the nineteenth century, a situation repeated both in the 1810s and 1820s. Those chiefdoms that had already developed their military capabilities through more systematic organization in regiments arranged on the basis of age-grades rather than villages were better prepared to raid others for cattle and crops and to defend their own territory, herds, and fields. Senzangakhona is said to have begun to raise age-based regiments in imitation of Dingiswayo, so that the AmaZulu were well prepared for any military contests that might arise with their neighbors.

The Legacy of Shaka's Reign

Senzangakhona began the process of consolidation that his son Shaka pursued so relentlessly after the chief's death.

Shaka's accession to the chieftaincy was achieved with the support of a some of his mother's family, members of the eLangeni royal family, and of Dingiswayo's advice and advisers. Shaka also received the support of many members of the AmaZulu royal family, including his aunts and numerous half brothers, Dingane and Mpande among them. Shaka first incorporated those chiefdoms who were not only nearby but also relatively weak. He waited to challenge larger and stronger chiefdoms until his regiments had grown from the accession of the young men of newly incorporated chiefdoms and their enrolment into AmaZulu regiments. Successful incorporation of chiefdoms through their voluntary submission or defeat gave Shaka control over their territory and possessions, allowing him to allocate land and herds of cattle in a system of patronage that ensured the continued loyalty, obedience, and support of the beneficiaries of his patronage. Ruling families of the chiefdoms he incorporated sent their men into his regiments and sent young royal women to live at his capital in his *isigodlo* where they not only served as concubines to Shaka but were also effective hostages preventing rebellion by their formerly powerful and still influential families. Shaka controlled the production and distribution of the weapons and accoutrements of war, including spears and shields, and the allocation of the spoils of war, primarily cattle, to individual warriors and to royal families and *indunas*.

An ivory trade that had emerged with Delagoa Bay during Dingiswayo's reign was diverted to Port Natal when the European traders arrived there in 1824. Shaka tried to exert control over the hunting and trade in ivory. His lack of success in doing so because of Fynn's success in acquiring ivory from the AmaMpondo and their neighbors far to the south fostered growing tension between Shaka and the European traders at Port Natal. There refugees from Shaka's expansionism collected around them for protection and security. Shaka continued to rely on his subordinate allies, including the AmaCele and AmaThuli chiefs of the Natal region and the uncontrollable Embo chief Zihlandlo whose ambitions remained a threat to Shaka.

To the end, Shaka remained vulnerable should any of his more powerful subordinates or military commanders enter into an alliance against him. It only remained for Shaka's counselor and his two leading (half) brothers to take advantage of the absence of his loyal military commanders and troops and with the widespread popular disaffection to succeed in their assassination plans finally in September 1828. Shaka's extension of AmaZulu rule, however tenuous, was marked by tribute payments in kind; the enrolment of men into AmaZulu regiments; the presence of the daughters of prominent men in the *isigodlo* at the capital; and demographic redistribution in new homesteads, regimental barracks, and cattle posts; and ceremonial acknowledgements on a huge scale at Bulawayo and then Dukuza.

Although he only ruled for a dozen years and his widespread extension of authority territorially was limited to only the second half of his reign, Shaka's rule left a presumption of AmaZulu authority over most of modern KwaZulu-Natal and its then diverse population. Dingane's suppression of rebellion following Shaka's death reasserted the authority of the AmaZulu royal house across much of the region of KwaZulu-Natal.[82]

The creation of the new AmaZulu kingdom did not occasion during Shaka's reign a new coherent recognition and acceptance of an AmaZulu identity among the diverse subject population that had been incorporated within its boundaries. On the contrary, even as Dingane and then Mpande repeatedly reasserted the authority of their ruling AmaZulu line of descent over the newly incorporated kingdom, the subjects of the kingdom remembered and passed down through oral history and oral traditions knowledge of their own diversity. The population of the region continued to be well aware of the diversity of their origins in terms of genealogical lineage, former sociopolitical organization in many chiefdoms, and varied cultural origins reflected in dialects, marks of identity, geography, and demographic settlement. These differences were remembered for generations afterward, even as the political needs of the subjects of AmaZulu authority in the kingdom prompted acceptance of and affiliation with a new more comprehensive AmaZulu identity. That acceptance provided a source of protection against the new intrusive European settler population and colonial authority.

This process of assimilation, yielding a new definition of AmaZulu identity in the generations after Shaka's rule, was reinforced by colonial policies of indirect rule in the nineteenth and early twentieth centuries and the continued policies of segregation and apartheid forged through most of the twentieth century.[83] The linguistic and cultural affiliations denoted as "ethnic" identities in the twentieth century have acquired meaning because they reflect residual practices and memories from the past, but these sociocultural identities are not of unknown, primordial origins, nor were the original identities ever bounded or inflexible with reference to genealogical, social, political, or cultural heritage and inheritance.

Peoples from the region of KwaZulu-Natal resettled and remained as thriving communities across southern Africa from the Transkei region in the south to the modern southern African countries north of contemporary South Africa. The legacy of Shaka's rule was the creation of the AmaZulu kingdom of the nineteenth century. The history of the peoples of the region of KwaZulu-Natal in the early nineteenth century reveals their capacity to create and recreate social and political communities, including people of diverse cultural origins, a legacy of inclusion that was mirrored over many centuries in chiefdoms across southern Africa.

Appendix

James Stuart Interviewees

BALEKA KA MPITIKAZI[1]

(v. I, 4-14)

Interview dates: July 15, 16, 25, 26, 1919.

She told James Stuart "she was born at the time of the Ndondakusuka fight between Cetshwayo and Mbuyazi (December 1856)," and she was given the name because so many people were running away.

She "grew up in Msinga Division, close to the Mzinyati. She seems to me to speak very good Zulu, and, although a member of the Qwabe tribe, she does not *tefula* [speak in the AbaQwabe dialect]."

Her paternal ancestry was of the royal family of the AbaQwabe chiefdom. The genealogy of Baleka's father Mpitikazi ka Nsila indicates he was directly descended from Qwabe ka Malandela, the brother of Zulu ka Malandela. Her grandmother, from whom she learned many oral traditions, was a daughter of the brother of the eLangeni chief and a first cousin of Nandi, Shaka's mother. Therefore, this interview reflects knowledge received and remembered by a woman whose genealogy indicates she is connected to the ancestors of the AmaZulu, AbaQwabe, and eLangeni chiefly families.

Her father Mpitikazi was of the Fasimba regiment. He was an *imbongi*, or praise singer, of chiefs, and she learned much of what she knew about the past from him. Her brother Mamgumguta (younger) was also considered to be a good *imbongi* in 1919.

Mpitikazi knew about Shaka's early life because "He grew up among the Langeni people, at his mother's kraal, like Tshaka. If Tshaka had been an ordinary person they would have been 'brothers'; their mothers were born at the same place" (v. I, 11).

BALENI KA SILWANA

(v. I, 16–52)

Interview dates: May 10, 12, 13, 14, 15, 16, 17, 18, 1914.

He was born at the White Umfolozi River in the Mahlabatini valley about 1838 and was of Dhloko regiment, formed of young men born circa 1838.

His paternal ancestry was the AmaMpungose chiefly line of descent. His father Silwana ka Ndhlovu was of the Siklebe regiment, formed circa 1816 by Senzangakona of youths born circa 1790. He died in battle at Maqongqo when Baleni was a small boy (1840). His mother was born about 1800 and lived in the household at Nobamba.

Baleni told Stuart "I heard most of my history from Siyongo of the Kanyile people. Siyongo was of the Sipezi regiment" [formed between 1821 and 1827 of youth born between circa 1800–1807].

DINYA KA ZOKOZWAYO

(v. I, 95–123)

Interview dates: February 27, 28, 1905; March 1, 2, 3, 29, 30, 1905; April 1, 2, 3, 5, 6, 8, 9, 17, 18, 1905.

He was born about 1827, his regiment was the Ingulube, and he was from the AbaQwabe who had *khonza*'d the AmaCele chief Magaye and lived south of the Thukela River. At the time of the interview, Dinya was from Ifafa mission station.

His paternal ancestry was of the royal family of the AbaQwabe chiefdom. The genealogy of Dinya's father Zokozwayo ka Mancenga indicates they were directly descended from Qwabe ka Malandela, the brother of Zulu ka Malandela.

Dinya had been the interpreter in Dutch and isiZulu when the Boers had their meeting with Mpande.

Dinya's testimony reflects the influence of European input, probably derived from missionary teaching because he lived on the mission station. For example, several times he draws comparisons between Zulu and Jewish cultural practices, which was a preoccupation of some missionaries at the time. He also explained some contemporary 1905 Zulu grievances to Stuart. Dinya said, "We do not care for the Tshaka regime. We were all killed off there,"103.

GIBA KA SOBUZA

(v. I, 149–154)
Interview date November 25, 1898.

Stuart wrote in these notes: "Per Giba ka Sobuza (king) and Mnkonkoni, two men sent by the Queen mother at my request for trustworthy information regarding the past history of the Swazis. See below for list of Swazi kings given by them and also for list of regiments. Giba is of the Tigogodolo regiment, Mnkonkoni of the Inyati, the one about 69, the other 72 years of age."

Later in his notes Stuart wrote: "The following is a list of Swazi kings given by Giba ka Sobuza (the king) and Mnkonkoni, the well-known Special Messenger, men who, when I asked the Queen Mother to send me someone to give me information of this point, were sent by her this day. She considers them trustworthy."(151)

HOYE KA SOXALASE

(v. I, 167–173)
Interview dates: September 12, 14,15,16, 20, 21, 1921.

He was born about 1869–1878. Hoye ka Soxalase ka Ngula ka Fukuzela ka Makasa ka Zombe of the "Ndhlela people – associated with" the AmaNdwandwe. Solomon ka Dinuzulu sent him with Mkebeni ka Dabulamanzi and Maqama ka Mzilikazi of the AmaMbata people to tell Stuart the AmaZulu kings' eulogies. He was of the Dakwaukwesuta regiment.

Hoye was Solomon ka Dinizulu's *imbongi* or praise singer ("professional herald") and had learned all of the *izibongo* of the Zulu kings and others from his own father. He did not know who had taught his father. Hoye recited numerous *izibongo* to Stuart and explained how praises were performed and their order according to the ceremony or circumstances of the performance. In addition to those of the Zulu kings, he knew the praises of Mnkabayi and those of Nandi but could not recite them himself.

JANTSHI KA NONGILA

(v. I, 174–207)
Interview dates: February 9, 10, 11, 12, 13, 14, 15, 16, 17, 1903.
He was born at Nyezane about 1848.

His paternal ancestry belonged to the Mabaso chiefdom from Nhlazatshe, near Ntabankulu and close to the White Umfolozi, and near the AmaZulu. He lived his entire life among the AmaZulu. His father Nongila was born about 1785–1790 and belonged to the Ntontela regiment formed in 1816 and served as a spy for four kings: Senzangakona, Shaka, Dingane, and Mpande.

KAMBI KA MATSHOBANA

(v. I, 208–212)

Interview dates: April 8, 11, 1903.

He was born about 1864. His paternal family was from the AbaQwabe chiefdom and had migrated with many other AbaQwabe to south of the Thukela River after an assassination attempt against Shaka in July 1824. This attempt was blamed on the AbaQwabe and caused many of them to be executed. Kambi, also known as Ntshokobela, worked as a day worker in Durban at the time of the interview. He had learned his information from his uncle Mnyaiza ka Maganga "who was well-informed and knew the tribal kings' *izibongo* [praises]," 210.

JOHN KUMALO

(v. I, 215–272)

Interview dates: October 12, 28, 29 1900; November 22, 24, 1900; December 8, 9, 10, 15, 16, 17, 29, 30, 31, 1900; January 1, 14, 1901.

Stuart estimated John was born about 1837.

He had previously lived in the Estcourt Division near Pasiwe, along the little Thukela. His father was Mayikana ka Mzondo, and his given name was Myeye. Before he became a Christian, his name was Myeye ka Mayikana. His father's family belonged to the AmaKhumalo chiefdom. Part of it was led away in flight from Shaka by Mzilikazi who founded the AmaNdebele kingdom in the Transvaal and then southern Zimbabwe. Apparently, John took the surname of Kumalo from this family connection. As a young man, he first migrated to work in the Cape Colony but returned and decided he wanted a Christian education. When he was about 36 or 37 years old, he sought out Bishop Colenso at Pietermaritzburg where he also found work. He learned to read and write and became a *kholwa* ("believer") Christian convert. At the time of the interviews, he was an important headman among the *kholwa* community at Roosboom, Klip River Division.

LUGUBU KA MANGALIZO

(v. I, 281–296)

Interview dates: March 4, 1909; May 29, 30, 31, 1916.

He was born about 1850–1853 of the AmaMbata people and was an *induna* (headman) of the AbaThembu chief Ngqambuzana. In 1916, Stuart wrote that Lugubu was a "Very intelligent, clear-headed man. Splendid at throwing light on meaning of *izibongo* [praises]. Has rather a thick headring, grey beard," 283.

LUNGUZA KA MPUKANE

(v. I, 297–353)

Interview dates: March 11, 12, 13, 14, 15, 16, 17, 18, 19, 20, 21, 22, 1909.

He was born about 1820 and was a member of the Kokoti regiment formed about 1838. His paternal family belonged to an offshoot of the AbaThembu known as the Madondo from an ancestor of that name. His grandfather Zikode was a very important man among the AbaThembu, allowed to hold the *umkosi* (first fruits) ceremony the day before the chief, Ngoza, held it.

Stuart wrote on March 22, 1909: "Lunguza seemed to me careful and accurate in everything he told me. The amount of detail he knows was surprising when compared with my other various informants. His memory for incidents and names is excellent, but his bump [knowledge] of locality is not strong, especially as regards Zululand, but this is explained by the fact that he left Zululand about 1837 or so, and seems not to have gone back, even on a visit," 345.

LUZIPO KA NOMAGEJE

(v. I, 354–357)

Interview dates: November 21, 23, 25, 1904.

There is no evidence of his age, but his father Nomageje ka Gaqa was of the iHlaba regiment and killed in battle in 1883, suggesting Luzipo may have been born in the 1870s.

His paternal family was of AmaNxumalo line of descent, a part of the AmaNdwandwe chiefdom.

MABONSA KA SIDHLAYI

(v. II, 11–41)

Interview dates: January 27, 28, 29, 30, 31, 1909; February 1, 2, 3, 1909.

He was born about 1829. His paternal family was of the AmaKubeka (or AmaHlatshwayo), and his father Sidhlayi ka Mbombosana ka Ntimane had migrated to the Phongolo River at the Ngcaka where Mabonsa was born. His father had joined (*khonza*'d) the AmaHlubi chief Mtimkulu there (between 1815 and 1821. Mabonsa was Langalibalele's envoy to King Cetshwayo and visited Langalibalele at Cape Town after Langalibalele was released from Robben Island.

MADHLEBE KA NJINJANA

(v. II, 45–46)

Interview date: May 13, 1905.

He was born about 1822. His paternal family was of AmaKhumalo origins. Madhlebe grew up at Shaka's capital at Bulawayo and knew Shaka's mother, Nandi; he was a young child when she died in 1827. The interview notes were apparently written by an amanuensis rather than by Stuart himself, as Webb and Wright noted.

MADIKANE KA MLOMOWETOLE

(v. II, 47–67)

Interview dates: July 8, 1903; August 15, 16, 17, 30, 1903; May 26, 27, 28, 29, 1905; June 27, 1905; July 11, 12, 1905; October 14, 1905.

He was born about 1828–1830. He was born at the Nsuze in the Nkandhla district but moved while he was a youth to south of the Thukela River where he lived along the coast.

His paternal family belonged to the AmaCele chiefdom of the AmaQadi or Maqadini line of descent. His father Mlomowetole ka Bobo gave his allegiance to Shaka, was of the Ntontela regiment formed about 1816, and lived at the Ntontela village.

At the time of the interviews, Madikane lived at eNanda under chief Mqawe and was a *kolwa* ("believer") Christian convert and teacher of the Bible. His son was studying in the United States where he had been seven years or more.

MAGEZA KA KWEFUNGA

(v. II, 68–76)

Interview dates: February 18, 19, 20, 1905.

He was born about 1830 at the Mhlali.

His paternal family was of the AmaCele chiefdom. His father Kwefunga ka Zwana ka Mkokeleli was a grandson of the AmaCele chief Mkokeleli who had led a portion of the AmaCele from the AmaMthethwa in a migration. They went south of the Thlukela in the eighteenth century. At the time of the interview, he lived in the Alexandra division on the south Natal coast.

MAGIDI KA NGOMANE

(v. II, 79–82)

Interview dates: May 7, 1903; February 8, 1904.

He was born about 1835. His father Ngomane ka Mqomboli ka Caya ka Sitole ka Nkomo ka Bumede ka Kuzwayo was a famous *induna* under the AmaMthethwa chief Dingiswayo. He later accompanied Shaka when he returned to usurp the AmaZulu chieftaincy. He remained an important *induna* of Shaka's and married a wife among the AmaZulu who was Magidi's mother. Magidi left Zululand with Mawa (Senzangakona's sister) in 1843 and never returned to live there but visited many times. He was chief of the emDletsheni or Caya (Lower Tugela division), according to Webb and Wright, 81 n.1.

MAGIDIGIDI KA NOBEBE

(v. II, 83–101)

Interview dates: May 5, 6, 7, 8, 9, 10, 12, 1905.

He was born about 1823 at the central AmaZulu village of Nobamba during Shaka's reign and grew up there. His paternal family belonged to the AmaChunu chiefdom. His maternal grandmother belonged to the Mabaso of the AmaKhumalo and came from Ndabankulu near Nhlazatshe. Magidigidi followed Mpande into Natal in 1839 and knew the AmaChunu chief Pakade well.

He was also known as Simeon Nobobe, and he came to the interview from Amanzimtoti. He was a policeman at Greytown and knew James Stuart's father.

MAGOJELA KA MFANAWENDHLELA

(v. II, 104-106)

Interview date: June 30, 1907.

He was born in the early 1850s. His paternal family was of the AmaZungu line of descent, from Mahlabatini and related to the AmaMpungose. His father Mfanawendhlela ka Manzini was a direct descendant of the founding ancestor Zungu ka Malendela (not to be mistaken for the Zulu progenitor named Malandela). His paternal grandfather Chief Manzini gave his allegiance to Shaka, but Shaka had him killed after Manzini's AmaNkentshane regiment demonstrated their strength in battle and therefore appeared to pose a threat to Tshaka.

MAHASHAHASHA KA PAKADE

(v. II, 107-109)

Interview date: May 8, 1910.

He was born in the early 1860s. His father was Pakade ka Mandhlesilo and his paternal family belonged to the eLangeni chiefdom. He was a sergeant in the Natal police in charge of the Pietermaritzburg jail.

MAHAYA KA NONGQABANA

(v. II, 110-139)

Interview date: August 25, 1905.

He was born about 1832 at the Mbatshe River, southwest of the Mthatha River, in the AmaXhosa chiefdom of the Transkei region. His paternal family was of the Imitwana chiefdom and had lived for many generations in the region. His father Nongqabana ka Ngciza traced his direct line of descent back thirteen generations to a man named Hohoho or Huhuhu of Sotho/Lobedu origins of the place of Mjantshi. His maternal grandfather's mother was a European woman stranded in a shipwreck. His uncle was among the AmaMpondo men who went to submit to Shaka after the second AmaZulu campaign against the AmaMpondo in 1828. Mahaya grew up at Kwelera across the Great Kei near East London and the sea.

MAKEWU

(v. II, 161-164)

Interview dates: October 8, 9, 1899.

Stuart did not include information about Makewu from this very early interview. According to Webb and Wright (163, n.1), he was chief of the AmaDube (Lower Tugela division) and six men accompanied him to the interview. Of these, Maruyi ka Sonyanga, born about 1830, contributed information to the interview.

MAKUZA KA MKOMOYI

(v. II, 165–172)

Interview dates: March 5, 6, 1921.

He was born in the early or mid-1840s. His paternal family was of the AmaCebu or Cebekulu line of descent, and his father Mkomoyi ka Pobo belonged to the Isimpohlo regiment stationed at the AmaZulu capital of Bulawayo. Makuza belonged to the Mbonambi regiment.

MANDHLAKAZI KA NGINI

(v. II, 174–198)

Interview dates: November 21, 1913; May 18, 20, 21, 22, 23, 24, 25, 1916; January 7, 8, 9, 1921; June 5, 8, 1921; February 2, 3 1922.

He was born in 1869. His paternal family was from the AbaQwabe chiefdom, and the famous warrior Zulu (Komfiya) ka Nogandaya was his maternal grandfather whom he had met once.

His father Ngini ka Mkongwa was of the Ndabankulu regiment and then the Izimpohlo regiment of esiKlebeni under Dingane. He was an *inceku* (servant) at the old AmaZulu village of isiKlebe (esiKlebheni).

MANGATI KA GOGIDE

(vol. II, 199–222)

Interview dates: June 29, 1918; July 1, 1918; June 12, 13, 14, 15, 26, 30, 1920; December 15, 1920; January 14, 1921.

He was born about 1848. His paternal family was of the AmaBele (AmaNtuli) chiefdom. His grandfather Ndhlela ka Sompisi was of the Intontela regiment. His father Godide was of the Inyosi regiment and was an *inceku* (servant) of Dingane's. Mangati belonged to the Indhluyengwe regiment. He had been a policeman in Greytown serving under the resident magistrate of Umvoti country, John Shepstone. There he also knew the clerk and Dutch interpreter in the Umvoti county court, James

Stuart's father Martinus Stuart (217, n.3). Stuart wrote in his notes that Mangati was "very smart."

MANKULUMANA KA SOMAPUNGA

(v. II, 226)

Interview date: September 14, 1905.

Mankulumana was the grandson of AmaNdwandwe Chief Zwide, and his father was Somapunga ka Zwide ka Langa.

He was Dinizulu's *induna*.

Mankulumana told James Stuart only one story, but it is significant because it connects Qwabe and Zulu as brothers and explains their separation into two different descent-based chiefdoms. It is also significant because it was told by a grandson of Zwide ka Langa, in 1905. This is the entire text of what Mankulumana told Stuart:

"Mankulumana says that Qwabe and Zulu's mother was Nozidiya [a point of disagreement in traditions told to James Stuart.] She had a quantity of amabele. People used to come and buy from her. She got a dark-brown beast in exchange for the amabele, and this beast gave birth to a number of white or whitish beasts. Either the dark-brown beast was given by Nozidiya to her younger son Zulu, or some of its [the dark brown beast's] progeny [its calves were given to him]. Qwabe [the elder son], seeing Zulu favoured, accordingly separated; hence the separation between the Qwabe and Zulu tribes." Bracketed comments mine.

MAQUZA KA GAWUSHANE

(v. II, 230–231)

Interview dates: February 2, 3, 4, 1905.

He was born about 1815–1818. His paternal family belonged to the AmaCele chiefdom. He was born at the Mhlali but was among the AmaCele who migrated to south of the Thukela river after Shaka's death. They resettled near the Matikulu below Magula hill.

MAYINGA KA MBEKUZANA

(v. II, 246–263)

Interview dates: July 8, 9, 10, 11, 1905.

He was born about 1839. His paternal family was from the AmaGasa chiefdom and related to the AmaBele. His father was given the name

Mbekuzana by Shaka and belonged to Shaka's umGumanqa regiment formed of men born in the 1780s-1790s. Mayinga's father was an *inyanga* ("doctor") who treated Shaka and later Mpande, and was referred to by Mayinga as "a hero of Tshaka's" (246). The umGumanqa village was at the White Mfolozi River at Mhalabatini. His father fought in the 1828 campaign against the AmaMpondo and died in the 1856 battle between Cetshwayo and Mbuyazi.

Mayinga was born and grew up in the Mahlabatini area south of the White Mfolozi, near the old AmaZulu capital of Nobamba. Then he lived at the Mamba stream near the junction of the Nsuze and Thukela rivers until he was recruited into his regiment. A year after he fought in the Ndondakusuka battle, Mayinga migrated to south of the Thukela river where he lived near Greytown at emaKabeleni.

Mayinga indicated that his father was not his only source of information, for on July 9, 1905, after relaying information about the AmaBele and uGasa people he said: "I was told this by Sobekase (deceased) ka Tshoba of the Bele people," 251.

MAZIYANA KA MAHLABENI

(v. II, 264-307)

Interview dates: April 20, 21, 22, 23, 24, 25, 26, 27, 30, 1905; May 1,1905.

He was born about 1827. His paternal family belonged to the AmaNdelu line of descent, of the AmaThuli chiefdom. He was born near the Mlazi river. Maziyana's father Mahlabeni remained in the region of modern Natal living with the AmaThuli chiefs Matubane and his successor throughout his life, including the entire period of Shaka's reign. Maziyana remembered an interpreter named Klaju whom he had known well, and who was evidently one of his most important sources about early Natal history, including information about the early European traders.

MBOKODO KA SIKULEKILE

(v. III, 1-22)

Interview dates: November 5, 6, 7, 8, 9, 10, 1913.

Born in the mid-1850s, he was of high rank, as indicated by the leopard skin he wore to the interview tied beneath his headring. His father was Sikulekile ka Sambela, of the Embo (Mkhize) chiefly line of descent.

Mbokodo was very cognizant of the importance of his own knowledge, which included praises he had been taught, as well as formal, stylized narratives and factual historical reports. He said, "My great informant was Ngwenyeni, also Sohayi ka Mdhlalose, who came from Zululand. Whilst still a lad I learnt especially from my father, who died when I was a young man (*ibungu*), say 25 years of age. My father directed me to go to Ngwenyeni and get him to teach me. My father and Ngwenyeni taught me the praises I have been reciting. Sohayi is living; he is of the Izinkuni regiment [born early 1830s]. He no longer leaves his hut. He never saw Tshaka or Zihlandhlo, being too young. He knew Dingana. He is of the [same age as the] Zulu Tulwane regiment or thereabout. My father was of the Izingulube regiment [born mid-1820s]," 16; 33 n.22.

MBOVU KA MTSHUMAYELI

(v. III, 23–50)

Interview dates: February 9, 1903; February 7, 8, 9. 1904; August 7, 29, 1904; September 11, 13, 16, 24, 25, 1904; November, 10, 13, 1904.

He was born about 1830.

His paternal family belonged to the AbaQwabe chiefdom, and his father Mtshumayeli ka Mnengwa ka Makanya was of the Makanya branch of the AbaQwabe ruling line of descent. As a youth, he had migrated with his family following Mpande to south of the Thukela in 1839 when he lived among the Embo (Abambo) people. In the early 1840s, he worked herding cattle for Boer farmers living south of Pinetown, so he remembered the events associated with the arrival of British colonial forces at that time. At the time of the interview, he lived at Kwa Davati and was a Christian.

Mbovu referred to Shaka as "an evil-doer," 37, and commented about Shaka's era that "We ought to be grateful that these cruel times of the past are no more. The white people have with their key locked that all up and established a lasting peace, but the young generation, oblivious of the past, may want to try and create unrest,"36.

MCOTOYI KA MNINI

(v. II, 53–70)

Interview dates: April 13, 14, 15, 16, 1905.

He was born in 1828. His family was the ruling line of descent of the AmaThuli chiefdom, his father being Mnini ka Manti ka Mzoywane ka Dole ka Sivuba ka Mayiya ka Lutuli ka Nkomo ka Zuba ka Mqayana ka Ncamuzakancane.

At the time of the interview Mcotoyi was chief of the AmaThuli people, Umlazi division, 63.

MELAPI KA MAGAYE

(v. III, 72–99)

Interview dates: April 27, 28, 29, 30, 1905; May 1, 2, 1905.

He was born about 1814 into the royal family of the AmaCele chiefdom. His father was Magaye ka Dibandhlela ka Mkokeleli ka Langa ka Sodi ka Ncumela (Nqumela) ka Maganga ka Ndosi ka Lubobo ka Cele ka Nyambose. His father Magaye was the chief of the AmaCele chiefdom during Shaka's reign and was a loyal subordinate ally of Shaka's. Melapi remembered seeing Shaka when he came to visit his father, Chief Magaye. Melapi knew well the man of AmaXhosa origins who served as an interpreter with Europeans for Shaka and for Magaye. He also knew Henry Francis Fynn and Henry Ogle well, and he knew Sotobe ka Mpangalala, the man who served as an emissary to the Cape Colony for Shaka in 1828. Melapi's half brother Mkhonto was designated by Dingane as their father Magaye's successor but later killed by him. Melapi went to live under Sotobe at oPisweni at the iNadi stream, a tributary of the Thukela River.

MESACH NGIDI

(v. IV, 116–124)

Interview dates: November 29, 1921; December 13, 1921.

Born about 1877, he was a direct descendent of Ngidi, of the AmaNgidi chiefly line of descent. He gave his name as Meshach (Mishaka) Ngidi ka Madhlakazi. His father was Madhlaka or Madhlakazi, and Mesach appears to have taken the surname Ngidi from his family line of descent, the name of the ancestor five generations earlier by whose name the chiefdom was known in the era of Shaka's reign. Early in his rule, Shaka attacked the AmaNgidi chiefdom when it was ruled by Mesach Ngidi's great-grandfather, Mnguni ka Kuzwayo. Shaka killed many before he and his followers migrated out of the region of modern KwaZulu.

Meshach got his information from his father and probably others. Meshach Ngidi told Stuart, "William Ngidi, Colenso's great informant, was *ubabekazi*, i.e. my uncle," 118. Later he said, "William Ngidi – Colenso's informant. Had home at Pomeroy, Umsinga. He had house at the place of Sobantu [Bishop Colenso], [at] Bishopstowe. Was Colenso's interpreter, also helped with Grammar and Dictionary. William was an uncle of mine, "123; 124, n.29.

MGIDHLANA KA MPANDE

(v. III, 102–113)

Interview dates: August 30, 1903; September 1, 1903; February 23, 1912; June 5, 7, 8. 1921.

Mgidhlana, born about 1828, was a son of King Mpande. At the time of the interview, he lived above oNgoye near the Mhaltuze.

Mgidhlana provided extensive information about Mpande's wives and children and contemporary information about the royal family at the time of the interviews. His mother was Nmcangce, a daughter of Tshandu.

MKANDO KA DHLOVA

(v. III, 145–194)

Interview dates: July 9, 10, 11, 13, 14, 15, 23, 29, 31, 1902; August 11, 4, 8, 9, 10, 12, 13, 14, 17, 19, 20, 21, 1902.

He was born about 1827 in the Nkandhla district near the Mhlatuze River. His father was from the AmaLuthuli, and Mkando went to give his allegiance at the eLangeni chiefdom when others of the AmaLuthuli migrated and fled in the era of Shaka's reign to south of the Thukela River. His mother was from the AmaCele chiefdom. His father was very wealthy, and had four villages and eighty wives. Shaka killed his father.

MKEBENI KA DABULAMANZI

(v. III, 195–209)

Interview dates September 12, 16, 17, 18, 19, 1921.

He was born in the late 1860s. His father was a son of Mpande, so he was in the direct line of descent of the AmaZulu royal family.

MKEHLENGANA KA ZULU

(v. III, 210–221)

Interview dates: April 18, 19, 21, 1905.

He was born about 1845. His father, Zulu or Komfiya ka Nogandaya ka Lujabu ka Manxeba ka Mnsunsula (Mntsuntsuya) ka Ndhlovu ka Dubula ka Ncwana, was Shaka's famous warrior who was given the name "Zulu" by Shaka for demonstrating his courage and ability in a battle. Komfiya was from the AmaNcwana line of descent of the AbaQwabe chiefdom and had come early in Shaka's reign to give his allegiance individually to Shaka. He rose from the position of *inceku* (servant) to that of renowned warrior. Komfiya had 80 wives, and died before the 1879 war at eMkunya near Springvale. Three of his wives were sisters of Stuart's interviewee Dinya ka Zokozwayo.

Mkehlengana had personal memories of his father, whom he called "awe-inspiring," 210. He cited his father as the source of his information about early AbaQwabe, AmaNcwana, and AmaZulu history.

MKOTANA KA ZULU

(v. III, 222–231)

Interview dates: April 10, 11, 12, 1905; May 28, 30, 1905; June 1, 1905; July 8, 11, 1905.

He was born about 1834–1836 at the Mvoti River.

His father, Zulu or Komfiya ka Nogandaya ka Lujabu ka Manxeba ka Mnsunsula (Mntsuntsuya) ka Ndhlovu ka Dubula ka Ncwana, was Shaka's famous warrior who was given the name "Zulu" by Shaka after demonstrating his courage and ability in a battle. Komfiya was from the AmaNcwana line of descent of the AbaQwabe chiefdom and had come to give his allegiance individually to Shaka early in Shaka's reign. He rose from the position of *inceku* (servant) to that of renowned warrior. Komfiya, who had 80 wives, died before the 1879 war at eMkunya near Springvale. Three of his wives were sisters of Stuart's interviewee Dinya ka Zokozwayo.

At the time of the interview, Mkotana lived at the Imfume mission station, having left Mahlongwa. He was a *kholwa*, a "believer," or Christian convert. Contradicting himself, Mkotana said both "I did not know my father well, for I quickly became a kolwa at Mahlongwa" and "I, of course, know my father [Komfiya/Zulu] well. I often saw and spoke to him. I never saw Nogandaya, my grandfather," 222.

MKUNGU KA MPANDE

(v. III, 232-233)
Interview date: January 4, 1914.
Mkungu ka Mpande, who did not tell Stuart when he was born, was a son of King Mpande. He was the youngest of eight children born to his mother Monase ka Mntungwa, of AmaNxumalo origin. The eldest child of his mother was Mbuyazi; his mother was given by Shaka to Mpande to bear an heir for Shaka. According to Webb and Wright, after the fight between Mpande's sons Cetshwayo and Mbuyazi in which Mbuyazi was killed, Mkungu was placed by his father King Mpande into the care of Anglican Bishop J. W. Colenso, 223, n.4. Stuart interviewed Mkungu at his village at Erabeni, near Emtandeni, the capital of the former AbaQwabe chief Phakathwayo.

MMEMI KA NGULUZANE

(v. III, 238-283)
Interview dates: September 8, 9, 1904; October 12, 13, 16, 17, 18, 19, 20, 21, 22, 23, 24, 25, 26, 1904.

17 January 1926: a genealogical table "put together" by Stuart, "based on Mangati, Tshingana, Cetshwayo, and especially Mmemi" is included in the text of Mmemi's interview, v. III, 273-276.

He was born about 1828-1830 at the Ematikulu River near where the Msunduze enters the sea.

His paternal family was descended from the ruling family of the AbaQwabe chiefdom. His father, born in the late eighteenth century, was Nguluzane ka Mbombo ka Zwana ka Dhlamuka ka Kuzwayo ka Sidinane ka Mahlobo ka Qwabe ka Mayandeya [Malandela]. His paternal grandfather Mbombo was the great *induna* of the AbaQwabe chief Khondlo, chief Phakathwayo's father.

Mmemi said his sources for stories of Shaka were his paternal uncle Mbokazi, whom he refers to often as his father, and other old men including his relative Makanda ka Mbombo ka Zwana, and so on, who was a body servant of Tshaka; both men were often with Shaka, giving credence to the information to which Mmemi had access. His uncle Mbokazi had been born perhaps as early as 1766 and had early childhood memories of the eighteenth century chief Simamane. He became an adult and put on the headring during the reign of Chief Kondhlo, Pakatwayo's father, making him a contemporary of Shaka's father

Senzangakona. Mbokazi died at a very old age in 1876, having relayed considerable information to Stuart's interviewee Mmemi over the years about the history of the AbaQwabe and AmaZulu.

Mmemi had personal memories of Shaka, who stayed at Ebuyiyaneni, the village of his "father" (uncle) Mbokazi, and later protected Mbokazi when the AmaZulu attacked the AbaQwabe under Phakathwayo. Mbokazi retained access to Shaka as a highly respected *induna*, giving great value to the information he later conveyed to Mmemi. Mmemi's family crossed the Thukela River into Natal along with several other prominent people including Shaka's paternal aunt Mawa ka Jama after Mpande had his brother, Gqugqu ka Senzangakona, killed. Mmemi was a little boy when his family moved into the region of modern Natal, where he grew up.

Mmemi knew and recited long genealogies and the praises of Pakatwayo and others. Stuart wrote, "Mmemi looks on himself as one of the best, if not the best, reciter in the Qwabe tribe," 263.

MQAIKANA KA YENGE

(v. IV, 1–33)

Interview dates: May 9, 10, 11, 13, 14, 16, 1916.

He was born about 1830–1831 at eMrolweni: a place of forests near Howick waterfall.

His paternal family belonged to the Zondi chiefdom, and were of the AmaMpumuza line of descent. His father was Yenge ka Nontshiza ka Mpumuza ka Makweta (Makweza) ka Sobangwa ka Luqa ka Gagatshe ka Nhlabitshileko [notice the *k* instead of *y* here] ka Lusibalukulu ka Dhlamini ka Mdhlovu, reflecting a genealogical link to the Dhlamini line of descent from whom the Zondi people were said by Mqaikana to have separated.

Mqaikana was also called Tomu. He grew up in Fodo's district, Umzimkulu. Mqaikana's father served as a messenger for Theophilus Shepstone, but he had had little contact himself with Europeans and disdained Africans who became Christian "*kholwa*s," or believers.

Mqaikana could recite the praises of Xesibe, Ngwane, Teteleku, Mpumuza, and Nobanda, and others. Stuart wrote that Mqaikana was "very intelligent, recollects affairs well; knows very little of Zulu affairs proper, but strong on Nhlangwini, Kuze and Mpumuza matters. He also knows much about Nxamalalas and Cunus," 28.

MRUYI KA TIMUNI

(v. IV 36–40)

Interview dates: January 7, 11, 18, 1903.

Brother of Ndhlovu ka Timuni. Their father Timuni was a son of Mudhli ka Nkwelo ka Ndaba, and Ndaba was the father of Jama, father of Shaka's father Senzangakona. Therefore Mruyi and Ndhlovu belonged to the left-hand (*ikohlo*) side of the royal AmaZulu house. Mruyi cited his father Timuni as the source for some of his evidence and stated that he had never lived in Zululand, indicating he had always lived south of the Thukela River.

MSIME KA BEJE

(v. IV, 49–60)

Interview dates: December 23, 26, 1906.

He was of the Izimpehlwa regiment. His father was Beje ka Manqe ka Mgubo ka Mtoto ka Ngidi ka Bopela ka Ludhloko; their family praise name, *isibongo*, was Ngidi, and they were of the AmaNyuswa.

Msime provided Stuart with genealogies, including of the AmaNyuswa and the AmaQadi branch of the AmaNyuswa. Most of his testimony relates to the 1906 rebellion.

MTSHAPI KA NORADU

(v. IV, 61–105)

Interview dates: April 1, 2, 3, 4, 6, 8, 9, 11, 1918; May 7, 8, 9, 10, 11, 1918.

He was born about 1846–1847. His paternal family belonged to the Magwaza chiefdom. His father Noradu (Nohadu) ka Mazwana ka Yengwayo ka Sibude ka Njinji was of the Magweza line of chiefs and was an *inceku* to Shaka.

Mtshapi explained the purpose of praises, saying, "The king makes up praises for his great warriors, but he himself has praises made up for him by the *izimbongi*." He also said, "Praises come to serve as a man's name," and "People die but their praises remain, Their praises will remain and mourn them where their homes once were," 73.

MTSHAYANKOMO KA MAGOLWANA

(v. IV 106–157)

Interview dates: January 10, 11, 12, 14, 15, 18, 20, 21, 22, 23, 1922.

Mtshayankomo was the son of King Mpandi's famous *imbongi* (praise-singer) Magolwana. Mtshayankomo reflected an attitude of loyalty to commands and willingness to perform order regardless of more contemporary values. According to his own account, he participated in killing thirty-one girls in their father's homes, shooting them with guns on the orders of King Cetshwayo because they had refused an order to marry older men instead of their younger lovers. He related these events without any evidence of regret or consciousness of wrongdoing.

In 1923, Stuart published an edited version of Mtshayankomo's testimony in his Zulu school reader *uTulasiqwe* in which, as Webb and Wright note, v. IV, 147, all references to Mtshayankomo were eliminated.

Mtshayankomo was an *imbongi*, as had been his father, from whom he learned the praises he could recite and perform. Throughout the interviews, he refers to his father's methods of performing the praises on public occasions and to his father's strategies for composing praises.

MTSHWAYIZA KA MAMFONGONYANA

(*JSA* v. IV, 163–164; also KCL, James Stuart Collection, File 60, NB [Notebook] 17, 11–12; see Kambi ka Matshobana, v. I, 208–212 (next interviewee of James Stuart) for additional testimony of Mtshwayiza)

Interview date: March 22, 1903.

Mtshwayiza, also known as Nkwatshakazi, ka Mamfongonyana ka Phakatwayo ka Godide, of the AbaQwabe people was a grandson of Phakatwayo; in Kambi interview, v. I, 208, he says his father, Mamfongonyana was Phakatwayo's heir.

"Mtshwayiza says he does not know much because he was obliged to treat his father with the greatest respect on account of his high rank. He had, for instance, to go behind the hut in which he was, and not before the door of it, and if he entered the hut there was a something about the place that was oppressive; one felt one's *mbombo* [forehead? bridge of nose (Colenso)] get hot," v. I, 209, Kambi interview. Bracketed annotation by Stuart.

At the time of the interview, James Stuart wrote "disputing with Ntshingumuzi," which appears to be a reference to a legal or other dispute of Mtshwayiza at the time he was interviewed by Stuart in 1903; Webb and Wright identify Ntshingumuzi as son of Mkhwethu, son of Bathintile, a brother of Qwabe chief Khondlo

"Mtshwayiza, est. about 42, is a borough police sergeant. He lives in Eshowe District, and is a son of Mamfongonyana, former chief of the tribe. He is more or less cut off, the main section of the tribe being Natal, i.e. that portion there lately under Zidumo (deceased). He now claims the chieftainship in Zidumo's place until the latter's children (heir) shall have grown up." "Mamfongonyana was a member of the Mdhlenevu regiment," v. I, 208; Kambi interview April 8, 1903.

NDABAMBI KA SIKAKANA

(v. IV, 175–179)

Interview dates: March 25, 26, 1909.

Ndabambi was born in the early 1850s. He was son of "Sikakana ka Mlisa of the Dhlamini people, of oDidini (royal kraal), Swaziland." He was of the Ngobamakosi regiment; his father from whom he had gotten most of his information and who was still living, was of the Kokoti (Khothothi) regiment; his grandfather had come from Swaziland to resettle in KwaZulu.

NDHLOVU KA TIMUNI

(v. IV, 198–238)

Interview dates: November 7, 8, 9, 10, 1902; January 1, 11, 1903; March 22, 1903; May 9, 1903; September 2, 1919.

Born about 1858, Ndhlovu was a chief in Mapumalo division and brother of Mruyi ka Timuni.

Ndhlovu's father Timuni was a son of Mudhli ka Nkwelo ka Ndaba, and Ndaba was the father of Jama, father of Shaka's father Senzangakona. Therefore, Ndhlovu belonged to the left-hand (*ikohlo*) side of the royal AmaZulu house. At the time of the interview, he was a chief at Mapumulo.

Ndhlovu learned his stories of the past from his father. Stuart wrote that Ndhlovu "frequently conversed with his father Timuni as to the far-off past," and Stuart commented that Ndhlovu was bright, talkative, agreeable, and intelligent, and had "a keen interest in larger questions," 200. His father had first-hand knowledge of Shaka and events during Shaka's reign.

NDUKWANA KA MBENGWANA

(v. IV, 263–406)

Interview dates: October 18, 19, 25, 1897; November 3, 1897; c. July 15, 1900; August 13, 1900; September 10, 11, 12, 13, 14, 15, 17, 18, 19, 20, 21, 22, 25–29, 30, 1900; October 1, 14, 15, 16, 18, 19, 20,

21, 22, 23, 27, 31, 1900; November 1, 3, 4, 9, 11, 12, 13, 16, 17, 18, 20, 25, 1900; December 2, 10, 12, 19, 22, 24, 26, 1900; December 22, 26, 28, 1901; July 6, 1902; October 12, 27, 28, 1902; November 7, 1902; January 18, 1903; March 30, 1903; April 4, 5, 18 1903; May 1, 2, 12, 17, 1903; June 21, 1903; September 3, 4, 6, 11, 12 ,1903; October 11, 1903.

Ndukwana was born about 1824. Stuart originally miscalculated his age as considerably younger because he appeared to be only about 57 years old in 1897 (putting his estimated date of birth at about 1840). Ndukwana was born before Nandi's death in 1827, and he thought he was about five years old because he could remember a comet that appeared at that time. That would have made Ndukwana 73 years old at the time of his first interview with Stuart, which is easily possible in spite of Stuart's misperceptions of his age, presumably based on his appearance. However, Ndukwana's estimates of his own age when certain events occurred is somewhat confused in his testimony.

Ndukwana's paternal family belonged to the AmaMthethwa chiefdom, of the Masondo people, and his maternal grandmother was of AmaNtshali origin. His father Mbengwana ka Matshotshwana had migrated with Mgudhlana ka Ntuli to Empangisweni near the sources of the Black Mfolozi River probably during the reign of Chief Jobe of the AmaMthethwa, father of Chief Dingiswayo.

The many subjects of these early interviews by Stuart included customs regarding coming of age, premarital relations, marriage, children, the *sisa* custom of loan cattle, traditional ceremonies such as first fruits, conscription into regiments, and cultural practices involving diviners and *izinyanga* "doctors," the uses of "medicines," and the function of an *inkata* symbolic large woven ring. Ndukwana also knew a lot of information about the early history of the region. At an interview of Ndhlovu Stuart wrote, "Ndukwana got his information from a fairly old man (say 72 now) of the Zulu tribe," v. III, 210.

NDUNA KA MANQINA

(v. V, 1–11)

Interview dates: April 19, 24, 25, 27, 1910,

He was born in 1879–1880. Nduna's father was Manqina ka Kepukepu ka Nogandaya ka Lujabu ka Manxeba ka Mnsunsula (Muntsuntsula) ka Ndhlovu ka Dubuyana ka Ncwana ka Malandela. His grandfather Kepukepu was therefore a brother or half brother of the famous warrior Zulu or Komfiya Nogandaya of the AbaQwabe chiefdom. His genealogy traces this family back to the AmaNcwana branch of the royal family, connected via Malandela to the AmaZulu and AbaQwabe, and taking their names from Malandela's sons Zulu, Qwabe, and Ncwana.

Stuart wrote, "Nduna's informants. The principal one was Sokwebula ka Mkobiso of the Swazi race. He was of the Mkulutshane regiment. He told me he went on the campaign in Mzilikazi's country. He saw Tshaka with his own eyes. My father [great uncle] Mkehlengana (deceased) also gave me some of my information," 31. Because Stuart also interviewed Mkehlengana, information that appears to be similar should be treated as second-hand information from the same source rather than as from two different sources and cannot be taken as independent for purposes of confirmation.

NGIDI KA MCIKAZISWA

(v. V, 28–124)

Interview dates: 11, 12 August 1904 with Mbovu ka Mshumayeli present; August 13, 14, 1904; November 3, 4, 5, 6, 7, 8 ,9, 10, 1904; October 17, 18, 21, 22, 23, 28, 29, 30,1905.

He was born about 1817–1818 at the Mfule near Melmoth and Kwamagwaza.

Ngidi (alias Magambukazi is his praise-name) was the son of Mcikaziswa ka Nombanda ka Mxabo ka Daleni ka Mhlongo ka Ncumela (Nqumela) ka Mavundhla (Sibidane) ka Nqetshe ka Lugoloza ka Sibiya ka Mzimaseli ka Langa. Ngidi therefore traced his paternal descent to the Langa chief Mhlongo, who was Mbengi's father and Nandi's grandfather (Shaka's great-grandfather) and to the founding ancestor Langa. He spent his early life living among the people of the AmaLanga at eLangeni where he was a member of the royal line of descent and closely related to Shaka's mother Nandi.

In 1838, he was 21 or 22 years old and fled, following Mpande into Natal following Dingane's defeat by the Boers. He knew Henry Francis Fynn and his son H. F. Fynn Jr. well and worked for John Dunn's father and other Europeans around Durban.

He named the people from whom he had learned his information several times, saying "I heard this from Dangazele, the great *induna* of ekuQobekeni, Tshaka's kraal (of the Langa tribe), from Bantwana, Tshangana, Gaxa, and Mseleli ka Ndina ka Mbengi (at whose kraal I grew up – at the eMazule stream, which enters the Mhlatuze near where

H. Osborn lives). Dangazele ka Qayiyana (Qayiyana's brother was Nombanda) ka Mxabu ka Daleni," 41.

Bantwana was Nandi's brother and Shaka's uncle, and Ngidilater he said, "Bantwana, Nsindwana, and Sizi ka Mbengi are my informants on these affairs [Nandi's marriage and pregnancy and the birth of Tshaka]."(59) Bantwana became a *kolhwa*, and in 1904 Ngidi said he had "died recently," (31) This is important, for it indicates one of Nandi's brothers was alive for several generations to sustain local knowledge of events concerning Nandi, Shaka, and the eLangeni people from the early nineteenth century. Ngidi was of the Isibubulungu regiment among the eLangeni, about the age of Mgabi, and Ngidi knew him personally. Ngidi said "I knew Bantwana. I lived with him at the Mbilo but we were in different kraals....He became a *kolwa*....His sons became *kolwa*s (were converted – *penduka*'d) and he did likewise. Bantwana was older than Tshaka, seeing he was Nandi's brother," 64.

Ngidi summarized his interpretation of the Zulu past as follows: "We were always in a state of unsettlement, unrest (*xobisekile*) in the Zulu country. We desired to get the cattle of our enemies to enrich ourselves, and in so doing killed the enemy. It was a good thing such a civilization or state of affairs came to an end. It greatly worried or inconvenienced us," 78.

Ngidi told Stuart, "I am 'The one who speaks without being heard; the ratel of the one who keeps guard of the assegai' [spear]," and Stuart noted that this was a praise or *isibongo*, but did not specify to whom it referred individually so it appears to be a group regimental praise. 81. He explained that the reference to ratel was from the mission of his regiment, the iMvoko, when they were sent to keep watch on the AmaSwazi.

NHLEKELE KA MAKANA

(v. V, 127–132)

Interview dates: June 2, 3, 1907, at Eshowe without attribution to an informant but presumed by Webb and Wright to be Nhlekele. However, Webb and Wright then note that in the middle of his interview notes for June 2,1907, Stuart recorded a diary entry on that date that indicates he was at Eshowe for a gathering of chiefs from the Empangeni (Lower Umfolozi), Mtunzini (Umlalazi) and Eshowe districts, which supports their conclusion that the second set of interview notes dated June 3 without attribution are from the same person, i.e. Nhlekele, 129.

He was born about 1852, according to Stuart's estimate.

Nhlekele's paternal family was of the emaCambini people from the AmaMthethwa chiefdom. His father was Makana ka Sobasa ka Sengeya.

Nhlekele said he learned the "old traditions" from an umMhtethwa chief, Myandeya ka Mbiya ka Tshangane ka Kayi ka Xaba ka Madango ka Ngxongo, whose son Sokwetshata became the umMthethwa chief of the Lower Umfolozi division (and died August 1, 1907).

NOMBASHINI KA NDHLELA

(v. V, 143–146)

Interview date: October 25, 1907.

He was born in 1843.

His father was of the AmaNcwabeni line of descent from the region of modern Transkei south of the Mzimvubu River where Nombashini's father Ndhlela was born. He gave his father's genealogy as Ndhlela (Mtakati) ka Novelezansi ka Mengezela ka Ndhlazi ka Zana ka Ncwabe ka Mdematoleni ka Nzima ka Bawoshana. His family had moved to the eNyamvubu stream at the Mooi River near Estcourt but fled to the Matatiele area when Shaka's attack against the AmaChunu under Chief Macingwane early in his reign. Later the family returned to the eMkuzana stream that enters the Umlazi River, where Nombashini was born and then lived at Pasiwe Mountain and eventually to eNgomankulu hill southeast of Pietermaritzburg. His father was known as Mtakati because he was forbidden to use his given name Ndhlela because it was the name of Dingane's *induna*.

NORMAN NEMBULA

(v. V, 12–19)

Interview dates: February 8, 1905; April 8, 1905; June 8, 9 30, 1905; July 1, 27, 29, 1905; October 19, 20, 1907; November 2, 1907.

Norman Nembula collected information for Stuart from other people whom Stuart sent him out to meet. Stuart attributed the brief reports of information to the individuals from whom Nembula received them.

The longest set of notes relates to an interview Norman Nembula had with a woman, Zitshibili, living 13 miles from Newcastle on the Ncandu River. She was from the ruling family of the AmaKhumalo chiefdom. Her father was Nyakanyakana ka Matshobana ka Mangete and therefore was a brother of the AmaKhumalo chief Mzilikazi who led a branch of the AmaKhumalo to form the AmaNdebele kingdom in the Transvaal and then southern Zimbabwe. Zitshibili was born in Mzilikazi's village named Mhlanhlandhlela on the Marico River in the Transvaal (modern Mpumalanga province). Her husband was Dube of the Intabazwe regiment of the AmaHlubi chief Langalibalele.

SINGCOFELA KA MTSHUNGU

(v. V, 338–358)

Interview dates: March 29, 39, 31,1910; April 1, 2, 3, 4, 1910.

He was born about 1848–1850 according to Stuart's estimate. His father was Mtshungu ka Myoli ka Matomela ka Ndhlovu from the AmaBomvu (AmaBomvini) chiefdom, closely related to the AmaNgwane chiefdom of Matiwane. His mother was of AmaZulu origins. His paternal grandfather Myoli was a brother of the AmaBomvu chief Zombane and had eight villages, indicating he was a man of wealth and standing. Chief Zombane of the AmaBomvu was killed by Shaka after being called to meet with him, causing the remainder of the AmaBomvu to emigrate to south of the Thukela River. Singcofela was a man of influence who had command of a section of warriors for battle. At the time of the interviews, he lived in a location about 20 miles from the town of Dalton.

SIVIVI KA MAQUNGO

(v. V, 367–383)

Interview dates: June 30, 1905; March 6, 7, 8, 10, 12, 13, 14, 1907.

He was born about 1820 and was a member of the uKokoti regiment formed about 1838.

His paternal family was from the people of kwaMalunga, originally of the AmaHlubi chiefdom from which they had broken away because of a quarrel although they traced their descent line to a common ancestor, Ndhlovu. Sivivi's father was Maqungo ka Nkweba ka Tulisa ka Nqondo ka Mwelase ka Mapanga ka Mbizankulu ka Gengezi ka Ndhlovu ka Mntungwa. He was an *induna* of Dingane's.

Sivivi fought in the battle between Mpande and Dingane in January 1840 when Dingane was defeated.

At the time of the interviews, Sivivi lived at eMzumbe under chief Charlie Fynn, along the Lower Mzimkulu River.

SOCWATSHA KA PAPU

James Stuart Collection, Killie Campbell Library (KCL), Durban, South Africa
  File 70, KCM 24398, interview notes of James Stuart 1901
  File 58, NB [Notebook] 24, KCM 24221, 31–34
  File 66, notes dated June 2, 1912
  Interview dates: December 28, 1901; January 24, 26, 1904; June 2, 4, 1912; October 26, 1913; October 2, 1921.

His father belonged to the chiefdom of chief Ngongoma who joined Shaka and gave their allegiance to the AmaZulu before Shaka began his campaigns of conquest. His father was a contemporary of Shaka, or perhaps a little older than Shaka.

TUNUNU KA NONJIYA

James Stuart Collection, Killie Campbell Library (KCL), Durban, South Africa
  The original interview notes are found in
  File 60, NB [Notebook] 22, KCM24258
  File 60, NB 23, KCM 24259
  File 60, NB 24, KCM 24260
  File 60, NB 27, KCM 24263.
  Subsequently, James Stuart rewrote his original notes of his interviews with Tununu from File 60, NB 22, KCM 24258, into full sentences, most of which is verbatim; it is found in File 70, KCM 24398.
  Interview dates: May 28, 29, 30, 31 1903; June 7, 9, 10, 1903.

Tununu was born about 1811–1812. His paternal family belonged to the AbaQwabe chiefdom. His father was Nonjiya ka Tuzuqu ka Mpotsho ka Myangatshe. His father Nonjiya had been given responsibility for Dingane by AbaQwabe Chief Pakatwayo when Dingane took refuge among the AbaQwabe as a young man at the time that Shaka went to live among the AmaMthethwa. Nonjiya belonged to the AbaQwabe regiment iZindonde. Because Dingane lived under Tununu's father Nonjiya, Tununu knew Dingane well. Dingane gave Tununu his name Sitununu at the time of his birth. Tununu became Dingane's *inceku* (servant) and milked for him at Dingane's capital at Mgungundhlovu. Tununu remembered the death of Nandi while he was Dingane's *inceku*. Dingane had Tununu's mother driven off. Dingane was Tununu's source for much of his information. Tununu was recruited into the Mkuluthana regiment and witnessed Piet Retief's death. Later Tununu followed Mpande instead of Dingane and fought against Dingane in 1840 because he was at Mpande's when the fighting began. Then Tununu's family lived at eTongati, and Tununu subsequently left Mpande. Later he returned to the Mlalazi near Eshowe.

ZITSIBILI KA NYAKANYAKANA KA MATSHOBANA

(v. V, 12–19: interview notes for Norman Nembula)

Interview date: June 1905 by Norman Nembula.

She was born about 1826, and her father was a brother of the AmaKhumalo/AmaNdebele chief Mzilikazi. See notes for Norman Nembula.

Notes

Chapter 1

1 Throughout the nineteenth century, the denomination "AmaZulu" was restricted to the original followers of the royal descent line but not extended to the subjects of the expanded kingdom whose distinct sociopolitical identities therefore remained well known for generations following the unification of the Zulu kingdom. See John Wright, "Turbulent Times: Political Transformations in the North and East, 1760s-1830s" in Carolyn Hamilton, Bernard K. Mbenga, and Robert Ross, eds., *The Cambridge History of South Africa* (Cambridge University Press, 2010), vol. I, 230.
2 A sense, sentiment, and political goal of Zulu nationalism did not emerge until the twentieth century, primarily in response to the political pressures of white domination. For an incisive analysis of the emergence of Zulu nationalism, see John Wright, "Reconstituting Shaka Zulu for the Twenty-First Century," *Southern African Humanities*, 18, no. 2 (2006), 139-153.
3 Adam Kuper, "The 'House' and Zulu Political Structure in the Nineteenth Century," *Journal of African History*, 24 (1993), 469-487, 474; Kuper analyzed the findings of archaeologist Thomas Huffman and revisited the work of J. F. Holleman on the Zulu *isigodi*, or district.
4 Ibid, 477.
5 Ibid, 479.
6 Ibid, 481.
7 Ibid, 483.
8 Ibid.
9 For further theoretical analysis and explanation of the importance of precolonial southern African women in their roles as daughters, wives, and mothers, see Elizabeth A. Eldredge, *A South African Kingdom: The Pursuit of Security in Nineteenth-Century Lesotho* (Cambridge University Press, 1993), 126-146.
10 John L. and Jean Comaroff, *Ethnicity, Inc.* (University of Chicago Press, 2009), have made the most incisive analysis of this problem.

11 Elizabeth A. Eldredge, "Deconstructing Ethnicity: Multicultural Origins of the AmaZulu Identity," Paper presented to the Annual Meeting of the African Studies Association, New Orleans, Louisiana, November 20, 2009.
12 For an analysis of the African and European origins and sources of images of Shaka and the AmaZulu, real, invented, and imagined, see Carolyn Hamilton, *Terrific Majesty* (Cape Town: David Philip, 1998).
13 Magidigidi ka Nobebe, in Colin de B. Webb and John B. Wright, eds., *The James Stuart Archive of Recorded Oral Evidence Relating to the History of the Zulu and Neighbouring Peoples* (hereafter *JSA*), 5 vols. (Pietermaritzburg: University of Natal Press and Durban: Killie Campbell Africana Library (hereafter KCL), 1976–2001), v. III, 96.
14 Hamilton, *Terrific Majesty*.
15 Dan Wylie, *Savage Delight: White Myths of Shaka* (Pietermaritzburg: University of Natal Press, 2000).
16 Leonard Thompson, "Co-operation and Conflict: The Zulu Kingdom and Natal," *The Oxford History of South Africa* (Oxford University Press, 1969), vol. I, 334–390.
17 Shula Marks, "The Traditions of the Natal 'Nguni': A Second Look at the Work of A. T. Bryant" in Leonard Thompson, ed., *African Societies in Southern Africa: Historical Studies* (London: Heinemann, 1969), 126–144.
18 Jeff Peires, *The House of Phalo: A History of the Xhosa People in the Days of Their Independence* (Johannesburg: Raven Press, 1981); Philip Bonner, *Kings, Commoners and Concessionaires: The Evolution and Dissolution of the Nineteenth-Century Swazi State* (Cambridge University Press, 1983); John Wright, "The Dynamics of Power and Conflict in the Late 18th and Early 19th Centuries: A Critical Reconstruction," Ph.D. dissertation, University of the Witwatersrand, Johannesburg, 1989.
19 John Wright and Carolyn Hamilton, "Traditions and Transformations: The Phongolo-Mzimkhulu Region in the Late Eighteenth and Early Nineteenth Centuries," in Andrew Duminy and Bill Guest, eds., *Natal and Zululand from Earliest Times to 1910: A New History* (Pietermaritzburg: University of Natal Press and Shuter & Shooter, 1989), 49–82.
20 John Wright, "Political Transformations in the Thukela-Mzimkhulu Region in the Late Eighteenth and Early Nineteenth Centuries," in Carolyn Hamilton, ed., *The Mfecane Aftermath: Reconstructive Debates in Southern African History* (Johannesburg: Witwatersrand University Press; Pietermaritzburg: University of Natal Press, 1995), 163–181.
21 John Wright, "Beyond the Concept of the 'Zulu Explosion': Comments on the Current Debate," in Hamilton, ed., *Mfecane Aftermath*, 107–121. In his more recent work, he has revised his position; see Wright, "Turbulent Times," 224.
22 Jeff Guy, "Ecological Factors in the Rise of Shaka and the Zulu Kingdom," in Shula Marks and Anthony Atmore, eds., *Economy and Society in Pre-Industrial South Africa* (London: Longman, 1980), 102–119.
23 Jeff Guy, *The Destruction of the Zulu Kingdom* (London: Longman 1979; Johannesburg: Raven Press, 1982). See also Eileen Jensen Krige, *The Social System of the Zulus* (London: Longmans Green, 1936; Pietermaritzburg: Shuter & Shooter, 1950); Keletso E. Atkins, *The Moon Is Dead! Give Us*

Our Money! The Cultural Origins of an African Work Ethic, Natal, South Africa, 1843–1900 (Portsmouth, NH: Heinemann, 1993); Nicholas Cope, *To Bind the Nation: Solomon kaDinuzulu and Zulu Nationalism, 1913–1933* (Pietermaritzburg: University of Natal Press, 1993).

24 J. D. Omer-Cooper, *Zulu Aftermath: A Nineteenth-Century Revolution in Bantu Africa* (Evanston, IL: Northwestern University Press, 1969).

25 Elizabeth A. Eldredge, "Sources of Conflict in in Southern Africa, ca. 1800–30: The 'Mfecane' Reconsidered," *Journal of African History*, 33, no. 1 (1992), 1–35; reprinted in Hamilton, ed., *The Mfecane Aftermath*, 123–161; Elizabeth A. Eldredge, "Slave Raiding Across the Cape Frontier," in Elizabeth A. Eldredge and Fred Morton, eds., *Slavery in South Africa: Captive Labor on the Dutch Frontier* (Boulder: Westview Press and Pietermaritzburg: University of Natal Press, 1994), 93–126; Norman Etherington, "Putting the Mfecane Controversy into Historiographical Context," in Hamilton, ed., *Mfecane Aftermath*, 13–19. See also Christopher Saunders, "Pre-Cobbing Mfecane Historiography," in Hamilton, ed., *Mfecane Aftermath*, 21–34 and Norman Etherington, "A Tempest in a Teapot? Nineteenth-Century Contests for Land in South Africa's Caledon Valley and the Invention of the Mfecane," *Journal of African History* 45 (2004), 203–219; John Wright, "Beyond the 'Zulu Aftermath' Migration, Identities, Histories," *Journal of Natal and Zulu History*, 24, no. 25 (2006–2007), 1–36; Elizabeth A. Eldredge, "Migration, Conflict, and Leadership in Early Nineteenth-Century South Africa: The Case of Matiwane," in Robert W. Harms, et al., eds., *Paths Toward the Past: African Historical Essays in Honor of Jan Vansina* (Atlanta: African Studies Association Press, 1994), 39–75; Elizabeth A. Eldredge, "Shaka's Military Expeditions: Survival and Mortality from Shaka's Impis," in Paul S. Landau, ed., *The Power of Doubt: Essays in Honor of David Henige* (Madison: Parallel Press/University of Wisconsin-Madison Libraries, 2011), 209–239.

26 Philip Bonner, A. B. Esterhuysen, M. H. Schoeman et al., "Introduction," in Natalie Swanepoel, Amanda Esterhuysen, and Philip Bonner, eds., *Five Hundred Years Rediscovered: Southern African Precedents and Prospects* (Wits University Press, 2008), 4–5.

27 John Wright, "Rediscovering the Ndwandwe Kingdom," in Swanepoel et al., eds., 217–238.

28 Ibid.

29 John Wright, "The Thuli and Cele Paramountcies in the Coastlands of Natal, c. 170–1820," *Southern African Humanities*, 21 (2009), 177–194.

30 John Wright, "Turbulent Times: Political Transformations in the North and East, 1760s–1830s," in Hamilton, Mbenga, and Ross, eds., *Cambridge History of South Africa*, vol. I, 211–252.

31 Benedict Carton, John Laband, and Jabulani Sithole, eds., *Zulu Identities: Being Zulu, Past and Present* (New York: Columbia University Press, 2009).

32 Paul S. Landau, *Popular Politics in the History of South Africa, 1400–1948* (Cambridge University Press, 2010), 1–41.

33 Ibid, 17.

34 Ibid, 59.

35 Swanepoel et al., eds, *Five Hundred Years*. Also articles in *Journal of Southern African Studies*, 38, no. 2 (2012), including Peter Delius and Shula Marks, "Rethinking South Africa's Past: Essays on History and Archaeology," 247–255; Carolyn Hamilton and Simon Hall, "Reading Across the Divides: Commentary on the Political Co-Presence of Disparate Identities in Two Regions of South Africa in the Late Eighteenth and Early Nineteenth Centuries," 281–290; Simon Hall, "Identity and Political Centralisation in the Western Regions of Highveld, c. 1770–1830: An Archaeological Perspective," 301–318; Jeff Peires, "'He Wears Short Clothes!': Rethinking Rharhabe (c. 1715–1782)," 333–354; Fred Morton, "Mephato: The Rise of the Tswana Militia in the Pre-colonial Period," 385–397.
36 Norman Etherington, *The Great Treks: The Transformation of Southern Africa 1815–1854* (Harlow: Pearson Education, 2001), 23, 43.
37 Popular fictionalized accounts include Thomas Mofolo, *Chaka* (Morija, Lesotho: Morija Sesuto Book Depot, 1926) (English translation, International Institute of African Languages and Cultures, 1931) (new translation by Daniel P. Kunene, London: Heinemann, 1981); E. A. Ritter, *Shaka Zulu* (London: Longman, 1955); Mazizi Kunene, *Emperor Shaka the Great: A Zulu Epic* (London: Heineman, 1979). The fictional elements in Mofolo's novel about Shaka are self-evident, including the invention of a "*sanusi*," or practitioner of "witchcraft"; that is, with supposed supernatural powers who is portrayed as advising Shaka throughout his life.
38 There are many points of disagreement between myself and Wylie, as will be made evident in the chapters that follow.
39 Dan Wylie, "Language and Assassination: Cultural Negations in White Writers' Portrayal of Shaka and the Zulu" in Hamilton, ed., *The Mfecane Aftermath*, 71–103.
40 Wylie, *Myth of Iron*, 4.
41 Wylie, "Language," 71.
42 Wylie, *Myth of Iron*, 1, 5–6. Wylie identifies himself as a Rhodesian or Zimbabwean of European descent by birth currently living in South Africa, teaching literature at Rhodes University in Grahamstown, and focusing his research on European mythologies of Shaka. He sometimes tries to disentangle, compare, and weigh evidence, but at other times resorts to dismissing contradictory evidence as merely "confusion," as in his misleading comments on the origins and changes of meaning of the terms *Nguni*, *Ntungwa*, and *Lala*. *Myth of Iron*, 16–21.
43 Ibid, 11–12.
44 Ibid, 40.
45 Ibid, 491.
46 A. T. Bryant, *A Zulu-English Dictionary* (Mariannhill Mission Press, 1905); A. T. Bryant, *Olden Times in Zululand and Natal* (London: Longmans, Green 1929). His other published works are *The Zulu People as They Were Before the White Man Came* (Pietermaritzburg: Shuter and Shooter, 1949) and a series of articles from 1911 to 1913 republished in *A History of the Zulu and*

Neighbouring Tribes (Cape Town: C. Struik, Africana Specialist and Publisher, 1964).
47 N. J. van Warmelo, "The Classification of Cultural Groups" in W. D. Hammond-Tooke, ed., *The Bantu-Speaking Peoples of Southern Africa* (London and Boston: Routledge and Kegan Paul, 1974), 61.
48 Monica Wilson, "The Nguni People" in Wilson and Thompson, eds., *Oxford History of South Africa*, vol. I, 87.
49 Wright and Hamilton, "Traditions," 50–57.
50 John Wright, "A. T. Bryant and 'The Wars of Shaka,'" *History in Africa*, 18 (1991), 409–425.
51 John Wright, "A T. Bryant and the 'Lala,'" *Journal of Southern African Studies*, 38, no. 2 (2012), 355–368.
52 KCL, James Stuart Collection, File 40 (ii), KCM 23756: handwritten notes by Stuart labeled "Conversations with Rev. A. T. Bryant 22 & 23 Jany 1924." Stuart was openly critical of Bryant's work as early as 1909 when Bryant was still so unsure of his information that he wrote to ask Stuart about the ancestry and origins of various peoples. Letter of A. T. Bryant to "Dear Mr. Stuart," dated July 7, 1909. P.O. Tongaat, KCL, James Stuart Collection, File 10, KCM 23448.
53 A. T. Bryant to J. Stuart, 39 Magdalen Road, St. Leonards, Sussex, July 4, 1929. KCL, JS File 40 item xiii, 11–14.
54 Ibid.
55 Brief biographies of James Stuart and explanations of his work are found in *JSA*, Webb and Wright, eds. and transl., "Introduction," v. I, xiii–xix; and Hamilton, *Terrific Majesty*, 130–167.
56 Webb and Wright, eds., *JSA*, 5 vols. The original interview notes, including the interviews now available in the Webb and Wright publication and additional unpublished interviews used in this bok, as well as Stuart's various unpublished essays and various other relevant holdings, are found in the Killie Campbell Library, hereafter cited as KCL. Interviews published in the five volumes edited by Webb and Wrights are cited as *JSA*, and individual interviewees are listed in the Appendix with full citations to their location. Unpublished interviews are cited as KCL using the assigned KCL archival reference. See also Carolyn Hamilton, "Backstory, Biography, and the Life of the James Stuart Archive," *History in Africa*, 38 (2011), 319–341; Benedict Carton, "Fount of Deep Culture: Legacies of the *James Stuart Archive* in South African Historiography," *History in Africa*, 30 (2003), 87–106.
57 Stuart lived in Natal until 1922 when he moved to London. He died in 1942, having spent the remainder of his years publishing several school readers in isiZulu that included some of the oral traditions he had collected and trying to portray a favorable image of the AmaZulu to British society with various lectures and writings. Webb and Wright, "Introduction," *JSA*, vol. I, xii–xix.
58 Hamilton, *Terrific Majesty*, 52, provides a similar critique of Julian Cobbing's position, "A Tainted Well: The Objectives, Historical Fantasies, and Working Methods of James Stuart, with Counter-argument," *Journal of Natal and Zulu History*, 11 (1988), 115–154. The very presence of the contradictory

and conflicting narratives indicates that neither those whose testimony he recorded nor Stuart himself had tried to or succeeded in imposing a hegemonic narrative and interpretation of the past in support of a specific personal or political motive or interest. That Stuart often noted he did not understand what he recorded and therefore pursued the question in later interviews indicates that he was accurately recording the testimony as it was received without distorting it according to prior knowledge or personal interest.

59 Hamilton, *Terrific Majesty*, 38–46, describes the circumstances of the early traders that influenced their perspectives and biased their production of images of Shaka.

60 *The Diary of Henry Francis Fynn* (hereafter *Diary*) compiled from original sources and edited by James Stuart and D. McK. Malcolm (Pietermaritzburg: Shuter & Shooter, 1986, first published 1951). The manuscript's history is provided in the two prefaces, one by each of the editors. The text appears to confirm Stuart's estimate that the manuscript for the "diary" portion of the *Diary* had been written about 1830 based on the actual diary he had previously kept and had unexpectedly lost because it was in the hands of his brother Frank who died and was buried with his personal effects.

61 The editors note that "this was probably written in or about 1832 or 1833 or even 1831 when Fynn was on the Cape Frontier. Two of the sheets of the revised version of these notes bear on them the watermark of 1827." Fynn, Diary, 131 n.1. In this passage in the text, Fynn wrote "there are now more than four thousand inhabitants under our protection" (i.e., in the vicinity of Port Natal).

62 Fynn's European wife bore him several children, including Henry Francis Fynn Jr., who gave his father's writings to Stuart for editing and publishing. Fynn senior also had numerous children with African wives, some of whom were murdered in a treacherous night surprise attack by a force sent out by Dingane.

63 "Mr. Fynn's Evidence," *The Natal Mercury*, April 14, 1853; typescript, Henry Francis Fynn Papers, KCL, KCM 14675. MS Fynn 1.04.

64 There is almost nothing with reference to history in Fynn's statement to the commission, however, and it contains nothing he did not say elsewhere. However, it was the first time any of these writings would have been made public because he had not yet published except in a few letters to the *Graham's Town Journal*.

65 Fynn, *Diary*, 15–16.

66 Wylie, *Savage Delight*, 105–135. Fynn's evidence and that of the other traders, including Nathaniel Isaacs, James King, and Charles Rawden Maclean ("John Ross") is not presumed to be accurate or honest in the historical narrative recreated below but is presented for consideration and comparison with oral traditions. Historians of Africa necessarily used extremely biased colonial and white settler sources but with skepticism and careful analysis to determine the reliability of each piece of evidence provided by these sources.

67 My perspective of Henry Francis Fynn has been strongly influenced by the scholarship of Julie Pridmore. I am grateful to her for the insights she gave me in conversations while I was conducting my research in 1994.

68 KCL, typescripts of The Fynn Letters, vol. [2 Incorrect AU change] II, pp. 59–63; original in the KwaZulu-Natal Provincial Archives in Pietermaritzburg.
69 *Isaacs Journal* published in the *South African Commercial Advertiser (SACA)*, beginning with no. 520, June 6, 1832, copied by James Stuart, typescripts, Extract 1, 89–119, and 3, 120–132. At the end of the series in the final journal entries published in *SACA* October 10, 1832 (James Stuart Extract 3, 127–132), the newspaper added: "Mr. Isaacs is now in Cape Town and intends, we understand, to communicate with the local Government respecting the utility of a settlement being formed at Natal." Wylie compares the two versions, Isaacs' unpolished *SACA* journal entries and the later two-volume book, Nathaniel Isaacs, *Travels and Adventures in Eastern Africa*, in Louis Herrman, ed. (Cape Town: The Van Riebeeck Society, 1956), vols. I, II); Wylie, 83–104. Wylie's critique is insightful and useful in the consideration of various pieces of evidence found in Isaac's journal, and as Wylie makes clear, the book evidently was heavily edited by someone else, if not ghostwritten. Isaac's well-known letter to Fynn cited above casts doubts on Wylie's assumption that Isaacs was unable to write even a letter unaided, as alleged by the colonial governor of Sierra Leone, but Wylie is certainly correct that an unidentified writer produced the version that was later published. Wylie, 94.
70 Isaacs, *South African Commercial Advertiser*, no. 521, June 9, 1832.
71 Charles Rawden Maclean, *The Natal Papers of "John Ross": Loss of the Brig Mary at Natal with Early Recollections of that Settlement and Among the Caffres*, Stephen Gray, ed. (Durban: Killie Campbell Africana Library and Pietermaritzburg: University of Natal Press, 1992), 132–133. Gray provides an excellent biography and insightful commentary but appears mistaken in thinking that Maclean/Ross wrote this work when it was originally published as a series of articles in the monthly *Nautical Magazine* in 1853–55; the text itself reveals that it was written between December 1838 and early 1839 based on Maclean's direct comments to the readership he was addressing at that time. From Grey's biography, it is self-evident that Maclean/Ross retained his sympathy for people of African origins and descent throughout his life and supported British antislavery efforts, even causing an incident to protect his free black sailors on the *Susan King* when it was docked at the port of Wilmington, North Carolina. Grey writes, "The unequal treatment of British subjects in foreign ports of call in treaty with Britain–meted out on the basis of skin-colour–obviously enraged him. Through an account made to his Lieutenant-Governor, Maclean entered the British press as something of a liberty man and he was much praised for his courage and conviction." Grey, "Introduction," 11.
72 Fynn, *Diary*, 131.
73 Maclean, 39. He wrote this while Dingane was still alive and "king" of the Zulu nation and after they had been "assailed" by the Boers in an incident that had made international news. This reference could only have been the events of the Day of the Covenant and the Battle of Blood River; hence, we know he wrote this no earlier than December 1838 and no later than Dingane's death the following year. Port Natal had not yet been named Durban, and there was not yet common usage in the spelling of the Zulu name and names of Zulus.

74 Maclean, 88.
75 Hamilton provides an excellent analysis of Shepstone's role as a colonial administrator and his use and propagation of Shaka myths. Hamilton, *Terrific Majesty*, 72–129.
76 Theophilus Shepstone, "Historical Sketch of the Tribes anciently inhabiting the Colony of Natal–as at present bounded–and Zululand." Sir T. Shepstone, K.C.M.G., "who has also supplied accompanying Sketch-Maps," Cape of Good Hope. *Report and Proceedings, with Appendices, of the Government Commission on Native Law and Customs*, G.4.-'83 (Cape Town: W. A. Richards and Sons, Government Printers, 1883 (January), 415–426.
77 Wright, "Dynamics," 100–104. Wright notes that a draft of the ninety-four "tribal" histories can be found in the Shepstone Papers at the Natal Archives, and the despatch (no. 34, Scott to Newcastle, 26 February 1864, and its enclosures [minus maps] were published as Sessional Paper no. 23 of the Natal Legislative Council, 1890, in *Correspondence Relating to…Tribal Titles to Land*, 95–117.
78 The interviewees are cited individually by name in the notes as specific information provided by them is used in the chapters that follow below. A full list of the interviewees of James Stuart cited in this book with basic biographical information is provided in the Appendix.

Chapter 2

1 Ndukwana ka Mbengwana, in Webb and Wright, eds., *The James Stuart Archive (JSA)*, v. IV, 279.
2 Ibid, 289.
3 Mtshayankomo ka Magolwana, *JSA*, v. IV, 122.
4 Mcotoyi ka Mnini, *JSA*, v. III, 53, 54, 64–65.
5 Maziyana ka Mahlabeni, *JSA*, v. II, 282, 292, 297–300.
6 Ibid, 274, 276–277.
7 Mcotoyi, *JSA*, v. III, 54–58.
8 Mageza ka Kwefunga, *JSA*, v. II, 69.
9 Maziyana, *JSA*, v. II, 300.
10 Mageza, *JSA*, v. II, 68–69, 73.
11 "Historical Sketch of the Tribes anciently inhabiting the Colony of Natal – as at present bounded – and Zululand," by Sir T. Shepstone, K.C.M.G., "who has also supplied accompanying Sketch-Maps," *Report and Proceedings, with Appendices, of the Government Commission on Native Law and Customs*, G.4.-'83 (Cape Town: W. A. Richards and Sons, Government Printers, 1883 (January), 415.
12 For early AmaMthethwa history, see Mabonsa ka Sidhlayi, *JSA*, v. II, 11–41; Ndukwana ka Mbengwana, *JSA*, v. IV, 263–406; Madikane ka Mlomowetole, *JSA*, v. II, 47–67; Magidi ka Ngomane, v. II, 79–82; Ndhlovu ka Timuni, *JSA*, v. IV, 198–238.
13 For early AmaHlubi history, see Mabonsa ka Sidhlayi, *JSA*, v. II, 11–41.
14 Sivivi ka Maqungo, *JSA*, v. V, 377.

15 Ndukwana, *JSA*, v. IV, 361. Dingiswayo's genealogy was alternatively given as Dingiswayo ka [of (i.e., son of)] Jobe ka Kali ka Xaba ka Madanga, or Dingiswayo ka Jobe ka Kali ka Madango; Magidi ka Ngomane, 79; Bunu at interview of Ndhlovu ka Timuni, 205; Ndhlovu ka Timuni, 210; Jantshi ka Nongila, 174-175; Ndukwana in interview of Jantshi, *JSA*, v. I, 174-175. Regarding the heartland of the AmaMthethwa and the name by which they were known in the early nineteenth century, Madikane said, "Nyambose is the name of a hill in the Mtetwa district, first built on by the Mtetwa people, and that is how they come to derive their [praise] name as abakwaNyambose." Madikane ka Mlomowetole, *JSA*, v. II, 53.
16 Shepstone, "Historical Sketch," 415-426.
17 The AmaZulu oral traditions were as insistent on this as were early Europeans who had heard it from AmaZulu informants earlier in the nineteenth century. See, for example, Socwatsha ka Papu, "Per Socwatsha, in the presence of Dhlozi; Ndkuwana was present during latter part of convn and assisted in giving information this day 28.12,1901 (Sat.)," unpub., 6-7, 15, 19: KCL, File 66 KCM 24365 on 2-6-1912 (Socwatsha); Madikane ka Mlomowetole, *JSA*, v. II, 50; Letter of John Shepstone to 'Jamie' James Stuart, 28 October, 1904 (Pietermaritzburg, KCL, JS File 40, item xvi, KCM 23770; Rupert Shepstone August 5, 1900; *JSA*, v. V, 328.
18 Dingiswayo was also known by various praise names, as was common for chiefs: "Dingiswayo, alias Makhlekezele or Sombangeya." Mmemi ka Nguluzane, *JSA*, v. III, 244.
19 Fynn *Diary*, "Historical Introduction," 7. Fynn had been told much of the information in this historical account by Shaka himself.
20 Mabonsa ka Sidhlayi, *JSA*, v. II, 12.
21 Ibid, 12.
22 Shepstone, "Historical Sketch," 415.
23 Ndukwana, *JSA*, v. IV, 289.
24 Ibid, 361.
25 Ibid, 326.
26 Fynn *Diary*, 7. For the trade link between the modern KwaZulu region and Maputo, see Alan K. Smith, "The Trade of Delagoa Bay as a Factor in Nguni Politics 1750-1835," in L. Thompson, ed., *African Societies in Southern Africa*, 171-189; Alan K. Smith, "Delagoa Bay and the Trade of South-Eastern Africa" in R. Gray and D. Birmingham, eds., *Pre-Colonial Trade in Central and Eastern Africa before 1900* (London, 1970), 265-89; David Hedges, "Trade and Politics in Southern Mozambique and Zululand in the Eighteenth and Nineteenth Centuries," Ph.D. dissertation, University of London, 1979.
27 Fynn *Diary*, 8.
28 Ibid, 9.
29 Mayinga ka Mbekuzana, *JSA*, v. II, 247.
30 Ibid.
31 Fynn *Diary*, 9.
32 Magidi ka Ngomane, *JSA*, v. II, 80.
33 Ngidi ka Mcikaziswa, *JSA*, v. V, 67.

34 Ibid.
35 Kambi ka Matshobana, *JSA*, v. I, 210.
36 Ibid.
37 Ibid, 212.
38 Ibid, 211.
39 Mmemi, 272.
40 Mbovu ka Mtshumayeli, *JSA*, v. III, 29-30.
41 Ibid, 35-36.
42 Ibid, 36.
43 Ibid.
44 Mbovu, 29.
45 Kambi, 210.
46 Mbovu, 36.
47 Kambi, 210.
48 Luzipo ka Nomageje, *JSA*, v. I, 354.
49 Giba ka Sobuza, 149.
50 Stuart's main informant about AmaNdwandwe history was Luzipo "of the Ndwandwe tribe," interviewed on November 19, 1904.
51 Luzipo, 354.
52 Ibid.
53 Ibid.
54 Madikane, 60.
55 Madhlebe ka Njinjana, *JSA*, v. II, 45; Luzipo, 354; Mkando ka Dhlova, *JSA*, v. III, 146; Jantshi, 186, confirmed by Mmemi according to annotation by Stuart.
56 Luzipo, 355.
57 Ibid, 354.
58 Baleka ka Mpitikazi, *JSA*, v. I, 13.
59 Luzipo, 354.
60 Mayinga ka Mbekuzana, *JSA*, v. II, 255.
61 Mmemi, 243.
62 Ngidi, *JSA*, v. V, 28; 45-47. *Elangeni* or *eLangeni* is the locative form derived from the name Langa (i.e., "at the place of Langa").
63 Ngidi, 30, 48, 49, 75, 79, 93; notes of Webb and Wright, v. V, 111 n.330 and n.337; v. V, 102, notes 145-148.
64 "Mkabayi *busa*'d [ruled] whilst Senzangakona was still young." "Per Socwatsha, in the presence of Dhlozi; Ndkuwana was present during latter part of convn and assisted in giving information this day 28.12,1901 (Sat.)", unpub., 9.
65 Madikane, 49.
66 See Chapter 3.
67 Ngidi, 49.
68 Ibid. Senzangakhona's wives were listed by Baleni ka Silwana, *JSA*, v. I, 23: "Langazana ka Gubetshe of the Sibiya people [not of the Nzimela as Bryant says] – mother of Gqugqu"; Songiya ka Ngotsha, of the Hlabisa, mother of Mpande; Mpikase ka Mlilela of the Maqungebeni, mother of Dingana; Nozibuku of the Nzumalo of the Ndwandwe, mother of Nzibe; Nandi, mother of

Tshaka; Ngcaka ka Mncinci; Magulana ka Ntshongolo of the Qwabe; Bibi ka Nkobe (Sompisi) of the Ntuli.
69 Baleni ka Silwana, 21; Kuba was Baleni's great-grandfather.
70 Ibid, 22.
71 Mayinga, 251.
72 Ngidi, 33, 36–37; Madikane, 50; Mkando ka Dhlova, 146.
73 Ibid.
74 Madikane, 50.
75 Ngidi, 37, listed Senzangakhona's children as Sigujana, Tshaka, Mhlangana, Dingana, Mpande, Nzibe, Mbudhlele, Ntikili (girl), Magwaza, Nongqobo (both sons of Langazana ka Gubetshe of the Beleni people of the Ntuli tribe, both of the iziNyosi regiment, and both killed at eNcome), Ngqojana, Mfihlo, Sopana, Somajuba, Mdungazwe, Nozilwana (girl, daughter of Mnkabi), Gqugqu ("of the house of Bandile, a girl of the left-hand house (*ikohlo*), of the people of Sigwebana and of Mudhli"), Nomkwayimba, and Nomzinhlanga. Ngidi's list of Senzangakhona's wives included Langazana ka Gubetshe, Mnkabi, Bandile, Ngoto ka Mhuyi, and Bidi (Bibi) daughter of Nkobe who was a brother of Sompisi of the AmaNtuli "tribe." Senzangakhona's sons listed by Baleni ka Silwana, 22, were Ndunge and Mhlangana, Dingana, Tshaka, Mpande, Nzibe, Gqugqu killed by Dingana, Sigujana (Mfokazi), and others. Baleni listed Senzangakhona's daughters as Ziwelile who married Jobe; Nomanqe who married Mlandela of the Mtetwa; Ntikili, Nomcoba, and Matenjwase who all also married among the AmaMthethwa; Sikaka who married an Mbata man; Nomzinhlanga who married among the AmaMthethwa; Mtembazi married in the Mgazini tribe; Maqukazi also married among the AmaMthethwa; Mantongela who married among the AmaButhelezi; and Zayi who married among the AmaMdhlalose. Baleni gave the names of many of the men they married, and said there were other daughters as well. Senzangakhona's sons listed in Stuart's notes without specific attribution were Mfokazana, Sigujana, Sopane, Kolekile, Dingane, Gqugqu, Mpande. Mkehlengana ka Zulu, *JSA*, v. III, 217.
76 Mkando ka Dhlova, 159. He told Stuart, "Ngqengelele's father was Mbulana. He was an iNtungwa and of the Butelezi people. He was brought to notice by Tshaka.... KwaGociza, Emantungweni, Emantungweni (2), eNsukaze, eMahlabaneni (where Mhlangana was killed) – these were Ngqengelele's kraals." Mkando, 159. See also Ndukwana, 317; Jantshi ka Nongila, 190–191.
77 Ndukwana in interview of Jantshi, 190.

Chapter 3

1 Ngidi, *James Stuart Archive (JSA)* v. V, 30. Information about Nandi's family members, including her mother's parentage, the names of other children of her father Mbengi, are found in the interviews of Ngidi, 29, 31, 54, 59, 64–65; Mbovu, *JSA*, v. III, 25. One of Nandi's brothers, Bantwana, became a Christian convert, *kolwa*, and in 1904 Ngidi said he had "died recently." This is important, because it indicates one of Nandi's brothers was alive for several generations to sustain local knowledge of events concerning Nandi, Tshaka,

and the eLangeni people from the early nineteenth century. He was of the Isibubulungu regiment among the eLangeni, about the age of Mgabi, and Ngidi knew him personally. Ngidi, 31; see also 64–65.
2 Mtshapi ka Noradu, *JSA*, v. IV, 87; Ngdi, 35, 90.
3 Mgidhlana ka Mpande, *JSA*, v. III, 105.
4 Ndhlovu, 202–3.
5 At his final interview with Stuart on September 20, 1919, with Munyana ka Somaloko also present, Ndhlovu told Stuart; "I heard the whole story of Tshaka from my father Timuni. I had many talks with him. I wanted particularly to hear stories of our tribe. I heard also from Sipika of the uMnkangala regiment. He was much older than my father. He died at eGilanyone, in the country of Ngunezi, of the Embo tribe. He died in 1880, i.e. the year that Cetshwayo returned from England." Ndhlovu, *JSA*, v. IV, 232.
6 Ndhlovu, 202–203.
7 When on February 11, 1903, Jantshi began telling Stuart about Senzangakona and Tshaka's personal early life, he underscored the reliability of the information he had learned from his father by saying, "my father told me he was in the Zulu country when Tshaka was born, and was a man at the time of his birth." Jantshi, 188.
8 Ibid, 177.
9 Ndhlovu, 219–220; also published in London 1919.
10 Ngidi, 59.
11 Ibid.
12 Mmemi, *JSA*, v. III, 248.
13 Mangati, *JSA*, v. II, 205.
14 Mkehlengana ka Zulu, *JSA* v. III, 218.
15 Madikane ka Mlomowetole, *JSA*, v. II, 51.
16 Mkehlengana, *JSA*, v. III, 218.
17 Madikane, 47; see also 51.
18 In his account, Fynn stated explicitly that Shaka was the primary source of his information but that he had corroborated it from other sources. Fynn's "Historical Introduction" was derived from oral versions of the past that he had heard from informants who are unidentified, had had variable access to accurate information of the past, and had intentions in conveying information to Fynn that cannot be determined or assessed.
19 Baleka ka Mpitikazi, *JSA*, v. I, 5.
20 Ndhlovu, *JSA*, v. IV, 198.
21 Ibid, 202.
22 Ibid.
23 Ibid. For evidence about where Shaka was born, see Mruyi, *JSA*, v. IV, 38; Ndhlovu, *JSA*, v. IV, 206; Mmemi, 248. Mbengi's kraals were Engugeni, Emhlanga, Obaneni, kwaNtsholo, and the Nguga, the largest and chief kraal. Ngidi, 30.
24 Madikane, 51.
25 Ibid, 47.
26 Ibid. Madikane's father Mlomowetole was old enough to know about the early history firsthand and had *khonza*'d Shaka, lending credibility to

information provided by Madikane about Shaka and early events associated with him. Madikane explained, "[m]y father heard all this Makobosi ka Ndhlovu, also from Hlati of the eMgazini people. My father lived with Hlati, a man belonging to one of Senzangakona's regiments." This provides a chain of transmission for Madikane's narrative that is more explicit than just with reference to his father Mlomowetole.

27 Ibid.
28 Jantshi, 178, 188–9.
29 Ibid.
30 Ndhlovu, 221.
31 Ibid, 223.
32 Ibid.
33 Ibid, 223, 1919 narrative; published in London 1919.
34 Ibid, 179; Webb and Wright, 203 n.16: these are "names for a beetle believed by the Zulu to cause intestinal disorders."
35 Ndhlovu, 232.
36 Ibid, 191.
37 Jantshi, 188.
38 Ibid.
39 Mkebeni ka Dabulamanzi, *JSA*, v. III, 199, in 1921.
40 Baleni, *JSA*, v. I, 32, 1914.
41 Ibid, 5, 1919.
42 Mmemi, 248.
43 Ngidi, 49.
44 Mayinga, 246; see also Sivivi, *JSA*, v. V, 375; Madikane, *JSA*, v. III, 47, 51.
45 Mayinga, *JSA*, v. III, 247.
46 Ibid.
47 Ibid.
48 Fynn, "Historical Introduction," *Diary*, 13. See also Mkebeni, *JSA*, v. III, 199–200; Ngidi, 29; Mruyi, 37; Jantshi, 179, 188, 199; Mmemi, 248; Jantshi, 189; Socwatsha, unpublished interview notes, James Stuart Archives, KCL; Ngidi, 30, 41; Mkando, 151.
49 Mkehlengana, 218.
50 Madikane, 48.
51 Ibid.
52 Ngidi, 94.
53 Baleka, 5.
54 Mayinga, 246.
55 Mkando, 151.
56 Ibid.
57 Ngidi, 29, 30.
58 Ndhlovu, 225.
59 Ibid.
60 Mkando explained the procedures associated with circumcision and related customs, and said, "A man who had been circumcised would not wash in the presence of others for he would be afraid of being laughed at. 'Look at the penistip, all by itself.'" I have never seen the ceremony. Tshaka put a stop

to the practice. My father, I hear, had been circumcised. Circumcised people put on the penis cover. Wearing of the penis cover is done so that if the front of the girdle parts, the penis should not be seen by women. I think this was the only reason. Formerly a piece of ox-hide would be sewn into a penis cover; this practice was discontinued in Dingana's reign and the stalk of the wild-banana leaf (*inkamanga*) used, i.e. the present-day penis cover, made of the *ingceba* (plants growing like bananas in bushes – edible fruit)." Mkando, 160.

61 Ndhlovu, 225.
62 Maziyana, 280.
63 Ngidi, 30.
64 Baleka, 4.
65 Ibid.
66 Ibid. See also Jantshi, 180; Mkebeni, 197; Ndhlovu, 203.
67 Ngidi, 29.
68 Ibid, 94.
69 Mmemi, 270; Ngidi, 29.
70 Ngidi, 36.
71 Ndukwana, 330. Webb and Wright note that "Zibhebhu kaMaphitha was head of the Mandlakazi, who were closely related to the Zulu royal house." *JSA*, v. V, 123 n.9.
72 Mruyi, 37.
73 Ngidi, 29.
74 Ibid, 30; see also 44, 53.
75 Madikane, 48. See also Mruyi, 217, in interview of Ndhlovu; Jantshi, 191; Mayinga, 246.
76 Ngidi 66, 78.
77 Ibid, 31; Ngidi ka Mcikayiswa, KCL, in File 61 NB [Note Book] 35, p. 3, 11 August 1904, from notes of interview with Ngidi (*isibongo* Magambukazi) ka Mcikayiswa, KCL File 61 NB 35 KCM24271, interview notes of James Stuart from 1904.
78 Ngidi, 78.
79 Ibid, 66.
80 Ibid.
81 Ibid, 60.
82 Ibid, 29.

Chapter 4

1 For Wylie's discussion of some of the evidence and events described in this chapter, see *Myth of Iron*, 140–147.
2 Ngidi ka Mcikaziswa, *James Stuart Archive* (*JSA*), v. V, 58.
3 Ibid, 78.
4 Ndhlovu, *JSA*, v. IV, 216.
5 Mruyi, *JSA*, v. IV, 37.
6 Ndhlovu, 216. This agrees with Fynn's narrative of these events: Fynn, "Historical Introduction," 13.
7 Ngidi, 58.

8 Ibid, 36, 78.
9 Ibid, 36. Dingane was said to have acquired the AbaQwabe dialect that remained with him his entire life, explaining why his exile there was so easily remembered.
10 Magidi, *JSA*, v. II, 79, in 1903, 1904.
11 Ndhlovu, 204.
12 Jantshi, *JSA*, v. I, 180
13 Ndhlovu, 205; Jantshi,180.
14 Ngidi, 94.
15 Ibid.
16 The narrative of Shaka's life that Ndhlovu told Stuart in 1919 was essentially unchanged from the narrative he had told sixteen years before, but in 1903, Stuart was primarily concerned with recording the events that he had been told in line with a factual narrative that would make sense to European readers. The 1919 version, published in 1924 in the original isiZulu and translated by Webb and Wright from Stuart's notes written in isiZulu, convey not only the narrative but also the idiom of the narrative as told by Ndhlovu. The substantial similarities in the two tellings of this narrative by the same person indicate faithfulness to the original content. Ndhlovu, 2 September 1919, 218–233.
17 Ndhlovu, 227, September 2, 1919.
18 Ibid.
19 Ibid.
20 Mandhlakazi ka Ngini, *JSA*, v. II, 187. He was interviewed in 1913, 1916, 1921, and 1922.
21 Madikane, *JSA*, v. II, 61.
22 Mayinga, *JSA*, v. II, 247.
23 Ibid.
24 Ibid, 246.
25 Ibid, 248.
26 Ibid, 256.
27 Ndhlovu, 216.
28 Mkebeni, *JSA*, v. III, 197–198, 1921.
29 Magidi, *JSA*, v. II, 80. Webb and Wright, 82 n.13, translate this in their text as "Tshaka had a headring. He put it on among the Mtetwa – he was authorized to do so by Dingiswayo."
30 Ndhlovu, 204.
31 Ibid, 206.
32 Ibid, 232.
33 Ibid, 204.
34 Ibid.
35 Ibid.
36 Ibid, 204–205. *Sic.* in original.
37 Ibid, 205, 206; Ngidi, 53.
38 Ibid, 206. Ndukwana and Mruyi were present and disagreed with specific points in Ndhlovu's narrative.
39 Ndhlovu, 227.

40 Ibid, 227–228.
41 Ibid, 229.
42 Magidi, 81.
43 For other versions, see Magidi, 80; Ngidi, 42.
44 Mruyi, 36.
45 Ibid, 37.
46 Ibid.
47 Jantshi, 181.
48 Ibid, 182.
49 Ibid. See also Mtshayankomo's version of events: Mtshayankomo ka Magolwana, *JSA*, v. IV, 122.
50 Ibid.
51 Ibid.
52 Madikane, 48.
53 Ibid.
54 Ibid.
55 Ngidi, 53.
56 Sivivi, *JSA*, v. V, 375.
57 Mkebeni, *JSA*, v. III, 198–199.
58 Ibid.
59 Ibid.
60 Ibid.
61 Magidi, 80.
62 Sivivi, 375. He added, "I do not know of Sigujana," but this was the same person, and Stuart's spelling suggests he used a close but different pronunciation.
63 Jantshi, 199, 15 February 1903.
64 Ndukwana in interview of Jantshi, 199.
65 Jantshi, 199.
66 Baleni, *JSA*, v. I, 16.
67 Ndhlovu, 205. See also Madikane, 48; Ngidi, 42.
68 Ngidi, 42. He listed the people who had returned with Shaka, 79.
69 Ibid, 59.
70 It is unlikely that Fynn's writing influenced these oral traditions because this did not appear in print until decades later when the *Diary* was published in 1951.
71 Fynn, "Historical Introduction," 14.
72 Fynn recorded the words of the song, which includes the lines "When we stab we proceed forward" and "Painful is it to be said I am a commoner." Fynn was told that Shaka himself composed this song. Fynn, "Historical Introduction," 14.
73 Ngidi, 42.
74 Webb and Wright, *JSA*, v. V, 100 n.118.

Chapter 5

1 Baleka ka Mpitikazi, *James Stuart Archive* (hereafter *JSA*), v. I, 10.
2 Ngidi ka Mcikaziswa, *JSA*, v. V, 67.
3 Ibid.

4 Ndhlovu, *JSA*, v. IV, 204–205; Jantshi, *JSA*, v. I, 180; Ngidi, *JSA*, v. V, 94; Madikane, *JSA*, v. II, 61; Mayinga ka Mbekuzana, *JSA*, v. II, 247.
5 Mayinga, 255.
6 For more about specific battles and military campaigns and their outcomes, see Chapter 6 and Eldredge, "Shaka's Military Expeditions."
7 Ndukwana, *JSA*, v. IV, 289.
8 Ngidi, 60.
9 Theophilus Shepstone, "Historical Sketch," par.13. There have been numerous studies of aspects of the Zulu military system in the nineteenth century, based on evidence from after Shaka's reign. See, for example, Ian Knight, *Anatomy of the Zulu Army from Shaka to Cetshwayo 1818–1879* (London: Greenhill Books, 1995). Evidence about AmaZulu regiments is included in R. C. Samuelson, *Long, Long Ago* (Durban, 1929), 233–245; his information about regiments from Shaka's reign is incomplete, however.
10 Nogandaya's father, i.e. Komfiya/Zulu's paternal grandfather, was Nkonjane. Mmemi ka Nguluzane, *JSA* v. III, 272.
11 According to Dinya, "[t]he Ncwane is the section to which Zulu ka Nogandaya belongs. This section seems to have come from the north say the Mtetwa tribe." Dinya ka Zokozwayo, *JSA* v. I, 101.
12 The three other men included Mandhlakazi's father Situnga and his brother Magutshwa. Mandhlakazi ka Situnga, *JSA*, v. II, 183.
13 Mandhlakazi ka Ngini, 179–183.
14 Dinya, 101–102.
15 The warrior hero Zulu ka Nogandaya lived into the reigns of both Dingane and Mpande. After quarrelling with King Mpande over a woman, Zulu was forced to leave and find protection from a European trader, Henry Ogle, whom he may have known from the earliest days of the traders at Port Natal.
16 Mmemi ka Nguluzane, 249.
17 Mmemi, 270; Jantshi ka Nongila, *JSA*, v. I, 190.
18 Mbovu, 37.
19 Mmemi, 270.
20 Jantshi ka Nongila, *JSA*, v. I, 186.
21 Jantshi, 193–194.
22 Ibid, 194–195.
23 Eldredge, "Shaka's Military Expeditions."
24 Melapi ka Magaye, *JSA*, v. III, 87.
25 Mbovu ka Mtshumayeli, 44.
26 Ngidi told Stuart, "What is known as the *umradu* [*umhadu*, violent] style of fighting began with Tshaka, which went to such extremes that children were impaled on posts and even the dogs of a kraal were killed." However, the only other references to impaling anyone on posts refer not to Tshaka but to another chief who terrorized southern Natal, raising important doubt about the accuracy of this information. Ngidi ka Mcikaziswa, 60.
27 Fynn, *Diary*, 17.
28 Lugubu ka Mangaliso, *JSA*, v. I, 290. See also Mkebeni ka Dabulamanzi, *JSA*, v. III, 196; Mmemi ka Nguluzane, *JSA*, v. III, 270; Fynn, *Diary*, 16.

29 Mayinga ka Mbekuzana, *JSA*, v. II, 247.
30 Ngidi, 68. Webb and Wright, v. V, 108 n. 269, note that "Sigananda was chief of the Cube, not the Chunu, until his death in 1906." See also Madikane ka Mlomowetole, *JSA*, v. II, 60; Ngidi, 66.
31 Baleni ka Silwana, *JSA*, v. I, 34–35.
32 Stuart was given information about "doctoring troops with flesh taken from 'deceased man' etc. Used was *umdidi*, *umtondo*, bone of right (throwing) arm and cartilege – *itamjana* – *uvalo* – these were taken by Zibebu in the case described." KCL File 66 KCM 24365: Mpatshana, Socwatsha, and Nsuze interviewed on January 2, 1912.
33 Mayinga, 248.
34 Baleni, 18.
35 Mmemi ka Nguluzane, *JSA*, v. III, 250.
36 Dinya ka Zokozwayo, *JSA*, v. I, 103. This term for the younger protective forces around the king, "*isibiba*", literaly means "antidote to snake poison." C. M. Doke et al., compilers, *English-Zulu Dictionary* (Johannesburg: Witwatersrand University Press, 1977).
37 Mkehlengana ka Zulu, 216.
38 Ibid, 216.
39 See another explanation from Baleni, 17.
40 Eldredge, "Shaka's Military Expeditions."
41 Socwatsha in interview of Maziyana ka Mahlabeni, 273.
42 Madikane ka Mlomowetole, 54.
43 Mtshapi, *JSA*, v. IV, 82.
44 Mkando ka Dhlova, *JSA*, v. III, 145. He lists the names of girls' regiments/age grades.
45 Ngidi, *JSA*, v. V, 41. Later he said, "Tshaka only gathered four classes of girls. They cut war-shields (*izihlangu*) and fought like men. Some of them earned and wore *iziqu* [emblems of bravery or killing in war worn in a necklace]." Ngidi, 69.
46 Second insert in brackets in original notes. Ngidi, 69.
47 Ngidi, 56.
48 Magidigidi ka Nobebe, 94.
49 A compilation of lists of regiments is found in Eileen Jensen Krige, *The Social System of the Zulus*, 2nd ed., Appendix VIII (Pietermaritzburg: Shuter & Shooter, 1957), 404–407. First edition published in 1936. Krige based the lists on one provided by A. T. Bryant, *Olden Times* with additions. Also cited is Samuelson, *Long, Long Ago* (1929). Lunguza ka Mpukane named Shaka's regiments, *JSA*, v. I, 303–304. Webb and Wright, 348 n.39, noted there are discrepancies between these lists and those of Samuelson, *Long, Long Ago*, 239–242, and Bryant, *Olden Times*, 645–646.
50 "There was a practice of *buta*ing in Zululand under which, though men were *buta*'d [*butha*'d, recruited or enrolled in regiments] all together, some would be cut off and established in some kraal, taking with them a separate name, although they were recruited at the same time as the main body. So later on confusion arises as to whether they were an independent regiment or merely a section of one, e.g. the Dhlangubo." Magidigidi, *JSA*, v. II, 94.

51 Lunguza ka Mpukane, *JSA*, v. I, 302.
52 Baleni ka Silwana, *JSA*, v. I, 17.
53 Ngidi, *JSA*, v. V, 61.
54 Ibid, 54. Ngidi knew Makedama's long genealogy, linking this royal eLangeni family all the way back to the founding ancestor Langa: "Makedama is a little younger than Tshaka. Makedama ka Mgabi ka Mbengi ka Mhlongo ka Ncumela ka Mavundhla ka Nqetshe ka Lugoloza ka Sibiya ka Mzimaseli ka Langa."
55 Ibid, 73.
56 Ibid. Referring to Makedama's father, Ngidi, 44, said, "Mgabi is about Senzangakona's age."
57 Ibid, 54, 55, 61–62.
58 Baleka, 5.
59 Ibid.
60 Ndukwana, 330. This is not a reference to the AmaQwabe chief Kondhlo.
61 John Gama, 132.
62 Shepstone, par. 13.
63 Maziyana in Melapi ka Magaye's interview, 81.
64 Shepstone, par. 13.
65 Jantshi, 183; Maziyana, Dinya, and Melapi in interivew of Melapi, 81; Fynn, *Diary*, 17.
66 Melapi, 81; Magudwini in 1905 interview of Madikane ka Mlomowetole, 61; Madikane, 61.
67 Lugubu ka Mangalizo, *JSA*, v. I, 283.
68 Shepstone, par. 13.
69 Ndhlovu ka Timuni, *JSA*, v. IV, 205.
70 Jantshi, 183, 176; Mandhlakazi, *JSA*, v. II, 185–186.
71 Ngidi, 54.
72 Ndhlovu, 232. This is a description from the oral traditions of the well-known cow's horn battle formation.
73 Ndukwana, *JSA*, v. IV, 279.
74 Fynn, *Diary*, 11.
75 Ndhlovu, 232.
76 Mandhlakazi, 176. A longer version of this story is found in Mandhlakazi, 186.
77 Ibid, 186.
78 Nhlekele ka Makana, *JSA*, v. V, 127.
79 Ibid.
80 Nhlekele, 127; Ngidi, 43; Fynn, *Diary*, 15.
81 Ngidi, 43.
82 Nhlekele, 130.
83 Jantshi, *JSA*, v. I, 186–7.
84 Lugubu ka Mangalizo, *JSA*, v. I, 282. He had gotten his information from his father, Mangalizo: "My father [Mmangaliso, of the Isipezi regiment], until he became an insizwa, grew up among the Tembu under Ngoza ka Mkubukeli. When an *insizwa* [young man], he went to *konza* [give his allegiance to] to the Zulu king [Tshaka]. The Tembu tribe at that time lived at Hlazakazi, and from

there to Isipezi. My earliest ancestor, Mlotsha, lived with the Tembu, and so for all the others." Lugubu, 283.
85 Ibid, 281–282.
86 Ibid, 284. This is not a reference to Mnguni, chief of the AmaNgidi.
87 Ibid, 284. This time the narrator Lugubu named the messengers sent by Ngoza.
88 Ibid, 282.
89 The later 1916 version included repetitions typical of oral narratives with more dialogue to carry the story forward and more details of some events but was the same story as Lugubu told in 1909.
90 Lunguza ka Mpukane, *JSA*, v. I, 298.
91 Lugubu , 284.
92 Lunguza, 298– 299.
93 Lugubu, 284.
94 Ibid, 284–285.
95 Ibid.
96 Ibid. Lugubu gave sketchy information of those Ngoza encountered, some names of chiefs, and details of where they went.
97 Ibid, 286.
98 Ibid, 282.
99 Ibid.
100 Lugubu, 287, noted, "[a]ll Ngoza's isigodhlo girls had their hands cut off by the Amampondo so that their brass armlets (*ingzota*) could be removed, for the metal was worked there." Lunguza, 298, said, "[o]ur mothers, when they went to Pondoland, had (some of them) their right hands cut off at the wrist to enable the Pondos to take off the metal ornaments they wore on the arm."
101 Lunguza, 299.
102 Lugubu, 284.
103 Ibid, 287.
104 Ngoza's regiments were named as the uNonyenge (the *ikanda* of Mkubukeli), the Ukudada (of the place of Mkubukeli's people), and the Ilangeni (of the place of Ngoza's people). "Each regiment fought separately from the others. My father Mpukane was of the Nonyenge regiment. There was no recruiting according to age, but father and son would be in the same regiment." Lunguza, 299.
105 Mqaikana ka Yenge, *JSA*, v. IV, 22.
106 Lugubu, 292, listed the sections of the amaMbata: ka Mbeje (in Zululand and Natal and other places); ka Dumisa (in Tembu country); ka Tshandu (in Zululand); ka Nsibankulu; ka Dhladhla (in Zululand); ka Mngeni, now in Pondoland, to which Lugubu went with Ngoza. Lugubu said the Mamata had been dispersed and broken up, that their warriors had been "bought" by other nations in exchange for cattle.
107 Lunguza, 298.
108 Eventually Shepstone appointed Lugaju as chief and assigned him land. Mqaikana, 17.
109 Magidigidi ka Nobebe, 87, described Phakade as "very tall and stout."

110 Lunguza, 307–308; Lubugu, 282, 288.
111 Lunguza, 307–308.
112 Baleka ka Mpitikazi, *JSA*, v. I, 5.
113 Madikane ka Mlomowetole, *JSA*, v. II, 60.
114 Mqaikana, 26.
115 Ibid, 23.
116 Ibid.
117 Magidigidi, 86.
118 Ibid.
119 "As Pakade was about the age of the amaWombe (Tshaka's and Dingana's), so he might have been born in 1788 and so have been 93 or 94 at the time of his death. His mother died a month or two before him, so she must have been about 115–120 years of age! I knew her well, says Magidigidi. Her *isibongo* was Ximba, of the Luvuno people, of the Cunu." Magidigidi, 89.
120 See Magididi, 86. Some of these royal *imizi* and regiments of Phakade's obviously postdate the era of Shaka. For the names of AmaChunu chiefs' indunas and the names of sections of the AmaChunu, 90.
121 Mqaikana, 26. This oral tradition suggests Mpongo was led to immoral acts by the "medicines" used against him and then was eaten by a leopard.
122 Ibid, 23.
123 Mahaya ka Nongqabana, *JSA*, v. II, 90.
124 Mqaikana, 24. Webb and Wright, v. IV, 33 n.86 and 87, reported that "[t]he Phateni hill lies to the north of the middle reaches of the Mkhomazi, some twelve kilometres north of present-day Richmond," and "[t]he Nsikeni hill lies some sixty kilometres north of present-day Kokstad."
125 Mqaikana, 26.
126 Ibid, 24. Mqaikana said that Mfusi had fled from his father Macingwane because his father had killed several of his own sons, and Mfusi's mother advised him to leave. According to this oral tradition, after Mfusi joined Shaka, Macingwane tried to have Shaka send him back in exchange for the gift of an ox, but Shaka refused.
127 Ibid. The articles of chiefship were "[t]he axe is what is used to strike the bull at the *ukutshwama* ceremony [first part of the first fruits ceremony];" "[t]he assegais are for the chief's personal use, and of course on his death must pass to the heir;" "[t]he pot for cooking the gourd was a small one – say about 10 inches in diameter;" and a ring, "[i]sonke – this seems to have belonged only to the amaCunu, and was copper."
128 Ibid, 17.
129 Ibid, 22.
130 Ibid, 23.
131 Ibid.
132 Ibid.
133 Ibid.
134 Ibid.
135 Ibid, 6. "After Ngwane died Mqaikana's grandfather Nontshiza crossed the Tukela and went to the emaKuzeni people, the place of Ngwane's chief wife. Some of the Mpumuza tribe accompanied him, but Xesibe remained behind.

They konza'd and stayed at the Nxamalala chief's which is why some descendants are still there," 11.
136 The oral evidence accords well with this assessment by Shepstone, 417–418, paragraphs 14–19.
137 Mqaikana, 8.
138 Ibid, 9.
139 Ibid.
140 Mesach Ngidi, 117. Stuart had interviewed the father of Mesach, Ngidi ka Mcikaziswa, in 1904 and 1905.
141 Ibid.
142 Singcofela ka Mtshungu, 341.
143 Mgidhlana ka Mpande, *JSA*, v. III, 107; Mayinga ka Mbekuzana, *JSA*, v. II, 251.
144 Singcofela, 342.
145 Ibid, 339.
146 Ibid, 339, 345–346. Singcofela provided extensive genealogies.
147 Mahaya ka Nongqabana, *JSA*, v. II, 130.
148 Lugubu, 287.
149 Maziyana, 277. He specified that Mangete died in hiding, and "his kraal was on the north side of the road to Pietermaritzburg from Durban and on the Berea. Its name was eBalwaneni. It was owing to Tshaka's wars that Mangete took to the bushes and died there alone, his own men and women having been either killed or having run off to Pondoland."
150 Ibid.

Chapter 6

1 Ngidi ka Mcikaziswa, *James Stuart Archive* (hereafter *JSA*,) v. V, 54; Ndukwana in interview of Jantshi ka Nongila, *JSA*, v. I, 201; Jantshi, 183; Mandhlakazi ka Ngini, *JSA*, v. II, 177.
2 Mmemi ka Nguluzane, *JSA*, v. III, 247.
3 Ibid, 240.
4 Ibid.
5 Ibid, 241.
6 Ibid, 21.
7 Ibid, 241.
8 Kambi ka Matshobana, *JSA*, v. I, 208.
9 Mandhlakazi ka Ngini, *JSA*, v. II, 177.
10 Ngidi, 54, and Lunguza ka Mpukane, *JSA*, v. I, 312, both reported that Shaka jumped over Phakathwayo who was seated, upon surrounding him successfully and ensuring his defeat.
11 Mmemi, 241; Jantshi, 183; Ngidi, 54; Kambi, 208. See also Baleni ka Silwana, *JSA*, v. I, 16.
12 Mmemi, 264.
13 Ibid, 241. "Pakatwayo's grave is near where the chief Mkungo now lives in the Eshowe District." Kambi, 209.
14 Ngidi, 54.

15 Mandhlakazi, 177.
16 Kambi, 210.
17 Mmemi, 242; Mbovu ka Mtshumayeli, *JSA*, v. III, 36.
18 Mmemi, 242.
19 Ibid, 242.
20 Ibid, 243.
21 Ibid, 242; Mbovu, 36. Fynn's account of Phakathwayo's death resulting in the subordination of the AbaQwabe to Shaka agrees in substance with the oral traditions but not in details. Fynn, *Diary*, 16–17.
22 Dinya ka Zokozwayo, *JSA*, v. I, 115.
23 Ibid, bracketed notes mine.
24 Ibid.
25 Ibid, 116.
26 Ibid, 115.
27 Ibid.
28 Ibid, 116.
29 Ibid.
30 Ibid, 117.
31 Melapi, 80.
32 Ibid, 78.
33 Ibid.
34 Ibid.
35 Ibid.
36 Ibid, 79; bracketed annotation in original.
37 Ibid.
38 Ibid, 92; Madikane ka Mlomowetole, 53.
39 Dinya, 117.
40 Ibid.
41 Ibid.
42 Maquza ka Gawushane, *JSA*, v. II, 237.
43 Ibid.
44 Melapi, 80.
45 Ibid, 72.
46 Ibid, 75.
47 Ibid.
48 Ibid.
49 Ibid.
50 Ibid.
51 Ibid, 72.
52 Ibid, 73.
53 Maquza, 236.
54 Melapi, 73.
55 Ibid, 80.
56 Maquza, 237.
57 Melapi, 80.
58 Ibid, 80–81.
59 Ibid, 81.

60 Ibid, 74.
61 Dinya, 116. Some of these had long before directly given their allegiance to Shaka.
62 For details of the marriages and family members of Magaye, see Dinya, 119–120.
63 Melapi, 73.
64 Ngidi, 68.
65 Mangati ka Godide, *JSA*, v. II, 209.
66 Fynn, *Diary*, 17; Jantshi, 184–186, 195; Mmemi, 270–271; Dinya, 102–103; Lugubu ka Mangalizo, *JSA*, v. I, 284–285; Nduna ka Manqina, *JSA*, v. V, 1–4; Baleni, 17; Mangati, 209; Ngidi, 68, 72–73; Mkotana ka Zulu, *JSA*, v. II, 223.
67 Nduna ka Manqina, *JSA, v.* V, 3–4.
68 Ibid, 4.
69 Shepstone, 417.
70 Luzipo, 355.
71 Madikane, 53. He reiterated, "The royal salutation of '*Bayede*! possibly came from Zwide and by him from the Swazis." This is historically plausible.
72 Maziyana ka Mahlabeni, *JSA*, v. II, 297.
73 Ibid, 297.
74 Ibid.
75 Maziyana, 297.
76 Ibid, 270.
77 Ibid, 269.
78 Ibid, 269–70.
79 Mcotoyi ka Mnini, *JSA*, v. III, 65. The evidence indicates the term "killed off" here refers to destroying the village at the site, breaking it up, and dispersing the people but not literally killing them all.
80 Maziyana ka Mahlabeni, 275.
81 Ibid, 297.
82 Ibid, 296.
83 Ibid.
84 Mahaya ka Nongqabana, *JSA*, v. II, 112–113. Mahaya traced his line of descent back sixteen generations to the Lovedu of the Transvaal, and the Imitwana remembered themselves as being of Sotho cultural and political origins: "We Imitwana are Basutos, but our elders say we are not the Basutoland Basutos but came from Mjantshi, whose country is in the Transvaal. I do not know how we came to leave Mjantshi's country. At Sangwana is where Sabela's people [twelve generations before Mahaya] increased in number. I hear we passed through Swaziland on our way south." Mahaya, 128.
85 Ibid, 126.
86 Maziyana, 275.
87 Mahaya, 112–113.
88 Ibid.
89 Ibid, 126.
90 Ibid,112–113. There were credible oral traditions of cannibals at the time of "Shaka's wars"; reported to be cannibal chiefs were Mdava, Sonkovana,

Simemezi, and Bulawayo who, according to one man, "lives in Tilonko's tribe, the Embo, but does not belong to the tribe really. Bulawayo is, I believe, of the Mbambo people." He explained, "Cannibals came into existence because of famine, no food, no cattle." Mbovu ka Mtshumayeli, *JSA*, v. III, 226–227. This explanation is also found for the historically remembered incidences of cannibalism among the BaSotho.
91 Maziyana, 297.
92 Nombashini ka Ndhlela, *JSA* v. V, 143.
93 Mabonsa ka Sidhlayi, *JSA* v. II, 18. See also Mqaikana ka Yenge, *JSA*, v. IV, 22; Maziyana ka Mahlabeni, *JSA*, v. II, 281; Elizabeth A. Eldredge, "Migration, Conflict and Leadership in Early Nineteenth-Century South Africa: The Case of Matiwane," in Robert W. Harms et al., eds., *Paths Toward the Past: African Historical Essays in Honor of Jan Vansina* (Atlanta: African Studies Association, 1994), 39–75.
94 Ibid, 16.
95 Ibid.
96 Ibid, 13–14, 16.
97 "They were driven out by Tshaka from the Pongolo, where they originated. They left and settled at the Mtshezi. Tshaka attacked again and they went over the Drakensberg," Maziyana, 281. Webb and Wright, v. II, 306 n.90 state that the Mtshezi was the Bushman's River.
98 Maziyana ka Mahlabeni, *JSA*, v. II, 281.
99 Mabonsa, 13–14, 16.
100 Ibid, 14. He also said, "The Iziyendane regiment, which was known as the Iziyendane of Nandi, was recruited in Tshaka's day, and Makata was the great *induna* [commander, officer] of that regiment. They were called Iziyendane because none of them had the headring on, i.e. their hair lay back on their heads. This regiment was composed of amaHlubi. Owing to this fact, Mtimkulu must have been killed early in Tshaka's reign, for the Iziyendane campaigned with Tshaka in the Mpondo country. It was only after Mtimkulu's death that the Iziyendane were made into a regiment. People went off in a body and *konza*'d Nandi and became her regiment." Mabonsa, 20.
101 Ibid, 17.
102 Mabonsa, 16.
103 Ngidi, 54.
104 Mabonsa ka Sidhlayi, 26.
105 Shepstone, par. 14, provides a summary of the history of the AmaNgwane that is in accord with other sources.
106 *Litaba tsa Lilemo* (Morija, Lesotho: Sesuto Book Depot, 1931). Mpangazitha is referred to as Pakalita in the sources of the BaSotho.
107 D. F. Ellenberger, *History of the Basuto Ancient and Modern*, edited and translated by J. C. Macgregor (London, Caxton, 1912), 170.
108 Ellenberger refers to the AmaNgwane and AmaHlubi here as "these Matebele," not to be confused with the people of Mzilikazi. Ibid, 154–156.
109 N.J. Van Warmelo, ed. *History of Matiwane and the Amangwane Tribe as told by Msebenzi* and supplemented by Archive Documents and other

material by Van Warmelo (Pretoria: Department of Native Affairs Ethnological Publications, 1938), vol. VII, 32; Mabonsa ka Sidhlayi, 16; Simeon Feko, "Bophelo ba Simeon Feko ke Moholo" ("Life of Simeon Feko, Sr."), unpub. ms., Lesotho Evangelical Church (Paris Evangelical Missionary Society) Archives, Morija, Lesotho; Ellenberger, 154–155. The battle was said to have taken place the same year as Moshoeshoe's migration to Thaba Bosiu, which was 1824.

110 Ellenberger, 155.
111 Sources for the later history of the AmaNgwane include Feko, "Bophelo"; Mabonsa ka Sidhlayi, 14; Fynn, *Diary*, 318; Ngidi, 54; Ellenberger, 176–180 and 185–89; Moloja, "The Story of the 'Fetcani' Horde," *Cape Quarterly Review*, 1 (1882), 267–275.
112 See Mqaikana ka Yenge, *JSA*, v. IV, 19; Mahaya ka Nongqabana, *JSA*, v. II, 113, 126; Mabonsa ka Sidhlayi, *JSA*, v. II, 17.
113 Maziyana, 295.
114 Mabonsa, 21.
115 Maziyana, 295–296.
116 The Embo or AbaMbo were also known as the Mkhize after a later ancestral chief and therefore the name that was of more recent adoption, but most references in the sources use the designation Embo.
117 Mbokodo ka Sikulekile, *JSA*, v. III, 19.
118 Maziyana ka Mahlabeni, 279–280.
119 Mandhlakazi ka Ngini, 175.
120 Mbokodo, 8.
121 Ibid, 9.
122 Ibid, 9–10.
123 Mandhlakazi, 175.
124 Mbokodo, 10.
125 Ibid, 6.
126 Madikane said that Shaka took Zihlandhlo's Inguqa regiment, but Maquza said he took the Mpiyake Embo regiment. Madikane ka Mlomowetole, 53; Maquza ka Gawushane, 237. Shaka also engaged in the exchange of luxury items with Zihlandhlo related to war and diplomacy, fancy monkey and genet skins worn by warriors, and oxen noted for their beauty. Mbokodo, 13.
127 Mbokodo, 11.
128 Ibid, 12.
129 Ibid.
130 Ibid.
131 Ibid, 13.
132 Ibid, 8.
133 Ibid.
134 Ibid, 12.
135 Ibid, 10–11.
136 Mandhlakazi ka Ngini, 193.
137 Ndukwana ka Mbengwana, *JSA*, v. IV, 285.
138 Fynn *Diary*, 127–130.
139 Ngidi, 79.

140 For a history of the AmaNdebele kingdom of Mzilikazi, see R. K. Rasmussen, *Migrant Kingdom: Mzilikazi's Ndebele in South Africa* (London, 1978); and J. D. Omer-Cooper, *The Zulu Aftermath: A Nineteenth-Century Revolution in Bantu Africa* (Evanston, IL: Northwestern University Press, 1969), 129–155.
141 Madikane ka Mlomowetole, 60.
142 Zitshibili ka Nyakanyakana ka Matshobana, interviewed by Norman Nembula, 13. AmaZulu oral sources about Mzilikazi include Luzipo ka Nomageje, 354; Ngidi ka Mcikaziswa, 44; Ndukwana ka Mbengwana, 278–279; Madikane, 60; Mabonsa, 25; Socwatsha (unpublished James Stuart notes), 24; Jantshi, 183. Mzilikazi is also referred to as Moselekatsi in some European sources.
143 Mabonsa ka Sidhlayi, 25.
144 Zitshibili, interviewed by Norman Nembula, 13.
145 "Sotshangana's followers were the Nxumalo i.e. Ndwandwes. Sotshangana ka Zikode ka Malusi, and Zwide ka Langa ka Malusi." Mbovu ka Mtshumayeli, 45. For the history of the AmaNdwandwe followers of Soshangane and of Zwangendaba, see Omer-Cooper, *The Zulu Aftermath*, 57–85.
146 Madikane, 59.
147 Ibid.
148 For the history of the Msene and Maseko chiefdoms see Omer-Cooper, *Zulu Aftermath*, 57–58, 65, 73, 75–78, 121–122, 127–128, on which I have based this summary.
149 Mbovu, 45. He added, "[i]t was Tshaka, not Dingiswayo who caused Nxaba to leave. Both Nxaba and Sotshangana made their way through Tongaland."
150 Mkehlengana ka Zulu, 216.

Chapter 7

1 Maziyana ka Mahlabeni, *James StuartArchive* (hereafter *JSA*), v. II, 272–273.
2 Ibid, 273.
3 Nduna, *JSA*, v. V, 4; Lugubu, *JSA*, v. I, 282, 287; Makewu, *JSA*, v. II, 163; Mkehlengana, *JSA*, v. III, 217; Maziyana, *JSA*, v. II, 2, 272–273; Mcotoyi ka Mnini, *JSA*, v. III, 55; Mbovu ka Mtshumayeli, *JSA*, v. III, 43; Fynn, *Diary*, 62.
4 Mbovu, 43.
5 Mcotoyi, 66.
6 Ibid, 55. Webb and Wright, v. III, 68 n.14 suggest "This is presumably a reference to Shaka's attack on the Mpondo in 1824. Mdlaka kaNcidi of the emGazini people was one of Shaka's chief *izinduna* [officers]."
7 Mkehlengana, 217.
8 Maziyana, 272–273.
9 Mayinga ka Mbekuzana, *JSA*, v. II, 249.
10 Mayinga, 249, said the Mkandhlwini regiment was "cut up" by the AmaMpondo and on account of their cowardice was "killed off" by Shaka.

Madikane also said that the Mkandhlu regiment was killed off after the AmaMpondo *impi*. Madikane ka Mlomowetole, *JSA* v. II, 61. See also Ngidi, *JSA*, v. V, 56, 58.

11 Farewell was the son of Rev. G. Farewell of Bristol and had served as midshipman in the Royal Navy from an early age. He had sailed in the Mediterranean, had received several wounds, had distinguished himself in several actions, and after his promotion to lieutenant, had been obliged to retire. Farewell then purchased a ship, the *Princess Charlotte*, to trade at Calcutta, Buenos Aires, and the Isle of France (Mauritius). On this trading voyage, he went next to the Cape Colony and then back to Rio, but the ship was then wrecked and Farewell lost almost everything. Before his trip to Delagoa Bay, Henry Francis Fynn had been in the Cape Colony where he had lived since coming from England in 1818. For four years, he worked on a government farm at Algoa Bay that provisioned British troops. Then he walked back to Cape Town where he found a British merchant, Henry Nourse, whom he had previously met on the frontier. Fynn accepted an offer from Nourse to serve as supercargo on the *Jane*, one of two brigs on their way to Delagoa Bay in the trading expedition of 1823. It was Henry Nourse's brother, Joseph Nourse, who commanded the British survey naval expedition up the east African coast. Lieutenant King was part owner with his mother in several ships engaged in the West Indian trade.
12 Fynn, *Diary*, 51–52.
13 Ibid, 52–53. Fynn was not present and this is a secondhand account from hearsay.
14 Ibid, 56.
15 Ibid, 58.
16 Ibid, 60–61.
17 Ibid, 61.
18 Ibid, 62.
19 Ibid, 63.
20 Ibid, 64.
21 Ibid, 66. Dying people were always removed from a village, so it is not surprising she was still alive but presumed to be dying. The death of a person within a village required that the entire village be removed to a new location, a strong incentive to instead remove dying people to outside the village.
22 Melapi ka Magaye, 73.
23 Fynn, *Diary*, 67.
24 Ibid, 66–67.
25 Ibid, 68.
26 Ibid, 71. The editors point out this discrepancy in Fynn's reports.
27 Ibid, 75.
28 Fynn was called Sofili. Ibid, 68–71.
29 Ibid, 73.
30 Melapi, 73.
31 Fynn, *Diary*, 83.
32 Ibid, 82.
33 Ibid, 86.

34 Ibid, 85.
35 Ngidi, 39.
36 Ibid. He repeated this later, 62–63.
37 Melapi, 80.
38 Ibid, 80.
39 Makewu, 161.
40 Melapi, 80.
41 Magidigidi ka Nobebe, *JSA*, v. II, 93.
42 Ngidi ka Mcikaziswa, 39–40.
43 Ndukwana, *JSA*, v. IV, 284.
44 Mbovu, *JSA*, v. III, 43.
45 Fynn, *Diary*, 87.
46 Ibid, 88–90.
47 Ibid, 85.
48 Ibid, 88.
49 Ibid, 91.
50 Ibid, 91–99.
51 Ibid, 101.
52 Ibid, 93.
53 Ibid.
54 Ibid, 110.
55 Ibid.
56 Ibid, 111.
57 Ibid.
58 Ibid, 111–113.
59 Ibid, 114–116.
60 Extract from Nathaniel Isaacs in Fynn, *Diary*, 117.
61 Ibid, 118.
62 Ibid, 119–120.
63 Fynn, *Diary*, 130–131. The editors note that "this was probably written in or about 1832 or 1833 or even 1831 when Fynn was on the Cape Frontier. Two of the sheets of the revised version of these notes bear on them the watermark of 1827." The contents definitely indicate this was originally written by Fynn at an early date and suggests the entire diary part of the *Diary* was written in 1831–1833 with the exception of perhaps one or two paragraphs as indicated. Ibid, 130–131.
64 Isaacs *Journal*, published in the *South African Commercial Advertiser*, beginning with no. 520, June 6, 1832, the final journal entries published in SACA October 10, 1832, copied by James Stuart, typescript copies, labeled as Extract 1, 89–119 and Extract 3, 120–132.
65 Charles Rawden Maclean, *The Natal Papers of 'John Ross': Loss of the Brig Mary at Natal with Early Recollections of that Settlement and Among the Caffres*, edited by Stephen Gray (Durban: Killie Campbell Africana Library and Pietermaritzburg: University of Natal Press, 1992). Maclean became apprenticed to James Saunders King, captain of the *Mary*. In 1825, he accompanied King on his ill-fated journey to "rescue" his partner, Lt. Francis Farewell, who had not been heard from since stranded at Port Natal in

1824. Maclean was about ten or twelve years old when they were wrecked at Port Natal in the *Mary* on September 30, 1825.
66 Fynn, *Diary*, 131.
67 Grey provides the evidence of the lifelong sympathy of Maclean for people of African origins and descent. Introduction, Maclean (John Ross), 11.
68 The first eleven "chapters" were each published as an article in *The Nautical Magazine* in 1853–1855 and were self-evidently written by Maclean in December 1838 to early 1839 as a single work. The editors of the magazine in which they were published later subdivided the long account, which accounts for the uniformity of the chapters' length. In his account of the "Loss of the Brig *Mary* at Natal with Early Recollections of that Settlement," Maclean refers to "the present Chief Dingane," indicating it was written before Dingane's death in 1840. Maclean (John Ross), 39.
69 Ibid.
70 Ibid, 49.
71 Ibid.
72 Ibid, 61.
73 Ibid, 71.
74 Ibid, 72.
75 Ibid.
76 Ibid, 73.
77 Ibid, 72–73.
78 Ibid, 73.
79 Ibid, 73, 86.
80 Ibid, 101.
81 Ibid, 102.
82 Ibid.
83 Ibid, 103–106.
84 Ibid, 113.
85 Ibid, 114.
86 Ibid, 132–133.
87 Fynn *Diary*, 130.
88 Ibid, 131. The content definitely indicates this was originally written by Fynn at an early date, and suggests the entire diary part of the *Diary* was written 1831–33 with the exception of perhaps one or two paragraphs.
89 Ibid, 93.
90 Ibid.
91 Ibid.
92 Ngidi, 79.
93 Ibid, 70. Ngidi said, "Sikunyana said to Zwide, 'Tshaka has overcome you, for you are an old man. He will not overcome my age-grade (*intanga*).' Upon this, Sikunyana returned and built at the Mhlongamvula river at the Ezindololwane hills."
94 Ibid, 79.
95 Nathaniel Isaacs, *Travels and Adventures*, 60 and Fynn, *Diary*, 122–128 left contemporaneous European accounts. Fynn's was an eyewitness account although he did not engage in the fighting. Shaka ordered the Europeans to

send men from Port Natal, and fearing the consequences should they refuse, they complied. Farewell became ill on the journey and did not go all the way to the battle.
96 Eldredge, "Shaka's Military Expeditions."
97 Fynn, *Diary*, 122.
98 The editors note that from Isaacs, the summons can be dated to on or about June 12, 1826.
99 Fynn, *Diary*, 123.
100 Ibid.
101 Ibid.
102 Ibid, 124.
103 Ibid.
104 Ibid, 124–126.
105 This decisive battle in which the AmaZulu defeated the AmaNdwandwe can be dated with some precision because just as the Europeans were returning to Port Natal from this battle against Sikhunyana, "a vessel that had arrived [at Port Natal] on 6th October, 1826, from Algoa Bay, proved to be the schooner *Anne*, with Mr. King and Mrs. Farewell on board."
106 Ndukwana, 276, 1897; see also Ngidi, 70, 79, 1904, 1905.
107 Fynn, *Diary*, 124–126.
108 Ngidi, 65, 70, 79; Webb and Wright, *JSA*, v. V, 107 n.255; Ndukwana, 276; Fynn, *Diary*, 124–126.
109 Mbokodo, 12.
110 Fynn *Diary*, 126.
111 Eldredge, "Shaka's Military Expeditions." The evidence suggests that 3,000 AmaNdwandwe, including both men and women, were killed in this battle.
112 Fynn *Diary*, 127.
113 Maclean (John Ross), 63, 67.
114 Ibid, 67–68.
115 Ibid, 68–69.
116 Ibid, 69.
117 Fynn, *Diary*, 124–126.
118 Mbokodo, 12.
119 Ngidi, 79; Jantshi ka Nongila, 186. See also Ndukwana, 276.
120 Magojela ka Mfanawendhlela, *JSA*, v. II, 104, 1907.
121 Mbokodo ka Sikulekile, *JSA* v. III, 11–12, 1913.
122 Ibid.
123 Maziyana, 269, 1905.
124 Ndukwana in interview of Jantshi, 186.
125 Maclean (John Ross), 67–69, citing the contemporaneous eyewitness reports of his European associates to him.
126 Fynn *Diary*, 127.
127 Ibid.
128 Ibid, 129.
129 Ndukwana in interview of Jantshi, 186.
130 Ibid.
131 Mbokodo, 12.

132 Eldredge, "Shaka's Military Expeditions."
133 Ndukwana, 277–278.
134 Fynn, *Diary*, 127.
135 Ibid, 127–129.
136 Ibid, 129.
137 For example, Ngidi, 64, told Stuart, "Beja ka Magozi of the Ngome and Sobuza ka Ndungunya of the Swazi defeated Tshaka by taking refuge in fortresses."
138 Fynn *Diary*, 129–130. The editors note that "this took place at the ingome forest, in the north-west of Zululand, February, 1827" and cite Isaacs, I, 197, 210, 211. Fynn commented, "[o]n our side, Mr. Isaacs was severely wounded. Shaka did not as much as thank them for their services; on the contrary, he took every opportunity of depreciating what they had done and minimising the value of fire-arms in the estimation of his people."
139 Maclean's confusion is evident in that he described the battle as having taken place at night, whereas the 1826 battle was during daylight as Fynn observed. Nevertheless, Maclean was certain that none of the men carrying firearms used them in this battle. Maclean (John Ross), 64, 67.
140 Maclean (John Ross), 67. In this instance, Maclean appears to have been correct in remembering this was a night-time attack, and "the services of the fire-armed men on that occasion were not called into requisition." Although this comment appears with reference to the battle against the AmaNdwandwe, the comment on a night attack suggests that it refers to the attack against Beje's people. However, Maclean later also reiterated that in the battle against Sikhunyana, firearms were not used in battle. His description of a Khoi ("Hottentot") firing his weapon and killing an assailant who turned out to be one of Shaka's warriors is the only instance of a shot fired that could refer to either attack.
141 Nathaniel Isaacs, *Travels and Adventures in Eastern Africa*, edited with footnotes and a biographical sketch by Louis Herman (Cape Town: Van Riebeeck Society, 1936), v. I, 163.
142 Ibid.
143 Ibid, 164–165.
144 Ibid, 166.
145 Ibid, v. I, 170–171.
146 Baleni ka Silwana, 18.
147 Mkehlengana ka Zulu, 215.
148 Ndukwana, 289.
149 Fynn, *Diary*, 131.
150 Ibid, 130–131.
151 Maziyana, 266–268.
152 Fynn, *Diary*, 131.
153 Wright and other scholars question whether this military expedition, known among the AmaZulu themselves as the *Eyobutshinga impi*, even occurred in spite of convincing reliable evidence that it did. They dismiss the evidence from BaSotho oral traditions that indicate the BaSotho were definitely aware of the identity of their attackers in early 1827 when the AmaZulu troops

carried off so many of their cattle and fought the famous battle of Ladybrand, and later in 1827 when Mzilikazi sent AmaNdebele troops into the region. Wright, "Turbulent Times," 243. The BaSotho were again attacked by Mzilikazi's forces in 1831.
154 Fynn *Diary*, 17.
155 Relying on the evidence of Thompson, who was present, Fynn referred to this military expedition in passing after explaining prior military encounters of the AmaNgwane.
156 Fynn, *Diary*, 318.
157 Mabonsa, 14; Ngidi, 54. The term *eyobutshinga impi* appears to derive from the transitive verb *ukutshinga* or *ukuntshinga*, to throw away or bury.
158 D.F. Ellenberger, *History of the Basuto Ancient and Modern* (London: Caxton Pub., 1912), 176–180.
159 Ellenberger, 176–177.
160 Eldredge, "Migration," 59.
161 Ellenberger, 177–178.
162 Moloja, "The story of the 'Fetcani horde'," *Cape Quarterly Review*, 1 (1882), 267–75. This story is retold almost verbatim by Ellenberger.
163 Ellenberger, 178.
164 Ibid.
165 Eldredge, "Migration," 56–60.
166 Moloja, "Story", also quoted in Eldredge, "Migration," 58; Van Warmelo, *History of Matiwane*, 29. The details of the description given by Isaacs of an expedition of warriors whose return he witnessed in March 1827 indicate this was the *impi* that had gone to the Caledon River valley and raided the AmaNgwane and some BaSotho cattle, the *eyobutshinga impi*. Isaacs believed mistakenly that they had gone to northwest of Delagoa Bay, but he reported correctly that they had reached a large river, the Orange River, and he named the BaSotho, or "Armasootoos," as people with whom they had fought. Isaacs, *Travels*, v. I, 179–180.

Chapter 8

1 For analyses of the indispensable contributions made by women to economic production and to social and political reproduction in precolonial southern Africa, see Elizabeth A. Eldredge, *A South African Kingdom: The Pursuit of Security in Nineteenth-Century Lesotho* (Cambridge University Press, 1993), 126–146; and Elizabeth A. Eldredge, "Women in Production: The Economic Role of Women in Nineteenth-Century Lesotho," *Signs: Journal of Women in Culture and Society* (Summer 1991; special issue on Women, Family, State, and Economy in Africa), 707–731. Carolyn Hamilton laid the groundwork for the study of the women of precolonial KwaZulu-Natal with a chapter on "Women's Labour and Social Stratification in the Early Zulu State" in her 1985 M.A. thesis. Her focus is on the status and roles of women in the *izigodlo* (segregated women's quarters). Carolyn Hamilton, "Ideology, Oral Traditions and the Struggle for Power in the Early Zulu Kingdom," M.A. thesis, University of the Witwatersrand, 1985, 422–464.

2 Jeff Guy, "Gender Oppression in Southern Africa's Precapitalist Societies" in Cherryl Walker, ed., *Women and Gender in Southern Africa to 1945*, 33–47, introduces some of the most salient issues in the study of precolonial women. See also Sifiso Ndlovu, "A Reassessment of Women's Power in the Zulu Kingdom" in Benedict Carton, John Laband and Jabulani Sithole, eds., *Zulu Identities: Being Zulu, Past and Present*, 111–121.
3 Jeff Guy, "Ecological Factors in the Rise of Shaka and the Zulu Kingdom" in S. Marks and A. Atmore, eds., *Economy and Society in Pre-industrial South Africa* (London: Longman, 1980), 102–119. In seeking to identify motive forces explaining the sociopolitical consolidation of the Zulu kingdom, Guy argued that overpopulation and the need for additional grazing land for cattle propelled political and military expansionism.
4 Guy incorrectly assumed that Shaka was attempting to correct a problem of overpopulation by delaying the marriage of women, but there is no evidence to support a condition of overpopulation relative to land resources used for both pastoral and arable production, and women continued to be married at the usual age of fourteen or fifteen. This allowed for normal rates of biological reproduction, although there may have been a difference between the marriage age of most women who did not live in an *isigodlo*, and the selective smaller group of girls from important families who did. Captain J. S. King, "Some account of Mr. Farewell's settlement at Port Natal, and of a visit to Chaka, King of the Zoolas, etc.," in George Thompson, *Travels and Adventures in Southern Africa* (London, 1827); reprint Cape Town: The Van Riebeeck Society, 1967), ii, 251. Guy's only evidence that women were not allowed to marry until the age of thirty is from 1872, fifty years later than the period under consideration. Guy, "Ecological Factors," 106. Krige similarly claimed, without evidence, that marriage was delayed for women in Shaka's era, and she tends to collapse evidence from across the entire century in her study. Krige, *Social System*, 38. This is also discussed in Sean Hanretta, "Women, Marginality and the Zulu State: Women's Institutions and Power in the Early Nineteenth Century," *Journal of African History*, 39, no. 3 (1998), 407–408.
5 Jeff Guy, "Analysing Pre-capitalist Societies in Southern Africa," *Journal of Southern African Studies*, 14, no. 1 (1987), 29.
6 Hanretta, "Women, Marginality and the Zulu State," 389–415.
7 Ndlovu, "A Reassessment of Women's Power."
8 Wylie, *Myth of Iron*.
9 A recent contribution to an analysis of "political philosophy" in precolonial KwaZulu-Natal as embedded in and represented by rituals and beliefs related to milk and to semen is limited and unconvincing because it neglects significant related issues with regard to beliefs in the supernatural effects of both male and female body fluids, excrement, hair, and internal body parts. Paul K. Bjerk, "They Poured Themselves into the Milk: Zulu Political Philosophy under Shaka," *Journal of African History*, 47, no.1 (2006), 1–19. This study is similarly incomplete in its consideration of many other related and significant issues, including the importance of cattle and cattle products beyond the production of milk, and ritualistic practices that do not relate to milk.

10 Adam Kuper, *Wives for Cattle: Bridewealth and Marriage in Southern Africa* (London: Routledge & Kegan Paul, 1982). See also Eileen Jensen Krige, *The Social System of the Zulus* (London: Longmans, 1936; reprint Pietermaritzburg: Shuter & Shooter, 1950); E. J. Krige, *The Realm of a Rain Queen: A Study of the Pattern of Lovedu Society* (London: Oxford University Press, 1943); Hilda Kuper, *An African Aristocracy: Rank among the Swazi* (London: Oxford University Press, 1947).
11 Mabonsa ka Sidhlayi, *James Stuart Archive* (hereafter *JSA*), v. II, 20.
12 Jantshi and Ndukwana in interview of Jantshi ka Nongila, *JSA*, v. I, 190. See Wylie, 96–98 for further discussion.
13 Sivivi ka Maqungo, *JSA*, v. 5, 376.
14 Magidi ka Ngomane, *JSA*, v. II, 81.
15 Krige, 264–265. Baleni said explicitly that "the girls cultivated their fields, also those of the king and those of Mpande's children. See Baleni ka Silwana, *JSA*, v. I, 38. Although this evidence is from a later period, it appears to have been true before and during Shaka's reign. Citing Hamilton's arguments that the women of the *amakhandla* cultivated the food that fed the men barracked there, Hanretta argues that this was unlikely on the grounds that they were too few to have accomplished such a huge task, and they were prevented from contact with the men. See Hanretta, 401–402. Hanretta's arguments are unconvincing, however, for the women kept in the *isigodlo* of an *ikhanda* to have cultivated crops does not preclude the assistance of other women from the area but not housed in the *isigodlo* in provisioning the personnel of the barracks, and evidence shows they did so. For about three years before they were enrolled in their own regiment, older boys or young men served to herd and milk the cattle at the *amakhandla*, and their work sometimes included work in the fields. Wylie, 335, citing evidence of Baleni, 34. The boys' mothers were expected to provide for them. Mcotoyi ka Mnini, *JSA*, v. III, 66. The younger regiments were said to have cultivated the fields at their *amakhanda*. In addition, it was not uncommon for men to assist in harvesting crops in the context of harvesting parties in which they were amply fed in exchange for their services. Hanretta also argues that *isigodlo* women were strictly forbidden contact with the regimental men and could not take food or other articles to them. Fertile women who might be menstruating were indeed not allowed contact with warriors before they went into battle for fear their military strength would be adversely affected, so that prohibitions of women entering the men's quarters for any reason were strictly enforced. Menstruating women, however, were sent to stay in an adjacent but separate village. See Sivivi ka Maqungo, *JSA*, v. V, 374. Hanretta fails to recognize that the service of the boys and young men of the *amakhandla* before being enrolled in regiments fulfilled just such roles but did not prevent women of the *izigodlo* from cultivating fields. Furthermore, there is plenty of evidence of contact between the women of the *izigodlo* of *amakhanda* and the military men barracked in them and even of the common practice of *ukuhlobonga* (or *ukusoma*), engaging in external sexual relations.
16 Baleni, *JSA*, v. I, 45.
17 Hamilton, "Ideology," 428–429; Wylie, 324.

18 Ngidi ka Mcikaziswa, *JSA*, v. V, 29, 30, 44, 53. Wylie discusses the evidence, 124–125.
19 Ngidi, 49.
20 They had merely been seen by the king and his council near where some women had just passed. Mkehlengana ka Zulu, *JSA*, v. III, 210, 1905; Mkotana ka Zulu, *JSA*, v. III, 225.
21 This was because the women and the men were both from the same branch of the royal house; Sopane and Nqetho "could not marry where the heir was produced." Mmemi ka Nguluzana, *JSA*, v. III, 249.
22 This occurred when the AbaQwabe were still independent of AmaZulu rule. Mmemi described their elopement and offering of allegiance to Shaka as "desertion" and assumed that "[a]s they deserted to a 'foreign' tribe [i.e., Zulu] I do not suppose anything was paid on account of lobola [bride-wealth]." Mmemi, 249.
23 Ngidi, 53, 90.
24 Ibid, 90.
25 Ibid, 53.
26 Shepstone, "Historical Sketch," par. 11; Ndukwana ka Mbengwana, *JSA*, v. IV, 289.
27 Lugubu ka Mangaliso, *JSA*, v. I, 284–287.
28 After their chief Ngoza died and their women had been killed and maimed by the AmaMpondo, many AbaTembu returned to give their allegiance to Shaka, who welcomed them back into his emerging kingdom. See Lugubu, 282, 287.
29 These were the followers of Chief Macingwane, and the battle occurred in a forest near Insikeni (Nsikeni) mountain (AmaMpondo territory). The chief and his favorite wife disappeared after the battle and were presumed to have died destitute. That not all of the women and children, nor all the men, were killed, is evident, however, because the survivors returned to live under Macingwane's heir Pakade, whom Shaka recognized as a subordinate chief, and was tributary to him. Mqaikana ka Yenge, *JSA*, v. IV, 24, 26; Magidigidi ka Nobebe, *JSA*, v. II, 85, 86, 89.
30 Ngidi, 65, 70, 79; Ndukwana, 276; Fynn, *Diary*, 124–126.
31 Ngidi, 67–68. It was remembered that Shaka ordered that none of Sikunyana's people be allowed to survive, including the women and children, and he was evidently targeting the royal family and Sikunyana's potential heirs. However, many AmaNdwandwe were incorporated after this battle as is evident in the presence of their men in the military regiments then and in future generations. See Mbokodo ka Sikulekile, *JSA*, v. III, 11–12; Ndukwana in interview of Jantshi, 186.
32 Mangati ka Godidi, *JSA*, v. II, 213.
33 Mkando ka Dhlova, *JSA*, v. III, 145. He lists the names of girls' regiments.
34 Mqaikana, 24, 26; Magidigidi, 85, 86, 89.
35 Tununu ka Nonjiya, 12, 18, interview of October 6, 1903, unpublished Stuart notebook, Killie Campbell Library (hereafter KCL); Ngidi, 69.
36 Ngidi, 41. Later he said, "Shaka only gathered four classes of girls. They cut war-shields (*izihlangu*) and fought like men. Some of them earned and wore *iziqu*."Ngidi, 69.

37 Ibid, 56.
38 Ndukwana, 297-298.
39 Eldredge, *South African Kingdom*, 126-146. Kuper provides insights into the ways in which marriages between royal families of different chiefdoms were a form of political intervention. These marriages provided control over the succession to the chiefdom where the royal woman would bear the heir whose loyalty would be tied to his maternal kin. Thus, these marriages were more than mere "alliances." See Kuper, "The 'House' and Zulu Political Structure," 484-485.
40 The traditions thus explain an historical relationship between the AmaZulu and AbaQwabe chiefly lines of descent, with reference to the mother of the brothers Zulu and Qwabe. See Ndhlovu ka Timuni, *JSA*, v. IV, 217. Carolyn Hamilton's argument in her master's thesis that the genealogies that link ancestors named Zulu and Qwabe were invented in the nineteenth century does not agree with the evidence. The independent retention of oral traditions by not only the AmaZulu and AbaQwabe royal houses but also unassociated royal lines of descent, linking them to a specific known ancestor, Malandela, is strong evidence of the traditions' reliability as generally assessed by historians using oral traditions of genealogies in African history. A grandson of the AmaNdwandwe royal house and their chief or king Zwide told Stuart one version of the oral tradition of AmaZulu and AbaQwabe common origins by virtue of two sons of the same woman, Nozidiya, wife of Malandela. Mankulumana ka Somapunga ka Zwide ka Langa, *JSA*, v. II, 226; Ndhlovu ka Timuni, *JSA*, v. IV, 217; Baleka ka Mpitikazi, *JSA* v. I, 4; Magidigidi ka Nobebe, *JSA*, v. II, 83; Mgidhlana, 105; Mtshwayiza ka Mamfongonyana (ka Pakathwayo), notes of James Stuart, File 60, notebook 17, pp. 11-12. Bryant was skeptical of the evidence about Nozidiya: *Olden Times*, 186, cited by Webb and Wright, Mgidhlana, 109-110. Stuart published Mkebeni's version of the story in his schoolbook reader, *Tulasizwe*, making it the best-known version to later generations. See Mkebeni ka Dabulamanzi, *JSA*, v. III, 195.
41 Mankulumana ka Somapunga ka Zwide ka Langa, *JSA*, v. II, 226.
42 A.C. Samuelson, *Long, Long Ago* (Durban: Knox Printing, 1929; republished Durban: T.W. Griggs & Co. Ltd., 1974), 255.
43 Melapi ka Magaye, *JSA*, v. III, 69, 73.
44 Ibid, 74.
45 Dibandhlela's eldest son Mande did contest the inheritance in this case, but when Magaye came of age, Magaye returned to his father's chiefdom to be welcomed by his people after a long absence and in open conflict defended his primacy as heir. See Dinya, in interview of Melapi, 78.
46 Shepstone, "Historical Sketch," 1864, par. 5.
47 Fynn, *Diary*, 5; Shepstone, par. 5 and 6. Shepstone compiled the information he had received directly through his own interviews with many knowledgeable informants, and his information is largely in accord with other sources, including Fynn.
48 After Jobe's death Dingiswayo returned to dethrone and kill his brother Mawewe and become chief. Fynn, *Diary*, 5.
49 Mabonsa, 13.

50 At this point, he mentioned the later marriages of Swazi royal women to Tonga chiefs. See Giba ka Sobuza, *JSA*, v. I, 149–150.
51 Ibid. It is not unlikely that the fate of this individual young woman would not have been remembered by the AmaZulu oral traditions. In addition, given the sophistication of the AmaSwazi oral traditions that easily distinguish between the early chiefs and the royal families with which their royal house interacted and intermarried, it is unlikely that this story was mistaken in referring to the fate of a woman married to a different chief. Wylie argues that the story referred to a daughter of Sobhuza who married the AmaNdwandwe chief Zwide. See Wylie, 328.
52 With her went girls to carry her belongings and later become her *tinhlanti*, or affiliated wives; they were her half sister File, Veya who was a daughter of Zidze's *ndvuna*; Lomawandla; and Lavumisa. Matsebula names their children here. Thandile was married to Sobhuza when she reached puberty. J. S. M. Matsebula, *A History of Swaziland*, 2nd ed. (Cape Town: Longman Penguin, 1976), 18–19.
53 Matsebula, 19–20.
54 Ibid, 18.
55 Mmemi ka Nguluzana, *JSA*, v. III, 263.
56 Mbovu ka Mtshumayeli, *JSA*, v. III, 36.
57 Mmemi, 243–244.
58 Ibid, 244.
59 Ibid, 245.
60 Baleka ka Mpitikazi, *JSA*, b. 1, 13.
61 See also Webb and Wright, v. I, 14 n.30 and n.31. n.30 and n.31.
62 Lugubu, *JSA*, v. I, 284–287; Mqaikana, *JSA*, v. IV, 23.
63 She is sometimes reported to have been his sister. This was the explanation for Dingiswayo's later bizarre behavior when he went out unprepared to meet Zwide in battle and was easily overcome. See Mandhlakazi ka Ngini, *JSA*, v. II, 185–186.
64 The old men refused to leave the homes they had already built in Zwide's territory. Eventually, Makedama returned to *khonza* Shaka and led several military expeditions before an open act of insubordination and defiance finally provoked Shaka to have him attacked and killed in spite of their maternal relationship. See Ngidi, 55, 61–62.
65 Senzangakhona's father was Jama son of Ndaba, and Jama's brothers included Mbuzo, Sidinane, and Xoko (Coko), and probably Ntopo, each of whose heirs retained significant influence socially and politically in later generations. See Luzipo ka Nomageje, *JSA*, v. I, 355–356; Mangati, 208.
66 These were sons Nkwelo, Sojisa, Zivalele (Sitayi), Manqe, Vubukulwayo, Mfolosi, Mkanyile, Mapasa, Mkonjile, Nobongoza, Nontshiza, Sigwebana, Maqunuza, and Jama's heir Senzangakhona, and daughters Mnkabayi, Mawa, Mmama, and Sikile. The sources are inconsistent but the genealogies are consistent with and appear to confirm the relationships described here. See Ndukwana in interview of Jantshi, 202; Luzipo ka Nomageje, *JSA*, v. I, 355; Ndhlovu ka Timuni, *JSA*, v. IV, 219; Mtshanyankomo ka Magolwana, *JSA*. v. IV, 145; Baleni, 29; Madikane, 49.

67 Jantshi, 178, 181, 182; Mruyi ka Timuni, *JSA*, v. IV, 37; Mangati, 210.
68 Ndhlovu, 200, 202–205, 214, 216; Mruyi, 37; Jantshi, 178, 182; Magidi, 81; Melapi, 84. Webb and Wright, v. I, 203 n.14, 357 n.18; v. III, 97 n.61, 282 n.128; v. IV, 39 n.5.
69 Ngidi, 42.
70 Baleni, 29.
71 Ibid, 28; Mangati, 208.
72 Socwatsha ka Papu, December 28, 1901, Stuart Interview notes, Killie Campbell Library, 6, 9, 16.
73 Madikane, 49. She was Mntaniya ka Singelwayo, "of the Sibiya people." Mgidhlana ka Mpande, *JSA*, v. III, 109. Although Wylie correctly identifies Mntaniya as Senzangakhona's mother, 30–31, 117, in an error that may have been made inadvertently by an editor, Wylie misidentifies her as Senzangakhona's sister and as regent during his youth, *Myth of Iron*, 99, 101. There is no corroboration of the events in this oral tradition, but the fact that they were included in a tradition passed down to a later generation suggests at least a kernel of truth to them.
74 Madikane, 49.
75 Wylie doubts that Vubukulwayo was a son of Senzangakhona because he does not appear elsewhere in the recorded oral traditions, whereas another man of the same name does. Any truth to the story that Vubukulwayo had tried to kill Senzangakhona would explain why the half brother who married Mntaniya did not appear in any later oral traditions. Perhaps Vubukulwayo indeed died from poison under the conditions related by the story, which would also explain his disappearance from the narratives of oral history. Wylie is primarily doubtful about the story, however, because he questions whether people really try to poison their closest kin. See Wylie, 30–31. Poison is an age-old and universal method that has been used to accomplish murder secretly without fear of discovery and is a common weapon used by women.
76 Ngidi, 49.
77 For Nozilwane, see a note of Stuart referring to the testimony of Mkungo, in interview of Baleni, 23; see Mmemi, 248, 260.
78 Wylie concludes that Bhibhi, rather than Mpikase, was Sigujana's mother although he acknowledges disagreement in the sources. Wylie, 118, 124, 146, 535 n.64. The evidence about the succession dispute after Shaka's death supports a conclusion that Mpikase was the mother of both Sigujana and Dingane, however. See below.
79 Melapi, 88–89, and comment of Norman Nembula.
80 Mangati, 208. This might refer to the conflict between Dingane and Mpande with Boer allies in 1840 or the civil conflict between Cetshwayo and Mbuyazi in 1856.
81 Mayinga ka Mbekuzana, 256; Baleni, 20.
82 Mayinga, 256.
83 Baleni, 23; Mayinga, 255.
84 His other known sons were Ndunge, Gqugqu, Nzibe, Ngqojana, Mfihlo, Mqubane, Sonkoye, Sigwebana, Mfokozana, Sopane, Kolekile, Mbludhlele, Magwaza, Nomgqobo, Somajuba, Mdungazwe, Ngqojana, Nomkwayimba,

and Ntunja (Mathunjana); Baleni, 22–23; Mkando, 166; Mkebeni ka Dabulamanzi, 206; Mkehlengana 217; Ngidi, 37–38; Mangati, 205; Jantshi, 179; Melapi, 84.
85 Jantshi, 196.
86 Mgidhlana ka Mpande, 105, 107; Ngidi, 37; Baleni, 22; Mmemi ka Nguluzane, *JSA*, v. III, 259.
87 Baleni, 22–3; Mghidhlana, 105; Sivivi, 372.
88 Magidi, 79; Mmemi, 259.
89 Mmemi, 243; Ngidi, 30. Information about Nandi's family members, including her mother's parentage and the names of other children of her father Mbengi, is found in the interviews of Ngidi, 29, 31, 54, 59, 64–65 and Mbovu, 25. One of Nandi's brothers, Bantwana, became a Christian convert, *kholwa*, and in 1904, Ngidi said that he had "died recently." This is important because it indicates that one of Nandi's brothers was alive for several generations to sustain local knowledge of events concerning Nandi, Shaka and the eLangeni people from the early nineteenth century. Bantwana was of the Isibubulungu regiment among the eLangeni, about the age of Mgabi, and Ngidi knew him personally. Ngidi, 31; see also 64–65.
90 For further details regarding these events surrounding Shaka's birth and early life, see Chapter 3.
91 Madikane, 51. Madikane's father Mlomowetole was old enough to know about the early history firsthand and had *khonza*'d Shaka. After telling the story of Shaka's life up to the time when he went to the Mtetwa, Madikane explained to Stuart, "My father heard all this from Makobosi ka Ndhlovu, also from Hlati of the eMgazini people. My father lived with Hlati, a man belonging to one of Senzangakona's regiments." This provides a chain of transmission for Madikane's narrative that is more explicit than just reference to his father Mlomowetole.
92 Ngidi, 53.
93 Jantshi, 199.
94 Ndukwana in interview of Jantshi, 199.
95 Ngidi, 42, 59.
96 Ibid, 42.
97 Ibid, 59.
98 Jantshi, 182; Melapi, 84; Mruyi, 37; Ndhlovu, 205.
99 Magidigidi, 91. Wylie, 236–237, provides information about the villages where the royal women presided.
100 Mangati ka Godide, 216.
101 Mgidhlana, 109.
102 Fynn, *Diary*, 121.
103 Ngidi, 79.
104 Mabonsa ka Sidhlayi, *JSA*, v. II, 20.
105 Jantshi, 191.
106 Ibid.; Mmemi, 248.
107 Baleka, 12; Jantshi, 191.
108 Tununu ka Nonjiya, unpublished interview, KCL, James Stuart Collection File 60 NB [Notebook] 22 KCM 24258; Jantshi, 195–196.

109 Maclean (John Ross), 118.
110 Ibid.
111 Mkando ka Dhlova, 151.
112 Baleka, 11.
113 Mkotana ka Zulu, 228.
114 Mabonsa ka Sidhlayi, 22. As Wylie, 325, points out, Gxubu told Stuart that his father lived in the village of a woman named Mzetepi, whom he said with certainty was a wife of Shaka. See also Gxubu ka Luduzo, *JSA*, v. I, 158.
115 Ngidi, 41, 90.
116 Ibid.
117 Tununu ka Nonjiya, interview, KCL James Stuart Collection File 60, NB 22 KCM 24258.
118 Socwatsha ka Papu, unpublished interview, KCL, James Stuart Collection, File 70 KCM 14398, interview notes 1904, p. 101.
119 Mkehlengana ka Zulu, 218.
120 Socwatsha ka Papu, unpublished interview, KCL, James Stuart Collection, File 70 KCM 14398, interview notes 1904, p. 101; Ngidi, 90.
121 Mkehlengana, 218; Socwatsha in interview of Mkehlengana, 218.
122 Socwatsha, File 70 KCM 14398, 101; Socwatsha in interview of Mkehlengana, 218.
123 Maclean (Ross), 111.
124 Melapi, 86.
125 Maclean (Ross), 111.
126 Ibid.
127 Ibid.
128 Ndukwana, 291; Mbovu, *JSA*, v. III, 31, 44; Baleka, *JSA*, v. I, 8; Mabonsa, *JSA*, v. II, 21, 22; Socwatcha, File 70 KCM 14398, 102; Melapi, *JSA*, v. III, 86; Lunguza, *JSA*, v. I, 31; Maquza ka Gawushane, *JSA*, v. II, 232; Magidi ka Ngomane, *JSA*, v. II, 81.
129 Mbovu, 31.
130 Baleka, 8; Mabonsa, 22.
131 Melapi, 86.
132 Ibid. Melapi's father was a trusted ally of Shaka and chief of the AmaCele chiefdom who had regular access to the highest levels of politics in the capital at Bulawayo and then Dukuza.
133 Ngidi at interview of Mbovu, 44; Jantshi, 195.
134 Mkehlengana, 218; Madhlebe ka Njinjana, *JSA*, v. II, 45.
135 Mabonsa, 14.
136 Ibid, 21.
137 Lunguza, 311.
138 Ibid, 311.
139 Mgidhlana ka Mpande, 109.
140 "Nandi fell ill at Bulawayo. Her brother Nxazonke was with her, also Mbikwana" (i.e., another brother). "There is general agreement in oral sources that she died shortly after being discovered by Tshaka with a small child purported to have been his." See Ngidi, 39.
141 Ngidi, 35.

142 Ibid. Stuart wrote an annotation here that "[Fynn gives quite a different version which appears more credible.]" This is a reference to John Bird, *The Annals of Natal*, 2 vols. (Pietermaritzburg: P. Davis and Sons, 1888; reprint Kessinger Publishing's Legacy Reprints, n.d.), 91–93, a work that was available from the 1880s.
143 Fynn, *Diary*, 131.
144 Ibid. The editor notes that it was a distance of 80 miles.
145 Ibid, 133.
146 Ibid, 135.
147 Ibid. Fynn later wrote, "Amidst this scene I stood unharmed, contemplating the horrors around me; and felt as if the whole universe was at that moment coming to an end. I stood there alone, a privileged being, not compelled to take part in this frantic scene; and I felt truly thankful, not only that I was a British subject, but that I had so far gained the respect of this tyrant as to hope for escape even from this horrible place of blood." This is one of the more revealing passages of Fynn's memoires with regard to his own character and perspectives.
148 Jantshi, *JSA*, v. I, 195.
149 Mbovu, 31. Similarly, Baleni, 19, "Mxamama of the Sibisi people told Tshaka that tears did not come from the eyes of certain people when Nandi died, upon which they would be put to death. It was said, 'They are being defiant.' As no tears flowed from their eyes."
150 Ndukwana, *JSA*, v. IV, 292–293. Stuart's annotation was, "[I fancy this means a comet appeared.]".
151 Ngidi, 72.
152 Fynn, *Diary*, 135–137.
153 Tununu ka Nonjiya, KCL James Stuart Collectiion File 60 NB[Notebook] 22 KCM 24258, 26.
154 Ngidi, 35.
155 Socwatsha, File 70 KCM 14398 interview notes, 102.
156 Mkando ka Dhlova, *JSA*, v. III, 51.
157 Melapi, 85; Dinya ka Zokozwayo, *JSA*, v. I, 100.
158 Lunguza ka Mpukane, v. I, 307.
159 Ibid, 337.
160 The details provided information about a ceremony held to help restore the fertility of women afterward because they had been adversely affected. This lends credibility to this account and indicates that Melapi believed it to be true. See Melapi, 86.
161 Socwatsha, File 70 KCM 14398 interview notes, 102.
162 Socwatsha, File 70 KCM 14398 interview notes, 102.
163 Ibid.
164 Ibid.
165 Ngidi, 35.
166 Fynn, *Diary*, 137.
167 Jantshi, 196.
168 Ibid.
169 Ibid, 197.

170 Ibid, 196.
171 Sivivi, 370–371.
172 Ibid, 372.
173 Ibid.
174 Baleni, 38. Hamilton, 444, rests her conclusion in part on the false assumption that "through their control over the *izigodhlo*, the *amakhosikazi* exerted a direct royal monopoly over access to the products of women's agricultural labour, and its redistribution to the men of the *amakhanda*." Hamilton and following her, Wylie, 236, 336, both draw unsupportable conclusions that the *amakhosikazi* had great power as well as prestige. Wylie refers to them as "extremely powerful figures."
175 Ngidi, 80–84.
176 Hoye ka Sozalase, *JSA*, v. I, 168.
177 Ngidi, 84.
178 For Nozilwane, see a note by Stuart referring to the testimony of Mkungo in interview of Baleni, 23; Mmemi, 248, 260.
179 Mangati, 204, 206.
180 These well-known events occurred in 1843. Mangati, 204–205; Mmemi, 243; Ndukwana, 332.
181 Mangati, 204–205.
182 The earliest theoretical contributions to the study of women's history and women in history in various contexts, both Western and non-Western, were made by Marxist-feminist scholars who sought to explain inequalities in the status of men and women with reference to Marxist definitions and explanations of class and class formation. Driven by a desire to reveal in world history a general tendency of the subordination of women by men, Marxist-feminist theorists adopted the terminology of domination and oppression that obscured the nuances and ambiguities in women's roles, initiatives, and options in exercising power in their own lives and over the lives of others and portrayed women as powerless and oppression as overt and deliberate.
183 Guy, "Analyzing Precapitalist Societies."
184 Sifiso Ndlovu, "Reassessment," 119.
185 Ibid.
186 Krige, *Social System*, 177.
187 Ibid, 229.
188 Kuper, *Wives for Cattle*, 76.

Chapter 9

1 Carolyn Hamilton and John Wright, "The Making of the *AmaLala*: Ethnicity, Ideology and Relations of Subordination in a Precolonial Context," *South African Historical Journal*, 22, 1, 3–23.
2 John Wright, "A. T. Bryant and the 'Lala,'" *Journal of Southern African Studies* 38, no. 2 (2012), 355–368.
3 Neil Parsons, "South Africa in Africa More Than Five Hundred Years Ago: Some Questions," *Five Hundred Years*, 48.

4 Hamilton and Wright, 13, citing C. A. Hamilton, "Ideology, Oral Traditions and the Struggle for Power in the Early Zulu Kingdom," M.A. thesis, University of the Witwatersrand, 1986), 112–131, 155–161, where the mistaken argument asserting the invention of KwaZulu-Natal genealogies and oral traditions is presented in detail.
5 Carolyn Hamilton, "Political Consolidation and the Making of Social Categories East of the Drakensberg in the Late Eighteenth and Early Nineteenth Centuries," *Journal of Southern African Studies*, 38, no. 2 (2012), 293–294.
6 Wright and Hamilton, "Ethnicity and Political Change Before 1840," in Robert Morrell, ed., *Political Economy and Identities in KwaZulu-Natal: Historical and Social Perspectives* (Durban: Indicator Press, 1996), 20.
7 Hamilton, "Political Consolidation."
8 Hamilton, "Ideology," 339–340.
9 Ibid, 330–421.
10 Ndukwana ka Mbengwana, *JSA*, v. IV, 303.
11 Ndukwana ka Mbengwana, Killie Campbell Library [hereafter KCL], File 74, KCM 24402.
12 Ibid.
13 Ndukwana, *JSA*, v. IV, 302.
14 Ibid, 320, 303.
15 Ibid, 296. He explained, "People became scattered when Tshaka formed the nation (*qoqa'd izwe*); that is, they went to *konza* (give allegiance to, join) various tribes in an indiscriminate manner."
16 For other examples, see Ngidi ka Mcikaziswa, *JSA*, v. V, 75; Mabonsa ka Sidhlayi, *JSA*, v. II, 13; Nombashini ka Ndhlela, *JSA*, v. V, 144.
17 Ndukwana, 363.
18 Mabonsa, 24.
19 Mgidhlana ka Mpande, *JSA*, v. III, 110.
20 Jantshi ka Nongila, *JSA*, v. I, 174.
21 Madikane ka Mlomowetole, *JSA*, v. II, 49.
22 Mruyi ka Timuni, *JSA*, v. IV, 37.
23 Mkando ka Dhlova, *JSA*, v. III, 146. A line of doggerel used that was evidently a mnemonic device is discussed in several additional sources: Ndhlovu ka Timuni, *JSA*, v. IV, 199–200; Mruyi, 37; Ndukwana in Jantshi interview, 202; Jantshi, 176; Webb and Wright, v. IV, 233 n.18 and v. I, 203 n.9.
24 Socwatsha, James Stuart Papers, KCL, 14; Lugubu ka Mangalizo, *JSA*, v. I, 292; Webb and Wright, 296 n.60. The substituted phrase thus left unspoken the implied and intended actual words or praise name.
25 Mmemi ka Nguluzana, *JSA*, v. III, 240; Mbovu ka Mtshumayeli, *JSA*, v. III, 25; Ngidi, 28; Mkebeni ka Dabulamanzi, *JSA*, v. III, 195.
26 Magidigidi ka Nobebe, *JSA*, v. II, 83, 84; Mbovu, 25.
27 They also recognized the peoples of the region of Maputo (Delagoa) Bay who were derogatorily referred to as "nHlengwe" as belonging to another distinct broad cultural group.
28 Mbovu, 42. For additional comments about these identities, see Mayinga, 254; Mkehlengana ka Zulu, *JSA*, v. III, 215.

29 Magidigidi, 84.
30 Magidigidi, 85; Socwatsha, 14; Mqaikana ka Yenge, 14.
31 Socwatsha in interview of Mkehlengana, 211.
32 Dinya ka Zokowayo, *JSA*, v. I, 117.
33 Mkehlengana ka Zulu, *JSA*, v. III, 213.
34 Dinya, 117.
35 Mruyi, 37.
36 Mkehlengana, 215.
37 Mayinga ka Mbekuzana, *JSA*, v. II, 254.
38 Ibid, 280–281. For versions of the grain basket myth, see Madhlebe ka Njinjana, *JSA*, v. II, 46; Mangati, 203.
39 Madikane, 57.
40 Michael Westcott and Carolyn Hamilton, *In the Tracks of the Swazi Past: A Historical Tour of the Ngwane and Ndwandwe Kingdoms* (Manzini: Macmillan Boleswa, 1992), 27, 56.
41 Mkehlengana, 215.
42 Sivivi ka Maqungo, *JSA*, v. V, 371.
43 Ndabambi ka Sikakana, *JSA*, v. IV, 176. He had heard this from his paternal grandmother who had AmaNtungwa relatives although she was not one herself.
44 Mgidhlana, 105.
45 Sivivi, 368.
46 Mkotana in interview of Mkehlengana, 215.
47 Socwatsha at interview of Mkehlengana, 211.
48 Mabonsa, 12. The AmaKhumalo were from the northern region of modern KwaZulu, inland from the coast but east of the prominent AmaHlubi and AmaNgwane chiefdoms.
49 Socwatsha in interview with Maziyana, 280; in a different interview Socwatsha, 14, said, "The Kumalo people have a *sibongo* [praise] which runs '*umNtungw'oluhlaza*.'"
50 Magidigidi, 97.
51 Maziyana, 277.
52 Mbovu, 25.
53 Mruyi, 37.
54 Mbovu, 42.
55 Mabonsa, 18; Mangati, 203.
56 Ndukwana, 348; Mahaya ka Nongqabana, *JSA*, v. II, 129; Mkehlengana, 21; Mbovu, 45; Magidigidi, 84; Mkehlengana, 213; Socwatsha at interview of Mkehlengana, 211; Socwatsha, 14; Mangati, 203; Maziyana, 277.
57 Madikane, 54–55. One man commented, "My belief is that the name amaLala came from the Cubeni people, i.e. the iron-smiths," Mqaikana, 14.
58 Socwatsha, 14.
59 Mbovu, 42.
60 Makewu, *JSA*, v. II, 161.
61 Mzukele ka Kuni, *JSA*, v. IV, 169.
62 Mmemi, 264.
63 Mbovu, 42.

64 Maziyana, *JSA*, v. II, 276, 279.
65 Mcotoyi ka Mnini, *JSA*, v. III, 56.
66 Ngidi, 49.
67 Msime ka Beje, *JSA*, v. IV, 50.
68 Mbokodo ka Sikulekile, *JSA*, v. III, 6; Dinya, 117.
69 Socwatsha, 6.
70 Mqaikana, 3.
71 Mkando, 150.
72 Mqaikana, 14.
73 Socwatsha, 14.
74 Ndukwana, 348.
75 Socwatsha, 14.
76 Ibid, 14.
77 Ibid, 14; also Dinya, 104.
78 Luzipo ka Nomageje, *JSA*, v. I, 354.
79 Magidigidi, 84.
80 For examples, see Mabonsa, 28; Mqaikana, 28.
81 Magidigidi, 97.
82 Ibid.
83 Mcotoyi noted that after their migration to the southwest, the AmaBhaca subsequently "...learnt a dialect of their own. They [their speech] were affected by the Mpondos [AmaMpondo]." Mcotoyi, 57.
84 Stuart's comment, *JSA*, v. II, 294.
85 Maziyana, 279.
86 Mcotoyi, 57.
87 Mageza ka Kwefunga, *JSA*, v. II, 69–70. For AmaLala vocabulary omitted by Webb and Wright but found in the original notebook for the interview of Mageza, 69–70, see File 61 NB [Notebook] 46, 20–22.
88 Mkando, 166–167.
89 Mmemi, 262, quoting Chief Phakade ka Macingwane.
90 Magidigidi, 84.
91 Socwatsha at interview of Mkehlengana, 211.
92 Dinya, 107; Ndukwana, 299.
93 Mcotoyi, 56.
94 Mbovu, 42; Mcotoyi, 56; Melapi ka Magaye, *JSA*, v. III, 75–76. For examples of the dialect spoken by the AmaCele, see Mcotoyi, 57 and Stuart's interview with Mageza and Magongo on February 19, 1905, File 61 NB [Notebook] 52 KCM 24288, 1–6.
95 Hamilton, "Ideology," 266.
96 Ibid, 266, 265.
97 Wright, "A. T. Bryant and the 'Lala,'" 355–368.
98 John Wright, "Politics, Ideology, and the Invention of the 'Nguni,'" in Tom Lodge, ed., *Resistance and Ideology in Settler Societies* (Johannesburg: Ravan Press, 1986, 96–118), 107.
99 Ibid.
100 This inconsistency in her acceptance or rejection of the integrity of oral sources reflects her own ideological agenda of demonstrating Gramscian

Marxist theories of ideological hegemony, which the Italian Marxist Antonio Gramsci developed to explain why the working class did not support revolution but instead was co-opted to support the ruling classes. Hamilton explicitly explains her adherence to Gramsci's theories, which she elaborated in an article published in 1987 but without reference to the Zulu or any historical evidence. C. A. Hamilton, "Ideology and Oral Traditions: Listening to the Voices 'from Below,'" *History in Africa*, 14 (1987), 67–86.

101 Carolyn Hamilton, "Political Centralisation and the Making of Social Categories East of the Drakensberg in the Late Eighteenth and Early Nineteenth Centuries," *Journal of Southern African Studies*, 38, no. 2 (2012), 291–300. Wylie correctly questioned the uses of identifying terminology and notes that their uses and meanings changed over time but failed to piece together the indigenous oral evidence to make sense of how they were understood by the peoples of KwaZulu-Natal before and during the era of Shaka. Wylie, *Myth of Iron*, 16–21.

102 Ibid, 266.

103 She refers to this as "the invention of the Malandela tradition"; Hamilton, "Ideology," 152–206.

104 Mageza, 70.

105 Dinya, 117; the same explanation was given by Mahaya, 130.

106 Mmemi, 263–4; Mahaya, 119; Wright, "Politics, Ideology, and the Invention of the 'Nguni,'" in Tom Lodge, ed., *Resistance and Ideology in Settler Societies, Southern African Studies*, 4 vols. (Johannesburg: Ravan Press, 1986). 107.

107 Ngidi, 31, 67.

108 Mahaya, 119, 130.

109 That is, isiXhosa, isiZulu, SeSwati, and all of their cognate dialects are now subsumed under those linguistic names.

110 John Wright traces the history of European references to the term *Nguni* and its adoption by Europeans as a linguistic term of reference and a convenient category adopted for administrative reasons by the Department of Native Affairs created in 1910. The white administration relied upon the faulty information they found in Bryant's work. Wright, "Politics, Ideology, and the Invention of the 'Nguni,'" 105–107. Wright asserts the association of the Zulu royal house with the term of identity *Nguni* is completely spurious (19) whereas oral traditions clearly identify it as an ancestral praise-name in the royal genealogy.

111 Socwatsha, 7.

112 Ibid, 7.

113 Wright, "Politics, Ideology," 107.

114 Magidigidi, 97.

115 Mkotana ka Zulu, *JSA*, v. III, 225; Mruyi, 37.

116 Madikane, 57.

117 Mruyi, 37.

118 Mmemi, 262.

119 Socwatsha, 14. He believed, "AmaNtungwa and abeNguni. These two names are for one and the same class of people.... The spelling abeNguni is the proper one, but the pronunciation abaNguni will also be heard."

120 Mbovu, 42, who also listed those he knew to be AmaNtungwa and AmaLala, said with certainty: "Abanguni: Qwabe, Makanya, Cunu, Zulu, Biyela, Langa, Ntombela, Magwaza. (The Zulu tribe were once spoken of as amaNtungwa because from the north.) [and] Mandhlakazi." He then named a few chiefdoms that he could not classify, including the AmaNdwandwe (AmaNxumalo).
121 Socwatsha in interview of Maziyana, 281; Mahaya, 116; Mayinga, 254.
122 Magidigidi, 97.
123 Mahaya, 115, 118.
124 Mruyi, 37.
125 Magidigidi, 97.

Chapter 10

1 Maziyana, *James Stuart Archive* (hereafter *JSA*), v. II, 277.
2 Lugubu ka Mangalizo, *JSA*, v. I, 292. From the AmaMbatha section of the AbaThembu chiefdom, he knew in detail the oral traditions of the AbaThembu under Chief Ngoza, related in Chapter 4.
3 Melapi ka Magaye, *JSA*, v. III, 80.
4 Maclean, 86.
5 Ibid, 98.
6 Ibid.
7 Ndukwana, *JSA*, v. IV, 285.
8 Ibid, 314.
9 Dinya in interview of Mayinga ka Mbekuzana, *JSA*, v. II, 257.
10 Mkotana in interview of Mayinga ka Mbekuzana, 257. He also listed the criteria for selecting a settlement site.
11 Mayinga ka Mbekuzana, 257. He added, "This separation is not due to quarrelling but simply to inclination. No district (*isigodi*) ever became full."
12 Ndukwana, 312; see also Mayinga, 257. Ndukwana also stated, "No woman was even given land to live on; such applications were unknown."
13 Ndukwana, 315; bracketed note written by Stuart.
14 Ndukwana, *JSA*, v. IV, 311–312. This long segment is labeled "Land and land tenure" in Stuart's notes.
15 Ibid. Ndukwana added, "For instance the country at Kwa Ndabenkulu, down the Black Mfolozi, behind Zibebu, this side of the Hluhluwe, where it flows into the Mfolozi, was land so set apart for Crown purposes. And again the land about Mpapala was similarly set apart and did not belong either to Ndhlela (father of Mavumengwana) or Zinti, for the izilomo or headmen Manyosi, Nhlebo, Sisinde, Ngqojana (ka Senzangakona) and others lived there. Ndukwana knows only of these two pieces of land set apart for Crown purposes."
16 Ibid. Ndukwana also said, "This making of boundaries (*imncelecele*) began in Mpande's time. These two tracts of country had no *umnumzana* [village or homestead heads] in charge, either one tract or the other. The *izilomo* were in charge of it all."
17 Baleni ka Silwana, *JSA*, v. I, 29.

18 Magidigidi ka Nobebe, *JSA*, v. II, 90.
19 Ngidi, *JSA*, v. V, 36–37. When listing Dingana's villages, Ngidi, 33, indicated that Senzangakhona's villages had also included Emahlabaneni (later Mnkabayi's village) and Ekloberi (later Gqugqu's village).
20 Baleni, 20; Ngidi, 33.
21 Ngidi, 36.
22 Ibid.
23 Magidigidi ka Nobebe, *JSA*, v. II, 91.
24 Other well known *imizi* found in the oral traditions, sometimes because of their associations with strong regiments, were Mkandhlu (previously known as Kwa Nogqogqa, having been Shaka's kraal among the AmaMthethwa), Mgumanqa (or Mgumanga, near Eshowe), Fasimba, Intontela, Isipezi, Mbonambi (first at Eshowe and later crossed over the Thukela), Dhlangezwa (near Eshowe), Gibabanye (first near Bulawayo and later rebuilt south of the Mzimkhulu River), Bekenya, Fasimba (also known as Nomagomba or uGobandwane), Ozweleni (or uZwewla, a "minor kraal"), Madadasa (or Mdadasa, at Mahlabatini), Kwa Guqu (at Emahlabatini), uMyehe (eMyeheni, built in Zwide's country, at Masipula ka Mamba's at the Black Mfolozi), Nomdayana (at Emahlabatini), Empangisweni (built in former AmaNdwandwe territory), Isipezi, and regimental villages including Ndabenkulu, and Injanduna. Stuart unpublished interviews of Socwatsha; Ngidi, 33, 36–7, 39; Baleni, 20.
25 Maclean, 118.
26 Ibid.
27 Ibid, 118–120. The measure of a yard refers to three feet, equal to 0.9144 meters.
28 Ndukwana, 278.
29 Mangati ka Godide, *JSA*, v. II, 216.
30 Magidigidi, 91.
31 Baleka ka Mpitikazi, *JSA*, v. I, 12.
32 Jantshi ka Nongila, *JSA*, v. I, 191. Bracketed note by Stuart in original notes: "Ngwadi was put to death by Dingana, Ndukwana says. Jantshi agrees."
33 Jantshi, 191, said of the father of Nandi's two other children besides Shaka, "I do not know how Gendeyana came by his death or what happened in regard to him, but I do not think he came to the Zulu country." Jantshi's uncle had once attacked Ngwadi's village but the latter had escaped harm; Jantshi did not know if Ngwadi had any children.
34 Magidigidi, 92.
35 Shaka may have had Sankoye killed. Jantshi, 191.
36 Tununu ka Nonjiya, interview, KCL, James Stuart Collection File 60 NB [Notebook] 22, KCM 24258.
37 Makewu, *JSA*, v. II, 162.
38 Mkungu ka Mpande, *JSA*, v. III, 232.
39 Ngidi, 90.
40 Ibid, 41.
41 Ibid, 41, 90.
42 Mangati, *JSA*, v. II, 213.

43 Maziyana ka Mahlabeni in interview of Melapi ka Magaye, 85.
44 Maziyana, 293. He also said, "Dingane killed Matubane because the king's cattle at Kwa Ndabenkulu had been eaten by hyenas."
45 Ndukwana, 316. He said specifically, "The boundaries of Zululand were the Income river on the north-west to where it enters the Mzinyate [River], from there along the Mzinyati [River] to the Tugela [River], then along the Tugela to the sea; on the north-east the Pongola [River] was the boundary (it was the first boundary in Tshaka's and Dingana's reigns, but it was afterwards crossed at the Ngcaka, Mhlongavula hill, and near the Swaziland 'Makosini ['place of kings']), thence to the uBombo [mountains] along the Pongolo, and then, on the east of the Ubombo, the Mkuze river to the sea was the boundary; the sea was the eastern boundary. The territory of Zululand was carried across the Pongolo when Sidubela ka Sobuza came to *konza* the king in Mpande's time. The Baqulusini also crossed and built near Makosini (Swaziland). Masipula drove the Swazis back and planted his kraal at Mkwakweni. (To this day Sitambi ka Masipula lives there; he *konza*'s the Zulu kings.) Tekwane also belonged to Masipula, but he afterwards re-*konza*'d the Swaziland king."
46 Maziyana, 297.
47 Wylie's analysis of the contradictory white myths of Shaka as both a monster and as noble and wise is excellent. Wylie, *Savage Delight*, 11–65.
48 Jantshi, *JSA*, v. I, 189. See also the comments of Mkando ka Dhlova, *JSA*, v. III, 160; Mangati, 213; Mayinga ka Mbekuzana, *JSA*, v. II, 248; Makewu, *JSA*, v. II, 163.
49 Baleka ka Mpitikazi, 8. Although she was one of Stuart's later interviews in 1919, her father had lived to a very old age and died in 1888.
50 Melapi, *JSA*, v. III, 87. He also referred to the way that Shaka would "mouth his words."
51 Jantshi ka Nongila, *JSA*, v. I, 195. To *tefula* is to speak with the distinctive accent associated with the AmaQwabe chiefdom; it is similar to the dialect of their neighboring AmaMthethwa with whom Shaka lived for a number of years as a young man. It is associated with peoples living in the lowland coastal areas.
52 Mcotoyi ka Mnini, *JSA*, v. III, 67.
53 Mbokodo ka Sikulekile, *JSA*, v. III, 19. Mangati ka Godide, *JSA*, v. II, 215, also knew that "Sikiti!" referred to Shaka but did not seem to understand it was one of his praise-names. Mbokodo, *JSA*, v. III, 5, said that Shaka took one of Sambela's praises and used it for himself. Socwatsho told Stuart, "M'tshongweni was the *imibongi ka Tshaka*" ["does not know Dingana's"]. "Per Socwatsha, in the presence of Dhlozi; Ndkuwana was present during latter part of convn and assisted in giving information this day 28.12,1901 (Sat.)" James Stuart Collection, interview notes, 9.
54 Baleka, *JSA*, v. I, 8.
55 Mcotoyi, 66.
56 Mqaikana ka Yenge, *JSA*, v. IV, 11.
57 Dinya ka Zokozwayo, *JSA*, v. I, 114.
58 Mandhlakazi ka Ngini, *JSA*, v. II, 179.
59 Maclean, 68.

60 Baleka, *JSA*, v. I, 11.
61 Fynn, *Diary*, 82.
62 Ibid, 154.
63 Maclean, 72–73. "*Mlungu* – Tshaka used this word. We used the word *abalumbi* at first, for Europeans *lumba* things." Mbovu ka Mtshumayeli, *JSA*, v. III, 26. Webb and Wright, 46 n.22 note that *ukulumba* means "to work wonders."
64 Maclean, 76–77.
65 Fynn, *Diary*, 80–82, 90, 120.
66 Jantshi ka Nongila, *JSA*, v. I, 200.
67 Lunguza ka Mpukane, *JSA*, v. I, 330. See also the accounts of Jantshi, 195; Ndukwana, *JSA*, v. IV, 317; Socwatsha, KCL, James Stuart Collection File 58 (AA) NB [Notebook] 23KCM24220, 16; Baleka, *JSA*, v. I, 9; Ngidi, 40.
68 Mtshapi, 69.
69 Makuza ka Mkomoyi, *JSA*, v. II, 166–167, who added, "I am in no doubt whatever as to this stick incident. It really occurred. I got the story from my father Mkomoyi. He also threw his stick, for he was one of Tshaka's warriors." Nduna ka Manqina, *JSA*, v. V, 7, told a similar story. He said Shaka challenged chief Zihlandhlo to throw sticks into the sea, and Shaka's did not return; he wanted to kill Zihlandlo but then instead called him "his brother" and desisted.
70 Melapi, 87.
71 Fynn, *Diary*, 24. This last sentence dates the writing of this passage as after 1836 if the reference to twelve years was accurate after he had arrived in 1824.
72 Mmemi ka Nguluzane, *JSA*, v. III, 246.
73 Baleka, 7.
74 Ibid, 7.
75 Socwatsha, 15.
76 Jantshi, 194.
77 Kambi ka Matshobana, *JSA*, v. I, 209.
78 Mmemi ka Nguluzane, 249.
79 Baleka, 8.
80 Ibid, 7.
81 Mangati ka Godide, 217.
82 For an example of an apparently apocryphal account that includes mystical or supernatural elements, see Mahashahasha ka Pakade, *JSA*, v. II, 107.
83 Lunguza ka Mpukane, *JSA*, v. I, 311.
84 Baleka, 12.
85 Ngidi, 69.
86 Ngidi, 40, gave his name as Madhlo (alias Mqakama) ka Nombanda ka Mxabu ka Daleni ka Mhlongo, the specific identification lending strong credibility to the story.
87 Ibid, 40, 69, 77.
88 They were also called the Mkandhlwini regiment. Mayinga, 249; Ngidi, 56, 58; Madikane ka Mlomowetole, *JSA*, v. II, 61. See also Baleni, 19.
89 Baleni, 19; see also Ngidi, 70.
90 Jantshi, 195.

91 Jantshi, 201–202. Jantshi told other stories of atrocities committed by Shaka but also misattributed to Shaka the action attributed by others to Dingane, that he killed people for the purpose of feeding vultures, prompting Stuart to write the annotation "no, it was Dingana did this." Jantshi, 195.
92 Fynn, *Diary*, 78.
93 Ibid, 28.
94 Makewu, 161–162.
95 Melapi, 86.
96 This is significant because it matches other descriptions of the killing of Nandi and killings ordered by Nandi. Maclean, 129.
97 Maclean, 112–113.
98 Ibid, 109.
99 Ibid, 111.
100 Mandhlakazi ka Ngini, 175.
101 Baleka, 12.
102 Ibid, 7, 10; Makewu, 161; Mbovu, 31; Mmemi, 245; Baleni, 30; Maziyana in interview of Melapi, 84; Melapi, 85; Maziyana, 294.
103 Maziyana, 294.
104 Ngidi, 62.
105 Ibid, 39.
106 Maclean, 101–102.
107 Ibid, 99.

Chapter 11

1 Makewu, 162.
2 Fynn, *Diary*, 141.
3 Ibid.
4 Maclean (John Ross), 72.
5 Maziyana ka Mahlabeni, *JSA*, v. II, 271.
6 Ndukwana, 282.
7 Makewu, 162.
8 Ndukwana, 332. Of course, this may have merely been given as a pretext for this decision in 1888 and may not accurately reflect Shaka's intentions sixty years earlier.
9 Maclean, 72–73.
10 Ibid, 73.
11 Jantshi, 200.
12 Jantshi added, "There is a general rumour in Zululand nowadays that Sotobe did not return and that the American negroes are his progeny. As a matter of fact he did return. His son and successor was Nobiya (killed by Zibebu at Ondini). Muntuwapansi, Nobiya's heir, is living on the other side of the Mhlatuze among the people of Qetuka and Siteku." Jantshi, 192–193.
13 Ibid, 198.
14 Melapi, 73.
15 Mayinga ka Mbekuzana, 257.
16 Ibid, 258.

17 Ibid, 252, 258.
18 Ngidi ka Mcikaziswa, 62.
19 Issacs journal, *South African Commercial Advertiser*, KCL, James Stuart Collection typescript copy, 97–98. Isaacs later republished the contents of this series of articles in book form with some embellishments designed to enhance the narrative; the earlier articles retain more value as a source because they were more contemporaneous and less influenced by subsequent personal and political agendas.
20 Mkando ka Dhlova, 145.
21 Maziyana ka Mahlabeni, 273.
22 Mbovu ka Mtshumayeli, *JSA*, v. III, 43. He added, "Tshaka, however, established colonies like Europeans."
23 Fynn, *Diary*, 141–142.
24 Ibid, 143.
25 Ibid.
26 In his report about his visit to chief Faku, Dundas wrote: "That Fynn was present with the invading army was verified to me beyond a doubt as a man who had been wounded by a shot from a gun in both thighs was brought to me, who said that the person who shot him afterwards saved his life and dressed his wounds, and then told him that his name was Fynn and that his father lived in the great town of the English, where Chaka's people intended to go. Though Fakoo informed me that there were other white people with Fynn, I have not been able to ascertain the point; perhaps he may have [mis]taken some Hottentots who are in that person's service for white people." KCL, James Stuart Collection File 17, KCM 23465. "Extracts of letters and information collected by Mr James Stuart on the early History of Natal. Extract No. 7" (Typescripts), 295–296, "Extracts from Dundas's report or statement."
27 If true, it is important to consider that this wounded man became a point of transmission of information not only of Fynn's purported presence. More importantly someone, supposedly Fynn, relayed through this injured man, who survived to tell the tale, what Shaka's plans were. The information, received and reported by Dundas and the British chain of command, is in accord with the information regarding Shaka's plans that Fynn provided in his record of the events, made only three or four years later. Although the accuracy of the report of the wounded man cannot be determined, it supports the conclusion that Fynn, forced by circumstances to be with Shaka during the time of the 1828 attack on the AmaMpondo, took advantage of his proximity to the people with whom he lived and engaged in friendly trade to send a warning to the AmaMpondo and any of their allies that the threat from Shaka was very real and part of a bigger and more ominous plan.
28 Fynn, *Diary*, 144.
29 Ibid.
30 Ibid.
31 Ibid.
32 Ibid.
33 Ibid, 145.
34 Ibid, 146.

35 Ibid.
36 Ibid, 146.
37 Ibid, 147.
38 Ibid, 148.
39 Ibid.
40 Ibid, 149.
41 Ibid, 153.
42 Ibid.
43 Mkehlengana, *JSA*, v. III, 217.
44 Mkando, *JSA* v. III, 145, 1902.
45 Mmemi, *JSA* v. III, 268, 1904; he names them.
46 Maziyana, 274.
47 Madikane, 61. This is a point of controversy in the sources, and Madikane's confident assertion of it is significant.
48 Stuart was told, "*Izinduna* [officers, commanders] that probably went with the *impi* to Pondoland with Tshaka: Mdhlaka ka Ncidi, *induna* of the nation (*induna yezwe*), but as he lived at Esiklebeni he would have been [commander] over a regiment; Ngomane ka Mqomboyo; Mxamana ka Sotshaya; Mbikwana ka Bebe [i.e., Mbengi] of the eLangeni people, *induna* of the Mgumanqa regiment; Sotobe ka Mpangalala; Seketwayo ka Nhlaka ka Dikane of the Mdhlalose people; Mvundhlana ka Menziwa ka Xoko of the Mdhlalose people, *induna* of m [sic]; Mapita ka Sojisa; Mbilini ka Cungeya ka Bakwanazi of the Mtetwa people, *induna* of the Mgumanqa regiment; Zulu ka Nogandaya of the Yinda alias Ncwana section of the Qwabe people." Mmemi, 268. Zulu ka Nogandaya's son said, "the *izinduna* in charge of the two *impi*s to the south (abeNguni and amaMpondo) were Mdhlaka ka Ncidi and Klwana ka Ngqengelele. Ngomane ka Mqomboli was also an *induna*, but he would appear not to have gone." Mkehlengana, 217. Ngidi, 55–56, provided miscellaneous details of the expedition.
49 Dinya in interview of Mcotoyi ka Mnini, 55.
50 Ibid, 55.
51 Dinya, 95.
52 Mcotoyi, 66.
53 Ibid. Mkehlengana added the information that his father had gone on the two southern campaigns, and "[h]e also started forth on the *Kukulela ngoqo impi* to the uBalule but was injured unexpectedly in the foot (right foot). This was reported to Tshaka, so he told him to come back, which he did." Melapi ka Magaye, a son of Shaka's subordinate ally the AmaCele chief during Shaka's reign and was also present on the second AmaMpondo campaign, said, "Tshaka gave orders to the Pondo *impi* south of the Mzimkulu and directed it to go to the north when he was there [with the *impi* in the south]. When he was assassinated he was said to have *bunguleka*'d, i.e. gone mad by giving such an order." Melapi ka Magaye, 83.
54 Mcotoyi, *JSA* v. III, 55. Elsewhere in the interview he said, "When Nandi died, later on, a further *impi*, known as the *ihlambo* one, was sent to attack Faku – [a chief who was] previously unknown [to Shaka]." Mcotoyi, 66.
55 Fynn, *Diary*, 149, 153.

56 *JSA*, File 17, KCM 23465.
57 Fynn, *Diary*, 149, 153.
58 Ibid, 154–155.
59 These reported comments became the basis for subsequent myths about Shaka.
60 Makewu, 163.
61 Dinya, 95.
62 Ibid.
63 Makewu, *JSA*, v. II, 163.
64 Mtshapi, *JSA*, v. IV, 80–81.
65 Makewu, 163.
66 Mtshapi, 80–81.
67 Madikane, *JSA*, v. II, 61. Webb and Wright, *JSA* v. II, 67 n. 83 and n. 84, note that the "Mphambanyoni river flows into the sea south of the Mkhomazi near present-day Scottburgh," and the "Chunu lived north of the Thukela near its confluence with the Mzinyathi.... The uPhasiwe or Karkloof range of hills is to the north-west of Pietermaritzburg; the amaNkamane hills are northwest or Pomeroy."
68 The evidence is somewhat ambiguous because in another interview, "Dinya says Hlangabeza and his people were absent from Tshaka's Pondo *impi*. From this it is clear the man intended eloping [absconding]. He did so. On the way back Tshaka ordered the *kukulela ngoqo impi*, not knowing of Hlangabeza's flight. Hlangabeza was chief of the amaNtshali tribe. The *impi* did not specially go after him, but it was ordered to overtake him and not allow him to reach Sotshangana, in which direction he was making." Dinya in interview of Mcotoyi, 56.
69 Dinya, 95.
70 Mayinga ka Mbekuzana, *JSA*, v. II, 249–250. He named warriors who had gone on the Balule impi: "Dhlemula and others from Natal – Jadilili ka Pudwa ka Ngozi ka Nyanise, Mrabula ka Msutu, Ndandane ka Mantiyane of the Mapumulo people, Ngungwini ka Mnganu, Funwayo da Mpopomo, Mruyi (alias Kofiyana) ka Mbengana, Sipongo ka – [sic] who was in charge of the Isihlenga company (*viyo*), i.e. Kam Kengi's, and others – went on this campaign to Balule, i.e. from Port Natal, from Esihlengeni (Kamu Kengi's kraal), Esinyameni (Febana's kraal). Europeans did not go on the Balule campaign. Ndandane was the *induna* of the two *amaviyo* [companies of warriors] sent from Port Natal to Balule." Maziyana, *JSA*, v. II, 297.
71 Ngidi, 75.
72 Madikane, 61, 1903, 1905.
73 Melapi, 83.
74 Mtshapi, 80–81.
75 Melapi, 88.
76 Ngidi, 75.
77 Mayinga, 249–250, 1905. He provides some details about the fate of individuals on this *impi*.
78 Melapi, 88.
79 Makewu, 163.
80 Madikane ka Mlomowetole, 61.

81 Mcotoyi ka Mnini, 66.
82 Mahaya ka Nongqabana, *JSA*, v. II, 111. He named them: "Myeki, chief of the Jali, Mbobo, and Mendu (my maternal uncle) went on to Tshaka."
83 Mbovu ka Mtshumayeli, 31.
84 Mcotoyi ka Mnini, 56.
85 For examples, see Mkehlengana ka Zulu, 217; Maziyana, 294; Ndukwana (1900), 291; Makewu, 163; Jantshi, 187. For related testimony, see Socwatsha in interview of Maziyana, 294; Ngidi, 43; Lunguza, 307; Dinya ka Zokozwayo, 95.
86 Fynn, *Diary*, 156–157. In several ways, Fynn's account diverges from those of the oral traditions collected by Stuart.
87 Ndukwana, 291, September 22, 1900.
88 Jantshi, 187.
89 Ibid. Jantshi's tale ends here with his direct reassertion of both the accuracy of his testimony, including an explicit statement of its sources and of the limits of his knowledge of events that fell beyond either what his father had witnessed, or what his father had been directly told. This narrative when told to Stuart in 1903 was not an imaginative oral "tradition" that had been subject to purposeful manipulation over several generations but was a memory of events fully believed by its transmitter Jantshi and his source, Nongila.
90 Ibid, 194.
91 Dinya, 95.
92 Socwatsha ka Papu, KCL James Stuart Collection File 58 (AA) NB [Notebook] 23, KCM 24220, 11. Interview of October 26, 1913, 34 Loop St., marked "Socwatsha ka Papu speaks." The notes begin "Matingwana ka Ndingizana, wa kwa Hlope, told me the following." He identified Matingwana's descendants: "Mantingwane died in Ndwedwe district at Umdhloti river – in about 1888 (Zululand disturbance). His sons living Mtomboli; Lokoza, and 'Pama (same age as myself [Socwatsha ka Papu] Sikova (in Zululand). The first three are at Ndwedwe, also another in Masende. They live in ground occupied by Tshevu *induna* (headman) of Chief Lokotwayo of Pinetown Office."
93 Ibid.
94 Ibid.
95 Ibid.
96 Ibid, 21. Stuart recorded Socwatsha's account based on the information he had heard from Matingwana in several places in his notebooks.
97 Maziyana also said that this referred to the commonly told report of Shaka killing a pregnant woman. Maziyana, 295, and KCL, James Stuart Collection File 58 (AA) NB [Notebook] 23 KCM 24220, 21, interview notes of James Stuart 1913. Bracketed translations mine; parenthetical reference to the Balule campaign written by Stuart in original.
98 Socwatsha, KCL James Stuart Collection File 40 (xxii) KCM 23776, 4. Per Socwatsha March 19, 1910, interview notes of James Stuart, 1910.
99 Socwatsha, KCL James Stuart Collection File 58 (AA), NB [Notebook] 23, KCM 24220. Interview notes of James Stuart, 1913.
100 Ngidi, 43.

101 Dinya, 95. Of course, because he said locusts *and* white, he obviously did not equate white people *with* locusts. Locusts may have been a literal or a metaphorical reference to the various AmaZulu-related peoples who had taken refuge under or near Fynn and the other European traders in Natal. Locusts generally appear following droughts because of their life cycle, and there had been several years of drought across the region during the era of Shaka's reign. So, predicting the arrival of locusts was as easy, or difficult, as predicting the arrival of rain. The inclusion of locusts in a supposed prophecy may have sounded convincing but could have applied to any decade of the nineteenth century.

102 Lunguza, 307. Bracketed note written by Stuart in original. It did not take a prophet to associate Europeans with the sea; in Shaka's era, it was widely known that with few exceptions, white people arrived in KwaZulu and Natal via the sea; overland journeys were still almost unknown because they were so dangerous for both Africans and Europeans. Even Sotobe's mission went to the eastern Cape Colony on a European ship. That Shaka felt threatened by Europeans' guns and was suspicious of European intentions was also widely known.

103 Fynn, *Diary*, 156–157.

104 Socwatsha, KCL James Stuart Collection File 58 (AA), NB [Notebook] 23, KCM 24220, 21. Interview notes of James Stuart, 1913.

105 Fynn, *Diary*, 157–158.

106 Socwatsha told Stuart, "After Tshaka's death Matingwane became Dingana's inceku – He died about 2 years ago [1903]." Socwatsha ka Papu, KCL, James Stuart Collection File 58 (AA), NB [Notebook] 23, KCM 24220, 21. Interview notes of James Stuart 1913.

107 Ngidi, 43, 64.

108 Socwatsha, KCL, James Stuart Collection File 58 (AA), NB [Notebook] 23, KCM 24220, 21. Interview notes of James Stuart 1913.

109 Ngidi, 43, 64.

110 Fynn, *Diary*, 157–158.

Chapter 12

1 Ndukwana in interview of Jantshi, *JSA*, v. IV, 100; Lunguza, 312.

2 Ndukwana, 291–292, September 22, 1900.

3 Ndukwana, 346; Mkehlengana, 217. Shaka's aunt Mnkabayi, like royal men as well as other royal women, did not have autonomous decision-making powers on this occasion, and the decision to name Dingane as heir and chief was made by the senior men of the kingdom. Nevertheless, her strong influence and the respect in which she was held is evident in their consultation with her. They agreed with her decision, endorsed it, and implemented it because her reasoning was in accord with long-standing and widely accepted customary standards of determining the succession.

4 Socwatsha ka Papu, KCL, James Stuart Collection File 58 (AA), NB [Notebook] 23, KCM 24220, 12. Interview notes of James Stuart, 1913.

5 Ndukwana, 291–292; Ndukwana in interview of Jantshi, 194.

6 Socwatsha in interview of Mkehlengana, *JSA*, v. III, 217; Socwatsha, KCL, James Stuart Collection File 58 (AA), NB [Notebook] 23, KCM 24220, 12–13. Interview notes of James Stuart, 1913.
7 Socwatsha, 13. This corresponds to Mkehlengana's narrative of these events.
8 Ndukwana, 291–292.
9 Ibid, 346.
10 Ibid, 292.
11 Mkehlengana, *JSA*, v. III, 217; Ndukwana, 291–292.
12 Mayinga, *JSA*, v. II, 254; Fynn, *Diary*, 158.
13 Melapi, *JSA*, v. III, 74; Socwatsha, KCL, James Stuart Collection File 58 (AA), NB [Notebook] 23, KCM 24220, 20. Interview notes of James Stuart, 1913. Jantshi, 191; Ndukwana in interview of Jantshi, 194; Mmemi, *JSA*, v. III, 266; Baleka, *JSA*, v. I, 6.
14 Note of James Stuart in interview notes of Ndhlovu, 217. Webb and Wright, 236 n.62, explain: "*Umsizi* means powdered medicines. At a certain point in the umkhosi ceremonies, the chief or king, daubed with *umsizi*, was required to spend the night in a specially prepared hut in the *isigodlo*. There he would be attended by a selected wife, or a girl from the *isigodlo*, with whom he might have [sexual] intercourse. A child born of this connection was held to be of inferior rank in the chiefly house."
15 MmemikaNguluzane in *JSA*, v. III, p. 266.
16 Baleka, 6. Mpande, a half brother who had been favored and trusted, evidently rightly, by Shaka, remained as a powerful and rising member of the royal family. In 1839, Dingane would regret that he had allowed him to live eleven years earlier.
17 Baleka, 5.
18 Ngidi, *JSA*, v. V, 90.
19 Magidi, *JSA*, v. II, 80. Webb and Wright cite Bryant, *Olden Times*, 107. Reference to Dingane's killing of Nzwakele of the Dube people in Webb and Wright, *JSA*, v. II, 82 n.16.
20 Mkebeni, *JSA*, v. III, 205.
21 Ndhlovu, *JSA*, v. IV, 217, interviewed on March 22, 1903, and May 19, 1903.
22 Ngidi, 90.
23 Ndhlovu, 217; Magidi, *JSA*, v. II, 80. Webb and Wright cite Bryant, *Olden Times*, 107. Reference to Dingane's killing of Nzwakele of the Dube people in Webb and Wright, *JSA*, v. II, 82 n.16.
24 Ndhlovu, 217.
25 Ngidi, 90.
26 Ibid, 90; Ndukwana, 301. Ndukwana told Stuart, "Mbuyazwe or Mbuyazi – both pronunciations common. N. says Mbuyazwe (and he was an isiGqoza) was fathered for Tshaka. This was a custom among kings, to father children for their brothers." Ndukwana also specified, "Dingana had no children, nor did Tshaka." When Mpande drove Dingane from KwaZulu and assumed the chieftaincy in 1840, his senior son was Cetwayo, who became his presumed heir. But both Mbuyazi and Cetwayo built their own factions of supporters, and the contest for the inheritance became a battle while Mpande held the position himself. Ndukwana explained, "Mpande, when questioned, said that

Cetshwayo was his chief son, as a man (*ngingumuntu*), but the chief of the land was Mbuyazwe."

27 For this period of AmaZulu history, see Peter Colenbrander, "The Zulu Kingdom, 1828–79," in Duminy and Guest, 83–115. For the later history of the AmaZulu, see Jeff Guy, *The Destruction of the Zulu Kingdom: The Civil War in Zululand, 1879–1884* (London: Longman, 1979, and Johannesburg: Ravan Press, 1982); Andrew Duminy and Charles Ballard, eds., *The Anglo-Zulu War: New Perspectives* (Pietermaritzburg: University of Natal Press, 1981); John Laband and Paul Thompson, eds., *Kingdom and Colony at War* (Pietermaritzburg: University of Natal Press and Cape Town: N & S Press, 1990); and Nicholas Cope, *To Bind the Nation: Solomon kaDinizulu and Zulu Nationalism 1913–1933* (Pietermaritzburg: University of Natal Press, 1993).

28 "Copy of a Despatch from Major General Bourke to Viscount Goderich. Government House, Cape Town, October 15th 1827," *JSA*, File 17, KCM 23465. "Extracts of letters and information collected by Mr James Stuart," 551. For the events associated with the battle of Lithakong, see Eldredge, "Sources of Conflict," and the evidence found in George Thompson, *Travels and Adventures in Southern Africa* in Vernon S. Forbes, ed. (Cape Town: The Van Riebeeck Society, 1967), v. I, 79–121. For additional analysis of the AmaNgwane under Matiwane, see Eldredge, "Migration, Conflict and Leadership in Early Nineteenth Century South Africa: The Case of Matiwane" in Robert W. Harms, et al., *Paths Toward the Past: African Historical Essays in Honor of Jan Vansina* (Atlanta: African Studies Association, 1994), 39–75.

29 "Copy of a Despatch from Sir George Murray to Sir G.L. Cole." No date given here, but it was written in response to the Bourke despatch of October 1827. *JSA*, File 17, KCM 23465. "Extracts of letters and information collected by Mr James Stuart," 553.

30 "Copy of a Despatch from Major General Bourke to Mr. Secretary Huskisson. Government House, Cape Town, June 29th, 1828," *JSA*, File 17, KCM 23465. "Extracts of letters and information collected by Mr James Stuart," 553.

31 "Copy of a Despatch from Major General Bourke to Mr Secretary Huskisson. Government House, Cape Town, August 1st 1828," *JSA*, File 17, KCM 23465. "Extracts of letters and information collected by Mr James Stuart."

32 "Copy of a Despatch from Major-General Bourke to Mr Secretary Huskisson. Government House, Cape Town, 26th August 1828," *JSA*, File 17, KCM 23465, 555. This letter contained false information: "This declaration has been the more necessary, as I have reason to believe the English at Port Natal have induced Chaca to suppose that his invasion of Caffreland would be favoured by the Colonial Government. On the late plundering expedition the Zoola leaders endeavoured to impress the tribes they attacked with this belief; and the presence in their ranks of an Englishman of the name of Fynn, and some other persons, either English or bastard Hottentots, armed with muskets, seemed to prove the assertion."

33 "Copy of a Despatch from Sir G.L. Cole to Sir George Murray. Government House Cape Town, 31st January 1829," *JSA*, File 17, KCM 23465.

34 Ibid, 305.

35 Fynn, *Diary*, 157.
36 "Copy of a Despatch from Sir G.L. Cole to Sir George Murray. Government House Cape Town, 31st January 1829." British Museum, Newspaper Room, Accounts and Papers (3), 1835 XXXIX. Press Mark 39 in *JSA*, File 17, KCM 23465, 306.
37 Ibid, 565 and 7/302. The rumors included reports that Shaka had ordered the killing of 2,000 of the wives after the defeat of the army that had gone north on the Balule campaign. It included the information that about 8,000 AmaZulu troops had been killed in the engagement, information that is not corroborated or confirmed by later reports or other sources.
38 Ibid, 7/302.
39 "Death of Chaka," *South African Commercial Advertiser* no. 169, January 24, 1829" *JSA*, File 17, KCM 23465, Extract III, 170–171. Stuart identified the writer as Henry Francis Fynn's father.
40 "Copy of a Despatch from Sir G.L. Cole to Sir George Murray. Government House Cape Town, 31st January 1829," *JSA*, File 17, KCM 23465, 306.
41 Ibid, 565.
42 Jantshi, 195–197.
43 The most famous revolt against Dingane upon his succession was led by the AbaQwabe chief Nqetho.
44 Elizabeth A. Eldredge, "Dingane: Violence and the Consolidation of Power in the Zulu Kingdom, 1828–1831," Paper presented at the Annual Meeting of the African Studies Association, Baltimore, Maryland, November 23, 2013.
45 These events are recounted by Fynn, *Diary*, 162–173; Maziyana ka Mahlabeni, 272, 279; Mbovu ka Mtshumayeli, 37; Ngidi, 63–64, 89–90; *South African Commercial Advertiser*, no. 258, December 2, 1829; no. 322; no. 325, July 24, 1830.
46 Fynn, *Diary*, 167.
47 Melapi, 82.
48 Dinya, 105.
49 Ibid, 106.
50 Maziyana, 293.
51 Ndukwana, 327.
52 Ibid, 360.
53 Baleni, 19.
54 Shepstone, 419.
55 Excerpt "[f]rom a fragmentary paper written by Mr. Fynn...after he had quitted it for the Eastern frontier of the Cape Colony (1834) and before the advent of the Boers (1838)," in John Bird, *The Annals of Natal, 1495 to 1845* (Pietermaritzburg: P. Davis & Sons, 1888, reprinted by Kessinger Publishing Legacy Reprints), v. I, 75.
56 Fynn, *Diary*, 175. In an unusual incident, a Portuguese slaver, the *African Adventurer*, bound for Sofala became lost at sea and came ashore at Port Natal (Durban) during which time sixty slaves were said to have been thrown overboard and others to have died of thirst. Dingane provided guides to return them all to Delagoa Bay but also said that he disliked the Portuguese. The anonymous writer of this report stated that the Port Natal Europeans would

have preferred to detain the slaves [to free them from the slavers] but because the Port Natal residents did not know whether the port was officially British by law (which it was not at the time), they determined that they did not have the authority to do so. *South African Commercial Advertiser*, no. 357, November 13, 1830, where part of a letter from Port Natal, June 21, 1830, sent from a correspondent in Graham's Town, was printed. The Portuguese later sent thanks to Fynn, who was evidently involved in nursing the survivors back to health but may or may not have been this correspondent; his brother William accompanied the party from Port Natal to Dingane's capital and is probably the author. Dingane began to turn his attention toward the reported wealth of the Portuguese at Maputo Bay. In 1833, he eventually sent troops there in an effort to impose trade terms with the Portuguese governor at Lourenço Marques; later that year he had a Zulu *impi* attack the Portuguese fort and kill the governor.

57 Nathaniel Isaacs, "Journal," *South African Commercial Advertiser*, beginning with no. 520, June 6, 1832, copied by James Stuart, typescripts, Extract 1, 89–119 and Extract 3, 120–132. Isaacs also wrote that "under the present Monarch Dingaan they have lost their fame as warriors, and say they do not intend to take up arms again unless to act on the defensive," and he expected the ivory trade would prosper.

58 Ibid.

59 Shaka had previously sent Cane to make overtures to colonial officials in the Cape Colony but had arrived at Cape Town on October 5, 1828, and delivered the message from Shaka, not yet knowing of his death a week before. "Copy of a Despatch from Sir G.L. Cole to Sir George Murray. Government House Cape Town, January 31, 1829," KCL, *JSA*, File 17, KCM 23465, 305. Cane had worked for Farewell and was present but fled and hid successfully when Farewell and his party were killed by Nqetho's men when they were returning to Port Natal overland from the Cape Colony. Fynn, *Diary*, 169–170.

60 "Letter from the Civil Commissioner of Albany and Somerset, D. Campbell, to the Hon. Lieutenant-Colonel John Bell, Secretary to Government, dated 26th November 1830" in John Bird, *The Annals of Natal, 1495 to 1845* (Pietermaritzburg: P. Davis & Sons, 1888, reprinted by Kessinger Publishing Legacy Reprints), v. I, 196–197.

61 Ibid.

62 Ibid.

63 Ibid.

64 Editor (Stuart and Malcolm), Fynn, *Diary*, 188, 190.

65 Fynn, *Diary*, 192–193.

66 Details of the interactions and communications between Fynn, Dingane, and others that convinced Fynn and the other traders that they were at risk for their lives are provided at length in Fynn, *Diary*, 195–205.

67 Fynn's earlier letter explaining his actions never reached the Cape Colony for unknown reasons. Later he wrote to defend his actions publicly in letters published in the *Grahamstown Journal*. "Extract of a letter from Mr. H. Fynn of Port Natal, Feb 21st 1832," *South African Commercial Advertiser*, no. 39,

September 21, 1832. In the letter, Fynn responded to disparaging letters about him that had been printed previously in the *Grahamstown Journal* concerning recent events and his decision, based on his judgment of an imminent threat, to leave Port Natal. "Letter of Henry F. Fynn to the *Grahams Town Journal (GTJ)* with "Port Natal, Ingoma, Sept 1832, published Nov. 29th 1832." Fynn proceeded to justify his own actions in light of scurrilous attacks against him that other traders including the Cawoods had made. The *GTJ* then published a paragraph supportive of Fynn and calling for the extension of British occupation to Port Natal for humanitarian and trade purposes; the paragraph refers to "the atrocious and hitherto inexplicable politics of the Zoolo Chief," "this systematic extermination of the tribes about Natal," and "the crooked policy of the Zoolo Chief, etc.," *Grahamstown Journal*, November 29, 1832. *GTJ* publications of July 27, 1832, no. 31, and August 23, 1832, no. 32, refer to the events later explained in the Fynn letter of September 1832 published in the *GTJ*, November 29, 1832. Fynn's letter further calls for official presence in Natal and includes references to atrocities committed by Dingane. A letter from John Cane dated July 4, 1832, also extracted for publication, explains the false report to Dingane that had alarmed the king (i.e., that Cane was bringing a commando to attack him from the Colony). Cane also explained the killing of the person who had disseminated the false rumor and denied a charge that he and Fynn had killed seventy or eighty Africans.

68 Fynn, *Diary*, 206–207. Fynn's followers were African, including more than one wife, and his mixed-race children.

69 In 1832, he assisted Dr. Andrew Smith in his journey to visit Dingane as a representative of the Cape Colony. Fynn returned to the British colony of Natal after seventeen years away and lived the rest of his life, 1859–1861, there.

70 *Grahamstown Journal*, no. 57, January 24, 1833. The Cawoods indicated they were taking their goods first to the AmaMpondo country, from where they planned to return to the colony; their safe arrival, with loads of ivory, was reported July 11, 1833. KCL File 17, no.81, KCM 23465.

71 *South African Commercial Advertiser (SACA)*, no. 256, November 25, 1829; no. 274, January 27, 1830; no. 280, February 17, 1830. Also *Grahamstown Journal*, June 1, 1832.

72 "Copy of a Despatch from Sir G.L. Cole to Sir George Murray. Government House Cape Town, 31st January 1829," *JSA*, File 17, KCM 23465, 306; Fynn, letter to the *Grahamstown Journal*, dated August 1832 and published September 21, 1832, in Fynn, *Diary*, 214–215.

73 This is the thesis of Okoye, "Dingane, A Reappraisal," 223.

74 In making his argument that Fynn and his people were never at risk, Okoye, 226, omits all reference to these deaths, only noting that Fynn arrived at Bunting with seventy of his dependents after they fled in May 1831. Okoye, 228, also makes the false claim that all of Fynn's cattle were returned. On the contrary, when Dingane put on trial those chiefs who had taken Fynn's cattle, they were tried not for that reason but because of the three hundred cattle taken, only thirty were turned over to Dingane. They were thus being tried for

the theft of cattle that were seen by the king to belong rightfully to him. Fynn, *Diary*, 217.
75 "Letter of Henry Francis Fynn to *Grahamstown Journal*, written August 1832, published 21st September, 1832," in Fynn, *Diary*, 213–215.
76 Fynn, 1852 Native Commission testimony, "Mr. Fynn's Evidence," *The Natal Mercury*, April 14, 1853.
77 Fynn *Diary*, 19.
78 Ibid.
79 Elizabeth A. Eldredge, "Shaka's Military Expeditions: Survival and Mortality from Shaka's Impis" in Paul S. Landau, ed., *The Power of Doubt: Essays in Honor of David Henige* (Madison: Parallel Press/University of Wisconsin-Madison Libraries, 2011), 209–239.
80 Ibid.
81 Ibid.
82 Ibid.
83 John Wright, "Reconstituting Shaka Zulu for the Twenty-First Century," *Southern African Humanities*, 18, no. 2 (December 2006), 139–153.

Appendix

1 Volume and page numbers refer to Webb and Wright, *The James Stuart Archive of Recorded Oral Evidence*, vols. I–V. Unpublished interviews are cited by their KCL references. The interview notes of James Stuart, both published by Webb and Wright and unpublished, are the source for the information compiled in this appendix. This list includes only those interviewees of James Stuart who are cited in this book.

Bibliography

Archives

Killie Campbell Library, Durban, South Africa
  James Stuart Collection
    James Stuart's original interview notes in notebooks; notebooks with Stuart's notes on various subjects; Stuart's unpublished essays.
  Fynn Collection
    Henry Francis Fynn Papers
    The Fynn Letters, KCM typescripts; originals in the KwaZulu-Natal Provincial Archives

KwaZulu-Natal Provincial Archives, Pietermaritzburg, South Africa
  Henry Francis Fynn Papers
  Shepstone Papers

Lesotho Evangelical Church (Paris Evangelical Missionary Society) Archives, Morija, Lesotho
  Simeon Feko, "Bophelo ba Simeon Feko ke Moholo" (Life of Simeon Feko, Sr.), unpublished manuscript.

Books and Articles

Arbousset, Thomas, *Missionary Excursion into the Blue Mountains being an account of King Moshoeshoe's Expedition from Thaba Bosiu to the Sources of the Malibamatso River in the Year 1840*, edited and translated, with an introduction and notes by David Ambrose and Albert Brutsch

(Morija: Morija Archives and Nairobi: Centre de Recherche, Mandeleo House, 1991).
Atkins, Keletso E., *The Moon is Dead! Give Us Our Money! The Cultural Origins of an African Work Ethic, Natal, South Africa, 1843–1900* (Portsmouth, NH: Heinemann, 1993).
Ballard, Charles, "Traders, Trekkers and Colonists," in" in Andrew Duminy and Bill Guest, eds., *Natal and Zululand from Earliest Times to 1910: A New History* (Pietermaritzburg: University of Natal Press and Shuter & Shooter Ltd., 1989), 116–145.
Bird, John, *The Annals of Natal*, 2 vols. (Pietermaritzburg: P. Davis and Sons, 1888, reprinted by Kessinger Publishing's Legacy Reprints, n.d.).
Bjerk, Paul K., "They Poured Themselves into the Milk: Zulu Political Philosophy under Shaka," *Journal of African History*, 47, no. 1 (2006), 1–19.
Bonner, Philip, *Kings, Commoners and Concessionaires: The Evolution and Dissolution of the Nineteenth-Century Swazi State* (Cambridge University Press, 1983).
Bryant, A.T., *A History of the Zulu and Neighbouring Tribes* (Cape Town: C. Struik, Africana Specialist and Publisher, 1964).
Olden Times in Zululand and Natal (London: Longmans, Green 1929).
A Zulu-English Dictionary (Mariannhill Mission Press, 1905).
The Zulu People as They Were Before the White Man Came (Pietermaritzburg: Shuter and Shooter, 1949).
Buthelezi, Mbongiseni, "The Empire Talks Back: Re-examining the Legacies of Shaka and Zulu Power in Post-apartheid South Africa," in" in Benedict Carton, John Laband, and Jabulani Sithole, eds., *Zulu Identities: Being Zulu, Past and Present* (New York: Columbia University Press, 2009), 23–34.
Cape of Good Hope. *Report and Proceedings, with Appendices, of the Government Commission on Native Law and Customs*, G.4.-'83, Cape Town: W. A. Richards and Sons, Government Printers, 1883(January), 415–426.
Carton, Benedict, "Fount of Deep Culture: Legacies of the *James Stuart Archive* in South African Historiography," *History in Africa*, 30 (2003), 87–106.
"Zuluness in the Post- and New-Worlds," in Benedict Carton, John Laband, and Jabulani Sithole, eds., *Zulu Identities: Being Zulu, Past and Present* (New York: Columbia University Press, 2009), 3–22.
Carton, Benedict, John Laband, and Jabulani Sithole, eds., *Zulu Identities: Being Zulu, Past and Present* (New York: Columbia University Press, 2009).
Cobbing, Julian, "The Mfecane as Alibi: Thoughts on Dithakong and Mbolompo," *Journal of African History*, 29 (1988), 487–519.
"A Tainted Well: The Objectives, Historial Fantasies, and Working Methods of James Stuart, with Counter-argument," *Journal of Natal and Zulu History*, 11 (1988), 115–54.
Colenbrander, Peter, "The Zulu Kingdom, 1828–79," in Andrew Duminy and Bill Guest, eds., *Natal and Zululand from Earliest Times to 1910: A New History* (Pietermaritzburg: University of Natal Press and Shuter & Shooter Ltd., 1989), 83–115.
Comaroff, John L. and Jean, *Ethnicity, Inc.* (University of Chicago Press, 2009).

Cope, Nicholas, *To Bind the Nation: Solomon kaDinuzulu and Zulu Nationalism, 1913–1933* (Pietermaritzburg: University of Natal Press, 1993).
Delius, Peter and Shula Marks, "Rethinking South Africa' Past: Essays on History and Archaeology," *Journal of Southern African Studies*, 38, no. 2 (June 2012), 247–255.
Duminy, Andrew and Charles Ballard, eds., *The Anglo-Zulu War: New Perspectives* Pietermaritzburg: University of Natal, 1981).
Duminy, Andrew and Bill Guest, eds., *Natal and Zululand from Earliest Times to 1910: A New History* (Pietermaritzburg: University of Natal Press and Shuter & Shooter Ltd., 1989)
Eldredge, Elizabeth A., "Delagoa Bay and the Hinterland in the Early Nineteenth Century: Politics, Trade, Slaves, and Slave Raiding" in Elizabeth A. Eldredge and Fred Morton, eds., *Slavery in South Africa: Captive Labor on the Dutch Frontier* (Boulder: Westview Press and Pietermaritzburg: University of Natal Press, 1994), 127–165.
"Migration, Conflict, and Leadership in early Nineteenth-Century South Africa: The Case of Matiwane" in Robert W. Harms, et. al, eds., *Paths Toward the Past: African Historical Essays in Honor of Jan Vansina* (Atlanta: African Studies Association Press, 1994), 39–75.
Power in Colonial Africa: Conflict and Discourse in Lesotho, 1870–1960 (Madison: University of Wisconsin Press, 2007)
"Shaka's Military Expeditions: Survival and Mortality from Shaka's Impis"in Paul S. Landau, ed., *The Power of Doubt: Essays in Honor of David Henige* (Madison: Parallel Press/University of Wisconsin-Madison Libraries, 2011), 209–239.
"Slave Raiding Across the Cape Frontier," in Elizabeth A. Eldredge and Fred Morton, eds., *Slavery in South Africa: Captive Labor on the Dutch Frontier* (Boulder: Westview Press and Pietermaritzburg: University of Natal Press, 1994), 93–126.
"Sources of Conflict in in Southern Africa, ca. 1800–30: The 'Mfecane' Reconsidered," *Journal of African History* vol. 33, no. 1 (1992), 1–35, reprinted in Carolyn Hamilton, ed., *The Mfecane Aftermath: Reconstructive Debates in Southern African History* (Johannesburg: Witwatersrand University Press, and Pietermaritzburg: University of Natal Press, 1995), 123–161.
A South African Kingdom: The Pursuit of Security in Nineteenth-Century Lesotho (Cambridge University Press, 1993).
"Women in Production: The Economic Role of Women in Nineteenth-Century Lesotho," *Signs: Journal of Women in Culture and Society*, special issue on "Women, Family, State, and Economy in Africa," 16, no. 4 (Summer 1991), 707–731.
Eldredge, Elizabeth A. and Fred Morton, eds., *Slavery in South Africa: Captive Labor on the Dutch Frontier* (Boulder: Westview Press and Pietermaritzburg: University of Natal Press, 1994).
Ellenberger, D. F., *History of the Basuto Ancient and Modern*, edited and translated by J. C. Macgregor (London, Caxton Pub., 1912).
Etherington, Norman, *The Great Treks: The Transformation of Southern Africa 1815–1854* (Harlow: Pearson Education Ltd., 2001).

"Putting the Mfecane Controversy into Historiographical Context" in Carolyn Hamilton, ed., *The Mfecane Aftermath: Reconstructive Debates in Southern African History* (Johannesburg: Witwatersrand University Press and Pietermaritzburg: University of Natal Press,1995), 13–19.

"A Tempest in a Teapot? Nineteenth-Century Contests for Land in South Africa's Caledon Valley and the Invention of the Mfecane," *Journal of African History*, 45 (2004), 203–219.

Fynn, Henry Francis, *The Diary of Henry Francis Fynn*, James Stuart and D. McK. Malcolm, eds. (Pietermaritzburg: Shuter & Shooter, 1986, first published 1951).

Gardiner, A. F., *Narrative of a Journey to the Zoolu Country in South Africa* (London: William Crofts, 1836, reprinted Cape Town: C. Struik Ltd., 1966).

Grey, Stephen, "Introduction," in Maclean, Charles Rawden, *The Natal Papers of "John Ross": Loss of the Brig Mary at Natal with Early Recollections of that Settlement and Among the Caffres*, edited by Stephen Gray (Durban: Killie Campbell Africana Library and Pietermaritzburg: University of Natal Press, 1992).

Grout, Lewis, *Zulu-land: Or Life Among the Zulu-Kafirs of Natal and Zulu-Land South Africa* (Philadelphia: Presbyterian Publication Committee, 1864).

Guy, Jeff, "Analysing Pre-capitalist Societies in Southern Africa," *Journal of Southern African Studies*, 14, 1 (1987), 29.

The Destruction of the Zulu Kingdom (London: Longman, 1979 and Johannesburg: Ravan Press, 1982).

"Ecological Factors in the Rise of Shaka and the Zulu Kingdom," in Shula Marks and Anthony Atmore, eds., *Economy and Society in Pre-Industrial South Africa* (London: Longman, 1980), 102–119.

"Gender Oppression in Southern Africa's Precapitalist Societies," in Cherryl Walker, ed., *Women and Gender in Southern Africa to 1945* (London: James Currey, 1990), 33–47.

Hall, Simon, "Identity and Political Centralisation in the Western Regions of Highveld, c. 1770–1830: An Archaeological Perspective," *Journal of Southern African Studies*, 38, no. 2 (June 2012), 301–318.

Hamilton, Carolyn, "Backstory, Biography, and the Life of the James Stuart Archive," *History in Africa*, 38 (2011) 319–341.

"'The Character and Objects of Shaka': A Reconsideration of the Making of Shaka as 'Mfecane' Motor," *Journal of African History*, 33, no.1 (1992), 37–63.

"Ideology and Oral Traditions: Listening to the Voices 'from Below'," *History in Africa*, 14 (1987), 67–86.

"Political Centralisation and the Making of Social Categories East of the Drakensberg in the Late Eighteenth and Early Nineteenth Centuries," *Journal of Southern African Studies*, 38, No. 2 (June 2012), 291–300.

Terrific Majesty (Cape Town: David Philip, 1998).

ed., *The Mfecane Aftermath: Reconstructive Debates in Southern African History* (Johannesburg: Witwatersrand University Press, and Pietermaritzburg: University of Natal Press, 1995).

Hamilton, Carolyn and John Wright, "The Making of the *AmaLala*: Ethnicity, Ideology and Relations of Subordination in a Precolonial Context," *South African Historical Journal*, 22: 1, 3–23.

Hamilton, Carolyn, and Simon Hall, "Reading Across the Divides: Commentary on the Political Co-Presence of Disparate identities in Two Regions of South Africa in the Late Eighteenth and Early Nineteenth Centuries," *Journal of Southern African Studies*, 38, no. 2 (June 2012), 281–290

Hamilton, Carolyn, Bernard K. Mbenga, and Robert Ross, eds., *The Cambridge History of South Africa*, vol. 1 (Cambridge University Press, 2010)

Hammond-Tooke, W. D., "Cattle Symbolism in Zulu Culture," in Benedict Carton, John Laband, and Jabulani Sithole, eds., *Zulu Identities: Being Zulu, Past and Present* (New York: Columbia University Press, 2009), 62–68.

Hanretta, Sean, "Women, Marginality and the Zulu State: Women's Institutions and Power in the Early Nineteenth Century" *Journal of African History*, 39, no. 3 (1998), 407–408.

Isaacs, Nathaniel, Travels and Adventures in Eastern Africa, Louis Herrman, ed. (Cape Town: The Van Riebeeck Society, 1956), vols. 1 and 2.

Kay, Stephen, *Travels and Researches in Caffraria* (New York: Harper & Brothers, 1834, reprinted Detroit: Negro History Press, n.d.).

King, Captain J. S. "Some account of Mr. Farewell's settlement at Port Natal, and of a visit to Chaka, King of the Zoolas, etc." in George Thompson, *Travels and Adventures in Southern Africa* (London, 1827, reprinted Cape Town: The Van Riebeeck Society, 1967), ii, 251.

Kinsman, Margaret, "'Beasts of Burden': The Subordination of Southern Tswana Women, ca. 1800–1840," *Journal of Southern African Studies*, 10, no. 1 (October 1983), 39–54.

Knight, Ian, *The Anatomy of the Zulu Army from Shaka to Cetshwayo 1818–1879* (London: Greenhill Books, 1995).

Krige, Eileen Jensen, *The Social System of the Zulus* (London: Longmans Green & Co., 1936, reprinted Pietermaritzburg: Shuter & Shooter, 1950).

Kuper, Adam, "The 'House' and Zulu Political Structure in the Nineteenth Century," *Journal of African History*, 24 (1993), 469–487.

Wives for Cattle: Bridewealth and Marriage in Southern Africa (London: Routledge & Kegan Paul, 1982).

Kunene, Mazizi, *Emperor Shaka the Great: A Zulu Epic* (London, Heineman, 1979).

Laband, John, "The Rise and Fall of the Zulu Kingdom," in Benedict Carton, John Laband, and Jabulani Sithole, eds., *Zulu Identities: Being Zulu, Past and Present* (New York: Columbia University Press, 2009), 87–96.

Laband, John and Paul Thompson, "The Reduction of Zululand, 1878–1904," in Andrew Duminy and Bill Guest, eds., *Natal and Zululand from Earliest Times to 1910: A New History* (Pietermaritzburg: University of Natal Press and Shuter & Shooter Ltd., 1989), 193–232.

Laband, John and Paul Thompson, eds., *Kingdom and Colony at War, The Anglo-Zulu War Series* (Pietermaritzburg: University of Natal Press and Cape Town: N & S Press, 1990).

Landau, Paul S., *Popular Politics in the History of South Africa, 1400–1948* (Cambridge University Press, 2010).
Litaba tsa Lilemo (Affairs/Events of the Years). (Morija: Sesuto Book Depot, 1931).
Maclean, Charles Rawden, *The Natal Papers of "John Ross": Loss of the Brig Mary at Natal with Early Recollections of that Settlement and Among the Caffres*, edited by Stephen Gray (Durban: Killie Campbell Africana Library and Pietermaritzburg: University of Natal Press, 1992).
MacKuertan, Graham, *The Cradle Days of Natal (1497–1845)* (London: Longmans, Green and Co., 1930).
Maggs, Tim, "The Iron Age Farming Communities" in Andrew Duminy and Bill Guest, eds., *Natal and Zululand from Earliest Times to 1910: A New History* (University of Natal Press and Shuter & Shooter, 1989), 28–48.
Marks, Shula, "The Traditions of the Natal 'Nguni': a Second Look at the Work of A.T. Bryant" in Leonard Thompson, ed., *African Societies in Southern Africa: Historical Studies* (London: Heinemann, 1969), 126–144.
Matsebula, J. S. M., *A History of Swaziland*, 2nd ed. (Cape Town: Longman Penguin, 1976).
Mazel, Aron, "The Stone Age Peoples of Natal" in Andrew Duminy and Bill Guest, eds., *Natal and Zululand from Earliest Times to 1910: A New History* (University of Natal Press and Shuter & Shooter, 1989), 1–27.
Mofolo, Thomas, *Chaka* (Morija, (Lesotho: Morija Sesuto Book Depot, 1926).
  Chaka, English translation. Translated from the original SeSotho by F.H. Dutton, International Institute of African Languages and Cultures (Oxford University Press, 1931).
  Chaka, translation by Daniel P. Kunene (London: Heinemann, 1981)
Moloja, "The story of the 'Fetcani horde,'" *Cape Quarterly Review*, 1 (1882), 267–275.
Nchakala, M., articles in *Leselinyana la Lesotho*, July 1, 15, 1891.
Ndlovu, Sifiso, "Zulu Nationalist Literary Representations of King Dingane" in Benedict Carton, John Laband, and Jabulani Sithole, eds., *Zulu Identities: Being Zulu, Past and Present* (New York: Columbia University Press, 2009), 97–110.
  "A Reassessment of Women's Power in the Zulu Kingdom" in Benedict Carton, John Laband, and Jabulani Sithole, eds., *Zulu Identities: Being Zulu, Past and Present* (New York: Columbia University Press, 2009), 111–121.
Omer-Cooper, J. D., *Zulu Aftermath: A Nineteenth-Century Revolution in Bantu Africa* (Evanston: Northwestern University Press, 1969).
Peires, Jeff, *The House of Phalo: A History of the Xhosa People in the Days of Their Independence* (Johannesburg: Raven Press, 1981).
Pridmore, Julie, "Henry Fynn and the Construction of Natal's History: Oral Recorder or Myth Maker?" in E. Sienaert, N. Bell and M. Lewis, eds., *Oral Tradition and Innovation: New Wine in Old Bottles?* (Durban: University of Natal Press, 1991).
  "H.F. Fynn and Oral Tradition: Debunking the Fynn Myths?" Edgard Sienaert, Meg Cowper-Lewis, and Nigel Bell, eds., *Oral Tradition and Its Transmission: The Many Forms of Message* (Durban: University of Natal, 1994), 188–199.

Rasmussen, R. K., *Migrant Kingdom: Mzilikazi's Ndebele in South Africa* (London: Rex Collings and Cape Town: David Philip, 1978).
Ritter, E. A., *Shaka Zulu* (London: Longman, 1955).
Samuelson, R. C., *Long, Long Ago* (Durban: Knox Printing & Publishing, 1929, republished Durban: T. W. Griggs, 1974).
Saunders, Christopher, "Pre-Cobbing Mfecane Historiography" in Carolyn Hamilton, ed., *The Mfecane Aftermath: Reconstructive Debates in Southern African History* (Johannesburg: Witwatersrand University Press and Pietermaritzburg: University of Natal Press, 1995), 21–34.
Scully, W.C., "Fragments of Native History," *The State*, September, October, and November 1909.
Shepstone, Theophilus, "*Historical Sketch of the Tribes anciently inhabiting the Colony of Natal – as at present bounded – and Zululand,*" *Cape of Good Hope, Report and Proceedings, with Appendices, of the Government Commission on Native Law and Customs, G.4.-'83* (Cape Town: W. A. Richards and Sons, Government Printers, 1883 (January), 415–426.
Shooter, Joseph, *The Kafirs of Natal and the Zulu Country* (E. Sanford, 1857, reprinted (New York: Negro Universities Press, 1969).
Smith, Alan K., "The Trade of Delagoa Bay as a factor in Nguni politics 1750–1835" in L. Thompson, ed., *African Societies in Southern Africa*, (London: Heinemann, 1969), 171–189.
  "Delagoa Bay and the Trade of South-Eastern Africa" in R. Gray and D. Birmingham, eds., *Pre-Colonial Trade in Central and Eastern Africa before 1900* (London, 1970), 265–289.
Stuart, James and D. McK. Malcolm, eds., *The Diary of Henry Francis Fynn, Compiled from original sources* (Pietermaritzburg: Shuter & Shooter, 1986, first published 1951).
Swanepoel, Natalie, Amanda Esterhuysen, and Philip Bonner, *Five Hundred years Rediscovered: Southern African Precedents and Prospects* (Johannesburg: Wits University Press, 2008).
Thompson, Leonard, "Co-operation and Conflict: the Zulu Kingdom and Natal," *The Oxford History of South Africa*, vol. 1 (New York and Oxford: Oxford University Press, 1969), 334–390.
  ed., *African Societies in Southern Africa: Historical Studies* (London: Heinemann, 1969).
Van Warmelo, N. J., ed. *History of Matiwane and the Amangwane Tribe as told by Msebenzi and supplemented by Archive Documents and other material by Van Warmelo* (Pretoria: Department of Native Affairs Ethnological Publications, 1938), vol. 7.
Webb, Colin de B. and John B. Wright, eds., *The James Stuart Archive of Recorded Oral Evidence Relating to the History of the Zulu and Neighbouring Peoples*, vols. I-V, (Pietermaritzburg: University of Natal Press and Durban: Killie Campbell Africana Library, 1976–2001).
Westcott, Michael and Carolyn Hamilton, *In the Tracks of the Swazi Past: A Historical Tour of the Ngwane and Ndwandwe Kingdoms* (Manzini: Macmillan Boleswa Publishers, 1992).

Whitelaw, Gavin, "A Brief Archaeology of Precolonial Farming in KwaZulu-Natal" in Benedict Carton, John Laband, and Jabulani Sithole, eds., *Zulu Identities: Being Zulu, Past and Present* (New York: Columbia University Press, 2009), 47–61.

Wilson, Monica and Leonard Thompson, eds., *Oxford History of South Africa* (Oxford: Oxford University Press, 1969), v. 1 .

Wright, John, "A T. Bryant and the 'Lala,'" *Journal of Southern African Studies*, 38, no. 2 (June 2012), 355–368.

"A.T. Bryant and 'The Wars of Shaka,'" *History in Africa*, 18 (1991), 409–425.

"Beyond the concept of the 'Zulu Explosion': comments on the Current Debate," in Carolyn Hamilton, ed., *The Mfecane Aftermath: Reconstructive Debates in Southern African History* (Johannesburg: Witwatersrand University Press, and Pietermaritzburg: University of Natal Press, 1995), 107–121.

"Beyond the 'Zulu Aftermath' Migration, Identities, Histories," *Journal of Natal and Zulu History*, 24, 25 (2006–2007), 1–36.

"Political Mythology and the Making of Natal's Mfecane," *Canadian Journal of African Studies*, 23, no. 2 (1989), 272–291.

"Politics, Ideology, and the Invention of the 'Nguni,'" Tom Lodge, ed., *Resistance and Ideology in Settler Societies* (Johannesburg: Ravan Press, 1986), 96–118.

"Political Transformations in the Thukela-Mzimkhulu Region in the Late Eighteenth and Early Nineteenth Centuries," in Carolyn Hamilton, ed., *The Mfecane Aftermath: Reconstructive Debates in Southern African History* (Johannesburg: Witwatersrand University Press, and Pietermaritzburg: University of Natal Press, 1995), 163–181.

"Reconstituting Shaka Zulu for the Twenty-First Century," *Southern African Humanities* 18, no. 2 (December 2006), 139–153.

"Rediscovering the Ndwandwe Kingdom" in Swanepoel, Natalie, Amanda Esterhuysen and Philip Bonner, eds., *Five Hundred Years Rediscovered: Southern African Precedents and Prospects* (Wits University Press, 2008), 217–238.

"Reflections on the Politics of Being 'Zulu,'" in Benedict Carton, John Laband, and Jabulani Sithole, eds., *Zulu Identities: Being Zulu, Past and Present* (New York: Columbia University Press, 2009), 35–43.

"Revisiting the Stereotype of Shaka's 'Devastations'" in Benedict Carton, John Laband, and Jabulani Sithole, eds., *Zulu Identities: Being Zulu, Past and Present* (New York: Columbia University Press, 2009), 69–81.

"The Thuli and Cele Paramountcies in the Coastlands of Natal, c. 1770–1820," *Southern African Humanities*, 21 (December 2009), 177–194.

"Turbulent Times: Political Transformations in the North and East, 1760s–1830s" in Carolyn Hamilton, Bernard K. Mbenga, and Robert Ross, eds., *The Cambridge History of South Africa*, vol. I (Cambridge: Cambridge University Press, 2010), 211–252.

Wright, John and Carolyn Hamilton, "Ethnicity and Political Change Before 1840" in Robert Morrell, ed., *Political Economy and Identities in KwaZulu-Natal: Historical and Social Perspectives* (Durban: Indicator Press, 1996), 15–32.

Wright, John and Carolyn Hamilton, "Traditions and Transformations: The Phongolo-Mzimkhulu Region in the Late Eighteenth and Early Nineteenth Centuries" in Andrew Duminy and Bill Guest, eds., *Natal and Zululand from Earliest Times to 1910: A New History* (Pietermaritzburg: University of Natal Press and Shuter & Shooter, 1989), 49–82.

Wylie, Dan, "Language and Assassination: Cultural Negations in White Writers' Portrayal of Shaka and the Zulu" in Carolyn Hamilton, ed., *The Mfecane Aftermath: Reconstructive Debates in Southern African History* (Johannesburg: Witwatersrand University Press, and Pietermaritzburg: University of Natal Press, 1995), 71–103.

Myth of Iron: Shaka in History (Pietermaritzburg: University of KwaZulu-Natal Press, 2006).

Savage Delight: White Myths of Shaka (Pietermaritzburg: University of Natal Press, 2000).

"White Myths of Shaka" in Benedict Carton, John Laband, and Jabulani Sithole, eds., *Zulu Identities: Being Zulu, Past and Present* (New York: Columbia University Press, 2009), 82–86.

Unpublished Sources

Eldredge, Elizabeth A., "Dingane: Violence and the Consolidation of Power in the Zulu Kingdom, 1828–1831," Paper presented at the Annual Meeting of the African Studies Association, Baltimore, Maryland, November 23, 2013.

"Deconstructing Ethnicity: Multicultural Origins of the AmaZulu Identity," Paper presented to the Annual Meeting of the African Studies Association, New Orleans, Louisiana, November 20, 2009.

Hamilton, Carolyn, "Ideology, Oral Traditions and the Struggle for Power in the Early Zulu Kingdom," M.A. Thesis, University of the Witwatersrand, 1985.

Hedges, David, "Trade and Politics in Southern Mozambique and Zululand in the Eighteenth and Nineteenth Centuries," Ph.D. dissertation, University of London, 1979.

Smith, Alan K. "The Struggle for Control of Southern Mocambique, 1720–1835," Ph.D. dissertation, University of California at Los Angeles, 1970.

Wright, John, "The Dynamics of Power and Conflict in the Late 18th and Early 19th Centuries: A Critical Reconstruction," Ph.D. dissertation, University of the Witwatersrand, Johannesburg, 1989.

Index

Zulu language words are indexed under their prefix, e.g., *isigodlo, isithakazelo*. Names of peoples and chiefdoms are indexed under the root name. For example, for AmaZulu, *see* Zulu, Ama- ; for BaSotho, *see* Sotho, Ba-.

AbaMbo, *see* Embo
abatakati, persons who use supernatural means to harm others, 36
Algoa Bay 257, 265 *See also* Port Elizabeth
Amabece Campaign, 122, 140–42, 144–5, 258, 262, 263
ancestors, importance of, 209–210, 21, 226, 230

Baleka ka Mpitikazi, 45, 50, 52, 55, 98, 190, 244, 246, 250, 298–9
Baleni (AmaNhlangwini chief), 101–2, 125, 126
Baleni ka Silwane, 50, 175, 286, 199
Balule Campaign, 121–2, 235, 251, 262, 263, 264, 265–9, 270, 283, 292
BaSotho, *see* Sotho, Ba-
Baleni, ema- (Beleni, ema-), 40, 50
Bantwana, 192, 195
Beje (AmaNtshali chief), 135, 165–8
Bele, Ama-, 88
Bhaca, Ama- (Baca, Ama-), 41, 86, 95, 96, 98, 99, 102–3, 123, 126, 140, 141, 181, 217, 221, 285
Bhibhi ka Nkobe (Bibi ka Nkobe), 72, 184, 200
Bryant, A.T., 8, 10, 14–15, 207, 223
Bhungane (Bungane) (AmaHlubi chief), 26, 29, 30–1, 32, 65, 91, 127, 174

Boers (Dutch-speaking farmers), 290
Bomvana, Ama- (segment of AbaTembu), 104, 151, 263
Bomvu, Ama-, 104
Bonner, Philip, 7
British colonial rule, 17, 18–19, 20, 23, 255, 260, 286, 287–8, 289
 colonial officials, 280–281
 troops and battle of Mbolompho, 130, 280–1
Bulawayo, 20, 123, 146, 155–6, 162, 187, 193, 195, 232, 235, 236, 245, 251
Bungane, *see* Bhungane
Buthelezi, Ama- (Butelezi, Ama-), 26, 33, 77, 85, 86, 88, 98, 214
butho (*ibutho*, pl. *amabutho*), *see* military regiments

Cane, John, 123, 157, 166, 265, 281–2, 284, 287–8
Cape Colony (Colony of the Cape of Good Hope), 17, 18, 25, 31, 141, 154, 242, 253–5, 258, 259, 261, 262, 264, 265, 280–84, 286, 287
Cape Town, 17, 19, 258, 287
cattle, 232, 238–9, 259, 262, 263, 264, 267, 284, 288, 295
ceremonies, 34, 36, 76, 91, 108, 121, 136, 161, 163, 169, 197, 200, 239, 249,

260, 262, 268, 274–5, 277–8, 337
  n.60, 366 n.160, 352 n.21, 382 n.14
 ancestral, 209–10, 212, 230
Cetwayo (Cetshwayo), 23, 279
Chase, J. Centlivres, 18,
chiefdom, definition of, 4, 5, 10, 28
chiefdoms, 1, 2, 4, 6, 26–41 See also names
  of individual chiefdoms
chiefs, 1, 2, 26–41, 97, 110, 111, 128, 133,
  134 See also inkosi
children, 80, 94, 100, 103, 120, 145,
  159–163, 189–90, 235, 248, 288, 291,
  292
Christians, 23
Chunu, Ama- (Cunu, Ama-), 39, 40, 77, 86,
  92, 97–100, 133, 164, 176, 181, 213,
  214, 222, 228, 229, 266–7
  See also Mcunu ka Malandela
Ci, Ama-, 27
CisKei region (west of the Kei River), 139,
  229
colonial rule, 1, 18–19
clan, 4, 231
Cube, Ama-, 8, 217

Daleni (eLangeni chief), 58, 59, 86
Delagoa Bay (Maputo Bay), 9, 17, 21, 28,
  32, 121, 135, 143, 151, 153, 154, 158,
  162, 168, 220, 254, 265, 268, 270,
  271, 287, 289, 290
descent, line of, 205, 206, 210
  clan, 205, 206
  exogamy, 210
  lineage, 205, 206
Dhlala, Ama-, 126
Dhlamini (Dlamini), ancestor of AmaSwazi,
  101, 215
Dhemula ka Mzucu, 121–22
dialects, 34, 214, 218, 219, 220–222, 223,
  227, 240 See also language; eZansi;
  Lala, Ama-; Ntungwa, Ama-
Dibandhlela (AmaThuli chief), 28, 110, 178
Dingane ka Senzangakhona, 3, 7, 23, 25,
  40, 41, 51, 55, 70, 79, 83, 104, 118,
  130, 134, 136, 158, 164, 168, 169–70,
  185, 186, 187, 198, 199–200, 234,
  237, 250, 263, 264, 267, 268, 270,
  271, 272, 273, 274, 276–7, 278, 279,
  283, 284–290, 294, 295, 296
Dingiswayo ka Jobe (AmaMthethwa chief),
  26–7, 29, 30, 31–3, 34, 35, 37, 52,

59–75, 78, 79, 87–90, 119, 127, 131,
  154, 174, 179, 180, 181, 291, 294–5
 sister of, 179
 Mawewe, brother of, 179
 Tana, brother of, 179
Dinizulu ka Cetshwayo, 255
Dinya ka Zokozwayo, 110–112, 227, 263,
  365, 266–7, 271, 272–3, 299–300
Diplomacy, 2, 3, 25, 288, 350 n.126
  See also Sotobe mission
Dole (AmaThuli chief), 27
Donda (AmaKhumalo chief), 70, 88
Dukuza, 112, 115, 118, 123, 148–9, 156,
  168, 193, 197–8, 217, 231, 235–6,
  241, 256, 262, 263, 264, 266, 269,
  274, 275
Dube, Ama-, 39, 61, 76, 77, 91, 111, 222,
  285
Dube (AmaQadi chief), 88
Dunge, Ama-, 126
Durban, 17, 118, 124, 139, 145
  See also Port Natal
Duze ka Mnengwa, 111–12

eLangeni (Langeni, Ma-; Langa, Ama-), 26,
  29, 33, 39, 41, 47, 49–50, 52, 54–5, 56,
  59, 77, 85–6, 124, 125–6, 181, 195,
  217, 218, 235, 237
Embo (eMbo; Mbo, Ama-), 11, 26, 86, 91,
  100, 106, 131–5, 160, 164–5, 207,
  217, 218, 221, 250, 295
Esiklebeni (Siklebi), 45, 47, 55–6, 234, 251
Etherington, Norman, 10
ethnic identity, 2, 6, 25, 205–230, 296
ethnicity, 2, 6, 25
Europeans in Natal, 143–4, 146, 150,
  289
Eyobutshinga Campaign, 169–70, 292
eZansi (abasezansi; Mzansi), 29, 34, 206,
  214, 219–220, 221

Faku (AmaMpondo chief), 96, 104, 139,
  140, 141–2, 145, 150–1, 157, 238,
  258, 260, 261, 262, 263, 264, 269,
  271, 278, 288
Farewell, Francis, 17, 19, 123, 124, 142,
  149, 150, 151, 152, 154, 156, 157,
  160, 168, 242, 255, 258, 282, 287,
  289, 352 n.11
Mrs. Farewell (wife), 20, 142
Fokeng, Ba-, 129

Index

Fynn, Henry Francis, 16, 17, 18–19, 32, 33, 45, 51, 74–5, 80, 89, 124, 143–7, 149–52, 156–7, 159–61, 163–4, 165–6, 168, 169, 191, 192–4, 197–8, 238, 241–2, 253–4, 258–62, 263, 264–5, 270, 273–4, 275, 282, 283, 284, 285, 287, 288–9, 290, 366 n.147, 385 n.67

Guqa ka Mendameli, 58
Gasa, Ama-, 39, 77
Gendeyana, 44, 50, 51, 187, 237
Godide ka Khondlo, 109–110
Godolozi ka Khondlo, 109–110
Godongwana, *see* Dingiswayo
Gqugqu ka Senzangakhona, 201, 235
Grahamstown, 282, 287
Grout, Lewis, 22
Gungunkhlovu, 287
Guy, Jeff, 9, 173

Hamilton, Carolyn, 8, 9, 10, 11, 14, 207–9, 223–7, 228, 229
Hanretta, Sean, 173
Hintsa (AmaXhosa chife), 139, 141–2, 260, 280, 282
Hlakoana, Ba-, 129
Hlangabeza ka Kondhlo (AmaNtshali chief), 87, 265, 267
Hlati ka Ncidi, 120
Hlengwa, Ama- (Nhlengwa, Ama-), 54, 137, 215, 220
Hlubi, Ama-, 26–7, 29, 30–1, 32, 39, 65, 77, 91, 124, 127–30, 160, 174, 179, 187, 215, 216 *See also* Bhungane; Mthimkulu; Mpangazitha; Iziyendane
Homesteads (*umuzi*, pl. *imizi*), 5, 35, 37–8, 60, 123, 187–8, 200, 209, 231, 233, 234–7, 373 n.24
  AbaQwabe, 35
  AmaCele, 110–11
  AmaChunu, 98–9
  AmaNdwandwe, 37–8
  AmaZulu, 39, 45, 55
  royal, 35

idlozi (pl. *amadlozi*), ancestor, ancestral spirit, x, 209–210
iHlambo Campaign, 177, 257–64
ikhanda, pl. *amakhanda*, regimental military barracks, x, 232
  See also military regiments

Imbuyeni, 39, 77
impi (pl. *izimpi*), military expedition, army, military force, xi, 2, 7 *See also* military campaigns
intelezi (pl. *izintelezi*), "medicine," concoctions used for harming enemies, 30
inceku (pl. *izinceku*), personal attendant, servant to a chief, xi
induna (pl. *izinduna*) person of authority, principal headman, commander, xi
inkosi (pl. *amakhosi*), chief, 4 *See also* chiefs
inyanga (pl. *izinyanga*), traditional "doctor," healer, xi
Isaacs, Nathaniel, 16, 18, 19, 152–3, 157, 166, 168, 170, 257, 287
isibongo (pl. *izibongo*), praises, xi, 210, 211
isigodlo (*isigodhlo*; pl. *izigodlo*), segregated women's quarters, xi, 36, 45, 47, 64, 72, 76, 107, 137, 174, 176, 188, 198–9, 236, 238
isikhulu (p. *izikhulu*), person of importance, great person, xi
isithakazelo (pl. *izithakazelo*), praise-greeting, xi, 205, 206, 211, 216
ivory trade, 20, 33, 151–2, 153, 156, 187, 287, 295
izangoma (diviners), 36
Iziyendane, regiment, 31, 114, 124, 126,k 131, 160, 187, 191, 349 n.100
  See also Hlubi, Ama-; military regiments

Jacob, also known as Hlambamanzi, 143, 149, 154–5, 254–5
Jali, Ama-, 27, 218
Jama ka Ndaba, father of Senzangakhona, 38–9, 40, 182, 183, 212, 213, 234, 257, 274
  genealogy of, 212 *See also* Zulu, Ama-, early history
Jantshi ka Nongila, 43, 47, 49, 50, 61, 70, 73, 79, 194, 199, 245, 256, 270–1, 300–301
Jobe, father of Dingiswayo, AmaMthethwa chief, 31
Jobe, AmaSithole chief, 104

Kambi ka Matshobana, 36
Kanyawo, Ama-, 218
Khala, Ama-, 218

Khondlo (Kondhlo), AbaQwabe chief, 26, 34, 35, 42, 107, 180, 185
Khumalo, Ama- (Kumalo, Ama-), 29, 39, 70, 77, 88, 135–6, 158, 169, 213, 214, 215, 216, 220 See also Donda; Mzilikazi; Ndebele, Ama-
King, James Saunders, (Captain King, Lieutenant King), 19, 20, 123, 142, 152, 154–5, 166, 168, 254–5, 256, 257, 265, 282, 287
kingdoms, 1, 2, 4–5, 6 see under individual kingdoms by name
Kanyawo, Ama-, 27
Kofiyana, 124
Komfiya ka Nogandaya, see Zulu ka Nogandaya
Komo, Ama-, 26, 123
Kondhlo ka Magalele, AmaNtshali chief, 87, 91
Kubung, Ba-, 130
Kuper, Adam, 5–6, 204
Kuyiwane, Ama-, 33
Kutshwayo, AmaDube chief, 91
Kuze, Ama-, 94–5, 101

Lala, Ama-, 86, 206, 207–8, 214, 215, 217–19, 220, 221–23, 224, 227, 229
land, 231–34
Landau, Paul, 10
Langa, Ama-, see eLangeni
Langalibalele, 179
Langeni, see eLangeni, Langa, Ama-
Langanzana, wife of Senzangakhona, 184, 237
Language, 222–23 See also dialects; eZansi; Lala, Ama-; Ntungwa, Ama-
Lazide, daughter of Zwide, wife of Sobhuza, mother of Mswazi, 180
lobola (ilobolo), bridewealth, x, 50, 51, 111, 174, 177, 189, 190, 239
Lubango, eLangeni chief, 86
Lucunge ka Nodinga, 117, 145
Lugubu ka Mangalizo, 80, 92, 302
Lukilimba (Lukwilimba), 122–3, 125
Lunguza ka Mpukane, 94, 96, 191, 273, 302
Luthuli, Ama- (Lutuli, Ama-), 27, 218

Mabonsa, AmaThuli chief, 121
Mabonsa ka Sidhlayi, 32, 191, 303
Macibise, female AmaBhaca chief, 95, 96, 99, 102, 181

Macingwane, AmaChunu chief, 86, 88, 92, 97–100, 126, 133, 164, 181, 213, 228
Maclean, Charles Rawden ("John Ross"), 2–21, 153–56, 168, 189–90, 231–2, 236, 242, 249, 251–2, 254–6, 294, 353 n.65
Madangala ka Zwide, 180
Madikane, AmaBhaca chief, 99, 126, 140, 141
Madikane ka Mlomowetole, 45, 47, 52, 56, 62, 71, 121, 263, 268, 303
Magaye ka Dibandhlela, AmaCele chief, 83, 84, 110–119, 124, 145, 146, 178, 231, 268, 284–5
Magidi ka Ngomane, 68, 73, 278, 304
Magidigidi ka Nobebe, 7, 97, 98, 220, 304
Magojela ka Mfanawendhlela, 162, 305
Mahaya ka Nongqabana, 125, 269, 305
Mahlangana ka Senzangakhona, 185
Mahlungwana, AmaBele (AmaNtuli) chief, 88
Majola, Ama-, 39, 77
Makanya, Ama-, 34–5, 36, 91, 110, 111, 114, 118
Makasane, AmaTembe chief (Delagoa/Maputo Bay region), 137
Makasane ka Jama, 40
Makedama ka Mbengi, brother of Nandi, 45, 52–8, 85–6, 124, 181, 251
Makewu, 255, 265, 269, 305–6
Makoba, Ama-, 39, 77, 88
Makuza ka Mkomoyi, 243–4, 306
Malandela ka Nnja, AmaZulu royal family progenitor, father of Zulu, 212, 213, 214, 216
Malcolm, D. McK., 17
Malusi, AmaNzumalo chief, 33, 76, 88
Mande ka Dibandhlela, 54, 91, 110–13, 115, 134
Mandhlakazi, Ama-, 56, 105
Mandhlakazi ka Ngini, 62, 90, 132, 192, 306
Mangati ka Godide, 44, 120, 306–7
'Mantathisi, female chief (regent) of BaTlokoa, 129
Mapita ka Sojisa, 182
Maputo Bay, see Delagoa Bay
Maqubana ka Senzangakhona, 70
Maseko, 137
Matingwana, 271–2, 274

Matiwane, AmaNgwane chief, 29, 30, 87, 98, 104, 119, 127–31, 169–70, 215, 280, 281, 290
Matubane, AmaThuli chief (regent), 110, 121–23, 125, 239, 258, 272, 285
Mawa ka Jama, 74, 186, 200, 236
Mawewe ka Jobe, 179
Mayinga ka Mbekuzana, 51, 62–3, 267, 268, 307–8
Maziyana ka Mahlabeni, 54, 168, 251, 263, 272, 274, 285, 308
Mbata, Ama-, 26, 33, 39, 62, 76, 77, 85, 88, 97, 213, 214, 215
Mbengi, eLangeni chief, 39, 42, 45, 53, 55, 86
Mbikwana ka Mbengi, 50, 55, 56, 58, 59, 145–6, 150
Mbili, Ama-, 26, 28, 114, 123–4
Mbo, *see* Embo
Mbokodo ka Sikulekile, 132, 162, 164–5, 308–9
Mbopha ka Zivalele (Mbopha ka Sitayi) (Mbopa), 149, 183, 197, 244, 250, 263, 266, 269, 270, 271, 273, 276
Mboto, Ama-, 126
Mbovu ka Mtshumayeli, 34, 36, 80, 309
Mbozamboza, 254, 261
Mbuyazi ka Mpande, 238, 279
Mcotoyi ka Mnini, 123, 264, 309–10
Mcunu ka Malandela, brother of Zulu ka Malandela, founding ancestor of AmaChunu, 222
Mcwana, 125, 126
Mdingi, 125, 126
Mdhlaka ka Ncidi, 87, 142, 183, 197, 263, 266, 267
Mdungazwe ka Senzangakhona, 56
Mendameli, 59
Menziwa ka Coko (Menziwa ka Xoko), 74, 183, 186
mfecane, 9
Mfihlo ka Senzangakhona, 56, 185, 199, 237, 271
Melapi ka Magaye, 112, 115–19, 145, 146, 148, 190–91, 251, 268, 310
Mfunda ka Khondlo, mother of Nandi, 42, 52, 185, 250–51
Mfundeko, 57, 58, 59
Mgabi ka Mapoloba, 55, 87
Mganga, Ama-, 27
Mgayi, 125

Mgazi, 180
Mgidhlana ka Mpande, 42, 311
Mgonambi, Ama-, 222
Mhlangana ka Senzangakhona, 40, 56, 70, 237, 263, 264, 266, 268, 269, 270, 271, 273, 274, 276, 277, 283
migration, 91–2, 98–9, 101–2, 103–4, 107, 127–8, 131, 135–8, 215
military, 3, 7, 106, 119, 124
 campaigns (expeditions), 25, 83, 106, 113–14, 119, 120, 121–2, 124, 128, 133, 137, 139, 140–42, 150, 158–64, 169–70, 177, 257–64, 265–9, 292;
   See also impi
 commanders, 378 n.48;
   See also Mdhlaka; Zulu ka Nogandaya
 regiments, xi, 31, 35–6, 38, 41, 55, 61, 83–5, 94, 95, 98–9, 106, 107, 114, 116, 117, 122, 123, 124, 126, 132, 133, 142, 146, 159, 164, 165, 198, 201, 231, 232, 235, 239, 247–8, 262, 266, 293, 342 n.50
 Mbonambi regiment, 247
 Mkandhlu regiment, 142
 Nobamba regiment, 263
 women's regiments, 83, 176–7, 263
   See also Iziyenane; war; warfare; warriors; wars
Mkabayi, *see* Mnkabayi
Mkebeni ka Dabulamanzi, 50, 51, 63, 72, 278–9, 311
Mkehlangana ka Zulu, 44, 45, 52, 214, 264, 312
Mkhize, Embo chief, 218
Mkhize, Ama-, 11, 131, 218 *See also* Embo, Zihlandlo
Mkokeleli, 27, 28, 110, 117, 178
 Ngwazi ka Zwana ka Mkokeleli, 110
 Nhlasiyana ka Nomunga ka Mkokeleli, 117
Mkando ka Dhlova, 52, 311
Mkungu ka Mpande, 238
Mlotshwa, chief, 125, 165
Mmama ka Jama, 74, 186, 187, 236, 277
Mmemi ka Nguluzana, 34, 44, 50, 107, 109–10, 278, 313–14
Mnguni, also known as Nnja, father of Malandela, grandfather of Zulu, founding ancestor of AmaZulu royal house, praise name for AmaZulu royal house, 224, 228

Mnguni, AmaNgidi chief, 103
Mnini ka Mabonsa, heir to AmaThuli chieftaincy, 121
Mnkabayi (Mkabayi) ka Jama, 40, 47, 48–9, 51, 73, 74, 76, 183–4, 185, 186, 187, 200, 235, 236, 277
Mnkabi, wife of Senzangakhona, 40, 44, 50–1, 74, 177, 184, 186
Mntaniya (Mtaniya), mother of Senzangakhona, 41, 183–4, 185
Monaheng, Ba-, 130
Mondisa, AmaMthethwa chief, 90
Moshoeshoe, Paramount chief of Lesotho, founder of BaSotho kingdom, 129, 169
Mozambique, 283 See also Balule Campaign; Delagoa Bay; Portuguese; Soshangane
Mpakeni, 37
Mpande ka Senzangakhona, 7, 23, 41, 70, 109, 124, 164, 185, 188, 200, 201, 216, 237–8, 167, 268, 271, 278, 279, 289, 295, 296
Mpandeze, daughter of Sobhuza, 179–80
Mpangazitha ka Bhungane, AmaHlubi chief, 30, 91, 127–130
Mpikase, wife of Senzangakhona, 40, 74, 184, 186, 277
Mpofana, Ama-, 27, 125
Mpondo, Ama-, 20, 25, 82, 95–6, 104, 115, 125, 139, 140, 141–2, 150–2, 157, 238, 257–63, 264, 269, 271, 272, 273, 277, 278, 279, 281, 288, 292
See also Faku
Mpukunyoni, Ama-, 222
Mpumuza, Ama- (Zondi, AmaXesibe), 101–2, 218
Mpungose, Ama-, 26, 40
Mqayana, 108
Mqaikana ka Yenge, 98, 100, 101–2, 314
Mqubane ka Senzangakhona, 185, 199, 237, 271
Mqumbela, 191
Mruyi ka Timuni, 56, 60, 68, 69, 214, 228, 315
Mtetwa, Ama-, see Mthethwa, Ama-
Mtetwa ka Nyambose, ancestor of AmaMthethwa royal family, 219
See also Dingiswayo, Jobe
Mthethwa, Ama- (AbakwaMthethwa), 26–7, 29, 30, 31–3, 35, 52, 58, 59–73, 76, 87–91, 124, 127, 131, 135, 181,
185, 207, 214, 219, 220, 222, 235, 240, 285, 291, 294
See also Dingiswayo
Mthimkulu, AmaHlubi chief, 30, 91, 127–8, 179
Mtoniya, mother of Ndaba, 178
Mtwana, see Twana, imi-
Mtshapi ka Noradu, 266, 268, 315
Mtshayankomo ka Magolwana, 72, 315–6
Mudhli ka Nkwelo, 44, 46, 47, 48, 52, 60, 64, 66, 67–8, 69, 70, 74, 183, 185, 186, 187
Myebu, 26
Mzilikazi ka Matshobana, AmaKhumalo chief, founder of AmaNdebele kingdom, 29, 88, 129, 130, 135–6, 158, 169, 216, 279, 288

Nandi ka Mbengi, mother of Shaka, 31, 39–40, 42- 7, 49–52, 55, 60, 74, 128, 131, 147, 148, 184, 185, 187, 198, 237, 245, 251
death of, 190–198, 253, 257–8, 263, 264, 265
Natal, Colony of, 9, 16, 19, 22, 27, 28, 124
Natal region (pre-colonial period), 122, 123–7, 131, 139, 140, 148, 231, 257, 259, 286
Ncapayi ka Madikane, AmaBhaca chief, 98
Ncwabeni, Ama-, 126
Ncwana, Ama-, AbaQwabe section, 214, 216
Ndaba ka Punga, father of Jama, grandfather of Senzangakhona, 38, 178, 212, 213,
Genealogy of, 212, 234 See also AmaZulu chiefdom, early history
Ndelu, Ama-, 28, 126, 218
Ndhlela ka Sompisi, 120, 184, 278
Ndhlovu, Ama-, 27, 214
Ndhlovu ka Kuba, 40
Ndhlovu ka Timuni, 42, 43, 46–9, 51, 53–4, 60, 61, 64, 69, 73–4, 279, 317
Ndlovu, Sifiso, 173, 202
Ndukwana ka Mbengwana, 23, 55–6, 73, 160, 194, 239, 255, 270, 276, 285–6, 317–18
Ndwandwe, Ama-, 10, 26, 29, 33, 37–8, 61, 76, 77–8, 82, 86, 87–91, 106, 109–10, 119–21, 127, 133, 135, 139, 147, 150, 152, 158–64, 168, 176, 181–2, 214,

215, 220, 264, 268, 269, 283, 291, 292
  See also Zwide
Nganga, Ama-, 124, 241
Ngati, Ama-, 27
Ngceba ka Nodanga, 59
Ngcobo, Ama-, 88, 91, 217, 218, 221
Ngidi, Ama-, 103
Ngidi ka Mcikaziswa, 44, 50, 52, 58, 59,
  61, 71, 74, 75, 86, 148, 186, 192, 195,
  247, 268, 272, 274, 275, 319-20
Ngomane ka Mqombolo, 57, 59-60, 73,
  195, 197
Ngoza ka Mkubukeli, AbaTembu chief, 92-
  7, 125-6, 140, 174, 176
Ngqengelele, 41, 60, 255, 277
Ngqojana ka Senzangakhona, 56, 70, 185,
  199, 237, 271
Nguboyencuga, AmaThembu chief, 140
Nguni, abe- (Nguni, Aba-), 126, 141, 206,
  220, 222, 223, 224, 227, 228, 229, 279
Ngwadi, son of Nandi, brother of Shaka,
  51, 75, 187, 237, 277
Ngwane, Ama-, chiefdom of KwaZulu-
  Natal region under Chief Matiwane,
  29, 30, 87, 98, 104, 127-31, 169-70,
  215, 280, 281, 292
Ngwane, Ama-, proto-Swazi, early name for
  AmaSwazi, 29, 30
Nhlanganiso, 267
Nhlekele ka Makana, 90, 320-21
Nhloko, Ama-, 28
Nkomo ka Tshandu, 26, 33
Nkwelo ka Jama, father of Mudhli, 182
Nnja, also known as Lugenulwenja,
  Mnguni, father of Malandela,
  progenitor of the AmaZulu royal
  house, 212-213, 228
  genealogy, 212
Nobamba (Lobamba), 39, 234
Nobongoza ka Jama, 74, 187
Nomagaga, AmaKuze chief, 94, 101
Nomagaga ka Dhlomo, AmaDhlamini chief,
  97
Nomahawu (Nomawaru), wife of
  Senzangakhona, queen wife at Dukuza,
  184, 199-200
Nombewu (Nombeu), AmaNhlangwini
  chief, 102, 126
Nomcoba (Nomcuba), daughter of Nandi,
  sister of Shaka, 44, 51, 60, 187, 237,
  277

Nomleti, 56
Nomo ka Khondlo, AmaQwabe chief, 34-5,
  109, 180
Nozidiya, wife of Malandela, mother of
  Zulu and Qwabe, progenitors of the
  AmaZulu and AmaQwabe royal
  houses, 178
Nozilwana (Nozilwane) ka Senzangakhona,
  40, 50, 177, 184, 185, 200
Nqetho, AbaQwabe chief, 35, 78-9, 108,
  109, 111, 115, 118, 175, 268, 284-5,
  287
Nqondo, Ama- (Nxondo, Ama-), 218
Nquhele ka Mgudhlane, 165
Ntombaze (Ntombazi), 37, 38, 89, 181
  See also Ndwandwe, Ama-
Ntombela, Ama-, 26
Ntopo ka Ndaba, 38
Ntshali, Ama-, 33, 76, 87, 88, 91, 135, 165-
  8, 215, 265, 267 *See also* Beje (chief);
  Hlangabeza ka Mabedhla (chief)
Ntshangawe, Ama-, 27
Ntuli, Ama-, 88, 214
Ntusi, Ama-, 151
Nxumalo, Ama-, section of
  AmaNdwandwe, 33, 76, 215
Ntungwa, Ama-, 53, 54, 206, 207, 208,
  214, 215-17, 218, 219, 220, 221, 222,
  223, 224, 227, 228, 229, 240, 267, 335
  n.76
Nxaba ka Mbekane (Ncaba, Nqaba),
  AmaMsene (AmaMsane) chief, 37,
  135, 136-8
Nxamalala, Ama-, 28, 101, 104, 131-2,
  217, 250
Nxazonke, eLangeni regent, 56, 57-8, 59,
  195 *See also* Makedama
Nzimela, Ama-, 229
Nyambose, ancestor of AmaMthethwa
  royal family, 219
Nyuswa, Ama-, (abakwaNyuswa), 33, 39,
  61, 76, 86, 87, 91, 217, 218
Nzibe ka Senzangakhona, 237, 267, 268
Nzobe, 198
Nzwakele ka Kutshwayo, AbaQwabe chief,
  115, 118, 278, 279, 285

Ogle, Henry, 157
Oral traditions, 11, 13-14, 16, 21-3, 28-9,
  30-2, 34-7, 39-40, 42-58,
  59-286 *passim*

Peires, Jeff, 7
Phakade, AmaChunu chief, 97, 99–100, 213
　genealogy, 213
Phakathwayo (Pakatwayo) ka Khondlo, AbaQwabe chief, 29, 33, 34–7, 53, 56, 106, 107–10, 174, 176, 180, 185, 284, 291
Pondoland, see Mpondo, Ama-
Port Elizabeth, 20, 152, 280, 281
　See also Algoa Bay
Port Natal, 17, 18, 19, 20, 28, 118, 121, 124, 139, 145, 150, 156–7, 164, 168, 232, 282, 283, 286–7, 288, 289
　European traders at, 18–19, 115, 139, 142–6, 150–8, 159, 166–8, 242–3, 254, 257–8, 265, 282, 286–9, 295
　See also Francis Farewell; Henry Francis Fynn; Nathaniel Isaacs; Charles Rawden Maclean
Portuguese, 17, 21, 153, 265, 384 n.56
Praises, see isibongo
Praise-greetings, see isithakazelo
Phumalo, Ama-, 124, 218, 241
Phuthi, Ba-, 129
Pungatshe, AmaButhelezi chief, 86, 88, 98

Qadi, Ama- (Qadini, Ama-), 33, 88, 217, 218
Qungebe, Ama-, 39, 77
Qwabe, Aba-, 26, 29, 33, 34–7, 39, 53–4, 56, 61, 63, 76, 77, 78, 80, 86, 106, 107–10, 112, 118, 147–9, 174, 176, 178, 180, 185, 213, 214, 216, 220, 221–2, 223, 226, 227, 228, 237, 245–7, 251, 284, 291, 293
Qwabe ka Malandela, brother of Zulu ka Malandela, founding ancestor of AbaQwabe royal family, 178, 213, 214

Ramokhele, Ba-, 129
regiments, see military regiments
Retief, Piet, 290
Rituals, see ceremonies
Ross, John, see Charles Rawden Maclean

Sambela, Embo chief, 11, 132, 124, 250, 285
San, 4
Sankoye ka Senzangakhona, 237
Senzangakhona ka Jama, father of Shaka, 26, 29, 37, 39–41, 42–52, 55–6,
　59–75, 78, 84, 107, 174, 175, 182–7, 234–5, 237, 257, 274, 277, 294–5
　daughters of, 185, 187, 199
　genealogy of, 212
　wives of, 184
Shaka ka Senzangakhona, founder of the Zulu kingdom, 2, 3, 7, 24–5
　accession to AmaZulu chieftaincy, 72–5, 235
　appearance of, 116–17
　assassination attempt against, 147–50, 245, 251
　birth, 42, 45–7, 49
　character of, 7, 21, 240–3, 293–4
　childhood and youth, 47–8, 51–8
　death of, 7, 25, 251, 269–75, 282–3
　Europeans, attitudes towards and relationships with, 253–6, 257–8, 260–1, 265, 272–3
　executions ordered by, 146, 147–9, 193–4, 244–251, 257–8, 160–1, 165, 272–3, 293
　genealogy, 212
　governance, 111–14, 116–17, 118, 123, 146, 223–6, 231–4, 238–40, 244–51, 269–70, 291, 295–6
　images of, 7, 11, 12–13, 18, 21, 225, 290–1
　Port Natal traders, relations with, 145–57, 159–60, 163–64, 166–68, 241–3
　praises of, 33, 116–17, 240–41, 249, 262
　praise names, 33, 206, 213, 224, 228, 229
　warrior, role as, 33, 52, 59–75, 76
　women and, 175, 180, 188–90, 196, 237–8, 241, 251, 279
Shepstone, Theophilus, 16, 21–2, 28, 31, 32, 78
Sigujana ka Senzangakhona, 40, 55, 56, 70–71, 73, 74, 186, 187, 237, 277
Sikakane, Ama-, 39, 77
Siklebi, see Esiklebeni
Sikhunyana ka Zwide, AmaNdwandwe chief, 38, 82, 120, 133, 135, 152, 153, 158–9, 161–4, 292
Simelane, 179
Sirayo ka Mapoloba, 87
Sitayi, see Zivalele
Sithole, Ama- (Sitole, Ama-), 104, 117
Sivivi ka Maqungo, 73, 199, 322
Siyingila, 145, 146

Index

Sobhuza (Sobuza), also known as Somhlolo, AmaSwazi king, 37, 121, 158, 179–80, 267
Socwatsha ka Papu, 83, 221, 229, 271–2, 274, 275, 323
Sojisa (Sojiyisa) ka Jama, 55, 74, 96, 182, 186, 187
Somajuba ka Senzangakhona, 56
Somaphunga ka Zwide, 159
Somhashi ka Zombane, AmaBomvu chief, 104
Somhlolo, see Sobhuza
Somveli, 90
Sondondonzima ka Luboko, 164
Songiya, wife of Senzangakhona, mother of Mpande, 184
Sopana ka Senzangakhona, 56
Sopane ka Mncinci, uncle of Nqetho, 78, 108, 175
Soshangana ka Zikode, AmaNdwandwe chief, nephew of Zwide, 38, 91, 135, 136–7, 158, 168, 262, 264, 265–6, 267, 268, 269, 270, 283, 292
Sotho, Ba- (Basuto), people of the kingdom of Lesotho, 129, 130, 169–70, 292
Sotobe ka Mpangalala, 20, 242, 253–5, 256–7
  mission to Cape Colony, 255, 259, 265, 280, 281
Stuart, James, 7, 11, 14–15, 17, 18, 22–3, 32, 34, 43, 50, 54, 77, 109, 110, 115, 194, 196, 197, 213, 214, 216, 217, 221, 225, 226, 234, 243, 251, 253, 256, 263, 267, 272, 285
Sutu, abe- (abeSutu), speakers of the Sotho-Tswana languages, 215, 219
Swazi, Ama- (Swati, Ama-), 9, 29, 30, 33, 37, 101, 158, 179, 206, 215, 216, 217, 218, 220, 221, 267, 268, 290
  AmaSwazi women, 179–80, 362 n.51, 362 n.52
Swazi kingdom, 4, 7, 121, 158
Swaziland, 110

Tana ka Jobe, brother of Dingiswayo, 31, 179
Taung, Ba-, 129
Tembe, Ama-, Delagoa Bay chiefdom, 28, 151
Tembu, Aba-, KwaZulu-Natal chiefdom, 27, 33, 39, 61, 76, 77, 92–7, 140, 174, 176, 215

Thembu, Ama-, neighboring chiefdom to the AmaXhosa, 130, 140, 280, 281, 283
Thuli, Ama- (Tuli, Ama-), 26, 28, 106, 110, 121–3, 124, 139, 145, 178, 218, 239, 258, 295
Tlokoa, Ba- (BaTlokoa) Caledon valley chiefdom, 129, 290
Tokotoko ka Sojisa, 182
trade, 32, 144, 151–2, 157, 282, 286–8, 350 n.1216 See also ivory trade; Port Natal traders
Trans-Kei region (east of the Kei River), 31, 125–6, 130, 139–42, 229, 260
Trans-Vaal region (north of the Vaal River), 136
tribe, European concept of, 1, 2, 6, 10, 28
tribute and tributary relations, 33, 91, 106, 129, 174, 188, 218, 286
Tshaba, Ama- (Tshabeni, Ama-), 123–4
Tshaka, see Shaka ka Senzangakhona
Tshangane, 90–1, 195
Tshangase, Ama-, 218
Tshange, Ama-, 28
Tshobeni, 125
Tsueneng, Ba-, 129
Tununu ka Nonjiya, 237, 323–4
Tsonga, Ama-, Delagoa Bay peoples, 54
Twana, Imi- (Mtwana), 27, 99, 125–6, 348 n.84

umuzi (pl. *imizi*), see homesteads

Van Warmelo, N.J., 14
Violence, 7, 24–5, 79–80, 91–2, 98, 106–7, 108, 112, 115, 120, 121, 123, 124, 131–4, 156–7, 161–4, 165, 170, 239–40, 244–52, 267, 284–6, 288–9, 291–94, 341 n.26, 344 n.100, 348 n.90
  See also Shaka – executions ordered by
Vubukulwayo ka Khondlo, 109–110, 183
Vundhle, Ama-, 126

war, 2, 3, 85, 92, 106, 112, 113–4, 115, 123, 124, 130, 162, 164, 170, 231, 260
warfare, 2, 7, 32, 33, 62, 67, 77–8, 79–80, 98, 159–62, 169–70
  tactics, 61, 79, 81–2, 98, 100, 103, 108–9, 113–4, 119–20, 124, 131–2, 160–61, 165–8, 258, 261, 266–7

weapons, 31, 57, 61, 81, 258
  See also military
warriors, 78, 116–7, 146, 156, 232, 247–8, 291, 379 n.70
wars, 61, 63, 76, 81–2, 86–91, 93–105, 108–9, 110–112, 113–114, 119–120, 121, 123–38, 150, 158–70, 260–62, 266–7, 291–3 See also military campaigns
Web, Colin, 15
women, 172–204
  AmaSwazi women, 179–80
  authority of, 172, 182–3, 185, 198, 199–204, 236, 276–7
  cultivation of fields by *isigodlo* women, 174–5, 359 n.15
  Dingiswayo and, 179
  marriage, women and, 79, 88–9, 99, 110–12, 235, 238
  military regiments, women's, 36, 83, 146, 263
  protection of, 175, 188
  royal, 72, 172–204, 236, 263, 276–7, 334 n.68, 335 n.75
  royal marriage alliances, 178–181, 185
  Senzangakhona and royal women, 182–5
  sexual relations, 175, 188–90, 199, 382 n.14, 359 n.15
  Shaka and, 175, 180, 188–190, 196, 237–8, 241, 251
  Sociopolitical roles, 5–6, 174–5, 177, 181, 236, 261
  sources about, 172–174
  subordination of women by men, 172, 202–204
  violence against, 175–6, 188, 200–201, 288
  war, women and, 80, 89, 94, 99, 100, 103, 120, 145, 159–64, 176–7, 181, 261, 263, 288, 291, 292, 344 n.100
  wives of Senzangakhona, 184
  See also Baleka; Bhibhi; Macibise; Mawa; 'Mantathisi; Mfunda; Mmama; Mnkabayi (Mkabayi); Mnkabi; Mntaniya (Mtaniya); Mpikase; Nandi; Nomahawu; Nomcoba; Nozidiya; Nozilwana; Ntombaze
Wright, John, 9, 10, 14–15, 207–208, 223–4, 226–7, 228
Wutshe, Ama-, 96
Wylie, Dan, 7, 11–13, 18, 173–4

Xabatshe, AmaXulu chief, 40
Xesibe, AmaMpumuza chief, 101–2

Xesibe, Ama-, (Zondi), see AmaMpumuza
Xhosa, Ama-, 7, 33, 115, 139, 141–2, 229, 260, 281, 283, 289
Xoxo ka Ndaba (Coko ka Ndaba), head of Biyela branch of AmaZulu royal house, father of Menziwa, 38, 183
Xolo, Ama-, 124
Xulu, Ama-, 39, 40, 57, 77

Yenge, AmaMpumuza chief, 101

Zibizendhlela, 238, 278, 279
Zihlandlo ka Gcwabe, Embo (Mkhize) chief, 11, 83, 86, 91, 100, 106, 111, 131–5, 158, 160, 164–5, 250, 285, 295
  See also Sombela ka Gcwabe
Zindhle, im-, 27
Zivalele ka Ndaba, also known as Sitayi, 38, 43, 69, 70, 74, 182, 186, 187, 245
Zombane, AmaBomvu chief, 104
Zomi, Ama-, 28
Zondi, Ama-, see Mpumuza, Ama-
Zuba, Ama-, 27
Zulu ka Malandela, founding ancestor of AmaZulu royal family from whom they take their name, 3, 29, 178, 207, 212, 213, 214, 216
Zulu ka Nogandaya, also known as Komfiya ka Nogandaya, 78, 137, 175, 214, 262, 278, 279, 285, 288
Zulu, Ama-,
  early history, 33, 38–41, 49–50, 214, 227, 228, 229
  praises, 212–213, 224, 228, 229
  royal family/royal house, 207, 226, 229–30, 362 n.65, 362 n.66
  royal family ancestral identity, 206, 208, 214, 216, 222, 223
  royal family genealogy, 212, 361 n.40
  See also individual chiefs by name, Senzangakhona, Shaka
Zungu, Ama-, 39, 77
Zungusi, mother of Phakathwayo, 180
Zwangendaba, AmaNdwandwe chief, 37, 136, 137
Zwide ka Langa, AmaNdwandwe chief, 26, 37–8, 78, 82, 86, 87–90, 106, 109–110, 119–121, 122, 127, 135, 139, 147, 152, 158, 181–2, 220, 239, 269, 291, 292
  daughter of, 181

Printed in Great Britain
by Amazon

58432673R00235